ELEMENTS OF
PROJECT MANAGEMENT

ELEMENTS OF
PROJECT MANAGEMENT

(as per UPTU Syllabus)

K. Nagarajan

PUBLISHING FOR ONE WORLD

NEW AGE INTERNATIONAL (P) LIMITED, PUBLISHERS

New Delhi • Bangalore • Chennai • Cochin • Guwahati • Hyderabad
Jalandhar • Kolkata • Lucknow • Mumbai • Ranchi

Published by New Age International (P) Ltd., Publishers
First Edition: 2005
Reprint: 2014

BRANCHES

- **Bangalore** 37/10, 8th Cross (Near Hanuman Temple), Azad Nagar, Chamarajpet, Bangalore-560 018 Tel.: (080) 26756823, Telefax: 26756820, **E-mail: bangalore@newagepublishers.com**
- **Chennai** 26, Damodaran Street, T. Nagar, Chennai-600 017 Tel.: (044) 24353401, Telefax: 24351463, **E-mail: chennai@newagepublishers.com**
- **Cochin** CC-39/1016, Carrier Station Road, Ernakulam South, Cochin-682 016 Tel.: (0484) 2377004, Telefax: 4051303, **E-mail: cochin@newagepublishers.com**
- **Guwahati** Hemsen Complex, Mohd. Shah Road, Paltan Bazar, Near Starline Hotel, Guwahati-781 008 Tel.: (0361) 2513881, Telefax: 2543669, **E-mail: guwahati@newagepublishers.com**
- **Hyderabad** 105, 1st Floor, Madhiray Kaveri Tower, 3-2-19, Azam Jahi Road, Near Kumar Theater Nimboliadda, Kachiguda, Hyderabad-500 027, Tel.: (040) 24652456, Telefax: 24652457 **E-mail: hyderabad@newagepublishers.com**
- **Kolkata** RDB Chambers (Formerly Lotus Cinema) 106A, 1st Floor, S.N. Banerjee Road, Kolkata-700 014 Tel.: (033) 22273773, Telefax: 22275247, **E-mail: kolkata@newagepublishers.com**
- **Lucknow** 16-A, Jopling Road, Lucknow-226 001 Tel.: (0522) 2209578, 4045297, Telefax: 2204098, **E-mail:lucknow@newagepublishers.com**
- **Mumbai** 142C, Victor House, Ground Floor, N.M. Joshi Marg, Lower Parel, Mumbai-400 013 Tel.: (022) 24927869, Telefax: 24915415, **E-mail: mumbai@newagepublishers.com**
- **New Delhi** 22, Golden House, Daryaganj, New Delhi-110 002 Tel.: (011) 23262368, 23262370, Telefax: 43551305, **E-mail: sales@newagepublishers.com**

ISBN: 978-81-224-1665-7

₹ 175.00

C-14-04-7543

Printed in India at Ajit Printing Press, Delhi.
Typeset at Shubham Graphics, Delhi.

PUBLISHING GLOBALLY
NEW AGE INTERNATIONAL (P) LIMITED, PUBLISHERS
7/30 A, Daryaganj, New Delhi-110002
Visit us at **www.newagepublishers.com**

Preface

Project Management, a multi-disciplinary subject, offers an interesting study. Projects are the backbone of any economy. It is through projects that the resources of an economy are put to productive use. Thus, wealth creation takes place in an economy only through projects. The scope of handling any assignment from the perspective of a project is increasing day by day and in the days to come, Project Management is going to take a prime position in the management of resources. Since Project Management aims at better utilisation of available resources, the scope for this discipline is bound to improve in the days to come as the future lies only in optimum resource utilisation.

Though there are many good books on this subject, the need for a book that covers the syllabus on the subject prescribed by the U.P. Technical University is long felt and this book is an attempt to fulfill this need. The language has been kept simple and the treatment of the subject made lucid with a view to offering a book to the students that is easy to read and comprehend and also proves user-friendly.

I shall feel amply rewarded if this book helps the students of U.P. Technical University in their pursuit to learn the intricies of Project Management, which I hope, this book will do. I earnestly look forward to suggestions from teachers and students for the improvement of the subject content and presentation of the book, which will be incorporated in the future edition of the book.

K. Nagarajan

Acknowledgements

I take this opportunity to thank Mr. Saumya Gupta, Managing Director, New Age International (P) Limited, Publishers, who prompted me [illegible] subject of Project Management [illegible] due to Mr. T. Karthikeyan for [illegible] preparation of the manuscript. I thank the publishers for [illegible] period of time. And I thank all my well wishers who have been [illegible]

K. Nagarajan

Acknowledgements

I take this opportunity to thank Mr. Saumya Gupta, Managing Director, New Age International (P) Limited, Publishers, who prompted me to write a book to meet the requirements of the syllabus on the subject of Project Management prescribed by the U.P. Technical University. My sincere thanks are due to Mr. T. Karthikeyan for preparing the typescript and for the secretarial help rendered by him in preparation of the manuscript. I thank the publishers for having brought out this book in a very short period of time. And, I thank all my well wishers who have been an inspiration to me.

K. Nagarajan

Contents

UNIT

I

PROJECT MANAGEMENT CONCEPTS

1.1 PROJECT

The term "Project" has a wider meaning. A project is accomplished by performing a set of activities. For example, construction of a house is a project. The construction of a house consists of many activities like digging of foundation pits, construction of foundations, construction of walls, construction of roof, fixing of doors and windows, fixing of sanitary fittings, wiring etc. The construction of a house is accomplished by performing the set of activities. Another aspect of "project" is the non-routine nature of activities. Each project is unique in the sense that the activities of a project are unique and non-routine.

A project conumes resources. The resources required for completing a project are men, material, money and time. The nature of resources is that they are limited and scarce. If a person wants to construct a house, the first thing that comes to his mind is the financial budget within which the work should be completed. Thus, resource constraint is a feature of all projects. If one wants to construct a house at an estimated cost of Rs. 10 lakhs and within a period of 6 months, the project should be completed subject to these constraints. Thus, we can define a project as an organized programme of pre determined group of activities that are non-routine in nature and that must be completed using the available resources within the given time limit.

According to Harison, a project can be defined as a non-routine, non-repetitive, one-off undertaking, normally with discrete time, financial and technical performance goals. Project Management institute, USA defines project as 'a system involving the co-ordination of a number of separate department entities through out the organization and which must be completed within prescribed schedules and time constraints.

According to the **Encyclocpaedia of Management**, project is 'an organized unit dedicated to the attainment of goal—the successful completion of a develolpment project on time, within budget, in conformance with pre-determined programme specifications'.

According to Little & Mirrless, a project is any scheme or part of a scheme for investing resources which can be reasonably analysed and evaluated as an independent unit.

Though Project Management is in the process of getting evolved as a separate branch of study, projects are not new to the earth. One of the seven wonders of the world, the Pyramids date back to

2650 BC, which stand as the hall mark of Egyptian civilization. The period of construction of the Taj Mahal, another wonder of the world is reported to be during 1626-1648 A.D. It is reported that about 20,000 persons worked for nearly 22 years to complete this spectacular structure, which stands today as mankind's proudest creation. One can imagine the extent of resources and expertise that would have been put forth for the completion of such magnificiant projects.

Project management is an organized venture for managing projects. It involves scientific application of modern tools and techniques in planning, financing, implementing, monitoring, controlling and coordinating unique activities or tasks to produce desirable outputs in accordance with the pre-determined objectives within the constraints of time and cost.

Project management consists of the following stages.

- Project planning
- Project scheduling
- Project implementation, controlling and monitoring

Every person, every organization and every nation is concerned with project management. An individual builds a house. It is his project. He performs marriages for his children. These are also projects that he undertakes in his life time. An organization sets up a new factory. It is a project for the organisation. The Government of a country builds highways, dams, thermal power plants, hydro power plants, airports etc. These are all projects that the country undertakes.

Project management as a technique is assuming greater importance since it aims at optimum utilization of resources. Every person is practising project management in his day to day life. When a person uses the shortest route to reach his office, it involves all the stages of project management, viz., planning, scheduling, implementing, controlling and monitoring. He plans for the shortest route; he schedules his starting time; he controls the speed of his vehicle to reach his destination in time. By choosing the shortest route, he tries to optimize the usage of fuel for his car and he also tries to reach the office at the shortest possible time. When a Government plans to build an express highway connecting two important cities covering a distance of several kilometers, it is a project of a greater magnitude than the project of house construction. As a project becomes larger in magnitude, its complexities with regard to planning, scheduling, implementing, controlling and monitoring increases. For effective management of larger and complex projects, systematically devised techniques are followed.

1.2 PROJECT CHARACTERISTICS

Major project characteristics are as below:

Objectives

A project has a set of objectives or a mission. Once the objectives are achieved, the project is treated as completed. For example the objective of a project may be construction of a highway connecting two cities 'A' & 'B', covering a distance of 20 kilometers. Once the construction of the highway is completed the project comes to an end.

Life cycle

A project has a life cycle. The life cycle consists of the following stages:

Conception stage : Where project ideas are conceived.

Design stage	: Where detailed design of different project areas are worked out.
Implementation stage	: Where the project is implemented as per the design.
Commissioning stage	: Where the project is commissioned after implementation. Commissioning of a project indicates the end of its life cycle.

Definite Time Limit

A project has a definite time limit. It can not continue forever. Construction of a highway connecting two cities is a project which is to be completed within a given time limit. Maintenance of the highway is an on going process and it will continue forever. Hence highway maintenance will not come under the purview of project.

Uniqueness

Every project is unique and no two projects are similar. Setting up a Cement plant and construction of a highway are no doubt two different projects having unique characteristics. Constructing a highway between cities A&B and construcing another highway between cities C&D are also unique in themselves, in view of the differences existing in the organization, infrastructure, location, technical specifications and the people behind the projects.

Team work

A project normall consists of diversed areas. There will be personnel specialized in their respective areas. Any project calls for the services of experts from a host of disciplines. Co-ordination among the diversed areas calls for teamwork. Hence a project can be implemented only with teamwork.

Complexity

A project is a complex set of activities relating to diversed areas. Technology survey, choosing the appropriate technology, procuring the appropriate machinery and equipment, hiring the right kind of people, arranging for financial resources, execution of the project in time by proper scheduling of the different activities etc. contribute to the complexity of the project.

Sub-contracting

This characteristic stems forth in view of the complexity of functions and activities of a project. Some of the activities are entrusted to sub-contractors to reduce the complexity of the project. Sub-contracting will be advantageous if it reduces the complexity of the project so that the project manager can coordinate the remaining activities of the project more effectively. In general, the greater the complexity of the project, the larger will be the extent to which sub-contracting will be resorted to. Sub-contracting is also helpful if the sub-contractors are specialized in their field of activity since this will improve the quality of the project.

Risk and Uncertainty

Risk and uncertainty go hand in hand with project. A risk free project cannot be thought of. Even if a project appears to be risk free, it only means that the risk element is not apparently visible on the surface and it will be hidden underneath. The risk factor will come to surface when conditions become conducive to it. Some of the risk elements can be foreseen and the project can be strengthened to encounter the risk as and when it emerges. Some other risk elements can not be foreseen. For example, assume that putting up a cotton yarn-spinning mill is the project on hand. If during the project feasibility study it is learnt that there has been a gradual shift among consumers from the usage of cotton yarn to the usage of synthetic yarn, and if it is apprehended that at one stage synthetic yarn will rule over, the machinery can be so chosen that they can be used for both types of yarns. If this is not entirely possible, the choice of machinery can be so done as to avoid major conversion cost while switching over from the manufacture of cotton yarn to the manufacture of synthetic yarn in case the need arises. Such eventualites can be foreseen and planned for. On the other hand the sudden entry of a strong competitor who can upset all our forecasts and projections can not be anticipated. Sudden fall of Government in a country, which is not anticipated may turn the calculations wrong and make the forecasts/projections meaningless.

Customer Specific Nature

A project is always customer specific. This is because the products produced or services offered by the project are necessarily to be customer oriented. It is the customer who decides upon the product to be produced or services to be offered and hence it is the responsibility of any organization to go for projects/services that are suited to customer needs.

Change

A project is not rigid in its life span. Changes occur throughout the life span of a project as a natural outcome of many environmental factors. The changes may vary from minor changes which may have very little impact on the project to major changes which may have a big impact or even may change the very nature of the project.

During the course of implementation, the technology would have improved further and equipments with the latest technology would have already started arriving. In such a case, if the equipment originally planned had not yet been procured, it would be wise to switch over to the equipment with the latest technology. There could also be latest technological innovations in the manufacturing process which may deserve a switch over. All such changes are necessitated in order to keep the project update.

Responsse to Environments

Projects take shape in response to environments. Indian Government soon after independence set up major projects in the public sector, in the sectors of iron and steel, coal, power generation, heavy equipments manufacture etc. This was in tune with the then need for the development of infrastrcuture and heavy industries.

Forecasting

Forecasting the demand for any product/service that the project is going to produce is an important aspect. Only if the forecast gives positive indications, the project is taken up for further study. Thus, all projects involve forecasts and in view of the importance attached to forecasts, they must be accurate and based on sound fundamentals.

Rational Choice

Since a project is a scheme for investing resources, the choice of a project is done after making a study of all the available avenues for investing resources and a rational choice among the available avenues is made.

Optimality

A project is always aimed at optimum utilization of resources for the overall development of the organization/economy. Resources are scarce and resources have a cost. Hence, optimum utilization of resources is a must for any project. Many project management concepts have evolved with the aim of achieving optimum utilization of available resources.

Control Mechanism

All projects will have pre-designed control mechanisms in order to ensure completion of projects within the time schedule, within the estimated cost and at the same time achieving the desired level of quality and reliability.

1.3 ATTRIBUTES OF A GOOD PROJECT MANAGER

An effective project manager is one who should have the following skills/capacities.

- PLanning and organizational skills
- Personnel management skills
- Communication skills
- Change orientation
- Ability to solve problems in their totality
- High energy levels
- Ambition for achievement
- Ability to take suggestion
- Understanding the views of project team members and having a sympathetic attitude towards them
- Ability to develop alternative actions quickly
- Knowledge of project management methods and tools
- Ability to make self-evaluation
- Effective time management
- Capacity to relate current events to the project/project management
- Ability to handle project management software tools/packages
- Flair for sense of humour
- Solving issues/problems immediately without postponing them
- Initiative and risk taking ability
- Familiarity with the organization
- Tolerance for difference of opinion, delay, ambiguity
- Knowledge of technology
- Conflict resolving capacity
- Team building skills
- Resource allocation skills
- Entrepreneurial skills

1.4 PROJECT CLASSIFICATIONS

The term 'taxonomy' refers to the science of classifying things by naming and identifying them. Projects can be classified under different heads, some of which are explained below.

Based on the Type of Activity

Under this category, projects can be classified as industrial projects and non-industrial projects. Industrial projects are set up for the production of some goods. Projects like health care projects, educational projects, irrigation projects, soil conservation projects, pollution control projects, highwawy projects, water supply projects etc. come under the category of non-industrial projects. Investments in non-industrial projects are made by the Government and the benefits from such projects are enjoyed by the entire society of people. It is difficult to quantify the benefits enjoyed by the society out of non-industrial projects.

Based on the Location of the Project

Under the category, projects can be classified as national projects and international projects. National projects are those set up with in the national boundaries of a country, while international projects are set up in other countries. International projects may be either projects set up by the Government or by the private sector. The following are the major forms of international projects.

- Setting up of fully owned subsidiaries abroad
- Setting up of joint ventures abroad
- Setting up of projects abroad by way of mergers & acquisitions

Handling of international projects needs more expertise and greater efforts in view of higher risk proportion and procedural formalities involved.

Based on Project Completion Time

Based on the constraints on project completion time, projects can be classified into two types, viz., normal projects and crash projects. Normal projects are those for which there is no constraint on time. Crash projects are those which are to be completed within a stipulated time, even at the cost of ending up with a higher project cost. For example, construction of canal lining with the condition that the work should be completed before the monsoon starts is a crash project.

Based on Ownership

Based on ownership, projects can be classified into private sector projects, public sector projects and joint sector projects. A private sector project is one in which the ownership is completely in the hands of the project promoters and investors. Profit maximisation is the prime objective of private sector projects since the investors invest their money in such projects only with the sole idea of earning better returns.

Public sector projects are those that are owned by the state. The evolution and growth of public sector enterprises is the natural consequences of the efforts of Governments for undertaking development in a country. The growth of public sector enterprises vary from country to country. In a country that follows only the system of private enterprises (USA, for example) there is hardly any public sector enterprise except for essential sectors like defense sectors, public utility services etc. In socialist countries (China, for example) public enterprises dominate the economy and they have become public property. In countries that follow a system of mixed economy (India, for example) both private and public sector enterprises exist.

An enterprise is considered as public enterprise when the state or any other national, regional or local authority holds at least 51% of its capital and the enterprise is under the control of the state. In India, public sector undertakings can be owned either by the Central Government or by the State Governments. Government undertakes investment in public sector enterprises due to many reasons.

- Both developing and under-developed countries need a planned economy for their sustained growth. The Government announces industrial and trade policies in tune with its plans to direct the growth of the economy in the desired direction. It becomes imperative for the Government to invest in growth sector.
- Private sector in developing and under-developed countries are not willing to take up investments in many planned sectors (sectors that the Government considers as thrust areas for the development of the economy) either due to huge investments required or due to un attractive returns from the investments in such projects. Hence it becomes the responsibility of the Government to invest and nurture industries in such planned sectors.
- Investment in strategic sectors (defense, space research, atomic research etc.) can not be given to the private sector for obvious reasons. Also, public utility services sectors can also be not left fully to the private sector since the private sector by nature is oriented only towards profit maximization and not in welfare maximization.
- The natural resources of a country are the properties of the Government. The natural resources can be exploited only by the public sector enterprises since the investment required is huge and the ownership of the resources rests with the Government. (example: mining, construction of dams for irrigation purposes, hydro power plants).

Joint sector projects are those in which the ownership is shared by the Government and by private entrepreneurs. The main consideration for the Government's investment in joint sector projects is to make use of the managerial talents, entrepreneurial capabilities and marketing skills of the private entrepreneurs. Joint sector offers hope to the private entrepreneurs since the Government shares the investment required for the project.

Based on Size

Projects can be classified based on the size into three categories, viz., small projects, medium sized projects and large projects. The size is normally expressed in terms of the amount of investment required. The investment limit for the different categories of projects are announced by the Government and this undergoes periodical changes keeping in view the inflation, the decision to offer certain incentives to projects categorized as 'small' scale projects etc. As per the directives of the Govt. of India, projects with investment on plant and machinery up to Rs. 1 crore are categorized as 'small scale projects' while those with investment in plant and machinery above Rs. 100 crores are categorized as 'large scale projects'. Projects with investment limit between these two categories are 'medium scale projects'.

Based on Need

Projects can be classified under the following groups, based on the need for project.

1. New project.
2. Balancing project.
3. Expansion project.
4. Modernization project.

5. Replacement project.
6. Diversification project.
7. Backward integration project.
8. Forward integration project.

New project: A new project idea is conceived and implemented to meet customer needs. The whole concept of business can be viewed as under:

(*i*) Finding a gap in terms of customer needs for goods and services.

(*ii*) Filling the gap.

A new project can be one that identifies a new product for which there is demand from the customers or it can be a project for the production of a product that is already in the market but the demand for which is in excess of the supply, leaving a gap to be filled in. Identification and formulation of a new project requires special knowledge and skill.

Balancing project: Projects in general have many production units that are linked with one another. The flow of material through different production units shall be such that the output of one production unit exactly matches the input requirement for the subsequent production unit. If this is so, the efficiency of the production line will be the maximum and there will not be any under utilization of production capacity. However, if the production capacity of any particular production unit is less, then this particular production unit sets the maximum limit of production possible for all other units.

Let us illustrate the above concept by an example.

Consider the production of steel furniture. For the simplicity of explaining the concept, let us assume a project for the manufacture of steel cupboards. Let the following are the types of operations involved in the production. (Again, for the sake of simplicity the operations are restricted to only four).

(*a*) Cutting of steel sheets to the required sizes.

(*b*) Folding of steel sheets as per the design requirements.

(*c*) Welding the parts.

(*d*) Painting.

Operation (*a*) above will need cutting machines (technically called shearing machines) operation (*b*) will need folding machines; operation (*c*) will need welding machines operation (*d*) will need air compressors, painting booth, paint spray guns and other related equipments.

If we plan to install a plant with a production capacity of say, 50 Nos. of steel cupboards per shift of 8 hours, it would be ideal if all the above four production departments have capacity to handle 50 Nos. of cupboards per shift. In such a situation, the production line is said to be perfectly balanced. However, this can not be the case in view of many limitations and practical problems. Most of the machinery are manufactured to standard specifications and sizes. In the example quoted above, the folding machine available in the market may be of certain standard capacity. For example purchasing of one machine may not be sufficient for the required production capacity, while purchasing two machines may be in excess of the planned capacity. A compromise is required to be made. If we plan a production capacity of 50 steel cupboards per shift and if the folding machines are available in the capacities of 80, 40 and 30 cupboards per shift (i.e., the folding capacity is adequate to produce 80, 40 and 30 cupboards per shift respectively), we have no necessarily go for the combinations of machines having 40 and 30 cupboards/shift capacity, in which case there will be an excess capacity of 20 cupboards (70-50) in the folding section.

As far as possible, the capacities of the other production units can be increased to match or at least to come nearer to the capacity of the folding section. But, other considerations like the total investment available for the project, the market demand for the product, the standard sizes in which other manufacturing facilities are available etc., impose limitations. Hence it is not uncommon to come across projects that have unutilized capacities in one or more production units.

Cost consideration of investments in manufacturing facilities and demand pattern of products are the two main reasons as to why projects that are newly set up have unutilized capacity in certain production units. A project may foresee a particular production capacity at which it can confidently market its entire production. Having decided upon a particular production capacity, the project is to be so designed that all the production facilities match the planned production capacity. In case a particular production facility (folding section, as in the example given above) can be installed only at a higher level of capacity than what is required, there is no other way except to accept the same. Increasing the production capacity of all other production units in tune with the increased capacity of such unmatched production units may not be practicable for implementation since this will mean both increase in production capacity and increase in investment limits. The management may be averse to both these options because of its own reasons based on other considerations. Hence the project implemented with such constraints will result in under utilization of production capacity of certain production units.

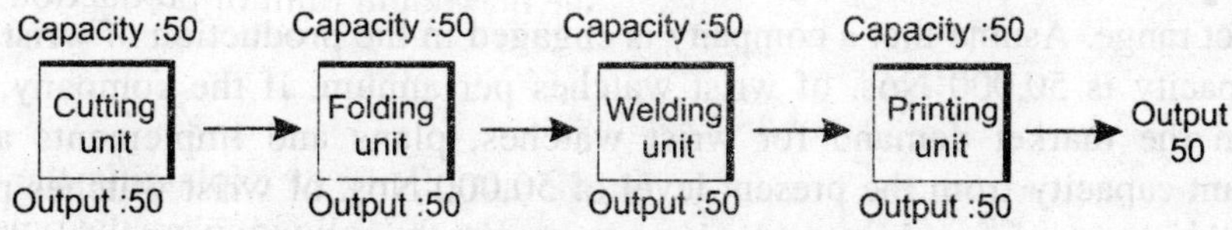

Fig. 1.1 *Balanced Production line*

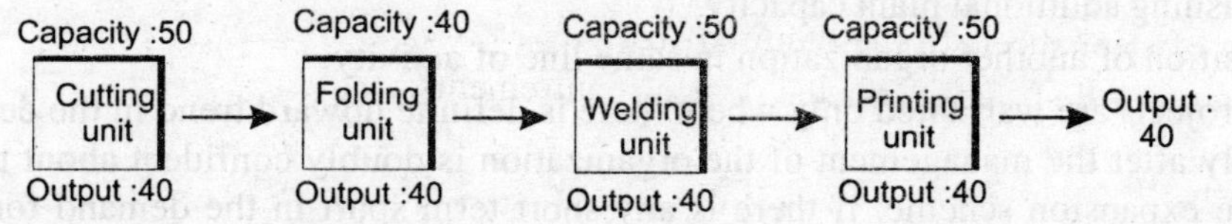

Fig. 1.2 *Unbalanced production line*

As seen from Fig. 1.2, though, the production capacity of cutting unit is 50 (i.e., the unit has cutting capacity needed for the production of 50 cupboards per shift), the cutting unit can not operate at its full capacity in view of the lower capacity of the following production unit viz., folding unit. If cutting unit is operated at its full capacity, stock will start piling up before the folding unit since the folding unit will be receiving additional jobs equivalent to 10 cupboards every shift.

Also, though the production capacity of Welding unit and painting unit is 50 each, these two units also can not operate at their full capacity since these two units will be receiving jobs below their capacity. Thus, in view of the lower capacity of one of the production units, all other production units in the production line (both upstream and down stream) operate at below their capacity.

What is the effect of such unbalanced projects?

Though perfectly balanced projects are rare to come across, attempts should be made to bring about near perfect balance as far as possible. The following are the effects of unbalanced projects.

(*a*) There is under utilization of production capacity.

(*b*) Idle production capacity will result in lower return on investment.

(*c*) If a project that can be balanced remains unbalanced, there is every possibility that a competitor may be able to offer his product at a comparatively cheaper price. The competitor may be a new entrant who sets up a balanced project or an existing producer who upgrades his project from an unbalanced to a balanced one. In such a situation, it is likely that the unbalanced project may face severe threat for its continued existence.

Having understood the concept, we can now define balancing project as under :

A project that is undertaken to improve upon the manufacturing capacity of one or more production units that will result in improvement in the overall production capacity of the project as a whole is called a Balancing project.

In the above example, if a project is undertaken to increase the production capacity of the folding unit from 40 units per shift to 50 units per shift, (provided such a proposal is technically feasible!) it amounts to a balancing project. After implementation of the balancing project, under utilization of capacity in certain production centres gets removed and utilization of production capacity of the remaining production centres improves, resulting in overall increase in production capacity and profitability of the project.

Expansion project : An expansion project is one that is aimed at increasing the plant capacity for the current product range. Asume that a company is engaged in the production of wrist watches and that the plant capacity is 50,000 Nos. of wrist watches per annum. If the company, anticipating further growth in the market demand for wrist watches, plans and implements a project for enhancing the plant capacity from the present level of 50,000 Nos. of wrist watches per to 75,000 Nos. per annum, the company is said to embark upon an expansion project.

Expansion of plant capacity can be done in two ways, viz.,

(*a*) by establishing additional plant capacity.

(*b*) by acquisition of another organization in same line of activity.

Expansion projects are warranted only where there is definite upward trend in the demand for the product and only after the management of the organization is doubly confident about the long term prospects of the expansion scheme. If there is any short term spurt in the demand for the product which is not expected to last long, is it advisable to plan for expansion? Prudence will indicate that such short term increase in orders is to be executed by diverting a part of the work to outsiders on jobs contract basis, rather than hurrying through an expansion project.

Modernisation project : Technological innovation is a continuous process. When a new technology is evolved and becomes commercially operative, the existing technology becomes obsolete. Any project is set up with the latest available technology. However with, the passage of time, in view of continuing technological upgradation, the projects, become obsolete in technology. There are two aspects of technological obsolescence that deserve consideration, viz,

(*a*) The production process would have become obsolete in view of the latest technological innovations. For example, for painting of metal components, 'brush painting' was used long ago which was replaced by 'spray painting'. Spray painting method gave improved finishing and also resulted in economical use of paint. 'Powder coating', a further advanced process of painting gave additional advantages and this replaced spray painting process in many important areas of application. 'Vapocure', which is another improvement over powder coating technology is now being used in many applications.

(*b*) More advanced features would have been incorporated in the plant and machinery, with the result the existing old plant and machinery might have become obsolete in technology. For example, CNC Lathes ("Computerized Numeric Control" Lathes) incorporate advanced features which facilitate improved machining operations. With the introduction of CNC lathes, the old-modeled lathes, which did not have any computerized automation features, become obsolete in technology.

Thus, whenever either the plant and machinery becomes obsolete or whenever the production process becomes obsolete there is a need for modernization.

Importance of Modernization

Ignoring the need for modernization will result in reduction of profit margin, which in the course of time may even lead to closure of the organization. Modernization when ignored will result in either of the following two situations.

(*a*) The organization that has ignored modernization will be producing products which are inferior in quality as compared to the products produced by its competitors.

(*b*) The cost of production would be higher than that of competitors, though there is no difference in quality.

It is also likely that both the above two factors may coexist. Hence for the survival of any organization, modernization of project keeping in tune with the latest developments is a must. Ignoring the need for modernization will only mean that the organization is moving towards its end.

Replacement project : Replacement project involves replacing some of the old machinery with new machinery of the same capacity. Due to ageing and wear and tear of machinery, the maintenance-cost starts mounting up and a stage will come when it will be no more advantageous to keep the worn-out machinery in the production line in view of abnormally high maintenance costs, poor quality of output, reduction in capacity of output, break-down etc.

Hence a replacement project is implemented to reduce the maintenance cost of old machinery and to keep the production going without any obstruction so that delivery schedules are met in time.

Thus, replacement projects are undertaken with a view to maintaining the same level of operational efficiency or even to better the level of operational efficiency wherever possible.

Diversification project : When a manufacturer wants to offer more than one product, it is described as product diversification and the project meant for this purpose is the diversification project. Diversification is generally of two types viz.,

(*a*) Related diversification.
(*b*) Unrelated diversification.

Related diversification means making closely related diversifications to the product line. A manufacturer in the line of manufacturing wrist watches may go for adding manufacturing facilities meant for the manufacture of time pieces and alarm clocks, which is an example for related diversification. When a company's proposed product range are different from the existing ones, we call that the company embarks upon unrelated diversification. Godrej, has a wide range of products like office furniture, cosmetics, edible oil, locks, agrofoods, office automation products etc., which is an example for unrleated diversification.

Diversification projects are necessitated by the urge to explore market potentials in unattempted areas with a view to improving upon the profitability of the organization. It may be noted that diversification project is almost like a new project for an organization but for the fringe benefits that the organization may derive from the infrastructure already available.

Backward integration project : Any manufacturing organization procures raw materials. The raw materials undergo a series of operations resulting into transformation to the form of finished product. The raw material that an organization purchases may be in different forms ranging from crude raw material to value added raw material. For example, iron ore is the raw material for a smelting unit. The smelting unit extracts iron out of the iron ore. Iron may become the raw material for a foundry. The foundry unit produces components of different nature using iron. Iron components molded in a foundry unit may become the raw material for a machinery manufacturing unit. The machinery manufacturing unit purchases components from foundry units, and finishes the components to suit the requirements, add addtional design features and use them in assembling a machinery. Thus the output of one industry becomes the raw material for another industry.

If an industry that uses a value added raw material goes for the implementation of a project for the production of this value-added raw material within its production line, the industry is said to be on backward integration. Consider a polythene bag making industry.

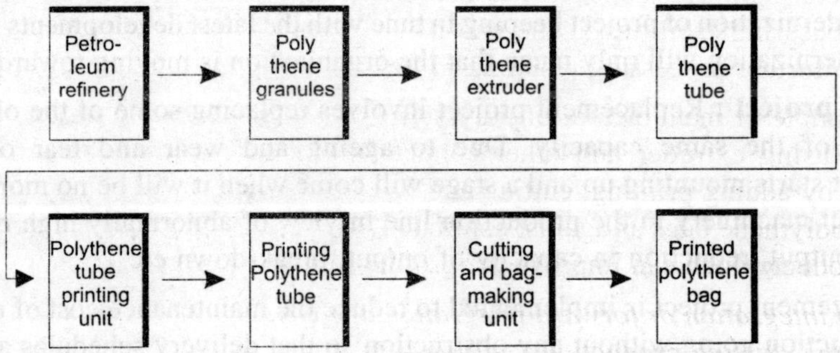

Fig 1.3 *Full production line for printed polyuthene bag manufacture*

Polythene granules are obtained as a by-product in petroleum refinery. These granules are the basic raw material for plastic industry. The granules are melted and blown in the form of tubes of continuous length. Conversion of polythene granules into polythene tube of continuous length is done with the help of a polythene extruder machinery attached with necessary blowers and other fittings.

The continuous polythene tube obtained from the extruder is passed through the printing machine where necessary printing is done on the tubes. The printed polythene tubes are passed through cutting and Bag making machine where the tube is cut into standard sizes, and the opening on one side is sealed, thus producing a printed polythene bag.

A polythene Bag-making unit if started with a smaller investment can have only a cutting and Bag-making machinery. Printed polythene tube will be the raw material for such a unit and this raw material, viz., printed polythene tube will be obtained from other manufacturers of this item. If this Bag-making unit wants to go for backward integration it can include a polythene tube printing machinery in its production line, in which case, plain polythene tube will be the raw material required. If after some time, the unit further wants to integrate its production facilities further backward, it can add an extruder machinery whereby it can procure polythene granules as raw material and produce continuous polythene tubes in-house using the extruder.

Thus, the process of backward integration can be continued till a stage is reached where further backward integration does not exist or may not be feasible in view of other constraints. In the example given above, adding production facility for the production of polythene granules in-house is not feasible since it is a different line of activity with very huge investment and more over the polythene granules are only a by-product, the main products being petroleum products meant for usage as fuel.

An organization opts for backward integration under the following circumstances.

(*a*) The availability of raw material is irregular in nature, which affects the production line and delivery schedule.

(*b*) Storing additional quantity of raw material to avoid stock-out situation results in heavy inventory carrying cost.

(*c*) Long lead time for the procurement of certain raw materials.

(*d*) High profit margin enjoyed by suppliers of raw material due to wide demand-supply gap.

Since the above pit falls are avoided with backward integration, the profitability and efficiency of the organization is bound to improve after the implementation of backward integration project.

Forward integration project: While backward integration is done by adding manufacturing/processing facilities at the beginning stages of a product line, forward integration is done by adding additional manufacturing/processing facilities at the end of the production line. By including additional manufacturing/processing facilities at the end of production line, the products that are currently produced undergo further processing resulting in further value addition.

Taking the example of manufacture of polythene bag, an organization that produces continuous polythene tubes (using extruder and other connected equipments) may integrate its production facilities forward by adding printing, cutting and bag making facilities so that the finished product becomes printed polythene bags as against continuous polythene tubes. Thus, there is value addition to the finished product which can improve the profitability of the organization.

Be it backward integration or forward integration, the capacity of the production facilities added must match with the existing production facilities.

Fig. 1.4 represents a schematic diagram for backward integration and forward integration. Considering the example already given, a backward integration project shall add extruder capacity to match the capacity of printing, cutting and bag making units while a forward integration project shall add printing, cutting and bag making capacity to match the capacity of extruder unit.

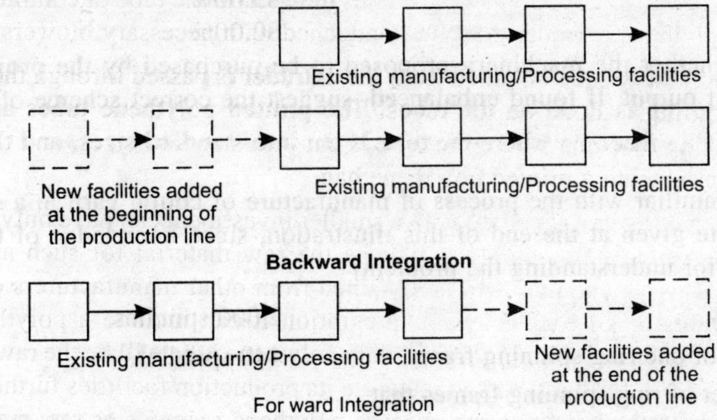

Fig 1.4 *Schematic diagram for backward and forward integrations*

Illustration 1.1

M/s Threadwell spinners, a new partnership firm has propsal to set up a new cotton yarn spinning unit with an installed capacity of about 2000 spindles, for the manufacture of 20's count cotton yarn. The project promoters, not being exposed to the technical details about the various machinery required for the project, have proposed to purchase the following machinery, after consultations with a few well wishers! (which is not infrequent in real life situations!).

Blow room (with one scutcher)	**1. no.**
Carding machines	**4. nos.**
Draw frame	**2. nos.**
Simplex frame	**2. nos.**
Ring spinning frames	**6. nos.**

The promoters have obtained licence for setting up a cotton spinning mill of 2000 spindles capacity. The following are the technical details of the machinery.

Rated capacity @ 100% efficiency:

Ring spinning frame	**: 213 grams per spindle per shift (8 hrs)**
Simplex frame	**: 3.59 kg. per spindle per shift (8 hrs)**
Draw frame	**: 329 kg per shift (8 hrs)**
Carding machine	**: 140.30 kg per shift (8 hrs)**
Blow room (with one scutcher)	**: 1,296 kg per shift (8 hrs)**

Ring spinning frames are available with 440 spindles capacity each and Simplex frames are available with 124 spindles capacity each.

Wastages at the different stages of processing are as under:

Wastage in ring spinning frame	**: 3.00%**
Wastage in simplex frame	**: 200%**
Wastage in draw frame	**: 1.00%**
Wastage in carding machine	**: 5.00%**

Capacity utilization of the ring spinning frame is 90%.

Machine efficiency of the different machines are as under:

Ring spinning frame	**: 84.50%**
Simplex frame	**: 84.00%**
Draw frame	**: 73.00%**
Carding machine	**: 85.00%**
Blow room	**: 80.00%**

Find out as to whether the machinery proposed to be purchased by the project promoters are balanced in terms of output. If found unbalanced, suggest the correct scheme of machinery.

Solution:

[Those who are unfamiliar with the process of manufacture of cotton yarn in a spinning mill may refer to the foot note given at the end of this illustration, since knowledge of the manufacturing process is essential for understanding the problem]

Licensed capacity	: 2,000 spindles.
Spindle capacity of one ring spinning frame	: 440 spindles.
Maximum number of ring spinning frames that	

can be purchased so that the licensed capacity is not exceeded	: 4 nos. : (4 × 440 = 1,760 spindles)
Hence,	
Installed capacity of the plant (expressed in terms of spindle capacity of ring spinning frames)	: 1,760 spindles
Effective utilization of spindles (1,760 × 0.90)	: 1,584 spindles
Machine efficiency of ring spinning frame	: 89.50%
Expected output of cotton yarn per shift (8 hrs)	: 0.895 × [1,584 × 213] grams 301.78 kg

[The expected output of 301.97 kg arrived at above is without taking into account the wastages in ring spinning frames. If the wastage of 3.00% is taken into account, the actual output of cotton yarn per shift will be 292.91 kg.]

Required output of simplex frame per shift (8 hrs)	: 301.97 kg.
Rated output of simplex frame per spindle per shift	: 3.59 kg.
Machine efficiency of simplex frame	: 84%
Number of spindles required for simplex frame	: $\left(\dfrac{301.97}{0.84 \times 3.59}\right)$
	: 100.14 say, 100 spindles

Since the simplex frames are available with 124 spindle capacity, one simplex frame need to be purchased to take up the required production. Though the spindles of simplex frame required are only 100, since machines are available only in standarized capacities, one simplex frame with 124 spindles is required to be purchased. The proposal of the project promoters to purchase 2 nos. of simplex frames is not well founded since even one simplex frame will have a spare capacity of 24 spindles (124-100).

Required input for simplex frame per shift for getting an output of 301.97 kg. per shift, taking into account wastage of 2.00% [301.197 ÷ 0.98)]	: 308.13 kg
Required output of draw frame per shhift (8 hrs)	: 308.13 kg
Machine efficiency of draw frame	: 73 %
Rated output of draw frame per shift (8 hrs)	: 329 kg.
Number of draw frames required	: $\left(\dfrac{308.13}{0.73 \times 329}\right)$
	: 1.28

The proposal to purchase 2 numbers of draw frames is in order. As seen from the actual requirement of 1.28 draw frames (which is not possible due to practical limitations), there will be spare capacity available in this section.

Required input for draw frame per shift for getting an output of 308.13 kg. taking into account wastage of 1.00% [308.13 ÷ 0.99)]	: 311.24 kg.
Required output of carding machines per shift	: 311.24 kg.
Machine efficiency of carding machines	: 85%
Rated output of carding machine per shift (8 hrs)	: 140.30 kg.

Number of carding machines required	:	$\left(\dfrac{311.24}{0.85 \times 140.30}\right)$
	:	2.61

The proposal of the project promoters to purchase 4 nos. carding machines is not well founded. As seen from the above, 3 nos. of carding machines are sufficient.

Required input for carding machines per shift for getting an output of 311.24 kg. taking into account wastage of 5.00% [311.24 ÷ 0.95]	:	327.62 kg.
Required input for blow room (with one scutcher) per shift	:	327.62 kg.
Machine efficiency of blow room	:	80%
Rated output of blow room (with one scutcher) per shift	:	1,296 kg.
Number of scutchers required for blow room	:	$\left(\dfrac{327.62}{0.80 \times 1{,}296}\right)$
Hence, blow room with one scutcher is sufficient.	:	0.32

The actual requirement of different machineries are as under. (Refer Fig. 1.5)

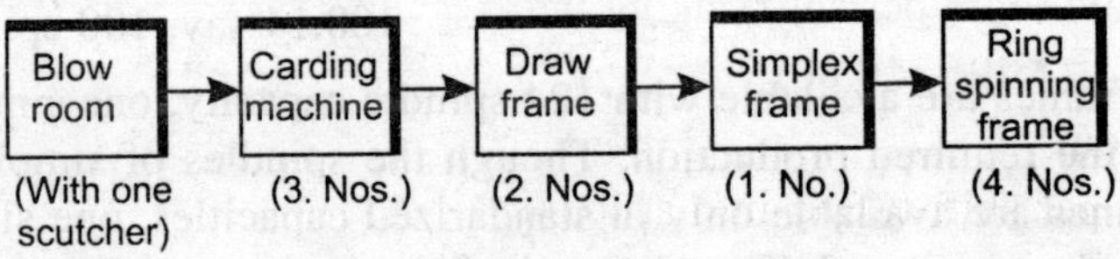

Fig. 1.5

[A comparison of the exact requirement of different machineries with the actual will reveal that there is spare capacity available in all the machineries except in ring spinning frames. This is because of the reason that machines are available only with standardized specifications. If the nature of machines are such that they can be made to order, then perfect balancing can be achieved in the sequence of proposed machinery.]

Note : (manufacturing process in cotton yarn spinning)

Cotton plucked from the fields is processed in ginning mills where cotton is cleaned by removing seeds and trash material. The ginned cotton is the raw material for cotton yarn spinning mill.

The ginned cotton is fed into the blow room machine where the cotton is opened up and cleaned further. The out-put from the blow room machine is in the form of cotton sheets rolled cylindrically. The part of blow room through which the sheet of cotton comes out is called 'scutcher'. There can be one or more scutchers in a blow room depending upon the capacity of the machine.

The sheet of cotton obtained from the blow room is fed into carding machine where the cotton is further cleaned by removing fine foreign material and trash. The output from carding machine is in the form of continuous untwisted strand. (called 'sliver'). The sliver is received in cylindrical drums ccalled 'carding cans' which are shifted to drawing machine (also called draw frame) for further processing.

The input into the drawing machine and also the output from the drawing machine are in the form of 'sliver'. The input into the drawing machine is again opened up inside the drawing machine and the cotton fibres are realigned to facilitate spinning. The cotton sliver obtained from the draw frame will have cotton fibres oriented properly so that further processing will be effective.

The ouptut from the draw frame is fed into the simplex frame (also called 'speed frame') where the thickness of sliver is reduced and a small amount of twist is introduced. The output from simplex frame is in the form of a thick thread which is wound over bobbins.

The output from the simplex frame is fed into ring spinning frame where the thread is reduced to cotton yarn of required thickness (technically called 'count') and twist. The output from the ring spinning frame viz., cotton yartn is also wound over bobbins).

Illustration 1.2

In the problem given in illustration 1.1. above, if there is no restriction on the installed capacity of spindles (i.e., if the industry is delicenced thereby the ceiling of 2,000 spindles is removed), ascertain the optimum combination of machinery for a blow room with one scutcher.

Solution :

Rated output of blow room (with one scutcher) per shift (8 hrs)	: 1,296 kg.
Machine efficiency of blow room	: 80%
Actual output of blow room per shift, taking into account the machine efficiency – (1,296 × 0.80)	: 1,036.80 kg.
Wastage in blow room	: 7.50%
Input to blow room per shift taking into account wastage (1036.80 ÷ 0.925)	: 1.120.86 kg.
Input to carding machines	: 1,036.80 kg.
Output from carding machines per shift taking into account wastage of 5% (1036.80 × 0.95)	: 984.96 kg.
Rated output of carding machine per shift	: 140.30 kg.
Machine efficiency of carding machine	: 85%
No. of carding machines required	: $\left(\dfrac{984.96}{140.30 \times 0.85}\right)$
	: 8.26
	say, 9 carding machines
Input to draw frames per shift	: 984.96 kg.
Output from draw frames per shift taking into account wastage of 1% (984.96 × 0.99)	: 975.11 kg.
Rated output of draw frame per shift.	: 329 kg.
Machine efficiency of draw frame	: 73%
No. of draw frames required	: $\left(\dfrac{975.11}{329 \times 0.73}\right)$
	: 4.06

say, 4 draw frames

Actual output from 4 draw frames (329 × 0.73 × 4) : 960.68 kg.

[Since four draw frames are proposed as against the requirement of 4.06, the actual output from draw frames works out to only 960.68 kg., as against the estimated output of 975.11 kg arrived at earlier.]

Input to simplex frames per shift : 960.68 kg.

Output from simplex frames per shift taking into account wastage of 2% (960.68 × 0.98) : 941.47 kg.

Rated output of simplex frame per shift : 3.59 kg. per spindle

Machine efficiency of simplex frame : 84%

No. of spindles of simplex frame required : $\left(\dfrac{941.47}{3.59 \times 0.84}\right)$

: 321.2

[Since simplex frames are available with spindle capacity of 124 spindles, two simplex frames will be insufficient while three frames will be more than adequate. We can opt for 3 simplex frames to avoid under-utilization of other back process machinery.]

Input to ring spinning frames per shift : 941.47 kg.

Output from ring spinning frames per shift, taking into account wastage of 3% (941.47 × 0.97) : 913.23 kg.

Rated output of ring spinning frame per shift : 213 grams per spindle

Machine efficiency of ring spinning frame : 89.50%

No. of spindles of ring spinning frames required : $\left(\dfrac{913.23}{0.213 \times 0.895}\right)$

: 4,790.

No. of ring spinning frames (with 440 spindles each) required (4,790 ÷ 440) : 10.88

say, 11 ring spinning frames

The desired combination of machinery that will more or less balance each other is as under. (Refer Fig. 1.6)

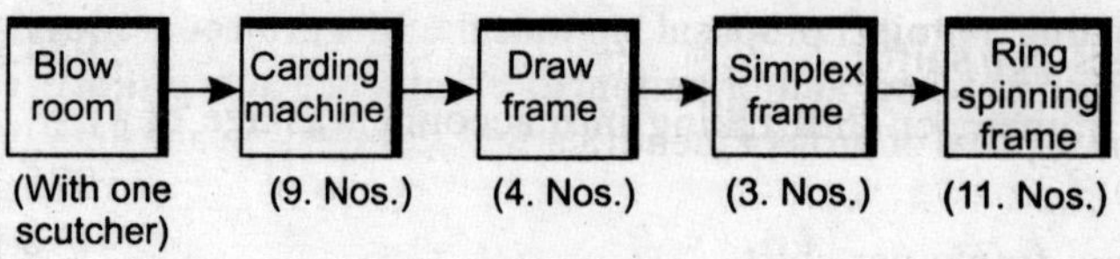

Fig. 1.6

1.5 PROJECT OBJECTIVES

The objectives (or goals) of any project will be,

- To complete the project within the allotted (or budgeted) funds.
- To complete the project within the scheduled time limit.
- To execute the project in such a way that the project meets the quality standards.
- To ensure that the project is completed to the satisfaction of the end users.

Project objectives are to be kept in mind by all the members of the project team through out the period of project implementation. All decisions, whether a major decision or a minor one are to be taken keeping in view the project objectives. The project objectives shall remain as the guiding force for the project team.

Social Objectives

There are certain projects that are implemented purely with social objectives. Such projects, though may have cost, time and quality objectives, rank social objectives as the prime objective. Public health projects, Rural Development projects, irrigation projects etc., are some of the projects that have social objective as the prime objective. In such social projects, the objectives other than the social objective may even be relaxed at times, if that could help achieve the social objectives. For example, if the social objective of irrigating 10000 hectares of land can be fulfilled only if the cost of the project is increased by say, 10% more than what was originally planned, a conscious decision to accommodate the increased cost can be taken as such a decision will help achieve the social objective.

1.6 ESTABLISHING THE PROJECT

The processes involved in establishing a project are:

- Initiating
- Planning
- Organising
- Executing
- Directing & Controlling

Planning, Organising, Executing, Directing and Controlling are applicable for all types of management activities irrespective of whether the management activity relates to project management or management of routine on-going operations. The first and the last processes, viz., initiating and closing are applicable only for project management. Since projects are one-time ventures, they have a beginning and an end which are denoted by the two processes, initiating and closing respectively.

Initiating

This is the starting phase. Initiating involves identification of projects, generation and development of project ideas, formulating a project proposal, appraisal of the project proposal chosen and getting the organisation's commitment and authorization to commence the project. (a detailed account of initiating covering the aspects of project identification, formulation and appraisal is given in para 1.7)

Planning

Planning is the process of deciding in advance about the future course of actions to be taken. In project environment, planning consists of defining all the works required to be carried out so that all the project participants will understand their role in the project team and carry out the work assigned to them. Planning acquires greater relevance to projects since projects consist of non-routine, non-repetitive tasks.

Project planning involves the following:

- Defining the scope of the project in terms of the product/services to be delivered by the project.
- Forecasting and estimating the resources (men, material, money, machines etc.,) required for the project.
- Breaking down the project into managebale activities and arriving at the logical sequence between the different activities. The logical ssequence between the activities is arrived at starting from the terminal activity of the project and working backwards towards the initial activity, deciding in the process, the activities that must be completed before the succeeding activities can be taken up for execution.
- Arriving at an appropriate organisational structure to implement the project .
- Planning for the tentative project completion time. This is done by preparing a master programme schedule that gives the critical dates of major events and control points.
- Scheduling the activities in such a way that the project is completed within the least possible time by carrying out CPM / PERT analysis. (a detailed account of scheduling techniques is given in Unit - III)
- Preparing detailed cost estimates for all the activities.
- Determining the required resources for all the activities.
- Considering the possibilities of adverse occurrences and keeping a contigency plan ready that gives the best cost / benefit results for the given resources.

Organising

Organising is the process of defining and analysing the activities of the enterprise, grouping the activities into distinct areas / departments and establishing the authority-responsibility relationships among them. It also involves organising the resources required for the accomplishment of organisational objectives. In project environment, organising consists of the following sub processes.

Arranging for financial resources

The financial resources required are to be arranged. This shall be done in such a way that availability of financial resources for the execution of the project are timely and adequate.

Building up a project organisation

A project that is well formulated can be of use only if the project is implemented as per the plans proposed. To facilitate execution of projects, the responsibility must be entrusted to a project manager, who must be responsible for coordinating, directing and controlling the implementation of the project. A suitable organisational structure is to be chosen for implementing any project. Personnel required for the project can be drafted from the different functional departments of the organisation. From among the employees of the organisation, those with the required expertise and skill for managing projects can be diverted from their respective functional departments to the project department to look after project related works. When the in-house expertise is not adequate, the work, either in part or full can be entrusted to contractors. Even when the work is entrusted to contractors, the responsibility of getting the work done through the contractors rests with the project team of the organisation. Since projects require time bound completion of activities, a suitable organisational structure to handle the project / projects at hand shall be devised, clearly establishing the authority relationship among the project team members. (a detailed account of organisational structures is given in para 1.8; a detailed account of organising human resources is given in para 1.9; a detailed account of organising contracts is given in para 1.10; a detailed account of organising systems and procedures for project implementation is given in para 1.11).

Team building

As mentioned above, the personnel required for the project can be drafted from within the organisation or the work can be entrusted to contractors as the nature of the project demands. Some times, experts from outside the organisation may be engaged and their services utilized on contract basis. Since execution of projects require special and unique skills, the personnel are to be given the required training, counseling etc., with a view to improving upon their individual and group skills so that they will function as a team for accomplishing the project objectives.

Tying up of material resources, service providers, contractors

The choice of material resources, suppliers of materials, specifications of materials, service providers, contractors etc., is be done by the Project Directorate with the approval of the competent authority (who may the Project Manager, Project Director or the General Manager of the organisation according to the powers entrusted by the organisational set up). These are to be defined in clear terms and documented and circulated among the project executives so that execution of project can proceed smoothly without any hiccup.

Dissemination of information

Effective communication of information among the members of the project team and other project stake holders is vital for the successful execution of a project. A suitable information system should be designed and implemented that is cost effective in collecting and disseminating all relevant information. Apart from being cost effective, the information system should also be accurate and should offer timely information.

Executing

Executing is the process of carrying out the project activities as per the plans. Though the project execution shall as far as possible be done according to the plans originally envisaged, changes / modifications required, if any, are to be incorporated wherever necessary. Since projects are dynamic in nature, flexibility is essential in execution of projects so that the overall objectives of the project are achieved.

Directing and Controlling

Directing is the process of guiding the subordinates towards achieving the organisational goals. It involves issuing orders, directives, instructions and commands. Directing aids the subordinates to know what they are expected to do. In a project environment, the project manager is expected to direct his subordinates through the tools of instructions, orders, requests, guidance, supervision, coaching, advice etc., and to inspire them to achieve the project goals (a detailed account of directing projects is given in para 1.12). Controlling is the process of comparing the actual performance of the project with the planned performance. In other words, it is checking up whether the project progresses exactly in line with what was planned and discovering deviations, if any. (The deviations are often called 'variances'). Once deviations in terms of time, resource and quality parameters are noticed, they must be analysed, the reasons for the deviations are to be identified and suitable remedial measures are to be taken to correct the deviations and to put the project back on the right track. It must be noted that the three important factors over which control is exercised are time, resource and quality. (a detailed account of controlling project implementation is given in para 1.13).

Closing

Projects are temporary endeavors. Hence, they have a beginning and an end. A project comes to an end when the execution is completed and the project objectives are fulfilled. For every project there must be a formal process called 'closing' for declaring the closure of the project. This formal process of closing consists of the following sub-processes.

- Studying and ensuring that the project gives the planned output.
- Closure of contracts, settlement of amounts due to contractors and resolution of any outstanding issues with them.
- Administrative closure which includes passing of information about closure of the project to all the stake holders, employees, executives and to all others who are involved in the project.
- Reallocating men and available material resources, if any to other projects or departments as the case may be.

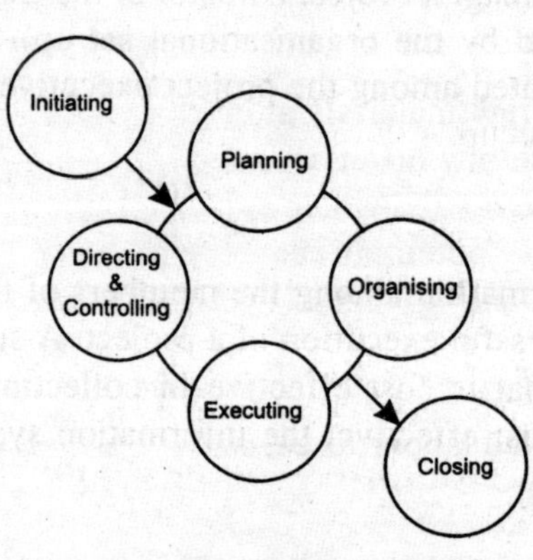

Fig. 1.7

It may be noted that part from initiating and closing that are the first and the last phases of projects, the intermediate four phases can form a cycle. At the exeuction phase, some difficulties or inconsistencies may be come across due to which certain activities of the project may be required to be replanned. Organising men and material resources may pose hurdles and this may necessiate modifications in the plans envisaged. Similarly, the directing & controlling phase may bring out some deviations from the plan and it may at times point towards revising the plans for correcting the deviations and bringing the project performance in tune with the original plan. (Refer Fig. 1.7)

1.7 INITIATING

The scope of initiating a project, which is the first step, is very wide. It involves identification and formulation of projects, appraisal of projects and getting formal approval from the competent authority. A detailed account of project identification, project formulation, project cost estimation and project appraisal are discussed in the following pages.

1.7.1 Project Identification

Identifying a new worthwhile project is a complex problem. It involves careful study from many different angles. Following are some of the sources from which new project ideas may emerge.

Performance of Existing Industries

Performance of existing industries provide a good indication about the health of a particular industry. An analysis of the profitability and break-even point of different industries will offer adequate information about the financial health of different industrial sectors. Though these provide on overall picture of industrial health, one should not be simply carried away by the present performance alone. One should be shrewd enough to read the stage of business cycle in which the different industries stand at a particular time. For example, a particular industrial sector might be performing well, but it might have already crossed its saturation stage and might have already fallen into the decline stage of its business cycle. Entering into such an industry will prove to be disastrous. Similarly, the financial performance of another industrial sector that is not so encouraging might have the potential to grow rapidly, since the industry is only in the beginning stage of its business cycle. Such factors are to be carefully analysed before making a final choice.

Availability of Raw Materials

Easy availability of good quality raw materials at cheaper prices is a definite indication that some projects that can make use of those raw materials may be through of. For example in an area where agriculture in the predominant activity and where agricultural produces (like cereals, vegetables and fruits) are available in plenty, the potential can be made use of by setting up food processing industries. Availability of minerals may give lead to chemical industries.

Availability of Skilled Labour

Based on the locally available skilled labour force, suitable industries that can make better use of the skilled manpower can be identified.

Import/Export Statistics

Import/Export statistics may reveal the potential that remain untapped. Higher proportion of import of a particular product and increasing trend in its import indicates that a product, which can serve as an import substitute can be produced locally. Similarly, higher proportion of export of a particular product and increasing trend in its export indicates high export potential for the product.

Price Trend

The trend in the price of various products/services may give an indication about the demand-supply relationship. If the general price level is rising during the past few years and if the rise in price level of a particular product is steeper than the rise in general price level, it may indicate a demand-supply gap. Further detailed study may be undertaken to ascertain the extent of demand-supply gap.

Data from Various Sources

Various publications of Government, banks and financial institutions, consultancy organizations, manufacturer's associations, export promotion councils, research institutions and international agencies contain data and statistic which may indicate prospective ventures. A study of the working results and balance sheets of existing companies will be useful in knowing the sectors of industry that are performing well. Study of profitability, break-even level, Earnings Per Share (EPS) of various industries may indicate those industries where opportunities exist for new investments.

Research Laboratories

Research laboratories that are engaged in identifying new products/processes often offer new avenues or commercial exploitation. However, proper care should be taken before attempting to go for large scale production of products that have been proved in the laboratory to ensure that conditions under which the products are developed in the laboratory can be simulated in the actual production line also. Failure to correctly simulate laboratory conditions may lead to failure when the product is produced in a large scale.

Consumption Abroad

Those entrepreneurs who are willing to take higher risks can identify projects for the manufacture of products or supply of services which are new to the country, but extensively used abroad. Thus, observing the consumption pattern abroad will help to identify projects with export potential.

Identifying Unfulfilled Psychological Needs

For well established, multi-brand product groups, there may be unsatisfied psychological needs, though the physical needs of the consumers might have been satisfied. Consumer goods like cosmetics, bathing soaps, toothpastes etc., come under this group. New products of this group being introduced and accepted by the consumers indicate the unfulfilled psychological needs of the consumers.

Plan Outlays and Government Guidelines

The Government plays an important role in the economy of a country. Government's plan of outlays in different sectors provide useful pointers towards possible investment opportunities. They indicate the potential demand for goods and services by the different sectors of the economy. The Department of Industrial Development, Government of India, publishes Guidelines to Industries annually which is a valuable source of information to identify the scope for new investments. This publication provides information about production performance of different sectors of industries, the licensed and installed capacity, scope for future exports, location and structure of industries etc.

Analysis of Economic and Social Trends

An analysis of the economic and social trends of the society will be very much helpful in identifying and projecting the demands for various goods and services. For example, the growing desire for leisure points to investment opportunity in recreational activities, rest-houses, resorts etc. The growing awareness of the value of time points to growing demands for fast-foods, high-speed vehicles, better mode of transport, ready-made garments etc.

Possibility of Reviving Sick Units

In any economy there are many industrial units that might have become sick, that are becoming sick, that are in the verge of death and that are weak. An industry that has become weak/sick might still have the capacity to become a financially viable proposition provided the reason for the weakness/

sickness are purely due to factors that are internal to the organization. A promising entrepreneur who has the required entrepreneurial skills can take over a weak/sick unit, revive it and make it to turn around. Infusion of further capital, provision of complementary inputs, revamping the organizational structure etc., are some of the corrective measures that need to be done to nurse an ailing industrial unit and to bring it back to life.

1.7.2 Project Preparation (or Project Formulation)

After having identified a project that prima-facie appears to be a worthwhile project, the project promoter has to further analyse the project to ensure that it has the potential and the investment on it would not go waste, but would yield attractive returns.

Project preparation consists of four stages viz.,

(*a*) Pre-feasibility study
(*b*) Functional studies (or support studies)
(*c*) Feasibility study
(*d*) Detailed project analysis (leading to the preparation of Detailed Project Report)

Pre-feasibility Study

A pre-feasibility study has be following main objectives.

(*a*) To determine whether the project offers a promising investment opportunity.
(*b*) To determine whether they are any aspects of the project that are critical requiring in-depth investigation by way of market surveys, laboratory test, pilot plant test etc.

The preliminary feasibility study should examine.

(*a*) The market potential for the selected product/service, the competitors in the field and their market share, the market forecast, the trading practices in the industry in terms of pricing, Credit, Distribution, Government controls etc.,
(*b*) The technologies available and the technology suitable for the project, the manufacturing facilities required in terms of plant and machinery.
(*c*) The availability, cost and sources of raw materials.
(*d*) The plant location.
(*e*) The plant capacity.
(*f*) The man power requirement in terms of labour, staff and management personnel, their availability and costs
(*g*) The investment required, the return on investment expected, the means of financing the project, the cost of production and commercial profitability.

Pre-feasibility study usually arrives at major parameters like location of project, production capacity, raw material and other inputs etc. It also provides rough estimates of project cost, means of finacning, cost of production, sales revenue, financial profitability, social benefits etc. If the pre-feasibility study indicates that the project is a worthwhile proposition, a feasibility study is taken up. If the pre-feasibility indicates certain areas of project that need a detailed study, such studies are taken up before taking up feasibility study. Such studies are also known as support studies or functional studies.

Support Studies (functional studies)

Support studies may be conducted in any of the following areas.

- Market study
- Raw material/input study
- Project location study
- Plant size study
- Equipment selection study etc.

Pre-feasibility study might arrive at a conclusion that the success of the venture depends upon successfully marketing the product in view of the stiff competition prevailing. In such a case, the need for a detailed market study arises. If the detailed market study reveals that marketing the proposed product successfully would be a difficult proposition, there is no point in taking up feasibility study and the project can be better shelved.

The need for a raw material sstudy might arise when there are many different raw materials available for producing the same product and whose cost of procurement, cost of transportation, continuous availability, quality etc., vary widely.

Project location study might look into aspects like nearness of raw material source, nearness of market for the finished product, cost of transportation of raw material/finished product, nearness to air ports/sea ports, availability of labour etc.

Plant size study is undertaken when there are several technologies available, each with a different economic plant size. The study should also take into account the cost of production with each technology, the extent of market that is available for the finished product etc.

Equipment selection study is undertaken when the sources of supply of equipments and the costs vary very much. The capital cost of the equipments, the operational cost, the after-sales support, the operational efficiency of the plant etc., are some of the factors that are studied under equipment selection study.

Note :

[Support studies can also be undertaken even before the pre-feasibility study when a basic input is a decisive factor in deciding the viability of a project. Support studies can also be done simultaneously with a pre-feasibility study or a feasibility study. When a feasibility study finds out the necessity of a more detailed analysis of certain aspects of the project, a support study for the same way be undertaken.]

Feasibility Study

Before making a final decision to take up a project, the technical, economic, commercial and financial justification of the chosen project shall be ascertained in concrete terms. Feasibility study is also known by the term 'techno-economic feasibility study'.

Technical feasibility : It is normally seen that while most of the projects get a fine screening on their financial prospects, the technical feasibility does not get the required attention. For projects concerning manufacturing activities, the technology proposed to be adapted needs careful consideration. In this connection, the technical feasibility can be evaluated by answering the following questions.

(*a*) Is the technology proposed to be adpated, the latest one?
(*b*) What is the likelihood of the proposed technology becoming obsolete in the near future?
(*c*) Is the technology proposed to be adapted, a proven technology?
(*d*) Is the technology proposed to be adapted available indigenously ?
(*e*) In case of imported technology, is the technology available freely?

In simple terms, Technical feasibility study aims to analyze whether the technology proposed to be adapted is capable of producing the intended goods/services to the requirement and specifications and to the complete satisfaction of the consumers without becoming obsolete in the near future and at the same time proving to be cost effective in the long run.

Economic viability : In simple terms, economy viability is a cursory examination as to whether the investment made on the project will give a satisfactory return to the economy. The major aspects to be looked into are as to whether the project will make better use of available raw material, whether the project will reduce/eliminate the use of some scarce/valuable resources, whether the community as a whole will stand to gain as a result of the project etc.

Commercial feasibility : Before embarking upon any product/service, the scope for successfully marketing the product/service shall be carefully and accurately assessed. If the product/service proposed is new to the industry, conducting a systematic market survey is a pre-requisite for assessing the probable estimates of likely sales. The likely sales estimated shall be well above the proposed plant capacity in order to overcome pitfalls if any that may remain unnoticed in the estimates made. If the product proposed to be manufactured is one that is already being manufactured by many others, the competitive edge that can be gained in terms of quality, price and consumer acceptability etc, needs to be studied.

Financial feasibility : The financial feasibility examines the workability of project proposal in respect of raising finance to meet the investment required for the project, be it equity, (by way of public issue of shares or by other means) or debt, (by way of term loans from financial institutions or by other means). This apart, the financial feasibility also consists of calculations of cost of debt, cost of procuring capital, cost of servicing the debt and equity and anticipated profits to checkup whether the financial benefits expected are in excess of the financial costs involved.

Detailed Project Report (DPR)

The DPR will contain almost the same information contained in the feasibility study (or techno-economic feasibility report), but in a more detailed format. The main idea of preparation of the DPR is to formally communicate the project promoter's decision of venturing a new project to financial institutions (from where financial assistance is sought for funding the project) for their perusal and to Government departments for getting their approvals.

The main sub divisions of a DPR are the following :

1. General information about the project
2. Background and experience of the project promoters
3. Details and working results of industrial concerns already owned/promoted by the project promoters
4. Details of the proposed project
    - plant capacity
    - manufacturing process

- technical known-how/tie-up
- management team for the project
- details of land, building and plant and machinery
- details of infrastructural facilities (such as power, water, transport facilities)
- raw material requirement/availability
- effluents produced by the project/effluent treatment arrangements
- labour requirements/availability

5. Schedule of implementation of the project
6. Project cost
7. Means of financing the project
8. Working capital requirement/arrangements made
9. Marketing and selling arrangements
10. Profitability and cash-flow estimates
11. Mode of repayment of term loan
12. Government approvals, local body consents and other statutory permissions
13. Details of collateral security that can be offered to the financial institution.

TAX INCENTIVES AND PROJECT INVESTMENT DECISIONS

Classical economists were generally of the view that the State should not intervene through its instruments of economic policy to influence the level of investment in the economic system. Till the 1920's, taxes were considered by the States only as resources to maintain internal law and order and to overcome external threats. The Great Depression that swept through the world during the 1930's brought about a radical change in the economic thinking. Lord Keneys, the proponent of monetary economics observed in his famous work "General theory of employment" as under:

....For my own part, I am now somewhat skeptical of the success of a merely monetary policy directed towards influencing the rate of interest. I expect to see the State which is in a position to calculate the marginal efficiency of capital goods on the basis of general social advantage, taking an ever-greater responsibility for directly organizing investment; since it seems likely that the fluctuations in the market estimation of the marginal efficiency of different types of capital, calculated on the principles I have described above, will be too great tobe offset by any practicable changes in the rate of interest....

During the course of time, tax became an effective weapon in the hands of the States of socialistic economies to induce and direct investments. Even in the capitalistic economies, the States started using tax as an instrument for inducing and regulating investments through various tax incentive and tax control measures. For inducing investments, incentives are offered by the States and these incentives for investment stem forth from the following policies of the state:

- Fiscal policy
- Monetary policy
- Commercial policy

Fiscal Policy

Fiscal policy is an important instrument to overcome recession and to control inflation in the economy. In India, fiscal policy of the Government are announced through Budgets. Budget proposals are eventually enacted as statutes by the parliament and periodical amendments are made thereof. (example: Income tax Act)

Examples of incentives that result due to fiscal policy are as under:

- Depreciation
- Tax holiday
- Investment allowance
- Amortisation of preliminary expenses

Monetary Policy

Monetary policy is concerned with changing the supply of money stock and the rate of interest, for the purpose of stabilizing the economy at full potential out put level. At times of recession, monetary policy is used to increase the money supply and reduce the interest rate in order to stimulate aggregate demand in the economy. At times of inflation, monetary policy is used to reduce the aggregate spending by reducing the money supply and raising the interest rate. Interest rate and lending policy are announced by the Central Bank of the country (in India, the Reserve Bank of India).

Examples of incentives that result due to monetary policy are as under:

- Interest rate concession
- Repayment moratorium
- Participation in risk capital
- Reduced security margin
- Refinancing facilities

Commercial Policy

Central Govt. announces major commercial policies. (example: Industrial Policy) These apart, Central and State Governments announce selective, adhoc policies.

Examples of incentives that result due to commercial policy are as under:

- Octroi exemptions
- Subsidised rate for electric power consumed by industries
- Capital investment subsidy
- Sale tax incentives for new industries

TAX PLANNING FOR PROJECT INVESTMENT DECISIONS

The ultimate test of business effectiveness and efficiency is the ratio of resources used to the results obtained, i.e., the ratio of after-tax profits to the share holders' equity.

The following aspects need consideration with regard to tax planning for new investment decisions:

The Income Tax Act

The Income Tax Act, 1922, 1961 and the periodical amendments there of attempt to serve the objectives of the Government by way of giving preferential treatment to selected sectors of the economy, in tune with the economic policy of the Government.

The prevailing income tax structure is as under:

Firms : A firm assessed as such is taxable at the rate of 35% for the assessment years 2005-06. Apart from this, surcharge at the rate of 10% of the income tax is also payable.

Comapnies : The following rates of income tax are applicable for the assessment year 2005-2006. (refer table 1.1)

Table 1.1

Company	*Rates of Income tax*
In the case of domestic company	35%
In the case of foreign company:	
(*a*) Royality received from Government or an Indian concern in pursuance of an agreement made by it with the Indian concern after 31/03/1961 but before 01/04/1976, or fees for rendering technical services in pursuance of an agreement made by it after 29/02/1964, but before 01/04/1976 and where such agreement has, in either case, been approved by the Central Government.	50%
(*b*) Other incomes	40%

Co-operative societies : The following rate are applicable for co-operative societies for the assessment year 2005-2006. (Refer table 1.2).

Table 1.2

Net income range	*Rates of income tax*
Up to Rs. 10,000	10%
Rs. 10,001 to Rs. 20,000	Rs. 1,000/- + 20% for the amount is excess of Rs. 10,000/-
Above Rs. 20,000	Rs. 3,000/- + 30% for the amount is excess of Rs. 20,000/-.

In the following pages we will go through some of imporant sections of the Income Tax Act that affect investment decisions:

Section 10A : A deduction of such profits and gains as are derived by an undertaking from the export of articles or things or computer software for a period of ten consecutive assessment years beginning with the assessment year relevant to the previous year in which the undertaking begins to manufacture or produce such articles of things or computer softward, as the case may be, shall be allowed from the total income of the assessee.

No deduction under section 10A shall be available from the assessment year 2010-11 onwards.

The undertaking must have begun to manufacture or produce articles or things or computer softward during the previous year relevant to the assessment year

(*a*) commencing on or after 01/04/1981, in any free trade zone (*b*) commencing on or after 01/04/1984, in any electronic hardware technology park, or, as the case may be, software technology park

(*c*) commencing on or after 01/04/2001 in any special economic zone

The benefit shall not be available when the undertaking is formed by splitting up, or reconstruction of a business already in existence, or by transfer to a new business of machinery or plant already used for any purpose.

Section 10B : Provisions similar to provisions in section 10A are available in section 10B in respect of deduction of such profits and gains as are derived by a 100% export oriented undertaking from the export of articles or things or computer software.

Section 30 : In respect of premises taken on rent, the actual rent paid by the assessee and, if he has taken to bear the cost of repairs, the expenditure on repairs are permissible deductions against profits and gains of business. In respect of premises owned by the assessee, no deduction is allowable on account of notional rent; amount spent on current repairs is, however, allowed as deduction.

Section 31 : The expenditure incurred current repairs in respect of the plant, machinery and furniture used for business purposes is allowable as deduction under this section. If however, expenditure is incurred to bring into existence an advantage of an enduring nature, or a new capital asset, it can not be regarded as an expenditure on current repairs. Similarly, the premium paid in respect of insurance against risk of damage of destruction of such assets is an allowable deduction.

Section 32 : This section deals with allowancce for depreciation.

From the assessment year 1988-89, depreciation is admissible on the basis of block of assets. To ascertain the amount of depreciation, one should find out the following :

(a) Written down value of block of assets

(b) Rate of depreciation

No depreciation is admissible where the written down value has been reduced to zero, though the. The term 'Block of assets' has been defined by section 2(11) to mean a group of assets falling within a class of assets, comprising (a) tangible assets, being buildings, machinery, plant or furniture and (b) intangible assets, being known-how, patents, copyrights, trade marks, licences, franchises or any other business or commercial rights of similar nature.

Refer table 1.3 for the block of assets and the applicable Rates of depreciation.

Table 1.3

Number	*Nature of Asset*	*Rate of Depreciation*
Block-1	Buildings: Residential buildings other than those covered under Block-3	5%
Block-2	Buildings: Office, factory, godowns or buildings which are mainly used for residential purposes and which are other than those covered under Block-3	10%
Block-3	Buildings: (*a*) used a hotels (*b*) dwelling units each with plinth area not exceeding 80 square metres	20%

Cont.

Table 1.3

Number	Nature of Asset	Rate of Depreciation
Block-4	Buildings: New buildings (Other than those covered under Block-3 with dwelling units each with plinth are not exceeding 80 square metres acquired after 31/03/1999 but before 01/04/2002	40%
Block-5	Buildings: Temporary erections such as wooden structures	100%
Block-6	Furniture: Any furniture/fittings not covered by Block-7	10%
Block-7	Furniture: Furniture and fittings used in hotels, restaurants and boarding houses, schools, colleges and other educational institutions, libraries, welfare centers, meeting halls, cinema houses/theatres and circuses and furnitures and fitting let out on hire for use on the occasion of marriages and similar functions.	15%
Block-8	Plant and machinery: Any plant and machinery not covered by Block 9, 10, 11, 12, 13 or 14.	25%
Block-9	Plant and machinery : (a) motor cars other than those used in a business of running them on hire, acquired or put to use on or after 01/04/1990. (b) Ocean-going ships including dredgers, tugs, barges, survey launches and other similar ships used mainly for dredging purposes and fishing vessels with wooden hull. (c) Vessels ordinarily operating on inland waters being speed boats	20%
Block-10	Plant and machinery: Buses, lorries and taxies used in the business of running them on hire, aeroplanes and machinery used in semi conductor industry and plant or machinery which satisfies conditions of rule 5 (2). Further, it includes commercial vehicle acquired after 30/09/1998, but before 01/04/1999.	40%
Block-11	Plant and machinery: Containers made of glass or plastic used as refills (applicable from assessment year 1997-98)	50%
Block-12	Plant and machinery: Computers (application from the assessment year 1999-2000) and commercial vehicle acquired in replacement of condemned vehicle of 15 years of age which is put to use before 01/04/1999 (if acquired during 01/10/ 1998 and 31/03/1999) or before 01/04/2000 (if acquired during 1999-2000)	60%
Block-13	Plant and machinery: Air pollution control equipments, water pollution control equipments, energy saving devices, renewal energy devices, solid waste control equipments, recyclcing and resource recovery systems, wooden parts used in artifciial silk manufacturing machinery, cinematograph films, bulbs of studio lights, rollers in flour mills, sugar works and steel industry, gas cylinders, wooden match frames, plant used in field operations by mineral oil concerns, some plants used in mines, quarries and salt works, direct fire glass melting furnaces and books owned by assesses carrying on a profession or carrying on business in running lending libraries.	100%

Cont.

Table 1.3

Number	Nature of Asset	Rate of Depreciation
Block-14	Plant and machinery: Ships being vessels ordinarily operating on inland waters other than speed boats.	10%
Block-15	"Know-how": Know-how acquired after 31/03/1998. [Know-how means any industrial information or technique likely to assist in the manufacture or processing of goods or in the working of a mine, oil-well or other sources of mineral deposits (including searching for discovery or testing of deposits for the winning of access thereto)	25%
Block-16	Patnets: Patents acquired after 31/03/1998	25%
Block-17	Copyrights: Copyrights acquired after 31/03/1998	25%
Block-18	Trade marks: Trade marks acquired after 31/03/1998	25%
Block-19	Licences: Licences acquired after 31/03/1998	25%
Block-20	Franchises: Franchises acquired after 31/03/1998	25%
Block-21	Other rights: Any other business or commercial rights of similar nature acquired after 31/03/1998	25%

Set Off and Carry Forward of Unabsorbed Depreciation

From the assessment year 1997-98 depreciation allowance will be set off and carried forward as follows:

(*a*) If in the assessment of the assessee full effect can not be given to depreciation allowance (including accumulated depreciation allowance) owing to profits or gains being less than the allowance or there being no chargeable profit or gain for that previous year, then that unabsorbed depreciation shall be set off against the profits and gains (if any) of any business of profession carried on by him.

(*b*) If the unabsorbed depreciation allowance can not be wholly set off under (a) above, the amount not so set off shall be set off against any other income of the taxpayer for the same year.

(*c*) If the unabsorbed depreciation can not wholly set off, the amount not so set off shall be carried forward to the following assessment year and it shall be set off against the profits and gains of any business or profession carried on by him.

(*d*) The unabsorbed depreciation can be carried forward for 8 assessment years. The time limit of 8 assessment years shall not apply in the case of a company for the assessment year beginning with the assessment year relevant to the previous year in which the said company has become a sick industrial company under section 17(1) of the Sick Industrial Company (Special provisions) Act, 1985 and ending with the assessment year relevant to the previous year in which the entire net-worth (i.e., paid-up, capital plus free reserves) of such company becomes equal to or exceeds the accumulated losses. "Free reserves" for this purpose means all reserves credited out of the profits and share premium account but does not include reserves credited out of revaluation of assets, write back of depreciation provisions and amalgamation.

(*e*) Carry forward of unabsorbed depreciation is possible only if the business or profession for which the allowance was originally computed is continuted to be carried on by him in the previous year relevant for the assessment year in which he wants to set off the unabsorbed depreciation.

Section 35D : This section deals with amortisation of preliminary expenses. Certain preliminary expenses [Section 35D(2)] incurred after 31/03/1970 by an Indian Company or a resident non-corporate assessee before the commencement of business or after the commencement of business in connection with the extension of an industrial undertaking or setting up of a new industrial unit, quality for amortisation. The aggregate amount of the expenditure can not exceed 5% of the cost of the project [as defined under section 35D(3)]. While the ceiling limit of 5% of the cost of the project applies to all assessies, an Indian company is given an option to elect an alternative limit of 5% of the capital employed [as defined under section 35D(3)]. One fifth of the qualifying expenditure is allowable as deduction in each of the five successive years beginning with the year in which the business commences or, as the case may be, the previous year in which extension of the industrial undertaking is completed or the new industrial unit commences production or operation.

Section 35-D2: Expenditures that can be considered as preliminary expenses are as under:

(*a*) expenditure in connection with
 (*i*) preparation of feasibility report
 (*ii*) preparation of project report
 (*iii*) conducting market survey or any other survey necessary for the business of the assessee
 (*iv*) engineering services relating to the business of the assessee;
 Provided the above works are carried out by the assessee himself or by a concern which is for the time being approved in this behalf by the Board.

(*b*) legal charges for drafting any agreement between the assessee and any other person for any purpose relating to the setting up or conduct of the business of the assessee.

(*c*) where the assessee is a company, also expenditure—
 (*i*) by way of legal charges for drafting the memorandum and Articles of Association of the company
 (*ii*) on printing the Memorandum and Articles of Association
 (*iii*) by way of fees for registering the company under the provisions of the Companies Act, 1956
 (*iv*) in connection with the issue, for public subscription, of shares in or debentures of the company,being underwriting commission, brokerage and charges for drafting, typing, printing and advertisement of the prospectus;

(*d*) such other items of expenditure (not being expenditure eligible for any allowance or deduction under any other provision of the Act) as may be prescribed.

Section 35-D3: the term 'Cost of the project' includes;

(*a*) When the assessee incurs the expenditure before the commencement of his business: "the actual cost of the fixed assets, being land. Buildings, leaseholds, plant, machinery, furniture, fittings and railway sidings (including expenditure on development of land and buildings), which are shown in the books of the assessee as on the last day of the previous year in which the business of the assessee commences.

(*b*) Where the assessee incurs the expenditure after the commencement of his business, in connection with the extension of his industrial undertaking or in connection with his setting up of a new industrial unit: "the actual cost of the fixed assets, being land, buildings, leaseholds, plant, machinery, furniture, fittings and railway sidings (including expenditure on development of land and buildings), which are shown in the books of the assessee as on the last day of the previous year in which the extension of the industrial undertaking is completed or, as the case may be, the new industrial unit commences production or operation, in so far as such fixed assets have been acquired or developed in connection with the extension of the industrial undertaking or setting up of the new industrial unit of the assessee.

The term "Capital employed" means:

(*a*) When the assessee incurs the expenditure before the commencement of his business: "the aggregate of the issued share capital, debentures and long term borrowings as on the last day of the previous year in which the business of the company commences".

(*b*) Where the assessee incurs the expenditure after the commencement of his business, in connection with the extension of his industrial undertaking or in connection with his setting up of a new industrial unit.

"...the aggregate of the issued share capital, debentures and long term borrowings as on the last day of the previous year in which the extension of the industrial undertaking is completed or, as the case may be, the new industrial unit commences production or operation, in so far as such capital, debentures and long term borrowings have been issued or obtained in connection with the extension of the industrial undertaking or the setting up of the new industrial unit of the company.

Section 80-IA : The section provides deductions in respect of profits and gainss from industrial undertaking or enterprises engaged in infrastructure development, telecommunication services, industrial parks and power generation, transmission and distribution.

An undertaking providing infrastructure facility must carry on business of

1. developling or
2. maintaining and operating or
3. developing, maintaining and operating any infrastructure facility.

Infrastructure facility means

(*a*) a road,bridge, airport, port, inland water ways and inland ports, rail system or any other public facility of a similar nature as may be notified by the board in this behalf in the Official Gazette.

(*b*) A highway project including housing or other activities being an integral part of the highway project and

(*c*) A water supply project, irrigation project, sanitation and sewerage system.

For undertakings engaged in providing infrastructure facility, subject to other conditions as specified in the Act, 100% of the profit is deductible for the first five years and 30% for the next five years.

An undertaking engaged in providing telecommunication services should have started providing telecommunication services whether basic or cellular, radio paging and domestic satellite service or network of trunking and electronic data interchange service at any time after 31/03/1995, but before 31/03/2000. The deduction of profits available for such undertakings is as under: (Table 1.4)

Table 1.4

Assessee-enterprises	*% of profit deductible*	*Period of deduction commecning from the initial assessment year*
Owned by a Company	100%	First 5 years
Owned by a Company	30%	Next 5 years
Owned by any other person	100%	First 5 years
Owned by any other person	25%	Next 5 years

An undertaking that develops and operates industrial parks must satisfy the following conditions:

(*a*) It develops and operates or maintains and operates an industrial park notified for this purpose in accordance with any scheme framed and notified by the Central Government.

(*b*) The industrial park must start operation during 01/04/1997 and 13/03/2002

The deduction of profits available for such undertakings is similar to the provisions as applicable for undertakings engaged in providing telecommunication services. (Table 1.4)

In respect of power generation/distribution, a new unit must be set up in any part of India for the generation or generation and distribution of power and it begins the operation at any time during 01/04/1993 and 31/03/2003. Alternately, it starts transmission or distribution by laying a network of new transmission or distribution lines at any time between 01/04/1999 and 31/03/2003. Deduction under this section is not available if the undertaking is formed by transfer of machinery or plant previously used for any purpose.

The deduction of profits available for such undertakings is also similar to the provisions as applicable for undertakings engaged in providing telecommunication serviced. (Table 1.4). However, the eligible profit is to be arrived at as under:

Activity	*Profit available for deduction*
Only power generation	Profit from generation of power
Generation and distribution	Profit from generation and distribution of power
Laying a network of new transmission Or distribution lines for starting transmission Distribution of power	Profit derived from laying of such network of new lines for transmission or distribution

Section 80-IB : Section 80-IB provides tax concessions to certain industrial undertakings other than infrastructure development undertakings. Deduction under this section is available for the following:

(*a*) Business of an industrial undertaking. (*b*) Operation of ship. (*c*) Hotels. (*d*) Industrial research. (*e*) Production of mineral oil and (*f*) developing and building house projects.

Refer table below (Table 1.5) for the details of deduction in profits allowed.

Income Tax Relief to Exporters and Foreign Exchange Earners

Section 80HHB: To encourage project exports, section 80HHB provides tax relief to an Indian company or resident tax payer as below :

Table 1.5

	Small Scale Industrial Undertaking	*Industrial under taking (including cold storage) set up in an industrial backward Stage (eight schedule)*	*Industrial under taking (including cold storage) set up in Category "A" Notified backward district*	*Industrial under taking (including cold storage) set up in Category "B" notified backward district*	*Cold chain facility for agricultural produce*
Nature of article to be produced	Any	Any	Other than those given in Eleventh Schedule	Other than those given in Eleventh Schedule	Cold chain facility for agricultural produce
Time limit for commencement of production or operation	Between 01/04/1991 and 31/03/2000		Between 01/10/1994 and 31/03/2000	Between 01/10/1994 and 31/03/2000	Between 01/04/1999 and 31/03/2003
Amount of deduction					
(a) Owned by a company	30% for the first 10 years next 5 years	100% for the first 5 years and 30% for the next 5 years	100% for the first 5 years and 30% for the next 5 years	100% for the first 3 years and 30% for the	30% for the first 10 years
(b) Owned by a co-operative society	25% for the first 12 years next 7 years	100% for the first 5 years and 25% for the next 7 years	100% for the first 5 years and 25% for the next 9 years	100% for the first 3 years and 25% for the	25% for the first 12 years
(c) Owned by any other person	25% for the first 10 years next 5 years	100% for the first 5 years and 25% for the next 5 years	100% for the first 5 years and 25% for the next 5 years	100% for the first 3 years and 25% for the	25% for the first 10 years

Deduction from profits of an amount equal to 50% thereof in computing the total income of the assessee is allowed. The profits and gains must have been derived from the business of

- The execution of a foreign project undertaken by the assessee in pursuance of a contract entered into by him
- The execution of any work undertaken by him and forming part of a project undertaken by any other person in pursuance of a contract entered into by such other person with the Government of a foreign state or any statutory or other public authority of agency in a foreign state or a foreign enterprise.

Section 80HHC : Under the provisions of section 80HHC, of the Income Tax Act, 100% deduction is allowed in respect of profits derived from export of goodsd or merchandise outside India, except mineral oil, minerals and ores and services. As a measure to provide incentive to supporting manufacturers/processors who sell goods to an Export House/Trading House for export, the benefit of deduction under section 80HHC was extended with effect 01/04/1989 to manufacturers and with effect from assessment year 1991-92 to processors.

Section 80RRA : Any remuneration received in foreign currency from any employer or for any service rendered outside India is entitled to a rebate of 75% on such remuneration as is brought into India in convertible foreign exchange with a period of six months from the end of the previous year.

Section 115J: This section deals with what is known as 'Minimum Alternate Tax'. According to this section, not withstanding anything contained in any other provision of the Income Tax Act, where in the case of an assessee being a company [other than a company engaged in the business of generation or distribution of electricity], the total income as computed under the Act in respect of any previous year relevant to the assessment year commencing on or after 01/04/1998 (but before 01/04/1991), is less than 30% of its book profit, the total income of such assessee chargeable to tax for the relevant previous year shall be deemed to be an amount equal to 30% of such book profit. This minimum tax of 30% of book profit is known as 'Minimum Alternate Tax' (MAT). Non-corporate exporters, i.e., proprietary and partnership firms have not to pay MAT.

Some of the other sections of the income tax act that are relevant as under:

- **Section 33AC:** deals with deductions available to an Indian Public Limited Company engaged in the business of operation of ship.
- **Section 35:** deals with deductions available for expenditure on scientific research.
- **Section 35-A:** deals with deductions available for expenditure on acquisition of patent rights and copy rights.
- **Section 36(1)III:** Interest paid on capital borrowed for the purposes of business or profession is allowed as deduction.

Zero Based Project Formulation

An entrepreneur who finds bright prospects for a particular project, goes further into the details about the project formulation in order to study its viability aspects. Any project has many intricacies that are to be carefully assessed for arriving at the formulation that offers the best alternative. There is an inherent instinct in the minds of many project promoters to visualize the project from a particular bench mark. For example, an entrepreneur who finds bright prospects for say 'plastic moulded chairs and furnitures' will start visualizing the capital investment required for the project in terms of cost of land, cost of construction of building, cost of plant and machinery etc., In doing so, he takes it for granted that the elements of the project cost (viz., land, building, plant and machinery, etc.) are essentially required for the project and he proceeds with further estimates and projections based on this assumption. A logical and rational project formulation is possible if the project promoter poses the question "Is it necessary"? to every component of the project cost. This may reveal an entirely different aspect of the project. Thus, the thinking in the minds of the project promoter should start from zero base in order not to err on project formulation.

Why to Invest in Fixede Assets at All?

When we say that the project promoter should ask the question "Is it necessary"? for all the components of the project cost, the same logic is also applicable for the project cost as a whole. Thus, the very first question to be posed is—"Is it worth investing in fixed assets for the creation of manufacturing facilities"? The product proposed to be manufactured may be such that there are already many manufacturers in the field and mere trading may work out to be a more profitable venture as compared to setting up a new plant by investing in fixed assets. In such a case, the project reduces to entering into tie-up with existing manufacturers for dealership/distributorship, arranging for godown for stocking the goods, arranging fleet of vehicles for procurement and delivery of goods etc. Such a venture may be a proposition with better return and lesser investment as compared to setting up the required manufacturing facility with heavy investment and not so attractive return.

Consideration of Investment on Components of Project Cost

When it is conceived that going for own production will offer a better return and competitive edge and will prove to be advantageous in the long run, the next step to be analysed is as to what are all the investments that are absolutely essential and what can be avoided/deferred. Investment in building is a major component of the project cost in many projects. It is to be studied as to whether construction of building is absolutely necessary. If the manufacturing facilities can be housed in a leasehold building, the chances of getting a suitable building on lease and its effect on project profitability vis-a-vis the project profitability considering investment on bulding need to be studied before taking a decision to go for investment on building. If the project needs a building of unique nature and getting such a suitable building on lease is not possible, the investment on building can be accepted and further considerations as to the nature of construction, area of construction etc., are to be studied with a view to bringing down the cost of construction to the minimum, without compromising on the functional requirements that are to be satisfied by the building.

Coming to the investment on plant and machinery, there are many aspects that need consideration. The cost of plant and machinery should be studied with reference to the available brands/models/specifications and those that are best suited for the project are to be chosen. A high precision, high cost machinery may not always be the one that is desirable for the project. The precision level required of the machine may be below that of the best available machine in the market, but still it may serve the purpose well. Such situations will lead to choosing machines of moderate cost with moderae precision level. Another aspect that needs consideration is the capacity utilization of the plant and machinery. The type and nature of plant and machinery chosen should be such that all the plant and machinery are utilized to their fullest capacity by the project. If any machine lies idle, it indicates inefficient planning and investment on plant and machinery.

Some machines may come with a certain minimum capacity. If the minimum capacity available for a particular machine is more than what is needed for the project, such machine, if included in the project, will remain mostly idle. The chances of getting such machining works done through job-order basis from other industrial units (i.e., sub-contracting) may be studied so that investment on such a machine can be avoided, which will improve the profitability of the project. Apart from studying the option of sub-contracting for those machines that will not be put into optimum use, the scope for sub-contracting other works also wherever it works out profitable is to be examined. For example, the cost of a particular machine might have increased heavily in the recent past and those industrial units that had acquired similar machines in the past could be in a position to undertake job-works at cheaper rates or could hire out such machines at cheaper rents in view of their comparatively lower capital investment. Thus, the pros and cons of new investment on plant and machinery vis-a-vis opting for sub-contracting is to be studied before arriving at the investment pattern on plant and machinery.

In respect of electricals, the investment of captive power plants (i.e., power generators) deserves major consideration. It is not always found necessary to have a captive power generator of capacity equal to the total connected power load. Some of the equipments need not be always in operation and power requirement for such equipments can be deducted while arriving at the capacity of powwer generator required. Careful analysis is required regarding the production processes, the power requirement of each process and the processes that can be stopped with out affecting the out put of the plant etc., in order to arrive at the capacity of captive power generator.

Thus, each element of the fixed cost requires an unbiased, rational study with out any pre-conceptions in order to arrive at a decision as to their necessity for inclusion in the project or otherwise and a project formulated with such an analysis will, in all probability, prove to be a successful venture since unwated costs are avoided.

1.7.3 Project Appraisal

Project appraisal is a process of detailed examination of several aspects of a given project before recommending the same. The institution that is going to fund the project has to satisfy itself before providing financial assistance for the project. The lending institution has to ensure that the investment on the proposed project will generate sufficient returns on the investments made and that loan amount disbursed for the implementation of the project will be recovered along with interest within a reasonable period of time. The concept of security oriented lending has given way for the introduction of purpose oriented lending. Purpose oriented lending can be successful only if a detailed appraisal of the project is done before committing funds on the project. The various aspects of project appraisal are explained in this chapter.

(a) Technical Appraisal

Technical appraisal broadly involves a critical study of the following aspects, viz.,

1. Selection of process/technology
2. Scale of operations
3. Raw material
4. Technical know-how
5. Collaboration agreements
6. Product mix
7. Selection and procurement of plant and machinery
8. Plant layout

9. Location of the project
10. Project scheduling and implementation.

Selection of Process/Technology

For manufacturing a product, more than one process/technology may be available. For example, steel can be manufactured either by the Bessemer process or by the open-hearth process. Cement can be manufactured either by the wet process or by the dry process.

The choice of technology also depends upon the quality and quantity of the product proosed to be manufactured. If the quantity required to be produced is large, mass production techniques should be followed and the relevant technology is to be adopted. The quality of the product depends upon the use to which it is meant for. A product of pharmaceutical grade or laboratory grade should have high quality and hence sophisticated production technology is required to achieve the desired quality. Products of commercial grade do not need such high quality and the technology can be chosen accordingly. There is no point in choosing a ophisticated technology meant for getting high quality products, where the product is meant for commercial use for which high quality is not required. Such unwarrented emphasis on quality will only land the project in trouble since the consumers will not be ready to pay higher price merely for the sake of high quality which they do not really need.

In the choice of technology, as for as possible, the latest technology should be chosen provided there are no other constraints. However, in choosing the latest technology it must be seen that the technology has been proved successful for large-scale production at factory level. Replying only on the technology proven in the laboratory is to be avoided.

A new technology that is protected by patent rights etc., can be obtained either by licensing arrangement or the technology can be purchased outright. Under licensing arrangement, the right to use the patented technology and to get the related technical know-how are mutually agreed upon between the licensor and the licensee. Getting a technology under licensing arrangement is suited when the cost of purchasing the technology outright is huge/when there is a rapid technological advancement in the field with the result that is every possibility of the technology becoming outdated shortly.

Technology can be purchased outright if the cost of acquisition is affordable, if there is no likelihood of significant improvement in technology in the foreseeable future and if the technology can be implemented and maintained without the need for continuous support from the seller of the technology.

Approrpriate technology: A technology appropriate for one country may not be the ideal one for another country. Even within a country, depending upon the location of the project and other features, two different technologies may be ideal for two similar projects set up by two different firms at two different locations. The choice of a suitable technology for a project calls for identifying what is called the 'appropriate technology'.

The term 'appropriate technology' refers that technology that is suitable for the local economic, social and cultural conditions. Appropriate technology can be identified by asking the following questions.

- Does the technology makes use of the locally available raw material ?
- Can the technology by implemented and maintained by the locally available man power ?
- Is the technology in tune with the local social and cultural conditions ?
- Does the technology protects ecologicalbalance etc. ?

For example, textile yarn spinning frames manufactured in Europe were designed in such a way that the manuallabour requirement to operate the machine is kept at the minimum while the electric power consumption by the machine is allowed to stand at a higher level. This technology is suited for European conditions where the cost of electric power is comparatively cheaper while getting manual labour is comparatively costlier. Indian conditions demand an opposite proposition since manual labour can be procured at a comparatively cheaper cost while the cost of electric power is comparatively higher. Hence, the choice of appropriate technology should be dealt with adequate care.

Scale of operations

Scale of operations is signified by the size of the plant. The plant size mainly depends on the market for the output of the project. Economic size of the plant varies from project to project. Economic size of the plant for a given project can be arrived at by an analysis of capital and operating costs as a function of the plant size. Though the economic size of the plant for a given project can be theoretically arrived at by the above process, the final decision on the plant size is circumscribed by a number of factors, the main factor being the promoter's ability to raise the funds required to implement the project. If the funds required to implement the project at its economic size is beyond ther promoter's capacity to arrange for and if the economic size is too big a size for the promoter to manage, the promoter is bound to limit the size of the project that will suit his finance and managerial capabilities. Whenever a project is proposed to be set up at a size below its economic size, it must be analyzed carefully as to whether the project will survive at the proposed size (which is below the economic size). Performance of existing units operating at below economic size (will throw some light on this aspect.

Other factors like special problems of fabrication of equipments, transportation and erection of equipments, problems associated with availability of production inputs on a sustained basis etc., also impose restrictions on the plant size.

Raw Material

Selection of raw material: A product can be manufactured using alternative raw materials and with alternative processes. The process of manufacture may sometimes vary with the raw material chosen. If a product can be manufactured by using alternative raw materials, the raw material that is locally available may be chosen. Since the manufacturing process and the machinery/equipment to be used also to a larger extent depend upon the raw material, the type of raw material to be used should be chosen carefully after analyzing various factors like the cost of different raw materials available, the transportation cost involved, the continuous availability of raw material etc. Since the process of manufacture and the machinery/equipments required depend upon the raw material used, the investment on plant and machinery will also to some extent depend upon the raw material chosen. Hence the cost of capital investments required on plant and machinery should also be studied before arriving at a decision on the choice of raw material.

For example, precipitated calcium carbonate can be produced using either lime stone or shell-lime as the raw material. Shell-lime will be available near seashore while lime store will be available in areas with lime stone deposit. Since the quantity of raw material to be handled is comparatively large, the cost of transporting the raw material from the place of availability to the factory site will also be considerable. Also, though the end product is the same, there will be minor changes in the plant and machinery requirement for processing the different raw materials viz., limestone and shell lime. All these factors are to be analyzed before choosing the raw material to be used and the appropriate process of manufacture.

Technical Know-how

When technical know-how for the project is provided by expert consultants, it must be ascertained whether the consultant has the requisite knowledge and experience and whether he has already executed similar projects successfully. Care should be exercised to avoid self-styled, inexperienced consultants. Necessary agreement should be executed between the project promoter and the know-how supplier incorporating all essential features of the know-how transfer. The agreement should be specific as to the part played by the know-how supplier (like taking out successful trial run, acceptable quality of final product, imparting necessary training to employees in the production process, taking out successful commercial production, perfomance guarantee for a specified number of years after the start of commercial production etc). The agreement should also include penalty clauses for non-performance of any of the conditions stipulated in the agreement. Payment of know-how fee should as far as posssible be made in stages along with the progress of the project and it is the normal practice to retain a portion of the know-how fee and to release the same only after compliance of all the conditions stipulated in the agreement.

Collaboration Agreements

If the project promoters have entered into agreement with foreign collaborators, the terms and conditions of the agreement may be studied as explained above for know-how supply agreement. Apart from this, the following additional points deserve consideration.

(*a*) The competence and reputation of the collaborators needs to be ascertained through possible sources including the Indian embassies abroad and the collaborator's bankers.

(*b*) The technology proposed to be imported should suit to the local conditions. A highly sophisticated technology, which does not suit local conditions, will be detrimental to the project.

(*c*) The collaboration agreement should have necessary approval of the Government of India.

(*d*) There should not be any restrictive clause in the agreement that import of equipment/machinery required for the project should be channelised through the collaborators. There should also be no clause for payment of commission and fee for the procurement of imported equipment/machinery.

(*e*) The design of the machinery should be made available to the project promoter to facilitate future procurement and/or fabrication of the machinery in India at a later stage. A knowledge of the design of the machinery will also help in proper maintenance of the machinery.

(*f*) The agreement should provide a clause that any dispute arising out of interpretation of the agreement, failure to comply with the clauses contained in the agreement etc., shall be decided only by courts with in India.

(*g*) The collaboration agreement should not impose any restriction on the exports of goods produced. It must be open to the project promoter to explore any market that is advantgeous to him, including export markets in any part of the globe.

(*h*) It must be ensured that the collaboration agreement does not infringe upon any patent rights.

(*i*) If there is financial participation in the projects by the collaborator, its effect on the management of the unit and transfer of payment/payment of interest to the collaborator may be studied.

(*j*) It is better to have a buy-back arrangement with the technical collaborator. This is to ensure that the collaborator would be serious about the transfer of correct know-how and would ensure quality of the output. Buy-back arrangement also helps the unit to release the pressure on the need for valuable foreign exchange. Since there is an assured market for the output, the promoter need not worry about identifying market for his product immediately after the project is on stream. Market for the product, both indigenous and export markets, can be explored duirng the course of time.

Product Mix

Customers differ in their needs and preferences. Hence variations in size and quality of products are necessary to satisfy the varying needs and preferences of customers. In order to enable the project to produce goods of varying size nature and quality as per the requirements of the customers, the production facilities should be planned with an element of flexibility.

Such flexibility in the production facilities will help the organization to change the product mix as per customer requirements, which is very essential for the survival and growth or any organization. Adding flexibility to the production facilities is not without any cost. It involves additional cost.

However, a cost benefit analysis keeping in view the long-term benefits will indicate the need for such additional cost to be incurred.

For example, a plastic container manufacturing industry can be planned to have more number of dies of different sizes, so that goods of different sizes can be produced according to the market requirement. This will give the unit a competitive edge.

Selection and Procurement of Plant and Machinery

Selection of machinery: The machinery and equipment required for a project depends upon the production technology proposed to be adopted and size of the plant proposed.

Capacity of each machinery is to be decided by making a rough estimate, as under; thumb rules should be avoided.

(*a*) Take into consideration the output planned.
(*b*) Arrive at the machine hours required for each type of operation.
(*c*) Arrive at the machine capacity after giving necessary allowances for machinery maintenance/ break down, rest time for workers, set up time for machines, time lost during change of shifts etc.
(*d*) After having arrived at the capacity of the machinery as above, make a survey of the machinery available in the market with regard to capacity and choose that capacity which is either equal to or just above the capacity theoretically arrived at.

In case of process industries, the capacity of the different machines used in various stages should be so selected that they are properly balanced.

The following points should be considered for selection of machinery.

(*a*) Apart from the main process machinery, equipments required for supply of utilities, quality control, effluent disposal, material handling equipments shall also be identified and purchased.
(*b*) Along with the purchase of main machinery, adequate numbers of tools and spares are also to be purchased and stocked.
(*c*) If necessary, stand by arrangements may be made for critical equipments.
(*d*) Where are investment on a particular machine is high and its utility does not justify the huge investment, the chances of getting such work done through job orders from other outside agencies should be explored so that the heavy investment can be safely avoided.

(*e*) As far as possible, machinery suppliers or their authorized agents shall be asked to attend to the erection work of the machinery since they will be knowing the intricacies involved.

(*f*) Practical constraints that exist are to be given due attention before selecting certain machinery. If availability of power is limited in the proposed location of the factory, care should be exercised in selecting power intensive equipments like electric ovens, electric furnaces etc., so that their power requirements matches with the power availability. If necessary, replacing such electric power intensive machinery with oil fired machinery (which use furnace oil as fuel instead of electricity) may be thought of. Similarly while selecting highly sophisticated machinery which require highly skilled personnel to operate them, the availability of skilled manpower should be studied.

(*g*) If the promoters propose to purchase second hand machinery, it's working condition, estimated future life and its value are to be ascertained through a competent engineer. It must be ensured that the machinery is free from any charge to banks, financial institutions or other creditors.

Procurement of machinery : Plant and machinery form the backbone of any indusry. The quality of output depends upon the quality of machinery used in processing the raw materials (apart from the quality of raw material itself). Uninterrupted production is again ensured only by high quality machines that do not break down so often. Hence no compromise should be made on the quality of the machinery and the project promoter should be on the look out for the best brand of machinery available in the market. The performance of the machinery functioning elsewhere may be studied to have a first hand information before deciding upon the machinery supplier. Comparison of price quoted by a few standard and reputed machinery suppliers is normally done before deciding upon the supplier. It is not always necessary to choose the supplier who has quoted the least price among all. Other factors like reputation of the supplier, delivery schedule, after sales-service offered, performance gurantee, payment terms etc., need consideration before choosing a supplier.

Plant Layout

The efficiency of a manufacturing operation depends upon the layout of the plant and machinery. Plant-layout is the arrangement of the various production facilities within the production area. Plant layout should be so arranged that it ensures steady flow of production and minimizes the overall cost.

The following factors should be considered while deciding plant-layout.

(*a*) The layout should be such that future expansion can be done without much alteration of the existing layout.

(*b*) The layout should facilitate effective supervision of work.

(*c*) Equipments causing pollution should be arranged to be located awy from other plant and machinery. For example generator is a major source of noise pollution. Generator can not be placed amidst other machinery since the noise generated will spoil the entire atmosphere of the plant. Hence generally generator is housed in a separate shed away from the main plant. Equipments that generate fumes are normally placed separately, preferably along the side of wlls so that proper exhaust and ducting arrangements can be made easily for driving out the fumes.

(*d*) There should be adequate clearance between adjacent machinery and between the wall and machinery to enable undertaking of regular inspection and maintenance work.

(*e*) The plant layout should ensure smooth flow of men and material from one stage to another.

(*f*) The plant layout should be one that offers maximum safety to the personnel working inside the plant.

(*g*) The plant layout should provide for proper lighting and ventilation.

(*h*) The plant layout should properly accommodate utilities like power and water connections and provisions for effluent disposal.

Location of Projects

Choosing the location for a new project is to be done taking many factors into account.

The study for plant location is done in two phases. First a particular region/territory is chosen that is best suited for the project. Then, within the chosen region, the particular site is selected. Thus, we may say that there are two major factors viz., Regional factors and site factors, to be considered.

Regional factors : (*a*) *Raw materials:* Raw materials normally constitute about 50 to 60 percent of the cost of the final product. Hence it is important that the cost of the raw material should be minimum. To procure raw material at minimum cost, the plant must be located nearer to the place where raw material is available so that transportation cost will be reduced and the number of middle men involved in the procurement process also will be reduced. The transportation cost will constitute a major portion of the raw material cost if the raw material is bulky and procured from distant places. This is the reason why sugar factories are located in sugarcane growing areas, cement factories are located nearer to areas where lime stone is available and steel mills are located nearer to places where iron ore and coal deposits are avalable. Another common example is brick and tile industry which is set up on the land where clay suitable for the manufacture of brick/tile is available. If the raw material is bulky and is imported from abroad, the ideal location of plant will be nearer to port. Thus, when the raw material is bulky nearness to the place of availability of raw material acts as a major deciding factor in choosing the plant location.

(*b*) *Proximity to market :* If transportation of the finished product is more difficult (due to the special nature of the finished product) than trasnporting the raw material and also if the cost of transporting the finished product is more as compared to the transportation cost of raw material, it is advantageous to locate the plant nearer to the consumers i.e., nearer to the market. 'Special nature of finished product' mentioned above deserves special consideration. The finisshed product may be one that is fragile and difficult to handle (glassware, clayware/porcelain products); the finished product may be one that is perishable in short duration (cake, bread, pastry products). Such products of special nature make it mandatory to locate the plant nearer to the market.

Soft drink bottling plant is another example for locating the plant nearer to the market. The soft drink concentrate which is the main raw material is not bulk in quantity and can be transported to the plant with ease, whereas after manufacture, the quantity of soft drink increases manifold (since the soft drink concentrate is diluted during the manufacturing process) and more over, transportation of soft drink in bottles is to be done with care.

(*c*) *Availability of labour :* Though unemployed people are in plenty in our country, this does not mean that there will be no problem in getting the labour force required for the project. Availability of skilled labour is what is the criterion rather than availability of unemployed who are unemployable! If the project needs skills of general nature, people can berecruited and trained to the requirement. If the project needs skills of special nature, getting adequate skilled labour will not pose any problem if the plant is located in areas where skilled labour force is available. People in different areas develop special skills in different activities by virtue of the work culture prevailing in their respective areas. Skilled labourers required for running hosiery garment making factories are available in plenty in Tirupur (a town situated near Combatore). This is because of the reason hosiery garment industry is in existence in Tirupur for over 40 years. It is not always impossible to hire skilled labourers from distant places. However, the following difficulties may be encountered.

1. The labourers may demand a higher wage since they would like to be compensated for leaving their birth place and migrating to a new location.
2. Continuous availability of skilled labourers may be affected.
3. The organization may have to provide additional benefits like housing and recreational facilities in order to retain the labourers.

This may add to the cost of the project as well as cost of production.

(*d*) *Availability of supporting industries :* If a firm has proposed to get some of the production operations done from out side, there must be suitable industries existing in the surrounding area to undertake such subcontracting works. For example, a project may envisage to produce a product that may require a smooth finish for which it may need a surface finishing machine. The promoter may feel that the cost of surface finishing machine is on the higher side and it is more economical to get surface finishing job done from outside by subcontractors, instead of investing heavily on the machine. This can be made possible only if there are firms around that are ready to undertake such subcontract works.

The reverse phenomenon is also true i.e., if a project is set up mainly with the idea of doing sub contract work to a major industrial establishment, the project should be located as for as possible nearer to the major industry that is going to offer sub contracts. This can be seen by the existence of many ancillary industrial units surrounding major industrial establishments like BHEL, NTPC, etc.,

(*e*) *Availability of infrastructural facilities :* Availability of power, water, and transport facilities are the important aspects to be considered under this head.

Power: Power intensive industries should be located at places where regular power supply is available. It must be seen wwhether power supply in the area is made available through industrial feeder line. (There are places where power lines may be agricultural feeder lines. Power supply through agricultural feeder lines are available only for a shorter period of time in a day).

If the manufacturing process is such that sudden power failure may disturb the manufacturing activities and may cause considerable losses, it is always advisable to keep power generators as a standby. In such cases, the cost of generator should be included in the project cost. For example in plastic goods manufacturing industries, if there is sudden power failure, the molten material in the extruder will get cooled and solidified. After the resumption of power supply, the extruder is required to be heated up for a considerable length of time to bring the machine into operation. This also will result in wastage of raw material. In such situations, if power generator is available, the production can be continued without any interruption even if there is sudden power failure. In case of power intensive industries, powwer supply is given from high tension power lines for which a voltage step-down transformer is required to be erected. The cost of the step-down transformer and other related installations are to be borne only by the project promoters and hence these should be provided for while arriving at the project cost.

Water : Water requirement for the project should be correctly arrived at. After having arrived at the water requirement, it must be checked if the required quantity of ground water can be obtained from the site. The level of ground water table may be checked by observing the open wells nearby. The likely depth of water table and the likely yield of water from the site can be ascertained with the services of qualified water diviners. Apart from the quantity of water, the quality of water also must be suitable. If the industry is going to use water in its manufacturing process and if the quality of water to be used has a bearing on the quality of the output, the quality of the ground water is to be tested in the laboratory to ascertain its suitability. For example, dyeing industries need soft water for their manufacturing process. If the ground water available is hard it can not be straightaway used for the dying process. The chances of getting soft water suitable for the process from outside is to be found out. Alternatively, the hardness of the groundwater can be removed by installing a water softening plant. The comparative cost advantages of the two alternatives are to be worked out before deciding upon the alternative best suited for the industry.

Steam boilers that are used in many processing industries need only soft water. If the water available is not soft in nature, a water softening unit to treat the feed water to be used in the boiler is to be necessarily included in the project. Using of hard water for boilers will lead to formation of scales inside the boiler will reduce the efficiency of the boiler and may even jeopardize the safety of boiler operation.

Transport Facilities : Transportation costs are incurred in two stages. Firstly, for the transport of raw materials and fuel into the factory site and secondly for the movement of the finished goods from the factory site. Thus, if a site is so located that the industry is to incur additional transportation cost.

(*f*) **Locating industries in backward/most-backward ares, growth centre areas :** Goverment identifies regions which are lacking in industrial development and notify them as backward areas most-backward areas, etc., Government also notifies growth centres which have potential for high growth. The Government offers many incentives in the form of capital subsidy, sale tax concessions, concessional financial assistance etc., for industries set up in these areas with the objective of ensuring dispersal of industrial activity throughout the country and to reduce regional disparities in industrial development. The incentives offered by the Government canbe availed by setting up projects in such notified areas. However, the project promoter should not merely get carried away by the attractiveness of the incentives and concessions available, but should make a judicious and unbiased analysis of all other factors. Normally such notified areas lack in infrastructure and other facilities, which is the reason why these areas remain undeveloped and industrially backward. If the advantages out weigh the shortcomings, locations coming under such notified backward areas can be chosen for the project.

(*g*) **Climatic factors :** Climatic factors have some influence in certain type of industries. Textile spinning mills, for example require high humidity for the spinning of cotton yarn. Hence places with high ranges of humidity are suitable for locating cotton-spinning mills. Though in areas of lesser humidity, cotton spinning mills can be set up by installing humidification plants, this will only add to the capital investment on plant and machinery and will also increase the cost of production due to increased expenses towards electric power for operating the humidfication plant. Similarly, paperboard industries find hot and dry climate more suitable since paperboards that are in wet condition immediately after production can be sun-dried inopen atmosphere.

Site Factors : After having chosen a region that iss comparatively more advantageous for the location of a project, for choosing a particular site in the chosen region, considerations like cost of land, suitability of land, availability and suitability of ground water, facilities for effluent disposal etc., are to be taken into account.

In general, industrial projects require considerable extent of land. If the unit cost of land is high, the investment required to be made on land may become prohibitively high, which should be looked into. Apart from cost of land, the soil suitability also plays a major orle. Since industrial projects mostly involve heavy machinery which need strong foundations, the load bearing capacity of the soil should be sufficient to withstand the pressure. Clay and black cotton soil are not suitable because of poor load bearing capacity and because of swelling nature when exposed to moisture.

The nature of effluent depends upon the type of the industry. If the effluent is of polluting nature, it has to be properly treated before disposal. Necessary consent for effluent disposal should be obtained from the concerned authorities. If the effluent is of polluting nature (as in the case of leather industries, chemical industries, paper plants etc.) there may be restrictions even for the dispoâl of the treated effluent if the location of the factory is nearer to water courses. Pollution control authorities some times tipulate conditions that major polluting industries should not be located within a minimum stipulated distance from natural watercourses. Hence, before choosing the site location for polluting industries, the possibility of getting consent from the concerned authorities should be ascertained beforehand. In case of projects that produce effluents that are permitted to be disposed off only after proper treatment, necessary effluent treatment plants should be included in the cost of the project.

Choice of location : Decision on the choice of location for the given project is to be made after considering the points enumerated above. In view of the number of factors involved, deciding upon the project location is a complex problem. The problem is compounded further because of the existence of both tangible and intangible factors. If there are only tangible factors, the solution to the problem can be arrived at by mathematical means. Arriving at a decision combining the tangible and intangible factors involve subjective estimate.

Choice of location based on tangible factors : When tangible factors alone are considered, an ideal location is one for which the cost of setting up the project, cost of procuring raw materials, cost of processing the raw material into finished product and cost of distributing the finished product to the customers are minimum.

Let us study the concept by way of an example.

Illustration 1.3

A team of five entrepreneurs have joined together and constituted a partnership firm for setting up a new project for the manufacture of dry cell batteries. They have studied many different locations for the project and finally, after weighing the pros and cons have arrived at four different locations A, B, C and D which rank in the top. The tangible and intangible factors related to the four locations are as under:

[Locations]

Factors	*A*	*B*	*C*	*D*
Tangible factors:-				[Amount in rupees]
a. Investment on land and land development	1,00,000	1,20,000	1,50,000	70,000
b. Investment on Building	7,00,000	8,00,000	7,50,000	8,00,000
c. Investment on plant and machinery including transport and erection charges	33,00,000	32,00,000	34,00,000	33,00,000
d. Expenses on raw materials (per annum)	20,00,000	24,00,000	26,00,000	22,00,000
e. Salaries and wages (per annum)	8,00,000	8,00,000	8,50,000	9,00,000
f. Expenses on utilities (per annum)	7,00,000	5,00,000	4,00,000	3,00,000
g. Distribution expenses (per annum)	3,00,000	1,00,000	2,50,000	50,000
h. Sales (per annum)	60,00,000	53,00,000	55,00,000	60,00,000

Factors	*A*	*B*	*C*	*D*
Intangible factors:-				
a. Attitude of labourers	Poor	Indifferent	Good	Good
b. Recreational facilities	Good	Good	Bad	Bad
c. Community facilities like hospital, education, communications, transportation	Fair	Poor	Fair	Good

Identify the suitable location considering only the tangible factors.

Solution:

When tangible factors of the different locations are considered, rate of return on investment comes handy as a leading indicator to decide upon the choice of the location.

Locations

[Amount in rupees]

Factors	*A*	*B*	*C*	*D*
Total expenses $[d+e+f+g]$	38,00,000	38,00,000	41,00,000	34,50,000
Profit [Sales – Total expenses]	22,00,000	15,00,000	14,00,000	25,50,000
Total investment $[a+b+c]$	41,00,000	41,20,000	43,00,000	48,00,000
Return of investment [%]	53.66%	36.41%	32.56%	53.13%
i.e., $= \dfrac{(\text{Profit} \times 100)}{[\text{Total investment}]}$				

Based on the return on investment, locations 'B' and 'C' score comparatively less and hence either of location 'A' or 'D' can be chosen. Out of these two locations, a final decision canbe arrived at taking the intangible factors into account.

Choice of location based on tangible and intangible factors: When the choice of location is to be made taking into account both the tangible and intangible factors, the solution to the problem takes the nature of a subjective decision in view of the reason that the intangible factors can not be accurately quantified. The technique devised by P.W. Bridgeman (called Bridgeman's Dimensional Analysis) can be best applied to arrive at a solution for the choice of location combining tangible and intangible factors.

Dimensional Analysis: This method of analysis is used for comparing two locations and deciding the better of the two locations, keeping in view both tangible and intangible factors.

Let

A and B are the two locations

CA_1, CA_2, CA_3 .... are the different costs associated with tangible factors of location 'A' and/or the different scores associated with intangible factors of location 'A'.

CB_1, CB_2, CB_3 .... are the different costs associated with tangible factors of location 'B' and/or the different scores associated with intangible factors of location 'B'.

W_1, W_2, W_3, ... are the weights given to the tangible and intangible factors.

Then the relative merit of location A and location B iss given by,

$$\left(\frac{CA_1}{CB_1}\right)^{W_1} \times \left(\frac{CA_2}{CB_2}\right)^{W_2} \times \left(\frac{CA_3}{CB_3}\right)^{W_3} \times .....$$

If the value of the above relationship is more than 1, it means that location 'A' gains more points when both tangible and intangible factors are combined which in turn means the location 'A' is comparatively costlier than location 'B' and hence location 'B' is preferable to location 'A'.

Illustration 1.4

In the illustration 1.3 and given above, choose the ideal location between 'A' and 'D' using dimensional analysis.

Solution:

For applying dimensional analysis, scores for the intangible factors (in the range of 1 to 10) and weights for the tangible and intangible factors are to be assigned.

Let us assign scores for the intangible factors for location A and D.

Intangible factors	*A*	*D*
Attitude of labours	Adequate (5)	Good (2)
Recreational facilities	Good (2)	Bad (8)
Community facilities	Fair (4)	Good (2)

Assigning scores is a subjective phenomenon and has to done judiciously. It is like giving marks to a feature. If a feature iss very good, excellent and rare to find it is treated as the best and score is assigned as 1. On the other extreme if a feature is very bad and highly unfavourable it is treated as the worst and score is assigned as 10. Features having qualities in-between the best and the worst conditions are assigned scores in the range of 2 to 9. After having assigned the scores for the intangible factors, wweights for the tangible and intangible factors are to be assigned. The weight for all tangible factors is assigned as '1' since all the tangible factors are measured in terms of the common unit, viz., money. The intangible factors are compared among themselves and weights are assigned depending upon their relative importance.

If we assume weights for the intangible factors as under,

Intangible factor	Weight
Attitude of labourers	2
Recreational facilities	3
Community facilities	2

[* The scores are allotted from 1 to 10, giving score 1 for the best condition and score 10 for the worst condition] then, the relative merit of site A to D is given by the following relationship.

$$\left[\frac{1{,}00{,}000}{70{,}000}\right]^1 \times \left[\frac{7{,}00{,}000}{8{,}00{,}000}\right]^1 \times \left[\frac{33{,}00{,}000}{33{,}00{,}000}\right]^1 \times \left[\frac{20{,}00{,}000}{22{,}00{,}000}\right]^1 \times \left[\frac{8{,}00{,}000}{9{,}00{,}000}\right]^1 \times \left[\frac{7{,}00{,}000}{3{,}00{,}000}\right]^1 \times$$

$$\left[\frac{3{,}00{,}000}{50{,}000}\right]^1 \times \left[\frac{5}{2}\right]^2 \times \left[\frac{2}{8}\right]^3 \times \left[\frac{4}{2}\right]^2$$

$$= 5.5239$$

Since the factor works out to be more than 1.00, location-D is preferable to location-A.

Observation

When only the tangible factors are considered location-A scored marginally higher over location-D, as evidenced by marginally higher return on investment. However, when both tangible and intangible factors are considered, location-D becomes preferable to location-A.

(b) COMMERCIAL APPRAISAL

The Commercial appraisal is concerned with market for the product/service. The very idea of promoting a project is to produce some product/service and to market the same to the consumers and earning a profit thereby. Hence, market appraisal occupies a prime place in project appraisal. In fact in modern management concept, marketing management receives more attention than in earlier years. This is because of the reason that the very survival and success of any project depends on the question as to whether the product/service offered by the project is successful commercially.

Commercial appraisal (or market appraisal) of a project is done studying the commercial successfulness of the product/service offered by the project from the following angles.

(*a*) Demand for the product.
(*b*) Supply position for the product.
(*c*) Distribution channels.
(*d*) Pricing of the product.
(*e*) Government policies.

Demand

Economists define demand for a commodity as the desire backed by the necessary purchasing power.

One of the most important determinants of a firm's profitability is the demand for its products. In spite of an efficient and technologically advanced production process and in spite of efficient financial management and cordial inter-personnel relationship between the employees and the management, the firm will find it difficult to earn profit if its products are not demanded by the consumers.

Because of the important role played by demand as a determinant of profitability, estimate of expected future demand for the product proposed to be manufactured consitutes a key element in all planning processes. Hence demand analysis forms a major part of project appraisal.

The term 'demand' can be defined as the number of units of a particular good or service that consumers are willing to purchase during a specified period under a given set of conditions.

Demand Forecasting Techniques

A forecast is a prediction or estimation of a future situation. No forecast can be cent percent correct, however scientifically designed the forecasting techniques are, in view of the reason that future is uncertain!

Broadly speaking, there are two approaches to the problem of business forecasting. One approach is to obtain information about the intentions of consumers through collecting views and opinions of experts in the field or by conducting interviews with the consumers. This approach is called 'survey method'. The other approach is to use the past experience as a guide and to arrive at the future demand by extrapolating the past 'statistical data'. this approach is called statistical approach. While the survey method is suitable for short term forecasting, the statistical method is suitable for long term forecasting. Estimating future demand for existing products can be done by either method. But, demand for a new product can be estimated only by the survey method since past statistical data are not available for extrapolation.

Survey Methods

(1) *Jury of expert's opinion method :* In this method, experts in the particular field are requested to give their views on the likely demand for the product in future. They are the persons who have been dealing in this product and in related products for a long time and thus are able to predict the future trend. This method is also called the hunch method since the experts give their opinions after weighing pros and cons of all factors affecting the product demand and arrive at an estimate, which is nothing but a hunch; the hunch of course is backed by knowledge and experience of the experts. If the views of more number of experts are obtained, and if their views differ significantly, then a forecast can be safely arrived at by taking the average of the expert's predictions. Though this method is simple and does not employ extensive statistical work, the disadvantage is that it is only a subjective approach and the experts may have their own personal bias. Also, in this approach, no regard is given to the relative importance of the opinions of different experts.

An alternative approach is to ask the experts to reach consensus in a face-to-face deliberation. In this approach, the experts can offer their opinions orally and arrive at a consensus after observing and deliberating the rationale behind the many different views. However, in this approach, the result may not be a highly reliable one due to problems associated with group interaction dynamics. A participant who has better communication skills may drive home his views more effectively and his views may get undue weight (though it may be neither the majority view nor the correct view). Similarly, one who is not able to present his view effectively may not impress the group though his view really requires active consideration.

(2) *Delhi technique :* This is a group decision by experts in which the individual experts act separately. Their views are pooled together and an attempt is made to arrive at consensus. If the views of the experts differ significantly, the individual experts are fed with the views of other experts in areas where there is distinct difference and they are asked to further analyze the problem and to revise/improve upon their views in the light of the views of the other experts in the group. The process can be repeated till a near coincidence of views is achieved. The important aspect of Delphi technique is that the experts who offer their opinions do not have face-to-face interaction and hence they are free to express their views. If at all they change their views in response to the views offered by other experts, it is only after due consideration and analysis without any external pressure from whomsoever. Hence, Delphi

technique is found to give more accurate results as compared to Jury of expert's opinion method.

(3) *Consumer's survey method :* This is the most direct approach to demand forecasting. In this method, consumers are approached and asked to express their opinion of a particular product. The survey can cover all the consumers if the consumers are smaller in number (eg. Medical practitioners). If the number of consumers is large, a selected group of consumers is chosen for the survey. The principal merit of this method is that the forecaster does not add any bias of his own. The forecaster merely collects information from consumers and aggregates the information collected. The sales forecast by this methhod is likely to be more accurate since no assumptions are made. Why do companies spend a lot of money, time and man power in customer survey, while simple, less expensive statistical forecasting techniques are available? Statistical data will only indicate the trend. It will not answer key questions like as to why consumers prefer a particular product etc., Surveying consumer intentions requires application of marketing research techniques. For forecasting the acceptancce and the likely demand for a new product, elaborate verbal and pictorial descriptions of the product are to be given to the prospective consumers; they must be demonstrated about its acual use and free samples may be offered for trials.

Analysis of survey response involves pooling of consumers' opinions on their planned purchases and arriving at a sales forecast using the following formula.

$$\text{Sales forecast} = \frac{\left[\begin{array}{c}\text{Total}\\ \text{population size}\end{array}\right]}{[\text{Sample size}]} \times \left[\begin{array}{l}\text{No. of}\\ \text{respondents}\\ \text{who said `yes'}\end{array}\right] \times \left[\begin{array}{l}\text{\% of those}\\ \text{who said}\\ \text{`yes' who}\\ \text{will actually}\\ \text{purchase}\end{array}\right] \times \left[\begin{array}{l}\text{Average}\\ \text{quantity}\\ \text{that will}\\ \text{be purchased}\\ \text{by a buyer}\end{array}\right]$$

4. *Sales forecast composite :* This method of sales forecasting relies on the judgement of sales personnel. The field level sales personnel are requested to offer their forecast in their respective geographic area, to their sales managers. The forecasts of salles personnel are pooled together and the estimate given by each person is adjussted by applying appropriate weights and the adjusted forecasts are combined to arrive at the composite forecast. It is likely that some of the sales personnel may be too optimistic and provide a higher estimate while the pessimistic sales personnei will offer a lower estimate. The past accuracy of each sales peron's opinion should be assessed to identify those who tend to offer consistently high or low estimates and suitable weights are applied to their estimates to correct the deviations in their estimates. In complex situations, the sales personnel may not be aware of the likely changes that may take place in the general economic conditions, likely advancements in technology which may have an impact on sales, the likely shift in the consumer preferences etc. Under such situations, the sales managers have to take into account such macro level indicators and adjust the estimates provided by the sales personnel accordingly.

Statistical Methods : Statistical methods made use of past data. The past data are arranged in a chronological order and some statistical method is used to identify the trend indicated by the past data. The trend is then extended to the future period. This process of extending the past trend to the future is called extrapolation. The statistical methods are of two types, namely, (1) *trend analysis and* (2) *regression technique.*

(1) *Trend analysis* : The following are some of the methods used in trend analysis to estimate the future demand based on the past data.

(*a*) Curve fitting.

(*b*) Moving average method.

(*c*) Weighted moving average method.

(*d*) Exponential smoothing method.

This basic assumption of trend analysis is that in future all the factors that were responsible for the past movements will be present and will exert influence in the same way as had been in the past. The relationship is often expressed in the form of a mathematical formula or model. With the help of the formula, the future trend is projected and forecasts are made on the assumption that the same trend would continue in the future also.

(*a*) *Curve fitting* : Suppose there are two variables '*x*' and '*y*' that are related to each other. For example, the consumption level ('*y*') of a particular good might increase with the increase of time ('*x*'). For instance, the consumption level in the year 1985 might be 2.00 tonnes, in the year 1986 — 2.4 tonnes, in the year 1987 — 3.3 tonnes, in the year 1998 — 4.7 tonnes, in the year 1989 — 5.9 tonnes and in the year 1990 — 7.10 tonnes. Such a trend in the consumption level indicates that there is a relationship between the consumption level ('*y*') and time ('*x*'). If we are in the year 1991 and if there are indications that the increasing trend in consumption would continue for another, say, 10 years, we can arrive at the demand pattern for the next ten years, by fitting a curve with the available data.

Fitting a curve using the available data can be done with minimum error, using the principle of least squares. The principle of least squares fits a straight line in such a way that the error of estimation is minimum.

Referring to Fig. 1.8 let 'AB' is the straight line that offers the best fit with minimum error. The sample points 1, 2, 3, 4, ... etc., lie on either side of the straight line.

Fitment error at point - 1 : $(y_1 - y_1^{\prime})$

Fitment error at point - 2 : $(y_2 - y_2^{\prime})$

Fitment error at point - 3 : $(y_3 - y_3^{\prime})$

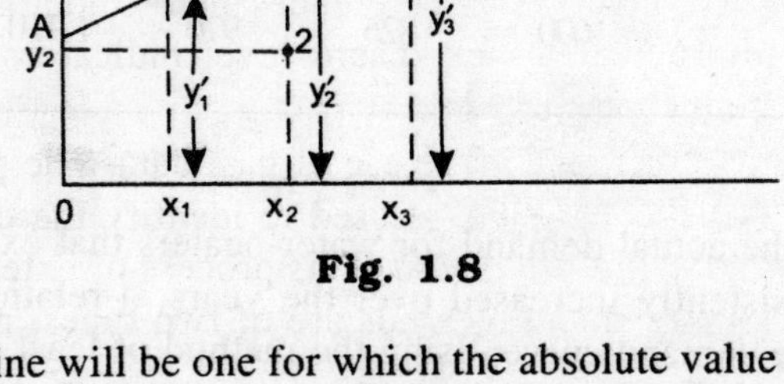

Fig. 1.8

The best fitting straight line will be one for which the absolute value of fitment error is minimum. In fact, the best line would be the line that passes through all the points. However, this is not possible. Hence, our aim would be to find a line that is closest to all the points. A line will be the closest to all the points if the total distance between the line and all the points is minimum. Since some of the points will be above the line and some below the line, the difference between the line and the points above the line would be positive, while the difference between the line and the points below the line would be negative. Thus, the differences would cancel out one another and hence total sum of differences as a measure of best fit would be incorrect. Instead, if we calculate the differences individually and square them up, this would eliminate the problem of positive and negative differences and the total sum of squares of differences would be positive. Since we are looking for a line that is closest to all the points, for such a line, the sum of squares of differences would be minimum. Hence, this method of arriving at the line of best fit is known as **"the method of least squares"**.

If $y = a + bx$ is the relation for the best fitting line, using the principles of least squares, the value of the parameters 'a' and 'b' can be determined. (Refer Fig. 1.9)

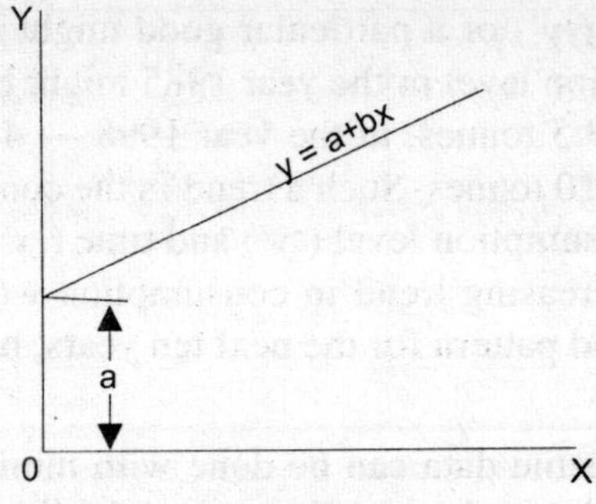

Fig. 1.9

It can be shown, using the principles of least squares that the values of 'a' and 'b' can be determined by the following two equations.

$$\Sigma y = n.a + b.\Sigma x$$

and
$$\Sigma xy = a.\Sigma x + b.\Sigma x^2$$

The above two equations are called 'normal equations' and these two equations can be used for arriving at the line of best fit from the available data.

Illustration 1.5

Fit a straight line trend to the following data, using the method of least squares. From the straight line trend, estimate the demand in the year 1995.

Year (x)	:	1979	1980	1981	1982	1983	1984	1985
Demand for house hold water heaters (y) (number in 1000's)	:	600	825	970	1,210	1,440	1,790	2,070

Solution:

The given data represents the actual demand for water-heaters that existed in the past seven years. Since the demand has consistently increased over the years, a relationship can be established by fitting a straight line for the demand curve, using the method of least squares.

Let $y = a + b.x$ is the line of best fit for the given data.

Using the principle of least squares, we have the following two relationships,

$$\Sigma y = n.a + b.\Sigma x$$

and $$\Sigma xy = a.\Sigma x + b.\Sigma x^2$$

Since Σx, Σx^2, Σxy etc., are to be calculated from the available data, the calculations can be made simpler by making simple assumptions as under:

Let $$X = x - 1982$$

and Let $$Y = y$$

With the above two assumptions, the normal equations take the following form

$$\Sigma Y = n.a + b.\Sigma X$$

and $$\Sigma XY = a.\Sigma X + b.\Sigma X^2$$

Year (X)	*Demand (Y)*	*X*	X^2	*XY*
1979	600	– 3	9	– 1,800
1980	825	– 2	4	– 1,650
1981	970	– 1	1	– 970
1982	1210	0	0	0
1983	1440	1	1	1,440
1984	1790	2	4	3,580
1985	2070	3	9	6,210
	Σ = 8905	0	28	6,810

Number of observations (n) = 7

$$\Sigma X = 0;\ \Sigma X^2 = 28;\ \Sigma XY = 6810 \text{ and } \Sigma Y = 8905$$

Substituting the values in the normal equations,

$$\Sigma Y = n.a + b.\Sigma X$$

$$8905 = 7a + 0$$

i.e., $$7a = 8905$$

$$a = 1272.14$$

$$\Sigma XY = a.\Sigma X + b.\Sigma X^2$$

$$6810 = 0 + b\ (28)$$

i.e., $$28b = 6810$$

$$b = 243.21$$

The equation for the trend line is,

$$Y = a + bX$$

$$Y = 1272.14 + 243.21X$$

Substituting (x – 1989) for 'X' and y for 'Y',

$$y = 1272.14 + 243.21\ (x - 1982)$$

$$= 1272.12 + 243.1\ x - 482042.22$$

i.e., $$y = 243.21x - 480770.88$$

Estimated demand in the year 1995:

$$y = 243.21x - 480770.88$$
$$= 243.21 \; . \; (1995) - 480770.88$$
$$= 485203.95 - 480770.88$$
$$= 4433.07$$

Since the demand is given in terms of 1000's,

$$y = 4433.07 \times 1000$$
$$= 44{,}33{,}070$$

∴ Estimated demand for household water heaters in the year 1995 = 44,33,070

say, 44,33,000 Nos.

(*b*) **Moving average method :** According to moving average method of forecasting, the forecast for the next year is arrived at by taking the average of the actual data for a few immediately preceding years. If the data of preceding three years are considered for arriving at the forecast for the fourth year, it is called a 'three year moving average'.

For example,

Actual Sales		*Forecast*
Year	*Sales*	
1994	2,219	
1995	2,302	
1996	2,007	
1997		(2,219 + 2,302 + 2,007) ÷ 3 = 2,176

The forecast made for the year 1997 is 2176, taking three year moving average. If the actual sale achieved in the year 1997 is , say, 2198, the three year moving average for the year 1998 is arrived at by taking the average of the actual sales during the immediately three preceding years.

Actual Sales		*Forecast*
Year	*Sales*	
1994	2,219	
1995	2,302	
1996	2,007	
1997	2,198	
1998		(2,302 + 2,302 + 2,198) ÷ 3 = 2,169

Determining the period of moving average is an important factor in calculating the trend values in the moving average method. This method is used when the past data do not exhibit a steady increase or decrease in trend over time, but show fluctuations. If the actual data of previous years show fluctuations in a uniform period, this uniform period is taken as the period of moving average. For instance, if the sales data of previous years indicate a steady growth for a continuous three years, followed by a drop in the fourth year, a 'four year moving average' can be assumed for forecasting. In other words, if the trend is cyclical in a period of every four years, a four year moving average is considered for arriving at the forecast.

Sometimes, though the actual data of previous years may be fluctuating, it may be difficult to find any distinct cyclical trend in the movement of data. In such cases, determining the period of moving average will be a difficult thing and can be done only on experimental basis, by making different trials and verifying the results of forecasts with the actuals before deciding upon the period of moving average.

(*c*) **Weighted moving average method :** In the moving average method of forecasting, only the simple arithmetic average of few previous years' data are taken as the forecast for the next year. It is likely that the more recent data might give a better indication of the trend than a past data. In a four year moving average, for example, the actual data of the immediate preceding year might have more relevance and the relevance of the previous three years data might decrease as we move backward to the past data. If this is so, in the calculation of moving average, weight of the past data will vary according to their period, the more recent data getting the maximum weight and vice versa. In a four year moving average, for example, the weight for the past four year data might be as under:

Actual Sales		*Weight*	*Forecast*
Year	*Sales*		
1989	2,555		
1990	2,761		
1991	2,999		
1992	1,999		
1993	2,182	0.6	
1994	2,219	0.7	
1995	2,302	0.8	
1996	2,007	0.9	
1997			$(0.6 \times 2{,}182 + 0.7 \times 2{,}219 + 0.8 \times 2{,}302 + 0.9 \times 2{,}007) \div 4$ $= 1{,}627.6$

Deciding the appropriate weight for the past data is a ticklish issue and can be arrived at only by extensive experimentation.

(*d*) **Exponential smoothing method :** The speciality of exponential smoothing method is that forecasts are modified in the light of observed errors. This method takes into account the decreasing influence of the past time periods as we move further into the past data. This decreasing trend as we move down into the past time period is found to be exponentially distributed and hence this method is designated as exponential smoothing method.

The forecasts for the next time period is given by the following relationship.

$$F_{(t+1)} = \alpha.A_t + (1 - \alpha).F_t$$

Where, $F_{(t+1)}$ = forecast for the time period $(t + 1)$

α = smoothing factor (which lies between 0 and 1, i.e., $\alpha \geq 0$ and ≤ 1.00)

A_t = Actual value for the time period 't'

F_t = forecast for the time period 't'

Referring to the relationship given above, the forecast for a particular time period depends on the forecast as well the actual value of the immediately preceding period. In any series of data, the forecast for the first data in the series will not be available as this is the starting point for the series. For instance, if we want to estimate the likely demand of a particular product for a particular period, say for year 1995, we may be having the actual data for the previous year, i.e., for the year 1994.

Since we want the forecast for the year 1995, the forecast for the previous year (1994) will not be available.

Since the forecast for the previous year is required as per the relationship given above, for assuming the forecasted value for the year 1994, the usual procedure is to make a few observations in the period prior to 1994 and the average of these observed values is taken as the forecasted value for the year 1994. For instance, if observations are done for the years 1989 to 1993, the forecast for the year 1994 is the average of the actual observed values during the period 1989 — 1993. This period of 1989 — 1993 is called the warm-up period and the sample of observations made during the warm-up period is called the warm-up sample. Thus, for the first period in the time series, we will be having both the actual value and a forecasted value (based on the warm-up sample).

Another parameter in the relationship that needs a careful assessment is the smoothing factor 'α'. The value of the smoothing factor is also determined with the help of the observations made during the warm-up period i.e., (the warm-up sample). Using different values of 'α' in the range "0 to 1.00", forecasted values for the warm-up period are calculated and are compared with the actual values. The value of 'α' that shows the minimum Mean Squared Error (MSE) is chosen.

Mean Squared Error (MSE) is given by the following relationship:

$$\text{MSE} = \frac{\Sigma\,(A_i - F_i)^2}{n}$$

Where, A_i = actual value for the period '*i*'

F_i = forecasted value for the period '*i*'

Suppose 1989 — 1992 is the warm-up period and the actually observed values during the warm-up period are 2005, 2920, 3210 and 3795 respectively. Different values for 'α' are assumed and the forecasted values for the warm-up period are calculated. The MSE for each set of forecasts are then calculated and the value of 'α' for which the MSE is minimum is chosen as the correct value for 'α'.

Warm-up period	A_i	F_i
1989	2,005	
1990	2,920	
1991	3,210	
1992	3,795	

Even while making forecast in the warm-up period, we come across the problem of 'F_i' for the first time period in the warm-up sample. 'F_i' for the first period in the warm-up sample is assumed to take the same value as 'A_i' for the first period. Accordingly,

Warm-up period	A_i	F_i
1989	2,005	2,005
1990	2,920	
1991	3,210	
1992	3,795	

The forecasts for the years 1990, 1991 and 1992 are made assuming a certain value of 'α'. The exercise is repeated for several assumed values of 'α' in the range of 0 to 1.00 and the value of 'α' for which the MSE is minimum is chosen for further forecast in the actual time series.

Illustration 1.6

The actual demand for a consumer product for the year 1991 is 20500. The value of 'α' is 0.32. The average demand of the warm-up period is 19980. Construct a table of forecasts using exponential smoothing method for the period 1992 — 2000. The actual demand for the period 1992 — 2000 are found to be 20,200, 20,310, 20,450, 20,610, 20,720, 20,815, 21,090 and 21,180 respectively.

Solution:

Year	A_i	F_i
1991	20,500	19,980

[the average demand for the warm-up period is taken as the forecast for the first year in the time series]

Year	A_i	F_i
1991	20,500	19,980
1992		20,146

Forecast for the year 1992 [F_{1992}] $= \alpha.A_{1991} + (1 - \alpha).F_{1991}$

$= 0.32\ (20{,}500) + (1 - 0.32)\ 19{,}980$

$= 20{,}146.4$

say 20146

The actual demand for the year 1992 will be known by the end of that year. The actual demand for the year 1992, as given in the problem is 20200.

Year	A_i	F_i
1991	20500	19980
1992	20200	20146

Forecast for the year 1993 [F_{1993}] $= \alpha.A_{1992} + (1 - \alpha).F_{1992}$

$= 0.32\ (20200) + (1 - 0.32)\ 20146$

$= 20164$

Year	A_i	F_i
1991	20,500	19,980
1992	20,200	20,146
1993		20,164

The forecast for the year 1993 is made at the end of the year 1992, after knowing the actual demand for the year 1992. The forecasted demand for the year 1993, of 20164 is made use of for all the managerial decisionb making purposes during the 1993. The actual demand for the year 1993 (which is known at the end of the year 1993) is 20130. The process of forecasting is repeated for further periods. It may be noted that as per the method of exponential smoothing, we can forecast only for the immediate next year.

The table of forecasts are as under:

Year	A_i	F_i
1991	20,500	19,980
1992	20,200	20,146
1993	20,310	20,164
1994	20,450	20,210
1995	20,610	20,287
1996	20,720	20,390
1997	20,815	20,496
1998	21,005	20,598
1999	21,090	20,728
2000	21,180	20,844

Regression Technique

A regression model is an equation relating a dependent variable to many independent variables. For example, anticipated sales (dependent variable) may be expressed as a function of independent variables like disposable income of consumers, price relative to the price of competitive products, level of advertising etc., and the relationship can be expressed as

$$Y = a_1 + (b_1 \cdot x_1) + (b_2 \cdot x_2) + (b_3 \cdot x_3) + \dots (b_n \cdot x_n)$$

where Y represents sales

$a_1, b_1, b_2 \dots b_n$ are constants

and $x_1, x_2, x_3 \dots x_n$ are independent variables which affect the dependent variable Y. With the time series data collected, a relationship is established as above. After establishing the relationship values for the independent factors for the future period are estimated. Substituting these values in the relationship, estimate for the future years can be made.

When the number of independent variables are more, multiple regression analysis can be undertaken with the help of computers.

Other Methods of Forecasting

(1) **End use method :** This method of forecasting is used for forecasting the demand for intermediate products. An intermediate product can have more than one uses, resulting in more than one final product. The demand for the various possible final products are projected. The likely consumption level at each of the final product is determined by determining the consumption co-efficient for the various uses. Consumption co-efficient is the number of intermediate products used in one final product

$$\begin{matrix}\text{Project demand for the} \\ \text{intermediary product}\end{matrix} = \sum_{1}^{n} \begin{matrix}\text{Consumption} \\ \text{co-efficient}\end{matrix} \times \begin{matrix}\text{Projected output for} \\ \text{the final product.}\end{matrix}$$

Where n = the number of final products in which the intermediate product finds its use.

For example two wheeler automobile horn is an intermediate product. It has no independent use of its own. It becomes useful when it is attached to the final product viz., the two wheeler automobile.

The horn can find its use in mopeds, scooters, motorbikes etc., which are the different end products. The consumption co-efficient for horns is 1 since every unit of the two wheelers is fitted with only one horn. If the output of different varieties of two wheeler automobiles are projected, the projected demand for the horns can be arrived at since the co-efficient of consumption is 1.

Final product	*Consumption Co-efficient*	*Projected output of final product*	*Projected demand for the intermediate product (Horn)*
Mopeds	1	25,000	25,000
Scooters	1	40,000	40,000
Motor cycle	1	45,000	45,000
	Total	1,10,000	1,10,000

If the intermediate product is say, indicator lamps used in two wheeler automobiles, since four numbers of indicator lamps are fixed to one two wheeler (two at the front and two at the rear) the consumption co-efficient is four i.e., for each unit of output of a two wheeler, four units of the indicator lamps would be consumed.

Final product	*Consumption Co-efficient final product*	*Projected output of product (indicator lamp)*	*Projected demand for the intermediate*
Mopeds	4	25,000	1,00,000
Scooters	4	40,000	1,16,000
Motor cycle	4	45,000	1,80,000
	Total	1,10,000	3,96,000

The consumption co-efficient can be also a fractional figure. For example paper board is an intermediate product which can have many uses. One such use is the manufacture of paper cones used in textile spinning mills for winding of yarn. If the weight of each finished paper cone is say 30 grams and if the weight of paper required for one paper cone is say, 40 grams (the difference is due to wastage of paper board in cutting the board to the required size for the manufacture of paper cone) the consumption co-efficient 1.33 (i.e., 40/30).

(2) **Leading indicator method:** In an economy there are many factors (or variables) that are interrelated and interdependent. The change in one variable affects the other interdependent variables. Those variables that change ahead of their dependent variable are known as leading indicators. The variables that change in response to a change in their leading indicators are known as lagging indicators.

A few examples will make the idea clear. If the personal income of a society increases, the demand for consumer goods is bound to increase. Here 'Personal income' is the leading indicator and 'demand for consumer goods' is the lagging indicator.

If the agricultural income increases, it is most likely that the demand for fertilizers, manures, agricultural implements etc., are bound to increase. Here 'agricultural income' is the leading indicator and demand for fertilizers, manures, agricultural implements etc., are the lagging indciators.

The idea can be extended to all areas of demand forecasting. The demand for educational books (a lagging indicator) depends on growth of educational institutions (a leading indicator). The demand for automobile spare parts (a laging indicator) is relfected by the number of automobiles being registered with the transport authorities (a leading indicator).

From the above, we get the understanding that the future demand for a lagging indicator can be predicted by observing the way in which its leading indicator behaves at present.

There are two steps involved in forecasting the demand by the use of leading indicator method, viz.,

(*a*) Identification of the appropriate leading indicator for a variable (laging indicator) whose demand is to be forecasted.

(*b*) Establishing a relationship between the leading and the lagging indicators and reducing the relationship in the form of a regression equation.

Merits

The main advantage of this method is that it does not require detailed market survey for the proposed product. As this method gives the trend and magnitude of movement of the lagging indicator based on the behavior of the leading indicator, in all probability, the prediction of the trend is not likely to be reversed if the leading indicators are correctly chosen. In otherwords, the direction of movement of market factors is well reflected by the leading indicators, though there may be minor deviations in the magnitude of movements in view of the difficulties involved in arriving at the exact lead-lag relationship.

Demerits

- The crux of the problem is fonding out the appropriate leading indicator. If a wrong leading indicator is chosen, the forecast may prove to be wrong.
- Since so many factors play in an economy, the lead-lag relationship, once established is not final, and requires continuous revision.

The leading indicators may change or the lead-lage relationship may get altered due to changes in market conditions. Hence the identifying the leading indicator and establishing the lead-lag relationship is to be a continuous process.

(3) **Chain-Ratio method :** This method makes use of secondary data for forecasting the demand for a particular product. Macro level data are gathered and the data are reduced sequentially by applying appropriated reduction factors until the required information is obtained. The method can be metter explained with the aid of an illustration.

Let a company has proposals to manufacture mopeds to suit the requirement of female customers and decides to use chain-ratio methhod to assess the demand. The following steps illustrate the method of assessment.

Total population of the targeted market	: 4,00,00,000
Proportion of females in the population	: 0.49
Total female population	: 1,96,00,000 [4,00,00,000 × 0.49]
Proportion of employed women in female population	: 0.15
Number of employed women	: 29,40,000 [1,96,00,000 × 0.15]
Proportion of college students in female population	: 0.19
Number of female college students	: 37,24,000 [1,96,00,000 × 0.19]

Proportion of employed women who do not own a moped : 0.68

Number of employed women who do not own a moped : 19,99,200 [29,40,000 × 0.68]

Proportion of female college students who do not own a moped : 0.78

Number of female college students who do not own a moped : 29,04,720 [37,24,000 × 0.78]

Proportion of employed women who can afford to buy a moped : 0.55

Number of potential customers from employed women : 10,99,560 [19,99,200 × 0.55]

Propotion of female college students who can afford to buy a moped : 0.30

Number of potential customers from college students : 8,71,416 [29,04,720 × 0.30]

Total potential customers for mopeds : 19,970,976 [10,99,560 + 8,71,416]

Proportion of market share that the firm is estimated to capture : 0.20

Estimated sales potential : 3,19,195 [0.20 × 19,70,976]
Say, 3,19,200 numbers of mopeds

Since the chain-ratio method arrives at the forecast on the basis of many factors/assumptions, the accuracy of the result depends upon the accuracy of different factors/assumptions made in the assessment.

Other Aspects to be Considered in Demand Forecasting of a Product

(*a*) There may be certain products thsat are entirely imported. If a project proposes to set up a unit for the manufacture of this kind of product, the demand pattern can be identified by studying the past trends in imports.

(*b*) The product proposed to be manufactured may have export potentials. If so, apart from the demand in the indigennous market, the demand from abroad can also be taken into account. For assessing the export potential for the product, the following details may be gathered and analyzed.

(*i*) Past trends in the volume of world trade for the product.

(*ii*) Major importing countries and the quantum of import by these countries.

(*iii*) Duties and tariff barriers/tariff concessions if any, existing in the importing countries.

(*iv*) The trends in international prices for the product etc.

Industry Demand vs Firm Demand

'Industry' refers to a particular line of activity, 'Steel industry, for example refers to the line of activity of producing steel and steel products. There will be many firms operating in a particular industry. There may be hundreds or thousands of firms producing steel/steel products. When we plan a project in a particular line of activity, we are interested in knowing only the demand that our proposed firm will get for its products i.e., we are interested in knowing the firm demand. The individual enterprises are known as firms and all the enterprises existing in a particular line of activity together constitute the industry. Hence firm demand and industry demand reflect two different parameters. While the industry demand refers to the demand for the product of the whole industry (say, for example the total demand for steel in particular country) the firm demand refers to the demand for the product of a particular firm in that industry.

Though we are interested in knowing the firm demand, it is only derived from industry demand. In otherwords it is a share of industry demand. Hence knowing the industry demand gives an overall picture. If there is good industry demand, the firm demand is also most likely to be good. This is because of the demand-supply gap existing for the product.

If there is no demand-supply gap for a particular product, it means that the output of all the existing enterprises producing that product is sufficient to meet the aggregate demand for that product. If the overall production capacity exceeds the aggregate demand, it means that there is excess production capacity in the industry. In both these situations, if a new enterprise is planned to be started in that industry, it is very unlikely that the firm's products will have any demand. If at all a new enterprise in such an industry is to be successful, it should deisgn its product in such a way that its product has different features than the products of other enterprises so that it can grab a portion of market share. However it will only be a risky venture and it will be very difficult to estimate a firm's demand in such a situation.

(c) Economic Appraisal

Economic appraisal measures the effect of the project on the whole economy. Developing countries and underdeveloped countries face scarcity of capital and foreign exchange. Hence in the overall interest of the country, the limited stocks of capital and foreign exchange should be put into the best possible use. Hence, policy makers are concerned as to where the scarce resources can be directed to maximize economic growth of the country. So, among the alternative projects, the policy makers make a choice based on the economic return. This is true irrespective of whether resources are committed to a large project under taken by the Government or to a smaller project under taken by an individual entrepreneur. But an individual entrepreneur, when left free to choose, is more likely to be interested in his profit rather than having a broader perspective of the economic returns of the project.

Consider the hypothetical example given below, which will make the idea clear.

Let an entrepreneur own a granite quarry consisting of high quality granite stone. If the entrepreneur is not aware of the potentials of granite stone as its use in the form of polished slabs/ tiles, he may choose to exploit the granite quarry by setting up a stone crushing unit which will produce stone jelly to be used as a raw material for say, laying of road, preparing concrete mix etc. Even if the entreprenur is aware of the potential of granite stone, if he is not mentally prepared to venture into a high-tech project for the production of polished granite slabs/tiles which can have very good export potential, he may settle for a low-tech stone crushing project, producing stone jelly. He may be even satisfied with the return from the stone crushing unit though setting up a unit for the production of polished granite slabs/tiles will maximize the economic growth of the country as a whole by earning valuable foreing exchange in view of its export potential. [This is only a hypothetical example.]

In otherwords a private entreprenur may not be interested in studying the social cost-benefit analysis of a project. Social cost-benefit analysis is also referred to as socio-economic analysis which deserves consideration especially in public projects.

In order to regulate the deployment of scarce resources for the economic upliftment of the country by channelising the use of scarce resources to the best possible use, the Government enforces control through its policies and regulations.

In India, the 'development banks function within the overall frame work of the Government's policies and regulations of industrialization and direct their lending to projects that are in accordance with the priorities of the Government.

(d) Financial Appraisal

Financial appraisal of project consists of two major areas viz., arriving at the cost of the project and arriving at the appropriate means of financing the project. By means of financing, we mean the combination of equity and debt. The proper equity-debt combination for a project depends upon the revenue earning capacity of the project. Though equity does not attract any interest and does not involve any repayment obligation, the debt obtained for financing the project is to be repaid along with interest. Hence, the revenue earning capacity of the project should be sufficient enough to meet the repayment of debt with interest. Moreover, the project should also generae additional revenue to meet the cost of equity capital. Though equity is contributed by the project promoters, it is not without any cost. An entrepreneur invests his capital in a project with a hope of getting returns on his capital invested apart from meeting debt obligations.

(e) Management Appraisal

Management is the most important factor that can either make a project a success or a failure. A good project at the hands of a poor management may fail while a not-so-good project at the hands of an effective management may succeed.

The American Institute of Management which conducted an appraisal of management as a method of ascertaining a company's health and propsects has assigned a weight of only 6% of the total to 'earnings'. A far greater weight of 22% has been assigned to the quality of the executive managing the affairs of the company. The board of directors of a company and its corporate structure gets a weight of 13%.

Hence, banks and financial institutions that lend money for financing projects lay more emphasis on management appraisal. Lending institutions look at two points before committing their funds to project financing. They look at the capacity of the project to repay the loan along with interest within the stipulated period of time and also they observe the willingness of the borrower to repay the loan. While the 'capacity to repay' is assessed by technical, commercial and financial appraisla,s the 'willingness to repay' (or propensity to repay or intension to repay) is assessed by way of management appraisal.

While other appraisal techniques are quantitative and objective in nature, management appraisal is purely qualitative and subjective in nature.

The persons who are to be evaluated for the purpose of management appraisal depends upon the constitution of the enterprise. Very small projects that are promoted by sole proprietors, are managed by the proprietors themselves. In such cases the management appraisal is to be done obviously on the proprietors. In respect of partnership firms, there may be partners who have only contributed capital, but keep themselves away from the day-to-day management of the enterprises. Hence, in the case of the partnership firms, the management appraisal shall be done on the managing partners of the firm (i.e., those partners who actually manage the affairs of the enterprise). Mutual understanding and trust among the partners is a key factor for the success of an enterprise.

Persons who maintained a cordial, long term relationship in the past either in business or in other areas, make good partners. Persons who join together for the first time with the sole intention of promoting a new project are often found to lack in mutual understanding and this will show up shortly after the project has taken shape, or at times, even during the implementation stage of the project itself. There are many instances where misunderstanding and dispute among the partners has led to the failure of projects than any other internal/external factors. Hence, mutual trust among the partners is a prerequisite for successful implementation and management of projects. The management appraisal shall give due importance to this aspect.

In private limited companies, it will be the managing directors/executive directors who are to be appraised. The affairs of closely held public limited companies are mostly looked after by the promoter directors. For such companies also, the managing directors/executive directors are the persons to be appraised who manage the affairs of the enterprises.

In respect of widely held public limited companies, the management appraisal shall be done on the directors who are in the board of the company, on the chief executive officer of the company and also on key functional managers. Appraisal of the chief executive officer carries more importance since he is the king-pin of a company.

Integrity, foresightedness, leadership qualities, Interpersonnel relationship, technical and financial skills, commitment, perseverance etc., are some of the parameters that need to be studied in management appraisal.

If management appraisal of persons who are already managing the affairs of some other enterprise(s) is required to be done, a visit to such enterprise(s) that is (are) managed by them will throw light. The industrial relations prevailing in that enterprise, morale of the employees, the prevailing superior-subordinate relationship, labour turnover, labour unrest, productivity of employees are some of the factors that will reflect the managerial capabilities of the persons concerned.

The importance of management appraisal is being increasingly felt now a days inview of the growing number of units that have become sick due to mismanagement. Though management appraisal is a vital aspect of project appraisal, it still remains more of a subjective exercise and it will continue to remain so, though refinements are possible. This is because, management appraisal is concerned with the appraisal of human qualities.

(f) Social Cost Benefit Analysis

The main objective of an individual, a firm or a company in investing on a project is to earn the maximum possible returns for the investment. Accordingly, the project promoters are solely interested in wealth maxmisation. Hence the project promoters tend to evaluate only the commercial profitability of a project.

There are some projects that may not offer attractive returns as far as commercial profitability is concerned, but stil such projects are undertaken since they have social implications. Such projects are public projects like road, railway, bridge and other transport projects, irrigation projects, power projects etc., for which socio-economic considerations play a significant part rather than mere commercial profitability. Such projects are analysed for their net socio-economic benefits and the profitability analysis of such projects is known as national profitability analysis, which is nothing but the socio-economic cost-benefit analysis done at the national level.

Every project imposes certain costs to the nation and produces certain benefits to the nation. The costs may be of two types viz., direct costs and indirect costs. So also, the benefit derived from any project will also be of two types, viz., direct benefits and indirect benefits.

For analysing the commercial profitability of projects, only the direct costs and direct benefits are taken into account. Further, for assessing the commercial profitability, the direct costs and direct benefits are reckoned at the market prices. The national profitability analysis, in other words, the social cost-benefit analysis differs from commercial profitability analysis in two ways viz.,

(*a*) As against the market prices of direct cost and direct benefits considered in commercial profitability analysis, the social cost-benefit analysis takes into account the 'real cost' of direct costs and 'real benefit' of direct benefits. For example, some of the inputs, (say, power charges) may be subsisided. Only the subsidised prices of inputs is what is relevant for assessing commercial profitability. However, the social cost-benefit analysis takes into account the real cost of inputs i.e., the cost of inputs had they not been subsidised. Accordingly, the required adjustments to direct costs of inputs are made for social cost-benefit analysis. Similarly, cost adjustments may also be required for the benefits. For example, the output may be a product whose price is controlled by the Government. The Commercial profitability analysis will take into account the controlled price (which is the market price fixed by the Government) while its actual benefit to the nation may be more or less than the controlled price, which is what is relevant for social cost-benefit analysis.

(*b*) As againsst the direct cost and direct benefits that are alone considered for commercial profitability analysis, socio-economic cost-benefit analysis takes into account the indirect costs and indirect benefits to the nation. While a nation bears the indirect cost, the people of the nation enjoy the indirect benefits. Hence, indirect costs/benefits are given due recognition and accounted for in social cost-benefit analysis. It is however difficult to assess exactly the quantum of indirect costs and indirect benefits (which has always remained as a subject for debate!). For example, consider a project of a pharmaceutical unit producing life saving drugs. For the pharmaceutical company, the benefit it derives out of the project is nothing but the returns that the project earns on the investment. Thus, the market price of the life saving drug is what the pharmaceutical company will be concerned with. As against this, the drug might be one that improves the well being of the society. It's contribution to the society might be more than what the society pays as price for the drug. Thus the social benefit might be much more than the benefit that accrue to the pharmaceutical company by way of returns.

Just as benefit has two different meansings of the project promoters and to the society, cost also has two different meanings of these two categories of persons. The cost, as far as the pharmacetucial company is concerned is only the financial cost which is nothing but the direct-cost. Apart from this, there are indirect costs to the society viz., the environmental pollution caused by the pharmaceutical industry, the harmful side effects of the drugs produced if any etc., Consider another example viz., construction of a bridge over a river. It's indirect benefits may include improved communication facilities, reduction in transportation costs, reduction in travelling time etc., while the indirect cost may include acquisition of private land by the State, removal of industrial/commercial/ agricultural activities that prevailed in the land that was acquired, disturbance of ecological balance etc.,

Social cost-benefit analysis can thus be regarded as a refinement over commercial appraisal, taking he hidden factors into account. Social cost-benefit analysis is mainly used for evaluating public investment projects.

Objectives of Social Cost Benefit Analysis (SCBA)

SCBA aims to appraise the total impact that a project will have on an economy. Accordingly, SCBA focuses on the following objectives that a project is expected to fulfill.

- Contribution of the project to the GDP (Gross Domestic Product) of the economy.
- Contribution of the project to improve the benefits to the poorer sections of the society and to reduce the regional imbalances in growth and development.
- Justification of the use of scarce resources of the economy by the project.
- Contribution of the project in protecting/improving the environmental conditions.

Approach to Social Cost Benefit Analysis

There are two main approaches to Social Cost Benefit Analysis, viz., the UNIDO Approach and the Little-Mirrlees Approach. Though the UNIDO approach is more popular, none of the approaches can be said to have universal applications. The suitability of an approach to a project depends upon many factors such us the present level of development of the country, the extent and nature of future development that the country strives to achieve etc. Sometimes modifications of the approaches are necessary to be in tune with the ground realities. A detailed approach to SCB analysis is beyond the scope of this book. This is an interesting and at the same time more involved area of study and readers who are interested to know more about this are referred to books on Welfare Economics by renowned economists.

Social desirability of a project for Indian conditions : The social desirability of a project depends upon the features of a country. A project that is socially desirably for one country may not be so for another country. In fact, a project that is socially desirable for one country may even socially undesirable for another country. This is because countries differ in many aspects such as the stage of development, the natural resources available, the population, the human resources avialble, climatic conditions, geographical location etc.

For Indian conditions, the following are some of the factors that decide upon the social desirability of a project.

- India being a country wigh a huge unemployed and under employed population, a project that offers substantial employment potential is a desirable one.
- India is a country with a vast area of land and the level of development varies widely across the country. There are under-developed and undeveloped regions as well as developed pockets. The unbalanced development across the country leads to unequal distribution of income. Hence, a project that comes up in a backward region is a socially desirable one as it will achieve the social objective of balanced development.
- Energy conservation projects and projects that tap alternative/non-conventional energy potential of the country are desirable projects.
- Compared to many highly industrailised countries, the environmental pollution caused by industries in India is low. However, this can not be taken for granted since the pollution level is likely to increase with the growth and development of new projects. As a developing country, the resources available at the disposal of the country to be spent on pollution control

measures is rather limited as compared to developed countries. Hence, obviously, pollution-free projects will be an added advantage to Indian conditions.

- India is a country that iss strong in natural resources. Any project that exploits are available natural resources of the country without having any adverse impact on the society/environment will be preferred.
- Projects that use indigenous technology are also worth considering since the required expertise will be locally available.
- In the arena of international business, the need for strengthening foreign exchange reserve can not be under estimated. Hence, projects that bring in foreign exchange for the country and projects that sop flow of foreign exchange out of the country are desirable projects.

1.7.4 Project Risk Analysis

In project appraisal, risk analysis play an import part. All projects are prone to some kind of risk or the other. All projects are appraised making certain assumptions. Assumptions in project appraisal are unavoidable sine no two projects are unique in all respects and hence a new project cannot be compared with an identical project that was executed in the past. Though there may be similarity between two different projects, exactly identical projects do not exit. There are many elements of a project which contain assumed values. The following list of elements will give an idea of the assumptions on which any project appraisal is based on.

- Periodic cash inflows (the cash inflows are assumed by assuming the selling price of the product over a period of time and the plant output over the said period)
- Periodic cash outflows (the cash outflows are assumed by assuming the purchase price of raw materials, the cost of power, labour etc.,)
- Life of machinery
- Salvage value of machinery

etc.,

Since a project is appraised making use of such assumptions, the appraisal is very much prone to the risk of yielding results that may deviate from reality.

Risk Vs Uncertainty

'Risk' can be defined as the variability of return from an investment. If the probabilities of possible outcomes of a given problem are known, we can conclude that the problem contains risk; in other words the problem is risky. On the other hand, if the probabilities of possible outcomes of a given problem are not known, we can conclude that the problem has an element of uncertainty, i.e., the outcome can not be predicted.

Kinds of Project Risks

Projects face a host of risks. Some important project risks are as under.

Project Completion Risk : Completing the project in time and within the estimated cost itself is a major achievement. A project that is delayed will result in time over-run which will consequently result in cost over-run. If the project promoters are not able to pump in additional funds required to meet the cost over-run, the project runs the risk of coming to a grinding halt. Also, delayed implementation means increase in interest commitments on the borrowed funds. When the project promoters find it difficult to meet the interest commitment during the implementation period, the lenders may not be prepared to fund the project additionally to meet the cost over-run. As the saying goes, ".... the banker will lend his umbrella when the whether is fine, but will get back the umbrella when it starts raining ....". Hence, once symptons of delay in project implementation surfaces, mobilizing additional funds becomes difficult which will add to the problem of project completion. There can be also technology failures, which may result in non-completion of projects. For projects with long gestation period in the fields of fast developing technology, there is risk of project not being completed due to technological obsolescene during the course of project implementation.

Resource Risk : Raw material, power, fuel, manpower etc., are the resources used by a project. Shortage of raw material may lead to reduction in capacity utilization and higher cost of production, which willmake all profitability estimates wrong. Similarly, shortage of power, fuel, and shortage of skilled manpower will also jeopardize the project profitability calculations and the project may run the risk of not earning the estimated returns.

Price risk : Price fluctuations of both inputs and outputs (i.e., raw material and finished products) affect the project. Unforeseen happenings such as Government's interventions in price fixation, ability of competitors to offer their product to customers at a comparatively cheaper price etc., are likely to have an adverse effect.

Technology risk : Technology risk may appear in two forms. A project that is based on unproven technology (i.e., a technology that is proved at laboratory level but not proved at commercial level) may have hidden defects which may make the project a non-starter. Rapid growth in technology may make a project obsolete in technology due to the evolution of latest technology.

Political risk : The saying goes .... "Do not fight with King and God ...." The King (i.e., the Government) acts as a which dog of the country's economy and frames rules and regulations for regulating the country's economy. The Government intervenes in many forms such as levying and regulating taxes, regulating monopolistic trade practices, imposing import duties, promoting exports, prohibiting export of certain commodities, issuing import licences, controlling foreign exchange transactions, price controls, expropriation, nationalization etc. Political risk is a major risk since it can not be predicted easily.

Interest rate risk : Fluctuations in interest rate may bring in an adverse effect. For example, if a project is funded by way of long-term borrowings at a particular rate of interest, and if the interest rate falls down subsequently, the project that availed long-term borrowing at a higher interest rate has to service the loan only at the higher rate of interest, unless it makes alternative arrangements to mobilize funds at the prevailing interest rate and swap the old borrowings which is a difficult proposition. New entrants who set up similar projects may have access to long-term loans at the prevailing rate of interest which may be cheaper. In such a situation, projects that were implemented with high-cost borrowings will find it difficult to compete with new entrants.

On the other hand, if the interest rate increases in future, the interest on working capital finance (which normally carries a floating interest rate) increases which will result in lower profit margins than estimated at the time of project appraisal. Interest rate risks can be managed to some extent by entering into interest rate heding agreements like 'interest cap', 'interest swap' etc.,

Exchange rate risk : Exchange rate risk (also called currency risk) is the risk arising from currency fluctuations. Volatile exchange rates can reduce cost and productivity advantages gained over years of hard work. Firms exposed to international economy face this risk. When a firm has already committed to a foreign currency denominated transaction (i.e., the firm has entered into an agreement agreeing to make foreign currency denominated payments or agreeing to receive payments in foreign currency), the firm is exposed to exchange rate risk. The firm will incur loss if the exchange rate of the foreign currency has moved adversely and will earn profit if the exchange rate has moved favourably. Many exchange rate risk hedging tools such as forward cover, leads and lags, currency options, currency swaps etc., are available which can be efficiently made use of to manoeuvre exchange rate risk.

Techniques of Risk Analysis

Though there are many mathematical techniques available for risk analysis, the following are the simple tools that come handy for analyzing small and medium sized projects.

- Break Even analysis
- Senstivity analysis
- Decision tree analysis
- Monte-carlo technique
- Game theory

Break Even Analysis : The financial viability of a project is estimated by making various assumptions like the cost of raw material, cost of consumables, cost of labour, expected sales realisation, expected capacity utilization of the plant etc. The proof of pudding is in eating. After implementation, the project starts earning profit or starts incurring loss depending on the actual sales volume that it could achieve, the actual cost of inputs, the actual sales realisation etc. Of these factors, the costs of inputs and the price of outputs are decided by the influence of market forces. The only thing that is under the control of the project promoter is the level of output (i.e., capacity utilization). Hence, it is very essential to know the level of operation below which the project will incur losses. Break even point (BEP) refers to the level of operation at which the project neither earns profit nor incurs loss. Calculation of BEP for the given cost and price levels indicate the minimum capacity utilization that the project should aim at in order to be in a no-profit, no-loss situation. BEP also helps in identifying the level of profit/loss for a specified level of operation and the level of operation required to attain a specified profit/to avoid a specified loss etc.

Break even analysis starts with dividing the costs into two broad heads, viz., fixed costs and variable costs.

Fixed costs : All projects incur certain costs that are fixed in nature. These costs remain constant irrespective of the changes in the volume of output. Following are some of the fixed costs:

- Rent payable for land
- Rent payable for factory/office premises
- Insurance premium on fixed assets
- Interest payable on long-term borrowing/deposits
- Administrative expenses
- Annual Maintenance Charges payable for machinery maintenance
- Depreciation
- Property tax

etc.

Variable costs : These are those costs that vary directly with the level of output. Raw material cost is a variable cost since it depends on the level of output. Some other variable costs are as under.

- Consumable stores
- Power, fuel, water charges
- Selling expenses

etc.,

Referring to Fig. 1.10

At the Break even point,

Sales realization = Fixed cost + variable cost

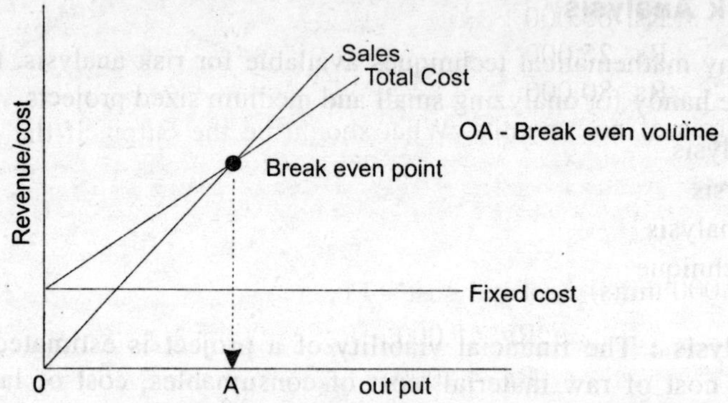

Fig. 1.10

Referring to Fig. 1.10

At the break even point,

Sales realization = Fixed Cost + Variable cost

i.e., (Output) × Selling price per unit = Fixed cost + (output) × Variable cost per unit

i.e., Output × (Selling price per unit – Variable cost per unit) = Fixed cost

i.e., $$\text{output} = \frac{\text{Fixed cost}}{(\text{Selling price per unit} - \text{Variable cost per unit})}$$

i.e., Break Even Point

$$(\text{in terms of no. of units}) = \frac{\text{Fixed cost}}{(\text{Selling price per unit} - \text{Variable cost per unit})}$$

Contribution : Contribution is the difference between the sales realisation and the variable cost. Excess of selling price over variable cost is called by the term 'contribution' since it contributes towards fixed cost and profit. For example, if the selling price per unit of a product is Rs. 12 and the variable cost per unit is Rs. 7, the contribution per unit is Rs. 5 (12 – 7) i.e., one unit of production contributes Rs. 5 onwards fixed cost and profit. If the fixed cost is say, Rs. 50,000, the BEP (in terms of no. of units) is 10,000 [50,000/5]. This means that at the level of output of 10,000 units, the contribution covers exactly the fixed cost. Hence, this is a no-profit, no-loss situation. Contribution first goes to meet the fixed cost up to BEP and subsequent to reaching of BEP, contribution adds to profit.

$$\text{BEP (in terms of no. of units)} = \frac{\text{Fixed cost}}{\text{(Selling price per unit – Variable cost per unit)}}$$

$$= \frac{\text{Fixed cost}}{\text{Contribution per unit}}$$

$$\text{B.E.P. (in terms of rupees)} = \frac{\text{Fixed cost}}{\text{Contribution per unit}} \times \text{Selling price per unit}$$

Illustration 1.7

The details of production costs and revenues of a project are as under:

Total cost : Rs. 65,000
Fixed cost : Rs. 25,000
Sales (8,000 units) : Rs. 80,000

Find the BEP in terms of no. of units. What should be the output if the profit desired is Rs. 20,000?

Solution:

Variable cost (for 8,000 units) : Total cost – Fixed cost
: Rs. 65,000 – Rs. 25,000
: Rs. 40,000

Variable cost per unit : Rs. 40,000/8,000
: Rs. 5

$$\text{BEP (in terms of no. units)} : \frac{\text{Fixed cost}}{\text{(Selling price per unit – Variable cost per unit)}}$$

$$: \frac{25000}{10-5}$$

: 5000 units

Output for a desired profit of Rs. 20,000

Let 'X' be the no. of units required to be produced for achieving a profit of Rs. 20,000

Profit = Sales – Total cost
= Sales – (Fixed cost + Variable cost)
= (10X) – (25,000 + 5X)

i.e., 20,000 = 15X – 25,000
15X = 45,000
X = 9,000

Therefore, the output required for achieving a profit of Rs. 20,000 is 9,000 units. (Refer Fig. 1.11)

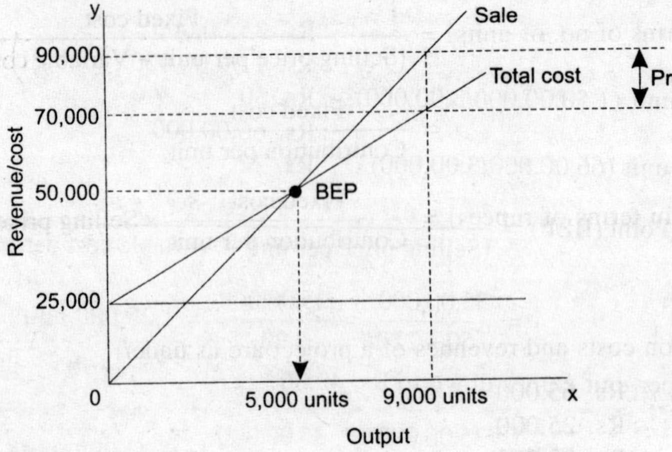

Fig. 1.11

Sensitivity Analysis: It is a technique that measures the change in the profitability of a project caused by changes in the factors that affect the cash inflows of the project. If a small change in one factors leads to a major change in the profitability of the proposed investment, the project is considered more sensitive to that factor; in other words, the project is more risky. Other things being equal, a project that is less sensitive is preferable to projects that are more sensitive. This is because a small change in a factor will affect a more sensitive project very much and may reduce the estimated profit, or may even change the estimated profit into loss. Sensitivity of a project is checked by observing the response of any measure of profitability (NPV, DSCR, BEP or any other measure) to changes in critical factors. For example, the sensitivity of a project can be studied as under.

- What happens to the NPV if the demand for the product drops down?
- What happens to the NPV if the economic life of the project reduces ?
- What happens to the DSCR if the selling price for the product falls down?

etc.,

Senstivity analyssis provides the management the much needed information as to which are the critical factors that are prone to affect the profitability of the project.

Illustration 1.8

ABC company limited proposes to start a new ventue for the manufacture of fluorescent bulbs. The estimates of the new venture are as under.

Output of bulbs per annum	: 3,00,000 nos
Expected sales revenue per annum	: Rs. 1,50,00,000
Fixed costs	: Rs. 35,00,000
Variable costs	: Rs. 66,00,000

(*a*) If the selling price comes down to Rs. 40.00 per unit, find out its effect on BEP

(*b*) If the fixed cost increases to Rs. 40,00,000, find out its effect on BEP

(*c*) If the variable cost increases by 10%, find out its effect on BEP

Solution:

Fixed cost	: Rs. 35,00,000
Sales revenue	: Rs. 1,50,00,000
Selling price per unit (1,50,00,000/3,00,000)	: Rs. 50
Variable cost	: Rs. 66,00,000
Variable cost per unit (66,00,000/3,00,000)	: Rs. 22

$$\text{Break Even Point (BEP)} = \frac{\text{Fixed cost}}{(\text{Selling price per unit} - \text{Variable cost per unit})}$$

$$= \frac{35{,}00{,}000}{50-22} = \frac{35{,}00{,}000}{28} = 1{,}25{,}000 \text{ units}$$

(*a*) Selling price per unit comes down to Rs. 40.00

$$\text{BEP} = \frac{35{,}00{,}000}{40-22} = \frac{35{,}00{,}000}{18} = 1{,}94{,}999 \text{ units}$$

(*b*) Fixed cost increases to Rs. 40,00,000

$$\text{BEP} = \frac{40{,}00{,}000}{50-22} = \frac{40{,}00{,}000}{28} = 1{,}42{,}875 \text{ units}$$

(*c*) Variable cost increases by 10%

Revised variable cost per unit

$(1.1 \times 22) = \text{Rs. } 24.20$

$$\text{BEP} = \frac{35{,}00{,}000}{50-24.20} = \frac{35{,}00{,}000}{25.80} = 1{,}35{,}659 \text{ units}$$

Results:

(*a*)

Selling price Per unit (Rs.)	*BEP*	*Reduction in (Selling price)*	*Increase in BEP*
50	1,25,000 units	$\frac{(50-40)\times 100}{50} = 20\%$	$\frac{(1{,}94{,}444 - 1{,}25{,}000)\times 100}{1{,}25{,}000} = 56\%$
40	1,94,444 units		

(*b*)

Fixed cost (Rs.)	*BEP*	*Increase in fixed cost*	*Increase in BEP*
35,00,000	1,25,000 units	$\frac{(40{,}00{,}000 - 35{,}00{,}000)\times 100}{35{,}00{,}000}$ $= 14.29\%$	$\frac{(1{,}42{,}875 - 1{,}25{,}000)\times 100}{1{,}25{,}000}$ $= 14.30$
40,00,000	1,42,875 units		

(c)

Variable cost per unit (Rs.)	BEP	Increase in variable cost	Increase in BEP
22	1,25,000 units	$\frac{(24.20-22)\times 100}{22} = 10\%$	$\frac{(1,35,659-1,25,000)\times 100}{1,25,000} = 9\%$
24.20	1,35,659 units		

Observations

- 20% increase in selling price results in 56% increase in BEP
- 14.29% increase in fixed cost results in 14.30% increase of BEP
- 10% increase in variable cost results in 9% increase of BEP

Out of three factors (selling price, fixed cost, variable cost), BEP is more sensitive to selling price.

Decision tree analysis: Decision tree approach is a graphical technique that can be used for analyzing the pros and cons of alternative decisions and choosing the best possible course of action. In real life situation, decisions are taken under conditions of uncertainty. In project management this is more so in view of the multiplicity of factors involved. A company, for example, might have to decide whether to go for investment in a large plant or a small plant, whether to invest in a new venture or to acquire an existing company; whether to produce goods indigenously or to import from abroad etc., All such decisions are taken keeping various factors in mind. The point to be noted is that the factors that have a bearing on a project are not constants but are subject to variations. Hence, there is always an element of uncertainty involved in any project decision.

A decision tree is a diagrammatic representation of the logical relationship between the different parts of a complex situation and the possible outcomes of different decisions.

A decision tree is made up of nodes and branches. Nodes are of two types, viz.,

Decision node (also called 'decision point')

and Chance node (also called 'chance point' or 'chance event')

A decision point is represented by a square '□' and a chance point is represented by a circle '○'. Different alternatives available for the given situation emerges from the decision point. At each chance point, the different possible outcomes of one of the alternative decisions are marked.

A small example will clarify this.

Example:

The chief executive of a company wants to introduce a new product in the market. He has, say, two alternatives available before him, viz., importing the product from abroad or setting up a plant for the manufacture of the product. The decision point is represented as under: (refer Fig. 1.12)

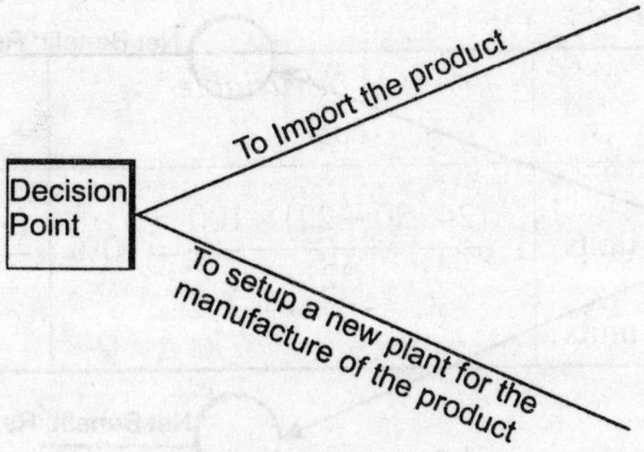

Fig. 1.12

The two alternative courses of actions available are marked as 'branches' emanating from the decision point.

Fig. 1.13 shows the chance points (or chance events) by way of circles. Each decision branch has got a chance point at its end. The different possible outcomes of each decision are noted at the respective chance points. For example, importing the product from abroad may result in a net benefit of Rs. 5,00,000/- while producing the product by investing on a new plant may result in a net benefit of Rs. 6,00,000/- which will be shown at the respective chance points. (refer Fig. 1.14)

A particular decision may have different possible outcomes. For example, when a company has investible surplus, it can either opt for investing the amount in long term securities that offer fixed returns or the company may opt for investing the surplus amount in a new venture. Any new venture always has risks associated with it. The risks cannot be accurately assessed since apart from internal factors, external (i.e., environmental) factors play a major role in deciding the magnitude of risk. We can only broadly assess the external environmental factors. In this regard, let us assume that if the company has opted to make investment in say, a consumer goods manufacturing plant, the success of the venture will depend upon the demand for the product. Let us assume that the probability for high demand is 50%, the probability for normal demand is 30% and the probability for low demand is 20%. We can tabulate the assumptions in the form of a table (as shown in the previous page) indicating the return on investment under different market conditions (i.e., under the conditions of high, normal, low demand for the product)

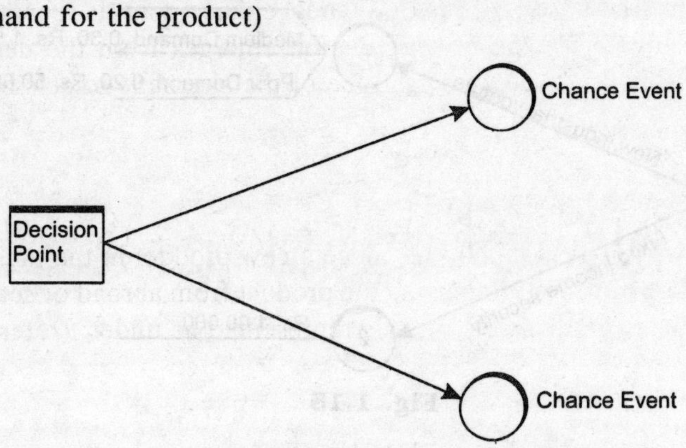

Fig. 1.13

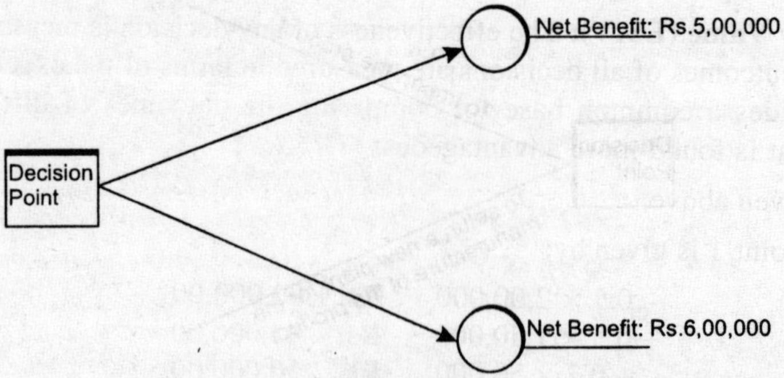

Fig. 1.14

Decision	*Return on investment*	*Risk weighted return on investment*
To invest in long term Fixed income security	*Rs. 1,00,000/-*	*Rs. 1,00,000/-**
To invest in a new industrial venture for the Manufacture of consumer Goods.		
(*a*) If the demand is high	Rs. 20,00,000/-	0.50×2,00,000 = Rs. 1,00,000/-
(*b*) If the demand is normal	Rs. 1,50,000/-	0.3×1,50,000 = Rs. 45,000/-
(*c*) If the demand is low	Rs. 50,000/-	0.2×50,000 = Rs. 10,000/-

(*Since there is no variability of income for a fixed interest bearing security, the risk weighted return is the same as the return on investment)

All the above explanations can be depicted in the form of a decision tree very easily and effectively. (refer Fig. 1.15)

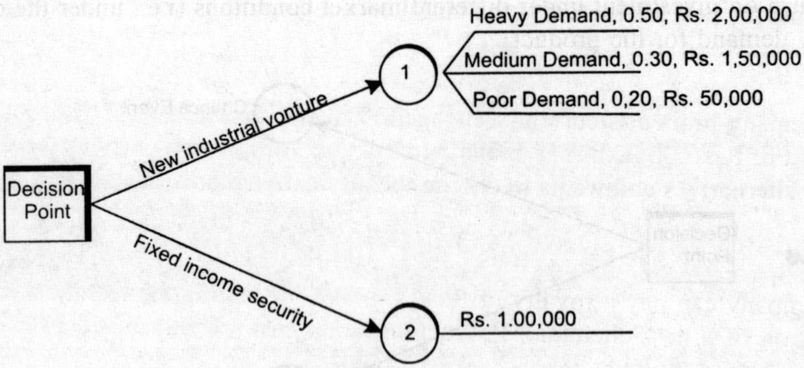

Fig. 1.15

0.5, 0.3, 0.2 are the respective probabilities

Expected Monetary Value (EMV): The effectiveness of any decision is measured only in terms of money. Hence, the outcomes of all decisions are measured in terms of the expected monetary value (EMV). EMV provides a common base for comparing the outcomes of different decisions and choosing the one that is found more advantageous.

In the example given above,

EMV at chance point-1 is given by:

0.5 × 2,00,000	Rs. 1,00,000.00
+ 0.3 × 1,50,000	Rs. 45,000.00
+ 0.2 × 50,000	Rs. 10,000.00
	Rs. 1,55,000.00

EMV at chance point-2 is given by:

1 × 1,00,000	Rs. 1,00,000.00

Having known the basic components of decision tree, let us see the rules for drawing decision tree. Since each decision can lead to further decision points, the decision tree will extend until all possible decisions are exhausted. Hence, for drawing the decision tree for a complex situation, one must know and follow certain rules.

Rules for drawing decision tree :

- Identify all the alternative decisions available at the initial decision point (i.e., at decision point-1)
- Identify all possible subsequent decision points.
- Identify all possible chance points and the likely outcomes at the chance points.
- Develop a decision tree diagram showing in sequence the decision points and chance points. Construct the decision tree diagram from the left to the right. Denote the decision point by a square and the chance points by a circle.
- After constructing the decision tree, work backwards (i.e., from the right to the left) computing the EMV of each chance point and each decision point till the initial decision point is reached.
- Determine the best alternative at the initial decision point.

Illustration 1.9

M/s ABC Company limited is currently engaged in the manufacture of industrial chemicals and is earning a profit of Rs. 5.00 lakhs per annum after paying for materials, labour etc. The company has the following alternatives and wants to choose the alternative that is most beneficial to it.

Alternatives

- The company can pay a royalty of Rs. 1.00 lakh for getting the technical know-how for the production of a new chemical. Production of the new chemical will bring additional gross income of Rs. 4.00 lakhs.

- The company can carry out research for identifying the formulation of the proposed new chemical. The research activity will cost the company Rs. 80,000/-. There is a u0% probability of achieving success in the research. Once the research comes out successful, the company will generate additional gross income of Rs. 8.00 lakhs.
- The company can invest Rs. 75,000/- in a special marketing programme to promote alternative uses for the chemicals presently being manufactured by the company. Such a venture, if successful, will generate additional gross income of Rs. 12.00 lakhs. The probability of success of such a venture is only 40% in view of the stiff competition from existing competitors who are already well established in the field.

The company can opt for only any one of the alternatives in view of the limited resources available with the company. Identify the strategy most suited for the company using decision tree analysis.

Solution:

The given problem can be convered in to a decision tree (refer Fig. 1.16)

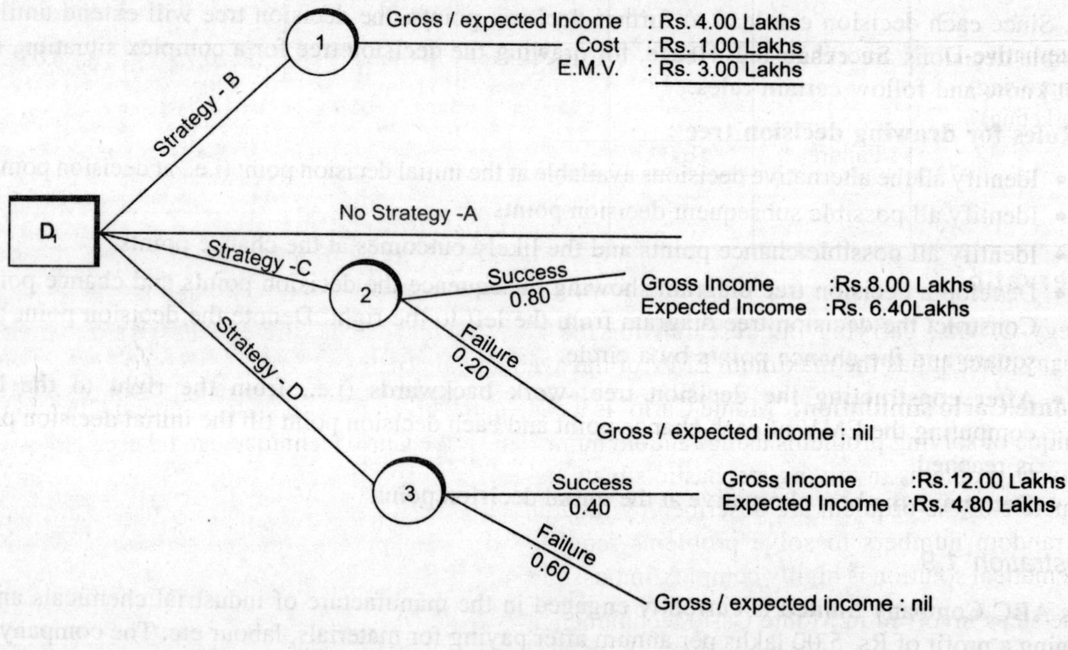

Fig. 1.16

There are three alternative strategies available as given in the problem. Infact, there are four strategies available, the fourth one being not choosing any of three given strategies.

The EMV for the four strategies are to be calculated and the strategy that has the highest EMV is the preferred strategy. The calculations can be given in the form of a table as shown below:

Alternatives (a)	*Event* (b)	*Proba-bility* (c)	*Gross income* (d)	*Expected income* [c × d] (e)	*Cost* (f)	*EMV* (e – f)
Alternative-A (not choosing any strategy)	—	—	—	—	—	—
Alternative-B (Payment of royalty)	Success	1.00	Rs. 4.00 lakhs	Rs. 4.00 lakhs	Rs. 1.00 lakhs	Rs. 3.00 lakhs
(Alternative-C (carrying out research)	Success	0.80	Rs. 8.00 lakhs	Rs. 6.40 lakhs	Rs. 0.80 lakhs	Rs. 5.60 lakhs
	Failure	0.20	0.00	0.00	(6.40 – 0.80)	
				Rs. 6.40 lakhs		
Alternative-D (improving) marketing)	Success	0.40	Rs. 12.00 lakhs	Rs. 4.80 lakhs	Rs. 0.75 lakhs	Rs. 4.05 lakhs (4.80 – 0.75)
	Failure	0.60	0.00	0.00		
				Rs. 4.80 lakhs		

Observation

Strategy-C, viz., carrying out research for the new product is the strategy best suited for the company since it has the maximum EMV of the available alternatives.

Monte Carlo simulation: 'Monte Carlo' is a code name given by Von Newmann and Ulam to the technique of solving problems using random numbers. Monte Carlo technique can be used to solve a variety of problems involving stochastic situations. (a stochastic situation is one where some or all parameters of the problem are described by random variables). It is a very popular technique and it uses random numbers to solve problems requiring decision making under uncertainty where a mathematical solution is highly complex/impossible.

The steps involved in Monte Carlo technique are as under.

- From the given probability of occurrence of events, establish cumulative probability
- Assign tag numbers to the events in such a way that the tag numbers represent the cumulative probability.
- Obtain random numbers from a random number table.
- Correlate the random numbers with the tag numbers assigned to the events and identify the value for the respective events.

Illustration: 1.10

It is observed that the demand for a product varies in a random fashion. The demand per day is observed to have the following probability.

Demand per day	:	25	33	42	51
Probability	:	0.15	0.25	0.45	0.15

Simulate the demand for the ensuing 30 days using Monte Carlo simulation technique.

Solution:

The demand is said to vary in a random fashion. The demand may get influenced by both internal and external factors. In the absence of any mathematical relationship to evaluate the demand over a period of time, the management of the firm would be very much interested to know the demand pattern for which Monte Carlo simulation technique is useful.

Demand per day	*Probability*	*Cumulative probability*	*Tag number*
25	0.15	0.15	0 to 14
33	0.25	0.40	15 to 39
42	0.45	0.85	40 to 84
51	0.15	1.00*	85 to 99

*Please note that the cumulative probability of all the events should always be equal to 1.00.

Tag numbers are assigned from 0 to 99, both numbers inclusive, so that there will be 100 tag numbers representing a cumulative probability of 1.00. A cumulative probability of 0.15 will have 15 tag numbers and accordingly tag numbers of 0 to 14 are assigned. Tag numbers for the subsequent events are assigned on similar lines.

After assigning tag numbers, the next step is to choose a set of two digits random numbers (two digits because the tag numbers are from 0 to 99) for conducting a series of trials. The number of random numbers to be chosen depends upon the accuracy required. More the number of random numbers, more the accuracy.

Let us choose, say, thirty random numbers.

(For choosing the set of random numbers from a random number table, one can start at any point on the table and proceed in any direction. A two digits random number table is given at the end of this chapter)

Referring to the two digits random number table given at the end of this chapter, let us choose arbitrarily any number, say, 40 (ninth row, first column of the table) and proceed, say, in the horizontal direction towards the right. The set of 30 random numbers chosen in this way are as under:

40, 92, 47, 01, 60, 05, 69, 79, 09, 66, 77, 69, 45, 18, 93

99, 17, 22, 62, 70, 28, 31, 07, 68, 22, 46, 30, 23, 76, 33

The first random number of 40 lies in the range '40 to 84' (the range of random numbers as referred from the range of tag numbers). Hence, the simulated demand for the first trial is 42.

The second random number of 92 lies in the range '85 to 99'. Hence, the simulated demand for the second trial is 51; the third random number is 47 which lies in the range '40 to 84' and hence the simulated demand for the third trial is 42. On similar lines, the demand is simulated by carrying out thirty trials. The simulated demand in thirty trials represent the simulated demand for a continuous period of 30 days.

Trial no.	*Random no.*	*Simulated Demand/day*	*Trial no.*	*Random no.*	*Simulated Demand/day*
1	40	42	16	99	51
2	92	51	17	17	33
3	47	42	18	22	33
4	01	25	19	62	42
5	60	42	20	70	42
6	05	25	21	28	33
7	69	42	22	31	33
8	79	42	23	07	25
9	09	25	24	68	42
10	66	42	25	22	33
11	77	42	26	46	42
12	69	42	27	30	33
13	45	42	28	23	33
14	18	33	29	76	42
15	93	51	30	33	33

Illustration 1.11

Company 'A' is considering the proposal to take over company 'B'. Based On the observations, company 'A' estimates the probability distributions of costs and revenues of the takeover proposal as under:

Cost per day (Rs.)	*Probability*	*Revenue per day (Rs.)*	*Probability)*
18,000.00	0.15	20,000.00	0.15
20,000.00	0.20	25,000.00	0.15
35,000.00	0.25	45,000.00	0.25
45,000.00	0.35	55,000.00	0.35
60,000.00	0.05	70,000.00	0.10

Obtain the probability distribution of net revenue to company 'A' if it takes over company 'B'.

Solution:

For arriving at the probability distribution of net revenue, we should first arrive at a simulated set of net revenues. Since the data available is with regard to cost and revenue, we can first simulate 'cost' and 'revenue' and then arrive at the simulated 'net revenue'.

The number of trails to be conducted is not given. Let us conduct, say, 20 trails.

Using two digits random number table, the following are the two sets of random numbers chosen. (one set for simulating 'cost' and another set for simulating 'revenue')

The first set of random numbers (for 'cost'):
40, 12, 82, 65, 74, 92, 47, 60, 01, 62, 28, 29, 69, 69, 00, 11, 81, 86, 05, 36

The second set of random numbers (for 'revenue'):
12, 98, 31, 86, 87, 38, 88, 19, 09, 44, 56, 35, 78, 02, 58, 06, 77, 23, 05, 01

Using the sets of random numbers, tag numbers are assigned to costs and revenues as under:

Cost	*Probability*	*Cumulative probability*	*Tag No.*
18,000.00	0.15	0.15	0 to 14
20,000.00	0.20	0.35	15 to 34
35,000.00	0.25	0.60	35 to 59
45,000.00	0.35	0.95	60 to 94
40,000.00	0.05	1.00	95 to 99

Revenue	*Probability*	*Cumulative probability*	*Tag No.*
20,000.00	0.15	0.15	0 to 14
25,000.00	0.15	0.30	15 to 29
45,000.00	0.25	0.55	30 to 54
55,000.00	0.35	0.90	55 to 89
70,000.00	0.10	1.00	90 to 99

Costs and revenues are simulated correlating the tag numbers with the random numbers which is given in the table below

Trial No.	*Random No.*	*Simulated cost*	*Trial No.*	*Random No.*	*Simulated revenue*
1	40	35,000	1	12	20,000
2	12	18,000	2	98	70,000
3	82	45,000	3	31	45,000
4	65	45,000	4	86	55,000
5	74	45,000	5	87	55,000
6	92	45,000	6	38	45,000
7	47	35,000	7	88	55,000
8	60	45,000	8	09	25,000
9	01	18,000	9	09	20,000
10	62	45,000	10	44	45,000
11	28	20,000	11	56	55,000
12	29	20,000	12	35	45,000
13	69	45,000	13	78	55,000
14	69	45,000	14	02	20,000
15	00	18,000	15	58	55,000
16	11	18,000	16	06	20,000
17	81	45,000	17	77	55,000
18	86	45,000	18	23	25,000
19	05	18,000	19	05	20,000
20	36	35,000	20	01	20,000

Trial No: 1 (Simulated cost)

The random number 40 lies in the range '35 to 59'. The corresponding cost is to Rs. 35,000.00 Other trials are conducted on similar lines and the costs for 20 days are simulated.

Trial No:1 (Simulated revenue)

The random number 12 lies in the range of '00 to 14'. The corresponding revenue is Rs. 20,000. Other trials are conducted on similar lines and the revenues for 20 days are simulated.

Using the simulated costs and revenues for 20 days, the simulated net revenue in view of the take over proposal can be obtained. (net revenue = revenue – cost)

Trial No.	*Cost*	*Revenue*	*Net revenue*
1	35,000	20,000	(–) 15,000
2	18,000	70,000	52,000
3	45,000	45,000	0
4	45,000	55,000	10,000
5	45,000	55,000	10,000
6	45,000	45,000	0
7	35,000	55,000	20,000
8	45,000	25,000	(–) 20,000
9	18,000	20,000	2,000
10	45,000	45,000	0
11	20,000	55,000	35,000
12	20,000	45,000	25,000
13	45,000	55,000	10,000
14	45,000	20,000	(–) 25,000
15	18,000	55,000	37,000
16	18,000	20,000	2,000
17	45,000	55,000	10,000
18	45,000	25,000	(–) 20,000
19	18,000	20,000	2,000
20	35,000	20,000	(– 15,000)

We have been asked to obtain a probability distribution for the net revenue. The table above gives the simulated net revenue for a period of 20 days. To arrive at the probability distribution of net revenue, note down the frequency of occurrences of same net revenues and tabulate them as under:

Net revenue	Frequency
(–) 25,000	1
(–) 20,000	2
(–) 15,000	2
0	3
2,000	3
10,000	4
20,000	1
25,000	1
35,000	1
37,000	1
52,000	1
	20

From the frequency of occurrences of each net revenue, the probability distribution for net revenue is arrived at as under:

Net revenue	*Frequency*	*Probability*
(–) 25,000	1	1/20 = 0.05
(–) 20,000	2	2/20 = 0.10
(–) 15,000	2	2/20 = 0.10
0	3	3/20 = 0.15
2,000	3	3/20 = 0.15
10,000	4	4/20 = 0.20
20,000	1	1/20 = 0.05
25,000	1	1/20 = 0.05
35,000	1	1/20 = 0.05
37,000	1	1/20 = 0.05
52,000	1	1/20 = 0.05
	20	1.00

Grame thoery : In real life situation, business firms compete with one another. Game theory deals with situations in which two intelligent opponents have conflicting interests compete. For example, two business firms may compete for attracting the consumers towards their products. To achieve their goals, the two firms will form strategies. The strategy that one firm forms will depend upon the strategy that the other firm has already formed/in the process of forming. The approach to such competitive problems was developed by Von Neumann who named it 'Game Theory'.

The following are the properties of a competitive game:

- The number of competitors are finite. (the competitors are also known as 'players')
- Each player has a finite number of strategies.
- All the players need not necessarily have the same number of strategies.
- Each player chooses a single course of action from the list of strategies available to him. All the players are assumed to make their choice simultaneously so that no player knows the choices of his opponents until he is already committed to his choice. When all the players select their strategy simultaneously, a play of the game results.
- The outcome of the play depends upon the strategies followed by the players.

The objective of the 'Game Theory' is to develop a rational criterion for the selection of a strategy/ strategies by each player. Since games are rooted in conflict of interests, the optimal solution selects one or more strategies for each player in such a way that any change in the chosen strategies does not improve the benefit to either player.

Explaining the mathematical treatment involved in 'Game Theory' is beyond the scope of this book. Interested readers are referred to standard books on 'Operations Research'.

SWOT analysis* : In a dynamic environment, a company must always keep vigil to ensure that its competitive position is maintained or improved upon so that it can exploit the situation for profit. Every organization operates in an environment that is subject to constant changes. Hence, unless an organization adapts itself to the changing environment, success can not be guaranteed. SWOT analysis provides an opportunity for introspection into the organisation's strengths, weaknesses, opportunities and threats. Of these four aspects, strengths and weaknesses refer to the organisation's inner strengths and weaknesses while opportunities and threats refer to factors external to the organization over which the organization has no control.

---

* **Source :** 'SWOT analysis is Project appraisaal'. The Management Accountant, Student Editon, Vol.3, No. 6, June, 2000.

SWOT analysis is done in many situations like mergers and acquisitions, takeovers, declining trends in profits, growing competition in the field, expansion/diversification of activities, product range extension, vertical integration etc. SWOT analysis can also be done in the absence of the above situations to improve upon the competitive edge of an organisation and also to avoid any pitfalls lying ahead that may hamper the growth of the organisation.

SWOT analysis applied to project appraisal : Project appraisal is an area where SWOT analysis is of immense help, particularly when project appraisal is done for expansion/diversification activities. Though SwOT analysis is primarily done as a subjective estimate of the strengths, weaknesses, opportunities and threats, it throws light on the important factors that are in support of the proposed project or that work against the interests of the proposed project so that the project can be planned suitably. Some of the factors that are worth considering with regard to strengths, weaknesses, opportunities and threats of an organization that envisages an expansion or diversification project arre enumerated below:

Strengths

- Locational advantage of the organization—nearness to the sources of raw material, nearness to location of end users etc.
- Goodwill developed among clients
- Buy-back arrangements
- Lower capital investment on the existing plant (i.e., setting up a similar plant would have become much costlier)
- Good network of dealers and distributors already established
- Qualified, committed, motivated, reliable work force
- Professional top management team
- Unutilized capacity utilization
- Globalised operations
- High-tech area/high initial investment required which act as a barrier to new entrants.

Weaknesses

- Technological obsolescence
- Scarcity of raw material
- Comparatively less international price for similar products
- Locational disadvantage resulting in higher freight costs for transportation of raw materials/ finished products
- Labour unrest
- Absence of entry barriers to new entrants

Opportunities

- Cost of raw material becoming cheaper
- Liberalisation of import of raw material (where the cost of imported raw material is cheaper)
- Growth in per capita income and growth in consumption level
- Advent of cost saving production technology
- Imports of competitive products becoming costlier
- Product finding alternate uses, leading to increase in demand

- Withdrawal of incentive offered by the Government to new entrants
- Chances of competitors changing their line of activity

Threats

- Import of competitive products becoming cheaper
- Liberalisation of import of competitive products (when the cost of imported goods is cheaper)
- Withdrawal of existing incentives by the Government
- Raw material becoming costlier
- General recession in the economy resulting in slowing down of consumption
- New entrants entering the field in a big way
- Stringent pollution control measures adopted by the Government
- Possible hike in electric power charges, hike in duties, taxes etc.
- Government's populist measures that may have adverse impact
- Product at the fag end of its life cycle
- Emergence of cheaper alternative products

Though SWOT analysis applied to project appraisal is subjective in nature, it throws light on important points that need to be considered before taking an investment decision. Certain factors like liberalization of import of competitive products that are cheaper might have a heavy implication and may even suggest shelving off the project idea. Factors like possible hike in the production expenses, possible reduction in selling price to fight the competition etc., will have to be accounted for while arriving at the profitability estimate by suitably adjusting the anticipated expenditures and incomes. SWOT analysis, thus comes first, before detailed financial projections are attempted upon.

Two Digit Random Number Table:

29	64	52	40	93	67	36	17	51	26	68	28	27	69	02
59	34	15	12	33	60	96	89	72	36	80	50	29	38	57
21	03	36	82	84	73	01	80	81	19	80	47	66	07	49
10	12	99	65	70	51	19	81	06	30	79	33	89	75	22
31	39	86	74	95	00	84	48	26	87	65	60	20	02	64
30	23	28	92	23	28	01	56	78	66	77	09	74	47	03
57	89	82	47	80	19	84	36	97	22	04	58	24	67	84
73	82	03	60	75	76	19	56	26	71	75	02	74	06	03
40	92	47	01	60	05	69	79	09	66	77	69	45	18	93
99	17	22	62	70	28	31	07	68	22	46	30	23	76	33
54	40	80	28	20	40	68	59	42	22	29	54	56	36	04
36	89	81	29	54	26	58	15	33	76	57	18	45	50	59
02	97	27	69	50	42	61	89	43	68	44	80	43	91	82
67	79	32	69	78	00	46	91	59	32	40	11	96	96	51
46	68	05	00	52	82	95	31	90	70	65	93	72	54	75
35	66	55	11	00	96	25	24	19	81	14	86	10	32	91
28	31	28	81	68	25	89	63	53	09	28	25	49	47	57
12	98	31	86	87	38	88	19	09	44	56	35	78	02	58
06	77	23	05	01	76	12	38	01	02	30	27	64	46	85
69	51	17	36	57	23	90	61	84	90	51	98	29	83	76

1.7.4 Project Cost Estimation

Cost of the Project

Correct estimation of the capital cost of a product is the foundation over which the edifice of financial appraisal stands. Resources for the project are tied up after the project cost is estimated. If the project cost is under-estimated, the project will run short of funds during implementation and there is risk of the project coming to a grinding halt if the promoter is not able to bring in additional capital to meet the increase in project cost or if the bank/financial institution that has extended financial assistance for the building up of fixed assets of the project does not come forward to extend additional loan to meet the increase in project cost. The emphasizes the need for a correct estimate of the project cost. On the other hand, if the project cost is over estimated, it leads to a situation where more funds (equity and debt together) are available than required and under these circumstances it is more likely that the promoters may divert the resources for other purposes which again is detrimental to the interests of both the promoters and the financing institutions.

Components of Capital Cost of a Project

The following are the components that constitute the capital cost of any project.

(*i*) Land
(*ii*) Land development
(*iii*) Buildings
(*iv*) Plant and machinery
(*v*) Electricals
(*vi*) Transport and erection charges
(*vii*) Know-how/consultancy fees.
(*viii*) Misscellaneous assets.
(*ix*) Preliminary and preopertative expenses.
(*x*) Provision for contigencies
(*xi*) Margin money for working capital.

We will discuss in detail about the individual components that make up the project cost, in the following pages. The aim in deciding upon the various components of project cost should be to reduce the cost to the minimum, keeping the functional requirements adequate.

(I) Land

Before deciding upon the extent of land required for the project, the cost of land etc., the first question to be asked it whether it is essential to invest on land and building. If the project is small in size, the possibilities of acquiring a building on lease may be thought of. The comparative cost advantages and the effect on profitability between the two options viz., starting the project in a leased building and starting the project in owned building by acquring land and constructing building thereon may be studied. Small projects can be started in leased building, which will reduce the cost of investment considerably. It may be noted that it is only the plant and machinery that are going to produce goods and building only acts as a shelter to house the production facilities and investment on building is not directlygoing to add to the production capacity. However, this can not be the case always. Building suitable for the chosen project may not be always available on lease. Some projects may require building of certain minimum sizes/specifications, in which case it will not be possible to identify a building on lease that is suitable for meeting the requirements of the project.

The component 'Land' comes into picture only after having decided to purchase land and construct building instead of starting the project in a leased premises.

The extent of land should be so chosen that it is neither too large as to inflate the cost of the project nor too small as to provide no leeway for making additions/alterations to the building and for future expansion.

The extent of land required for a project can be stimated after deciding upon the building plan. Sufficient allowances for open space around the building should be provided for. Also open space shall be provided to take up expansion proposals that may come up in the near future. In respect of industries where raw materials are stored in the open, sufficient vacant land should be available. For example, wood working units store a large volume of wooden logs in open space. Similarly, steel foundries and steel re-rolling mills also stock raw materials in huge quantity in open yards. Sufficient vacant land surrounding the building should be available to take care of the above requirements. If there are plans to go for expansion/diversification in the near future, say within a span of three years or so, the extent of land should be chosen accordingly, since it may not be possible to acquire additional land when required, if the adjacent lands have already been put into some use by the owners. The cost of land includes the legal charges payable for registration of sale deeds.

(II) Land Development

Land development charges include cost of levelling of land, cost of laying internal roads, cost of providing fencing and gates. Land development charges deserve to be carefully assessed since this is an area where there is a likelihood of under estimation if detailed and correct estimates are not made.

(III) Building

Provisions for different types of buildings shall be envisaged and provided for. The following are the types of buildings that are normally required for any project.

- Main factory building.
- Ancillary factory buildings.
- Administrative buildings.
- Laboratory.
- Godowns.
- Toiler blocks.
- Overhead/Underground water storage tanks.
- Canteen, rest rooms, guesthouses.
- Quarters for essential staff etc.

The plant layout suited for the proposed project should be studied and analyzed. The size of the main factor building depends upon the plant layout. It must be ensured that the built-up area of different buildings proposed are sufficient to meet the requirements and that no unnecessary construction is done. Type of roofing plays a major role in determining the cost of building since the nature of super structure (walls, columns, beams etc.,) depends upon the type of roofing. Office/ Administrative buildings are normally constructed with reinforced concrete slab roofing as this gives a dust proof and sound proof environment and is also suitable for air-conditioning of rooms. Factory hall, godowns and other buildings are normally provided with industrial roofing, which may be a combination of steel/concrete trusses and A.C.C. sheet/G.I. sheet roofing sheets. This type of roofing reduces the cost of construction considerably as compared to a building with refinforced concrete roofing. The height of factory building should also be correctly decided after taking into account the height of machinery proposed to be erected, the headroom required for operating the plant and machinery, the requirements of overhead cranes if any etc. After having arrived at the size and design of different buildings, their cost of construction can be arrived at by preparing a detailed estimate, entrusting the work to a qualified civil/structural engineer.

(IV) Plant and Machinery

Indigenous Plants : While choosing machinery suppliers, their reputation and past performance act as the leading indicators. Performance of machinery supplied by them earlier are to be seen to have a first hand knowledge. Quotations from a few reputed machinery suppliers can be obtained and a comparative study of the prices quoted by them can be done before deciding upon a particular supplier. Cost of indigenous plants include basic price plus sales tax, octroi and other taxes, if any. Apart from price, other factors like the market reputation of the supplier, the differences in machinery specifications of different suppliers, their service network to effect after-sales-service are also to be considered and these factors are tobe properly weighed before arriving at a decision.

Imported plants: The cost of imported plant and machinery is the sum of the F.O.B. (Free-on-board) value of the plant to be imported, the shipping/Air cargo freight charges, marine/air insurance charges, import duty payable on the machinery, clearing charges, loading and unloading charges at different places etc. It is always advisable to import necessary spares along with the main machinery since identifying spare parts for imported machinery may be time consuming. While the cost of new imported machinery can be arrived at fairly accurately as mentioned above, caution should be exercised when second hand machinery are proposed to be imported. In such cases, apart from getting quotation for machinery price from the machinery dealers, the price of the machinery should also be assessed by an independent, competent engineer after duly inspecting the machinery. The unexpired future life of second hand machinery is also to be got estimated by the engineer.

Cost of power generator is to be included in the cost of plant and machinery, whenever it is felt essential to have a generator as a stand-by source of power. Apart from main machinery, the requirement of items like laboratory equipments, tool room machinery etc., are also to be carefully assessed and included in the scheme of plant and machinery proposed for the project.

(V) Electricals

The cost of electrical items include the cost of cables, panel boards, voltage stabilizers etc. Whenever the industry is to draw electric power from a high tension power line, necessary voltage step-down transformer should be included in the project and it's cost should be accounted for.

(VI) Transport and Erection Charges

Transportation charges till the plant and machinery reaches the factory site, including loading and unloading charges are to be accounted for. Erection charge includes machinery foundation cost and machinery assembling and erection expenses.

(VII) Know-how/Consultancy Fees

The following are the expenses that are included under this head.

(*a*) Know-how fee to technical consultants.

(*b*) Expenses of training employees in the production process.

(VIII) Miscellaneous Assets

These are the assets that are allied to industrial activity, but that do not form part of plant and machinery. For example, office equipments, furnitures, fire fighting equipments, water coolers, air conditioners etc., come under this category. These assets, though not form part of industrial equipments, are to be included in the project and adequately provided for in the project cost. Cash deposits with Electricity Boards for getting power connection, advances made to lessor while taking building on lease etc., which are in the nature of refundable deposits are also included under this head.

(IX) Preliminary and Preoperative Expenses

These are micellaneous expenses that are incurred before the project takes shape and starts commercial production. The following expenses come under this head.

- Investigation fee, service charge etc., to banks/financing institutions.
- Commitment charges payable on loans offered by banks/financial institutions.

(Bank/Financial institutions, after having sanctioned loans for a project, disburse the loan in stages, in proportion to the progress of project implementation. If, for example, the implementation period for a project is say one year, the bank/financial institution that has sanctioned loan to the project should be in a position to release the loan as and when required so that the project implementation is not delayed due to shortage of funds. This being so, the bank/financial institution has to maintain sufficient liquid cash to meet the loan disbursement as and when needed. Since maintaining such cash reserve involves cost, the banks/financial institutions charge a fee called commitment charges).

- Interest on term loans during implementation period.

[The term 'Term loan' is nothing bu t along term loan given by banks/financial institutions for setting up of projects. Term loans are granted for the acquisition of fixed industrial assets. As mentioned above, the loan is disbursed in stages during the implementation of the project. Banks/ financial institutions offer holiday period (technically called as 'Moratorium') for the repayment of principal loan amount. The moratorium for the repayment of principal loan amount will depend on the project implementation schedule and is normally fixed in such a way that the first instalment of term loan repayment starts after allowing reasonable period beyond the date of commencement of commercial production. However, interest on term loan is pauable right from the date of disbursement of term loan. If a project has drawn term loan in stages during a particular period of time, interest on the term loan amount is payable in quarterly or half yearly installments as decided by the financing institution. Since by now the project would be only under implementation stage and would have not yet started generating revenue, the project promoter should tie-up necessary sources of funds to meet the interest on term loan during the implementation period. Hence the interest amount payable to the term-loan lending institution during the period of implementation of the project is to be worked out and included in the project cost].

- Mortgage expenses.
- Expenses on capital issues.
- Other miscellaneous expenses during the project implementation stage.
- Insurance charges.

Both fixed assets and current assets (inventory) are to be insured against possible damage by fire accident. Though the project promoters may sometimes consider this is an unwanted expense it can not be viewed so. Any project is started with the plan of reaping benefits over a longer period of time. For the project to survive till its economic life, it is imperative that the assets should be safeguarded by insuring them. Banks and financial institutions insist that the assets financed by them be insured. Normally the insurance premium is paid once in a year. Assets are to be insured as and when they are created. Insurance premium for the fixed assets will be fully paid by the time the fixed assets are created and the project is about to go for production, while the insurance premium on inventory will be paid after this period. Thus the insurance premium payable on the fixed assets is an expense that is incurred during the project implementation stage and accordingly the same is to be included in pre-operative expense.

During the project implementation period, insurance premium is payable on the fixed assets that are being created. This is taken to the head 'pre-operative expenses'. Once the project implementation is completed, insurance premium is payable on the inventory also apart from the insurance premium on the fixed assets created. Hence, from the first year of operation of the plant onwards, insurance premium is payable on the fixed assets as well as on the inventory.

(X) Provision for Contingencies

The cost estimates of land, land development, building, plant and machinery, electricals, transport and erection etc., that are made are based on certain assumptions. While actually implementing the project, it is more likely that there may be deviations between the estimated cost and the actual cost. For example, (*a*) the price of plant and machinery may rise; the sales tax, excise duty etc., may get revised on the higher side (*b*) in the case of imported plant and machinery, the cost in terms of rupee may increase due to adverse fluctuations in foreign exchange rates (*c*) during implementation of the project there may be minor deviations required to suit the field conditions—some equipments which were not originally envisaged may be required to be included etc.

In order to meet such unexpected but unavoidable cost increase, there must be a provision in the project cost. This is done by making a contingency provision in the project cost which may vary from 5% to 15% of the cost of non-firm items. A higher contingency provision is required if the implementation period is longer since the chances of increase in cost increases with the passage of time.

(XI) Margin Money for Working Capital

This head which forms part of the project cost needs some explanation. Any project needs funds for two purposes. First, for the setting up of the project and then for maintaining the operation of the plant. The funds required for setting up the project consists of investment on fixed assets while the funds required for maintaining the operations of the plant consists of investment on working capital. Banks/Financial institutions extend Term loan for investment on fixed assets while financing of working capital requirement is done mainly by banks. In both the type of financing viz., financing of fixed assets and working capital, the financier expects a margin to be brought in by the promoters. The entire requirement is not financed by way of loan. If the total working capital requirement is say Rs. 50.00 lakhs and if the bank that finances the working capital requirement of the project stipulates a promoter's contribution of 25%, the promoters are to bring in Rs. 12.50 lakhs towards their share of working capital and the bank can finance the remaining 75% of the requirement i.e., Rs. 37.50 lakhs. The share of promoter's contribution to be brought in for availing working capital assistance from bank is the margin money for working captial.

For funding fixed investments meant for the project, the financing institutions stipulate a minimum promoter's contribution. The margin money brought in by the promoters towards working capital is also taken into account for arriving at the promoter's contribution required to be brought in for availing term loan. Hence the margin money for working capital is included as a component of the project cost.

The margin money brought in by the promoters to meet the working capital requirement is out of equity capital which is a long-term source and hence it is included in the capital cost of the project.

Method of arriving at the margin-money for working capital:

$$\text{Margin money for working capital} = \text{Working capital requirement} - \text{Probable working captial loan that can be obtained from bank}$$

Working capital requirement consists of the funds required for maintaining the working capital cycle. A working capital cycle may be depicted as shown in Fig. 1.17

Funds are locked up in
Raw material
Work-in progress
Finished goods
and Debtors

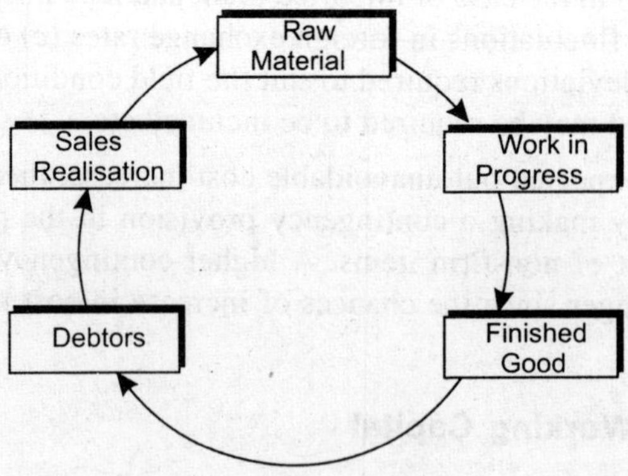

Fig. 1.17

Raw material : If the raw material is freely available from nearby sources, it need not be stocked heavily. In such situations, it is enough to stock, say a week's requirement of raw material to meet unforeseen, emergency situations. On the other hand, if the raw material is a scarce commodity, it should be adequately stocked. A stock of, say, 2, 3 or more months requirement may be needed depending upon the situation. Further, if raw material is required to be transported from a far off place, the holding period for raw material will be more in order to maintain production even if transportation of raw material is delayed beyond the scheduled time due to any unexpected reasons. Also there may be situations where the raw material is sold only in bulk quantities. This often happens when the raw material is imported from abroad. In such situations, the quantity of raw material to be stocked is the minimum quantity of raw material that can be purchased in one order.

Work-in-progress : By the term 'work-in-progress", we mean the 'Goods-in-progress', i.e., the goods that are undergoing the production process. At any point of time, the goods are in different stages of production. Some may be nearing completion and some may have just been introduced in the production line. The cost of goods-in-progress (or work-in-progress) thus lies between the cost of raw material and the cost of finished goods.

We can visualise finished goods as 'value added raw material'. While the value addition is complete for finished-goods, the value addition is incomplete for goods-in-progress. This is because the value addition is underway and goods are in different stages of production.

Cost of work-in-progress = Cost of raw material + Expenses

= Cost of raw material + (Direct expenses + Overheads)

The work-in-progress (or goods-in-progress) period is ascertained by carefully studying the production process and the time taken by the raw material to get converted into finished product after passing through the different stages of production.

The break-up details of direct expenses and overheads deserve careful consideration. The different components that form part of the cost of production and profitability estimate will be of use in identifying the direct expenses and over heads. A specimen format of cost of production and profitability estimate is furnished for ready reference. [Refer Table 1.6]

Table 1.6 Cost of Production and Profitability Estimate

	I year	*II year*	*III year*	......
Capacity Utilisation				
A. Sales realization				
B. Cost of production				
Raw material				
Power				
Fuel				
Consumables				
Wages and ssalaries				
Repairs and maintenance				
Rent and insurance				
Factory supervision				
Depreciation (As per Companies Act)				
C. Administrative and selling Overheads				

	I year	II year	III year	.. ..
Administrative expenses				
Selling expenses				
D. Gross profit before Interest and tax [A—B—C]				
E. Financial charges				
Interest on term loan				
Interest on working capital loan				
F. Profit after Interest				
[D—E]				
G. Preliminary exp. written-off				
H. Profit/loss before tax [F—G]				
I. Provision for tax				
J. Profit/loss after tax [H—I]				
K. Less: Dividend				
L. Retained profit [J—K]				
M. Add: Depreciation				
(as per Companies Act)				
N. Add: Preliminary exp. Written off				
O. Net cash accrual [L + M + N]				

The following components (Refer Production and Profitability Estimate for easy identification) form part of Direct Expenses.*

- Power.
- Fuel.
- Wages and Salaries.
- Repairs and Maintenance.
- Factory supervision.

The following components form part of the overheads.

- Administration expenses.
- Selling expwenses (includes advertisement expenses also)

out of the overheads, it is enough if only administrative expenses are taken into account for arriving at the cost of work-in-progress.

Stock of finished goods : This component of working capital refers to the cost of goods produced and stored in the godown, before being despatched to the customers. This intrun depends upon the demand-pattern. Even if a product has a high demand, some finished stock will be usually maintained to meet orders from unexpected/new customers, to provide samples to new customers, to meet unexpected and sudden increase in quantity demanded by existing customers etc.

Cost of stock of finished goods = Cost of raw material and consumables + Expenses

= Cost of raw material + (Direct expenses + Over heads)

Both administrative expenses and selling expenses can be taken into account for arriving the overheads. Though selling expenses in strict sense arises only by the time the goods are sold, the company will be incurring some selling expenses like advertisement and promotion expenses etc., even while the finished goods are in stock but no sale has taken place yet. Hence if selling expenses are also included, we only err on the safer side.

Sales bills (or book debts) : Certain products can be sold on cash and carry basis. If so, there won't be any sales-bills outstanding i.e., there will be virtually no book debts. On the other hand, if as per the prevailing customs and practice, goods are sold on credit for some period, the same should be taken into account for working capital assessment. A period of say, one month provided for book debts means that goods produced would be sold to customers on credit and the sale proceeds would be paid by the customers to the seller after a period of one month. Till such time the sale proceeds are received back, the plant can not be kept idle for want of working capital. The operations of the plant will continue without break if there are working capital funds available to offer one-month credit to the customers.

Book debts are calculated either on the basis of

(*a*) Cost of raw material + Expenses (as in the case of finished goods) or on the basis of

(*b*) Sales price:

While the first method indicates the actual funds required, the second method includes profit also. Of the two methods, the first method (viz., Books debts = Cost of raw material + expenses) is more accurate since 'Profit' does not form part of funds requirement in strict sense.

Creditors for raw materials and consumables (suppliers credit) : Just as produced goods are sold on credit to the customers, raw materials and consumables can be purchased on credit from the sellers. The credit period available for raw materials and consumables is to be assessed by keeping in view the practice prevailing in the industry. Obviously, the availability of credit facilities from the suppliers of raw materials and consumables reduces the working capital requirement to that extent. Suppliers credit is calculated on the basis of raw material/consumable costs.

Thus the components of working capital requirement may be summarised as under.

Component	*Period of requirement*	*Cost*
(*a*) Raw materials and consumables	________month*	
(*b*) Work-in-progress	________months**	
(*c*) Finished goods	________months***	
(*d*) Book debts (or debtors) or sales bills)	________months****	
	Total	
Less: Supplier's credit available for raw Materials and consumables	________months*****	
Working capital requirement		

* Period for which raw materials/consumables are to remain in stock.

** Time taken by raw material to get converted into finish product.

*** Period for which finished goods are to be stocked.

**** Credit period allowed to debtors.

***** Credit period allowed by suppliers of raw materials/consumables.

[The period of requirement for each of the above components of working capital is to be carefully arrived at by studying the prevailing industrial/market trend.]

After having arrived at the working capital requirement, the next step is to arrive at the working capital margin. It is the working capital margin that forms part of the capital cost of the project.

Working capital margin = Working capital requirement – Probable working capital finance that can be arranged.

For working capital finance, companies normally approach commercial banks. Hence, it is essential to know the approach generally followed by banks for arriving at the component of working capital finance for a given project. Let us devote some time to understand some of the norms followed by commercial banks in assessing the working capital requirement and working capital finance for projects.

Tandon committee recommendations : In the year 1974, Reserve Bank of India appointed a study group named "Study Group for framing guideline for the follow up of Bank Credit" under the Chairmanship of P.L. Tandon, who was the Chairman of Punjab National Bank. RBI accepted the major recommendations made by the committee and advised the banks to implement the recommendations accepted by the RBI.

The major areas of recommendation covered by the Tandon Committee are as under:

(*a*) Stipulation of norms for holding of inventory and for receivables.

(*b*) Style of bank credit towards working capital.

(*c*) Maximum possible bank finance towards working capital. and

(*d*) Follow-up and supervision of bank credit.

The Committee prescribed norms for 15 selected industries and these 15 industries together accounted for about 50% of the total industrial bank credit. Though the committee suggested norms only for 15 selected industries it suggested to the RBI to make regular review of the norms and to make necessary changes that are deemed necessary and also suggested to include other industries. RBI has been accordingly revising the norms based on the requirement.

Out of the recommendations of the Tandon Committee, the areas most relevant to the determination of working capital finance/working capital margin is the "Maximum Permissible Bank Finance".

Tandon Committee suggested three different method of arriving at the Maximum Permissible Bank Finance, which are reproduced below:

First method		*Second method*		*Third method*	
Total current assets	--	Total current assets	--	Total current assets	--
Less: Current Liabilities other than Bank borrowings	--	Less: 25% of the total current assets (to be met out of long term sources)	--	Less: Core current assets (to be financed from long term sources)	--
	______		______		______
Working capital gap	--		--	Real current assets	--
Less: 25% of Working capital gap (to be met out of long term sources)	--	Less: Current Liabilities other than bank borrowings	--	Less: 25% of real current assets	--
				Less: Current liabilities other than	--

(Cont)

First method		*Second method*		*Third method*	
				bank borrowings	
Maximum Permissible Bank Finance	– –	Maximum Permissible Bank Finance	– –	Maximum Permissible Bank Finance	– –

One of the recommendations of CHORE COMMITTEE (a committee appointed by the RBI in the year 1979 to suggest further guidelines to fine-tune the working capital financing pattern) is that all the borrowrs enjoying working capital credit limit of Rs. 50.00 lakhs and above will have to bring gradually additional contribution based on the second method of lending as prescribed by the Tandon committee.

Accordingly, Method—I is adopted for projects with working capital limit of Rs. 10.00 lakhs and above, but less than Rs. 50.00 lakhs.

Method—II is adopted for projects where the total working capital limit is Rs. 50.00 lakhs and above.

Method—III deals with a component known as 'Core Current Assets'. This represents the minimum level of current assets that a company should hold during course of operations and it varies from one company to another. This method requires higher proportion of working capital requirement to be funded by long term resources and hence the maximum permissible bank finance will be less under this method, as compared to the other two methods. Fig. 1.18 indicates the composition of fixed assets and currents assets of a company.

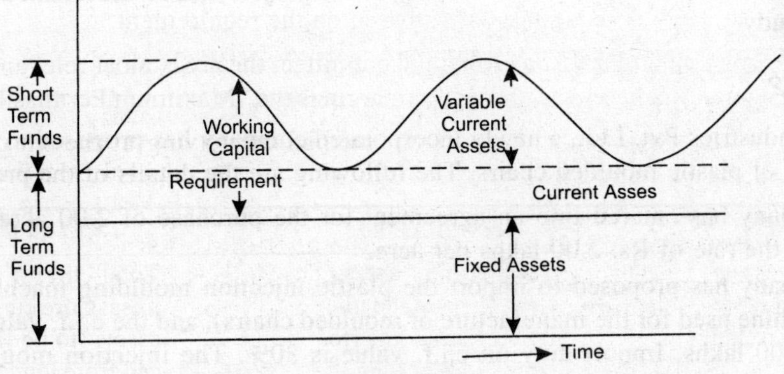

Fig. 1.18

Method—III is applicable only for companies that are in operation for some time and whose operations have stabilized.

Hence only the first two methods are relevant for arriving at the working capital margin for new projects. (Though norms have been prescribed by Tandon Committee, they are not rigid and deviations from the prescribed norms are allowed if the situations warrant and if the bankers are convinced).

RBI directives to banks for lending working capital assistance: Since the Government has taken to the option of economic liberalisation, consistent with the Government's Policy, the RBI, in the year 1997, had withdrawn in the prescription given to banks regarding assessment of working capital requirements/finance based on the Tandon Committee recommendations and the banks have been given optional freedom to decide upon the quantum of working capital finance based on their assessment of the borrowers and their credit requirements. After the dissolution of Tandon committee guidelines, State Bank of India has come out with some guidelines for arriving at the working capital finance limits to borrowers. However, most banks are still either following the Tandon Committee Guidelines or are using the Tandon Committee guidelines as a reference to recheck their assessment in case they follow some other techniques.

For our purpose of arriving at the working capital margin we can follow method—I of Tandon committee guidelines if the working capital credit limit is less than Rs. 50.00 lakhs and method—II if the working capital credit limit is Rs. 50.00 lakhs and above.

General remarks on project cost: The project cost is arrived at by adding the estimated cost of the individual components as explained above. It is always worthwhile to have the project cost cross checked with industry standards. This will help in identifying major deviations, if any. For example, the cost of setting up a cotton yarn-spinning mill can be arrived at in terms of cost per spindle. The cost per spindle serves as a reference since this can be compared with other similar projects.

The cost of setting up a cement plant may be reduced to the cost per tonne of installed capacity. Such yard sticks of cost per unit of output serve as reference, especially to banks/financial institutions who can compare the unit cost of similar projects that they appraise for extending term loans.

It may be noted that such yard sticks only act as thumb rules and one should not get carried away by this. If the industry yard stick is Rs. 10,000/- per unit of output, and if a project that is being appraised has a project cost of Rs. 8,000/- per unit of output, the project cost is prima-facie less and hence it is likely that the project's profitability would be good. However, this is only an indicator and not the final word. The profitability and viability of the project can be ascertained only by carrying out a detailed study.

Illustration 1.12

M/s Excellent Industries Pvt. Ltd., a newly incorporated company has proposed to set up a plant for the manufacture of plastic moulded chairs. The following are the details of the proposed project.

(*a*) The company has entered into an agreement for the purchase of 2.00 acres of land for the project at the rate of Rs. 2.00 lakhs per acre.

(*b*) The company has proposed to import the plastic injection moulding machine (which is the main machine used for the manufacture of moulded chairs), and the c.i.f. value of the machine is Rs. 80.00 lakhs. Import duty on c.i.f. value is 30%. The injection moulding machine is capable of producing moulded chairs at the rate of one chair per minute. Though the machine can be used for the manufacture of chairs of different sizes, the company has proposed to concentrate only on the manufacture of chairs of normal size, which has got good market. The average weight of normal sized chair is 2.50 kg.

(*c*) The company proposes to acquire the following machinery indigenously.

(*i*) Scrap Grinder (at a price of Rs. 5.00 lakhs)
(*ii*) Mixing machine (at a price of Rs. 4.00 lakhs).
(*iii*) Power Generator (at a price of Rs. 35.00 lakhs).

(*d*) The cost of electric motors, starter, switches, cables and other electrical items is Rs. 7.00 lakhs.

(*e*) The cost of dies required for the plant is estimated at Rs. 30.00 lakhs.

(*f*) The company has proposed to construct the following buildings.

(*i*) Main factory building with Asbestos Corrugated Cement Sheet (A.C.C.) roofing over steel trusses— with a built-up area of about 375 square metres

(*ii*) Store room (for the storage of rw material and for the storage of finished products), with Asbestos Corrugated Cement Sheet (A.C.C.) roofing over steel trusses—with a built-up area of about 95 square metres.

(*iii*) Office and administrative blocks with Reinforced cement concrete (R.C.C.) roofing—with a built-up area of about 70 square metres.

(*iv*) Other amenities like Toilet block, compound wall, gate, underground water tank to suit the requirements.

(*g*) The raw material required for the project is polypropylene granules, which is costing around Rs. 60/- per kg. The wastage of raw material during the manufacturing process is estimated at about 3%.

(*h*) The total power requirement (connected load) is estimated at 200 H.P.

(*i*) The selling price of moulded chair is around Rs. 350/- per chair in the retial market. The company has tied up a selling price of Rs. 280/- per chair with a network of dealers across the country.

Estimate the cost of the project. Make suitable assumptions wherever necessary.

Solution:

For arriving at the project cost, each component of the project cost is to be taken up separately and assessed.

(a) Land:

Extent of land proposed	:	2.00 acres
Cost of land (at the agreed price of Rs. 2.00 lakhs per acre)	:	Rs. 4.00 lakhs
Add : Registration charges at 3% of the Consideration (13% of Rs. 4.00 lakhs)	:	Rs. 0.52 lakh
		Rs. 4.52 lakhs

(*b*) Land development charges: It has not been indicated that the land needs any developmental work. Hence no provision is made.

(*c*) Building:

(*i*) *Main factory building;*

Built up area : 375 sq.m.

Cost of construction at the rate of Rs. 3,750/- per sq.m. (estimated cost per sq.m. of construction is to be arrived at based on either detailed estimate or by making an assessment of the prevailing construction cost of similar constructions).

= 375 × 3,750 Rs. 14,06,250/-

Say Rs. 14.06 lakhs (A)

(*ii*) Store room:

Built-up area : 95 sq.m.

Cost of construction at the rate of Rs. 3,750/- per sq.m

= 95 × 3,750 : Rs. 3,56,250/-

Say Rs. 3.56 lakhs (B)

(*iii*) Office and Administrative Blocks:

Built-up area : 70 sq.m.

Cost of construction at the rate of Rs. 5,300/- per sq.m.

= 70 × 5,300 : Rs. 3,17,000/-

Say Rs. 3,17 lakhs (C)

(*iv*) Other amenities:

Toilet block (Lumpsum)	Rs. 1.50 lakhs	
Compound wall (Lumpsum)	Rs. 3.00 lakhs	
Gate (Lumpsum)	Rs. 0.50 lakh	
Underground water tank (Lumpsum)	Rs. 1.25 lakhs	
	Rs. 6.25 lakhs	(D)

Note:

The cost of construction of amenities can be obtained by getting detailed estimates from a qualified civil engineer. Under this head, the actual requirement of amenities should be studied carefully, because this is an area where there is likelihood of under estimation due to not envisaging all the amenities required for the project. For example, if water is required for the manufacturing process and if water supply is to be made available at different points in the production line, this will necessitate construction of an overhead water tank. The capacity of overhead water tank is to be ascertained based on the storage capacity required.

Other amenities that may be required include, loading/unloading platforms, canteen, restromm for workers, power distribution room, etc. The actual requirement is to be arrived at after giving a thought over the needfs of the project.]

Total investment required for building (A + B + C + D): Rs. 27.58 lakhs

(*d*) **Plant and machinery :**

(*i*) *Imported machinery*

c.i.f. value	:	Rs. 80.00 lakhs
Customs duty at 30%	:	Rs. 24.00 lakhs
*Clearing charges	:	Rs. 0.50 lakh
		Rs. 104.50 lakhs

(*Clearing charges are the charges payable to the clearing agents for their services rendered in clearing the goods from the port and this may be in the range of ½% to 1%).

(*ii*) *Indigenous machinery :*

Scrap grinder	:	Rs. 5.00 lakhs
Mixing machine	:	Rs. 4.00 lakhs
Power generator	:	Rs. 35.00 lakhs
Dies*	:	Rs. 30.00 lakhs
		Rs. 74.00 lakhs

Total investment on plant and machinery

(Rs. 140.50 lakhs + Rs. 74.00 lakhs) : Rs. 178.50 lakhs

[*The project is for the manufacture of plastic moulded chairs of normal size. Such projects require dies of different designs to suit the taste of the customers. How much is to be invested for dies is a crucial decision. If the plant has say 100 dies of different designs, it means that the plant can produce chairs of 100 different models, which means that the company will have an edge over its competitors in view of the product variety that it can offer. However, if the investment on dies becomes exhorbitant, it would even affect the viabiity of the project proposition. Dies are in general costly items and hence a proper balance should be struck in arriving at the actual requirement. Too many dies means to much investment and most of the dies will remain idle since only one die willbe used in the machine at a time. On the other hand, if only a very few dies chosen, the product may lack variety and the product may find it difficult to penetrate through the market.

In the given problem, no mention has been made about the number of dies proposed, but only the total investment proposed for dies has been given as Rs. 30.00 lakhs. Let us presume that the optimum requirement of dies has been correctly assessed and provided for.]

(*e*) **Transport and erection charges :** Expenditure under this head is to be estimated by studying to real situation. The main machine is proposed to be imported. Hence this machine is to be carried to the factory site from the nearest port.

Indigenous machines are to be lifted from the supplier's site to the factory site. The transportation expense depends on the weight and volume of the machinery and the distance to be covered. Apart from transportation charges, loading and unloading expenses and also to be accounted for under this head. Freight carriers will be in a position to indicate the approximate amount that may be required for transporting the machinery to the factory site.

Erection charges depend upon the nature of the machine. Heavy machines and machines that generae strong vibrations need special machine foundations. The opinion of structural engineers may be used in arriving at the likely erection charges. The machinery suppliers themselves will be in a position to indicate this amount, since, after all, they are the people who know the ground realities in view of their constant exposure to such situations.

Let us assume that the transport and erection charges has been arrived at Rs. 8.00 lakhs after giving due consideration to the factors explained above.

(*f*) **Electrical :**

Electric motors, starters, switches, cables
and other electrical items : Rs. 7.00 lakhs

Note:

In respect of projects that use high tension electric power, the State Electricity Board authorities insist that the consumers have to install their own 'Step-down electric transformer' which is meant for reducing the high voltage of the incoming electric current to a low voltage meant for actual consumption. There may be also instances where the promoters have to meet expenses for bringing electric power line from nearby locations (like cost of cables, cost of poles etc). These aspects are to be carefully studied.

(*g*) **Contingency :** Contigency provision is made to take care of probable increase in cost due to new additions and/or due to escalation in prices. The provision allowed ranges from 5% to 15% and it is allowed on the following heads.

- Land.
- Land development expenses.
- Building.
- Plant and machinery.
- Transport and erection.
- Electricals.
- Technical know-how fee.
- Miscellaneous assets.

For other heads in the project cost, contingency provision is not normally made. The above elements of the project cost can be grouped under two categories viz, firm items and non-firm items. Firm items are those elements whose cost are more or less fixed and are not likely to increase and hence do not require any contingency provision. Other elements whose cost are likely to fluctuate and hence require contingency provision are called non-firm items. For example, if an agreement has already been entered into for the purchase of the required extent of land at a certain price, within a certain period, the investment required to be made towards the purchase of land is tied up, provided purchase of land is not delayed beyond the agreed date. This cost of land is a firm cost and hence does not need any provision of contingency.

Among other items, it is the normal practice to provide a contingency provision of about 5% on the cost of building and about 10% on the cost of plant and machinery and electricals. However, this is not a hard and fast rule and the judgement of the appraiser plays an important rule in arriving at the appropriate contingency provision. If the project involves imported machinery, there is a higher element of cost fluctuation in view of likely fluctuations in foreign exchange rate, and likely change in import duty, apart from increase in machinery price.

In the given problem, the company has already entered into an agreement for the purchase of land. Hence it can be assumed that the land cost is tied up (i.e., it is not likely to increase).

We can provide 5% contingency on building and say 10% on plant and machinery (indigenous) electricals, transport and erection and say 15% on plant and machinery (imported). It is assumed that the cost of miscellaneous assets is firmed up and does not require any contingency provision.

Thus, the required contingency is,

$$5\% \, (27.58) + 10\% \, (7.400 + 7.00 + 8.00) + 15\% \, (104.50)$$
$$= \text{Rs. } 1.374 + 8.900 + 15.675$$
$$= \text{Rs. } 25.954$$
$$= \text{Say Rs. } 26.00 \text{ lakhs}$$

(*h*) **Miscellaneous fixed assets:** The given data does not contain any information on the investment towards this head. The following assumptions are made

Miscellaneous assets	*Price*
Office furnitures	Rs. 1.25 lakhs
Office equipments	Rs. 1.40 lakhs
Deposit to electricity board	Rs. 0.75 lakhs
	Rs. 3.40 lakhs

(i) Preliminary and preoperative expenses: The following assumptions are made

(*i*)	Service charge on term loan	: 0.75%
(*ii*)	Commitment charges on term loan	: 1.00%
(*iii*)	Rate of interest on term loan	: 15% per annum
(*iv*)	Project implementation period	: 11 months
(*v*)	Insurance premium on fixed assets	: 0.75% per annum

The outlay required to meet items (*i*), (*ii*), and (*iii*) depends upon the term loan amount. We have not yet arrived at the term loan component. The value of fixed assets assessed so far is given below:

		[Rs. in lakhs]
Land	—	4.52
Land development	—	—
Building	—	27.58
Plant and machinery		
(*a*) Imported	—	104.50
(*b*) Indigenous	—	74.00
Transport and erection	—	8.00
Electricals	—	7.00
Contingency	—	26.00
		251.60

The term loan component is not known at present.

The following is assumed.

Term loan component (at 80% of fixed assets)

i.e., 0.80 × 251.60) = Rs. 201.28 lakhs

Say = Rs. 200.00 lakhs*

Interest during implementation period (for a term loan of Rs. 200.00 lakhs)

$$\frac{15}{100} \times \frac{11}{12} \times 200 \times \frac{1}{2} ** = \text{Rs. } 13.75 \text{ lakhs}$$

Commitment charges at 1.00% of loan amount=Rs. 2.00 lakhs

Service charge at 0.75% of loan amount = Rs. 1.50 lakhs

= Rs. 17.25 lakhs

Insurance premium on fixed assets @ 0.75% per annum

[0.75/100 × (27.58 + 178.50 + 7.00 + 8.00 + 26.00] = Rs. 1.85 lakhs***

Other startup expenses (Say) = Rs. 0.90 lakhs

= Rs. 20.00 lakhs

* The loan component assumed is only a rough estimate and if the loan component arrived at after tying up the means of finance differs from this assumed figure by a larger extent, the figures of preliminary expenses are to be reworked.

** It is assumed that the loan amount of Rs. 200.00 lakhs is drawn during the implementation period of 11 months at a uniform phase and hence the interest is arrived at by multiplying simple interest for 11 months by 1/2.

*** Transport and erection charges for machinery are also included for arriving at the insurance charges. The entie contingency provision of Rs. 26.00 lakhs is also included on the assumption that the entire contingency will be used.

(j) **Working capital margin :** Before arriving the working capital margin, which is the last component of the project cost, the working capital requirement for the first year of operation is required to be arrived at. From the working capital requirement, if the likely working capital loan component is deducted the balance represents the working capital margin. For arriving at the working capital requirement/margin, usually, the data relevant to the first year of operation are taken into account. Let us assume the capacity utilisation as under.

Year	*I**	*II*	*III*	*IV*	*V*	*VI*
Capacity utilisation	50%	60%	70%	80%	80%	80%

The working capital requirement/margin is to be arrived at for the first year of operation viz., for 50% capacity utilisation.

The format for arriving at the working capital margin/working capital finance is as under (for working capital limit about Rs. 50.00 lakhs).

	Total current assets	– – –
Less	: 25% of the total current assets (to be met out of long term sources)	– – –
		– – –
Less	: Current liabilities other than bank borrowings	– – –
	Maximum permissible bank finance	– – –

Thus, as per the above method, the working capital margin is nothing but 25% of the total current assets. The different current assets/current liabilities and their period of requirement (assumed) are as under.

Current Assets

Raw material and consumables	— 1 month
Goods in progress	— 2 days
Stock of finished goods	— 1 month
Debtors	— 2 months

Current Liabilities

Supplier's credit for raw materials and Consuambbles	— 1 month

Let us calculate the total current assets using the above data.

* • Capacity utilisation in the initial years is less due to the following reasons:

- Workers used time to get trained in the machine.
- Some machines normally require to be operated at a slower speed than the designed speed for some time.
- The product is at the beginning stage and capturing market share will take some time.

Raw Material and Consumables

The raw material used for the production is 'polypropylene' and there are virtually no 'consumables' and hence 'consumables' is ignored.

Average weight of one chair : 2.50 kg.
Quantity of raw material required for one chair, taking into account wastage of 3% : 2.50 × 1.03
= 2,575 kg.
Output per day (for 3 shifts) = 1,440 chairs
Output per day for the first year of operation (at 50% capacity) = 720 chairs
Output per month (assuming 25 working days per month) [720 × 25] = 18,000 chairs
Raw material requirement for one month (18,000 × 2,575) = 46,350 kg
Cost of stock of one month requirement of raw material at the rate of Rs. 60/- per Kg.: (46,350 × 60) = Rs. 27,81,000/-
i.e., Rs. 27.81 lakhs

Expenses

(*a*) Direct expenses:

(*i*) Power:

Power charge : Rs. 3.50 per unit (assumption)
Connected power : 200 H.P.
: 149.20 kilowatt

(1 HP = 0.746 kilowatt)

Power consumption per month at the rate of 24 hours of working per day and for 25 working days per month = 149.20 × 24 × 25
= 89,520 units.

[1 kilowatt-hour = 1 unit i.e., if one kilowatt of power is used for a period of one hour, the power consumption is one unit].

Power consumption per month for the first year of operation at 50% capacity utilisation (0.50 ´ 89,520) = 44,760 units.

Power charges per month for the first year of operation at the rate of Rs. 3.50 per unit (44,760 b 3.50) = Rs. 1,56,660/-
Say = Rs. 1.57 lakhs

(*ii*) *Fuel:* Certain industries may need fire-wood, coal, furnace oil etc., in their production process. In the given project, the production process requires only electric power and hence no provision is made under this head. Though power generator envisaged in the project will consume diesel which can be provided for under this head, since frequent electric power cut/shortage is not envisaged, provision for fuel is not made.

(*iii*) *Wages and salaries:* The following personnel and wages/salaries are assumed for the first year of operation.

Personnel	*Salary per person per month [Rs.]*	*Toal salary per month [Rs.]*
General Manager—1 person	20,000/-	20,000/-
Production incharge—6 persons (at the rate of 2 persons per shift)	15,000/-	90,000/-
Skilled technicians—12 persons (at the rate of 2 persons per shift)	9,500/-	1,14,000/-
Semi skilled persons—15 persons (at the rate of 5 persons per shift)	5,000/-	75,000/-
Unskilled workers—18 persons (at the rate of 6 persons per shift)	4,000/-	72,000/-
Wages for persons who are not regularly employed (Lumpsum)		10,000/-
		3,81,000/-
		= Rs. 3.81 lakhs

(*iv*) *Repairs and maintenance:* The following assumptions are made for the first year of operation.

(*a*) Repairs and maintenance charges for building for the first year of operation = 0.5% of the cost.

(*b*) Repairs and maintenance charges for plant and machinery for the first year of operation = 4% of the cost.

Hence, Repairs and maintenance charges per month for both building and plant & machinery = 1/12[0.5/100 × 27.58) + (4/100 × 178.50)]

= Rs. 0.61 lakh

(*v*) *Rent, Insurance:*

'Rent' does not apply since the project is not set up in leasehold premises. Insurance consists of insurance on fixed assets as well as insurance on inventories. [**Note:** Insurance premium on fixed assets was already included in the pre-operative expenses. This is the insurance premium paid on the fixed assets for the period of implementation]. Once the project implementation is over, both the fixed assets and the inventores need to be insured.

As far as insurance premium on Fixed assets is concerned, only the premium for industrial assets are included under this head. Thus the insurance premium payable on office/administrative buildings are excluded. [These are considered under the head Administrative overheads]

Total estimated cost of building	:	Rs. 27.48 lakhs
Less: Cost of office and administration block and Other amenities [3.71 + 6.25)	:	Rs. 9.96 lakhs
Estimated cost of industrial building	:	Rs. 17.62 lakhs

Out of the total contingency provision of Rs. 26.00 lakhs, the proportionate contingency for office and administrative buildings and other amenities is to be excluded.

Total contingency	:	Rs. 26.00 lakhs/annum.
Less : Contingency on office and administrative Building and other amenities at 5% [5/100 × 9.96]	:	Rs. 0.50 lakhs/annum
Contingency allowed for industrial assets	:	Rs. 25.50 lakhs/annum

Insurance premium on industrial assets at the rate of 0.75% [assumption]

$$= [\frac{0.75}{100} \times (17.62 + 104.50 + 74.00 + 8.00 + 7.00 + 25.50)]$$

= Rs. 1.77 lakhs per annum.

i.e., = Rs. 0.15 per month

(*vi*) **Factory supervision**

The following are assumed for the first year of operation

Personnel per month [Rs.]	*Salary per person per month [Rs.]*	*Total salary*
Factory supervisors—3 Nos. (at the rate of one person per shift)	12,000/-	36,000/- i.e., Rs. 0.36 lakh

Total direct expenses (1.57 + 0.00 + 3.81 + 0.61 + 0.15 + 0.36) = Rs. 6.50 lakhs

(*b*) *Overheads :*

(*i*) **Administrative overheads**

The following are assumed:

Salary to administrative staff per month : Rs. 0.46 lakh

Director's fee, audit fee per month : Rs. 0.20 lakh

Insurance premium on office and administrative Buildings and miscellaneous office assets at the rate of 0.75% p.a. on building and 1.00% p.a. on miscellaneous office assets

(*a*) 0.75/100 × (9.96 + 0.50*) + 1/100 × (1.25 + 1.40) = Rs. 0.105 lakhs p.a

i.e., Say : Rs. 0.01 lakh per month

(*b*) Insurance premium for inventory Rs. 0.03 lakh per month (assumption)

Rs. 0.70 lakh per month

*Rs. 0.50 lakh represents proportionate contingency for office and administrative buildings.

(*ii*) *Selling overheads:*

The following assumptions are made.

Packing expenses = 0.50% of sales turnover (assumption)

Selling and advertisement expenses = 2.00% of sales turnover (assumption)

Total = 2.50%

Sales turnover per month for the first year of operation at 50% capacity and for 25 working days in a month (25 × 720 × 280) i.e., : Rs. 50,40,000/- Rs. 50.40 lakhs

Selling over heads per month at 2.50% of sales turnover Rs. 1.26 lakhs

Total over heads per month
(0.70 + 1.26) Rs. 1.96 lakhs

Goods in Progress

Cost of goods-in-progress for 2 days = Cost of raw materials for 2 days + Expenses for 2 days
= 2/25 (27.81) + 2/30 (6.50 + 0.70)*
= 2.22 + 0.48 = Rs. 2.70 lakhs

* Raw material requirement for 2 days is arrived at aby considering the monthly requirement as the requirement for 25 working days. However monthly expenses are considered to be the expenses for 30 days.

Stock of Finished Goods

Cost of stock of finished goods = Cost of raw material + Expenses.
Cost of stock of finished goods = Cost of raw materials per month + Expenses per month
= 27.81 + (6.50 + 1.96)
= 27.81 + 8.43 = Rs. 36.24 lakhs

Debtors

(**Note:** Profit component is excluded for the computation of sales bills)

Sales bills per month = Cost of war material per month + Expenses per month
= 27.81 + (6.50 + 1.96)
= 27.81 + 8.43 = Rs. 36.24 lakhs
Sales bills for 2 months = Rs. 72.48 lakhs

Total Current Assets

Raw material and consumables	–	1 month	–	Rs. 27.81 lakhs
Good-in-progress	–	2 days	–	Rs. 2.70 lakhs
Stock of finished goods	–	2 months	–	Rs. 36.24 lakhs
Debtors	–	2 months	–	Rs. 72.48 lakhs
	–			Rs. 139.23 lakhs

Working capital margin at 25% of total current assets (0.25 × 139.23) = Rs. 34.81 lakhs
Say = Rs. 35.00 lakhs

Note :

Maximum Permissible Bank Finance for working capital is not required for the computation of capital cost of the project. However the same is worked out below to give an exposure.

Total current assets	—	Rs. 139.23 lakhs
Less: 25% of the total current assets	—	Rs. 34.81 lakhs
		Rs. 104.42 lakhs
Less: Current laibility other, than bank borrowings (suppliers credit of one month for raw material is assumed)	—	Rs. 27.81 lakhs
Maximum Permissible Bank Finance		Rs. 76.61 lakhs

Since all the components of project cost have been arrived at, it can be summarised as under.

Project cost		[Rs. in lakhs]
(a) Land	—	4.52
(b) Land development	—	—
(c) Building	—	27.58
(d) Plant and machinery		
(a) Imported	—	104.50
(b) Indigenous	—	74.00
(e) Transport and erection	—	8.00
(f) Electricals	—	7.00
(g) Contingency	—	26.00
(h) Miscellaneous assets	—	3.40
(i) Preliminary and Pre-operative expenses	—	20.00
(j) Working capital margin	—	35.00
		310.00

Note:

The method of arriving at the working capital margin as explained in illustration 4.1 above, is a fairly accurate method. But, we know that however accurate our assessments are, it is all based on certain assumptions and the assumptions may go wrong. To take care of any underestimation in the costs of fixed assets, we have included a head called 'Contingency' in the project cost estimate. How about contigency for working capital assessment?

Financial institutions adopt the following format for the assessment of working capital requirement/working capital margin.

(i) Raw material	- - - - month's requirements	: Rs.- - - -
(ii) Stock-in-progress	- - - -week's/month's requirements	: Rs.- - - -
(iii) Finished goods	- - - -month's requirements	: Rs. - - - -
(iv) Sundry debtors	- - - -month's requirements	: Rs. - - - -
(v) Working expenses	- - - -month's requirements	: Rs. - - - -
Total for (i) + (ii) + (iii) + (iv) + (v)		: Rs. - - - -
(vi) Less: Credit available for raw materials	- - - -month's requirements	: Rs.- - - -
(vii) Less: Advance payment on order received		: Rs.- - - -
(viii) Working capital required [(i) + (ii) + (iii) + (iv) + (v) – (vi) – (vii)]		: Rs.
(ix) Less: Probable Bank Loan for working capital		: Rs. - - - -
(x) Working capital margin		: Rs.- - - -

In the above format, item – (v) viz., working expenses deserves consideration. It represents the manufacturing and administrative expenses. A question might be raised as to why expenses should be included separately while the expenses likely to be incurred have already been taken into account at every stage viz., in items II, III and IV above. It is customary to provide for one month's working expenses (both direct and indirect expenses) as a cushion to take care of any underestimation in the working capital assessment and to take care of any bottlenecks that may prop in while production process is on. In a way this additional provision acts like a contingency provision for working capital assessemnt. If the operation cycle is very long (say more than a year) the provision for working expenses may have to be increased (to say, two or three months) to take care of contingencies.

Illustration 1.13

M/s A.B.C. Industries, a registered partnership firm proposes to set up a new industrial unit for undertaking machining job works. The firm proposes to set up the unit in a rented premises. There are firm orders in hand from reputed customers. The customers will supply components to be machined (i.e., Raw material) and take back machined components, paying the charges quoted by the firm. The firm proposes to purchase an indigenous CNC milling machine for the purpose. The other relevant detials about the project are as under.

- Monthly lease rent payable for the factory premises : Rs. 8,000/-
- Cost of machine (including taxes), including electricals : Rs. 25,22,000/-
- Transport and erection charges (estimated) : Rs. 1,05,000/-
- Miscellaneous assets proposed to be purchased : Rs. 19,000/-
- Advance payable to lessor of the premises : Rs. 80,000/-
- Electricity power charges per month (estimated) : Rs. 6,750/-
- Wges and salaries per month (estimated) : Rs. 55,000/-
- Administrative and other overhead expenses per month (estimated) : Rs. 9,000/-
- Insurance premium for machine : 0.6%

The customers are not expected to make any advance payment, but are expected to pay the charges quoted for executing orders immediately after receiving the finished products. The partners of the firm have decided to invest their own capital for both meeting the fixed cost of the project and for meeting the working capital requirements of the project.

Estimate the capital cost of the project. Make suitable assumptions wherever required.

Solution:

Let us reproduce the components of project cost for the sake of easy reference.

Project cost		[Rs. in lakhs]
(*a*) Land	—	
(*b*) Land development	—	
(*c*) Buildings	—	
(*d*) Plant and machinery	—	
(*e*) Electricals	—	
(*f*) Transport and erection charges	—	
(*g*) Contingency	—	
(*h*) Know-how/consultancy charges	—	
(*i*) Miscellaneous assets	—	
(*j*) Preliminary and Pre-operative expenses	—	
(*k*) Working capital margin		

Most of the required data are given straight away in the problem.

(*a*) Land :
(*b*) Land development :
(*c*) Buildings :

} Not applicable; There is no fixed investment required under this head as the unit is proposed to be located in a rented premises.

(*a*) Plant and machinery Including electricasl	:	Rs. 25.22 lakhs (from the given data).
(*e*) Electrical	:	Rs. Nil (since electricals are stated to be included in plant and machinery).
(*f*) Transport and erection	:	Rs. 1.05 lakhs (from the given data).
(*g*) Contingency (assuming a provision of 10% on plant and Machinery Transport and erection)	:	Rs. 2.63 lakhs
(*h*) Know-how/Consultancy Charges	:	Rs. Nil
(*i*) Miscellaneous assets	:	Rs. 0.99 lakh

[(*i*) Miscellaneous assets proposed to be purchased — Rs. 0.19 lakh

*(*ii*) Advance payable to lessor — Rs. 0.80 lakh

Rs. 0.99 lakh]

(*j*) Preliminary and pre-operative expenses : Rs. 0.21 lakh

[(*i*) Insurance premium on fixed assets at 0.6% per annum.

$$\frac{0.6}{100} \times (25.22 + 1.05 + 2.63) = : \text{Rs. } 0.17 \text{ lakh}$$

(*ii*) Interest/other financial charges payable during project implementation (since no loan component is envisaged for funding the project) : Nil

Rs. 0.17 lakh

(*iii*) Other start up expenses (say) — Rs. 0.04 lakh

Rs. 0.21 lakh]

* Advance payable to lessor is treated as an asset since it will remain with the lessor and it is always refundable when the lessee vacates the premises.

(k) Working Capital Margin

This head requires some clarification. We know that working capital margin is the difference between working capital requirement and working capital finance. In otherwords, it is the promoter's contribution towards working cqpital requirement. In the given problem, the firm is stated to be going to undertake only job orders. It is further stated that the raw material will be supplied by the customers. Hence, the part played by the firm is adding value to the raw material supplied by the customers. Hence, the part played by the firm is adding value to the raw material supplied by the customers. Thus, the question of different components of working capital viz., raw materials, goods-in-progress, stock of finished goods etc., does not arise. However, the promoter must have to meet the working expenses and administrative expenses for which he should make necessary provision in the project cost. A minimum of one month rent, wages and salaries, repairs/maintenance charges, power charges etc., are to be provided for.

These items in effect from part of the working capital funds required for running the unit. It is stated in the problem that the customers are expected to pay the charges immediately on taking delivery of the finished products. If, for example, the customers are likely to pay only after two months, the unit will start earning only two months after it first despatches the finished products. In such a case the working and administrative expenses shall have to be provided for a minimum period of over two months (i.e., two months plus the processing time required for the despatch of the first batch of finished products). Since in the given problem, it is given that the customers will pay immediately and as the processing time required for finishing the raw material is also not indicated, we can assume one month requirement and provide for one month working and administrative expenses. For units that undertake purely job orders, working capital limits are not sanctioned by banks (except in cases where the working expenses alone form a predominant portion of the total expenses like the software industry etc.). Hence, the entire requirement is expected to be brought in by the promoters.

In respect of projects that are set up exclusively to undertake job orders, the component 'working capital margin' can be replaced by the component 'working capital requirement' in the project cost.

Thus, the working capital requirement for M/s A.B.C. Industries is given by,

Rent	—	1 Month	: Rs. 0.08 lakh
Wages and salaries	—	1 Month	: Rs. 0.55 lakh
Administative and other overheads	—	1 Month	: Rs. 0.09 lakh
Power charges	—	1 Month	: Rs. 0.07 lakh
Repairs and maintenance charges [Assumed @ 5% on machinery cost, per annum, [(5/100 × 25.22) × 1/12)]	—	1 Month	: Rs. 0.11 lakh
Total working expenses	—	1 Month	: Rs. 0.90 lakh

Thus, the estimated project cost is as under:

Project cost		[*Rs. in Lakh*]
(*a*) Land	—	Nil
(*b*) Land development	—	Nil
(*c*) Buildings	—	Nil
(*d*) Plant and machinery (including electricals)	—	25.22
(*e*) Transport and erection charges	—	1.05
(*f*) Contingency	—	2.63
(*g*) Know-how/consultancy charges	—	Nil
(*h*) Miscellaneous assets	—	0.99
(*i*) Preliminary and Pre-operative expenses	—	0.21
(*j*) Working capital requirement	—	0.90
Project cost	—	31.00

Order of Magnitude Estimate

We have so far seen the method of arriving at the project cost by estimating the cost of individual components of the project. This is done after having decided upon a project and after forming a rough idea about the size of the project. At the initial stage of project formulation, a project promoter may like to know about the approximate cost of the project that he envisages. Only after knowing the approximate cost of the project that he has in mind, he can go for further detailed study. There are some methods available that are useful to estimate the likely cost of a proposed project. These methods of estimating the project cost (known by the term 'Order of magnitude Estimate') are very rough, approximate but quick estimates. They serve the purpose of giving a first hand information about the capital investment required without going into the finer details of the project.

The following are some of the methods used for arriving at a rough estimate of project cost.

(a) Investment Per Unit of Output

The investment pattern of similar existing projects are compared with the proposed project. For example, if the likely investment on a project for setting up a cement plant is required to be estimated, the investment made on an existing cement plant is taken as reference.

Let

I_e = Investment made on an existing project

C_e = Installed capacity of the existing project

I_p = Investment required for the proposed project

C_p = Installed capacity of the proposed project

Then,

$$I_p = \frac{I_e}{C_e} \times C_p$$

The technology / process of manufacture used in the project taken for reference should be the same as the technology / process of the proposed project. This method assumes that the investment required is proportionate to the installed capacity and that the project cost for a certain capacity will hold true for all capacities provided the technology / process is the same.

(b) Turnover Ratio

This method takes the ratio of sales turnover to investment as the reference.

Let

T_e = Turnover achieved by an existing project

I_e = Investment made on the existing project

T_p = Turnover of the proposed project

I_p = Investment required for the proposed project

Then,

$$I_p = \frac{I_e}{T_e} \times T_p$$

(c) Inflation Index

This metod gives fairly accurate result. This method compares the investment made on a similar project with the same capacity as that of the proposed project. The investment made on an existing project (of similar nature and similar capacity) is taken as reference and this investment is corrected for the inflation that has taken place during the time gap of investment on the two projects.

Let

I_e = Investment made on an existing project (of the same capacity as the proposed project)

I_p = Investment required for the proposed project

Then,

$$I_p = I_e \times \frac{[\text{Consumer price index (present)}]}{[\text{Consumer price index (at the time of investment on the project that is taken as reference)}]}$$

(d) Six-tenth Factor

This method is a variation of the 'Investment per unit of output'. In this method, the investment is asumed to vary as a power of 0.6 of the ratio of installed capacity of the proposed project to the installed capacity of the existing project.

As per the 'Investment per unit output' method,

$$I_p = \frac{I_e}{C_e} \times C_p$$

As per 'Six-tenth Factor' method. $I_p = I_e \times \left(\frac{C_p}{C_e}\right)^{0.60}$

(e) Location Index

When similar projects are not avialable within the country for comparison, similar projects implemented abroad can be taken as reference for arriving at a tentative estimate of the cost of the proposed project. For example, when a nuclear power project is set up in a country for the first time, the likley investment on the project can be judged only by compring similar projects existing in other countries. The tentative estimate of project cost arrived at may be corrected by applying suitable correction factors to account for the difference in cost of material and cost of labour between the two projects.

(c) Financial Appraisal

C-I: Fianncial Analysis of Projects

A project should earn sufficient return on the investment. The very idea of promoting a project by an entrepreneur is to earn attractive returns on investment on the project. Projects sponsored/undertaken by Government may take into account social cost benefits of the proposed project and in such cases, financial return alone need not be the criterion. But for such Government projects, all other projects have the prime motive of getting maximum return on investment. If there are many alternative projects, all of which, prima facie, appear to be more or less equal in profit eawrning capcity, the investor should make a comparative study of the return on the different alternative proposals before choosing one.

Such financial analysis broadly falls under two categories viz.,

Non-discounted cash flow techniques.

Discounted cash flow techniques.

The further subdivisons within these two tecniques are as under:

Non-discounted cash flow techniques:

- Payback period (PB) method.
- Accounting rate of return (ARR) method.

Discounted cash flow techniques:

- Net Present Value (NPV) method
- Profitability Index (PI) method
- Internal Rate of Return (RR) method
- Benefit Cost Ratio (BCR) method

Payback Period Method

This is one of the widely recognized and simple method of evaluating investment proposals. Payback period is defined as the length of time required to recover the original investment on the project, through cash flows earned. The cash inflow includes operating profit, less income tax payable, plus depreciation.

The following illustration explains the method.

Illustration 1.14

The likely investment on a project is Rs. 14,00,000.00. It is expected to take 2 years for implementation of the project and the project is expected to earn profits from the third year onwards. The estimated profits; tax; depreciation are as under:

		3rd year	*4th year*	*5th year*	*6th year*	*7th year*
Operating profit	[Rs.]	1,50,000.00	1,75,000.00	2,00,000.00	2,25,000.00	2,00,000.00
Tax	[Rs.]	50,000.00	60,000.00	68,000.00	75,000.00	68,000.00
Depreciation	[Rs.]	3,30,000.00	2,21,000.00	1,48,000.00	99,000.00	67,000.00

Solution:

	3rd year	*4th year*	*5th year*	*6th year*	*7th year*
[Profit − Tax + Depreciation]: [Rs.]	4,30,000.00	3,36,000.00	2,80,000.00	2,49,000.00	1,99,000.00

	Year	*Cumulative cash inflow [Rs.]*
1.	3rd year	4,30,000.00
2.	4th year	7,66,000.00
3.	5th year	10,46,000.00
4.	6th year	12,95,000.00
5.	7th year	14,94,000.00

The initial investment of Rs. 14,00,000/- is likely to be received after the sixth year (i.e., four years after the project implementation period).

Cumulative profit (4 years after implementation)	: Rs. 12,95,000.00
Cumulative profit (5 years after implementation)	: Rs. 14,94,000.00
Difference	: Rs. 1,99,000.00

$$\text{Payback period} = 4 \text{ years} + \frac{[12 \times (14{,}00{,}000 - 12{,}95{,}000)]}{1{,}99{,}000} \text{ months}$$

$$= 4 \text{ years} + \frac{[12 \times 1{,}05{,}000]}{1{,}99{,}000} \text{ months}$$

$$= 4 \text{ years} + 6.33 \text{ months}$$

Say, = 4 years and 6 months.

Limitations of pay back period method : Pay back period method ignores the time value of money. The following example illustrates this draw back.

	Cash inflow				
	1st year	*2nd year*	*3rd year*	*4th year*	*5th year*
Project A	20,000.00	25,000.00	25,000.00	30,000.00	10,000.00
Project B	40,000.00	30,000.00	20,000.00	10,000.00	10,000.00

If the two projects A and B require investment of Rs. 1,00,000/- each the payback period for both projects is exactly 4 years. Hence pay back period method, rates both these projects equally. However projects 'B' would be a better proposition than project 'A' since the cash inflow out of project 'B' is more in the initial years. However, the pay back period method fails to recognize the time value of money and rates both the above projects equally.

Pay back period method also ignores the cash flow beyond the payback period.

The following example illustrates this drawback.

	Project A Investment Rs. 1,00,000/-		*Project B Investment Rs. 1,00,000/-*	
	Annual cash inflow	*Cumulative cash inflow*	*Annul cash inflow*	*Cumulative cash inflow*
1.	20,000.00	20,000.00	40,000.00	40,000.00
2.	25,000.00	45,000.00	30,000.00	70,000.00
3.	25,000.00	70,000.00	20,000.00	90,000.00
4.	30,000.00	1,00,000.00	10,000.00	1,00,000.00
5.	30,000.00	1,30,000.00	10,000.00	1,10,000.00
6.	20,000.00	1,50,000.00	—	—
7.	20,000.00	1,70,000.00	—	—
8.	10,000.00	1,80,000.00	—	—

Since the payback period for both the projects is 4 years, both the projects will be rated equally by pay back period method. If the cash flows after the pay back period are considered, Project 'A' may turnout to be superior to Project 'B'.

Obviously pay back period method, though simple, lacks in-depth analysis and hence may lead to inaccurate results. However, this method comes handy in situations where projects to be compared relate to industries where the rate of technological obsolescence is vary fast, requiring investment on projects to be recovered at the shortest possible time.

Average Rate of Return (ARR) Method (or Accounting Rate of Return Method)

The average rate of return is also called the accounting rate of return.

$$\text{Average rate of return} = \frac{(\text{Profit after tax})}{(\text{Book value of investment.})}$$

Profit after tax is the average annual post tax benefit over the life of the roject. Unlike pay back period method, under ARR method, the entire life of the project is taken into account.

The following illustration explains the comparison of projects by ARR method.

Illustration 1.15

There are three projects A, B and C. The details about the three projects are as under. Compare the three projects by ARR method and choose the one that is most attractive among the three.

	Profit after tax [Rs.]		
Life of the project	*Project—A* *4 years*	*Project—B* *5 years*	*Project—C* *6 years*
Ist year	Rs. 4,00,000/-	Rs. 3,00,000/-	Rs. 2,50,000/-
IInd year	Rs. 4,50,000/-	Rs. 4,50,000/-	Rs. 3,00,000/-
IIIrd year	Rs. 5,00,000/-	Rs. 5,00,000/-	Rs. 4,00,000/-
IVth year	Rs. 4,50,000/-	Rs. 5,50,000/-	Rs. 5,00,000/-
Vth year	—	Rs. 5,50,000/-	Rs. 3,00,000/-
VIth year	—	—	Rs. 2,50,000/-
	Rs. 18,00,000/-	Rs. 23,00,000/-	Rs. 20,00,000/-

Book value of investment	*Project—A* *4 years*	*Project—B* *5 years*	*Project—C* *6 years*
Ist year	Rs. 15,00,000/-	Rs. 12,00,000/-	Rs. 10,00,000/-
IInd year	Rs. 13,50,000/-	Rs. 10,80,000/-	Rs. 9,00,000/-
IIIrd year	Rs. 12,15,000/-	Rs. 9,72,000/-	Rs. 8,10,000/-
IVth year	Rs. 10,93,000/-	Rs. 8,74,800/-	Rs. 7,29,000/-
Vth year	—	Rs. 7,87,320/-	Rs. 6,56,100/-
VIth year	—	—	Rs. 5,90,490/-

Solution:

	Project—A	Project—B	Project—C
Total profit over the life of the project	Rs. 18,00,000/-	Rs. 23,00,000/-	Rs. 20,00,000/-
Average annual Profit	Rs. $\frac{18,00,000/-}{4}$	Rs. $\frac{23,00,000/-}{5}$	Rs. $\frac{20,00,000/-}{6}$
	i.e., Rs. 4,50,000/-	Rs. 4,60,000/-	Rs. 3,33,333/-
Average Investment	[15,00,000/- + 13,50,000/- + 12,15,000/- + 10,93,500/-] ÷ 4	[12,00,00/- + 10,80,000/- + 9,72,000/- + 8,74,800/- + 7,87,320/-] ÷ 5	[10,00,000/- + 9,00,000/- + 8,10,000/- + 7,29,000/- + 6,56,100/- + 5,90,490/-] ÷ 6
	i.e., Rs. 12,89,625/-	Rs. 9,82,824/-	Rs. 7,80,932/-
Return on average investment	$= \frac{4,50,000}{12,89,625} \times 100$	$\frac{4,60,000}{9,82,824} \times 100$	$\frac{3,33,333}{7,80,932} \times 100$
i.e.,	= 34.89%	46.80%	42.68%

As per ARR method, Project 'B' gives a higher return on investment than projects A and C.

Limitations of ARR method:

- This method also does not take into account the time value of money.
- This method is based on accounting profit and not on cash inflow.

Net Present Value (NPV) Method

This method is one of the discounted cash flow techniques and it recognizes the time value of money.

Net present value (NPV) of cash flow = [Present value of future cash in flows over the life of the project.] — [Present value of all cash out flow]

The present value of future cash inflows is arrived at by discounting the future cash inflows at an interest rate equal to the cost of capital.

Symbolically it can be expressed as

$$NPV = \left[\frac{CF_1}{(1+r)^1} + \frac{CF_2}{(1+r)^2} + \frac{CF_3}{(1+r)^3} + \ldots\ldots + \frac{CF_n}{(1+r)^n}\right] - CF_0$$

Where,

CF_1, CF_2.....Future cash inflows occurring at the end of the first year, second year.... etc.,

n = life of the project in years.

r = discount rate (cost of capital)

CF_0 = Present cash out flow.

If

NPV = 0, it indicates that the present cash outflow and the present value of future cash inflows are equal.

NPV < 1, it indicates that the present value of future cash inflows is less than the present cash out flow.

NPV > 1, it indicates that the present value of future cash inflows is more than the present cash out flow.

The following illustration explains the application of NPV method.

Illustration 1.16

Compare projects A and B using the given data. Use NPV method of evaluation

Project—A

Investment on the project : Rs. 10,00,000/-
Life of the project : 5 years.
Period of implementation : 1 year.
Cost of capital : 15%.

Year	*1*	*2*	*3*	*4*	*5*
Cash inflow	*2,00,000/-*	*3,00,000/-*	*4,00,000/-*	*3,00,000/-*	*1,00,000/-*

Project—B

Investment on the project : Rs. 10,00,000/-
Life of the project : 5 years.
Period of implementation : 1 year.
Cost of capital : 13%.

Year	*1*	*2*	*3*	*4*	*5*
Cash inflow	*3,00,000/-*	*4,00,000/-*	*4,00,000/-*	*3,00,000/-*	*2,00,000/-*

Solution:

Project—A

Present value of future cash inflows is given by

$$= \frac{CF_1}{(1+r)^1} + \frac{CF_2}{(1+r)^2} + \frac{CF_3}{(1+r)^3} + \frac{CF_4}{(1+r)^4} + \frac{CF_5}{(1+r)^5}$$

$$= \frac{2,00,000}{(1+0.15)^1} + \frac{3,00,000}{(1+0.15)^2} + \frac{4,00,000}{(1+0.15)^3} + \frac{3,00,000}{(1+0.15)^4} + \frac{1,00,000}{(1+0.15)^5}$$

= 1.73,913 + 2,26,843 + 2,63,002 + 1,71,527 + 49,717

= Rs. 8,85,002/-

$$\text{NPV} = 8{,}85{,}002 - 10{,}00{,}000$$

$$= -1{,}14{,}998/-$$

The net present value is negative and hence the project should not be taken up.

Project B

Present value of future cash inflows is given by

$$= \frac{CF_1}{(1+r)^1} + \frac{CF_2}{(1+r)^2} + \frac{CF_3}{(1+r)^3} + \frac{CF_4}{(1+r)^4} + \frac{CF_5}{(1+r)^5}$$

$$= \frac{3{,}00{,}000}{(1+0.13)^1} + \frac{4{,}00{,}000}{(1+0.13)^2} + \frac{4{,}00{,}000}{(1+0.13)^3} + \frac{3{,}00{,}000}{(1+0.13)^4} + \frac{2{,}00{,}000}{(1+0.13)^5}$$

$$= 2{,}65{,}487 + 3{,}13{,}259 + 2{,}77{,}219 + 1{,}83{,}993 + 1{,}08{,}548$$

$$= \text{Rs. } 11{,}48{,}506/-$$

$$\text{NPV} = 11{,}48{,}506 - 10{,}00{,}000$$

$$= \text{Rs. } 1{,}48{,}506/-$$

Since the net present value is positive, present 'B' is comparatively better than Project 'A' and hence out of the two projects, Project 'B' can be selected for implementation.

Profitability Index (PI) Method

If there are two projects that require the same amount of investment, the project with a higher net present value can be chosen. If the two projects have different investment outlays, comparing the net present value of the projects will not give a correct picture since net present value only indicates the excess of present values of cash inflows over cash outflow in absolute terms.

Illustration 1.17

Consider the following two projects:

	Project—A	Project—B.
Initial value of investment (cash out flow)	Rs. 5,00,000/-	Rs. 11,00,000/-
Present value of cash inflows	Rs. 6,00,000/-	Rs. 12,50,000/-
Net Preesent value	Rs. 1,00,000/-	Rs. 1,50,000/-

The net present value of Project—B is higher than that of Project—A. Hence if we compare the N.P.V. alon, Project—B will score high. However, NPV is only an absolute figure. For an investment of Rs. 5,00,000/-, project 'A' offers a NPV of Rs. 1,00,000 whereas Project 'B' offers a NPV of Rs. 1,50,000/- for an investment of Rs. 11,00,000/-.

In such a situation, profitability index is used as a measure for comparing the profitability of projects.

$$\text{Profitability Index (P.I.)} = \frac{(\text{Present value of cash inflows})}{(\text{Initial cash outflow})}$$

$$\text{P.I. for Project 'A'} = \frac{6,00,000}{5,00,000} = 1.200$$

$$\text{P.I. for Project 'B'} = \frac{(12,50,000)}{(11,00,000)} = 1.136$$

Since Profitability Index of Project—A is more than of Project—B, it can be concluded that Project—A is better as compared to Project—B.

Internal Rate of Return (IRR) Method

The internal rate ofreturn of a project is the discount rate that makes the net present value equal to zero.

In other words, internal rate ofreturn is that rate of discount which would equate the present value of cash out flows (investments on the project) to the present value of cash inflows (the benefits over the life of the project).

In the calculation of net present value of a project, the discount rate (cost of capital) is assumed and the net present value is calculated by discounting future cashinflows at the assumed discount rate. In the calculation of internal rate ofreturn from a project, the net present value is set equal to zero and the corresponding discount rate is determined; the discount rate at which the net present value is zero is the internal rate of return.

The following illustration will explain the method of arriving at the IRR.

Illustration 1.18

For a project with the given data, calculate the internal rate of return

Year	*Cash outflow*	*Cash inflow*
0	Rs. 10,00,000/-	
1	—	Rs. 4,00,000/-
2	—	Rs. 2,50,000/-
3	—	Rs. 2,50,000/-
4	—	Rs. 2,00,000/-
5	—	Rs. 2,00,000/-
6	—	Rs. 1,50,000/-

Solution :

Let 'r' be the internal rate of return. The IRR is arrived at by equating the presence value of cash outflow and the present value of cash inflows.

i.e.,

$$10,00,000 = \frac{4,00,000}{(1+r)^1} + \frac{2,50,000}{(1+r)^2} + \frac{2,50,000}{(1+r)^3} + \frac{2,00,000}{(1+r)^4} + \frac{2,00,000}{(1+r)^5} + \frac{1,50,000}{(1+r)^6}$$

The IRR is arrived at by trial and error.

Let uss first assume r = 12% p.a.

Present value of

$$\text{cash inflows} = \frac{4,00,000}{(1+0.12)} + \frac{2,50,000}{(1+0.12)^2} + \frac{2,50,000}{(1+0.12)^3} + \frac{2,00,000}{(1+0.12)^4} + \frac{2,00,000}{(1+0.12)^5} + \frac{1,50,000}{(1+0.12)^6}$$

= 3,57,143 + 1,99,298 + 1,77,949 + 1,27,105 + 1,13,488 + 75,996

= Rs. 10,50,979/-

The present value of cash inflows is nearly equal to the present value of cash outflow at a discount rate of 12% p.a. If we want a more accurate result, we can arrive at the present value of cash inflows assuming a slightly higher discount rate than 12%.

Let us assume a discount rate ofsay, 13% p.a.

Present value of cash inflows at a discount rate of 13% p.a.

$$= \frac{4,00,000}{(1+0.13)^1} + \frac{2,50,000}{(1+0.13)^2} + \frac{2,50,000}{(1+0.13)^3} + \frac{2,00,000}{(1+0.13)^4} + \frac{2,00,000}{(1+0.13)^5} + \frac{1,50,000}{(1+0.13)^6}$$

= 3,53,982 + 1,95,788 + 1,73,263 + 1,22,664 + 1,08,552 + 72,048

= Rs. 10,26,297/-

Though $r =$ 13% p.a. is a closer approximation than r = 12% it can further be improved.

Assume $r =$ 14% p.a.

Present value of cash inflows at a discount rate of 14%p.a.

$$= \frac{4,00,000}{(1+0.14)^1} + \frac{2,50,000}{(1+0.14)^2} + \frac{2,50,000}{(1+0.14)^3} + \frac{2,00,000}{(1+0.14)^4} + \frac{2,00,000}{(1+0.14)^5} + \frac{1,50,000}{(1+0.14)^6}$$

= 3,50,877 + 1,92,368 + 1,68,743 + 1,18,416 + 1,03,874 + 68,309

= Rs. 10,02,587

The difference between the present value of cash outflow and the present value of cash inflows (discounted at a rate of 14% p.a. is only Rs. 2587/-). Hence the IRR can be taken as 14% p.a.

However, for academic interest let us workout the present values of cash inflows at a discount rate of 15% and see the results.

Present value of cash inflows at a discount rate of 15% p.a.

$$= \frac{4,00,000}{(1+0.15)^1} + \frac{2,50,000}{(1+0.15)^2} + \frac{2,50,000}{(1+0.15)^3} + \frac{2,00,000}{(1+0.15)^4} + \frac{2,00,000}{(1+0.15)^5} + \frac{1,50,000}{(1+0.15)^6}$$

= 3,47,828 + 1,89,035 + 1,64,380 + 1,14,350 + 99,436 + 64,850

= Rs. 9,79,879/-

At a discount rate of 15% p.a., the present value of cash inflows fall short of the present value of the cash out flow by Rs. 20,121.00 (10,00,000 – 9,79,879).

Thus, the correct value of '*r*' lies between 14% and 15%. The correct value of '*r*' at which the present value of cash outflows is equal to the present value of cash inflows can be arrived at by interpolating between 14% and 15%.

$$\text{IRR (r)} = 14\% + \frac{(15-14)\times(10{,}02{,}587-10{,}00{,}000)}{(10{,}02{,}587-9{,}79{,}879)}\%$$

$$= 14\% + \frac{(1\times 2{,}587)}{22{,}708}\%$$

$$= 14\% + 0.1139\%$$

$$= 14.1139\%$$

$$\text{Say} = 14.114\%$$

Comparison Between NPV Method and IRR Method

Both NPV method and IRR method appear to be the same structurally. Prima facie, it appears that if two projects are compared using NPV method and IRR method, both the methods would rank the projects in the same order. Though in most cases the decision based on either of the methods would be similar, there are certain instances wherein the ranking by the two methods may differ from each other. Though it sounds not logical, the following illustration will clear the apprehensions.

Illustration 1.19

Compare the projects 'A' and 'B' using net present value method, assuming a discount rate of 11% p.a.

Year	*Project 'A' (Cash flow)*	*Project 'B' (Cash flow)*
0	– 10,00,000/-	– 10,00,000/-
1	8,00,000/-	4,00,000/-
2	6,00,000/-	4,00,000/-
3	—	3,00,000/-
4	—	3,00,000/-
5	—	2,00,000/-

Note:

Negative figures indicate cash outflow

Solution:

N.P.V. Method:

For arriving at the present value of future cash inflows, instead of working out the reduction factor $\left[\frac{1}{(1+r)^n}\right]$, the same can be directly obtained from present value factor tables. [Refer P.V. factor table 1.7 at the end ofthis chapter.

		Project 'A'		*Project 'B'*	
Year factor at 11%	*Discount flow*	*Cash value*	*Present flow*	*Cash value*	*Present*
0	1.000	–10,00,000	–10,00,000	–10,00,000	–10,00,000
1	0.90090	8,00,000	7,72,720	4,00,000	3,60,360
2	0.81162	6,00,000	4,86,972	4,00,000	3,24,648
3	0.73119	—	—	3,00,000	2,19,357
4	0.65873	—	—	3,00,000	1,97,619
5	0.59345	—	—	2,00,000	1,18,690
			2,07,692		2,20,674

As seen from the above table, project 'B' gives a higher net present value and hence out of the two projects, Project 'B' can be chosen.

Let us workout the internal rate of return of the two projects by IRR method and see if the results obtained by NPV method matches with the results of IRR method.

Project 'A'

Let us assume an IRR of 25%.

Present value of cash inflows:

Year	*Discount factor at 25%*	*Cash inflow of cash inflow Rs.*	*Present value Rs.*
1	0.80000	8,00,000	6,40,000
2	0.64000	6,00,000	3,84,000
			10,24,000

Let us assume an IRR of 26%.

Present value of cash inflows:

Year	*Discount factor at 26%*	*Cash inflow of cash inflow Rs.*	*Present value Rs.*
1	0.79365	8,00,000	6,34,920
2	0.62988	6,00,000	3,77,920
			10,12,840

Still the present value of cash inflows is higher than the present value of cash outflow (i.e., Rs. 10,00,000).

Let us assume an IRR of 28%.

Present value of cash inflows:

Year	Discount factor at 28%	Cash inflow of cash inflow Rs.	Present value Rs.
1	0.78125	8,00,000	6,25,000
2	0.61035	6,00,000	3,66,210
			9,91,210

The present value of cash inflows when discounted at the rate of 28% works out to Rs. 9,19,210/ which is below the present value of cash out flow by Rs. 8,790/- (10,00,000 – 9,91,210).

The correct value of IRR can be obtained by interpolating between 26% and 28%.

$$\text{IRR} = 26\% + (28 - 26) \times \frac{(10{,}12{,}840 - 10{,}00{,}000)}{(10{,}12{,}840 - 9{,}91{,}210)}\%$$

$$= 26\% + 2 \times \frac{12{,}840}{21{,}630}\%$$

$$= 26\% + 1.1872\%$$

$$= 27.1872\%$$

Project 'B'

Let us assume an IRR of 27%.

Present value of cash inflows:

Year	Discount factor at 27%	Cash inflow Rs.	Present value of cash inflow Rs.
1	0.78740	4,00,000	3,14,960
2	0.62000	4,00,000	2,48,000
3	0.48819	3,00,000	1,46,457
4	0.38440	3,00,000	1,51,320
5	0.30268	2,00,000	60,536
			8,85,273

Since the present value of cash inflows falls short by Rs. 1,14,727/- (10,00,000 – 8,85,273), the IRR will be below 27%.

Let us assume an IRR of 21%.

Present value of cash inflows:

Year	*Discount factor at 21%*	*Cash inflow Rs.*	*Present value of cash inflow Rs.*
1	0.82645	4,00,000	3,30,580
2	0.68301	4,00,000	2,73,204
3	0.56447	3,00,000	1,69,341
4	0.46651	3,00,000	1,39,953
5	0.38554	2,00,000	77,108
			9,90,186

Since the present value of cash inflows when discounted at a rate of 21% is also below Rs. 10,00,000/- the IRR for project B is even below 21%.

Let us assume an IRR of 19%.

Present value of cash inflows:

Year	*Discount factor at 21%*	*Cash inflow Rs.*	*Present value of cash inflow Rs.*
1	0.84034	4,00,000	3,36,136
2	0.70616	4,00,000	2,82,464
3	0.59342	3,00,000	1,78,026
4	0.49867	3,00,000	1,49,601
5	0.41905	2,00,000	83,810
			10,30,037

Since the present value of cash inflows when discounted at 19% exceeds the present value of cash outflow, the correct value of IRR can be obtained by interpolating between 19% and 21%.

$$\text{IRR} = 19\% + (21 - 19) \times \frac{(10{,}30{,}037 - 10{,}00{,}000)}{(10{,}30{,}037 - 9{,}90{,}186)}\%$$

$$= 19\% + 2 \times \frac{(30{,}037)}{(39{,}851)}\%$$

$$= 19\% + 1{,}5075\%$$

$$= 20.5075\%$$

Observations :

As seen from the above example the following are the observations.

	Project 'A'	*Project 'B'*	*Result*
Net present value	Rs. 2,07,692/-	Rs. 2,20,674/-	Project 'B' ranks higher than Project—A
Internal rate of return	27.1872%	20.5075%	Project 'A'' ranks higher than Project—B

The difference in the results obtained by NPV method and IRR method can arise due to two reasons,viz.,

(*a*) When the size of the projects are different, requiring different capital outlays.

and

(*b*) When the times of the cash inflows are different.

In the example given above, though the cashoutflow for both the projects are the same, still the two methods gave different results which is due to the time difference in cash inflows. This is because of the reason that the IRR method assumes that the cash inflow at the end of each year is reinvested at the same rate of internal rate of return. Thus, when the IRR is higher, the cash inflows are assumed to be reinvested at a higher rate and vice versa whereas in NPV method the rate of reinvestment is the same for all the projects that are compared since all the projects are evaluated at the same rate of discount (viz., the cost of capital.)

Benefit—Cost ratio method

This is only another version of Net Present Value method. Under this method, the benefits from the project (i.e., cash inflows) are reduced to their present value at a specified rate of discount (cost of capital) and this figure is divided by the present value of the cost of the project (i.e., cash out flows). Thus,

$$\text{Benefit-cost ratio} = \frac{\text{Present value of cash inflows}}{\text{Present value of cash outflows}}$$

It may be noted that Benefit-cost ratio (BCR) is similar to profitability index (PI). However the difference between BCR and PI is that in calculating BCR, the cash out flows that occur over a period are also reduced totheir present value. As against this, for the calculation of PI, the period over which cash outflows occur are ignored and it is assumed that the entire cash outflow occurs at one point of time in the initial period.

Since cash out flows also occur over a period of time in practice, Benefit cost ratio (BCR) is a better measure than profitability index. (PI).

Net Benefit-cost Ratio (NBCR) is another measure that is used in practice which is given by

$$\text{NBCR} = \text{BCR} - 1$$

If BCR is more than one (or if NBCR is more than zero), it indicates that the benefits from the project are in excess of the cost incurred towards the project.

Data Required for the Calculation of NPV/PI/IRR/BCR/NBCR—Certain Points for Consideration.

For the calculation of the above factors the following information are relied upon

(*a*) Life of the project.

(*b*) Cash outflow.

(*c*) Cash inflow.

(*d*) Cost of capital.

The above factors need further elaboration for proper assessment of projects.

(a) Life of the Project

In calculating present value of cash-inflows from a project, the life of the project is assumed and the cash inflows during the life of the project are discounted at an appropriate rate of interest. How to estimate the life of a given project is a point requiring consideration.

Any project has a physical life, a technological life and a product market life. Life depends on the nature of the project. For example, an industrial project may have a physical life of say around 10 to 15 years. This is the duration till such time the industrial project will survive, had there been no technological obsolescence and no product obsolescence. By the end of the life (or 10 to 15 years) the plant and machinery would have become worn-out, requiring replacement. Infrastructure projects like construction of highways, bridges etc., will have a longer physical life than industrial projects. On the other hand chemical industries have a shorter physical life (in order of say 5 to 7 years) because of the nature oftheir product which will have an adverse effect on the plant and machinery.

Technological life depends upon technological obsolescence. In the sectors of industries that have rapid technological growth, technological obsolescence will set in even before the physical life of the project expires.

Product market life depends upon product obsolescence. If the product becomes obsolete even when the project has unexpired physical life, the project will become unproductive and can not sustain its operations.

Thus the project life is the least of its physical life, technological life and product market life. The project life may be higher in case there are no possibilities of technological and product obsolescene. If a project has a long life of say 40 to 50 years, it is only the initial 20 to 25 years of the life of the project that is relevant for appraisal since the present value of income streams received in the later years will be negligible.

(b) Cash Outflow

To understand the heads under which cash outflow takes place for a project, consider the components of project cost.

Project cost

(*a*) Land :
(*b*) Land development :
(*c*) Building :
(*d*) Plant and machinery :
(*e*) Electricals :
(*f*) Contingency :
(*g*) Miscellaneous assets :
(*h*) Preliminary and Pre-operative expenses :
(*i*) Know-how/consultancy fee :
(*j*) Working capital margin :

Out of the above ten components consider the amount spent towards components except working capital margin. These components consist of the fixed assets required for the project, the miscellaneous assets and start up expenses. When the amount against these heads are invested the project reaches a 'ready to start' stage. The amount against these heads are invested/spent during the implementation period of the project. Apart from this, the project needs funds to be invested on working capital to commence production. Regarding the cash out flow towards working capital, the same is arrived at as under.

Cash outflow towards

Working capital = Current assets – Current liabilities other than Bank borrowings

(The current assets, current liabilities and bank borrowings relate to the period just before commencement of commercial production).

Thus the total cash outflow consists of cash out flow towards creation of fixed assets, miscellaneous assets and startup expenses (i.e., preliminary and pre-operative expenses) as well as cash out flow towards working capital.

(c) Cash Inflow

Cash inflow includes the profits earned by the project out of its operations during its lifetime and the residual value of the project at the end of its life time.

The treatment of interest, lease rentals, depreciation, and tax in arriving at the cash inflow needs a closer look. A project may be funded entirely by equity capital or by a combination of equity and debt capital. Since interest on debt capital is a deductible item of expenditure for the purpose of direct tax, if there are two projects with the same level of initial investment and if one of these two projects is funded entirely by equity while the other by a mix of equity and debt, the project which is funded with a mix of equity and debt would be paying lesser amount of tax in view of its taxable profit getting reduced to the extent of interest paid on debt capital. Thus if interest payable on debt capital is taken into account, it will not indicate the correct picture regarding the profit actually earned by the projects. Hence profit before payment interest, lease rentals and also before payment of tax is considered for arriving at the cash inflow. So also, depreciation is not deducted from profit since the amount of depreciation remains within the organization and it does not constitute cash outflow. Thus, cash inflows for the purposes of arriving at NPV, IRR, etc., of projects should be taken to mean the profit before interest, lease rentals, depreciation and tax for each year during the estimated life of the project.

(d) Cost of Capital

While arriving at the present value of cash inflows, the cash inflows during the life of the project are discounted at an appropriate rate of interet, normally at a rate equal to the cost of capital.

(i) Cost of Equity Capital

Equity Capital is the capital contributed by the project promoters in the case of proprietory/partnership concerns. In respect of limited companies it is the capital contributed by the project promoters and shareholders.

Though it is not legally binding on companies to pay dividend to ordinary shareholders, equity capital is not without any cost. The project promoters and the shareholders contribute capital with the expectation of getting continuous dividends. This apart, they also expect capital appreciation commensurate with the risk that they take in investing their money in the project.

The market value of the shares which is determined by the demand and supply forces, reflects the return expected by ordinary shareholders. Cost of equity capital may be defined as the rate of discount

(Ce) that equates the present value of all expected future dividends per share with the current market price of the share.

Let D_1 is the present dividedn per share and P_1 is the present market price of equity share. If it is assumed that the dividend D_1 is likely to remain the same in all future years, then the cost of equity capital is given by

$$Ce(\%) = \left[\frac{D_1 \times 100}{P_1}\right]\%$$

However the shareholders expect the dividend to increase with the passage of time. If we assume that the dividends are expected to grow at a constant rate of G% every year, the cost of equity capital (Ce) is given by

$$Ce(\%) = \left[\frac{D_1 \times 100}{P_1}\right]\% + G(\%)$$

(ii) Cost of Debt Capital

The cost of debt capital (or cost of borrowing) is given by the interest on borrowings. Since interest on loan is tax deductible, it is the after-tax cost of borrowing that correctly represents the cost of debt.

Hence, the cost of debt capital may be expressed as under:

$$(C_d)\% = C(1 - t)\%$$

Where $C_d(\%)$ is the after-tax cost of debt capital.

C is the before tax cost of debt capital.

and t is the tax rate.

i.e., if the interest rate on debt capital is 15% and if the tax rate applicable for the company is 50%, the after tax cost of debt capital would be

$$= 15\,\frac{(1-50)}{100}\%$$
$$= 15\,(1 - 0.5)\%$$
$$= 7.5\%$$

(iii) Cost of Retained Earnings

A company that earns profit distributes a portion of the profit earned to its shareholders and the remaining portion of the profit is retained by the company to be used for its business operations. This retained surplus is referred as 'retaining earnings' or 'reserves'. A company with considerable retained earnings can use a portion of its retained earnings for fundingan expansion project. Just because this amount is the surplus generated by the company out of its own operations, it does not mean that retained earnings is available free of cost for funding the expansion project.

The retained earnings can be used either for payment of dividend to shareholders or can be invested elsewhere. Thus the retained earnings will have the same cost as if the same have been raised as equity shares from the public.

Though there are different methods available for arriving at the cost of retained earnings, for all practical purposes the cost of retained earnings can be taken to be equal to the cost ofequity capital for our purpose.

(iv) Cost Preference Share Capital

The cost of preference share is a function of its stated dividend. Unlike in equity shares where it is assumed that the shareholders expect a growth in the dividend rate, in respect of preference share, no such growth in dividend rate exists since the dividend is fixed.

Hence cost of preference share capital can be given by

$$C_p(\%) = \frac{\text{Div} \times 100}{P} \ (\%)$$

Where Cp is the cost of preference share.

'Div' is the stated preference dividend.

'P' is the issue price of preference share.

Weighted Average Cost of Capital

Any project is funded by a combination of capital from different sources. As we have seen, each type of capital has a cost depending upon its nature. The overall cost of capital is nothing but the weighted average cost of various sources of funds, the weight for each source of fund being the proportion of that source of fund in the overall capital structure. It is the weighted average cost of capital that is of use for financial decision making.

The cost of after-tax debt capital is less as compared to the cost of before-tax debt capital. However in respect of equity capital, the cost before-tax and cost after-tax are the same. In financial decision making, it is the after-tax cost of capital that is considered. Hence, the weighted average cost of capital should also be arrived at a based on the after-tax costs.

The following illustration explains the method of arriving at the weighted average cost of capital.

Illustration 1.20

The funding pattern proposed for an expansion project is as under:

Equity capital	Rs. 40,00,000/-
Retained earnings	Rs. 10,00,000/-
Reference capital	Rs. 15,00,000/-
Debt capital	Rs. 25,00,000/-
	Rs. 90,00,000/-

The after-tax cost of equity capital and retained earnings is 17% p.a. The after-tax cost of preference capital is 10% p.a. while that of debt capital is 8% p.a. Calculate the weighted average cost of capital

Solution:

Source capital	*Equity capital*	*Retained earnings*	*Preference*	*Debt capital*
Amount [Rs.]	40,00,000/-	10,00,000/-	15,00,000/-	25,00,000/-
Proportion of each Source of capital [Rs.]	$\frac{40{,}00{,}000}{90{,}00{,}000}$ = 0.444	$\frac{10{,}00{,}000}{90{,}00{,}000}$ = 0.111	$\frac{15{,}00{,}000}{90{,}00{,}000}$ = 0.167	$\frac{25{,}00{,}000}{90{,}00{,}000}$ = 0.278
After tax cost	17%	17%	10%	8%
Weighted average cost of each source of capital	(0.444×17%)	(0.111×17%)	(0.167×10%)	(0.278×8%)
	i.e., = 7.548%	1.887%	1,670%	2.224%
Weighted average cost of capital for the given mix. of funding		=	7,548% + 1,887% + 1,670% + 2,224% = 13,329%	
		Say = 13.33%		

General remarks: Inthe search for a viable project, the project promoters may, after their intensive efforts, come to a stage where they have identified a few projects that are equally promising. The financial evaluation techniques explained above may be used to compare these few projects and decide upon the project that can be taken up for further in-depth investigation. After having chosen a project based on its comparative cost advantages, further financial investigation of the chosen project is required to be done. Financial projection techniques are used to study in depth, the financial aspects of the chosen project.

Table 1.7 Present Value of one rupee due at the end of '*n*' years

'*n*'	*5%*	*6%*	*7%*	*8%*	*9%*	*10%*	*11%*	*12%*
1	0.95238	0.94340	0.93458	0.92593	0.91473	0.90909	0.90090	0.89286
2	0.90703	0.89000	0.87344	0.85734	0.84168	0.82645	0.81162	0.79719
3	0.86384	0.83962	0.81630	0.79383	0.77208	0.75131	0.73119	0.71178
4	0.82270	0.79209	0.76290	0.73503	0.70843	0.68310	0.65873	0.63552
5	0.78353	0.74726	0.71299	0.68058	0.64993	0.62092	0.59345	0.56743
6	0.74622	0.70496	0.66634	0.63017	0.59627	0.56447	0.53464	0.50663
7	0.71068	0.66506	0.62275	0.58349	0.54703	0.53132	0.48166	0.45235
8	0.67684	0.62741	0.58201	0.54027	0.50187	0.46651	0.43393	0.40388
9	0.64461	0.59190	0.54393	0.50025	0.46043	0.42410	0.39092	0.36061
10	0.61391	0.55839	0.50835	0.46319	0.42241	0.38544	0.35218	0.32197

(Contd.)

'n'	*5%*	*6%*	*7%*	*8%*	*9%*	*10%*	*11%*	*12%*
11	0.58468	0.52679	0.47509	0.42888	0.38753	0.35049	0.31728	0.28748
12	0.55682	0.49697	0.44401	0.39711	0.35553	0.31863	0.28584	0.25667
13	0.53032	0.46884	0.41496	0.36770	0.32618	0.28966	0.25651	0.22917
14	0.50507	0.44230	0.38782	0.34046	0.29925	0.26333	0.23199	0.20462
15	0.48102	0.41726	0.36245	0.31524	0.27454	0.23939	0.20900	0.18270
16	0.45811	0.39365	0.33873	0.29189	0.25187	0.21763	0.18829	0.16312
17	0.43630	0.37136	0.31657	0.27027	0.23107	0.19784	0.16863	0.14564
18	0.41552	0.35034	0.29586	0.25025	0.21199	0.17986	0.15282	0.13004
19	0.39573	0.33051	0.27651	0.23171	0.19449	0.16351	0.13768	0.11611
20	0.37689	0.31180	0.25842	0.21455	0.17843	0.14363	0.12403	0.10367

'n'	*13%*	*14%*	*15%*	*16%*	*17%*	*18%*	*19%*	*20%*
1	0.88496	0.87719	0.86957	0.86207	0.85470	0.84746	0.84034	0.83333
2	0.78315	0.76947	0.76614	0.74316	0.73051	0.71818	0.70616	0.69444
3	0.69305	0.64797	0.65762	0.64066	0.62437	0.60863	0.59342	0.57870
4	0.61332	0.59208	0.57175	0.55229	0.53365	0.51490	0.49867	0.48225
5	0.54276	0.51937	0.49718	0.47611	0.45611	0.43711	0.41905	0.40188
6	0.48032	0.45559	0.43243	0.41044	0.38984	0.37043	0.35214	0.33490
7	0.42506	0.39964	0.37594	0.35383	0.33320	0.31392	0.29592	0.27908
8	0.37616	0.35056	0.32690	0.30503	0.28478	0.26604	0.24867	0.23257
9	0.33288	0.30751	0.28426	0.26295	0.24340	0.22546	0.20897	0.19381
10	0.29459	0.26974	0.24718	0.22668	0.20804	0.19106	0.17560	0.16151
11	0.26070	0.23662	0.21494	0.19542	0.17781	0.16192	0.14756	0.13459
12	0.23071	0.20756	0.18691	0.16846	0.15197	0.13722	0.12400	0.11216
13	0.20416	0.18207	0.16253	0.14523	0.12989	0.11629	0.10420	0.09346
14	0.18068	0.18971	0.14133	0.12520	0.11102	0.09855	0.08757	0.07789
15	0.18989	0.14010	0.12289	0.10793	0.09489	0.08352	0.07359	0.06491
16	0.14150	0.12289	0.10686	0.09304	0.08110	0.07078	0.06184	0.05404
17	0.12522	0.10780	0.09993	0.08021	0.06932	0.05998	0.05196	0.04507
18	0.11080	0.09456	0.08080	0.06914	0.05925	0.05083	0.04367	0.03756
19	0.09806	0.08295	0.07026	0.05961	0.05064	0.04308	0.03669	0.03130
20	0.08678	0.07256	0.06110	0.05139	0.04328	0.03651	0.03084	0.02608

C-II Financial Projections

The followingfinancial projects are done in financial appraisal of projects to ascertain the financial viability.

(*a*) Cost of production and profiabilityestimate

(*b*) Cash flow estimate.

(*c*) Projected balance sheet.

The above three projections are interrelated.

Profitability Estimate : This is an estimate of expected sales realizations and expected expenses tobe incurred by the enterprise. If the expected sales realization is greater than the expected expenses, the unit is expected to earn profit.

The format of cost of production and profitability estimate containing the various heads of incomes and expenditures is given below :

Cost of production and profitability estimate

	I Year	II Year	III Year	IV Year
Capacity Utilisation				
A. Sales realization				
B. Cost of production				
Raw material				
Power				
Fuel				
Consumables				
Wages and salaries				
Repairs and maintenance				
Rent and insurance				
Factory supervision				
Depreciation (as per Companies Act)				
C. Administrative and selling Overheads				
Administrative expenses				
Selling expenses				
D. Gross profit before interest and tax [A – B – C]				
E Financial charges				
Interest on term loan				
Interest on working capital Loan				
F. Profit after interest [D – E]				
G Preliminary exp. written-off				
H. Profit/loss before tax [F – G]				
I. Provision for tax				
J. Profit/loss after tax [H – I]				
K. Less: Dividend				
L Retained profit [J – K]				
M. (Add: Depreciation (as per Companies Act)				
N. Add: Preliminary exp. Written off				
O. Net cash accrual [L + M + N]				
P. Term loan repayment				

The vaious items included in the cost of production and profitability estimate are to be correctly chosen. The cost of production and profitability estimate is projected for a period equal to the life of the project (Life of the project is the least of its physical life, technological life and product market life). The assumption to be made for the individual items of the cost of production and profitability estimate are given below:

Capacity utilization : A plant may have a capacity to produce say 1,000 unit of a proposed product in a year. This is called the installed capacity of the plant. In cost of production and profitability estimate what we are interested in projecting is the likely actual output for the different years. This will be less than the installed capacity for various reasons. A plant, however well-maintained may operate at a capacity close to its installed capacity, but will never reach its installed capacity due to various factors like fatigue of workers, relaxation time needed for workers, time spent by workers in attending to their personal needs (like drinking water, attending to calls of nature etc.,). Also, workers who operate machines need some time to get themsleves familizarized with the different operations involved in the production process. This means that in the initial years, the production output is likely to be less than the plant capacity. (In Production Management, this concept of learning by workers to adopt to the factory work situation is recognized and accepted by the concept called learning curve concept).

Apart from the technical constraints to operate the plant at its installed capacity as explained above, there may be also marketing constraints. A new product (or a product from a new firm) will take time for customer acceptance and hence the sales can only buildup gradually. This also enforces a limitation on the output in the initial years.

The normal capacity utilization assumed for different years in cost of production and profitability statement are as under.

Ist year	:	50%
IInd year	:	60%
IIIrd year	:	70%
IVth year on wards	:	80%

(The capacity utilization for different years given above is only a broad indication and it has to be decided taking into account the type of the industry, the complexities involved in the production process, the market demand for the product etc.,).

Raw Materials : The requirement of raw material depends upon the projected output. If the capacity utilization of the plant for the first year of operation is assumed at, say 50%, then, the raw material requirement for the production of products equal to 50% of the installed capacity of the plant is to be arrived at. Necessary allowances for the normal wastage of raw material during the production process are to be accounted for while arriving at the quantum of raw material. If more than one raw material is required for the production, the requirement of each raw material for the production of one unit of output is tobe assessed correctly and the total requirement should be arrived at accordingly. This information can begathered from consultants, from existing similar industries, by conducting trial production in existing plants etc. Even the suppliers of raw materials themselves can give correct information of this, because they are the people who are in constant touch with production units.

The cost of raw material is arrived at by multiplying the total raw material (s) requirement with the present price of raw material (s).

Power, fuel, water : Electric power requirement is to be calculated keeping in view of the manufacturing process. Some of the equipments may be in operation only for a few hours in a shift while some equipments may be running throughout. These factors are to be carefully looked into while arriving at the power requirement. The expenses required to be spent on power charges is arrived at by multiplying the total power requirment with the prevailing power tariff.

Fuel may consist of coal/firewoo/diesel required for boilers, diesel required for power generators, furnace oil required for furnaces/ovens etc. The cost of fuel isarrived at by estimating the requirement and multiplying the same with the present fuel price. Since transportation cost of fuel is generally considerable, care should be taken to include the cost of transporting the fuel to the plant site.

Cost of water is of relevance only if water is to be purchased from outside.

Consumables : These are materials that are consumed during production process and they can not be traced in the final product. Consuambles depend upon the nature of production process and type of machinery. The following are some of the examples for consumables.

(*a*) Welding electrodes used in Arc welding components.

(*b*) Welding wires and oxy-acetelene gas used in gas welding.

(*c*) Drill bits used in drilling machines.

(*d*) Graphite electrodes used in Arc furnaces.

(*e*) Grinding stones.

(*f*) Grease, emergy sheets, etc.

Wages and salaries : Wages and salaries for all the employees in the production and allied departments are to be accounted for. It may be noted that the planned capacity of the plant in the first year of its operation will be very much below the installed capacity. The planned capacity will increase in second and subsequent years till a practically achievable capacity is reached, which may be in the order of 80% to 90% of the installed capacity. Thus, though the planned capacity for the initial years is less, it does not necessarily mean that proportionately lesser number of employees would be employed initially. In fact, the lesser capacity utilization in the initial years is more due to factors like, workers not getting tuned to the work environment, product in the process of findingcustomer acceptance etc., than due to lesser number of people employed.

Hence if at all there is any increase in the volume of work force with the increase in capacity utilization in the later years, it is only marginal and can be ignored. However, employees deserve to be paid additional salary as they put up service, by giving periodical hike in their basic salary, by giving periodical increments, etc., which means that the expenses under 'wages and salaries' head will be on the rise every year.

The amount required for wages and salaries in the first year of operation is arrived at by ascertaining the total number of employees required in different cadres and the present level of salary payable to them. An increase of 5% in the wages and salaries payable is normally provided every year to cover the normal increase under this head.

Repairs and maintenance : Both building and machinery require periodical maintenance. If the building is a leased building, it is the responsibility of the lessor to take care of maintenance of the building. The lessee's laibility is only to pay the rents and other charges as contained in the lease agreement.

In the first year, repairs and maintenance charges on building may be taken at around 0.5% of the cost of building if the building is owned by the business enterprise. For plant and machinery, the repairs and maintenannce charges may be in the range of 0.5% to 5% of the cost of plant and machinery. Chemical equipments and machinery that are subjected to high wear and tear will require higher repairs and maintenance charges. It is evident that the plant and machinery (even building) nees higher maintenance as the years pass by due to continuous use/wear and tear they are put into. Hence to account for the increase in expenses under this head with the increase in life of assets, expenses are incremented every year by a fixed percentage of around 10%.

Rent, Insurance: Rent for leased premises shall be calculated as per the terms of the lease agreement.

Fixed assets of the project (Building, Plant and machinery) are to be insured. Building is to be insured against the risk of fire, while plant and machinery is normally insured against the risks offire and burglary. The insurance premium payable can be calculated by ascertaining the premium rates from the insurance companies. When financial institutions have financed for the creation of fixed assets, they insist that the fixed assets be insured since the fixed assets form part of their security for the term loan given bythem. Though as per books of accounts, fixed assets will depreciate in value with the passage of time, it is better toinsure fixed assets for the depreciated value or the market value whichever is higher. Though in the preparation of cost of production and profitability estimate we project the revenue and expenditure for the future period, the market value of fixed assets in the future years is a figure that can not be easily ascertained at present. Hence for all practical purposes, and tobe on the safer side, the insurance expenditure can be taken based on the purchase price of the fixed assets for the present year and also for all the future years.

Factory supervision : This is the salary payable to factory supervisory staff and it shall be ascertained in the same lines as it is arrived at for the head 'wages and salaries'.

Depreciation : The term depreciation denotes the decrease in the value of fixed assets with the passage of time. Depreciation is not applicable for land. Except land, all other fixed assets depreciate in value with the passage of time. Any fixed asset (other than land) once required by a business enterprise can not be used for an indefinite period of time. Every fixed asset has limited economic useful life. It is during this economic useful life that the business enterprise derives benefit from the use of the asset. After its economic useful life is over, the asset becomes useless. Hence, the investment made in a fixed asset spreads over a number of years equal to its economic useful life. The fraction of investment on fixed asset that is allocated for an accounting year is known as depreciation. Depreciation is chargeable as an expense to the profit and loss account in each of the accounting year in which the asset is used.

Provisions in the Companies Act. As per the Companies Act, 1952, while determining distributable profits for the purpose of declaring dividend, depreciation was required to be provided at the rates specified for the various assets by the Income Tax Act. With the steep increase in the depreciation rates under the income tax during the course of time, companies were not left with sufficient profits, after providing for depreciation, to enable declaration of reasonable dividend by them to their shareholders. Therefore, section 205 of the Companies Act, 1952 was amended by the Amendment Act of 1988 and the relevant clause of the Amendment Act of 1988 reads as under:

"This clause seeks to amend section 205to provide that in future, depreciation shall be calculated in accordance with the rates specified in schedule XIV to the act, thus delinking depreciation under the Companies Act from the under the Income Tax Act....".

Thus,the Amendment Act of 1988 has the effect of delinking the provisions for depreciation required to be make for determining the distributable profits for the declaration of dividend.

In schedule XVI of the Act, depreciation rates have been prescribed under two alternative methods viz., written down value method (WDV) and straight line method (SLM). Please refer table (table 7.1) at the end of this chapter for the rates of depreciation application under Companies Act. It is open to a company to adopt any of the said two methods of depreciation and apply appropriate rate of depreciation. However, having chosen one of the two methods, the same shall be maintained.

Provisions in the Income Tax Act : Income Tax Act considers Block of Assets for the purpose of allowing depreciation. The term 'block of assets' has been defined by section 2(11) of the Income Tax Act to mean 'a group of assets falling within a class of assets, being building, machinery, plant or furniture in respect of which the same percentage of depreciation is prescribed. As per the definition, assets falling within a class of assets (i.e., building, furniture or plant and machinery) in respect of which the same rate of depreciation is admissible will form "block of assets".

Please refer table 1.3 for Block of assets and the applicable rate of depreciation. The amount of depreciation admissible is calculated as under.

Depreciation allowance = [Written down value of block of assets] × [Rate of depreciation]

Apportionment of Contingency Provision Towards Fixed Assets for the Purpose of Depreciation

We have seen earlier that while arriving at the project cost, a contingency provision is included to take care of unexpected, but an avaoidable cost escalation. The contingency provision provided in the project cost is to be added to the different fixed assets in proportion to their value, for the purpose of arriving at the depreciation on fixed assets. The following table illustrates the method of apportioningcontingency. [estimated costs of fixed assets and contingency provision have been assumed arbitrarily]

[Rs. in lakhs]

*Fixed assets [excluding land]**	*Estimated cost*	*Proportion of contingency*	*Cost of fixed asset to be considered for depreciation (2 + 3)*
(1)	(2)	(3)	(4)
Building	6,00,000	$\frac{1,98,000}{18,00,000}$ × 6,00,000 = 66,000/-	6,66,000/-
Plant and machinery	10,00,000	$\frac{1,98,000}{18,00,000}$ × 10,00,000 = 1,10,000/-	11,10,000/-
Electricals	1,00,000	$\frac{1,98,000}{18,00,000}$ × 1,00,000 = 11,000/-	1,11,000/-
Transport and Erection	1,00,000	$\frac{1,98,000}{18,00,000}$ × 1,00,000 = 11,000/-	1,11,000
	18,00,000	1,98,000	19,98,000

* Assuming that there is no increase is the cost of land, the contingency provision of Rs. 1,98,000/- is apportioned among the other fixed assets.

Apportionment of Preliminary and Pre-Operative Expenses Towards Fixed Assets for the Purpose of Depreciation and Amortization of Preliminary Expenses

As per Sec. 35-D of the Income Tax Act, preliminary expenses, upto a limit of 5.00% of the project cost can be written off from proits over a period of 5 years. 'Project cost' for the purpose as per explanation to section 35 D(3) of the Income Tax Act means the actual cost of the fixed assets,being land, buildings, leaseholds, plant, machinery, furniture, fittings and railway sidings (including expenditure on development of land and buildings) which are shown in the books of the assessee as on the last day of the previous year in which the business of the assessee commences. Hence, for all practical purposes, cost of the project for this purpose may be taken to be equal to the project cost excluding working capital margin and preliminary and preoperative expenses. As per Section 35D(2), the following are the eligible heads of preliminary expenses which can be written off from the profits.

(*a*) Expenditures in connectionwith:
preparation of feasibility report;
preparation of project report;
conducting market survey orany other survey necesary forthe business of the assessee;
engineering services relating to the business of the assesee;

(*b*) Legal charges for drafting of any agreement between the assessee and any other person for any purpose relating to setting up or conduct of the business of theassessee;

(*c*) Where the assessee is a company, also expenditure—
by way of legal charges for drafting of Memorandum of Association and Articles of Association of the company;
on printing of the memorandum and Articles of Association;
by way of fees for registering the company under the provisions of the Companies Act, 1956;
in connection with the issue, for public subscription of shares/debentures of the company, being underwriting commission, brokerage charges for drafting, typing, printing and advertisement of the prospectus.

(*d*) Such other items of expenditure (not being expenditure eligible for any allowance, or deduction under any other provision of the Act) as may be prescribed.

If the preliminary expenses are more than 5.00% of the capital cost, the excess portion of preliminary expenses over and above 5.00% of the capital cost and also the pre-operative expenses shall be added to the fixed assets in proportion to the cost of the fixed assets. This increased cost of fixed assets after adding the share of amortized preliminary and pre-operative expenses is taken into account for calculating depreciation on fixed assets.

Administrative expenses: Salary to administrative staff, director's fees, audit fees, printing, stationery and other miscellaneous administrative expenditure to be incurred are included under this head. Apart from this insurance premium payable on current assets are also normally included under this head. [Note: Insurance premium payable on fixed assets is included in thecost of production as we have already seen under the head 'Rent and Insurance'.] Apart from the fixed assets, stock of goods (raw material, goods in progress, semi finished and finished goods) are also required to be insured. When banks extend financial assistance for working capital, they insist that the current assets be insured. This is because the assets financed by the Banks form part of security mortaged to the banks over which they advance loan. The expenses likely to be incurred towards insurance premium can be arrived at by knowing the insurance rates and knowing the value of the assets.

Selling expenses : Selling expenses is normally provided at a certain percentage of sales. The percentage of selling expenses to sales is decided upon after a careful study of the distribution system, type of the product and market conditions prevailing in the industry etc. The normal selling expense is in the range of 3% to 5% of the sales.

Interest on term loan : Interest on term loan is calculated at the rate of interest for term loan stipulated by the bank/financial institution. Since interest is charged on the balance loan outstanding, the interest component for a particular year is to be arrived at after taking into account the schedule of loan repayment. Thus if the term loan component is Rs. 10.00 lakhs which is repayable in a span of 8 years with an initial moratorium of 2 years,the total loan of Rs. 10.00 lakhs would be repaid in a span of 10 years. In the first two years (moratorium period) there will be no repayment of term loan and hence the term loan outstanding will be Rs. 10.00 lakhs for the first two years.

Hence interest on term loan for thefirst two years shall be calculated for the loan outstanding of Rs. 10.00 lakhs at the appropriate rate of interest. If the loan to be repaid during the third year is Rs. 2.00 lakhs, the loan outstanding as the end of the third year would be Rs. 8.00 lakhs. Since interest on term loan is charged on the loan outstanding on a diminishing balance method, the interest on term loan payable for the third year would be on a loan outstanding of Rs. 9.00 lakhs.

i.e.,

Loan outstanding at the beginning of the third year	:	Rs. 10.00 lakhs
Loan outstanding at the end of the third year	:	Rs. 8.00 lakhs
	:	Rs. 18.00 lakhs

Average balance for the third year on which interest is payable = 18/2
= Rs. 9.00 lakhs

The interest component of the subsequent years is arrived at on similar lines, by gradually reducing the loan outstanding according to the loan repayment schedule.

Interest on working capital loan: As against term loan which is repaid over a period of time, the borrowings to meet working capital requirement will remain under the head of 'Current liabilities' in the balance sheet of an enterprise for ever. This is because, working capital is needed to meet the operating expenses for which funds are required as long as the enterprise is engaged in its production operation. We have already seen under 'Capacity utilization' that the operating capacity of the plant will be below its installed capacity. We have also seen that in the initial years the capacity utilization will be lower and it will increase in the later years. As the working capital requirement depends on the volume of operation, the requirement of funds to meet the working capital requirement will keep on increasing as the volume of operation of the enterprise increaes. Hence the interest on working capital borrowings will be less in the initial years and will be more in the later years. The interest component on working capital borrowings is arrived at by finding the requirement of working capital borrowings for each year and multiplying the same with the appropriate rate of interest.

Tax: Tax is deducted from the 'Profit before tax' [DBT]*, to arrive at the Net profit [EAT]**. The tax component will vary according to the constitution of the firm [proprietory, partnership, limited company, etc.,]. For proprietary and partnership firms, there is also difference in tax structure for different slabs of taxable income. These data can be taken from the latest income tax act for arriving at the tax component. The tax concessions available to specific industries are also to be taken into account. [**EAT = Earnings after tax *EBT = Earnings before tax]

Illustration 1.21

M/s XYZ Company private limited, a newly incorporated company proposes to set up a new project for the manufacture of motors and pumps.

- The cost of land and land development charges is estimated at Rs. 1.00 lakh.
- The cost of construction of building is estimated at Rs. 10.00 lakhs.
- The estimated cost of plant and machinery including electricals is Rs.39.00 lakhs.
- Transport and rection of machinery is expected to cost Rs. 1.00lakh.
- Miscellaneous assets are expected to cost to Rs.1.00 lakh.
- Preliminary and pre-operative expenses are estimated at Rs. 7.50 lakhs which include interest on term loan payable during the period of implementation.
- A Contingency provision of Rs. 4.60 lakhs is considered adequate.
- The company proposes to approach a financial institution for availing a term loan of Rs. 45.00 lakhs towards creation to fixed assets. The company had a preliminary discussion with the financial institution and the institution has shown its willingness to lend term loan of Rs. 45.00 lakhs for the project. It also indicated that the term loan is to be repaid in a period of eight years which is inclusive of one year moratorium for the repayment of principal amount. Interest on term loan, is however payable even during the period of moratorium.
- The sales turn over at 100% capacity utilization is estimated at Rs. 215.00 lakhs. The plant is expected to operate at 60% capacity in thefirst year of operation, at 70% capacity in the second year and at 80% capacity from the third year onwards.
- The cost of raw material required for the first year of operation is Rs. 52.00 lakhs; power and fuel expenses for the first year of operation are estimated at Rs.2.00 lakhs and Rs. 3.00 lakhs respectively; consumables will account for Rs. 5.00 lakhs during the first year of operation; wages and salaries for the first year of operation will be Rs. 30.00 lakhs and it is estimated to increase at the rate of 10.00% every yer; repairs and maintenance charges for the first year of operation is estimated at Rs. 2.00 lakhs and it is expected to increase at the rate of 5.00% every year; factory supervision charges for the first year of operation is Rs. 4.00 lakhs and it is expected to increase at the rate of 10.00% every year.
- Insurance charges on fixed assets, being meagre, may be ignored.
- Depreciation will be provided on straight line method for the purpose of profitability estimate and on written down value method for tax calculations. The applicable rates of depreciation for profitability estimate, as per schedule—XIV of the Companies Act are as under:

Building	: 3.34%
Plant and machinery, electricals, (including transport and erection)	: 7.42%
Miscellaneous assets	: 6.33%

The rates of depreciation for tax calculation, as per the Income Tax Act are as under:

Building	: 10.00%
Plant and machinery, electricals (including transport and erection)	: 25.00%
Miscellaneous assets	: 10.00%

- Administrative expenses for the first year of operation is Rs. 2.50 lakhs and it is expected to increase at the rate of 5% every year.

- Selling expenses can be assumed at 3% of the sales turnover.
- Rate of interest for term loan is 17.00% per annum and for working capital loan is 18.00% per annum
- The company is required to hold two months stock of raw materials, three weeks stock of goods in progress and one and a half months stock of finished goods. The normal duration of accounts receivable (book debts) as per the practice prevailing in the industry is one month. Trade credit is available on raw material and consumables for a period of one month.
- The company has preliminary discussions with bank and the bank has in principle agreed to sanction working capital laon to the company. It is learnt that the bank would insist a margin of not less than 25.00% on the current asssets to bebrought in by the project promoters to meet the working capital margin.
- The company proposes to pay dividend at the rate of 12.00% in thesecond year of operation and it also proposes to increase the dividend by 2.00% every alternate year during the first tenyears.

Arrive at the project cost for the project

Arrive at the profitability estimate for the project for a period of eight years of operation.

Arrive at the projected cash flow statement for the project for a period of eight years of operation and

Arrive at the projected balance sheets for eight years of operation.

Solution:

The components of profitability estimate are discussed below before the preparation of the statement.

Raw material : It is given that the raw material requirement for the first year of operation is Rs. 52.00 lakhs. The consumption of raw material is in proportion to the level of production. The capacity utilization of the plant for the first year of operation has been given as 60%, for the second year. 70% and from the third year onwards, 80%. Based on the capacity utilization, the raw material consumption will be as under:

Miscellaneous assets	: 10.00%
• For the second year of operaton	: 52 × (70/60)
	: Rs. 60.67 lakhs
• For the third year of operation	: 52 × (80/60)
	: Rs. 69.33 lakhs
• For the fourth and subsequent years	: Rs. 69.33 lakhs (since the capacity utilization of the plant is given to remain at 80% from the third year onwards.)

Power, Fuel, consumables : The consumption level of these also depend on the level of operation. Hence, on similar lines as the estimate for raw material was made, the expenses towards power, fuel and consumables can be done for thesecond and subsequent years.

• Expenses for power for the second year	: 2.00 × (70/60)
	: Rs. 2.33 lakhs
• Expenses for power for the third and Subsequent years	: 2.00 × (80/60)
	: Rs. 2.67 lakhs

Similarly, the expenses for fuel and consumables are arrived at as under:

	II year	III year onwards
• Feul	Rs. 3.50 lakhs	Rs. 4.00 lakhs
• Consumables	Rs. 5.83 lakhs	Rs. 6.67 lakhs

Wages and salaries : The expenses under this head is expected to increase at the rate of 10% everyyear.

II year	*III year*	*IV year*	*V year*	*VI year*	*VII year*	*VIII year*
33.00	36.30	39.93	43.92	48.32	53.15	58.46

Repairs and maintenance : This is estimated to increase at the rate of 5% every year. Hence, the repairs and maintenance charges from the second year onwards will be as under:

II year	*III year*	*IV year*	*V year*	*VI year*	*VII year*	*VIII year*
2.10	2.21	2.32	2.43	2.55	2.68	2.81

Factory supervision : This is estimated to increase at the rate of 10% every year. Hence, the factory supervision charges from the second year onwards will be as under:

II year	*III year*	*IV year*	*V year*	*VI year*	*VII year*	*VIII year*
4.40	4.84	5.32	5.86	6.44	7.09	7.79

Administrative expenses : Can be arrived at by giving 5% increase every year over the previous year.

Selling expenses : Since this depends upon the sales turnover, it can be easily assessed for all the years as a percentage of (3%) of the projected sales for the respective years.

Interest on term loan : The company proposes to repay the term loan in a span of eight years, which includes a moratorium (i.e., repayment holiday for the repayment of principal) of one year. The termloan is normally repayable either in half-yearly or quarterly, or even in some cases in monthly instalments. The interest payable on term loan will go on reducing, since the term loan gets repaid as the year progresses. The company is required to pay interest on term loan only for the loan amount out-standing. As the term loan repayment progresses, the company will be required to pay less and less of interest on term loan since the term loan out-standing gets reduced with the repayment of term loan. The exact amount of interest payable on term loan can be arrived at only if the number of instalments of repayment for all the years and their quantum are known. In the given example, the term loan of Rs. 45.00 lakhs is proposed to be repaid in a period of eight years. The intalments of term loan repayment will be structured in such a way that the cash generation is sufficient to meet the repayment obligation. The following repayment pattern is assumed for the purpose of arriving at the interest component.

Rs. in lakhs

I year	*II year*	*III year*	*IV year*	*V year*	*VI year*	*VII year*	*VIII year*
NIL	10.00	14.00	8.00	6.00	4.00	2.00	1.00

In the first year of operation, the entire term loan of Rs. 45.00 lakhs will be out-standing. Hence, the interest for the first year can be taken as 17% on Rs. 45.00 lakhs, which works out to Rs. 7.65 lakhs. At the beginning of the second year, the term loan balance will be Rs. 45.00 lakhs. Since, term loan of Rs. 10.00 lakhs will be repaid during the second year of operation, the term loan balance at the end of the second year will be Rs. 35.00 lakhs. The interest paid can be taken to be on the average balance of Rs. 40.00 lakhs [(45.00 + 35.00)]/2]. Interest at 17% on Rs. 40.00 lakhs works out to Rs. 6.80 lakhs, which can be taken as correct for all practical purposes for thesecond year of operation. If the term loan is repayable in quarterly or in monthly instalments, the average balance will differ slightly. However, the error can beignored as it will be nominal. Also, the term loan repayment schedule that will be fixed by thefinancial institution is not known beforehand. This apart, financial institutions also demand interest on term loan in half yearly or quarterly instalments. Hence, some asumption is necessarily tobe made regarding this. The average balance method illustrated above can be used without much error.

On similar lines, the term loan balance at the beginning of the third year will be Rs. 35.00 lakhs. Since, term loan of Rs. 14.00 lakhs is to be repiad during the third year, the balance at the end of the third year will be Rs. 21.00 lakhs. For calculating the interest component for the third year the average term loan balance can be taken as Rs. 28.00lakhs [(35.00 + 21.00)/2]. Interest at17% on Rs. 28.00 lakhs works out to Rs.4.76 lakhs, which is the interest on term loan for the third year of operation.

The term loan interest for the remaining years can be arrived at on similar lines.

Interest on working capital loan : Unlike the term loan which will be repaid in a span of some years, the working capital loan will not be repaid. The company is to pay only interet on the loan component. Repayment of principal component of working capital loan does not arise, in the first year to its capcity utilization. Since the capacity utilization increases in the subsequent years, the working capital loan that the company would avail will also increase in the subsequent years. Accordingly, the interest payable on working capital loan will normally keep on increasing from year to year until the capacity utilization becomes stagnant. In the given problem the capacity utilization is asumed to increase from 60% in the first year to 80% in the third year. But, it remains at 80% in the subsequent years. Hence, the interest payable on working capital loan is likely to remain the same from the third year onwards. The exact calculation of working capital loan are shown subsequently.

Depreciation:

[as per Companies Act]

It is given in the problem that straight line method is to be followed for profitability estimate. Referring to schedule XIV of the Companies Act, the rates of depreciation are taken as under: (these rates are in fact given in the problem explicitly. In case the depreciation rates are not given, they can be found out referring to schedule XIV of the Companies Act. Refer table 1.8 given at pages 159-164.

- Building : 3.34%
- Plant and machinery, including electricals, Transport and erection charges : 7.42%
- Miscellaneous fixed assets : 6.33%

Loan and land development cost will not be eligible for depreciation. There is a contingency, provision of 5.00% on the cost of building and 10.00% on the cost of plant and machinery, electricals, transport and erection charges and also there is a contingency provision of 10.00% on miscellaneous assets.

Contingency provision : The contingency provision of Rs. 4.60 lakhs is to be apportioned between the assets before arriving at depreciation.

	Cost (Rs. in lakhs)	*Proportionate Contingency (Rs. in lakhs)*
Building	*10.00*	*0.90*
Plant and machinery Including electricals and Transport and erection Charges.	40.00	3.61*
Miscellaneous assets	1.00	0.09
	51.00	4.60

*[4.60 × (40.00/51.00) = 3.61]

As per the provisions of the Income Tax Act, a portion of preliminary expenses qualify for amortization. Such expenditure can not exceed 5.00% of the project cost ('project cost' under this section of the Act refers to the cost of fixed assets, i.e., land and building, plant and machinery, furniture, fittings etc., refer section 35D(2) of the Income Tax Act). The balance preliminary expenses and pre-operative expenses qualify for depreciation. The amortised preliminary expense can be written off in five succesive years.

Preliminary and pre-operative expenses as given in the project cost	:	Rs. 7.50 lakhs
5.00% of the project cost (i.e., cost ofland, building, plant and machinery, electricals, miscellaneous assets and contingency provision) [0.05 × 56.60]*	:	Rs. 2.83 lakhs
Amount that can be apportioned Towards fixed assets for the Calculation of depreciation [7.50 – 2.83]	:	Rs. 4.67 lakhs

[*5.00% of the project cost (as defined bythe Act) of Rs. 2.83 lakhs can be amortised in five instalments.]

The preliminary and pre-operative expenses of Rs. 4.67 lakhs that can be apportioned towards fixed assets for depreciation purposes can be allocated to the different assets on a proportionate basis as under:

	Cost (Rs. Lakhs)	*Proportionate share of Preliminary and pre-operative expenses (Rs. in lakhs)*
Building	*10.00*	*0.92*
Plant and machinery including electricals and Transport and erection Charges	40.00	3.66
Miscellaneous assets	1.00	0.09
	51.00	4.67

[*4.67 × (40.00/51.00)= 3.66]

	Cost (Rs. in lakhs) (Rs. in lakhs)	*Proportionate contingency Pre-op. expenses*	*Proportionate Preliminary and Depreciation (Rs. in lakhs)*	*Total Cost Eligible for (Rs. in lakhs)*
Building	*10.00*	*0.90*	*0.92*	*11.82*
Plant and machinery including electricals and transport and erection charges	40.00	3.61	3.66	47.27
Miscellaneous assets	1.00	0.09	0.09	1.18
	50.75	4.60	4.67	60.27

After arriving at the value of assets eligible for depreciation as shown above, depreciation as per Companies Act can be arrived at as under:

Depreciation on straight line method at 3.34% on building [0.0334 × 11.82]: Rs. 0.39 lakhs
Depreciation on straight line method at 7.42% on plant and machinery, electricals, transport and erection [0.0742 × 47.27] : Rs. 3.51 lakhs
Depreciation on straight line method at 6.33% On miscellaneous assets [0.0633 × 1.18] : Rs. 0.07 lakhs
: Rs. 3.97 lakhs

Administrative Expenses : Administrative expenses for the first year of operation has been given as Rs. 2.50 lakhs and it has also been indicated that it is expected to increase at the rate of 5.00% every year.

I year	*II year*	*III year*	*IV year*	*V year*	*VI year*	*VII year*	*VIII year*
2.50	2.63	2.76	2.89	3.04	3.19	3.35	3.52

Selling expenses : Selling expenses are estimated at 3.00% of the sales turn over.

	I year	*II year*	*III year*	*IV year*	*V year*	*VI year*	*VII year*	*VIII year*
Turn-over	129.00	150.50	172.00	172.00	172.00	172.00	172.00	172.00
3.00%→	3.87	4.52	5.16	5.16	5.16	5.16	5.16	5.16

Interest on term loan : Interest is calculated on the average term loan balance in every year. For example, the term loan balance at the beginning of the second year is Rs. 45.00 lakhs. Since term loan of Rs. 10.00 lakhs will be repaid during the second year, the term loan balance at the end of the second year will be Rs. 35.00 lakhs. Hence, the average balance of term loan for the second year of operation will be (45 + 35)/2 i.e., 40.00 Interest payable during the second year can be calculated on this balance of Rs. 40.00 lakhs which will be reasonably accurate.

	I year	*II year*	*III year*	*IV year*	*V year*	*VI year*	*VII year*	*VIII year*
Term loan repayment	Nil	10.00	14.00	8.00	6.00	4.00	2.00	1.00

Average Term loan balance	45.00	$\frac{(45+35)}{2}$ = 40.00	$\frac{(35+21)}{2}$ = 28.00	$\frac{(21+13)}{2}$ = 17.00	$\frac{(13+7)}{2}$ = 10.00	$\frac{(7+3)}{2}$ = 5.00	$\frac{(3+1)}{2}$ = 2.00	$\frac{(1+0)}{2}$ = 0.50
Interest at The rate of 17.00% p.a. on the average term loan balance	7.65	6.80	4.76	2.89	1.70	0.85	0.34	0.09

Interest on working capital loan : Before arriving at the interest on working capital loan, we must know the working capital loan component.

The components of profitability estimate so far calculated can be filled up in the respective places and the cost of production can be arrived at.

Referring to the profitability estimate, the cost of production for the first three years are as under:

First year : Rs. 101.97 lakhs (52.00 + 2.00 + 3.00 + 5.00 + 30.00 + 2.00 + 4.00 + 3.97)

Second year : Rs. 115.80 lakhs (60.67 + 2.33 + 3.50 + 5.83 + 33 00 + 2.10 + 4.40 + 3.97)

Third year : Rs. 129.99 lakhs (69.33 + 2.67 + 4.00 + 6.67 + 36.30 + 2.21 + 4.84 + 3.97)

	Period of requirement	*I year*	*II year*	*III year*
Raw material	6 weeks (1.5 months)	(52/12)×1.50 = 6.50	(60.67/12)×1.50 = 7.58	(69.33/12)×1.50 = 8.67
Goods in progress*	3 weeks (0.75 months)	(101.97/12)×0.75 = 6.37	(115.80/12)×0.75 = 7.24	(129.99/12)×0.75 = 8.12
Stock of Finsihed Goods*	2 weeks (0.50 months)	(101.97/12)×0.5 = 4.25	(115.80/12)×0.50 = 4.83	(129.99/12)×0.50 = 5.42
Accounts receivables (Book Debts)*	4 weeks (1 month)	129.00/12 = 10.75	150.50/12 = 12.54	172.00/12 = 14.33
Total current Assets		27.87	32.19	36.54
Less: Margin for Working capital (at 25% of current assets)		6.97	8.05	9.14
		20.90	24.14	27.40

*Refer 'Remarks on working capital assessment' in page 157–158

Period of requirement	I year	II year	III year
Less: Trade credit Avaialble for Raw material and 1 month Consumables (1 month)	(52.00 + 5.00)/12 = 4.75	(60.67 + 5.83)/12 = 5.54	(69.33 + 6.67)/12 = 6.33
Working capital Loan to be Availed from Bank	16.15	18.60	21.07

Having known the working capital margin, the project cost can be summarized as under. [please note that the working capital margin included in the project cost is the margin required for the first year of operation.]

Project Cost : *(Rs. in lakhs)*

Land and land development	:	1.00
Building	:	10.00
Plant and machinery and Electricals	:	39.00
Transport and erection	:	1.00
Miscellaneous assets Preliminary and pre-operative Expenses	:	1.00
		7.50
Contingency	:	4.60
Working capital margin	:	6.97
		71.07

Means of finance : *(Rs. in lakhs)*

Capital	:	26.07
Term loan	:	45.00
		71.07

Interest on working capital loan:

	I year	II year	III year	IV year	V year	VI year	VII year	VIII year
W.C. loan (estimated)	16.15	18.60	21.07	21.07	21.07	21.07	21.07	21.07
Interest rate	18%	18%	18%	18%	18%	18%	18%	18%
Interest on W.C. loan	2.91	3.35	3.79	3.79	3.79	3.79	3.79	3.79

All the above figures arrived at under different heads can be entered in the profitability estimate statement and 'profit/loss before tax' can be arrived at (refer profitability estimate). After this, the tax component is to be arrived at. Since the Income Tax Act provides for depreciation only on Written down Value basis and also as the rates of depreciation allowed by the Income Tax Act for different blocks of assets are different from that of Companies Act, a re-adjustment of the profit/loss is required before arriving at the income tax component which is explained below:

Depreciation as per the provisions of the Income Tax Act.

Year →	*I*	*II*	*III*	*IV*	*V*	*VI*	*VII*	*VIII*
Building at 10% On WDV (starting Value: Rs. 11.82* Lakhs)	1.18	1.06	0.96	0.86	0.78	0.70	0.63	0.57
Plant and machinery, Electricals, transport and erection at 25% on WDV (starting value: Rs. 47.27 lakhs)m	11.82*	8.86	6.65	4.99	3.74	2.80	2.10	1.58
Miscellaneous Assets at 10% on WDV (starting Value: Rs. 1.18 lakhs)	0.12	0.11	0.10	0.09	0.08	0.07	0.06	0.06
	13.12	10.03	7.71	5.94	3.65	3.57	2.79	2.21

*Coincidence of these two figures is accidental.

Calculation of tax :

Year →	*I*	*II*	*III*	*IV*	*V*	*VI*	*VII*	*VIII*
Profit/loss before tax (after providing for depreciation as per companies Act)	9.53	16.83	24.97	22.49	18.91	15.06	9.80	3.74
Add:								
Depreciation as per Companies Act	3.97	3.97	3.97	3.97	3.97	3.97	3.97	3.97
	13.50	20.80	28.94	26.46	22.88	19.03	13.77	7.71
Less:								
Depreciation for tax Purposes	13.12	10.03	7.71	5.94	3.65	3.57	2.79	2.21
Taxable income	0.38	10.77	21.23	20.52	19.23	15.46	10.98	5.50
Income tax at the Rate of 35% with a Surcharge of 10% (net: 38.50%)	0.15	4.15	8.17	7.90	7.40	5.95	4.23	2.12

Cost of production and profitability estimate of M/s XYZ company limited **Rs. in lakhs**

	Years							
	I	*II*	*III*	*IV*	*V*	*VI*	*VII*	*VIII*
Capacity Utilisation	60%	70%	80%	80%	80%	80%	80%	80%
A. Sales realization	129.00	150.50	172.00	172.00	172.00	172.00	172.00	172.00
B. Cost of production								
Raw material	52.00	60.67	69.33	69.33	69.33	69.33	69.33	69.33
Power	2.00	2.33	2.67	2.67	2.67	2.67	2.67	2.67
Fuel	3.00	3.50	4.00	4.00	4.00	4.00	4.00	4.00
Consumables	5.00	5.83	6.67	6.67	6.67	6.67	6.67	6.67

Year →	*I*	*II*	*III*	*IV*	*V*	*VI*	*VII*	*VIII*
Wages and salaries	30.00	33.00	36.30	39.33	43.92	48.32	50.74	53.27
Repairs and maintenance	2.00	2.10	2.21	2.32	2.43	2.55	2.68	2.81
Factory supervision	4.00	4.40	4.84	5.32	5.86	6.44	7.09	7.79
Depreciation (as per Companies Act)	3.97	3.97	3.97	3.97	3.97	3.97	3.97	3.97
C. Administrative and Selling Overheads								
Administrative expenses	2.50	2.63	2.76	2.89	3.04	3.19	3.35	3.52
Selling expenses	3.87	4.52	5.16	5.16	5.16	5.16	5.16	5.16
D. Gross profit before Interest and tax [A – B – C]	20.66	27.55	34.09	29.74	24.95	19.70	13.93	7.62
E. Financial charges								
Interest on term loan	7.65	6.80	4.76	2.89	1.70	0.85	0.34	0.09
Interest on working capital Loan	2.91	3.30	3.79	3.79	3.79	3.79	3.79	3.79
F. Profit after Interest (D – E)	10.10	17.40	25.54	23.06	19.46	15.06	9.80	3.74
G. Preliminary exp. Written-off	0.57	0.57	0.57	0.57	0.55*	—	—	—
H. Profit/loss before tax [F – G]	9.53	16.83	24.97	22.49	18.91	15.06	9.80	3.74
I. Provision for tax	0.15	4.15	8.17	7.90	7.40	5.95	4.23	2.12
J. Profit/loss after tax [H – I]	9.38	12.68	16.80	14.59	11.51	9.11	5.57	1.62
K. Less : Dividend	Nil	3.13	3.13	3.65	3.65	4.17	4.17	4.69
L. Retained profit (J – K]	9.38	9.55	13.67	10.94	7.86	4.94	1.40	-3.07
M. Add: Depreciation (as per Companies Act)	3.97	3.97	3.97	3.97	3.97	3.97	3.97	3.97
N. Add: Preliminary exp. Written off	0.57	0.57	0.57	0.57	0.55*	—	—	—
O. Net cash accrual [L + M + N]	13.92	14.09	18.21	14.83	12.38	8.91	5.37	0.90
P. Term loan repayment	Nil	10.00	14.00	8.00	6.00	4.00	2.00	1.00

* Preliminary Expenses Written off in the fifth year = 2.83 – (0.57 × 4) = 0.55

$$\text{Debt service coverage ratio} : \frac{\text{Profit after tax + Depreciation + Interest on term loan}}{\text{Term loan + Interest on term loan}}$$

i.e.,

$$9.38 + 12.68 + 16.80 + 14.59 + 11.51 + 9.11 + 5.57 + 1.62 = 81.26$$
$$3.97 + 3.97 + 3.97 + 3.97 + 3.97 + 3.97 + 3.97 + 3.97 = 31.76$$
$$7.65 + 6.80 + 4.76 + 2.89 + 1.70 + 0.85 + 0.34 + 0.09 = 25.08$$
$$138.10$$

$$\text{D.S.C.R.} = \frac{138.10}{45.00 + 25.08} = 1.95 : 1.00$$

Note:

Net cash accrual indicates whether sufficient cash is available for the repayment of the term loan. Though dividend is deducted for arriving at the net cash accrual, the D.S.C.R. is calculated for the profit before payment of dividend. In the case of proprietary and partnership concerns the question of dividend does not arise. Financial institutions normally stipulate a condition in the sanction of term loans that the borrowing company shall obtain theprior consent of the financial institution for the declaration of dividend. This is to ensure that the company has sufficient cash available for the repayment of term loan and interest on term loaneven after the payment of dividend.

Cash flow estimate for M/s XYZ company limited — Rs. in lakhs

	Im-plemen-tation period	*I Year*	*II Year*	*III Year*	*IV Year*	*V Year*	*VI Year*	*VII Year*	*VIII Year*
Source of funds:									
Increase in share capital	26.07	—	—	—	—	—	—	—	—
Profit after depreciation And pre. exp., but before interest and taxes [H + E]	—	20.09	26.98	33.52	29.17	24.40	19.70	13.93	7.62
Depreciation	—	3.97	3.97	3.97	3.97	3.97	3.97	3.97	3.97
Preliminary expenses Written off	—	0.57	0.57	0.57	0.57	0.55	—	—	—
Increase in term loan	45.00	—	—	—	—	—	—	—	—
Increase in W.C. loan [Bank borrowings]	—	16.15	2.45	2.47	—	—	—	—	—
Govt. subsidy		—	—	—	—	—	—	—	—
(A)	71.07	40.78	33.97	40.53	33.71	28.92	23.67	17.90	11.59
Disposition of funds:									
Increasing in capital expenditure	61.27	—	—	—	—	—	—	—	—
Increase in working capital	—	23.12	3.53	3.56	—	—	—	—	—
Preliminary expenses	2.83	—	—	—	—	—	—	—	—
Repayment of term loan	—	—	10.00	14.00	8.00	6.00	4.00	2.00	1.00
Interest on term loan	—	7.65	6.80	4.76	2.89	1.70	0.85	0.34	0.09
Interest on W.C. loan	—	2.91	3.35	3.79	3.79	3.79	3.79	3.79	3.79
Tax	—	0.15	4.15	8.17	7.90	7.40	5.95	4.23	2.12
Dividend	—	—	3.13	3.13	3.65	3.65	4.17	4.17	4.69
(B)	64.10	33.83	30.96	37.41	26.23	22.54	18.76	14.53	11.69
Opening balance of cash	—	6.97	13.92	16.93	20.25	27.53	33.91	38.82	42.19
Net surplus/deficit (A – B)	6.97	6.95	3.01	3.12	7.48	6.38	4.91	3.37	(0.10)
Closing balance of cash in hand and at bank	6.97	13.92	16.93	20.25	27.53	33.91	38.82	42.19	42.09

Projected Balance Sheet for M/s XYZ Company Limited — Rs. in lakhs

	Implementation period	*I year*	*II year*	*III year*	*IV year*	*V year*	*VI year*	*VII year*	*VIII year*
Liability:									
Share Capital	26.07	26.07	26.07	26.07	26.07	26.07	26.07	26.07	26.07
Reserves and Surplus	—	9.38	18.93	32.60	43.54	51.40	56.34	57.74	54.67
Term Loan	45.00	45.00	35.00	21.00	13.00	7.00	3.00	1.00	—
W.C. Loan	—	16.15	18.60	21.07	21.07	21.07	21.07	21.07	21.07
Unsecured loans	—	—	—	—	—	—	—	—	—
Sundry creditors	—	4.75	5.54	6.33	6.33	6.33	6.33	6.33	6.33
	71.07	101.35	104.14	107.07	110.01	111.87	112.81	112.21	108.14
Assets:									
Gross fixed assets	61.27	61.27	61.27	61.27	61.27	61.27	61.27	61.27	61.27
Less: Accumulated Depreciation	—	3.97	7.94	11.91	15.88	19.85	23.82	27.79	31.76
Net fixed assets	61.27	57.30	53.33	49.36	45.39	41.42	37.55	33.48	29.51
Current assets (inventory + books debts)	—	27.87	32.19	36.54	36.54	36.54	36.54	36.54	36.54
Preliminary expenses	2.83	2.26	1.69	1.12	0.55	—	—	—	—
Cash/Bank balance	6.97	13.92	16.93	20.05	27.53	33.91	38.82	42.19	42.09
	71.07	101.35	104.149	107.07	110.01	111.87	112.81	112.21	108.04

Working Notes :

Cash flow statement :

Increase in working capital loan for the second year of operation : (18.60 – 16.15) = 2.45

Increase in working capital loan for the third year of operation : (21.07 – 18.60) = 2.47

There is no increase in the working capital loan from the fourth year onwards since the loan component remains at Rs. 21.07 lakhs from the fourth year onwards.

Increase in capital expenditure (Implementation period)
: Cost of the project – W.C. Margin – Pre. Exp. written off
: 71.07 – 6.97 – 2.83
: 61.27

Increase in working capital (I year) : W.C. Loan + W.C. Margin
: 16.15 + 6.97
: 23.12

Increase in working capital (II year) : Additional W.C. loan + Additional W.C. margin
: 2.45 + 1.08
: 3.53

Increase in in working capital (III year) : Additional W.C. loan + Additional W.C. margin
: 2.47 + 1.09
: 3.56

Interest on term loan (Implementation period)	:	Not provid;ed for since it is included in the preliminary and pre-operative expenses.
Net surplus (implementation period)	:	71.05 – 64.10
	:	6.97 (This is the working capital margin brought in and kept ready for utilization during the first year of operation.)
Net surplus (I year)	:	40.78 – 33.83 = 6.95
Net surplus (II year)	:	33.97 – 30.96 = 3.01
Net surplus (III year)	:	40.53 – 37.41 = 3.12
Net surplus (IV year)	:	33.71 – 26.23 = 7.48
Net surplus (V year)	:	28.92 – 22.54 = 63.8
Net surplus (VI year)	:	23.67 – 18.76 = 4.91
Net surplus (VII year)	:	17.90 – 14.53 = 3.37
Net surplus (VIII year)	:	11.59 – 11.69 = (0.10)

Projected Balance Sheet : Reserves and surplus is nothing but the cumulative retained profit. The retained profit for the first year is Rs. 9.38 lakhs. (refer profitability estimate). This figure is taken as the Reserves and surplus for the first year of operation.

The retained profit for the second year as per the profitability estimate is Rs. 9.55 lakhs. Hence, the cumulative retained profit up to the end of second year is Rs. 1893 lakhs (9.38 + 9.55). Hence, the figure for reserves and surplus for the second year is taken as Rs. 18.93 lakhs. On similar lines, the reserves and surplus for the third year is Rs. 32.60 lakhs (18.93 + 13.67), reserves and surplus for the remaining years are calculated on the same basis.

Gross Fixed Assets:

Land	:	1.00
Building	:	10.00
Transport and erection	:	1.00
Miscellaneous assets	:	1.00
Contingency	:	4.60
Preliminary and pre-operative expenses	:	4.67 (Out of the total provision of Rs. 7.50 lakhs, the amount that can be amortised in a period of five years, viz., Rs. 2.83 lakhs is deducted and the balance of Rs. 4.67 lakhs is considered. It may be recalled that this amount of Rs. 4.67 lakhs was also added to the cost of fixed assets for the purpose of calculating depreciation.)
		61.27

Refer working capital assessment calculations for 'current assets' which has already been arrived at Rs. 27.87 lakhs, Rs. 32.19 lakhs and Rs. 36.54 lakhs for the first, second and third year of operations respectively.

Remarks on Working Capital Assesment

In illustration 1.12, while arriving at the working capital requirement/working capital margin, depreciation was not taken into account (as it is a non-cah expenditure item). Also, only administrative overheads are included for arriving at the cost of "goods-in-progress". Further, profit was excluded from the head "debtors". Though this is a reasonably correct method of arriving at the working capital requirement, it is considered as a conservative approach. In practice, the method followed in illustration 1.21 is widely followed where both administrative and selling overheads are excluded from the cost of "goods-in-progress" and "finished goods" but depreciation is included. More over, sales turnover is taken as the basis for arriving at 'accounts receivables (debtors)'. The method followed in illustration 1.21 though approximate, is considered as a reasonably good estimate. It may be noted that more efforts are to be taken for correctly arriving at the likely capacity utilisation for the different years, rather than dwelling on the intricacies of correct working capital assessment since a minor deviation between the estimated and actual capacity utilisation will affect the working capital calculations considerably.

Table 1.8 Rates of Depreciation under Companies Act
SCHEDULE-XIV
[See sections 205 and 350]
RATES OF DEPRECIATION

Nature of assets	*Single shift*		*Double shift*		*Triple shift*	
	WDV	*SLM*	*WDV*	*SLM*	*WDV*	*SLM*
1	2	*3*	*4*	5	6	7
I. (*a*) BUILDINGS (Other than factory building) [NESD]	5%	1.63%	—	—	—	—
(*b*) FACTORY BUILDINGS	10%	3.34%	—	—	—	—
(*c*) PURELY TEMPORARY ERECTIONS such as wooden structures	100%	100%	—	—	—	—
II. PLANT AND MACHINERY						
(I) **General rate applicable to:**						
(*a*) Plant and machinery (not being a ship) other than continuous process plant for which no special rate has been prescribed under (*ii*) below :	13.91%	4.75%	20.87%	7.42%	27.82%	10.34%
(*b*) continuous process plant for which no special rate has been prescribed under (ii) below [NESD]	15.33%	5.28%	—	—	—	—
(II) **Special rates**						
A.1. Cinematograph films—Machinery used in the production and exhibition of cinematograph films, [NESD]						
(*a*) Recording equipment, reproducing equipment, developing machines, printing machines, editing machines, synochronisers and studio lights except bulbs.	20%	7.07%	—	—	—	—
(*b*) Projecting equipment of film exhibiting concerns						
2. Cycles [NESD]						
3. Electrical machinery, X-ray and electrotherapeutic apparatus	20%	7.07%	—	—	—	—

1	2	3	4	5	6	7
and accessories thereto, medical, diagnostic equipments, namely, catscan, ultrasound						
4. Juice beling pans (karhals) [NESD]	20.00%	7.07%	—	—	—	—
5. Motor-cars, motor-cycles, scooters and other mopeds [NESD]	25.89%	9.50%	—	—	—	—
6. Electrically operated vehicles including battery powered or fuel cell powered vehicle [NESD]	20%	7.07%	—	—	—	—
7. Sugarcane crushers (indigenous kolhus and belans) [NESD]	20%	7.07%	—	—	—	—
8. Glass manufacturing concerns except direct fire glass melting furnaces-recuperative and regenerative glass melting furnaces	20%	7.07%	30%	11.31%	40%	16.21%
9. Machinery used in the manufacture of electronic goods and components	15.62%	5.38%	23.42%	8.46%	31.23%	11.87%
B1. Aeroplanes, aero engines,simulators, visual system and quick engine change equipment (NESD)	16.20%	5.60%	—	—	—	—
2. Concrete pipes manufacture-moulds [NESD]	30%	11.31%	—	—	—	—
3. Drum containers manufacture -Moulds [NESD]	30%	11.31%	—	—	—	—
4. Earth-moving machinery employed in heavy construction works such as dams, tunnels, canals, etc., [NESD]	30%	11.31%	—	—	—	—
5. Glass manufacturing concenrs except direct fire glas melting furnaces-moulds [NESD]	30%	11.31%	—	—	—	—
6. Moulds in iron foundries [NESD]	30%	11.31%	—	—	—	—
7. Mineral oil concerns-field operations (above ground)-Portable boilers, drilling tools, well-head tanks, rigs, ec., [NESD]	30%	11.31%	—	—	—	—
8. Mines andquries-Portable under ground machinery and earth moving machinery used in open cost mining [NESD]	30%	11.31%	—	—	—	—
9. Motor buses and motor lorries other than those used in business of running them on hire [NESD]	30%	11.31%	—	—	—	—

1	2	3	4	5	6	7
10. Motor tractors, harvesting combines [NESD]	30%	11.31%	—	—	—	—
11. Pattern, dies and templates [NESD]	30%	11.31%	—	—	—	—
12. Ropeway structure-ropeways, ropes and trestle sheaves and connected parts [NESD]	30%	11.31%	—	—	—	—
13. Shoe and other leather goods fabrics-Wooden lasts used in the manufacture of shoes.	30%	11.31%	45%	18.96%	60%	29.05%
C. 1. Motor buses, motor lorries and motor taxis used in a business of running them on hire [NESD]	40%	16.21%	—	—	—	—
2. Rubber and plastic goods factories Moulds [NESD]	40%	16.21%	—	—	—	—
3. Data processing machines including computers [NESD]	40%	16.21%	—	—	—	—
4. Gas cylinders incluidng valves and regulators [NESD]	40%	16.21%	—	—	—	—
D. 1. Artificial manufacturing machinery wooden parts	100%	100%	—	—	—	—
2. Cinematograph films-Bulbs of studio lights	100%	100%	—	—	—	—
3. Flour mills—Rollers	100%	100%	—	—	—	—
4. Glass manufacturing concerns—Direct fire glass melting furnace	100%	100%	—	—	—	—
5. Iron and steel industries—Rolling mill rolls	100%	100%	—	—	—	—
6. Match lactories—Wooden match frames	100%	100%	—	—	—	—
7. Mineral oil concern—(a) Plant used in field operations (below ground)—Distribution—returnable packages; (b) Plant used in field operations (below ground) but not including assets used in field operations (distribution)-Kerbside pumps including under-ground tanks fittings	100%	100%	—	—	—	—
8. Mines and quaries—						
(a) Tubs, winding ropes, haulage ropes and sand slowing pipes.	100%	100%	—	—	—	—
(b) Safety lamps	100%	100%	—	—	—	—

1	2	3	4	5	6	7
9. Salt works—Salt pans, reservoirs and condensers, etc., made of earthy, sandy or clay material or any other similar material	100%	100%	—	—	—	—
10. Sugar works—Rollers	100%	100%	—	—	—	—
III. FURNITURE AND FITTINGS						
1. General Rates (NESD]	18%	6.33%	—	—	—	—
2. Rate for furniture and fittings used in hotels, restaurants and boarding houses; schools, colleges and other educational institutions, libraries; welfare centers; meetings halls, cinema, houses; theaters and circuses; and for furniture and fittings let out on hire for use on the occasion of marriage and similar functions [NESD]	25.88%	9.50%	—	—	—	—
IV. SHIPS						
1. Ocean-going ships—						
(i) Fishing vessels with wooden hull [NESD]	27.05%	9.50%	—	—	—	—
(ii) Dredgters, fugs, barges, survey launches and other similar ships used mainly for dredging purposes (NESD]	19.80%	7%	—	—	—	—
(iii) Other ships [NESD]	14.60%	5%	—	—	—	—
2. Vessels ordinarily operating on inland waters—						
(i) Speed boats [NESD]	20%	7.07%	—	—	—	—
(ii) Other vessels [NESD]	10%	3.34%	—	—	—	—

* WDV means written down value.

* SLM means straight line method.

Notes

1. Buildings include roads, bridges, culverts, wells and tube-wells.
2. Factory buildings does not include offices, godowns, 'officers and employees' quarters, roads,bridges, culverts, wells and tube-wells.
3. Speed boat means a motor boat dirven by a high speed internal combustion engine capable of propelling both at a speed exceeding 24 kilometres per hour in still water and so designed that when running at a speed it will plane, i.e., its bow will rise from the water.
4. Where, during any financial year, any addition has been made to any asset, or where ny assets has been sold, discarded, demolished or destroyed the depreciation on such assets shall be calculated on a pro-rata basis from the data of such addition or, as the case maybe up to the date on which such asset has been sold, discarded, demolished or destroyed.
5. The following information should also be disclosed in the accounts:
   (i) Depreciation method used; and
   (ii) Depreciation rates or the useful lives of the assets, if they are different from the principal rates specified in the Schedule.
6. The calculations of the extra depreciation for double shift working and fro triple shift working shall be made separately in the proportion while

1	2	3	4	5	6	7

the number of days for which the concern worked double sbhift or triple shift, as the case may be, bears to the normal number of working days during the year. For this purpose, the normal number of working days during the year shall be deemed to be—

(a) in the case of a seasional factory or concern, the number ofdays on which the factory or concern acually worked during the year or 180 days, whichever is greater.

(b) in any other case, the number of days on which the factory or concern actually worked during the year or 240 days whichever is greater. The extra shift depreciation shall not be charged in respect of any item of machinery or plant which has been specifically expected by inscription of the letters NESD (meaning "no extra depreciation") against it in sub-items above and also in respect of the following items of machinery and plant to which the general rate of depreciation of 4(13.91) per cent applies.

1. Accounting machines.
2. Air-conditioning machinery including room air-conditioners.
3. Building contractor's machinery.
4. Calculating machines.
5. Electrical machinery—Switchgear and instruments, transformers and other stationery plant and wiring and fitting of electric light and fan installations.
7. Locomotives, rolling stocks, tramways and railways used by concerns, excluding railway concerns.
8. Mineral oil concerns—field operations;
   (a) Prime movers.
   (b) Storage tanks (above ground)
   (c) Pipelines (above ground)
   (d) Jetties and dry docks.
9. Mineral oil concerns—field operations (distribution)—Kerbside pumps, including underground tanks and fittings.
10. Mineral oil concerns—refineries:
   (a) Prime movers.
   (b) LPG Plant
11. Mines and quarries:
   (a) Surface and underground machinery other than electrical machinery and portable underground machinery)
   (b) Head gears.
   (c) Rails
   (d) Shafts and inclines
   (e) Tramways on the surface
12. Neo-post franking machines.
13. Office machinery
14. Overhead cables and wires.
15. Railway sidings.
16. Refrigeration plant container, etc., (other than racks).
17. Ropeway structures:

1	2	3	4	5	6	7
(a) Trestle and station steel work.						
(b) Driving and tension gearing.						
18. Salt works—Reservoirs; condensers, salt pans delivery channels and piers if constructed of masonry, concrete, cement, asphalt or similar materials, barges and floting plant, piers, quays and jeties; and pipelines for conveying brine if constructed of masonry, concrete, cement, asphalt or similar materials.						
19. Surgical instruments.						
20. Tramways electric and transways run by internal combustion engines—permanent way, cars-car trucks, car bodies, electrical equipment and motors, tram cars including engines and gears						
21. Typewriters.						
22. Weighing machines.						
23. Wireless apparatus and gear, wireless appliances and accessories.						
7. Continuous process plant means a plant which is required and designed to operate 24 hours a day.						
8. Not withstanding anything mentioned in this Schedule, depreciation on assets, whose actual cost does not exceed five thousand rupees, shall be provided at the rate of hundred per cent].						
[Provided that where the aggregate actual individual items of plant and machinery costing Rs. 5,000/- or less constitutes more than 10 per cent of the total actual cost of plant and machinery, rates of depreciation applicable to such items shall be the rates as specified in item II of the schedule].						

1.8. ORGANIZATIONAL STRUCTURE

Organizing is the function of dividing and grouping the activities of the organization and establishing the authority-responsibility relationship between them.

Organizational structure is concerned with the allocation of task and establishment of authority-responsibility relationship between the members of the organization.

Broadly speaking, organizational structure can be of three types. They are,

- Functional organization
- Product organization and
- Matrix organization

Functional Organization

Functional organization is the most basic and logical form of organizational structure. Functional organization brings together in one department all those who are engaged in one activity or in one or more related activities. Fig. 1.19 depicts the structure of a functional organization.

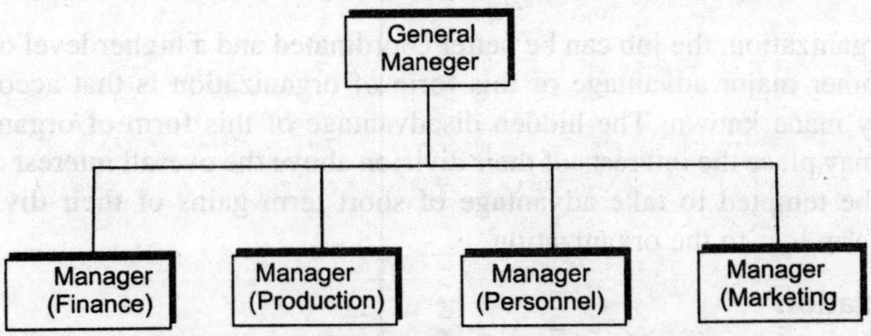

Fig. 1.19 (Functional organization)

Referring to Fig. 1.19, the manager (Marketing) for example, wiil be responsible for marketing of all the products manufactured by the firm. This type of organizational structure is suitable for smaller organizationss that offer a limited line of products. As the organization grows by expanding its product line or when the organization expands geographically, the weakness of functional organizational structure will become apparent since controlling will become ineffective. Another disdavantage of functional organization is that it is difficult to fix accountability and difficult to judge the performance of the memebrs. If for example, a new product introduced in the market turns out to be a failure, no department will assume responsibility. Instead, the different functional departments will blame one another. The manager (Marketing) may hold that the product failure is due to poor financial decisions; the manager (Finance) may in turn assert that the product failure is to be attributed to the poor product features and thus blame the production department and so on. Coordination of the functional members of the entire organization will pose a big problem to the top management.

Product Organization

For organizations with a longer product line, the form of organizational structure suited is the Product Organisation structure. Fig. 1.20 depicts the structure of a product organization. The advantage of product organization is that all the activities, skills and expertise required to produce and market a particular product (or a group of related products) are grouped together under a single head. Fig.

1.20 shows a line diagram of product organization. Referring to Fig. 1.20 can observe that a manager of a particular product is in charge of all activities relating to that product. For example, manager (pharmaceutical products) will be responsible for production, marketing, research, financial aspects, personnel requirement etc., connected to pharmaceutical products produced by the firm.

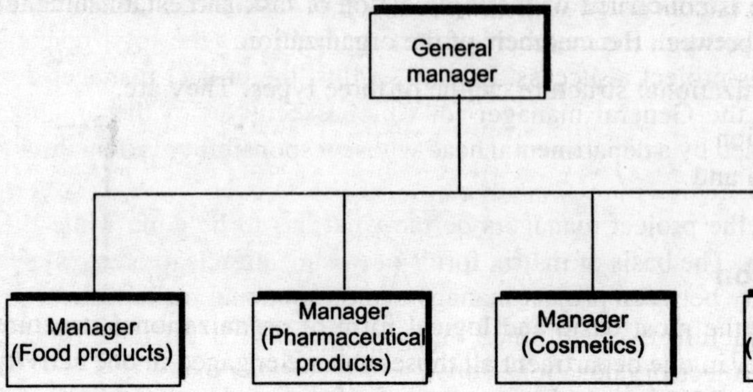

Fig. 1.20 (Product organization)

In a product organization, the job can be better coordinated and a higher level of performance can be achieved. Another major advantage of this form of organization is that accountability of each division is clearly made known. The hidden disadvantage of this form of organization is that the divisional heads may place the interests of their division above the overall interest of theorganization. Thus, they may be tempted to take advantage of short term gains of their divisions even at the expense of long term loss to the organization.

Matrix Organization

The matrix form of organization is an attempt to combine the merits of functional and product forms of organizations.

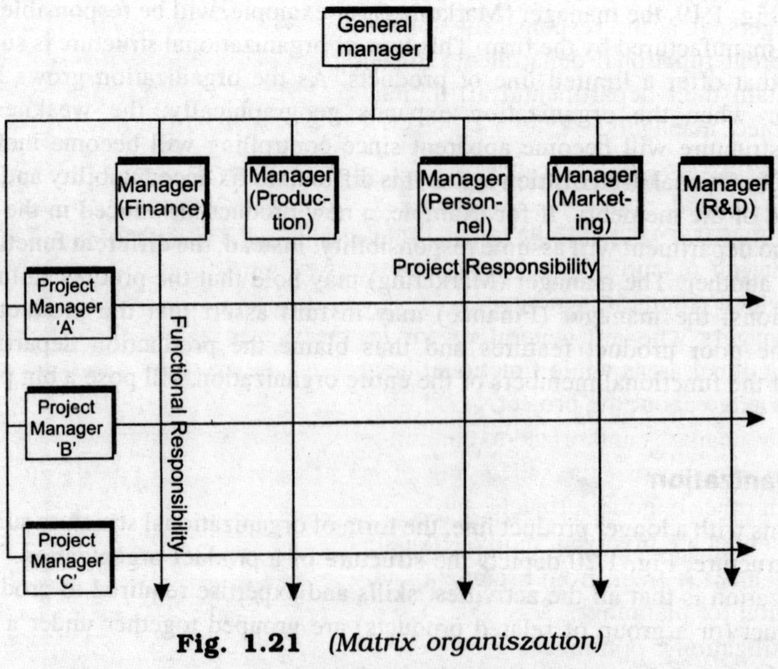

Fig. 1.21 *(Matrix organiszation)*

This form of organization is ideally suited for enterprises that are "project-driven", i.e., enterprises whose activities centers around handling projects like construction companies, companies offering turn-key projects etc., Fig. 1.21 depicts a typical matrix structure of an organization. Let the organization undertake three different construction projects concurrently. There are three project managers (A, B and C) who are in charge of the three different construction projects. Each project represents a potential profit center. Hence, each project manager has the total responsibility and accountability for making his project a success. In view of this, the project manager derives power and authority directly from the General manager (or Chief Executive) of the organization. Each functional department is headed by a departmental head whose responsibility is to maintain functional excellence in all the projects.

In a matrix organization, the project managers define what has to be done while the functional managers decide how to do it. The basis of matrix forms of organization is to create synergy through mutually shared responsibility between project managers and functional managers.

Matrix organisational structure evolved since organisations felt it difficult to bear the huge expenses of creating pure project organisations separately for each project that is being handled. Hence, the concept of matrix organisation was thought of and brought into practice with the objective of creating synergy by the involvement of functional and project team members.

For the successful functioning of a matrix organization.

- The project managers and the functional managers must coordinate with each other and must be willing to negotiate for resources keeping the overall interest of the organisation in view.
- Both functional and project managers must provide input to the planning process.
- Though there are two lines of controls (vertical line of control by the functional departments and horizontal line of control from project departments), the horizontal line of control must be allowed to operate freely as a separate entity except for administrative purpose.

The point to be noted in a matrix organization is that the personnel working in the project are under the control of their respective functional managers and are also under the control of project managers. In other words, authority over the personnel is shared between the functional managers and project managers. It is the responsibility of the project manager to coordinate the efforts of personnel in different functional departments towards reaching project objectives. The personnel continue to maintain their departmental affiliation though they come under the control of both functional and project managers.

Advantages of a Pure Matrix form of Organization

- The project manager is able to have maximum control over the project.
- There is sharing of authority and responsibility between project managers and functional managers which results in synergy.
- Project managers who are generalists (or technical specialists) acquire knowledge about specific functional areas while functional heads who are specialists in their areas acquire all round knowledge about the project.
- The project manager is authorized to commit resources of the organizations for the project,the only condition being that the scheduling of his project does not cause conflicts in resource sharing with other ongoing projects.
- All the personnel are involved, motivated and are prepared to face the challenge.
- Top management is freed from organizing and coordinating resources and can hence devote more attention for planning.
- Resource utilization is optimized.

Disadvantages of Pure Matrix form of Organization

- Since project managers have an edge over functional managers, it is likely that the functional managers might become biased which will create conflicts and power struggles between the project department and functional departments.
- There is danger of dual reporting since the personnel are under the dual control of project and functional managers.
- Since each project wing operates independently, there are chances for duplication of efforts.
- Managers and employees are made more susceptible to role ambiguity which results in more discussions than actions.
- It is costly to implement matrix form of organization since more people than otherwise required are employed.
- Emergence of conflicts and resolution of conflict will be a continuous process and this may require the continuous support of a person who is a specialist in inter-personnel relationships and organization development.

Modified Matrix Structures

In a pure matrix form of organization, the General manager (or the chief executive) of the organization directly controls the project managers as well as the functional managers. As the organization grows in size and as the number of projects handled by the organization increases, it will be difficult for the General manager to have direct control over all the project managers and functional managers. Another form of organization evolved to handle such a situation in which a manager of project managers (or a Director of projects) was entrusted with exclusive charge of the projects handled by the organization. The Director (projects) will report to the General manager and will control all the project manages. The General manager is freed of monitoring the daily routine of on-going projects. Fig. 1.22 depicts a line diagram of matrix organization in which the Director (projects) has control over all the project managers.

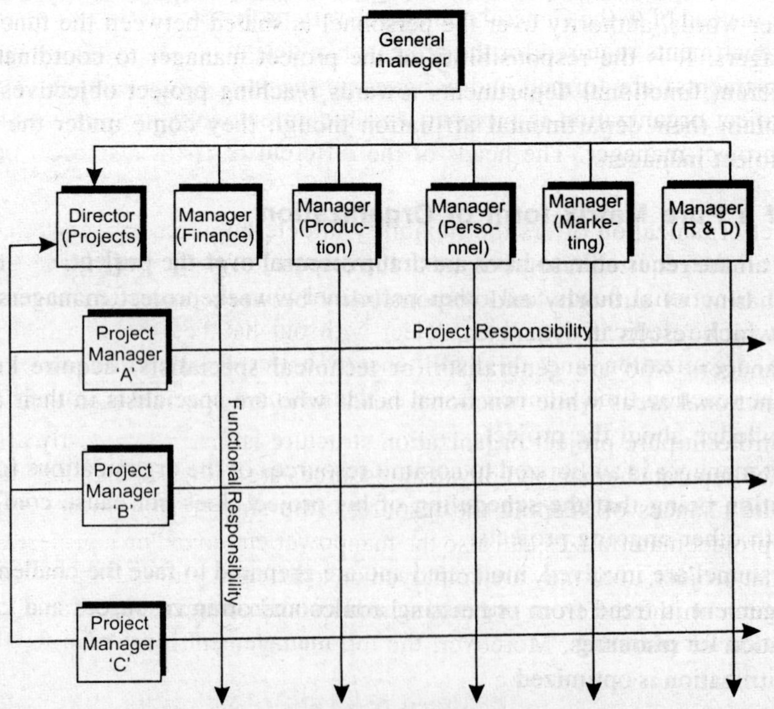

Fig. 1.22 *(Modified matrix organization)*

The role of Director (projects) is different from the role of project managers. While project managers look at their respective projects on their own merits, the project director evaluates all the projects under his control to see if they are in tune with the overall objectives of the organization.

Pure Project Organization Structure

A pure project organization structure is one in which the project manager is in total control of all other departments. It is like a mini company or an autonomous division of a parent company. The project manager in a pure project organization has full authority and maximum control over the men and material resources assigned to the project. Fig. 1.23 indicates a pure project organization structure.

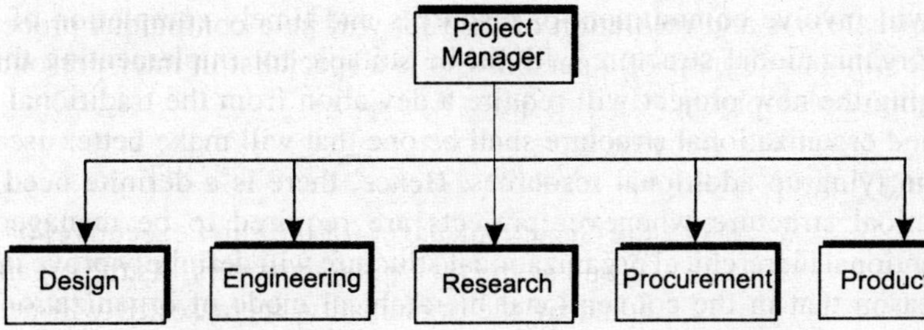

Fig. 1.23 *(Pure project organization)*

This form of organizational structure is suited if the organization has a complex project whose resource requirements are large. In such situations, all the resources for the project are left at the disposal of the project manager. The project manager has complete authority and full control over all resources (both physical and human resources) assigned to the project. The organizational structure resembles the traditional functional form of organization, but the functional heads report to the project manager instead of to the General manager. Every project is treated as a separate entity and all the functional departments required for the project (like design, engineering, procurement, research, production departments) are formed and assigned to the project manager for his overall control. Thus, a pure project organization is more or less like an autonomous division of the organization headed by the project manager. The heads of the different departments report only to the project manager.

A pure project organization offers the flexibility in determining cost, schedule and performance trade-offs since all the required resources are at the disposal of the project manager. Under this form of organization, functional heads and other personnel who are qualified and inclined towards a specific project canbe dedicated to that project with out having to share their services to other projects of the organization and this will ensure better work performance. In pure project organizations, the reaction time is much faster as there is no ambiguity in authority relationships.

The major hurdle in pure project organization structure is that it is a costly affair for the parent organization since separate human and physical resources are to be assigned and maintained for each project. There are chances of keeping the resources idle since resources are acquired in advance even before the project materializes and also the manpower employed on a project will remain idle on completion of that project, until they are employed on a different project. Unless the top management keeps a close watch on the different projects schedules and optimize resource allocation, there will be under utilization of resources. Moreover, the top management must plan for the deployment of personnel in other projects once the on-going projects come to an end and this planning should be done well in advance. Otherwise, as projects approach completion, the project team members will become highly apprehensive and anxious about their future assignments and this may bring down their morale and enthusiasm.

Selection of Product Organization Structure

We have seen five major organizational structures. The next question that may arise is how to choose an organizational structure to suit the given project. Let there be a company engaged in the production of product — A. If the company embarks upon launching a totally different, new product — B and plans to bring out the new product within a stipulated time limit, the existing organizational structure may not be conducive to implement the project for launching the new product — B. Producing the new product — B will involve commitment of resources and timely completion of activities. The existing functional organizational structure will not be suitable for implementing this project. The approach for managing the new project will require a deviation from the traditional organizational form and the modified organizational structure shall be one that will make better use of the existing resources, apart from tying up additional resources. Hence, there is a definite need to modify the traditional organizatioal structure whenever projects are required to be managed. Under such situations, the conventional hierarchical organizational structure will definitely prove inadequate. This is because of the reason that in the conventional hierarchical mode of organization, the authority flows from the top to the bottom in a systematic way and hence the roles of the organizational members are well defined and no deviation is allowed; such a rigid organizational structure will not suit for handling of projects that are one-time, unique, non repetitive ventures.

1. For "project-driven" enterprises, the matrix form of organizational structure is the best suited. This is because the main activity of such enterprises is project implementation and new project/ projects are taken up once ongoing project/projects are completed. Construction companies and companies undertaking turnkey projects are the organizations that can be benefited by matrix organizational structure since the resources would be put to effective and optimum use. The choice of suitable project organizational structure depends upon the frequency of new projects handled by the organization and the duration of the projects. If the organisation handles long term projects and also if the frequency of new projects is such that the organizational resources can always be put to maximum use, a matrix organizational structure will give better results.
2. In functional organizational structure, the integration between the functional units is achieved by formal rules, regulations, plans, budgets etc. This form of organisation is suitable for stable and repetitive environments. For example, a project involving construction of 5,000 similar houses can be handled by a functional organizational structure effectively without the use of a matrix structure of organization.
3. Other organizations that are not "project-driven" also come across situations where they are to manage projects. For example,consider an enterprise engaged in the production of heavy machinery that proposes to expand its manufacturing facilities. Construction of additional buildings, purchase and erection of new machinery, acquisition of new technical know how etc.,may form part of the expansion plan. Thus, the expansion plan is a new project for the existing organization. Any organization will try to utilize the existing resources as far as possible to implement the new project. Hence, it can be said in general terms that the project

organizational structure is to be chosen in such a way that it satisfies the requirements of the project management and also it does not disturb the organizational structure of the parent organization. Departmental project management structure is one that explains this aspect well. Under this structure, section-level personnel are temporarily designated as project leaders and are assigned with project responsibility. Once the project is completed, the project leaders will return back to their former positions. (refer Fig. 1.24 for departmental project management structure.)

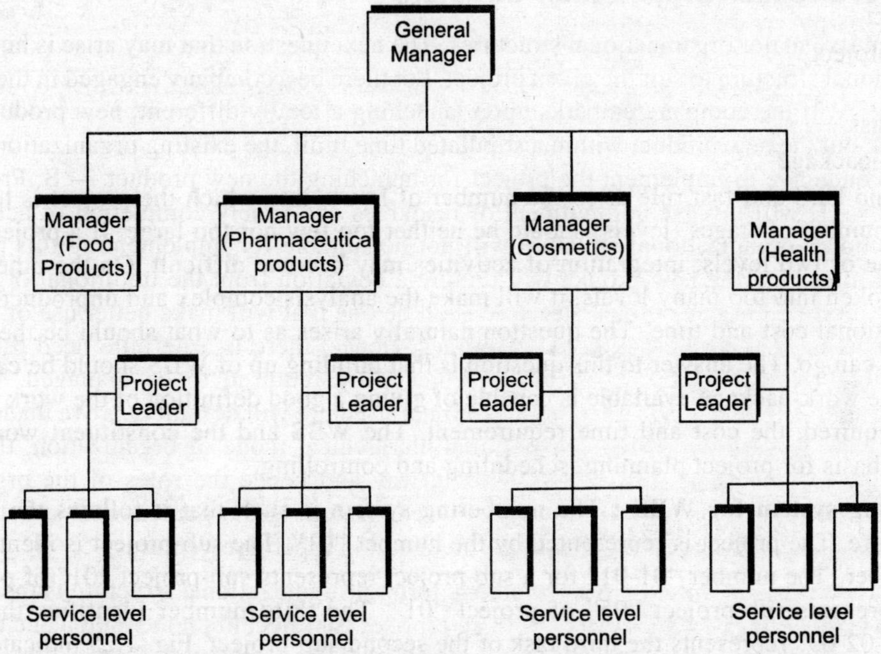

Fig. 1.24 *(Department project management structure)*

4. Pure project organizational structure and matrix organisational structure work better for the control of human resources and hence these structures are more suited for labour intensive projects.
5. Projects involving high complexity and requiring huge resources can be better handled by a pure project organization structure.
6. Project management involves integrating the activities across functional boundaries andultimately it is the top management that decides theauthority structure that will control the integration mechanism. The authority structure ranges from pure functional authority to product authority and finally to dual authority. Under pure functional authority, the organizational structure takes the form of a functional (or traditional) organization; under product authority, the organizational structure takes the form of a product (or market) organization; under dual authority, the organizational structure takes the form of a matrix organization. The organizational forms are selected based on how much authority the top management is prepared to delegate.

Break Down Structures

Modern methods of project management uses breakdown structures for work and organization.

Work Break Down Structure is a process by which the whole project is divided (i.e., broken down into various sub-projects, the sub-projects into various tasks, the tasks into various sub-tasks and finally the sub-tasks into work-packages. In the process of building up WBS, the project manager, all connected functional managers and all the connected staff work together and analyse all aspects of the project so that their collective wisdom will prevail. Thus, we have the following stages or levels:

1. Project
2. Sub-project
3. Task
4. Sub-task
5. Work-package

There is no hard and fast rule as to the number of levels into which the project is to be broken down. The number of stages (levels) should be neither too few nor too large. If a project is broken into only one or two levels, integration of activities may become difficult. On the other hand, if a project is broken into too many levels, it will make the analysis complex and unproductive and will lead to additional cost and time. The question naturally arises as to what should be the level up to which WBS can go. The answer to this question is that building up of WBS should be carried on till such time the work-package available is capable of giving a good definition of the work content, the resources required, the cost and time requirement. The WBS and the constituent work-packages become the basis for project planning, scheduling and controlling.

Numbering system for WBS : The numbering system is such that it follows the work break down structure. The project is represented by the number "01". The sub-project is identified by the second number. The number "01-01" for a sub-project represents sub-project "01" of project "01", "01-05" represents sub-project "05" of project "01". The third number identifies the task. The number "01-02-03" represents the third task of the second sub-project. Fig. 1.25 indicates the WBS numbering system.

Types of work breakdown structures: Work Break down Structure can be of two types, viz.,

- Product oriented WBS
- Functionally oriented WBS

Product oriented WBS : In this type of orientation, the project is subdivided in to sub-projects on the basis of 'products'. The sub-projects are again subdivided on the basis of 'products' and so on till tiny work packages are obtained. Fig. 1.26 indicates the diagram of a product oriented WBS for a hospital project.

Functionally oriented WBS : In this type of orientation, the project is broken down on the basis of functional departments (or functional tasks). Fig. 1.27 indicates the diagram of a functionally oriented WBS for the hospital project.

In practice, a combination of product oriented and a functionally oriented WBS can be used, the only requirement being that the project should be divided into meaningful, independent work packages.

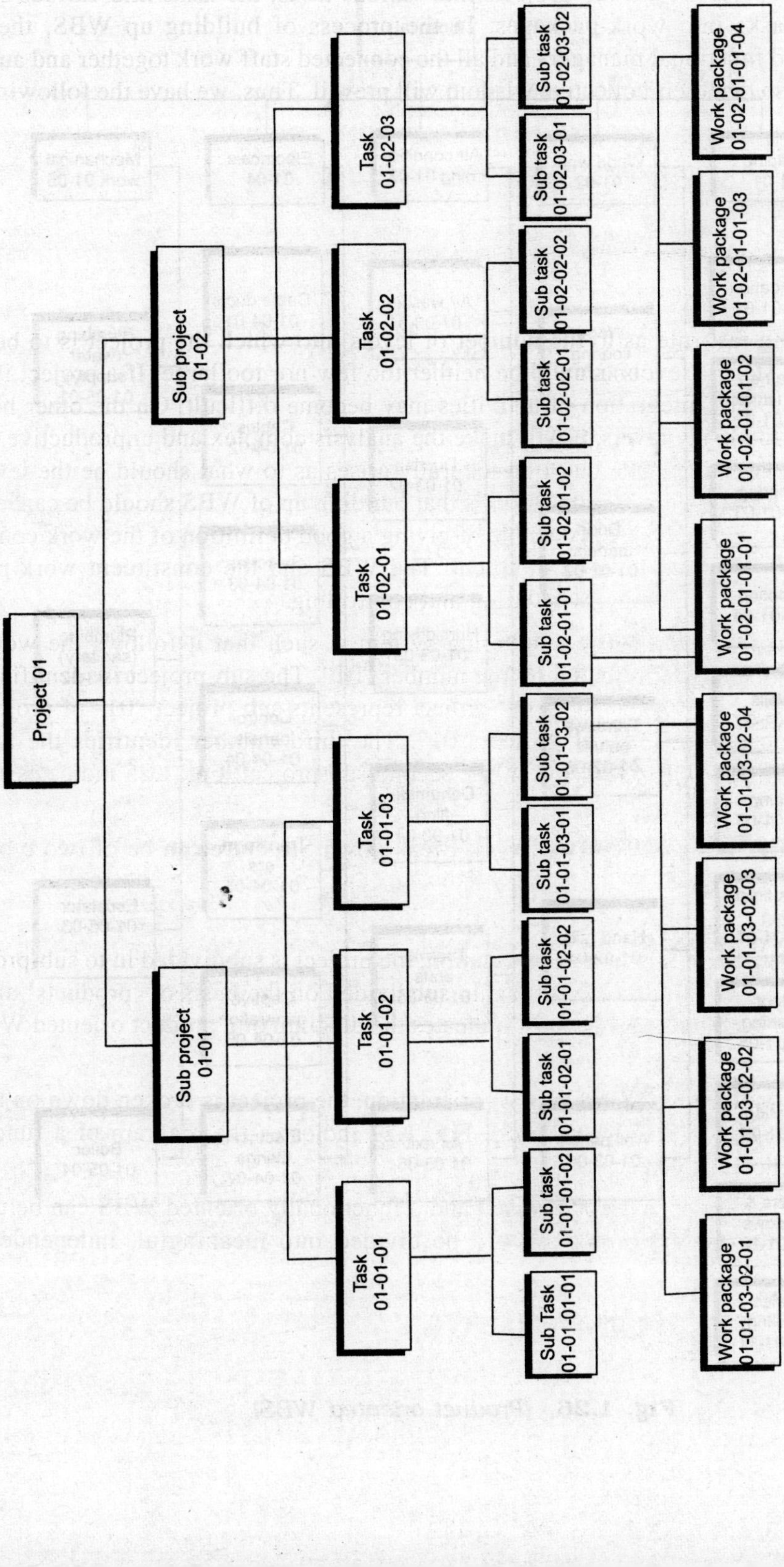
Project 01
Sub project 01-01
Sub project 01-02
Task 01-01-01
Task 01-01-02
Task 01-01-03
Task 01-02-01
Task 01-02-02
Task 01-02-03
Sub Task 01-01-01-01
Sub task 01-01-01-02
Sub task 01-01-02-01
Sub task 01-01-02-02
Sub task 01-01-03-01
Sub task 01-01-03-02
Sub task 01-02-01-01
Sub task 01-02-01-02
Sub task 01-02-02-01
Sub task 01-02-02-02
Sub task 01-02-03-01
Sub task 01-02-03-02
Work package 01-01-03-02-01
Work package 01-01-03-02-02
Work package 01-01-03-02-03
Work package 01-01-03-02-04
Work package 01-02-01-01-01
Work package 01-02-01-01-02
Work package 01-02-01-01-03
Work package 01-02-01-01-04

Fig. 1.25

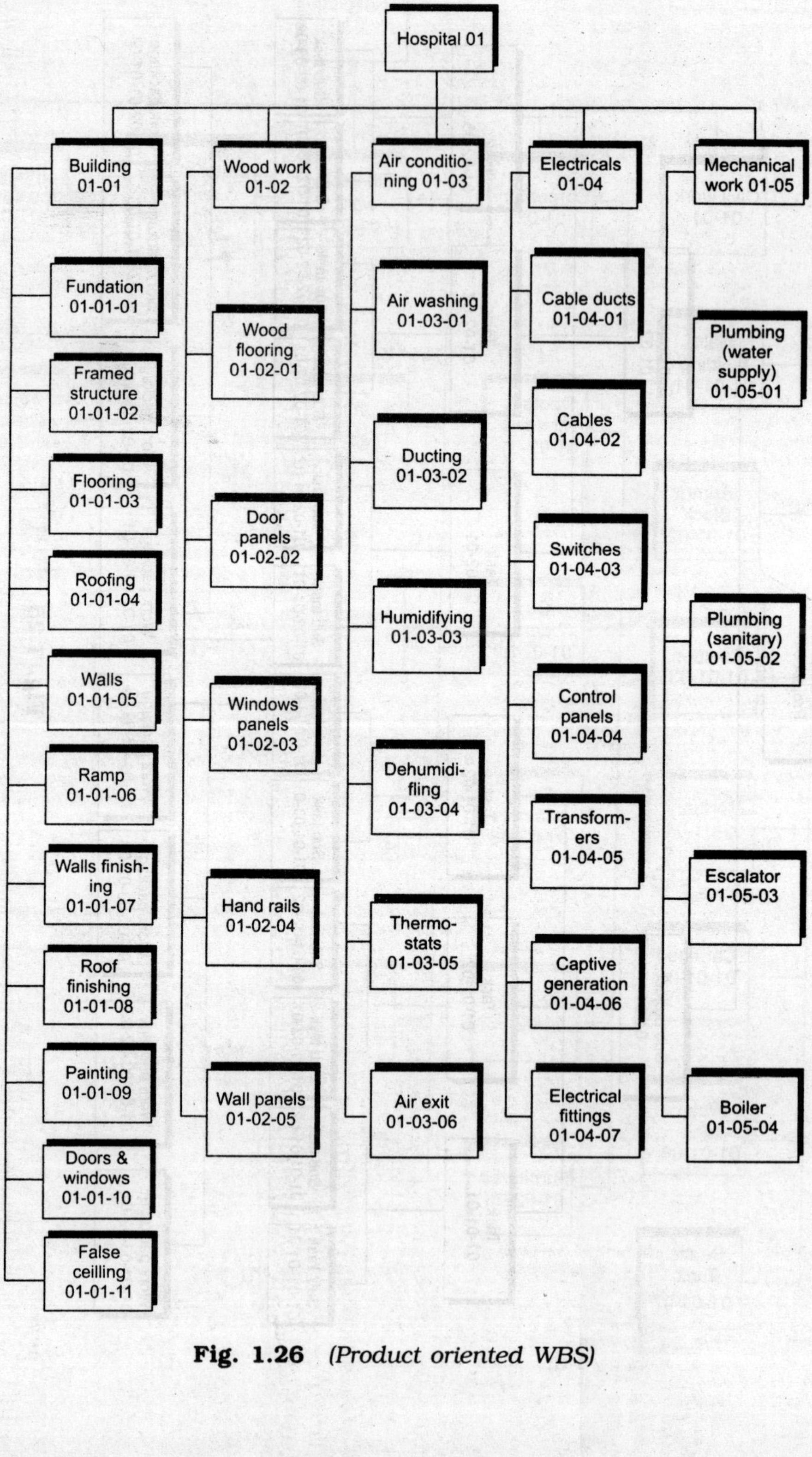

Fig. 1.26 *(Product oriented WBS)*

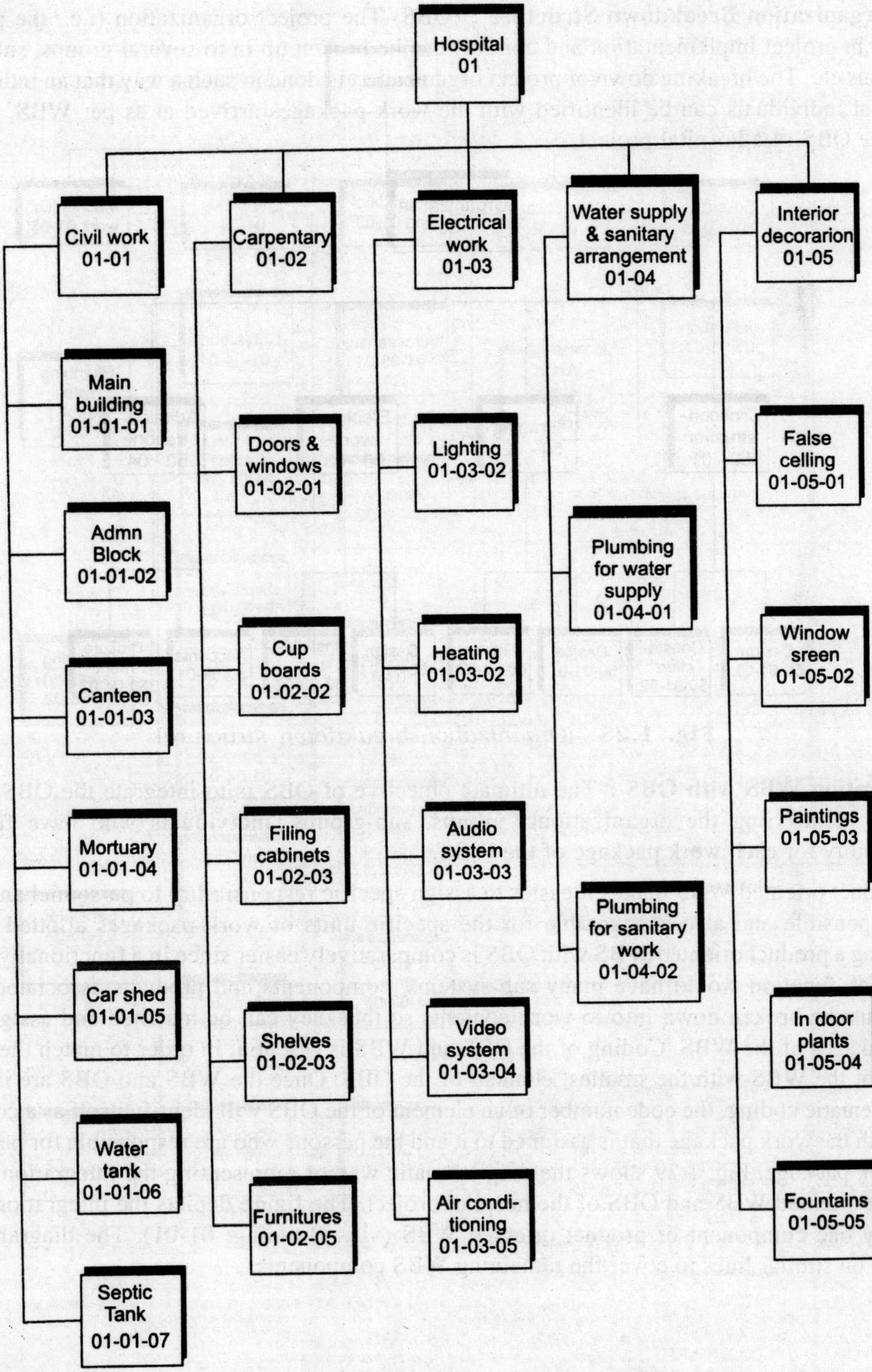

Fig. 1.27 *(Funtional oriented WBS)*

(b) **Organization Breakdown Structure :** (OBS) The project organization (i.e., the personnel involved in project implementation and control) can be broken up in to several groups, sub-groups, individuals etc. The breaking down of project organization is done in such a way that an individual or a group of individuals can be identified with the work packages arrived at as per WBS. Fig. 1.28 shows the OBS of a hospital project.

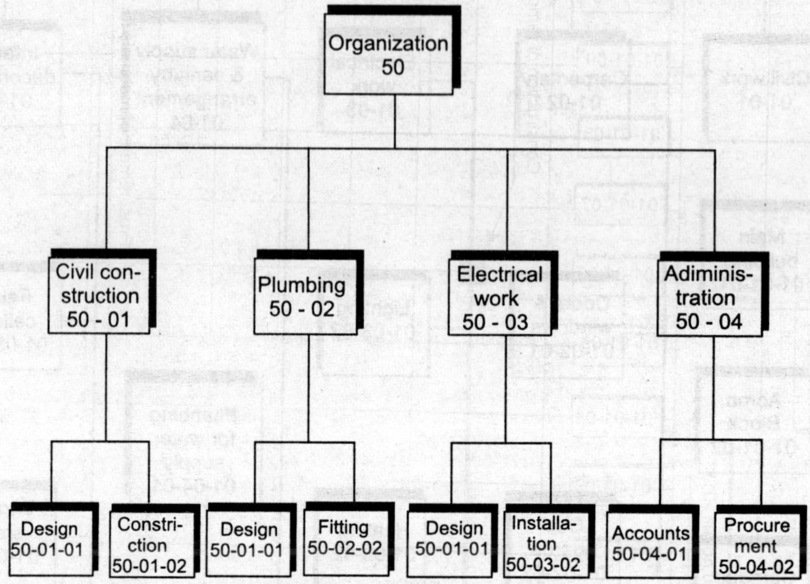

Fig. 1.28 *(Organization breakdown structure)*

Integrating WBS with OBS : The ultimate objective of OBS is to integrate the OBS with the WBS by identifyiing the organizational groups, sub-groups, individuals who have functional responsibility for each work package of the WBS.

A product oriented WBS makes it easier to assign specific responsibility to personnel and to hold them responsible and also accountable for the specific units of work packages allotted to them. Integrating a product oriented WBS with OBS is comparatively easier since in a functionally oriented WBS, each function would have many sub-systems, components and products associated with it, which must be broken down into to work contents so that they can be matched and assigned with work packages of the WBS. Coding of the OBS and WBS is essential in order to match the smallest element of the WBS with the smallest element of the OBS. Once the WBS and OBS are integrated with systematic coding, the code number of an element of the OBS will identify itself as a cost centre along with the work package that is assigned to it and the persons who are responsible for performing such work package. Fig. 1.29 shows the diagrammatic way of representing the integration between a product oriented WBS and OBS of the hospital project. The figure depicts the integration of OBS with only one component of product oriented WBS (viz., Building: 01-01). The diagram can be extended on similar lines to cover the remaining WBS components.

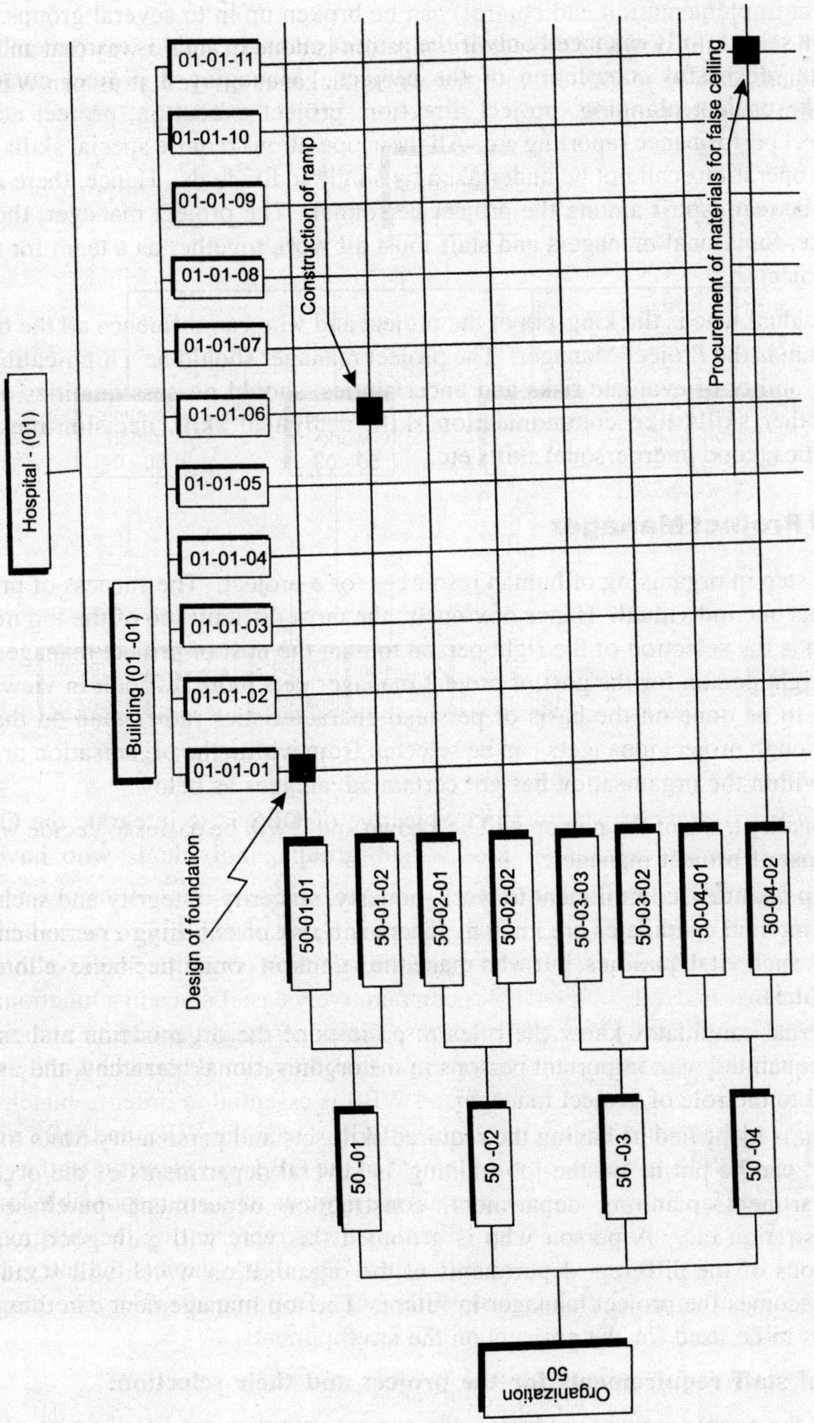

Fig. 1.29 *Integrating OBS with WBS*

1.9 ORGANISING HUMAN RESOURCE

A project can be successfully managed only if the project manager and his team members are totally dedicated to the successful completion of the project. Managing a project contains different requirements like project planning, project direction, project execution, project control, project evaluation, project performance reporting etc. All these operations require special skills and collective wisdom. These operations can not be undertaken by single individuals. Hence, there is a great need that there must be team spirit among the project personnel. The project manager, the personnel of the project office, functional managers and staff must all work together as a team for the successful execution of projects.

The one individual who is the king-pin of the project and who can influence all the other members of the project team is the Project Manager. The project manager should be a high-calibre person. He should have the ability of evaluate risks and uncertainties, should possess qualities of honesty and integrity, and other skills like communication skill, analytical skill, decision-making capacity, leadership qualities, good interpersonal skills etc.

Selection of Project Manager

This is a crucial step in organising of human resources for a project. The success of project depends very much on this one individual. Hence obviously, the most difficult job of the top management of any organisation is the selection of the right person to man the post of project manager. The task of identifying the right person for the post of project manager gets more difficult in view of the reason that selection is to be done on the basis of personal characteristics rather than on the basis of job descriptions. Though project managers can be selected from within the organisation or from outside, selecting from within the organisation has got certain advantages as below:

- The personality traits of the person will be known and it will be easier to decide whether he will suit the post of project manager.
- Leadership qualities, commitment to work, honesty, sincerity, integrity and such other factors about the internal candidates are known. There is a risk of choosing external candidates who really lack such vital qualities, but who make the selection committee believe that they possess these qualities.
- Since internal candidates know the rules & policies of the organisation and as they will be already acquainted with important persons in the organisational hierarchy, they will be able to adapt well to the role of project manager.

A person who is identified as having the required skill sets and personality traits to make a good project manager, can be put in 'on-the-job training' in several departments of the organisation like production department, planning department, construction department, purchase department, contract administration etc. A person who is groomed this way will gain good exposure to the working conditions of the different departments of the organisation which will stand him in good stead when he becomes the project manager in future. The top management can thus groom future project managers to be used for the projects on the anvil.

Identification of staff requirements for the project and their selection:

To decide upon the people resource required, the project activities are listed down. Description of the project activities listed is done and job descriptions of the individuals required for the different activities are defined.

Once the job descriptions are defined, the type and number of people required under different categories is arrived at. After this, a staffing plan is drawn which answers the following questions.

- How many people are required full time and what are the skill sets required of them?
- How many people are required who can continue to remain attached to their respective functional departments but can participate in project execution at times of requirements?
- When will the people be required?
- Is only internal man-power resource adequate or is there need for acquiring human resources from outside?
- How long will the people be attached to the project and when will they be released?

The successful implementation of a project depends upon the efficiency and effectiveness with which the project team members perform the tasks assigned to them. The manpower requirements for the projects are complex and varied. Personnel of varying qualifications, experience and calibre are present in any project team. The man power requirement for the project is determined by assessing the man power requirement for the individual activities and adding up. While arriving at the man power requirement for the individual activities, the optimum number of persons required for each activity is to be assessed keeping in view the time-cost trade-off relationship. Further, man-power leveling technique can be employed wherever possible so that the requirement of man-power will be uniform through out the project implementation period, which will consequently reduce the cost of man-power in the long run. Once the man-power requirement during the different points of time are estimated, steps should be taken for recruitment and selection of the required man-power and the availability of man-power at the required points of time should be ensured.

Project Office

Project team is a combination of personnel attached to project office and field-level employees attached to the project. The personnel in the project office are assigned to the project as full time employees. The project office members should be dedicated individuals who support the project manager in his endeavour to complete the project successfully. Some of the responsibilities of the personnel of project office are as under.

- To gather project related data & information and to disseminate them across the project team members.
- To assist the project manager and the top management by providing project related information periodically.
- Monitoring the progress of the project and controlling time, cost and performance / quality parameters.
- To follow the stipulated guidelines for awarding of contracts and to act according to the terms of contracts in connection with monitoring and controlling the work entrusted to contractors, to make payment to contractors etc.
- To ensure creation of proper documents for the works executed by contractors/ departmentally.
- To obtain required authorisation from the top management for all the works being performed/ entrusted to contractors.

Selection of team members from within and from outside the organisation:

Project team members are selected both from within the organisation and from outside as the situation demands. Persons selected from within the organisation for the purpose of forming the project team have the advantage that they will be already acquainted with the organisational members and this will help in moulding a unified project team . Moreover, they will be acquainted with the policies, work procedures and work culture of the organisation . Persons recruited from outside for projects (either on contract basis or on permanent basis) will lack familiarity with the organisational culture . However, it may become necessary to recruit people from outside, if special skills required for the project are not available with the existing members of the organisation.

One of the major problems that project manager faces in staffing the project by choosing personnel from within the organisation is the reluctance on the part of the employees to join the project team. This may be due to the following reasons :

- The employees chosen for the project team may be required to be transferred to the project site. Most of the employees may resist such a transfer unless the change of place is something that they have been waiting for.
- There may be fear in the minds of the employees that once the project is completed they may go out of job and the management may either dump them in insignificant posts or may even terminate their services.
- Employees maybe reluctant to work under the dual authority of the project manager and the functional manager.
- Since project managers mostly do not enjoy the delegation of powers to fix the salary for the members of the project team or to give them perks / incentives, the employees who are given the option to join the project team may feel that their efforts may not be rightly rewarded.

In order to encourage the employees to switch over to the project team, the top management may devise ways and means. Hike in salary may be given to those who accept project assignments. They may be explained about the longevity of the project and this may remove their fear of 'going out-of-job' in the near future. The long term plans of the organisation with regard to undertaking new projects in future may be explained to the employees so that they can gain confidence in working with challenging projects. This will prove advantageous to them in the long run as they can learn different skills and build their career.

Team Building

A team is a collection of individuals who work towards a common goal. A project team consists of all the individuals who contribute towards the success of the project. Project leaders should have the required skills to build an effective team. A project team has the special nature that it consists of individuals from diverse functional areas and specialists / experts.. Apart from those who are employees of the organisation, outsiders (like, technical consultants, financial advisors, machinery / equipment suppliers and erectors etc.,) are also part of the project team. Hence, in order to coordinate the efforts of all such individuals with diverse qualifications and experience, the project leader should be a person with good team-building skills.

Tips for Building Successful Teams

- Selecting people with the required talent and skills, offering them with right monetary benefits, designing a right organisational structure are necessary for building up a good team. But, these alone are not sufficient. These factors will not work in the absence of a friendly, cordial and intimate relationship among the team members.

- Though there will be complex hierarchy of work relationships in a project environment (which can not be avoided), it must be flexible and to some extent informal. The relationship among the project team members should be akin to the relationship among the members of a family. In a family, there is a hierarchy. The father (or the grand father / the eldest member in a joint family) is the head of the family. This, of course may not be so in the families of the western countries, but the hierarchy is very much present in Indian families, even today. In spite of the hierarchy, there is informality in a happy family. This is possible because of the mutual trust, affection and closeness among the family members. A similar relationship among the team members is what is expected. Under such favourable conditions, there won't be any communication gap. The communication will be perfect, though informal. Designing any type of sophisticated formal information system will not work unless there is intimate emotional relationship among the team members.
- Synergy is possible in a team only when the team members have cordial interpersonal relationships.
- The team leader must be prepared to share power and responsibility. This will make the team members involved and committed to the task and they will be prepared to bear accountability. Team members who share responsibility and bear accountability will make the team a successful one.

Motivating the Project Team Members

A project manager shall have the ability to understand the motivational needs of his team members. While selecting people as members of the project team, it is important to know their needs and only if their needs could be satisfied, they must be selected as project team members. Selecting a person, whose needs, the organisation can not satisfy, will be of no use and he / she will leave the organisation at the earliest. If at all he / she continues to remain with the organisation, he / she will remain only as an unmotivated individual and won't contribute what he /she is capable of contributing. The greater the likelihood of fulfilling the needs of project team members, the greater will be the chances for the successful implementation of the project.

Many motivational theories have been proposed by eminent sociologists, psychologists and management thinkers like Abraham Maslow, V.H.Vroom, J.D.MOooney, Douglas McGregor, Herzberg and M.E.Dimock . The motivational theory that is suitable for the situation can be applied and motivational techniques can be devised accordingly. Whatever be the motivational technique adopted, the following four factors contribute towards motivating people at work.

(a) Nature of the Job

Among all the motivating factors, the nature of the job plays a major role. If the job is made interesting and demanding, thus giving a sense of satisfaction and a sense of achievement, the job itself will act as a major motivator. An artist is motivated to paint not just because he could sell his paintings at a fancy price, but because he likes painting and it gives him mental satisfaction. Hence, the artist is totally involved in painting. As he is wholeheartedly involved, he produces master pieces. But for the involvement, achieving quality is not possible. Hence, the job content of work packages should be such that they give a sense of satisfaction to those who perform the works. Grouping of unrelated, fragmented and discrete works into a work package and assigning such works to individuals will kill their motivation.

(b) Synchronizing Individual's Goals with Project Goals

If the goals of the project team members can be identified with the goals of the project, successful projects are ensured. The management must strive to provide environments suitable for such synchronization of goals and should also offer suitable training programmes, if required.

(c) Status Advancement

The successful project team members should be offered facilities to learn more, to develop their skills further and should be offered higher status in the organisation. This will encourage all the team members to become performers.

(d) Organisational Environment

Organisational environment refers to the working atmosphere. A free, open, friendly, considerate and refreshing organisational climate is a must not only for successful project management, but for managing any affair for that matter. The top management should be aware of this and should cultivate a pleasing organisational culture. This is easier said than done. For achieving this, all the key executives through out the organisational hierarchy should be persons with human touch, apart from their technical and managerial capabilities. Once the organisational environment is conducive, results are sure to follow.

De-motivators

The management shall see to it that de-motivating factors are identified and removed. This should be a continuous exercise since the de-motivating factors might find their way into the organisation unless the top management consciously look for such factors and remove them as and when found. Some of the de-motivating factors are as below:

- Jobs those are highly impossible to perform.
- Jobs those are too easy to perform.
- Jobs those are routine in nature.
- Restrictions on freedom to act.
- Negative criticism.
- Lack of recognition of good work done.
- Lack of support and guidance at times of crisis.
- Unsympathetic approach to human problems.
- Poor physical working conditions.
- Bad pay structures.
- Poor and ineffective communication system.

The project manager should aim at making the jobs of project team members as satisfying as possible. He can do this by entrusting his team members with specific tasks from start to finish so that they will feel having done a fruitful job. Indiscriminate splitting of jobs will take the wholeness out of them and such fractional tasks will not induce interest to perform. Moreover, only when specific tasks from start to finish are offered, the team members will have the chance to make changes in the way the work can be done that will improve efficiency. Such a working condition will also allow room for creativity and innovation which all will help the project in a big way. After all, people produce best results when their own methods and ideas are encouraged.

Characteristics of a Good Team

- The atmosphere will be pleasing, comfortable and informal.
- All the members of the team will be committed to the task.
- The members of the team will be receptive to the ideas of others.
- There will be freedom for the expression of views. Members will feel free to express their opinions honestly and openly.
- Disagreements might arise between the views of the team members. However, there will be only constructive criticisms and the members will still feel comfortable amidst criticisms and differences of opinions. They will work together for resolving any issues between themselves amicably.
- Since the team members approach the problems objectively and discuss with an open mind before arriving at decisions, all decisions will be accepted in the right spirit. Hence implementation of the decisions taken will not suffer due to want of cooperation.
- The team leader will set an example for his team members to emulate.
- Difficult situations will be managed constructively, without passing the blame on others.

Skills Required of a Project Manager

Leadership Skills

A project manager must possess leadership skills. Leadership is a quality that a person possesses by virtue of which he could influence his team members to work together in the way the leader wants them to work. Thus, leadership skill is the ability to influence the behaviour of others. Though a person may possess professional skills, it is his ability to influence the behaviour of others that makes him a leader. In order to influence the behavior of others, a leader should possess qualities of sympathy, empathy, generosity, broad-mindedness, honesty, integrity, sincerity, fair-play, affection towards fellow human beings etc., so that his team members will repose their confidence in him and will be willing to carry out his instructions.

A project manager, as a leader, shall be capable of guiding and motivating the team members. He should also have the ,acumen to understand the feelings of his subordinates, their problems, hardships, expectations and limitations. For understanding his subordinates and their requirements, the project manager should lead his team by working with them, instead of sitting at top and merely issuing directions. He should make his team members feel that he is one among the team members. Once he wins the confidence of his team members, communication (both upward and downward & formal and informal) will flow freely and this will help make right decisions.

Team Building Skills

A project manager must be a good team builder. Since a project team consists of people of varied skills, knowledge, experience and background and as they are drawn from diverse disciplines, uniting them into a team is a great task. Unless they function as an unified team, the project goals can not be reached. As the project team members possess varied skills that are complementary to one another, synergy can be achieved only if there is strong and cordial interpersonal relationships among the members. The team building skills of the project manager plays an important role in bringing about this synergy. The team building skills of a project manager acquires more importance in view of the fact that all the project team members are not under the direct organisational control of the project manager and quite often even persons who occupy higher positions than the project manager in the organisational hierarchy are also part of the project team. For building an effective team, the project manager must create a working atmosphere that is informal and free from conflicts. He should ensure free flow of communication (both formal and informal), permit discussions without any inhibition / apprehension, inculcate among the team members, the habit of listening and understanding the views of other team members, make all the team members aware of the team's goals and objectives and extract whole-hearted commitment of all the team members towards achievement of the objectives.

Conflict Resolution Skills

Conflict is a psychological state of mind. It is the outcome of behavioural differences. Conflicts in organisations is a common occurrence. Situations where superiors do not appreciate the way their subordinates work and subordinates finding fault with the decisions taken by their superiors are very often come across almost in all organisations. A project organisation is more prone to conflicts due to its multifunctional components and due to the matrix form of superior-subordinate relationships.

Conflicts will create a climate of mistrust among the organisational members and it may distract their attention from the goals set to be achieved. A lot of time and energy will be wasted in the perpetuation of conflicts. Conflicts will lead to taking wrong decisions, delay in taking decisions, disruption of team work and all these will have their adverse impact on project performance. A project manager must act diligently and prudently to resolve conflicts. He must have the patience to listen to the conflicting views of the parties to the conflict and must take rational, unbiased decisions. He should have the knack of seeing to it that resentment does not creep in among any one while attempting to resolve conflicts. Correct understanding of the behavioural patterns of organisational members goes a long way in monitoring and resolving conflict situations. Implementing an effective communication system, free from any barriers will help avoid misunderstanding of issues/problems by the organisational members and this will bring about smooth working conditions which will stop breeding of conflicts.

Technical Skills

It will be good if the project manager is a technocrat so that he will have good understanding of the technical aspects of the project. Since almost all projects involve technology to a greater or a lesser extent, the project manager is expected to possess appropriate technical skills for handling projects effectively. Choice of production process, choice of technical know-how, choice of equipments / machinery etc. can be correctly made only if the project manager as technical knowledge. Though a project manager may not be expected to be an expert in all the technical aspects of projects, his exposure to critical technical areas and his skill in handling technical problems will be highly useful, especially for engineering projects.

Managerial Skills

The project manager shall have the managerial skills of planning, organising, delegating and controlling. Planning is the first function performed by any manager and project manager is no exception to this. In fact, a project manager requires effective planning skills in the areas of resource allocation, project scheduling, cost control, information processing etc., Since projects are dynamic in nature, planning is an on-going activity in projects. Moreover, since projects compete for resources, planning for the negotiation and allocation of resources required for the execution of projects is an important activity of a project manager. Plans are made into realities by organising the required resources and utilizing the resources to give concrete shape to the plans, by executing the plans to perfection. Once the required resources are organized, the project manager should direct the resources towards accomplishment of project objectives. The objectives framed can be achieved only if there is a control system by which the actual results are periodically measured, compared with the planned performance and corrective actions are taken wherever and whenever required. Hence, the project manager should have necessary skills for carrying out the control functions effectively.

Duties and Responsibilities of Project Managers

The prime responsibility of making a project a successful one rests with the project manager. The following are some of his duties and responsibilities. The list, however, is not exhaustive and the project manager is responsible for any other duties that are contingent upon the nature of the project.

- To plan for all project tasks.
- To plan for the allocation of resources for all the project activities.
- To ensure that the project activities are realistically scheduled.
- To ensure that the resources required for implementing the projects are made available in time.
- To motivate and direct the project team members towards fulfillment of project objectives.
- To monitor the project continuously.
- To identify deviations between the actual progress and the planned progress in terms of time, cost and performance; to arrive at and suggest remedies for correcting such deviations.
- To ensure that the corrective actions required to bring back the project to the status that was originally planned for are taken and the project progresses as per the plans, without any deviations and shortcomings.
- To maintain an effective communication system.
- To keep vigil over the possible chances for conflicts and to resolve conflicts at the earliest possible instant.
- To maintain good liaison with the members of functional departments, external project participants and consultants / experts connected with the project
- To prepare periodical progress reports and to send the same to the top management.
- To participate in contract negotiations, to coordinate with contractors on finalization of contract agreements, to settle contractors' payments, to handle litigations with contractors etc.
- ,To take decisions as and when warranted with regard to procurement of resources, assignment of tasks to project team members, delegating authority to subordinates etc., to ensure compliance of project plans.

- To coordinate with Government / statutory authorities with regard to obtaining necessary clearances / approvals required for the project.
- To exercise control over the funds allotted for the project.

1.10 PROJECT CONTRACTS

Introduction

A project is ready for execution when the required funds are arranged and necessary statutory approvals are obtained. In the case of Government/Public sector projects, the execution is taken up after administrative approval and technical sanction are accorded and after the funds required for the project are allotted through budgetary allocations.

Small sized projects promoted by private entrepreneurs are normally executed by employing workers directly.

Medium sized projects promoted by private entrepreneurs can be executed either

- by executing all the works by employing work force directly

  or
- by entrusting some work to contractors and executing the remaining work directly.

  or
- by entrusting the entire work to contractors.

A large sized project is normally executed by entrusting to contractors.

Government/Public sector projects are also executed by any of the two methods, viz., a) Contract system and b) Departmental execution depending upon the complexities involved in the project.

Though an organisation may have reasonably good in-house resources, the need for entrusting some work to contractors rises under the following circumstances:

- If the type of work to be carried out is of special nature and the required expertise to carry out the work is available with contractors while the resources and expertise available in-house are inadequate to carry out the work.
- Even though the required resources/expertise are available in-house, there may be time constraints and the project may be required to be completed within a certain deadline which may be impossible to accomplish unless a part of the work is assigned to contractors.

Contract

A contract is a legal agreement. It is an exchange of promises by two or more persons.

Section 2(b) of the Indian Contract Act, 1872 defines contract as "an agreement enforceable by law". The definition given by the Indian Contract Act has two distinct parts. viz.,

- a contract is an agreement
- the agreement must be one enforceable by law.

Thus, though contract is necessarily an agreement, all agreements are not contracts. Only those agreements that are enforceable by law are contracts. For an agreement to become enforceable by law, it must satisfy certain essential elements called "essentials of valid contract"

The contractor is a person, a firm or a company who undertakes contract.

The essentials of a valid contract are as under:

- There must be an offer and an acceptance of that offer (Public notice inviting tenders for the execution of a work on contract basis is an offer and if a contractor submits his tender documents in response to the public notice and in accordance with the terms and conditions stipulated, it amounts to acceptance of the offer.)
- There must be an intention to create a legal relationship on the part of the parties to the contract.
- The consent of the parties to the contract shall be free and genuine.
- The parties to the contract shall be competent persons. (For example, minors and lunatics do not have the capacity to enter into any contract.)
- There must be a lawful consideration between the parties to the contract.
- The object of the contract must be lawful and not one which the law disapproves.
- The contract must not have been declared as void by any law in force in the country.
- The meaning of the contract must be certain without any room for ambiguity or different interpretations.
- The terms of the contract shall be capable of performance.
- A contract shall fulfill the necessary legal formalities. (For example, a contract, as such, may be oral or in writing. However, if the law stipulates that a particular contract shall be in writing, the same shall be complied with. Similarly, if the law requires certain contracts to be registered/ attested etc., such legal formalities are to be carried out. Else, the contract will not be enforceable at law.)

Types of Contracts

Broadly contracts can be divided into two types. They are:

- Turnkey contracts
- Non-turnkey contracts

Turnkey Contracts

In a turnkey contract, the entire responsibility of project execution is entrusted to the contractor. It is as if the owner comes into the picture only when the project is completed and he turns the key of the plant to start production. Till such time the project reaches a 'ready-to-start' stage, the contractor takes care of all aspects of project execution.

This type of contract is entered into when the project involves high technology, the know-how is not available with the project promoter and the contractor is fully conversant with the technology and know-how. There may by some projects that involve integration of many areas, of which, the project promoter is conversant only with certain areas while he has to depend on others for some other areas of the project. In such situations also, turnkey contract is preferred in order to fix the responsibility for execution and completion of entire activities to a single point.

Since the contractor of a turnkey project is expected to do everything right from scratch, the scope of contract covers all areas of the project, viz., design, Engineering, construction, structural work, supply and erection of plant and machinery, supply of spares, testing and commissioning. Since the entire work is done by a single contractor, turnkey contract agreements invariably have a clause on performance guarantee.

Turnkey contracts may be for the whole project or even for a sub-unit of a main project. Turnkey contract for a sub-unit is undertaken when such sub-unit is a separately identifiable component of the total project and whose performance can be assessed independent of other units of the project.

Non-Turnkey Contracts

Non-turnkey contracts are preferred when the projects are small sized, the know-how for the project is available with the promoters and when there is a strong, competent and capable project team available with the organization.

In non-turnkey arrangement, the total project is divided into suitable work packages. The packages that need to be given to contractors are identified. A contractor may be entrusted with one or more work packages. However, the responsibility for overall supervision and performance of the project will rest with the in-house project department.

For example, in a project for the construction of an industrial shed, the total project may be divided into the following packages.

- Site clearance & leveling
- Engineering design of the industrial building
- Construction of foundation for the building
- Construction of super-structure
- Construction of flooring
- Construction of machinery foundation inside the building at the places where machinery will be housed.

Out of the above work packages, construction of foundation for the building and construction of machinery foundation may be entrusted with a contractor who is specialized in foundation work, engineering design work may be entrusted with a contractor who has expertise in the line, and so on. Identification of different work packages is to be done carefully. A work package should be comprehensive. It should be such that the responsibility for poor performance, if any, can be easily attributed to a particular contractor. For example, in Reinforced Cement Concrete (R.C.C.) work, if the work of fixing reinforcement of steel bars is taken as a work package and assigned to one contractor while laying of cement concrete is assigned to some other contractor as a separate work package, it will become difficult to identify the contractor who has not carried out the work as per the specifications, if it is found at a later stage that the R.C.C. construction has defects. Thus, laying of cement concrete and fixing of reinforcement in the form of steel bars of the given design and specifications are to be treated as one work package.

The objective of breaking down a project into a number of work packages is to break down complex projects into smaller number of well identifiable and easily manageable units that will facilitate smooth execution. This will also help in entrusting the project activities to different contractors who have expertise in different lines of activities.

The following are some of the types of non-turnkey contracts:

- Piece-work contract
- Lump sum contract
- Cost-plus percentage contract
- Labour contract

Piece-Work Contract

This type of contract is suited for small works like site-clearance, maintenance/repair works, earthwork excavation etc., In this method of contract, the contractor agrees to execute a specific work for a specified rate with out reference to the quantity/magnitude of the work involved, or the time taken for completing the specified work. Obviously, the cost of works for such contracts will be very small, say, within about Rs 1.00 lakhs or so.

Lump Sum Contract

This is the system of contract that is used for all major non-turnkey contracts. In this system, the contractor agrees to execute the work completely in all respects, within the stipulated time, in accordance with the drawings, designs and detailed specifications and for an agreed sum. Once the contractor completes the work as per the drawings and specifications, no measurements of actual work done are taken, but the work done is only compared with the drawings and specifications. Payment of the agreed sum to the contractor is made on the strength of a work-completion certificate issued by the engineer- in-charge. Since this type of contract is used for major projects, time of completion of work is a crucial factor. The time limit with in which the work is to be completed is given in the contract and penalty for slow progress is also included as one of the conditions of the contract.

Lump Sum Up-front Contract

Under this agreement, the client pays a fixed sum to the contractor even before the contractor commences his work. This method is advisable only when the client has full confidence on the contractor. The contractor will use the initial payment received from the client for the purpose of purchase of materials required for carrying out the work. This is a risky way to contract since the project will suffer if the contractor backs out after receiving the initial payment. Though legal remedies are available to the client, this will only be a delayed process and will affect the project implementation.

Cost-Plus Percentage Contract

Under this method of contract, the contractor uses his own materials and labour and execute the work according to the given drawings and specifications. The contractor keeps proper accounts of material and labour charges. The project promoter exercises close control during execution to ensure that right quality of materials are used and right specifications are maintained. After completion of the work, the contractor is paid by the project promoter at a certain percentage above the actual cost of execution. The cost plus percentage is predetermined and provided in the contract and is meant to take care of overhead charges and also to provide the contractor with some profit margin.

Labour Contract

In this system, the project promoter arranges for the supply of all required material at the work site and the contractor arranges the labour. Thus, the contract is entered into only for the labour portion of the project. This type of contract is chosen when the project promoters do not want to compromise on the quality of material to be used.

Turnkey Vs. Non-Turnkey Contracts

Turnkey contract is preferred when the project involves high technology for which the in-house resource/expertise is inadequate while non-turnkey contract is preferred for smaller projects with known/familiar technology.

In turnkey contract, the entire responsibility for the execution of a project as per the plans is entrusted to a single contractor. Thus, the responsibility for executing the project to perfection lies solely with the contractor.

In non-turnkey mode, the various work packages are entrusted to different contractors. The responsibilities of the contractors are restricted to the scope of the different contracts. Thus, it becomes the responsibility of the project department to properly coordinate the different contractors in such a way that the project is executed as per the plans and gives the desired output.

Since the contractor bears the total responsibility in a turnkey contract, the cost of such contracts is generally higher as compared to that of non-turnkey contracts.

Sub-Contract

When a major work is undertaken by a main contractor, he can entrust some of the works to be executed by sub-contractors. There will be separate contracts between the main contractor and his sub contractors. Such sub-contracts should provide for the execution of work by the sub-contractors as per the requirements of the original contract. The project promoter is not liable to make any payment to the sub-contractor, which is the liability of the main contractor. In some sensitive works, if it is felt that sub-contracts shall not be permitted, suitable clauses to this effect should be incorporated in the main contract.

Preparation of Specifications for Project Activities

Specifications are required to be prepared before initiating contracting process and the specifications should form part of the contract documents. Specifications are to be prepared both for materials / equipments to be supplied and for works to be executed. The dictionary meaning of specifications is 'a standard of workmanship, materials etc., required to be met in a piece of work '. Specifications include general requirements like standards to be adhered to, inspection & testing methodology, delivery schedule, guarantee and penalty clauses, erection and commissioning parameters and technical requirements like design features, drawings, schedules, material properties, equipment standards, equipment performance characteristics, preferred makes of equipments, if any etc.,

The purpose of preparing specifications is to give in writing the requirements of materials/ equipments / services to all the tenderers so that all the tenderers can quote their bids on the basis of same parameters. Putting the specifications in black and white will help avoid disputes and misinterpretations at a later stage. If the specifications required are spelt out in clear terms, the contractors will know what is expected of them and clients (the project promoters) can check the project quality and performance taking the specifications as the reference.

Tenders

Tender is an offer in writing by the tenderer (the person who offers the tender) to execute some specified work or to supply some specified good at certain rates within a fixed time frame under certain conditions of agreement.

Tender Notice

It is a notice inviting tenders from interested parties (contractors). The tender notice is a public notice and is published in leading newspapers to give wide publicity. This is a popular method used by Government Departments and Public sector Enterprises. The tender notice contains the following information:

(*a*) Name of the organization calling for tenders and the designation of the officer concerned who is inviting tenders.

(b) The nature of work, the place of work and the estimated cost of work.

(*c*) Cost of tender documents and drawings/plans.

(*d*) Last date and time of receipt of tenders, place and availability of tender forms

(*e*) Type of contract and time of completion.

(*f*) Amount of Earnest Money Deposit (EMD) to be paid and the method of payment of E.M.D.

(*g*) Amount of security deposit to be deposited by the successful tenderer.

(*h*) Date, time and place of opening tenders.

Tender Documents

Tender documents are meant to keep the tenderers informed about the General and Specific conditions applicable for tender Tender documents usually consist of the following:

- A letter of invitation to the tenderers
- Specimen tender form
- General instruction to the tenderers
- Details of civil/structural work along with complete set of civil/structural drawings.
- Details and equipments of machinery/equipment to be supplied, if any
- Details of specifications for each item of the activities of project.
- Draft contract agreement
- Arbitration authority who will decide in case of dispute
- Time schedule for completion of work.
- Amount of earnest money to be deposited and the form in which it is to be deposited.
- Amount of security deposit to be made by the successful tenderer.

Pre-Qualification of Tenderers

Pre-qualification of tenderers is done only in bigger and complex projects. The objective of pre-qualification is to ensure that only competent tenderers participate in the tenders. The following information are gathered from the intending tenderers for deciding as to whether they are competent enough to participate in the tenders:

- The financial capacity of the contractors for carrying out the work.
- Infrastructure available with the contractors in terms of machinery, equipment, qualified personnel, man-power etc.,
- Previous experience in having handled projects of similar nature.

After assessing the qualifications of the intending tenderers, those who are found competent are chosen and only the selected persons are allowed to participate in the tenders.

Earnest Money Deposit (EMD)

It is the amount to be deposited by all the tenderers when they submit their tender. The EMD amount varies from 1% to 3% of the tender value. Once the contract is finalized, the EMD remitted by all the unsuccessful tenderers are returned back. The EMD of the successful tenderer is retained as a measure of caution so that he will not withdraw his offer. In the event of the successful tenderer withdrawing his offer, or refusing to take up the work, the EMD retained will be forfeited. A tenderer can withdraw his offer before acceptance of the tender. Once a particular tender is selected and communicated and if the successful tenderer withdraws his offer after the communication, he has to forego his EMD.

The EMD is payable normally in the form of pay-order/Demand Draft from a nationalized / scheduled bank. When the EMD amount is large, EMD is also accepted in the form of Bank Guarantee from a nationalized/scheduled bank.

Security Deposit

Security Deposit is the amount to be deposited by the successful tenderer after the contract is finalized. Normally it is about 15% of the total value of the contract. This amount is collected as a safety measure so that the contractor (successful tenderer) fulfills all the terms and conditions of the contract and completes the work in accordance with the terms of the contract. Security Deposit amount willl be forfeited in case the contractor fails to fulfill any of the terms of contract . The security deposit amount will be refunded to the contractor on completion of the work and after observing the work for defects, if any, till the 'defects liability period' which is normally around six months.

Acceptance of tenders

On the appointed date, the sealed envelopes containing tenders and E.M.Ds. are opened. The envelopes containing E.M.Ds are first opened and if found in order, the other envelopes containing the tender documents are opened. Opening of tenders is usually done in the presence of the tenderers

The valid bids received are scrutinized and evaluated by a committee of experts designated for the purpose. The tender evaluation committee will have representatives from all then departments (like legal department, finance department, operations department, purchase department etc.,) and special invitees who have specialized knowledge in the concerned field.

Before accepting one among the tenders received, the following aspects are to be given consideration:

(*a*) The financial capacity of the tenderer

(*b*) The technical infrastructure available with the tenderer

(*c*) Past performance of the tenderer in executing similar works

(*d*) Specifications (both general and technical) quoted by the tenderers and deviations in specifications, if any.

Apart from the above, the draft contract is to be examined and its terms studied, before accepting a tender.

The lowest tender is usually accepted provided the tenderer who has quoted the lowest amount satisfies the above criteria. For valid reasons, a tender other than the lowest can also be accepted.

Letter of Intent (LOI)

This is a letter issued to the successful tenderer intimating about his/her offer being accepted. LOI is issued before signing of the contract by the two parties. The successful tenderer is required to intimate any pre-condition within the stipulated time. Issue of LOI by the project promoters and acceptance of the same by the successful tenderer does not obviate the need for signing a contract. Since LOI is not a legal document, the two parties have to necessarily execute the contract by signing the contract agreement.

Execution of Deed of Contract

Strictly speaking, a contract, as such, can be oral or in writing. But, if a contract is required by law to comply with certain legal formalities, it must comply with the necessary formalities as to writing, registration and attestation, if necessary. If these legal formalities are not carried out, then the contract is not enforceable at law.

Liquidated Damages

One of the important clauses in contract is the schedule for completion of work/schedule for delivery. As we are aware, any delay in implementation over the pre-determined schedule results in time-overrun which may lead to cost-overrun. Moreover, a delayed project means, delay in getting back return on investment which will also affect the financial viability of the project. To ensure that the project implementation is carried out as per the original schedule, a clause known as 'liquidated damages' clause is incorporated in the contracts, which stipulates deduction of certain percentage of payment due to the contractor in case of delays. The clause can have provisions to assess the delay on monthly, weekly or even on daily basis for very critical projects and provide for deduction of payment from the R.A.bill for every month/week/day of delay.

Penalty Clause for Non-Performance of Guarantee Parameters

Apart from the clause on liquidated damages, a penalty clause for non-performance of guarantee parameters is also included in the contract. This clause provides for deduction of a certain pre-determined percentage of price from the contract price for non-performance of any guarantee parameters. The percentage of deduction is to be carefully decided in consultation with the consultants and contractors in such a way that it sufficiently covers the loss due to non-performance. The percentage of deduction should be such that it neither affects the clients nor the contractors.

Types of Payments to Contractors

Bill

Bill is an account of work done or supplies made specifying the actual quantities of work done or supplies made, their rates and the amount due to the supplier.

The following are the different modes of payment to contractors that are in vogue.

(*a*) First and Final Bill
(*b*) Running account Bill

(*a*) First and final bill:

This method of payment is suitable for very small, petty works. There is only a single payment to the contractor on his completion of the work.

(b) Running account bill (R.A.bill):

Running account bill refers to the accounts prepared at frequent and regular intervals for payment for the work done or supplies made at intervals. During the progress of the work, the contractor is paid from time to time, while the final payment is made on completion of the work. On a particular date when the bill is prepared, it is prepared for the quantity of work executed till that date and at the rates agreed in the contract. Payments are made for about 90% of the bill amount, retaining about 10%. Every time the bill is raised, it is raised for the cumulative value of the works executed and from this value the payment received till that date is deducted. Thus, there will be many intermediate bills and one final bill. Final bill is the last bill raised on completion of the work and in full settlement of the account. Sometimes advance payment is made on running account under special circumstances where measurements can not be taken for certain valid reasons, but the work has progressed sufficiently.

Voucher

Voucher is a written document as a proof of payment. Normally payment made to the contractor is acknowledged by the contractor by putting his signature on the bill on a revenue stamp. A bill, thus becomes a voucher after payment.

1.11 ORGANISING SYSTEMS AND PROCEDURES FOR IMPLEMENTATION

For realizing the objectives of projects, the execution should be done as planned and this can be better achieved if proper systems and procedures are devised. Since projects are dynamic in nature and as pitfalls / deficiencies / constraints will come to notice only during the course of implementation, the project plans should have the flexibility to suit field conditions / requirements. Hence, the systems and procedures devised for project execution should also have a built-in flexibility to cope with continuous changes and uncertainties that may be come across. Some of the systems and procedures to be organized are summarized below:

The project activities that are to be performed are identified and defined and resource requirement for carrying out the activities are estimated.

After the activities are identified and defined, the suitable organisational structure that can effectively handle the project is decided upon and formed. The ideal organisational structure will depend upon the nature of the project. Once the ideal organisational structure is defined, those who are responsible for implementing the project (i.e., the members of the project team and those who are indirectly involved in the project) are designated and their roles and duties are defined. The organisational relationship among the project team members are defined clearly to ensure smooth flow of activities. The authority and responsibility of project team members is defined in clear terms. Once these are completed, a framework for executing the project is drawn. The authority and responsibility among the various functionaries are to be clearly defined by the top management and this, inter alia, should address the following issues.

- Who can modify / change the project objectives?
- Who is responsible for the procurement of project resources?
- Who has the authority to change the project schedule and to change the activity durations?
- Who has the authority to decide upon substitutes of resources at times when the project faces resource constraints?
- Who has the authority to give orders for premature termination of the project? etc.

Standards and Schedules

Before the project team members go for the execution of the project activities, necessary standards and schedules are to be prepared and communicated to them. These standards and schedules will act as bench marks for monitoring and controlling the implementation and performance of projects.

When works are entrusted to the contractors, there must be standardized procedures for finalizing contracts. The contractors should be given to understand the project, the project organisation, the project environment and terms of contract clearly through a systems of effective communication. All contracts, be they small or big, must be granted formal approval through contract agreements. The contract agreements should be prepared in consultation with all departmental heads and specialists in the field.

All the activities of the project should be well documented. Some of the areas were accurate and detailed documentation is required are as under:

(1) Engineering specifications
(2) Project schedules
(3) Layouts of plant and machinery
(4) Process flow charts
(5) Electrical line diagrams
(6) Process design
(7) Safety requirements and procedures
(8) Statutory requirements
(9) Detailed drawing structures
(10) Machinery foundation drawings / specifications, etc.

The above documents will be of use to more than one person. For example, the project manager, the civil engineer, the contractor, the production engineer, the electrical wiring contractor, the machinery erector etc., should all have a layout plan of the plant and machinery with them for their respective use. After the documents are prepared, the recipients of all such document should identified and listed down. The requirement of copies of different documents are to be prepared and handed over to the respective persons. A small table showing the types of documents and the names of the recipients will be of use to identify all the recipients without leaving out any of them. (Refer Fig. 1.30)

	RECEIPIENTS OF DOCUMENTS												
LIST OF DOCUMENTS		G. M.	Project Manager	Works Engineer	Civil Contractor	Machine Erector	Production Manager	Electrical Contractor	Legal Manager	Purchase Manager	......	......	......	......
	Engineering. Specification												
	Project schedules												
	Plant layout												
	Process flow chart												
	Electrical line drawings												
	......												
	......												
	......												

Fig. 1.30

Activity Lists

Distributing schedules in the form of network indicating critical activities can be use only if the persons concerned have the capacity to read the charts and make out meaning full interpretation. This, of course, can not be taken for granted and will invariably prove ineffective. Schedule of the works to be completed can be better let known to the persons concerned by preparing a table of activity lists, showing the start and finish dates and the estimated man power & material requirements (Refer fig.1.31). Such a table can be easily understood by all concerned and will serve as a useful tool at their hands for implementing the project as per the schedule.

Project name : ____________________

Project code : ____________________

Activity code	Activity name	Schedule		Resource estimate		Code no. of work group that is responsible for the activity
		Start date	Finish date	Man hour	Materials	

Fig.1.31 *Activity List Table*

The activity list table gives a picture of what has been planned. The phase of actual implementation may vary from the plans made and hence there must be a reporting system to report the actual progress as against the plan so that the deviations from the plans will come to notice. For this, activity progress table can be of use and should be submitted periodically by persons / work groups in charge of execution (refer fig.1.32).

Project name : ________________

Project code : ________________

Work group code : ________________

Activity code	Activity name	Start schedule		Finish schedule		Resource estimate				Comments
						Man hour		Material		
		Planned	Actual	planned	Actual	Planned	Actual	Planned	Actual	

Fig. 1.32 *Activity Progress Table*

1.12 PROJECT DIRECTION

Directing refers to guiding people as to what to do and ensuring that they do their work to the best of their ability. Thus, directing includes assignment of jobs to the individual employees, explaining them the procedures to be followed in carrying out their jobs, giving guidance and instructions on the job, issuing directives and guidelines to be followed and correcting errors noticed, if any, in time. In other words, directing refers to giving the correct orientation. Since personnel from different functional departments with different skills and calibre are involved in executing a project, they must be given the right direction. It is the responsibility of the project manager to give the right direction to his team mates. If a project has many project managers headed by a project director, the project director is responsible for giving proper direction to the project managers who work under his control. If a close observation of the way in which the project activities are proceeding is not made, it will be difficult to provide the correct direction. Project direction becomes crucial and complicated if the organisational structure is such that the project personnel are under the dual control of the project department and the functional departments. Under such conditions, unless the project personnel are carefully and properly directed, the project implementation will suffer.

A project manager directs his team by virtue of the formal authority that he derives from the organisation. In an organisational structure, every manager draws formal authority by way of delegation of authority from those who occupy organisational positions at higher levels. Power is often used along with authority. Power is the ability to influence the behaviour of others. A project manager's ability to direct his team is a combination of his organisational authority and power. While a project manager derives authority through the organisational structure, he uses his authority along with his power to exact obedience. While authority is official in nature, power is something personal. The organisational structure can provide a project manager with an official authority. The project manager should possess the ability to lead, should have intelligence and expertise, should possess moral values and should set examples for his team mates to emulate. These qualities give the project manager the power to use his authority effectively in directing his team mates towards the achievement of project objectives.

Though project management structure creates a web of relationships that can cause chaos in the internal authority structure and in delegation of authorities, it is the project manager's responsibility to direct his team members in the right path towards the accomplishment of project objectives. Regarding completion of the project in time, the project manager has to give the required direction to his team. In this connection, he should give attention to the following aspects.

- Top priority shall be given to complete the critical activities since any delay in completion of the critical activities will delay the project completion time leading to time over-run, which in turn may lead to cost over-run.
- Apart from the critical activities, among the non-critical activities, the project manager shall identify those activities that consume expensive resources and that are of longer durations and he should study the scope for reduction of cost and time respectively so that the resources saved can be profitably deployed in other activities. Proper direction to this effect can be given only by the project manager.
- Trade-off between time and cost as well as trade-off between performance and cost are the two aspects that require conscious decisions to be taken based on the prevailing conditions. A project may be required to be finished earlier than planned even if it involves additional cost. Similarly, there may be shortage of men and/or material resources and time constraint may not prevail. Such situations will need reallocation of resources. The revised time schedule for the completion of activities and the revised allocation of resources are to be made known to the project team members. Without right direction being given to the persons on the field who are in charge of execution of project activities, the desired results can not be achieved.
- Since projects are dynamic in nature, the project manager should keep vigil on the project performance and watch for the warning signals. He should accordingly introduce the required changes in project implementation and should direct his team members in such a way that the required changes are recognised and acted upon.
- The project manager should see to it that directions for project execution do not emanate from any other person in the hierarchy who do not have the authority to do so. Especially, outsiders should not be allowed to direct the team members. Though those from functional departments and external specialists / consultants can given their suggestions, recommendations and views, the directions to the team members should emanate only from the project manager.

1.13 PROJECT COORDINATION

Coordination is a process by which the efforts of the members of a team are synchronized in such a way that the desired goals are achieved easily. To coordinate means to unite all the activities.

Coordinating the activities of a project is highly complex in nature and the success of a project lies in proper coordination. Coordinating the activities of a project is a difficult task because of the reason that several agencies/departments are responsible for the different components of a project. Hence, unless the mode of coordinating the different agencies / departments is pre-planned and monitored, implementation of project will get affected and this will lead to both wastage of resources and delay in project implementation. The first thing that the top management should do for proper coordination of project activities is to appoint the project manager at the earliest, identify the project team early and to assign them with clearly defined responsibilities. Project manager's prime responsibility is to coordinate the efforts of all the project participants and it is due to this responsibility that is cast upon him, the project manager is given the authorization to cut across several organisational lines in order to get things done.

Some of the activities to be coordinated in managing projects are as under:

- Tying up men and material resources and making the resources available at the right point of time.
- Tying up of contractors.
- Engagement of consultants.
- Receipt and storage of materials/equipments and release of materials/equipments from the store to the project sites in time

There must be periodical meetings between the project manager and the functional heads to sort out problem areas and out-standing issues. Since the authority structure of project management has the inherent nature of creating confusion in the delegation of authority, identifying the person concerned who has the authority to deal with certain problem areas will be an elusive task and such issues can be solved by informal discussions between the project manager and the functional heads.

The project manager has to pay attention to the following areas for effective coordination of the activities.

- Carrying out adequate pre-contract appraisal and choosing the appropriate contract strategy.
- Setting up an effective communication network between the project team members, functional heads, outside stake holders and other key participants before the commencement of the project.
- Ensuring that then different activities of the project are carried out in their logical sequence, in relation to their importance and without any conflict..
- Continuous evaluation of progress on comparison with the plans and re-planning on a periodical basis as per the needs.
- The project manager shall keep in mind that he has to coordinate three different types of participants, viz., the direct participants, the indirect participants and the external participants. All the three groups of participants need to be given equal importance. Ignoring any one group will jeopardize the project. Direct participants in the project include all those who are involved in project planning and implementation like the project team members who are in charge of execution, the contractors, the experts / consultants, material / equipment suppliers etc., The indirect participants are those who are indirectly responsible for the project execution, like the personnel in the project directorate, personnel of other functional departments like finance, marketing, sales, planning, HRD etc., The external participants include statutory and regulatory authorities like labour officers, inspector of factories, pollution control authorities, town planning authorities, ESI/Health department personnel etc., and other institutions like banks, financial institutions and insurance companies.

- Since the project manager is required to cut across several organisational lines / authorities to get his work done, he must establish good rapport with the employees and heads of all the functional departments so that smooth coordination of project activities can be achieved.
- Since the external experts / specialists / consultants also have their role to play in the execution of projects, the project manager should build good rapport with them and should act as a bridge between the external participants and the internal project team members.

1.14 PROJECT CONTROL

The term 'control' refers to verifying if the project progresses as per the plan and to regulate deviations found, if any. In managing of projects, the three aspects to be controlled are,

(*a*) the cost

(*b*) the time &

(*c*) the quality / technical performance.

For effectively controlling a project, suitable control plans are to be formulated well in advance, suitable standards for project work packages are to be developed and suitable information system is to be set up. Project can be controlled by gathering the required information from the project information system and comparing the actual performance with the planned performance. When deviations between the actual performance and the planned performance are noticed, immediate corrective actions are to be taken to realign the project back on the right track.

Control System

Control system is an arrangement that offers the project manager with details about deviations of the project from what was planned and also recommends corrective actions needed for rectifying the deviations.

Control systems are designed to monitor three major factor, viz., cost, time and quality parameters. In other words, control systems help in identifying cost over-run situations, time over-run situations and deviations from quality parameters. Since projects are dynamic in nature, project control systems are to be more sophisticated than the control systems meant for functional departments. The sophistication of the control system depends on the nature and complexity of projects and also on the ability of the project participants to administer it.

Requirements of a Good Control System

- It must be easy to understand by those who use it.
- It must be easy to extract data / information by those who use the systems and the control system must act as an indicator for pointing out deviations.
- It must be reduced to the form of tables / graphs / charts so that it will offer a visual display of the happenings. Since visual displays are easy for interpretation this feature will improve the utility of the control system.
- The control system should report deviations (of time, cost and quality) from the plan on a timely basis and must have the capacity to anticipate or predict deviations so that timely action can be taken to correct the deviations.
- The control system is to be designed by the active participation of all the major executives of the project team so that the system can satisfy the actual requirements.

Some of the Control Systems are as Under

- Work breakdown structure
- Bar chart / Mile stone chart
- Programme-progress chart
- Monthly status reports
- Line of Balance (LOB) chart
- Earned Value analysis
- PERT-Cost system
- Net work plans (Precedence diagrams , CPM /PERT net works)
- Graphical Evaluation Review Technique (GERT)
- Net work simulation
- Review meetings

Use of Work Breakdown Structure (WBS) for Project Control

Having seen what a WBS is and how it is organized (refer para 1.8 (*a*) for detailed explanation on WBS), the use of WBS for exercising control over projects is to be understood. The objective of WBS is to break down the whole project into smaller work packages that are easily identifiable and that can be defined, planned, budgeted, scheduled and controlled accurately.

For each work package in the WBS, the budgeted direct cost for the completion of the package, the time taken for its completion, the time schedule (i.e., the start and end dates), and the man-power requirement are calculated. This becomes the basis for project control. The sum of the budgeted direct cost for all the work packages gives the direct cost for the project as a whole. When project overheads are added to the direct cost, it gives the total budgeted cost of the project. Having prepared the time; cost and man-power requirements for each work package, the actual time spent, the actual cost incurred and the actual man-power used are compared for each work package and the deviations can be noted. Since the Work Break down structure (WBS) is integrated with the Organisation Break down Structure (OBS), the persons responsible for each work package is known and control can be exercised directly over the persons / work groups who are responsible for the work package where deviations from time / cost / man-power planned are come across.

A table showing the individual work packages, the persons responsible for the work packages, the direct cost budgeted for each work package, the time duration planned for each work package, the time schedule of carrying out each work package etc., can be prepared for easy reference and control. (Refer Table 1.9)

Bar Chart

A bar chart is a pictorial representation showing the various activities involved in a project. (Refer Unit-III, para 3.3.1 for further details)

Table 1.9 Project control using WBS

Sl. No.	*Code No. of work package*	*Code No of work group responsible*	*Direct cost*		*Time duration*		*Time schedule*																							
							Year 2000												*Year 2001*											
			Budgeted	*Actual*			*January*	*February*	*March*	*April*	*May*	*June*	*July*	*August*	*September*	*October*	*November*	*December*	*January*	*February*	*March*	*April*	*May*	*June*	*July*	*August*	*September*	*October*	*November*	*December*
1	01-01-01	50-01-01				Planned																								
						Achieved																								
2	01-01-01	50-01-02				Planned																								
						Achieved																								
3	01-01-02	50-01-01				Planned																								
						Achieved																								
4	01-01-02	50-01-02				Planned																								
						Achieved																								
5	.....	.....				Planned																								
						Achieved																								
6	.....	.....				Planned																								
						Achieved																								

Programme—Progress Chart

A programme - Progress chart is also a bar chart; but apart from depicting the activities with their proposed duration, this chart also incorporates the actual progress of the different activities (Refer Unit-III, para 3.3.1 for further details)

Monthly Status Reports

The monthly status reports shall cover all the important areas of operations of projects. Some of the major status reports are as under:

Financial Reports

- Planned vs. actual expenditure report.
- Planned vs. actual cash flow report.
- Report on outstanding payments to creditors. (suppliers of raw materials, equipments, consultants etc.,)

Procurement Reports

- Orders placed during the month.
- Orders executed / pending.
- Status of processing of bids.
- Stock position of materials.
- Forecast of delivery of materials / equipments.

Engineering Reports

- Report on adherence to specifications.
- Preparation and release of construction and erection drawings.
- Technical scrutiny of bids.

Inspection Progress Reports

- Inspection reports of works executed.
- Inspection reports on vendors' facilities, premises and reputation.
- Reports on technical constraints and suggestions to overcome them.

Construction and Erection Reports

- Job wise progress of constructions.
- Erection of equipments- planned vs. achieved.
- Modifications done in construction / erection, if any to suit field conditions.

Over all Review Reports

- Over all review reports covering all major issues.
- Exception reports.
- Suggestions and recommendations

Line of Balance (LOB) Chart

This is the chart for ascertaining the progress of various activities of a project on any particular date it is an extension of bar chart. (Refer Unit-III, para 3.3.1 for further details)

Earned Value Analysis (EVA)

Effective control over a project can be exercised only by performing periodic and systematic performance analysis. Modern method of performance analysis provides an analytical framework for project control by estimating factors like cost variance, time variance, schedule variance, cost performance index, schedule performance index, estimated cost performance index etc.

Arriving at the above parameters for a project needs the understanding of the following terms.

BCWS (Budgeted Cost for Work Scheduled)

It is the value of the work that should have been completed as of the date of review. The value is arrived at using the originally budgeted cost schedule.

BCWP (Budgeted Cost for Work Performed)

It is the budgeted cost for completed work. This is computed by taking the sum of the budgeted costs of all work packages completed thus far plus the estimates of the costs of 'open' work packages (work packages that have been started but not yet completed).

ACWP (Actual Cost for Work Performed)

It is the cost actually expended in completing the work accomplished within a given time period.

BCTW (Budgeted Cost for Total Work)

It is the total budgeted cost for the entire project.

ACC (Additional Cost for Completion)

It is the estimated additional cost required for completing the project.

CV (Cost Variance)

It is the difference between the actual expenditure made in the project till the date of review to the value of work accomplished for the expenses incurred.

$$\text{CV} = \text{ACWP} - \text{BCWP}$$

Cost Performance Index

$$\text{CP Index} = \text{BCWP}/\text{ACWP}$$

SV (Schedule Variance)

It is the difference between the value of work that has actually been completed and the value of the work scheduled to have been completed.

SV = BCWP – BCWS

The above formula gives the schedule variance in cost terms

Schedule Performance Index

This parameter gives the schedule variance in the form of an index.

SP Index = BCWP/BCWS

TV (Time Variance)

The Time Variance gives the time lag, at the date of review, by indicating the time equivalent of the value of work which has to be completed to stay on schedule.

TV = (Date of review) – (Date on which BCWP = BCWS)

Estimated Cost Performance Index

ECP Index = BCTW/(ACWP + ACC)

Illustration 1.22:

XYZ Company has bagged a fixed cost contract for the supply, installation, testing and commissioning of 200 computers of same specifications at a cost of Rs. 600 lakhs. The company had estimated that it could supply, install, test and commission 10 computers per day so that the entire work would be completed in 20 days time. The project status was reviewed after the completion of 16 days. It was noted at the time of review that only 120 computers have been installed and the cost incurred was Rs. 380 lakhs. It was estimated at the time of the review that a sum of Rs. 260 lakhs would be required for completing the pending work, viz., installation of the remaining 80 computers. Make a performance analysis by arriving at the various connected parameters.

Solution:

BCWS:

Work scheduled per day	:	10 computer installations
Work scheduled for 16 days (16 X 10)	:	160
Budgeted cost of one installation(600/200)	:	Rs. 3 lakhs
BCWS	:	160 X 3
	:	Rs. 480 lakhs

BCWP:

After 16 days, only 120 computers have been installed.

Hence, BCWP : 120×3

: Rs. 360 lakhs

Cost Variance:

CV : BCWP – ACWP

: $(120 \times 3) - 380$

: Rs (–) 20 lakhs*

(*The negative figure indicates that the actual cost is more than the budgeted cost)

Cost Performance Index :

CP Index : BCWP/ACWP

: 360/380

: 0.947

Scheduled Variance (in cost terms):

SV : BCWS – BCWP

: 480 – 360

: Rs. 120 lakhs

Schedule Performance Index:

SP Index : BCWP/BCWS

: 360/480

: 0.75

Time Variance:

No. of installations that ought to have been completed after 16 days (16 X 10) : 160

No. of installations actually completed after 16 days : 120

Short fall : 40

TV is the time equivalent of work which has to be completed to stay in schedule, i.e., the number of days required to make good the short fall of 40 , the rate of installation per day as planned being 10.

Therefore,

TV : 40/10

: 4 days

Estimated Cost Performance Index:

ECP Index : BCTW/(ACWP + ACC)

: 600/ (380 + 260)

: 0.9375

Forecasting Funds Requirement (PERT-COST System)

PERT-COST system helps to forecast the funds required during the implementation of the project. Once the actual funds required for carrying out the project activities during the course of project implementation is correctly forecasted, the required funds can be mobilized at the required points of time and this will help to carry on project implementation without getting struck up for want of funds. Thus, PERT-COST system helps in exercising control over the execution of projects. (PERT-COST system is explained in para 3.7 of unit - III. Readers are advised to study the PERT network given in unit - III before going through PERT-COST system, for better understanding).

Network plans:

For bigger projects involving a large number of activities, the project scheduling becomes very complex and the use of conventional methods of scheduling like bar charts and mile stone charts will not be effective. Complex projects, if not correctly scheduled, will most probably result in either under estimation or over estimation of project implementation period, both of which will have serious consequences. If the project completion time is under estimated, the actual implementation period will be more than the estimated period of time resulting in what is technically called 'time over-run'. Invariably, time over-run leads to cost over-run of projects. If the additional costs due to cost over-run are not made available in time, the project completion will suffer a set back.

Net work based scheduling of projects come handy in solving complex project scheduling problems.

There are two popular net work-scheduling techniques. They are

a. Critical Path Method (CPM)

& b. Programme Evaluation Review Technique (PERT)

(Refer Unit-III, para 3.3.2 for further details on CPM and PERT techniques)

GERT:

Graphical Evaluation and Review Technique (GERT) is a technique for the analysis of networks which takes into account the probalistic nature of occurrence of events. In a way, PERT also takes into account the probalistic nature of time taken for the completion of activities and it recognises three probable time estimates (Optimistic, pessimistic and most-likely). However, PERT is deterministic in arriving at the critical path since the PERT arrives at the critical path without any regard to the uncertainty of the actual materialization of the critical path. As against this, GERT takes into account the uncertainties that are inherent in real projects and arrives at the critical path duly incorporating the uncertainties.

GERT is not widely used for small / medium sized projects in view of the sophistication that it contains and the enormous computer resource that it demands for its application.

Net Work Simulation:

PERT assumes three probable time estimates for each activity and assumes a specific distribution for arriving at the expected time of the completion of each activity. However, in actual practice, the distribution of time estimates is not fixed, but will vary according to the real life situations. Net Work Simulation models permit assuming any activity-time distribution. For a given set of activity-time distributions, the model simulates 'Project duration distribution'. The project duration distribution is the output of Net Work Simulation models while the activity-time distributions of the different activities of the project form the input to the Net Work Simulation Model. Since a Net Work Simulation model can accept any type of distribution for the activity-time, it resembles real life situations and permits assignment of any realistic activity-time distribution so that the project completion time can be more realistically assessed.

Review Meetings

Apart form the use of control tools like charts, reports, analytical evaluations etc., review meetings at frequent intervals will help achieve proper control of project activities. Review meetings can be arranged for overall review of projects by the top management and also for specific reviews like Technical reviews, Design reviews, Progress reviews etc., by the middle management.

The following are the uses of review meetings:

- Since projects consist of multidisciplinary activities, coordination and control of the different functions can be achieved by the direct involvement of the top management and this can be made possible by discussions at the review meetings.
- Review meetings will help bring solution to the outstanding issues due to the direct involvement of all the key personnel.
- Technical shortcomings of the project can be discussed and alternative courses of actions can be arrived at.
- Consensus can be arrived at on issues that remain unsolved.
- Since review meetings offer an opportunity for interaction among the key personnel, easy and early identification of potential problems can be made and suitable preemptive steps can be taken.
- Since execution of projects involve active participation of personnel from different disciplines, the synergism required to take the project in the right direction can be achieved by discussing the issues openly and by motivating the participants towards the achievement of project objectives.

Tips for Efficient Implementation of Projects :

- Ensure proper planning of the project, project activities and the resources required.
- Correctly assess the man power requirement; recruit and select the required man power and ensure timely availability of the required man power for the different activities.
- Establish clear authority and responsibility relationships among the project team members.
- Keep the project team personnel always motivated to reach the goal.

- Don't commit the error of unrealistic scheduling of project activities.
- Establish effective communication.
- Introduce an effective, easy to understand, easy to interpret information system.
- Plan for the timely availability of material resources and have a predetermined procurement plan that will avoid 'out-of-stock' situations.
- Continuously assess the project priorities and introduce changes required, if any as and when warranted.
- Establish proper control mechanism.

1.15 PROJECT MANAGEMENT PERFORMANCE

The performance of a project is evaluated both during the course of its implementation (which is known as project evaluation) and after its completion (which is known as post audit or post project evaluation)

Project Evaluation

To evaluate means to assess. Thus, project evaluation is an assessment of the project during the course of implementation. It is an interim assessment at major milestones. Evaluating the project at major milestones during the course of implementation will steer the project in the right direction. Project evaluation is an attempt to determine if the overall status and progress of the project is acceptable as compared to what was planned earlier and if the objectives are being achieved. The ultimate aim of project evaluation is to bring about all-round improvements in project planning and execution.

Project Evaluation Objectives

- To verify if the progress of project implementation is as planned to take corrective measures if the project progress lags behind the schedule.
- To ascertain whether the actual costs are within the budgeted costs at the different stages of implementation and to take steps to contain costs if the actual costs escalate over the budgeted costs.
- To ensure that the quality standards of the project are reached without any compromise.
- To identify any unexpected problem areas and to plan for managing such situations appropriately.
  (for example, during the course of implementation of a project, the macro economic factors might have changed drastically and unfavourably and this might have changed the project into an unviable proposition. In such situations, it may even be wiser to abandon the project if going ahead with implementation proves to be 'throwing good money after bad money')
- To appraise the clients about the progress of the project and to keep them informed about the project status.
- To bring about overall improvement in project performance.
- To watch whether the project objectives are met and to suggest corrective measures if the objectives are found to get defeated.
- To give confidence to the project team memebrs and to reassure the organisation's commitment to the project.

Evaluation Methods

Smaller projects may be evaluated by direct observation and by getting first-hand information from the field staff, specialists and others connected with the project implementation. Evaluated based on periodic written reports is done for major projects. The written reports may be supplemented with charts, graphs and illustrations to add value to the reports.

Post Project Evaluation (Post Audit)

Post project evaluatiion is also known as Post Audit or Post Completion Audit. It is an evaluation of the project after its completion. At the time of project appraisal, estimates are made for project cost and for project completion time. After the project is completed, project audit is carried out to assess the actual project cost and the actual time taken for project completion. Thus, while project appraisal is an estimate for the 'future', post project evaluation is an assessment of the 'past'. In respect of public projects, apart from studying the variations in project cost and project completion time, post project evaluation also makes an assessment of the actual social cost-benefit factors and the extent up to which the project's objectives are achieved.

Objectives of Post Audit

Experience is the greatest teacher. The knowledge gained during the process of project implementation is of great value to all concerned. The project owner and the project management team learn a lot during the course of project implementation and they become a store house of knowledge which they can share with others or use them in their future ventures.

By carrying out post project evaluation, the financial institution that has funded a project can identify the pitfalls, if any, in its project appraisal and the control mechanism that should have been followed for effective project monitoring. For example, the financial institution might have estimated the project implementation time for a particular project during its appraisal, based on which it would have provided for 'interest during implementation' as a component of the project cost. Further, the financial institution would have fixed the commencement of loan repayment schedule, keeping in view the estimated project implementation time. If the actual project implementation period exceeds the estimate made, the time-overrun would result in cost-overrun of the project. The loan repayment schedule alsomight need rephasement in view of delayed project implementation. The financial institution can learn from reality, the factors to be considered for correctly assessing the project implementation time. Post project evaluation by fianancial institutions will also throw light on the following aspects.

- The adequacy of 'contingency' provision made in the project cost estimate to take care of unforeseen expenditures
- The normal project implementation time for different projects
- The comparative project cost for similar projects

A contractor who has executed a project and completed the project in time might have incurred additional expenditures than what was originally envisaged by him. This will enlighten him to be cautious while quoting his bid for subsequent projects. He can also make use of his experience to guard against uncertainities in future.

Based on the points discussed above, the objectives of post audit can be summed up as under.

- Educating all those concerned with the project about the realities of project management.
- Establishing correct time-cost relationship.
- Creation of appropriate standards for work based on suitable work techni-ques.
- Sharing of project audit information among all concerned, in order to build up better understanding and better comprehension of the project and its problem areas so that lapses could be avoided in future.

Phases of Post Audit

Post audit is carried out in two phases, viz., immediately after the completion of the project and after the lapse of some time (say 2 or 3 years) since the completion of the project.

Post audit that is carried out immediately after project completion is done

1. for studying the differences between the actual project cost and the estimated project cost.
2. for studying the difference between the actual time taken for project implementation and the estimated time.
3. for locating the areas that have contributed to the variances in project cost and time.
4. for identifying the reasons for such variances,classifying them into avoidable and unavoidable variances.
5. for analyzing the steps that could have been taken to avoid the avoidable variances
6. for analyzing in depth the factors that have caused the unavoidable variances and examining the possibilities of their removal in future by adopting suitable methodology.

Post audit that is carried out after the lapse of 2 to 3 years is done with a wider perspective. This study is done;

1. for studying whether the product goals and objectives are achieved.
2. for knowing whether the project produces products of acceptable quality.
3. for knowing whether the estimated output is achieved.
4. for knowing whether the product is accepted by the market and whether the production volume is commensurate with the market share planned toachieve.

The post project evaluation, whether done immediately after the project completion or after the lapse of some time has the main aim of studying the pitfalls and gray areas and identifying the required corrective measures.

Types of Post Audit

Technical evaluation (or Technical Audit) : Technical evaluation refers to the evaluation of quality and quantity of production, the operating costs in production etc. A comparison of these factors is done between what is presented in the feasibility report/detailed project report and what has been the actual achievement. As regards the rated output, certain projects are expected to give the estimated rated output immediately on commissioning. Such projects can be evaluated, for the variations inoutput if any, immediately after commissioning. In respect of certain other projects, the output will stabilize only after some time. These are the cases where the output depends upon the quality of raw materials, the skill of the personnel operating the plant etc. The operation of the plant is to be studied by varying these parameters and observing the out put till the production is stabilized at the maximum level. Evaluation of output can be done only after this i.e., only after all the inputs are synchronized and the production stabilized.

Apart from evaluating the actual output vis-a-vis the rated out put, the other areas of interest are the evaluation of utilities consumed by the plant, like power, fuel, water, steam, consumables, spares etc. An evaluation of these aspects is made and compared with what was estimated/projected at the time of project appraisal. Technical evaluation also includes evaluation of the quality of the output and checking-up if the quality standards as envisaged are reached.

Financial evaluation (or Financial Audit) : Financial projection/estimates are made at the time of project appraisal as to the project cost under various heads, operating cost of the project, maintenance costs, profitability estimates, cash-flow and fund-flow estimates, sources and application of funds for the project etc. Financial evaluation is done to verify whether the actual project cost, operating costs, profitability, cash/fund flows etc., are as per the estimates and projections made at the time of appraisal. While the assessment of actual project cost canbe done immediately after the completion of the project, other financial parameters can be studied only after the lapse of say, two to three years since the record of actual operating costs, profits etc., would be available only after the project is in operation for some time.

Economic evaluation (or Economic Audit) : Economic evaluation is the most difficult to make since it involves many subjective aspects which are difficult tobe quantified. The evaluator should have an 'eye' for identifying the social costs and benefits of the project. Economic evaluation is more relevant for public sector and community development projects since such projects are undertaken with social objective in mind, apart from financial and other objectives.

A public sector project would have been implemented with the aim of achieving certain social benefits. The social costs and social benefits, though subjective in nature, are quantified using some techniques while doing Social Cost Benefit Analysis (SCBA) at the appraisal stage of the project. The project audit from Social Cost Benefit angle should analyse whether the social benefits envisaged are achieved andwhether there are any adverse effects that the project has brought in, which were not originally foreseen. Such unforeseen adverse effects have the nature of adding to the social cost of the project. Though SCBA at the appraisal stage has grown into a well laid out system of appraisal in the recent past, post project evaluation from social cost-benefit angle is yet in an infant stage.

Agencies for Project Audit (Indian Scenario)

For private sector projects, the post audit is normally done by the project promoter and/or the financial institution that has funded the project. Post audit work can be better entrusted to a team of specialists drawn from different functional areas so that the evaluation can be done objectively and the grey areas can be identified.

For community development projects, Programme Evaluation Organisation (PEO) of the planning commission carries out the audit. The PEO is entrusted with the task of evaluating the impact of community development projects on the lives of the people and on the economy of the community and to offer suggestions/recommendations for rural development. Apart from the PEO which is under the control of the Central Government, every State has a State Evaluation Organisation (SEO) under its control to evaluate the projects sponsored by the State Government.

For public sector projects the post project evaluation is done by the respective ministries along with the Department of Public Enterprises (DPE) and Bureau of Public Enterprises (BPE). Besides, public sector projects are also audited by the Comptroller and Auditor general of India.

Specimen Project Evaluation Form

Name of the project :

Audit done by : Date of audit : / /

Period of audit : From .... To ....

Evaluation : [Tick ** whichever is applicable]

Progress of implementation	Budget vs. actual expenditure	Quality aspects of project
☐ Proceeding as per target	☐ Expenditure is as per budget	☐ As planned
☐ Proceeding ahead of target	☐ Expenditure is below budget	☐ Better than planned
☐ Lags behind target	☐ Expenditure is above budget	☐ Worse than planned
If lags behind target, reasons thereof:	If expenditure is above target, reasons thereof:	If quality is worse than planned, reasons thereof:
Corrective steps to be taken to overcome the above:	Corrective steps to be taken to overcome the above:	Corrective steps to be taken to overcome the above:
Problems anticipated, if any that may delay implementation:	Problems anticipated, if any that may increase expenditure:	Problems anticipated in Furture if any, that may affect quality:
Precauations to avoid the above:	Precauations to avoid the above:	Precauations to avoid the above:

Changes experienced, if any, in business climate:
Change/modification needed in project objectives in view of the above:
Additional / unanticipated problems that are come across:
Comments:

UNIT II

PROJECT INFORMATION SYSTEMS

2.1 INTRODUCTION

The importance of project management is being widely recognised and is gaining more and more importance as an organisational structuring concept meant for efficient utilisation of organisational resources. Unlike in an organisation with traditional organisational structure in which the flow of work is vertical, in a project organisation, the work flows both vertically as well as horizontally. While it is relatively easier to monitor the vertical flow of work, it is a highly complex affair to monitor the flow of work in a project environment wherein work flows through the organisation both vertically and horizontally. In project environment, smooth flow of activities can be made possible only if a conflict-free work atmosphere is created. This is possible only if there is cordial interpersonal relationship among the team members and an effective communication system between them.

The importance of good communications in a project environment should not be underestimated. Absence of communication and poor / distorted communication leads to misinterpretation and misunderstanding of issues among the project team members and this will act as the main reason for the origination and propagation of conflicts. A correctly designed information system avoids conflicts and aids in accomplishment of project objectives. Success or failure of projects very much depend upon the ability of project director, project managers and other key personnel to take decisions. Right decisions can be made only if the decision-makers are provided with all the relevant information and this can be made possible only by devising an effective, efficient, fool-proof and intelligent project information system.

Broadly speaking, the Project Information System (or Project Management Information system) serves the following purposes:

(*a*) for controlling the project implementation

(*b*) for reporting about the progress of the project to the top management and to the external agencies concerned.

The Project Information System, for being effective, should, apart from giving details about the progress of the project implementation, also indicate areas of future troubles in the project. Such capacity to foresee potential problem areas is an essential characteristic of a project Information System.

Project managers are often tempted to design Project Information Systems to suit their specific requirements. Such information systems, which are designed by the project managers will normally act as stand-alone systems, without the capacity to be integrated into the information system of the organisation.

A well designed Project Information System is an integrated system that will meet the information requirements of the project managers, the functional managers, the top management, the consumers and other external agencies concerned. Another characteristic of a good Project Information System is that it must be adaptable to many different projects. In bigger and complex organisations, where there may be many projects going on at the same time, the Project Information System should have sufficient flexibility so that it can be easily modified to suit the requirements of the different project managers.

2.2 ESSENTIALS OF A GOOD PROJECT INFORMATION SYSTEM

- Should be an integrated information system package so that it meets the requirements of all concerned.
- Should have the needed flexibility.
- Should be flexible enough to serve the requirements of different Project managers.
- Should offer information on the cost, time and performance parameters of a project; this apart, should also expose the interrelationships among the three vital parameters, viz., cost, time and performance.
- Should be decision oriented; the information reported should be focused towards the decisions required to be taken by the project managers, the functional managers and the top management.
- Should be capable of providing exception reports so that project managers can focus more attention on critical areas that need greater attention.
- Should fit into the over all information system of the organisation so that duplication of work and taking of conflicting decisions at different levels of the organisation can be avoided.
- Should have built-in warning signals in order to offer early warning on potential problem areas.
- Should be easier to handle by those who feed in data / information and easier to interpret by those who analyse the data / information.

2.3 COMPUTER BASED PROJECT MANAGEMENT

2.3.1 Computerised Project Management System

When the size of the project increases, it becomes difficult and at times even impossible to plan, schedule, budget and control project activities using manual techniques. Hence, for large projects the task is made easier with the use of computers. It is therefore necessary to have Computerised Project Management System (CPMS) for projects of bigger size and complex nature. The advantages of using a CPMS are as under:

- A CPMS can analyse the problem at a very high speed as compared to manual analysis. Because of its high speed, any number of permutations and combinations can be handled with ease which can not be done manually. For example, sensitivity analysis of profitability estimate can be done using computers by varying the different parameters and studying their impact on profit. Carrying out such an analysis manually is very difficult and.tiresome task.

- Since computers can store and process large volumes of data, CPMS is best suited for large and complex projects that require handling and analysis of voluminous data.
- Accuracy of results produced by CPMS can be relied upon while there is an element of committing mistakes in manual computations.
- A CPMS reduces the human resource requirements considerably. A well versed computer programmer can replace many of the clerical and support staff and thus CPMS improves efficiency and economy of projects.
- Since a project manager who is in direct control of the project can himself directly interacts with computers and analyse the problem rather than depending upon too many of his subordinates, he can plan properly and arrive at optimum decisions. It also relieves the project manager of daily routines and makes more time available at his disposal so that he can plan and act efficiently.

2.3.2 Essential requirements of Project Management Softwares

Some of the common, but essential requirements of project management softwares are as under :

- The project management software should be able to handle multiple projects together. In other words, it should have the capacity to integrate the different projects that are in progress at during the same time and to produce consolidated reports of all the on-going projects.
- It should support a variety of graphs and reports in different formats.
- It should have filtering capacity to extract a set of tasks and milestones from a scheme for the purpose of analysis and for producing the required reports.
- It should support a range of file formats for importing and exporting data.

Some of the features of project management software that are desired are as under :

- The project management software should be, as far as possible, one that is compatible with the software currently being used by the organization.
- It should be easy to learn and easy to implement.
- It should have extensive on-line help so that the learner will gain confidence in putting the software to use without apprehension.
- It should have the capacity to solve a wide range of problems.
- It should have the capacity to produce the reports required by the management and in the desired format.
- As far as possible, it should have the facility to operate on the existing network environment.

2.3.3 Software Packages for CPMS

The first project management software tools were developed in the late 1960s. The early software tools developed were mainly for the mainframe computers. During the 1970s and 1980s project management software packages suitable for micro computers were developed and by 1990 there were over 100 project management software packages available for use. Though there are many software packages available today, only a few are widely used since many project management software packages are not comprehensive in their coverage, but were mainly meant for specified project management areas. Some of the popular software packages used in project management are as under:

Microsoft Project

Harvard Total Project Manager

Project Planner

PRISM
YOGNA
INSTA PLAN
Quick Net
PC-projaks
Proman
Project Scheduler 8
Etc.

PRISM, the software package developed by Tata Consultancy Services and INSTA PLAN, the package developed by WIPRO are popular among Indian project managers.

PRISM determines the sequence of activities and the duration with in which each activity must be completed in order to meet a given project schedule. For a given budget, PRISM can determine the minimum time within which the project must be completed. The details of all the available resources can be fed into a resource pool. PRISM automatically schedules activities based on the resource requirement of each activity and referring to the resource pool for the availability of resources . PRISM provides many pre-designed reports like the list of critical activities, the list of activities that are currently in progress, variations in the duration of activities completed so far, activities that lag behind the schedule and many other useful reports. PRISM also supports a powerful graphic generator that provides the user with many useful charts like Bar charts, time-cost trade off curves, resource histograms, cash flow graphs, network diagrams etc.

INSTA PLAN provides project planning facilities and also has presentation features.

It provides four types of reports and three types of presentation charts INSTA PLAN is gaining acceptance because of its simplicity for use.

2.3.4 Microsoft Project 2000

Microsoft Project is the most popular among the available project management software packages. Project 2000 software supports many project management areas like scheduling, budgeting, resource management, charting, performance monitoring, risk management, analysis, reporting and communication.

Project 2000 also offers the facility to manage multiple projects. It also provides for sharing of resources between the projects and export/import of project data among the multiple projects being handled.

The various features and facilities available in Project 2000 package are explained below.

Gantt Chart

A Gantt chart shows the sequence of activities. While a traditional Gantt chart shows only the relationship between various activities, Project 2000 uses a modified Gantt chart that includes links to show the relationship between the activities. Adding link lines to Gantt chart clearly indicates the series and parallel relationships between the activities.

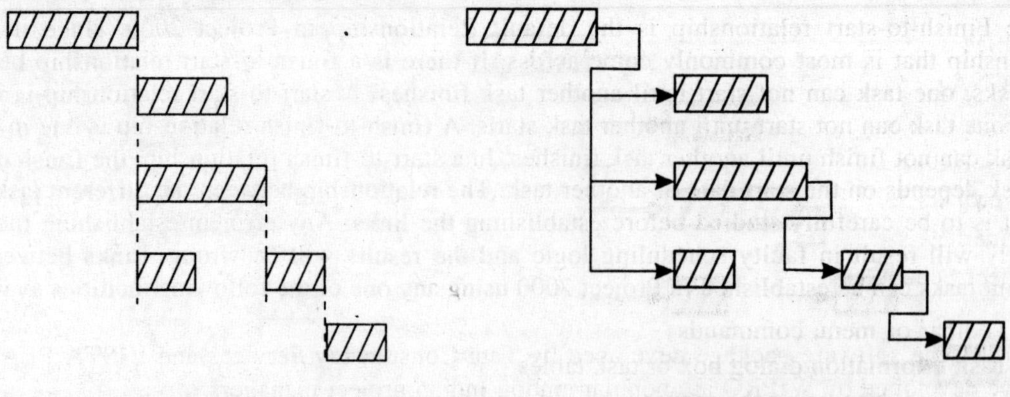

Fig. 2.1.

Project Baseline

Any project plan is finalized after a lot of deliberations, corrections, modifications and revisions. Once the project plan is finalized, it is to be 'stored' as a reference. Project 2000 uses a 'baseline' for storing the project plan. A baseline is a project plan containing the original estimates for tasks, resources, assignments and costs. Data as per the plan like start & finish dates of tasks, duration of tasks, splits in tasks, costs of tasks etc., are captured in a baseline. Once a baseline is formed and stored, it is used as a reference for comparing the actual progress with the planned progress. The comparison can be made either in terms of cost or in terms of time.

Splitting Tasks

When a project is under implementation, a task may need to be splitted. Suppose person who is attending to a particular task requiring two months duration, goes on leave after one month. Instead of waiting for one month till the person rejoins, the task can be split so that a portion is completed before the person goes on leave and the remaining portion after the person rejoins the team. The rest of the tasks can be accordingly realigned provided that such splitting of a task does not bring forth any error in the logical sequence of tasks. Project 2000 provides facilities for splitting tasks and revising the project schedule suitably.

Schedule Processing (or Relating tasks with one another)

Tasks in a project are to be properly linked. Once proper link is established between the different tasks, the project schedule can be altered suitably whenever there are changes in the start/completion time(s) of some of the tasks. Project 2000 links the tasks by establishing the relationship between the different tasks. When tasks are linked, the task that must be started or completed first is called the predecessor and the task that depends on the predecessor is called the successor. Project 2000 uses the following relationships for linking the tasks.

- Finish-to-start
- Start-to-start
- Finish-to-finish
- Start-to-finish

The Finish-to-start relationship is the default Relationship in Project 2000, since it is the relationship that is most commonly come across. If there is a finish-to-start relationship between two tasks, one task can not start until another task finishes. A start-to-start relationship is one in which one task can not start until another task starts. A finish-to-finish relationship is one in which one task can not finish until another task finishes. In a start-to-finish relationship, the finish date of one task depends on the start date of another task. The relationship between the different tasks of a project is to be carefully studied before establishing the links. Any error in establishing the links properly will result in faulty scheduling logic and the results will be wrong. Links between the different tasks can be established in Project 2000 using any one of the following facilities available:

1. Toolbar or menu commands
2. Task information dialog box or task tables
3. Drag and drop using the mouse

Project 2000 also provides facilities for modifying the task relationships. It may be likely that the task relationship is not correctly established for all the tasks at the first instance itself, especially for bigger projects. Further, when a task is removed or a new task is inserted or a task is moved, Project 2000 automatically repairs the broken links created due such modifications when 'Autolink' option is Enabled.

Project Cost Estimation

Project 2000 arrives at the project cost by arriving at the costs of individual tasks indirectly. Every activity consumes resources. Costs are assigned to resources and resources are in turn assigned to tasks. Cost of a task is arrived at by the software by multiplying the resource required to complete a task with the cost of the resource. A resource pool is created that includes all the resources used in the project. Resources are grouped into two categories, viz., Work resources and material resources. Work resources are the people and equipment assigned to a task. Material resources are supplies, stock and other consumable items used to complete the tasks. Details about the work resources and material resources are entered in the 'Resource Sheet'. The resource sheet contains, interalia, fields like resource name, resource type (work or material), standard rate etc. Apart from creating a resource pool, the resources must be assigned to tasks so that cost of each task can be arrived at. 'Resource assignment' relates a task to the resources responsible for the task. Resources can be assigned to tasks by using the 'Assign Resources Dialog Box' or by using the 'Task Form'.

After tasks, resources and their costs and resource assignments are entered, project budget (i.e., estimated project cost) can be arrived at easily.

Monitoring the Progress of Project (Earned Value Analysis)

Project 2000 includes tools for Earned Value Analysis, also called BCWP (Budgeted Cost of Work Performed) analysis. Earned Value Analysis measures key performance indicators and compares them to the baseline parameters. The difference (or variance) between the baseline and actual performance can be calculated which indicated whether the project is being implemented as planned. Project 2000 can measure both Cost Variance (the difference between the task's planned cost and actual cost) and Schedule Variance (the difference between the actual progress and the scheduled progress of a task).

For calculating the variance, the up-to date progress of the project is to be entered into the package. Project data can be updated using 'Tracking Table' in the 'Task Sheet View'. This table contains fields like actual start date, actual finish date, percentage of actual completion, actual duration, remaining duration, actual cost and actual work. Once all the required data on the actual progress of the project are entered, Project 2000 can calculate the variances. Variances can be viewed by switching to 'Tracking Gantt View' and selecting 'Variance Table'.The variance table gives the baseline data and the variances of all tasks.

'Earned Value Table' of Project 2000 gives the following estimates at any point of time.

BCWS : Budgeted Cost of Work Scheduled

BCWP : Budgeted Cost of Work Performed

ACWP : Actual Cost of Work Performed

SV : Schedule Variance [BCWP-BCWS]

CV : Cost Variance [BCWP-ACWP]

EAC : Estimate At Completion (i.e, the estimate of cost if the remainder of the task's work is completed as budgeted.)

BAC : Baseline cost At Completion

VAC : Variance At Completion [BAC-EAC]

Using the above information furnished by Project 2000, two important indices can be calculated, viz.,

Schedule Performance Index (SPI) : BCWP/BCWS

and

Cost Performance Index(CPI) : BCWP/ACWP

When SPI is greater than 1, the actual cost incurred is more than the budgeted cost; when CPI is greater than 1, the actual cost incurred is less than the budgeted cost.

Resource Leveling

Project 2000 provides two options for resource leveling. Resource leveling can be done within a specified range of dates or for the entire project. Project 2000 allows two methods of leveling, viz., 'automatic' and 'manual' leveling. When automatic leveling option is chosen, the project will adjust tasks as soon as a task is changed or assigned a resource that results in over allocation, i.e., the software checks for over allocation after each entry. Hence, choosing automatic leveling option will slow down the overall performance of the software. If manual option is chosen, the discretion to level the resources is given to the project manager. When he chooses to level the resources, he can open "Resource leveling Dialog Box' and click 'Level now' to level the resources.

Project 2000 will not delay tasks that have the following constraints.

- Must finish on ______
- Must start on ______
- As late as possible (for projects scheduled from the start date)
- As soon as possible (for projects scheduled from the finish date)

It may be noted that when the constraint 'Must finish on _____' is not given to any of the tasks, it means that there is no constraint on project completion time. In this case, the resource allocation will be optimum and the resource allocation will amount to 'resource smoothing' (Refer Unit III for Resource Smoothing Techniques).

Before using Project 2000's leveling feature, the constraints and priority settings for the critical tasks are to be defined. Priority setting for tasks can be given in the range 0 to 1000. If a task is set a priority of 1000, Project 2000 will not delay this task.

Resource Pool

A resource pool is a project file that contains resource information of an organization. The main idea behind creating a resource pool is to facilitate sharing of resources among multiple projects. When an organization handles multiple projects at a time, it becomes efficient to distribute resources from the resource pool instead of allocating resources for the individual projects exclusively. The multiple projects that are under implementation/to be implemented can be assigned priority, by assigning a number from 0 to 1000 in order to rank them in the order of their relative importance. A project that is given the highest priority (i.e., assigned the highest number) will receive top consideration while allocating resources from the resource pool; projects with lower priority will receive lower consideration while allocating resources. This arrangement will help to handle situations in which there is a conflict for resource sharing among the multiple projects.

PERT

As we know three time estimates are used in PERT, viz., the optimistic time, the pessimistic time and the most likely time. The three time durations are weighted and averaged to determine the expected duration of the tasks. Weights are to be assigned to the three time estimates so that Project 2000 can arrive at the expected time of the tasks and use the same in PERT calculations. The default settings for weights are as under:

Optimistic : 1

Expected* : 4

Pessimistic: 1

[Project 2000 uses the term 'Expected' time for the 'Most Likely' time.]

The above default settings for the weights of the three time estimates are based on the assumption of normal distribution for the time estimates. If there is evidence that the distribution of time estimates will not follow normal distribution, the weights can be altered. Project 2000 permits allocation of different weights by the user depending on his perception of the distribution of time estimates. For example, the user can alter the weights for the three time estimates as under:

Optimistic : 0.50		Optimistic : 1.50		Optimistic : 0.40
Expected : 4.00	(or)	Expected : 4.00	(or)	Expected : 3.60
Pessimistic: 1.50		Pessimistic: 0.50		Pessimistic: 2.00 etc.,

After the three time estimates and their weights are fed in, Project 2000 provides views of Gantt charts based on the three time estimates, i.e., views of optimistic Gantt chart, pessimistic Gantt chart and expected Gantt chart can be seen. Critical path can be viewed by choosing 'View' and further choosing 'Net work diagram' from 'View' menu. Project 2000 also provides filter facility to view network diagram. When the filter facility is used, the network diagram will display only the critical tasks on the screen (called 'slipping' tasks by Project 2000) that require the attention of the project manager.

Reports

Project 2000 provides the following built-in reports

- Overview reports
- Current activity reports
- Cost reports

- Assignment reports
- Workload reports

Overview Reports

An overview report provides an overview of the following aspects of the project at a fixed point in time.

1. **Project summary.** [This report compares the actual dates, durations, work, total costs and task status with the project baseline.]
2. **Top level tasks.** [This report provides the name, duration, start date and finish date for the highest level tasks and summary tasks, based on the outline.]
3. **Critical tasks.** [This report provides the start and end dates for all critical tasks, including the preceding and succeeding tasks for each critical task.]
4. **Milestones.** [This report shows the milestone tasks sorted in ascending order by start date; the sort order can also be changed by the user. Note: Mile stones are tasks that usually have no duration and mark the completion of a significant phase of the project.]

Current Activity Reports

The current activity reports are task-focused reports. If desired, the user can add resource information to these reports by customizing the reports. Project 2000 provides the following reports under this head.

1. **Unstarted tasks.** [This report shows the tasks that have not yet begun. The immediate predecessors of such tasks are also given.]
2. **Tasks starting soon.** [This report gives the tasks that are scheduled to start within the date chosen by the user.]
3. **Tasks in progress.** [This report shows the tasks that have already started. The resource information associated with these tasks are also given.]
4. **Completed tasks.**[This report shows the tasks that have been completed. The start and finish dates of the completed tasks are also given.]
5. **Should have started tasks.**[This report shows the tasks that should have started by the time chosen, but have not yet started.]
6. **Slipping tasks.** [This report shows the tasks that have been rescheduled beyond the baseline start date.]

Cost Reports

Cost of project is a main consideration for the project manager. A project might have been completed within the pre planned completion date. However, if the cost of completion has doubled as compared to the budgeted cost, there is no merit in having completed the project in time. Thus, cost reports help the project manager to identify the deviations in cost and provide an opportunity to correct the discrepancies in order to contain the cost.

Project 2000 provides the following reports under this head:

1. **Cash flow.** [This report shows the weekly cost of the project, giving the break up details of the cost of different tasks. The report can be customized to show different time units, say, in terms of monthly cost, biweekly cost etc.]
2. **Budget.** [This report shows the actual cost vs. the budged cost per task.]

3. **Over budget tasks.** [This report shows the tasks whose actual costs has exceeded the baseline costs.]
4. **Over budget resources.** [This report shows the resources whose actual costs has exceeded the baseline costs]
5. **Earned Value.** [This report shows how much of the budget should have been spent by this time (i.e., as of current date) based on total work and resource costs.]

Assignment Reports

Resource reporting is the focus of the assignment reports. Project 2000 provides the following reports under this head:

1. **Who does what.** [This report shows each resource and the tasks assigned for each resource.]
2. **Who does what when.** [This report shows each resource and the tasks assigned for each resource along with a calendar showing the daily work assigned for each task.]
3. **To do list.** [This report shows the list of tasks for the chosen resource along with start and finish dates, duration, predecessor task and other assigned resources. If a task has already been completed. It is checked off in the report.]
4. **Over allocated resources.** [This report shows the list of over allocated resources with their assigned tasks, including start and finish dates, duration and delay.]

Workload Reports

There are two forms of workload reports, viz., the task usage report and the resource usage report. The task usage report lists the tasks and their assigned resources in the first column. The rest of the columns are dates in increments of one week. Under the date columns, the work scheduled for each task and for each resource are displayed. The resource usage report is similar to 'Who does what when' report.

2.4 ENTERPRISE-WIDE PROJECT MANAGEMENT

It is a web based project management system in which multiple project summaries are monitored from one central location. It allows for collaborative planning among project managers and project executives, thus facilitating web based resource management and reporting. 'Microsoft Project Central' and 'Project Communicator' are the two popular web based project management software tools. The interaction between the project manager and the different project teams located at different locations is achieved through web. (refer fig. 2.2)

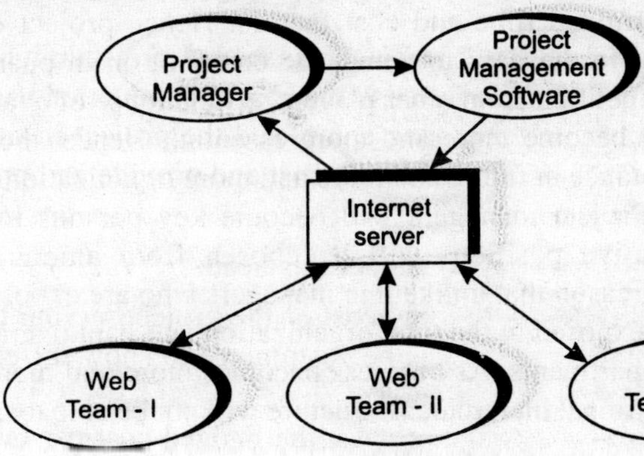

Fig. 2.2

The project manager prepares project schedule, resource allocation plans etc,. with the help of a project management software and puts the data on the internet server. The team members, who are in charge of actual execution of projects at different locations access the web site and collect the required data sent by the project manager. The team members submit actual work times, actual resource requirements etc., back to the project manager through the internet server. The project manager accesses the responses from the team members, revises his estimates if need be and resubmits the revised plan of action. Thus, the system provides for continuous interaction between the different personnel involved in project execution at different project sites, which helps in better monitoring and efficient utilization of resources.

2.5 USING SPREAD SHEETS FOR FINANCIAL PROJECTIONS

Spread sheet packages like Lotus-123 and MS Excel help in developing financial projections like profitability estimates, cash flow estimates, break even estimates etc., The design of spread sheet software that provides cells in which formulae and functions can be embedded is best suited for easily developing software packages for financial projections. The greatest advantage of a spread sheet package is that it helps in carrying out sensitivity analysis of financial projections. Any or all of the parameters used in financial projections can be altered and the variations in the results can be studied. Such 'what-if' analysis can be done using other software packages only with a great level of programming skills. Spread sheet also supports a variety of graphical views which can be used to depict the financial projections in graphical form.

2.6 FUTURE OF PROJECT MANAGEMENT

Project management is different from functional management in that project management aims to achieve specific goals within a given time using the available resources in the best possible way. The time limit specified for achieving a goal distinguishes project management. While functional management is an on-going activity, project management is a one-time affair.

2.6.1 Organizational Structure

The functional structure of an organization which is the traditional form of organizational structure relies more on hierarchy. Reliance on hierarchy breeds bureaucracy and delays taking decisions. In the traditional form of organization the chain of command from the top to the bottom is very much unwieldy. A project management structure, on the other hand relies much less on hierarchy and relies on team work among the members of the project team. Since the project team works for achieving short term goals within predetermined time and cost factors. Hence project organization makes better use of available resources. In the days to come, the competition in business is going to be stiffer and to meet the stiffer competition from other players, efficient use of available resources and achieving time bound goals will become more and more essential. Hence, the concept of project management will get wider acceptance in future and more and more organizations will switch over to project management structure. Project managers will become key persons in organizations and persons who occupy top executive positions will be chosen from among successful project managers. This is because of the reason that unlike line managers who are exposed to only their line of activity, project managers are exposed to the total organization and gain overall knowledge about the operations of the different departments. As business becomes more and more complex the style of management that relies on traditional hierarchical structure will not be able to cope op with the fast changing business conditions.

2.6.2 Role of Computers in Project Management

With continued reduction in the cost of computer hardware microprocessors and 'smart terminals' will be used for controlling of projects. If the trend of rapid increase in technology continues, in the near future, the physical organizational structure might disappear and project managers might be located at different places, relying totally on telecommunication facilities. A number of computers that are linked together by an interdependent system of network might be used for controlling a number of projects handled by an organization. Computers might replace many clerks, accountants and other operational employees in the project office. Many middle level managers may also lose their positions to computers. With men and material resources becoming scarce, optimum utilisation resources will be given top priority. For optimizing the use of available resources, improved techniques of project control would become operational and more accurate time-cost trade-off analysis would be carried out. For optimization and trade-off analysis sophisticated computers might be used in future.

2.6.3 The Role of Project Managers

The role of project manager would become a crucial and important one in the organization. More rigorous selection techniques would be used for selecting project managers. Psychological testing would receive more attention, as project managers will be expected to display very good interpersonal relationship among their team members. The project managers will interact more frequently with the top management and will gain first hand knowledge of strategic goals set by the organization. This will help them to know how the organizational goals are transformed into project objectives and how the non-achievement of project objectives will affect the strategic goals of the organization. The project managers will be expected to possess the following skills / qualities for helping the organization survive.

- Project managers will be expected to possess high calibre leadership qualities and team building skills.
- Project managers will be expected to deliver the goods at any cost within the constraints of available resources, within the time constraints and satisfying the performance requirements.
- Project managers will be expected to have the ability to learn new skills continuously throughout their career. To cope up with the changing conditions, they will be expected to learn new developments in all related fields. They will be expected to know how major policy decisions are made and will be exposed to the economic environment of the country and of the world, so that they can make their projects globally competitive.

2.6.4 Reporting and Control Systems

In view of advancement in communication and information technology, the reporting system and control systems will become highly automated. Thus, reporting of the results from lower levels to higher levels and directions from higher levels to lower levels on the basis of reports received will take place with the aid of computers in a highly automated environment and will require relatively less effort. Both for preparing and sending the reports and for preparing and sending feed-back / control instructions, 'smart terminals' will play an increasing role in project control.

2.6.5 Shortage of Physical Resources

As projects consume naturally available physical resources, the pressure on exploitation of physical resources will increase. A stage may reach where the naturally available inorganic mineral resources will get nearly depleted. Hence, the stage will be set for recycling of resources. Projects that produce recyclable resources and projects that use such resources will become more in number. The availability of naturally available organic fuel (in the form of crude oil, natural gas) will become more and more reduced and the need for developing alternative fuel will be very much felt. Fuel developed from vegetation (example: Jetropa Oil produced from seeds of Jetropa plants) will find their application as industrial fuel and will substitute crude oil based fuel. Based on the characteristics and cost of alternative fuels developed, the process of manufacture of goods will undergo changes. Fuel will become a key resource for the project manager to control.

2.6.6 Globalization

The process of globalization will become complete and there will be boundary-less trade and transfer of resources between the countries of the world. Since any change that takes place in one part of the world will have its immediate impact on a project at a different part of the world, contingency planning will become the way of executing projects. Though a project may have a shorter duration, its objectives may have to be redefined / realigned even during the course of its implementation due to continuously changing business environment. The project manager may be required to procure men and material resources from different parts of the world, may be required to coordinate people from different countries who have different skill sets / culture and thus the task of the project manager will become increasingly demanding.

UNIT

III

DEVELOPMENT OF PROJECT NETWORK

3.1 INTRODUCTION

Planning is nothing but deciding in advance the future course of actions. Planning is a primary function of management.

The process of project planning involves the following main steps.

(*a*) Defining the objectives of the project.

(*b*) Making forecasts for achieving the goals.

(*c*) Identifying the alternative courses of action for achieving the goals.

(*d*) Evaluating the resources available to the organization.

(*e*) Evaluating the available alternative courses of actions and selecting the course of action/actions that are most suited to achieve the desired results, taking into account resource constraints, if any.

During the process of planning, the various operations involved in the project, their sequences and their logical inter relationships are established.

3.2 PROJECT SCHEDULING

Project scheduling refers to the process of laying out all the actual activities of the project in the time order in which they are to be performed, keeping in view of the logical sequence of the activities.

The logical sequence of activities of a project would be as under :

- Company registration.
- Obtaining industrial licenses/import licenses.
- Appointment of consultant.
- Resource mobilization.
- Land acquisition and site development.
- Preparing civil work designs, plans and estimates and entrusting the construction work to civil contractors.
- Preparing design specifications and placing order for plant and machinery.
- Transport of plant and machinery to the project site.
- Erection of machinery.
- Commissioning the plant and taking trial run.
- Commencing regular commercial production.

3.3 SCHEDULING TECHNIQUES

As we have seen above, a project consists of many activities, which have some logical interrelationship between themselves. All activities consume resources of three kinds viz., time, men and materials (or money). The project scheduling techniques are concerned with the resource 'time'. One of the objectives of project management is to optimize the use of resources. Scheduling techniques offer solutions to optimatisation of project time.

3.3.1 Bar Charts

Bar chart is a pictorial representation showing the various activities involved in a project. The chart has two co-ordinate axes; one axis represents the activities and the other axis represents the time required for completion of the individual activities. Bar chart was first conceived and developed by Henry L. Gantt and hence bar chart is also sometimes referred as Gantt chart, in the name of the person who popularized the concept.

A typical bar chart [or Gantt chart] is shown in Fig. 3.1

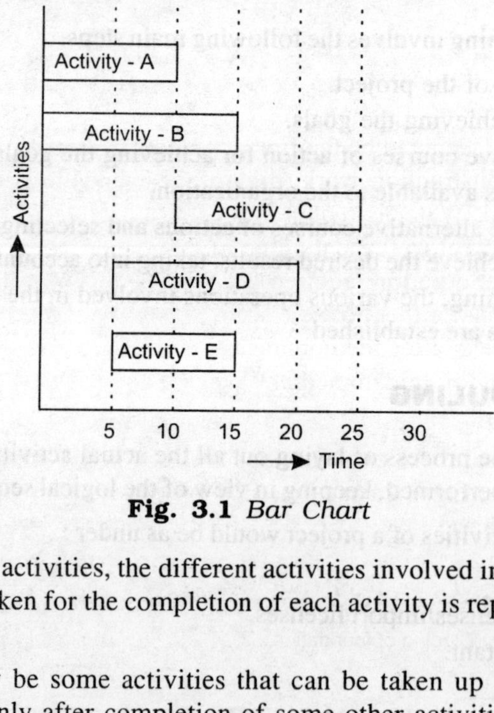

Fig. 3.1 *Bar Chart*

In the axis that represents activities, the different activities involved in a given project are drawn in the form of bars. The time taken for the completion of each activity is represented by the length of the bar.

In any project there may be some activities that can be taken up simultaneously, while some activities can be taken up only after completion of some other activities. There may be also some activities, which are independent of all other activities.

Consider the example of construction of a residential house. The following are some of the activities involved in the construction of a residential building.

Activities	*Time required*
Digging of foundation	3 weeks
Pouring foundation concrete	1 week
Construction of walls	10 weeks
Construction of roof slab	3 weeks
Fixing of doors and windows	1 week
Digging of well	1 week
Plastering and finishing of walls	2 weeks

The above activities can be depicted in a bar chart, after identifying their logical sequence.

If water required for the construction work is not available at the project site, the activity "digging of well" takes priority. [If water required for the construction work can be obtained without much difficulty, digging of well can be deferred to a later time and it need not be the starting activity].

Let us assume that water required for the construction work is not available at the project site and it is also not easy to procure water from outside. Under these circumstances consider the following two activities.

- Digging of foundation

  and
- Digging of well.

Though digging of well is seems to be the first activity that should be started since requirement of water is essential for the construction work, digging of foundation activity need not wait till the digging of well is completed. Water is required only for concrete work, brickwork etc., and hence both the activities viz., digging of well and digging of foundation canbe done simultaneously. As seen from the data given, the time duration required for digging of foundation is 3 weeks while that for digging of well is 1 week. Hence either both the activities can be started at the same time or digging of well can commence two weeks after the commencement of digging of foundation. In either of the options, the commencement of the immediate succeeding activity, viz., pouring of foundation concrete will not get affected.

Hence we can conclude that these two activities are concurrent activities but need not necessarily start at the same point of time. Fig. 3.2a and Fig. 3.2b indicate the pictorial representation of these two options in the form of bar chart.

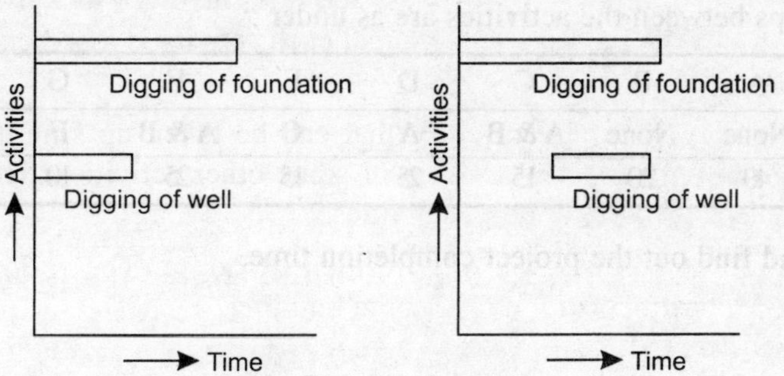

Fig. 3.2 (a) and (b)

Let us now complete the bar chart for the remaining activities for the following precedence/ succession relationship.

Construction of walls	–	Succeeds pouring foundation concrete.
Construction of roof slab	–	Succeeds construction of walls.
Fixing of doors and windows	–	Succeeds construction of roof slab.
Plastering and finishing of walls	–	Succeeds fixing of doors and windows.

Fig. 3.3 depicts a bar chart for the construction of residential building with the given data and given precedence/succedence relationships.

As seen from the bar chart, the total time required for the completion of the project is 20 weeks.

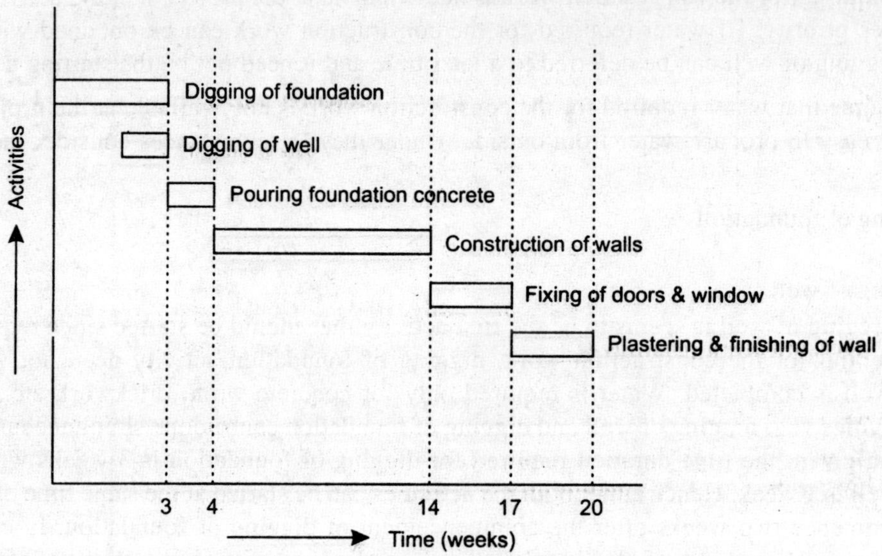

Fig. 3.3 *(Bar chart representing construction of a residential building)*

Illustration 3.1

A project has 10 activities (A, B, C .. J). The time required for each of the ten activities and the precedence relationships between the activities are as under :

Activity	A	B	C	D	E	F	G	H	I	J
Proceeding activity	None	None	A & B	A	C	A & B	F	G	G	I
Time days	40	20	15	25	15	25	10	15	10	15

Draw a bar chart and find out the project completion time.

Solution :

Activities A & B have no preceding activities i.e., they do not depend on any other activity for their commencement. Thus, these two activities can be done simultaneously. The decision as to whether A & B shall commence simultaneously or B shall commence subsequent to A depends on the precedence relationship of subsequent activities. The two activities that depend on A & B are activities C & D.

Activity 'C' shall commence after completion of activities A & B.

The above relationship means that irrespective of whether activities A & B are commenced at the same time or not, activity 'C' shall have to wait till both the activities A & B are completed. Hence both the options viz., simultaneous commencement of activities A & B and delayed commencement of activity B are equally vaild and choosing any one option will not alter the total project implementation time. Refer figure 3.4 (a) and Fig. 3.4 (b) for the two different options.

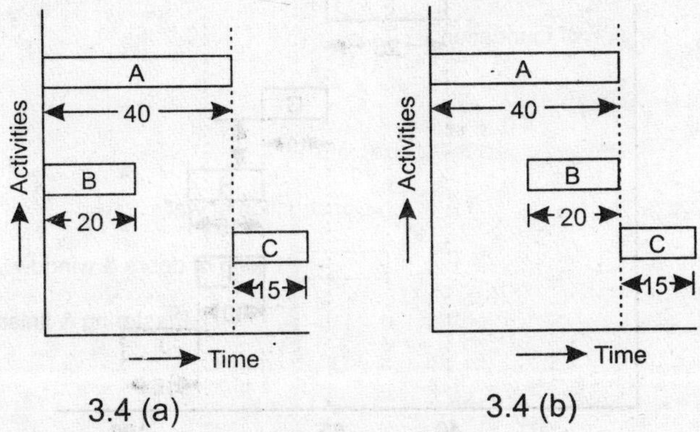

Fig. 3.4 (a) and (b)

In both the options, activity 'C' can commence, 40 days after the commencement of activity 'A'.

Fig 3.5 depicts the bar chart for the given problem incorporating all the ten activities. The duration for completion of the given project is 100 days.

Programme-progress Charts: The Bar chart that we have discussed in the previous paragraph depicts the proposed activities of a project with their estimated time duration. A bar chart is drawn in order to have a pictorial view of the logical sequence of operations and their interrelationships and to have an estimate as to when the project is likely to be completed. It is only a projection in the future.

A programme-process chart is also a bar chart; but apart from depicting the activities with their proposed duration, this chart also incorporates the actual progress of the different activities. Both the estimated time and the actual time taken for the completion of different activities are incorporated in the programme—progress chart. This chart helps in knowing the time lag between the estimated and actual progress of work and also helps in controlling the progress of workduring the implementation of the project.

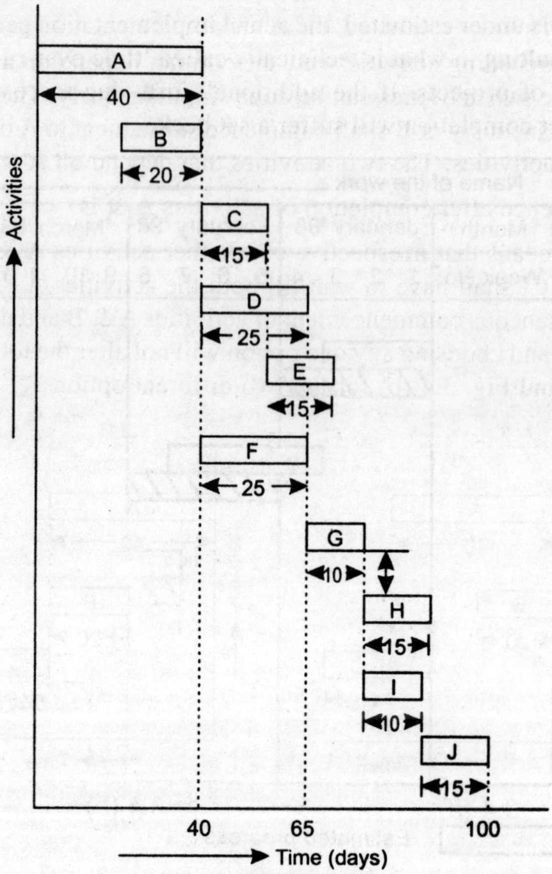

Fig. 3.5

Fig. 3.6 shows a typical programme—progress chart.

Limitations of Bar Chart

- **Bar charts are difficult to update when there are many changes.**
- **When there are changes between the plan and the actual achievement, bar charts become quickly obsolete.**
- **Bar charts do not equate time with cost; hence time-cost relationship can not be derived from them.**
- **Bar charts do not provide methods for optimizing resource allocation.**
- **In view of the above limitations, bar charts are useful only for small projects and can not be effectively used for medium sized and large projects.**

3.3.2 Net Work Based Scheduling

For bigger projects involving a large number of activities, the project scheduling becomes very complex and the use of conventional methods of scheduling like bar charts will not be effective. Complex projects, if not correctly scheduled, will most probably result in either under estimation or over estimation of project implementation period, both of which will have serious consequences. If

the project completion time is under estimated, the actual implementation period will be more than the estimated period of time resulting in what is technically called 'time over-run'. Invariably, time over-run leads to cost over-run of projects. If the additional costs due to cost over-run are not made available in time, the project completion will suffer a set back.

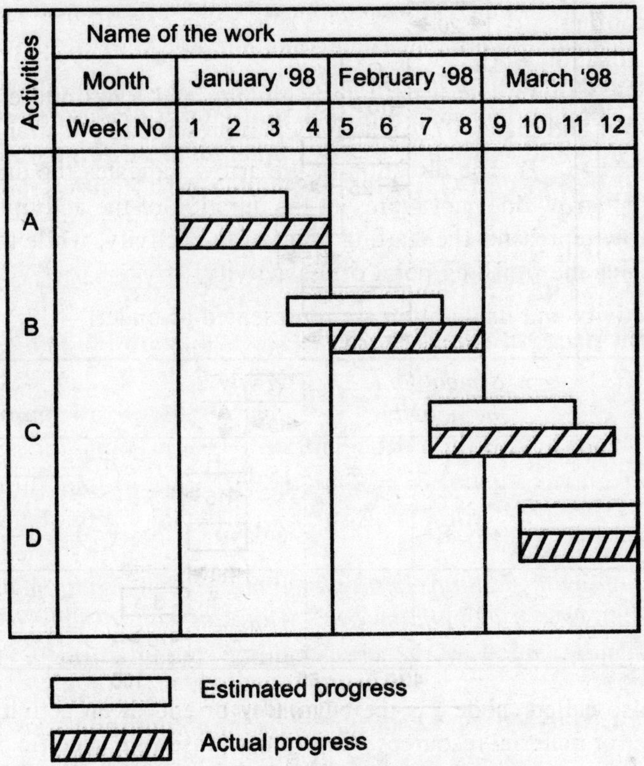

Fig. 3.6 *(Program-progress chart)*

Net work based scheduling of projects comes handy in solving complex project scheduling problems.

There are two popular net work-scheduling techniques. They are

(*a*) Critical Path Method (CPM) and

(*b*) Programme Evaluation Review Technique (PERT)

CPM was developed in the year 1957, by Morgan R. Walker of DU Pont and James E. Kelly of Remington Rand.

PERT was developed in the year 1958 by the US Navy.

Though the two methods are conceptually similar except for certain minor differences, they were developed independently.

For understanding as to how a network for a project is drawn, we should get ourselves familiarized with the following terminologies.

Activity : An activity is any identifiable job that has a beginning and an end. An activity consumes time, manpower and material resources.

The following are some examples of activities.

- Excavation of foundation.
- Placing of foundation concrete.
- Construction of walls.
- Construction of roofing.
- Wiring and electrification work.

As seen, all the above activities have definite beginning and a definite end and they consume resources (time, manpower and material). An activity is represented by a straight arrow with circles at both the ends (). The direction of the arrow indicates the direction of flow of the project. The length of the arrow does not represent the duration of the activity. The circle placed at the beginning of the arrow represents the starting point of the activity, while the circle placed at the end of the arrow represents the finishing point of the activity.

The symbol of the activity and its duration are represented as under.

Activity	*Symbol for the activity*	*Activity time*	*Symbolic representation*
Excavation of foundation	A	15 days	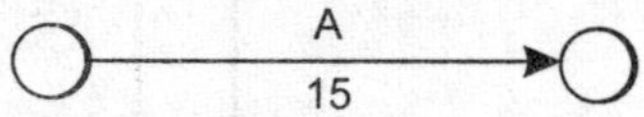
Placing of foundation concrete	B	6 days	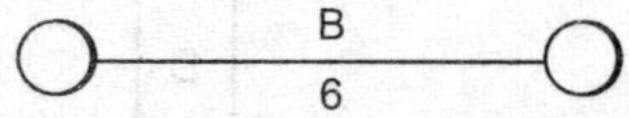
Construction of walls	C	21 days	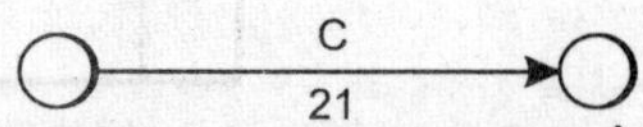

Event : An event (also called 'node') is the beginning or end of an activity. An event does not consume time,manpower or material resources. An event represents a specific point in time. Event is represented by a circle. Thus, the two circles placed at the beginning and at the end of an activity are called events.

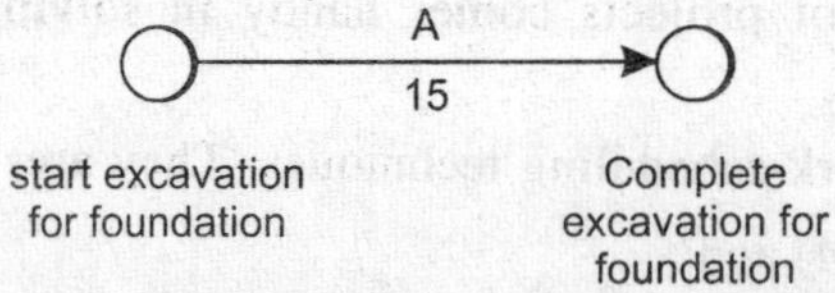

Event is symbolically represented by numbers or alphabets written inside the circle.

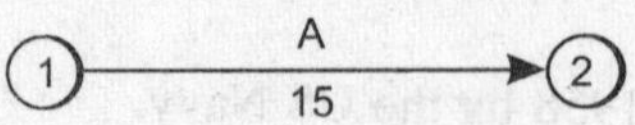

As seen, event (1) stands for starting of foundation excavation and event (2) stands for completion of foundation excavation. Thus, each activity has two events.

The name of the activity (or symbol of the activity) is indicated above the arrow, while the duration of the activity is indicated below the arrow.

Relationship Among Activities : As we have already said, a network is a graphical representation of the logical sequence of all the activities of a project. A project is a collection of various activities and the activities are interrelated among themselves. There are three possible relationships between the different activities.

Concurrent Activities : The activities that can be carried out concurrently are called concurrent activities. As we had seen earlier, digging of well and excavation of foundations are concurrent activities. These two activities can be carried out concurrently since they do not depend on each other.

Preceding Activity : For a given activity, the activity that occurs immediately before it, is its preceding activity.

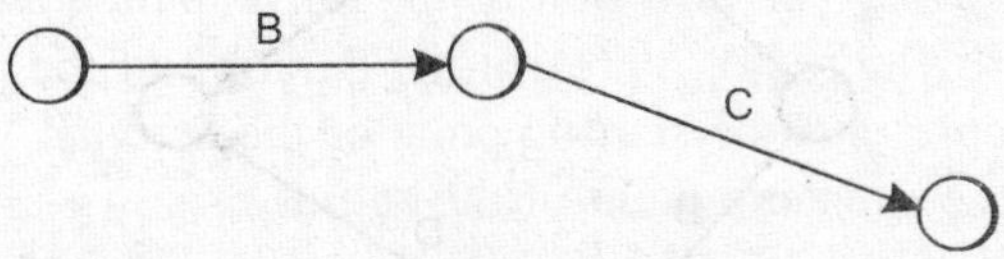

Activity 'B' is the preceding activity for activity 'C'.

Succeeding Activity: For a given activity, the activity that follows immediately after it, is its succeeding activity.

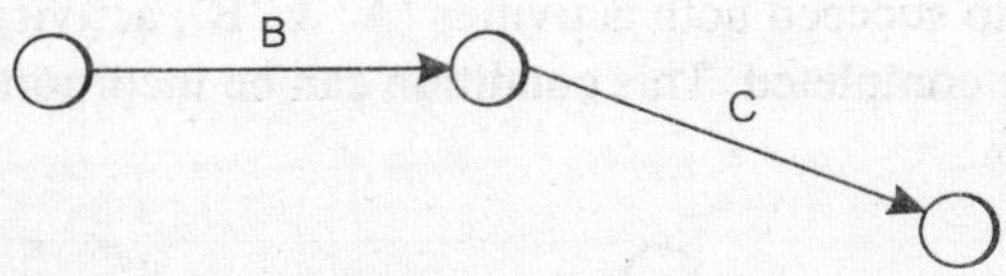

Activity 'C' is the succeeding activity for activity 'B'.

Dummy Activity: A dummy activity is an imaginary activity included in a network. Since it is not a real activity, it does not consume time manpower and material resources. It is included in a network to maintain the network logic and to avoid ambiguity. A dummy activity is represented by a dotted arrow, as under.

Illustration 3.2

Consider the following illustration to understand the use of dummy activity.

- Activity 'A' and Activity B are concurrent activities.
- Activity 'C' follows activity 'A'.
- Activity D succeeds activities A & B.
- C & D are the last activities.
- Draw a net work

Solution :

If we draw a network for the given problem without introducing a dummy activity, the diagram will look like as in Fig. 3.7.

Out of the four conditions given, the following three conditions are satisifid by Fig. 3.7, viz.,

(*a*) Activity 'A' and Activity 'B' are concurrent activities.

(*b*) Activity 'C' follows activity 'A'

and

(*c*) C& D are the last activities.

However the condition that activity D succeeds activities A & B is not satisfied. Hence the network given in Fig. 3.7 is not the correct one. Had it been given that the activity'D' succeeds only activity 'B' the net work diagram shown in Fig. 3.7 would be correct since it satisfies all the four conditions.

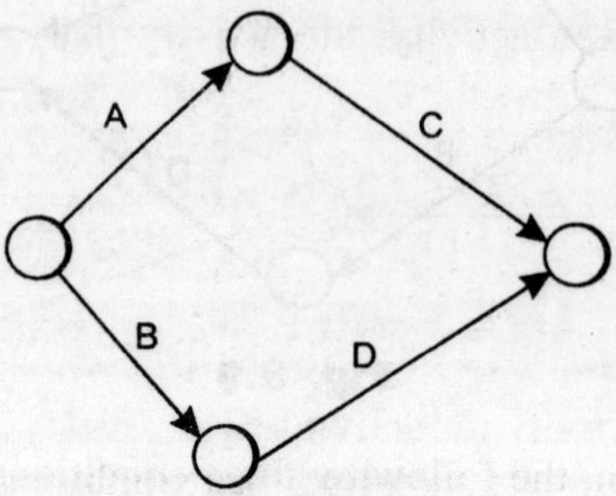

Fig. 3.7

Since activity 'D' is said to succeed both activities 'A' & 'B', activity D can commence only after both the activities A & B are completed. This condition can be incorporated by introducing a dummy activity as shown in Fig. 3.8.

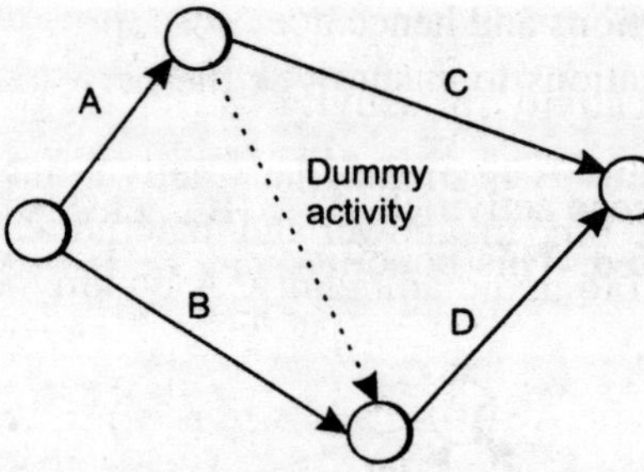

Fig. 3.8

Since activity 'D' can start only after the activities A & B are completed the direction of the dummy activity is marked accordingly.

Illustration 3.3

Draw a net work for the problem given below; use dummy activities if required.

A & B are concurrent activities; Activity 'D' follows activity 'B'. Activity 'C' succeeds activities 'A' & 'B'.

C & D are the last activities.

Solution :

If we draw a network for the given problem without introducing dummy activity, the diagram will look like as in Fig. 3.9.

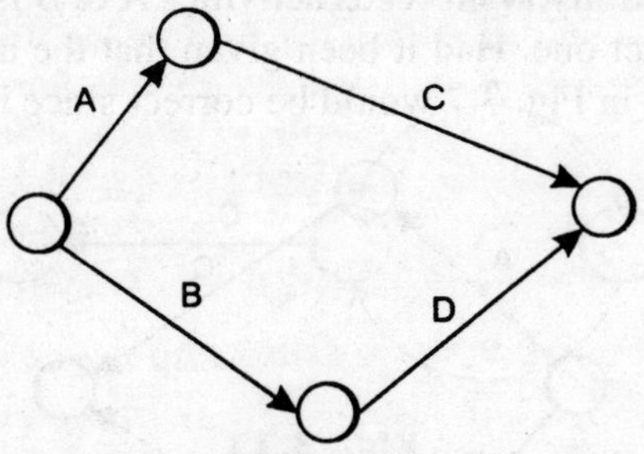

Fig. 3.9

Out of the four conditions given, the following three conditions are satisfied by Fig. 3.9 viz.,

(a) A & B are concurrent activities.
(b) Activity 'D' follows activity 'B', and
(c) C & D are the last activities.

However the condition that activity 'C' succeeds activities 'A' & 'B' is not satisfied. As per Fig. 3.9, activity 'C' succeeds only activity 'A'. Hence the net work diagram given in Fig. 3.9 does not satisfy one of the given four conditions and hence does not follow the given logic. The use of dummy activity comes handy in such situations to ensure that the network satisfies the logical sequence of operations.

Since activity 'C' is said to succeed activities 'A' & 'B', activity 'C' can commence only after both the activities A & B are completed. This condition can be incorporated by introducing a dummy activity as shown in Fig. 3.10.

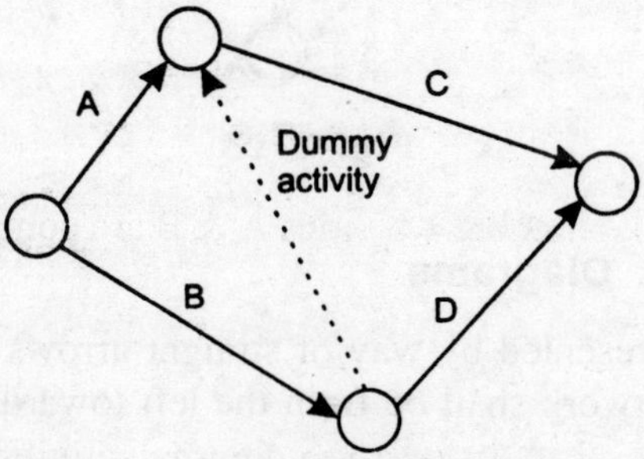

Fig. 3.10

Since activity 'C' can start only after activities 'A' & 'B' are completed, the direction of the dummy activity is marked accordingly.

The need for dummy activity in a network can be also viewed from another angle. One of the network logics is that two activities can not have common start and common finish points. They can have either a common start point or a common finish point, but not both.

Accordingly, the net work as represented in Fig. 3.11 is an incorrect representation. The correct representation will be as indicated in Fig. 3.12 or as in Fig. 3.13, by introducing a dummy activity. Having known the meaning of activity, event and dummy activity, let us understand some of the rules to be followed in preparing a network diagram.

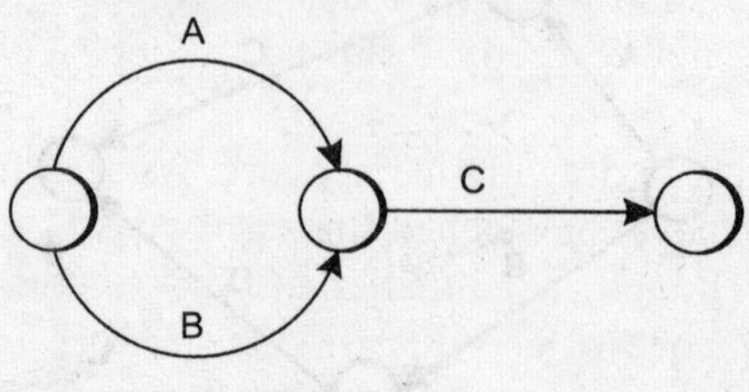

Fig. 3.11

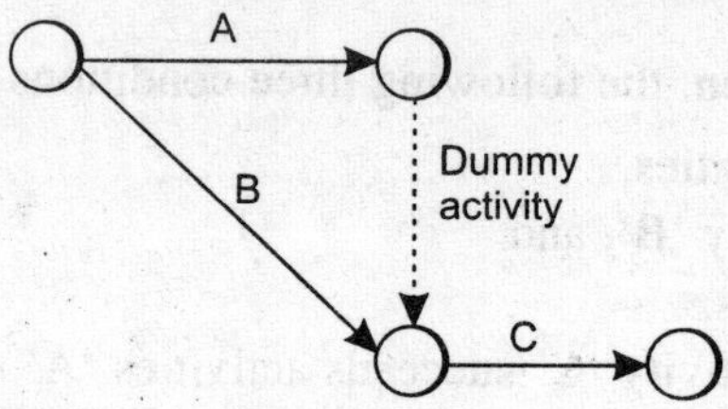

Fig. 3.12

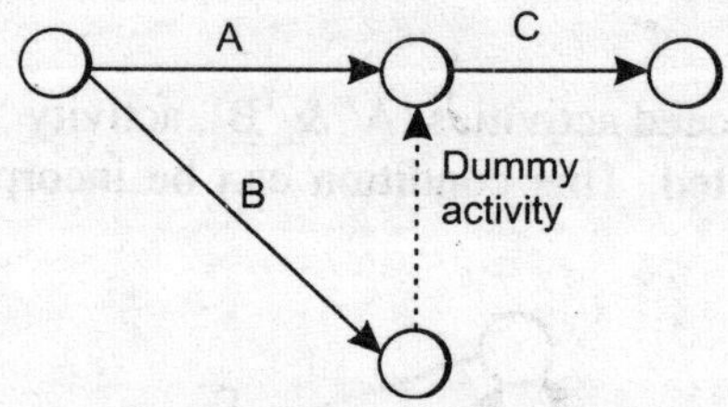

Fig. 3.13

Rules for Drawing Network Diagrams

(*a*) All activities shall be represented by way of straight arrows pointing towards the right. This means that the flow of network shall be from the left towards the right. (Refer Fig. 3.14).

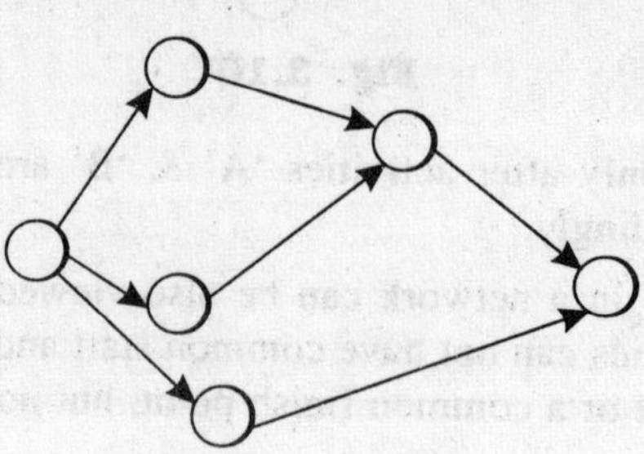

Fig. 3.14

(*b*) There shall not be any criss-crossing of arrows. Fig. 3.15 shows a network in which two arrows cross each other, which is not permitted. A network following the same logic as followed by Fig. 3.15 can be drawn as per Fig. 3.16 without any criss-crossing of arrows which is the correct method of drawing the network.

(*c*) The arrows of a network shall not form loops. In complex network problems, if the logical sequence of activities is not correctly followed, a loop network may be formed. Fig. 3.17 shows a loop network.

A loop network indicates error in drawing the network. As seen from Fig. 3.17, activities B, C, D & E form a loop. Activity F can never be reached since activities B, C, D & E will occur repeatedly in view of the loop formation. Though in a smaller network looping can be avoided by a careful observation of the logical sequence of activities, if the network is large, a systematic method of drawing the network shall be followed to avoid getting loop formation. This will be ensured if the events are logically numbered. Fulkerson's rule for numbering of events is useful in this connection, which is explained later in this chapter.

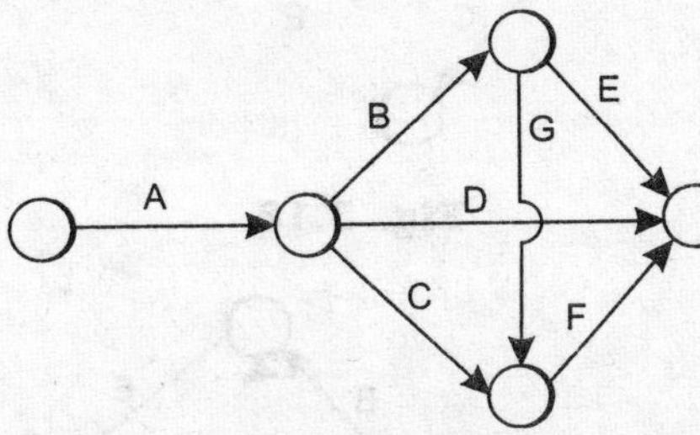

Fig. 3.15

(*d*) There shall not be unnecessary dummy activities in the network. Dummy activities shall be introduced only when it is absolutely necessary and without which the network diagram can not be completed.

Fig. 3.18 shows two dummy activities D & E. These two dummy activities indicate that the last activity F can be started only after the completion of activities 'B' & 'C'. This logic can be represented as in Fig. 3.19 with the use of only one dummy activity 'D'. As seen in Fig. 3.19 the last activity 'E' succeeds activities B & C which is the required logic.

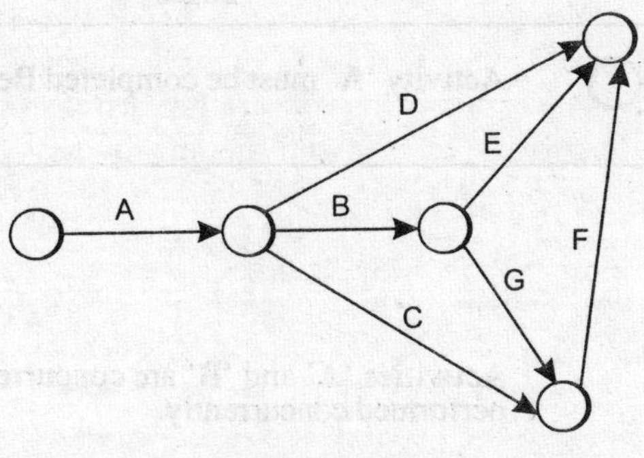

Fig. 3.16

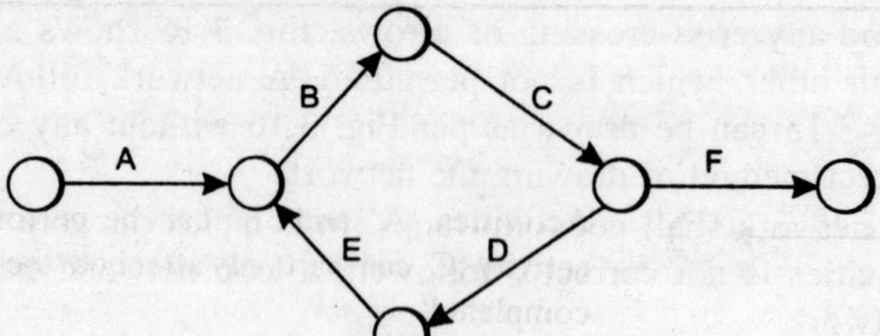

Fig. 3.17

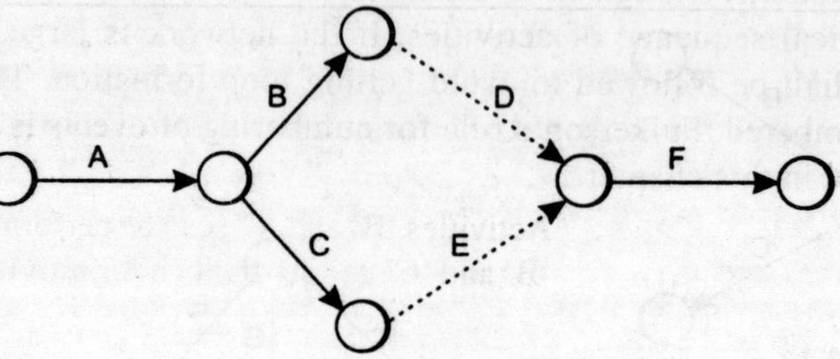

Fig. 3.18

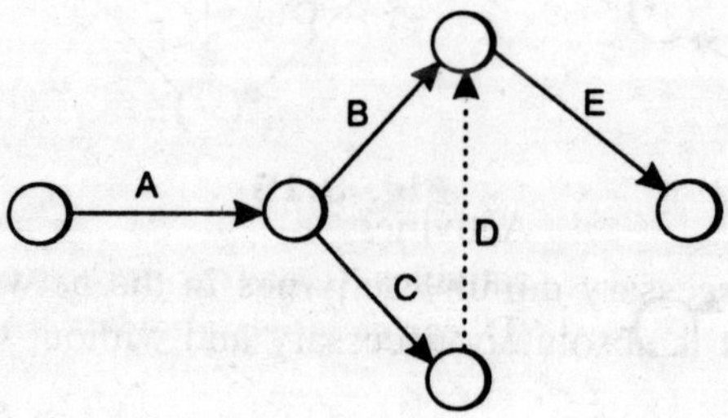

Fig. 3.19

The following diagrams give a summary of the interpretation of arrow diagrams in a network.

Diagram	*Logic*
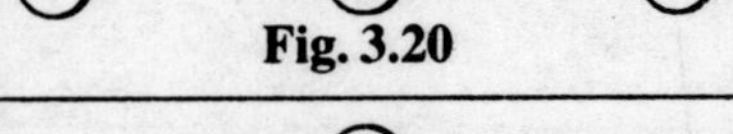 **Fig. 3.20**	Activity 'A' must be completed Before activity 'B' can begin
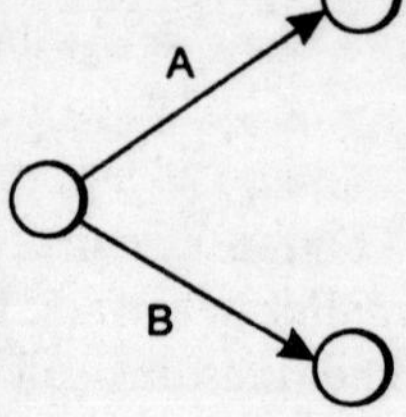 **Fig. 3.21**	Activities 'A' and 'B' are concurrent activities, *i.e.*, they can be performed concurrently.

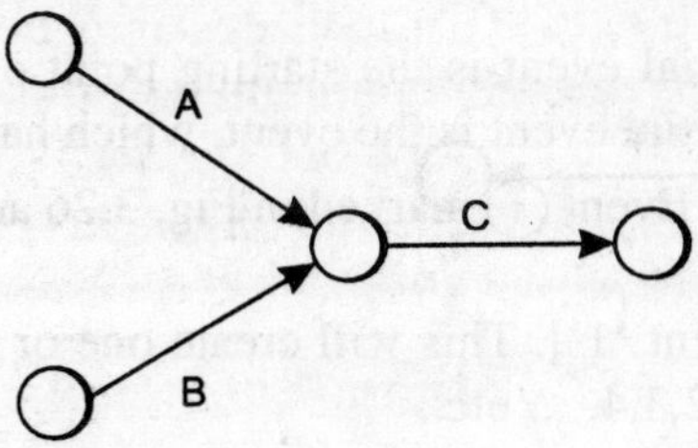

Activities 'A' and 'B' can be performed concurrently. But activity 'C' can start only after both the activities 'A' and 'B' are completed.

Fig. 3.22

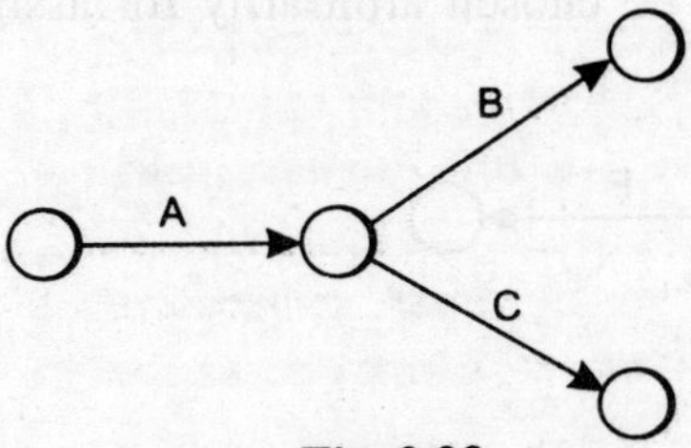

Activities 'B' and 'C', can be performed concurrently. But both 'B' and 'C' can start only after activity 'A' is completed.

Fig. 3.23

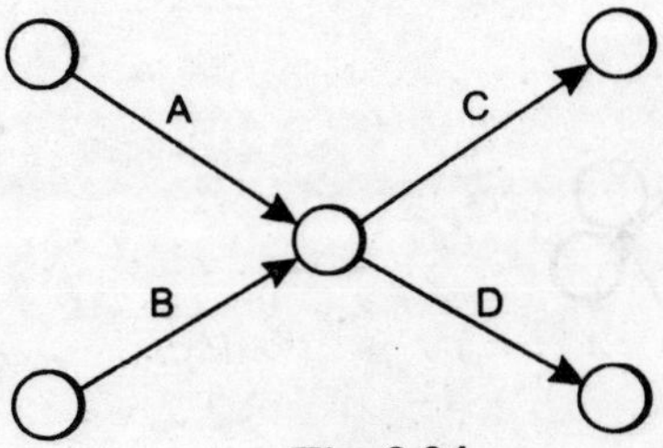

Activities 'A' and 'B' are concurrent activities. Similarly, activities 'C' and 'D' are also concurrent activities. But, 'C' and 'D' can start only after both 'A' and 'B' are completed.

Fig. 3.24

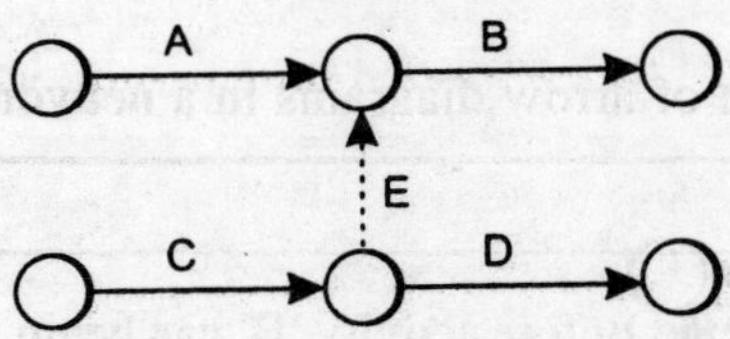

'E' is a dummy activity. Activity 'D' can start after 'C' is completed. But for activity 'B' to start, both 'A' and 'C' should be completed.

Fig. 3.25

Numbering of events (Fulkerson's rule): Every activity in a network is given a name or symbol. The events are represented by circles at the beginning and at the end of an activity and are assigned numbers. Numbering of events help in drawing the network correctly. Numbers should be so assigned to the events that they reflect the logical sequence of events in the network. Though numbers to events following the logical sequence of activities can be assigned directly for smaller networks, for larger networks the problem of assigning numbers to events can be made easier if the rules devised by D.R. Fulkerson are followed.

Fulkerson's Rule :

(*a*) Identify the "Initial event" and assign it number '1'. Initial event is the starting point of any project. Defining from the angle of a network diagram, initial event is the event, which has one or more arrows emerging from it and no arrow entering it. Event (1) marked in Fig. 3.26 are the initial events.

(*b*) Delete all the emerging arrows from the initial event [event '1']. This will create one or more 'new initial events'. Number these new initial events as 2,3,4, ... etc.,

In Fig. 3.27 initial event is numbered as '1'. When all the emerging arrows from the initial event are deleted, we are left with three new initial events (Refer Fig. 3.28). These new initial events are numbered as 2,3, & 4. The new initial events can be chosen arbitrarily for assigning numbers 2, 3 & 4 respectively.

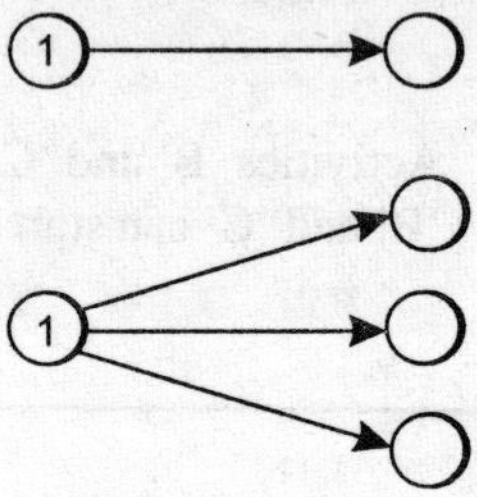

Fig. 3.26

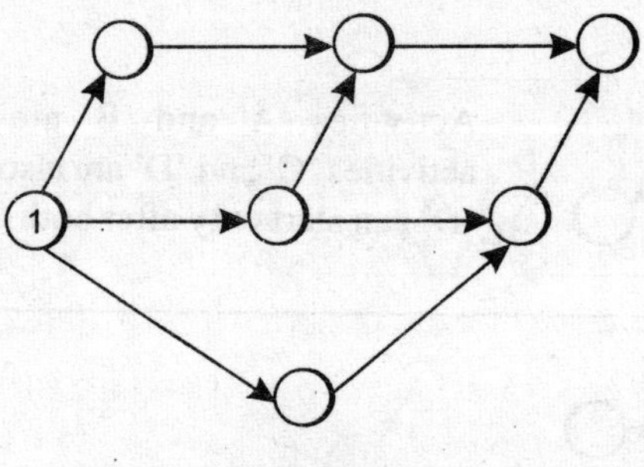

Fig. 3.27

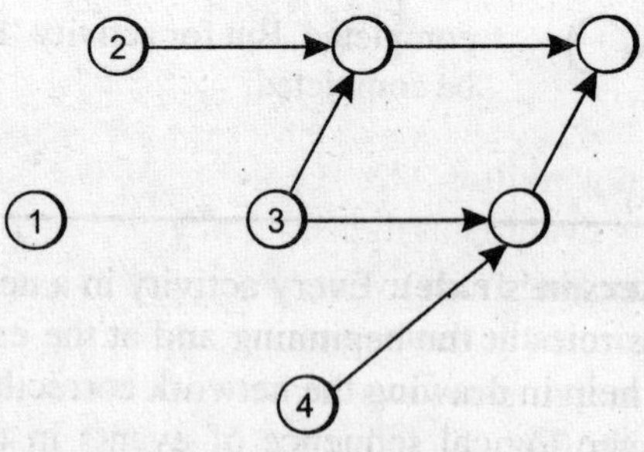

Fig. 3.28

(Refer Fig. 3.28)

(*c*) Delete all the emerging arrows from the new initial events, which will create a new set of new initial events. Assign numbers to these initial events starting from the number next to the number that has so far been assigned.

Fig. 3.29 is obtained after deleting all the emerging arrows from the events 2, 3, & 4. This leads to two new initial events that are numbered as 5 & 6.

(*d*) Follow the above procedure till the end of the network is reached. The last event of the network is the one from which no arrow emerges and into which one or more arrows enter (s). The last event is assigned with the highest number in the network.

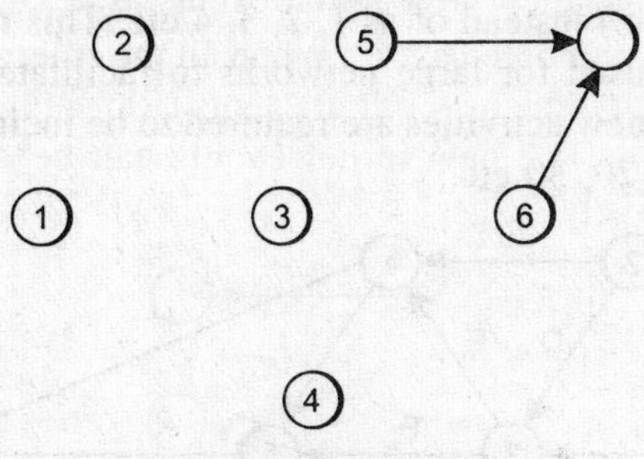

Fig. 3.29

Illustration on Numbering of Events

A network diagram having 12 activities (A to L) is given in Fig. 3.30. A sign numbers to the events applying Fulkerson's rule.

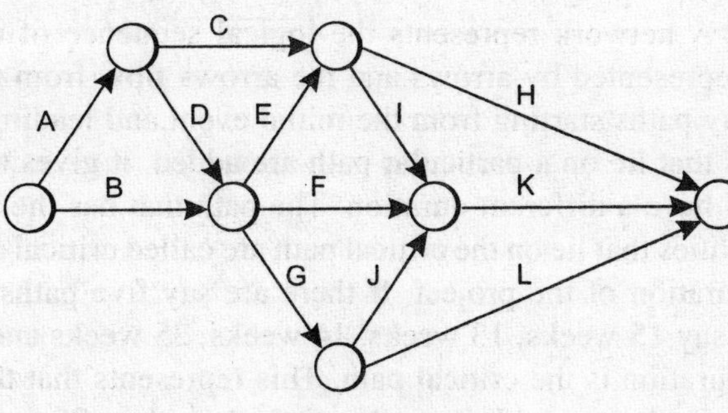

Fig. 3.30

Solution :

Step 1 : The event from which activities A & B emerges is the initial event since it has no activity entering it. Hence this event is assigned number '1'.

Step 2 : Delete the arrows emerging from event '1' (i.e., arrows representing activities 'A' & 'B'). This leads to two new initial events. Assign numbers 2 & 3 to these two new initial events.

Step 3 : Event '2' has two emerging arrows and event '3'has three emerging arrows. Delete all these five emerging arrows, which leads to a three new initial events. Assign numbers 4, 5 & 6 to these three new initial events.

Step 4 : The event that is left unnumbered is the event into which three arrows enter, but no arrow emerges from. Hence this is the last event and hence it is numbered as '7'.

This procedure completes the numbering process and the network diagram in Fig. 3.31 shows the numbers assigned to the events as per Fulkerson's rule.

Skip numbering: Large projects involve a large number of activities. Since all the activities can not be correctly foreseen and included in the network, the network for large projects may need modifications during execution of projects. The modifications may be in the form of addition of a few new activities or deletion of few activities originally included. Renumbering of events due to modifications will be a tedious task. This problem will be overcome if the events are numbered in steps of 10 (like 10, 20, 30, 40 etc.) instead of as 1, 2, 3, 4 etc. This method of numbering of events is called skip numbering and is used for large networks to facilitate addition/deletion of activities during execution. For example if new activities are required to be included, the new additional events can be numbered in between 10, 20, 30 etc.,

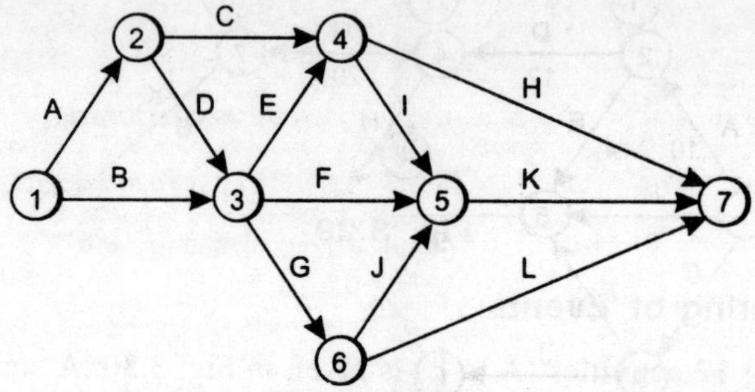

Fig. 3.31

Critical path method : A network represents the logical sequence of activities contained in a project. The activities are represented by arrows and the arrows flow from the left to the right. In a net work, there may be many paths starting from the initial event and leading to the last event. If the duration of all the activities that lie on a particular path are added, it gives the duration of that path. Each path in a network will have a different duration. The path that has the longest duation is called the critical path and the activities that lie on the critical path are called critical activities. It is the critical path that sets the overall duration of the project. If there are say five paths in a network and if the duration of these paths are, say 15 weeks, 13 weeks, 14 weeks, 25 weeks and 26 weeks respectively, the path having 26 weeks duration is the critical path. This represents that the project duration is 26 weeks. Though other paths in the network have durations less than 26 weeks, the project will be completed in all respects only by the end of the 26th week. This path that has duration of 26 weeks is the critical path.

Illustration 3.4

Fig. 3.32 represents the network of a project. The duration of each activity (in number of days) is given along the respective activity. Identify all the paths through the network. Find out the critical path and the project duration.

Solution :

A, B, C...............N are the activities.

1, 2, 3, ...9 are the events.

The following are the paths in the given net work.

A → D → G → K
A → D → H → L
A → E → I → L
B → I → L
C → J → N
C → J → M → L
C → F → I → L

The duration along these paths are obtained by adding up the durations of all the activities that lie on the path.

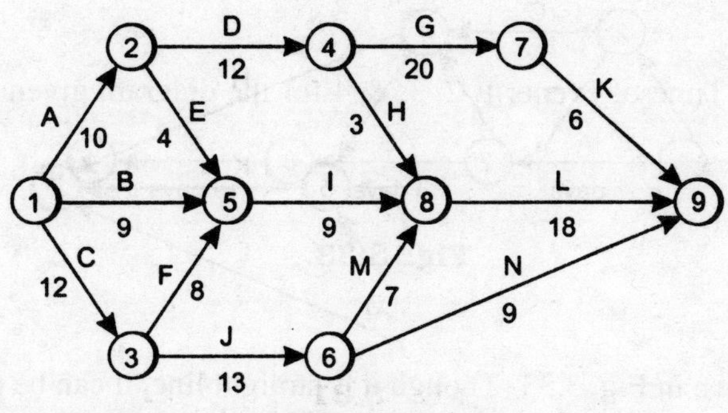

Fig. 3.32

Path	*Duration*
1. A → D → G → K	10 + 12 + 20 + 6 = 48 days
2. A → D → H → L	10 + 12 + 3 + 18 = 43 days
3. A → E → I → L	10 + 4 + 9 + 18 = 41 days
4. B → I → L	9 + 9 + 18 = 36 days
5. C → J → N	12 + 13 + 9 = 34 days
6. C → J → M → L	12 + 13 + 7 + 18 = 50 days
7. C → F → I → L	12 + 8 + 9 + 18 = 47 days.

Out of the seven paths, C → J → M → L has the longest duration and this is the critical path. The project duration is the duration of the critical path, which is equal to 50 days.

Characteristics of Critical Path

(*a*) A critical path is the longest path (time-wise) connecting the initial and final events.

(*b*) A critical path may run though dummy activity/activities.

(*c*) Since critical path is the path having the longest time duration, it does not mean that the critical path will have the maximum number of activities. The number of activities lying on a critical path may be less than the number of activities in other non-critical paths.

(*d*) It is possible that a network may have more than one critical path *i.e.*, if two or more paths have the same time duration which is maximum then all such paths will be critical paths.

Finding critical path in large network: The method of finding out the number of paths available in a given network connecting the initial and end events, finding the time duration of all the available paths and identifying the critical path is suitable for smaller networks. If the network is relatively larger in size, there will be a larger number of paths available connecting the initial and the end events. In such cases, it would be cumbersome to find out all the possible paths. Hence in the case of large networks a more systematic procedure is followed to identify the critical path. The method uses two series of computations *viz.*, Forward pass computation and Backward pass computation.

Forward pass computation: This is a method of computation of starting time of events. The computation begins from the initial event and moves towards the final event. This series of computation is done to arrive at the Earliest Start Time of all the events.

The concept of Earliest Start Time (T_E) is explained below, with the help of an illustration.

Illustration 3.5

Find out the Earliest Start Time of events 1, 2, 3, & 4 for the diagram given in Fig. 3.33.

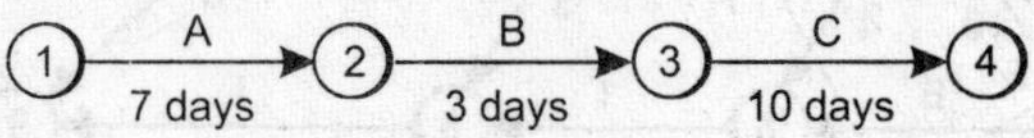

Fig. 3.33.

Solution :

Consider the net work shown in Fig. 3.33 (Though it is straight line, it can be regarded as the simplest form of a net work since it satisfies the requirements of a net work). There are three activities and four events. 'A' is the initial activity and hence the starting time of 'A' does not depend on any other activity *i.e.*, there are no constraints for the start of activity 'A'. Hence the Earliest Start Time (T_E) of event '1' is taken as '0' *i.e.*, T_E (for event-1) = 0.

Event-2 represents the end of activity 'A' and it also represents the beginning of activity 'B'. In the given net work, there is no difference between the two event times viz., end of activity 'A' and start of activity 'B' *i.e.*, activity 'B' can start at the very same moment when activity 'A' ends. Therefore the Earliest Start Time of event-2 is 7 days.

i.e., T_E (for event-2) = 7

On similar lines, we can say that event-3 *viz.*, start of activity 'C' can commence immediately after activity 'B' is completed. Thus the Earliest Start Time for event-3 is 10 days (7 days + 3 days).

T_E (for event-3) = 10

Event-4 is the last event. Though the net work does not extend beyond event-4, for the purpose of computation of Earliest Start Time, the same logic is followed. Thus, the Earliest Start Time for event-4 is 20 days (7 days + 3 days + 10 days)

i.e., T_E (for event-4) = 20

Fig. 3.34 represents the net work with the Earliest Start Time of events indicated at the respective nodes.

The illustration that we have taken for calculating T_E is the simplest one. Since all the three activities A, B & C follow one another resulting in a straight line.

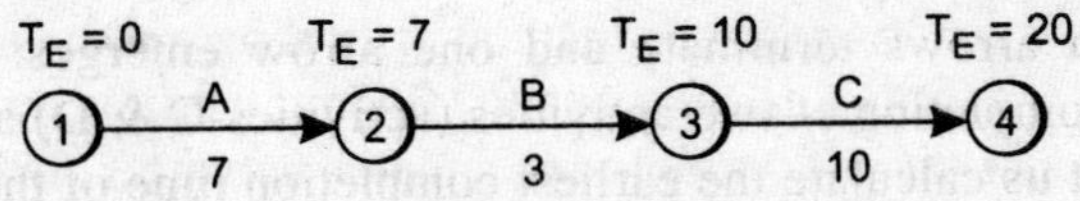

Fig. 3.34

Let us move on to a real network of activities and arrive at the Earliest Start Time of events (T_E).

Illustration 3.6 (calculation of T_E)

Find out the Earliest Start Time of events (T_E) of events 1 to 8 shown in Fig. 3.35. The duration of each activity (in number of days) is given along each activity.

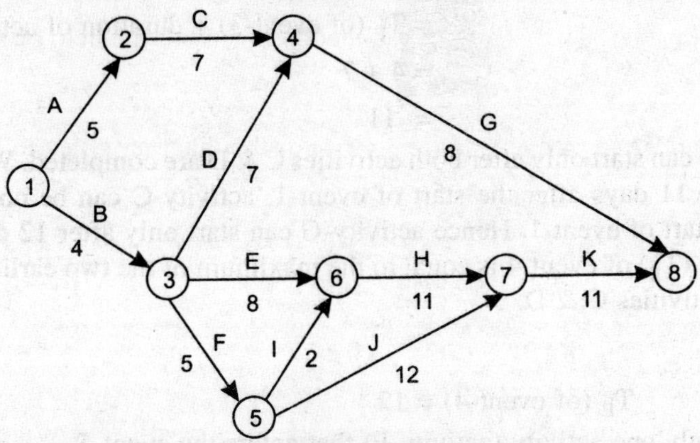

Fig. 3.35

Solution :

Event-1 : This is the start event or initial event. Hence its Earliest Start Time is Zero.

i.e., T_E (of event-1) = 0

Event-2 : Event 2 represents the end of activity 'A' as well as the beginning of activity 'C'. There is no difference between these two moments, i.e., activity 'C' can start at the very same moment when activity 'A' comes to an end.

Hence the Earliest Start Time of event-2 is given by

$$T_E \text{ (of event-2)} = T_E \text{ (of event-1)} + \text{duration of activity-A}$$
$$= 0 + 5$$
$$= 5$$

Event-3 : Activities D, E & F can start at the very same moment activity 'B' comes to an end. Therefore, the Earliest Start Time (T_E) of event-3 is given by

$$T_E \text{ (of event-3)} = T_E \text{ (of event-1)} + \text{duration of activity-B}$$
$$= 0 + 4$$
$$= 4$$

Event-4: At event-4 two arrows terminate and one arrow emerges. This means that event-4 represents the completion of two activities (activities-C & D) and the start of one activity (activity-G). Let us calculate the earliest completion time of the two activities C & D.

Earliest completion time of activity-C

$= T_E$ (of event-2) + duration of activity-C

$= 5 + 7$

$= 12$

Earliest completion time of activity-D

$= T_E$ (of event-3) + duration of activity-D

$= 4 + 7$

$= 11$

Activity G can start only after both activities C & D are completed. While activity-D can be completed 11 days after the start of event-1, activity-C can be completed only 12 days after the start of event-1. Hence activity-G can start only after 12 days. Thus the Earliest Start Time (T_E) of event-4 is equal to the maximum of the two earliest completion time of the two activities C & D.

Therefore

T_E (of event-4) = 12

Event-5: There is only one activity (activity-F) that enters the event-5.

Hence,

T_E (of event-5) = T_E (of event-3) + duration of activity-F

$= 4 + 5$

$= 9$

Event-6: There are two activities (activities E & I) entering the node-6 and one activity (activity-H) leaving from the node-6 (events are also some times referred as 'nodes').

Activity-H can start only after both the activities E & I are completed. Hence the Earliest Start Time (T_E) of event-6 is given by the maximum of the following two time estimates *a* & *b*.

(*a*) T_E (of event-3) + duration of activity-E.

$= 4 + 8$

$= 12$

(*b*) T_E (of event-5) + duration of activity-1.

$= 9 + 2$

$= 11$

Therefore activity-H can start only after 12 days from the commencement of the project. Hence the Earliest start time (T_E) of event-6 is 12 days.

i.e., T_E (of event-6) = 12

Event-7: Working on the similar lines as explained for event-6, T_E (of event-7) is the maximum of the two time estimates *a* & *b*.

(*a*) T_E (of event-6) + duration activity-H

i.e., = 12 + 11

= 23

(*b*) T_E (of event-5) + duration of activity-J

= 9 + 12

= 21

Therefore T_E (of event-7) = 23

Event-8: This is the final event. Since there are two activities entering this node. T_E for this event is the maximum of the two time estimates *a* & *b*.

(*a*) T_E (of event-4) + duration activity-G

= 12 + 8

= 20

(*b*) T_E (of event-7) + duration activity-K

= 23 + 11

= 34

Therefore, T_E (of event – 8) = 34

Fig. 3.36 shows the earliest Start time (T_E) of all the events at the respective nodes.

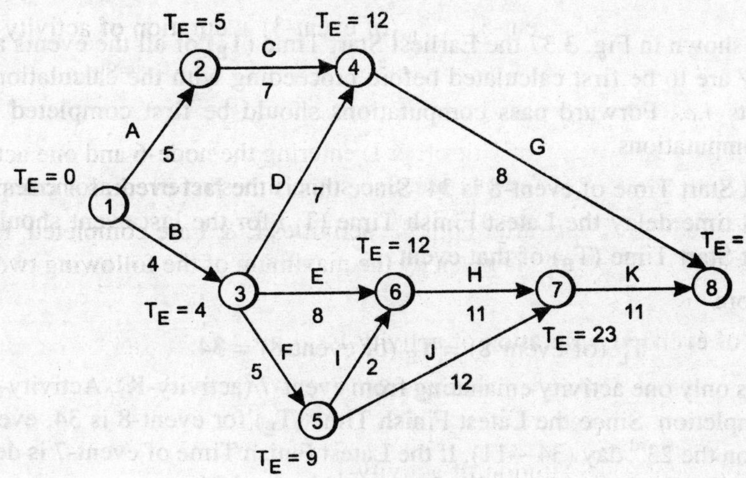

Fig. 3.36

Backward pass computation. This is a method of computation of the finishing time of events. The computation begins from the final event and moves towards the initial event. This series of computation is done to arrive at the Latest Finish Time (T_L) of all the events. Latest Finish Time is also referred to as Latest Allowable Event Time, or Latest Allowable Occurrence Time, or Latest Allowable Completion Time.

Latest Finish Time (T_L) is the latest time by which an event should be completed so that the project completion will not be delayed.

The concept and method of arriving at the Latest Finish Time (T_L) of events is explained with the help of an illustration.

Illustration 3.7 (Calculation of T_L)

The same net work that was used for the calculation of T_E is used for this illustration. The net work is reproduced below (Fig. 3.37)

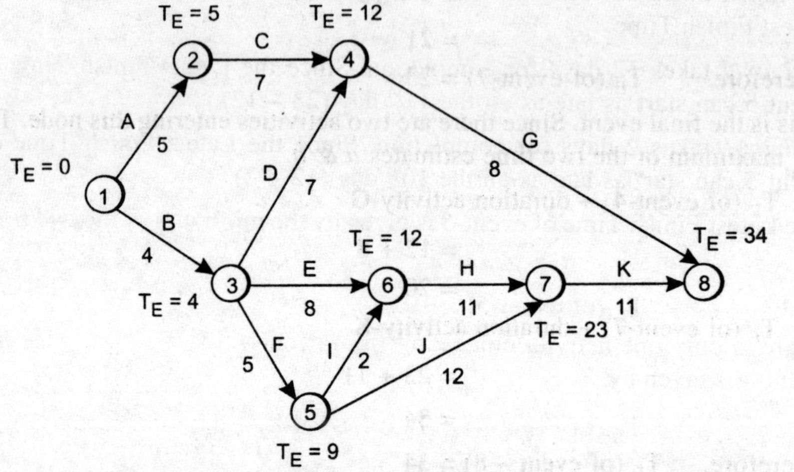

Fig. 3.37

In the net work shown in Fig. 3.37 the Earliest Start Time (T_E) of all the events are given. If these are not given, they are to be first calculated before proceeding with the calculation of Latest Finish Time (T_L of events *i.e.*, Forward pass computations should be first completed before taking up Backward pass computations.

Event-8: Earliest Start Time of event-8 is 34. Since this is the last event, for completing the project without time delay the Latest Finish Time (T_L) for the last event should be equal to the Earliest Start Time (T_E) of that event.

Therefore

$$T_L \text{ (of event-8)} = T_E \text{ (of event-8)} = 34$$

Event-7: There is only one activity emanating from event-7 (activity-K). Activity—K takes 11 days for completion. Since the Latest Finish Time (T_L) for event-8 is 34, event-7 can occur as late as on the 23rd day (34—11). If the Latest Finish Time of event-7 is delayed beyond 23, the project completion time will also extend beyond 34.

Hence

$$T_L \text{ (of event-7)} = T_E \text{ (for event-8) - duration of activity-K}$$

$$= 34 - 11$$

$$= 23.$$

Event-6: Again, there is only one activity emanating from event-6 (Activity-H), which takes 11 days for completion. As per the logic applied to event-7, the Latest Finish Time of event-6 is given by,

$$T_L \text{ (of event-6)} = T_L \text{ (of event-7)} - \text{duration of activity-H}$$
$$= 23 - 11$$
$$= 12$$

Event-5: There are two activities emanating from event-5. Hence there will be two time estimates for finish times out of which the minimum of the two time estimates will represent the Latest Finish Time.

Activity-J takes 12 days for completion. Since the Latest Finish Time of event-7 is 23, event-5 can start as late as on the 11th day (23 – 12).

Activity-I takes 2 days for completion. Since the Latest Finish Time of event-6 is 12, event-5 can start as late as on the 10th day (12 – 2).

The Latest Finish Time of event-5 is given by the minimum of the two time estimates, viz., 10.

$$T_L \text{ (of event-5)} = 10.$$

Event-4: There is only one activity emanating from event-4. Therefore the Latest Finish Time of event-4 is given by

$$T_L \text{ (of event-4)} = T_L \text{ (of event-8)} - \text{duration of activity-G}$$
$$= 34 - 8$$
$$= 26$$

Event-3: There are three activities emanating from event-3 (activities-D, E & F). Hence three time estimates of finish times are available out of which the minimum time represents the Latest Finish Time of event-3.

T_L (of event-3) is the minimum of

(*a*) T_L (of event-4) – duration of activity-D

$$= 26 - 7$$
$$= 19$$

(*b*) T_L (of event-6) – duration of activity-E

$$= 12 - 8$$
$$= 4$$

(*c*) T_L (of event-5) – duration of activity-F

$$= 10 - 5$$
$$= 5$$

Therefore, T_L (of event-3) = 4 (being the minimum of the three time estimates).

Event-2: There is only one activity emanating from event-2.

Therefore

T_L (of event-2) = T_L (of event-4) – duration of activity-C.

= 26 – 7

= 19

Event-1: There are two activities emanating from event-1. Hence T_L of event-1 is the minimum of the following two time estimates.

(*a*) T_L (of event-2) – duration of activity-A

= 19 – 5

= 14

(*b*) T_L (of event-3) – duration of activity-B

= 4 – 4

= 0

Therefore, T_L (of event-1) = 0

If the backward pass computations are done correctly, the Latest Finish Time of the start event (event-1) will be equal to its Earliest Start Time.

In our example, we have arrived at T_E (of event-1) = T_L (of event-1) = 0

The Latest Finish Time of all the events (along with the Earliest Start Time) are given in Fig. 3.38.

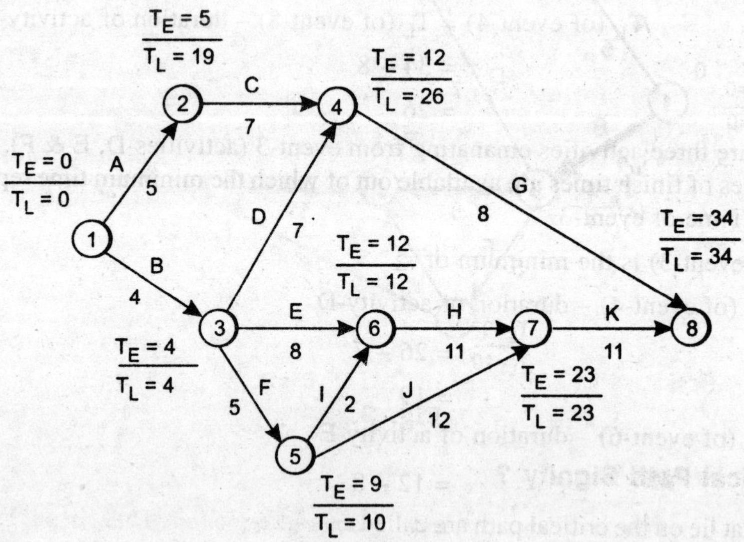

Fig. 3.38

Slack time and critical path : We have calculated the Earliest Start Time (T_E) of all events by doing forward pass computations. We have also calculated the Latest Finish Time (T_L) of all events by doing backward pass computations. Thus T_E & T_L of all the events of the network is known.

Slack Time (or Slack) of an event is the difference between the Latest Finish Time (T_L) and the Earliest Start Time (T_E) of that event.

The path connecting events with zero slack is the critical path.

The following table reproduces the T_L, T_E & Slack of all events of the net work that we have considered in our illustration (Refer Fig. 3.38)

Event	T_L	T_E	*Slack* $(T_L - T_E)$
1	0	0	0
2	19	5	14
3	4	4	0
4	26	12	14
5	10	9	1
6	12	12	0
7	23	23	0
8	34	34	0

We find that events 1, 3, 6, 7 & 8 have zero slack. The path connecting these events is the critical path. *Critical path is denoted in the net work by bold line*. Fig. 3.39 indicates critical path in the given net work.

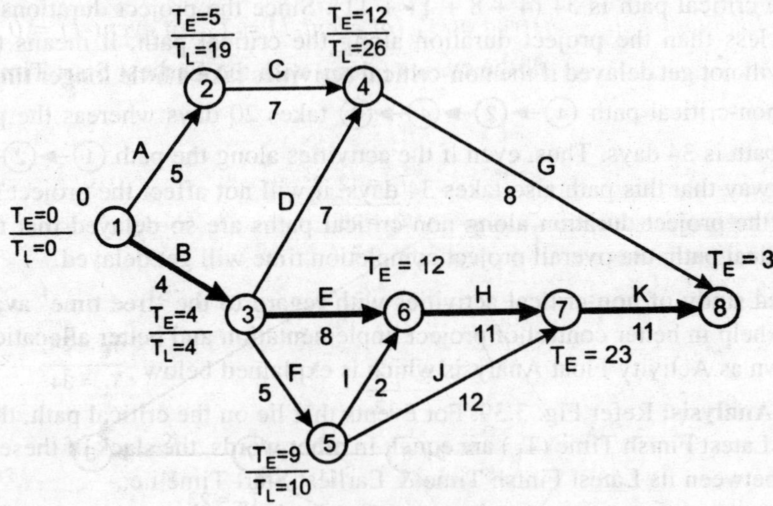

Fig. 3.39

What does Critical Path Signify ?

The activities that lie on the critical path are called critical activities. Thus, in our example, activities B, E, H & K are the critical activities.

Since the two time estimates of all the nodes in the critical path are the same, it means that a succeeding activity in a critical path shall commence immediately after its proceeding activity is completed.

In our example, activity-K shall start immediately after activity-H is completed; activity-H shall start immediately after activity-E is completed and activity-E shall start immediately after activity-B is completed. If there is any delay in either starting a critical activity or if the time taken for completing a critical activity exceeds the estimated time, the project implementation period will get extended.

Thus it is obvious, that only the critical activities deserve more attention and control by the management. Any delay in critical activities will lead to time-overrun of the project. Since every time-overrun invariably results in cost-overrun, delay in critical activities will also more likely to result in cost-overrun of projects.

All paths in a network other than the critical path are called non-critical paths. A non-critical path may have only non-critical activities or a combination of both critical and non-critical activities.

The table below is a summary of the non-critical paths in our example.

Non Critical path	*Activities lying on the non-critical path*	*Non-critical activities*	*Project duration along the non-critical path*
①→②→④→⑧	A, C, G	A, C, G	20
①→③→④→⑧	B, D, G	D, G	19
①→③→⑤→⑥→⑦→⑧	B, F, I, H, K	F, I	33
①→③→⑤→⑦→⑧	B, F, J, K	F, J	32

We have seen in the example that ①→③→⑥→⑦→⑧ is the critical path and the project duration along the critical path is 34 (4 + 8 + 11 + 11). Since the project durations along the non-critical paths are less than the project duration along the critical path, it means that the project completion time will not get delayed if the non-critical activities take a little longer time than planned. For example the non-critical path ①→②→④→⑧ takes 20 days whereas the project duration along the critical path is 34 days. Thus, even if the activities along the path ①→②→④→⑧ are delayed in such a way that this path also takes 34 days, it will not affect the project implementation time. However if the project duration along non-critical paths are so delayed that they exceed the duration of the critical path, the overall project completion time will get delayed.

Hence a detailed study of non-critical activities with regard to the 'free time' available is worth doing since it will help in better control of project implementation and better allocation of resources. This study is known as Activity Float Analysis which is explained below :

Activity Float Analysis: Refer Fig. 3.39. For events that lie on the critical path, the Earliest Start Time (T_E) and the Latest Finish Time (T_L) are equal. In other words, the slack of these events is given by the difference between its Latest Finish Time & Earliest Start Time i.e.,

$$\text{Slack} = (T_L - T_E)$$

The free time available for an activity is called 'float'. Thus 'float' for an activity is similar to 'slack' for an event. (Some times the words slack and float are used interchangeably for activity and event also).However, in our study we will restrict the use of the word 'slack' to events and the word 'float' to activities.

An event has only one estimate of slack (which may be either zero or may be of some value). However, an activity has three types of estimates for float viz.,

Total float,

Free float,

and Independent float.

Total float: Total float represents the maximum time by which the completion of an activity can be delayed without affecting the project completion time.

If an activity is delayed by a time equal to its total float, that activity and all other subsequent activities in that path become critical activities.

Let us study this concept, using the same net work that we used for explaining critical path. The net work is again reproduced in Fig. 3.40 for ready reference.

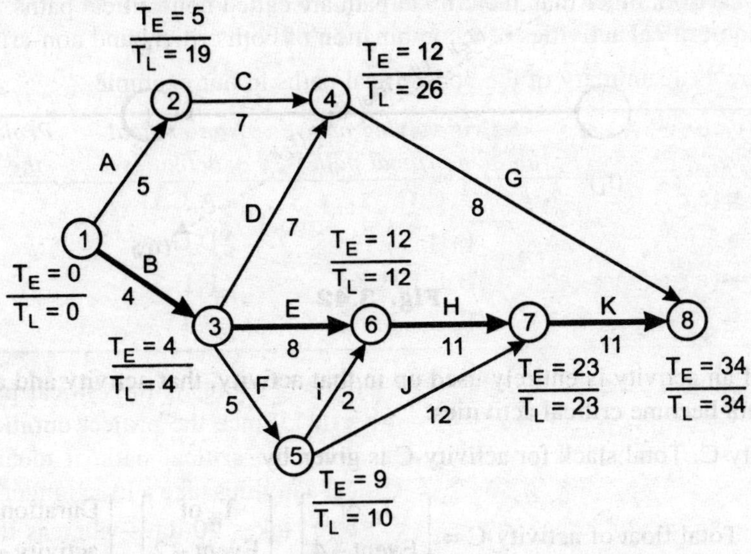

Fig. 3.40

Let us consider any one of the non-critical activities, say activity C. (Refer Fig. 3.41)

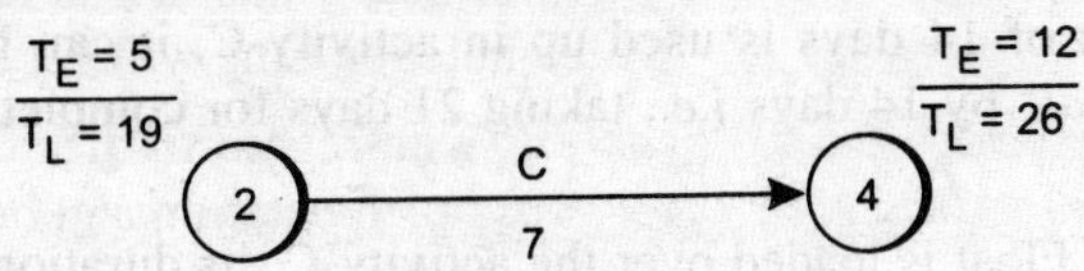

Fig. 3.41

For the calculation of Total float of a particular activity, it is assumed that all its proceeding activities start at their respective Earliest Start Times. If this is so, the Earliest Start Time of activity C is 5 (which is the Earliest Start Time of event-2). Similarly the Latest Finish Time of activity-C is 26 (which is the Latest Finish Time of event-4).

Thus from the Earliest starting moment of activity-C to the latest finishing moment of activity-C, there are 21 days (26 – 5). The duration of the activity is 7 days. Thus the total float available for activity-C is 14 days (21 - 7).

For the ease of understanding, we can reduce the calculation of Total Float in the form of a formula as under:

Total float of an activity	=	T_L of the head event	–	T_E of the tail event	–	Duration of the activity

In general,

Total float of activity-(i-j) = $(T_L)\ j - (T_E)\ i - t\ ij$

Where (T_L) j is the Latest Finish Time of the head event, (T_E) i, is the Earliest Start Time of the tail event and t ij is the duration of the activity.

The formula can be represented pictorially as under (Refer Fig. 3.42)

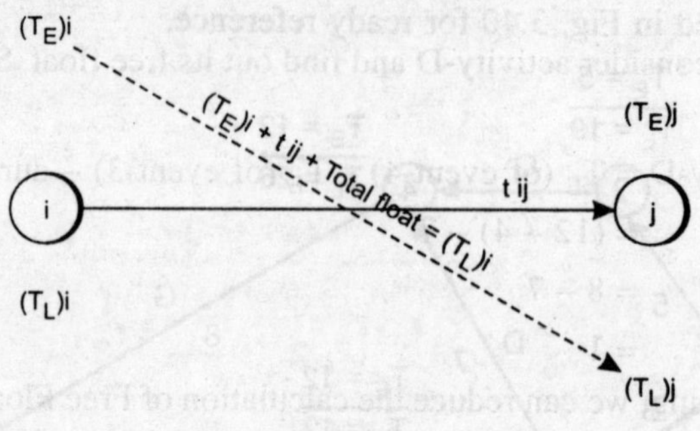

Fig. 3.42

Remarks

If the total float of an activity is entirely used up in that activity, that activity and all the subsequent activities in the path become critical activities.

Consider activity-C. Total slack for activity-C is given by

$$\text{Total float of activity-C} = \begin{bmatrix} T_L \text{ of} \\ \text{Event} - 4 \end{bmatrix} - \begin{bmatrix} T_E \text{ of} \\ \text{Event} - 2 \end{bmatrix} - \begin{bmatrix} \text{Duration of} \\ \text{activity} - C \end{bmatrix}$$

$$= 26 - 5 - 7$$

$$= 14$$

If the entire Total float of 14 days is used up in activity-C, it can be viewed as delaying the completion time of activity-C by 14 days *i.e.*, taking 21 days for completion of activity instead of 7 days planned.

Thus, if the entire Total Float is loaded over the activity-C, its duration is extended up to 21 days and the modified network is shown in Fig. 3.43.

Referring to Fig. 3.43 we find that both activities-C & G have now become critical activities. (Incidentally activity-A has also become a critical activity, after the total float of activity C is utilized fully).

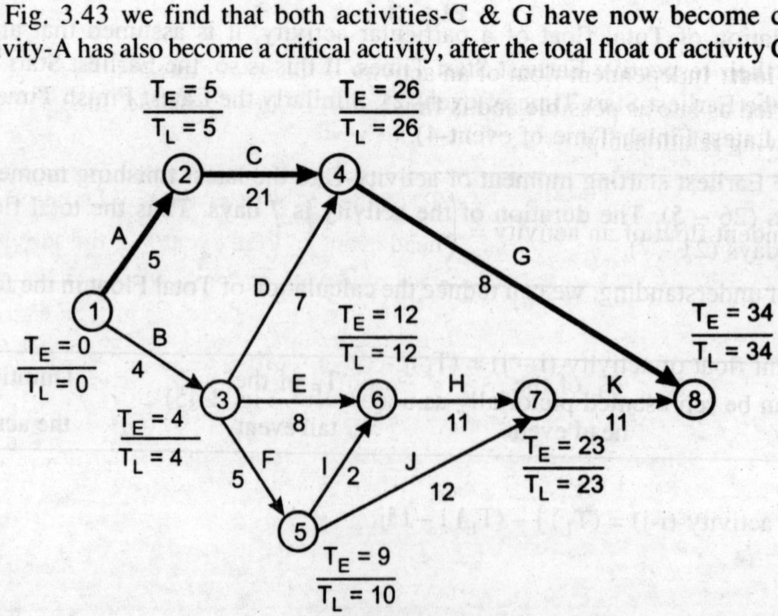

Fig. 3.43

Free Float: Free float of an activity is the delay that can be permitted in an activity so that succeeding activities in the path are not affected. If the succeeding activities are to remain un-affected by the delay in a particular activity the Earliest Start Time (T_E) of the head event of that activity shall not be exceeded.

Refer to Fig. 3.39. Let us consider activity-D and find out its free float. Since T_E (of event-4) is not to be exceeded,

$$\begin{aligned}\text{Free float of activity-D} &= T_E \text{ (of event-4)} - T_E \text{ (of event-3)} - \text{duration of activity - D}\\ &= (12 - 4) - 7\\ &= 8 - 7\\ &= 1\end{aligned}$$

For the ease of understanding, we can reduce the calculation of Free Float in the form of a formula, as under.

$$\text{Free float of an activity} = \left(\begin{matrix}T_E \text{ of the}\\ \text{head event}\end{matrix}\right) - \left(\begin{matrix}T_E \text{ of the}\\ \text{tail event}\end{matrix}\right) - \left(\begin{matrix}\text{Duration of}\\ \text{the activity}\end{matrix}\right)$$

In general,

$$\text{Free float of activity-(i-j)} = (T_E)j - (T_E)i - t\,ij$$

The formula can be represented pictorially as under (Refer Fig. 3.44)

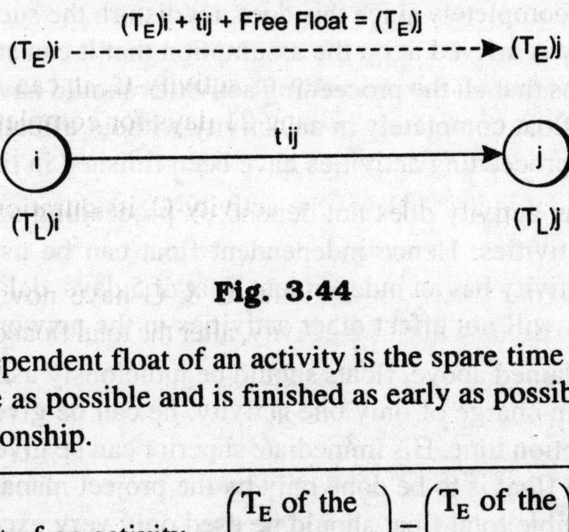

Fig. 3.44

Independent Float: Independent float of an activity is the spare time available for that activity, if that activity is started as late as possible and is finished as early as possible. Independent float can be given by the following relationship.

$$\text{Independent float of an activity} = \left(\begin{matrix}T_E \text{ of the}\\ \text{head event}\end{matrix}\right) - \left(\begin{matrix}T_E \text{ of the}\\ \text{tail event}\end{matrix}\right) - \left(\begin{matrix}\text{Duration of}\\ \text{the activity}\end{matrix}\right)$$

In general,

$$\text{Independent float of activity-(i - j)} = (T_E)j - (T_L)i - t\,ij$$

The formula can be represented pictorially as under (Ref. Fig. 3.45)

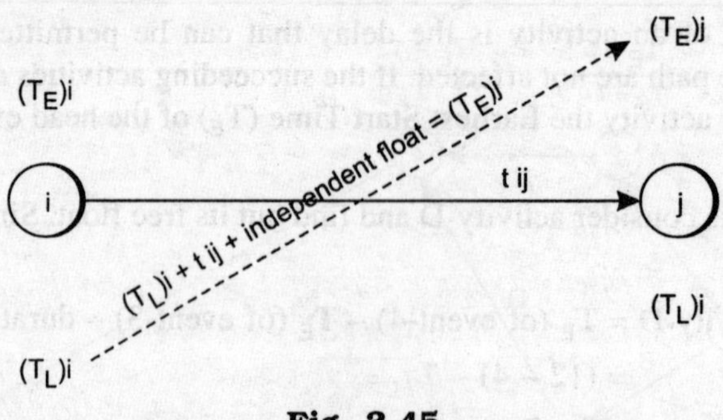

Fig. 3.45

Use of Different Floats for Management Decisions :

(*a*) All the activities that lie on the critical path have their total floats equal to zero.

[Hence critical path may also be defined as the path passing through activities having zero total float. This definition may prove to be wrong if the T_E & T_L of the last event are not made equal. However, situations where T_E & T_L of the last event differ are rarely come across. Hence treatment of floats where T_E & T_L of the last event differs are not explained in this book.]

(*b*) If the total float of an activity is used entirely in that activity, it would make that activity and all the succeeding activities in the path critical. Hence it is not advisable to use the total float completely in an activity as this will leave no cushion available if subsequent activities need additional time for completion than originally planned.

(*c*) Free float can be used completely since this does not disturb the succeeding activities. However free float of an activity is arrived at on the assumption that it can start at its Earliest Start Time (T_E). This in turn means that all the proceeding activities should have been finished by this time. Hence the use of free float completely in an activity without affecting the succeeding activities is possible only if the proceeding activities have been finished in time.

(*d*) Independent float of an activity does not depend on proceeding activities and it also does not disturb succeeding activities. Hence independent float can be used with out any constraint. Thus, if a particular activity has an independent float of 5 days, delaying the completion time of that activity by 5 days will not affect other activities in the network.

In view of the factors explained above, floats should be judiciously used while managing a project. If a first level supervisor is in charge of only one activity, he can be given only independent float to maneuver his activity completion time. His immediate superior can be given the option to excercise the use of free float. Use of total float is to be done only by the project manager who is in overall charge of the project. As far as possible total float should be used only very exceptionally.

Illustration 3.8

For the network shown in Fig. 3.46 work out the total float, free float and independent float of all the activities.

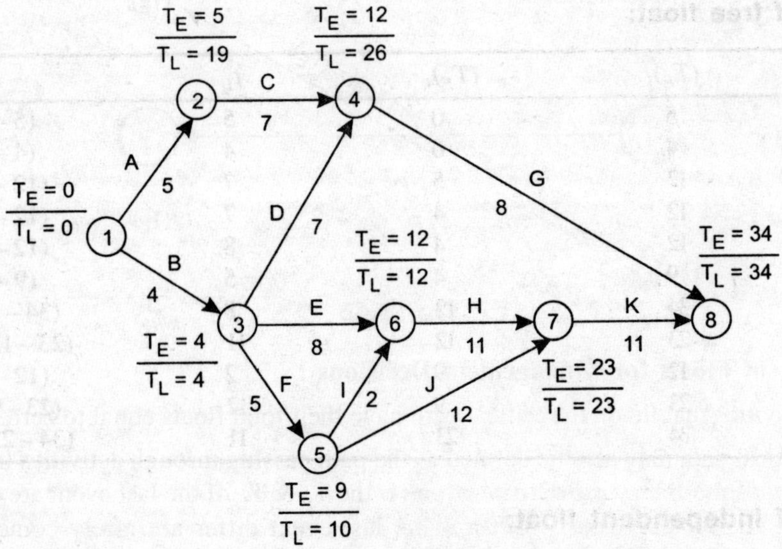

Fig. 3.46

Solution :

Let us reproduce the formula for Total float, free float and Independent float.

Total float of activity-(i-j) = $(T_L)j - (T_E)i - t_{ij}$

Free float of activity-(i-j) = $(T_E)j - (T_E)i - t_{ij}$

and Independent float of activity-(i-j) = $(T_E)j - (TL)i - t_{ij}$

Calculation of Total float:

Activity	$(T_L)_j$	$(T_E)_i$	t_{ij}	*Total float*
A	19	0	5	(19 – 0 – 5) = 14
B	4	0	4	(4 – 0 – 4) = 0
C	26	5	7	(26 – 5 – 7) = 14
D	26	4	7	(26 – 4 – 7) = 15
E	12	4	8	(12 – 4 – 8) = 0
F	10	4	5	(10 – 4 – 5) = 1
G	34	12	8	(34 – 12 – 8) = 14
H	23	12	11	(23 – 12 – 11) = 0
I	12	9	2	(12 – 9 – 2) = 1
J	23	9	12	(23 – 9 – 12) = 2
K	34	23	11	(34 – 23 – 11) = 0

Activities B, E, H and K have zero total floats. Hence, all these four activities will lie on the critical path. As we have already seen, the critical path for the given net work is ①→③→⑥→⑦→⑧ which confirms that these four activities are the critical activities and they lie on the critical path.

Calculation of free float:

Activity	$(T_E)_j$	$(T_E)_i$	t_{ij}	*Free float*
A	5	0	5	(5 – 0 – 5) = 0
B	4	0	4	(4 – 0 – 4) = 0
C	12	5	7	(12 – 5 – 7) = 0
D	12	4	7	(12 – 4 – 7) = 1
E	12	4	8	(12 – 4 – 8) = 0
F	9	4	5	(9 – 4 – 5) = 0
G	34	12	8	(34 – 12 – 8) = 14
H	23	12	11	(23 – 12 – 11) = 0
I	12	9	2	(12 – 9 – 2) = 1
J	23	9	12	(23 – 9 – 12) = 2
K	34	23	11	(34 – 23 – 11) = 0

Calculation of Independent float:

Activity	$(T_E)_j$	$(T_L)_i$	t_{ij}	*Independent float*
A	5	0	5	(5 – 0 – 5) = 0
B	4	0	4	(4 – 0 – 4) = 0
C	12	19	7	(12 – 19 – 7) = 0*
D	12	4	7	(12 – 4 – 7) = 1
E	12	4	8	(12 – 4 – 8) = 0
F	9	4	5	(9 – 4 – 5) = 0
G	34	26	8	(34 – 26 – 8) = 0
H	23	12	11	(23 – 12 – 11) = 0
I	12	10	2	(12 – 10 – 2) = 0
J	23	10	12	(23 – 10 – 12) = 1
K	34	23	11	(34 – 23 – 11) = 0

*A negative float has no real meaning and it can be assumed as zero float.

Illustration 3.9

For the network shown in Fig. 3.47 find out the critical path and the project duration, using forward pass and backward pass calculations.

Solution:

Forward pass :

Event	*Earliest Start Time* (T_E)
1	0
2	0 + 3 = 3
3	0 + 4 = 4

(Cont.)

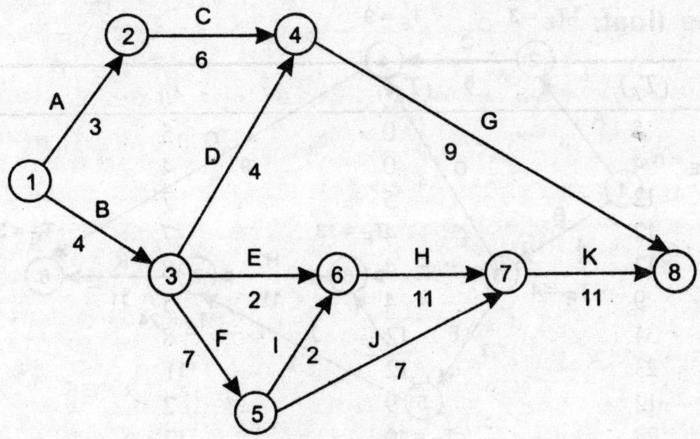

Fig. 3.47

(Cont.)

Event	*Earliest Start Time* (T_E)
4	Higher of (*a*) 3 + 6 = 9 and (*b*) 4 + 4 = 8 *i.e.*, = 9
5	4 + 7 = 11
6	Higher of (*b*) 4 + 2 = 6 and (*b*) 11 + 2 = 13 *i.e.*, = 13
7	Higher of (*c*) 13 + 11 = 24 and (*b*) 11 + 7 = 18 *i.e.*, = 24
8	Higher of (*d*) 9 + 9 = 18 and (*b*) 24 + 11 = 35 *i.e.*, = 35

The Earliest Start Times of events (T_E) are indicated in the network shown below: (Fig. 3.48)

Backward Pass

Event	*Latest Finish Time* (T_L)
8	35 (Kept equal to T_E)
7	35 – 11 = 24
6	24 – 11 = 13
5	Smaller of (*a*) 13 – 2 = 11 and (*b*) 24 – 7 = 17 i.e., = 11

(Cont.)

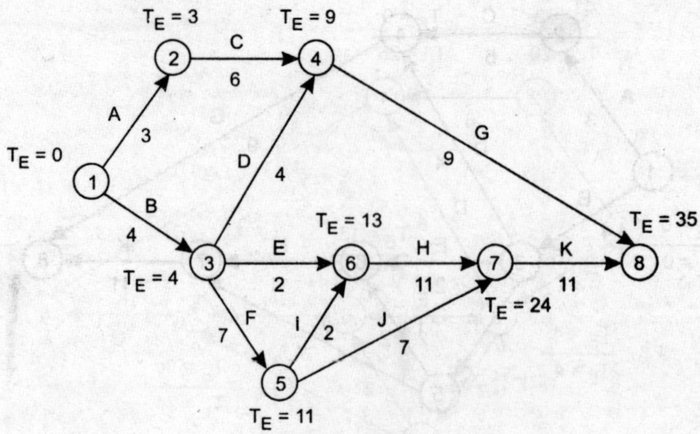

Fig. 3.48

Event	*Latest Finish Time (T_L)*
4	$35-9=26$
3	Smaller of (*a*) $26-4=22$ (*b*) $13-2=11$ and (*c*) $11-7=4$ i.e., $=4$
2	$26-6=20$
1	Smaller (*a*) $20-3=17$ and (*b*) $4-4=0$ i.e., $=0$

The Latest Finish Time of all events (along with their respective Earliest Start Times) are given in the network shown below: (Fig. 3.49)

As seen from the above network, the following events have zero slack (i.e., the T_E and T_L for these events are equal).

Event-1
Event-3
Event-5
Event-6
Event-7
and Event-8

We have seen already that all the events lying on the critical path have zero slack. However in the given example there are three paths connecting zero slack events. They are

①→③→⑤→⑦→⑧ : 29 days

①→③→⑤→⑥→⑦→⑧ : 35 days

and ①→③→⑥→⑦→⑧ : 28 days

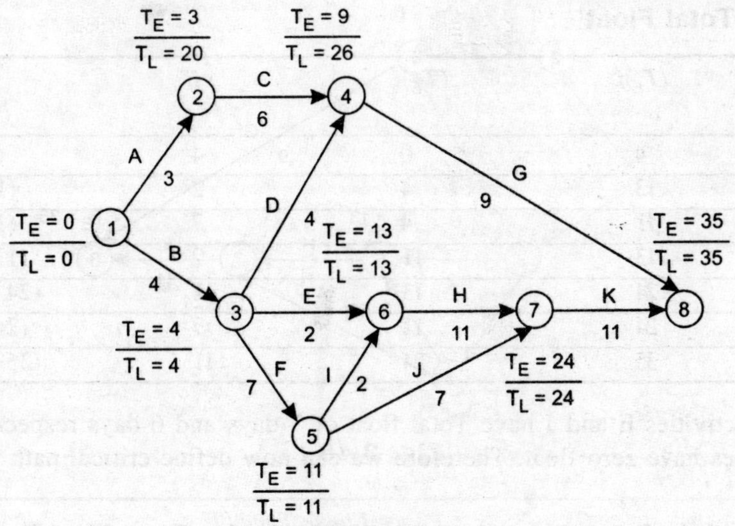

Fig. 3.49

Out of the above three paths, the critical path is the one that takes the longest time i.e., ①→③→⑤→⑥→⑦→⑧ is the critical path. *The critical path is marked in bold line in the network shown below:* (Fig. 3.50). The project duration is 35 days.

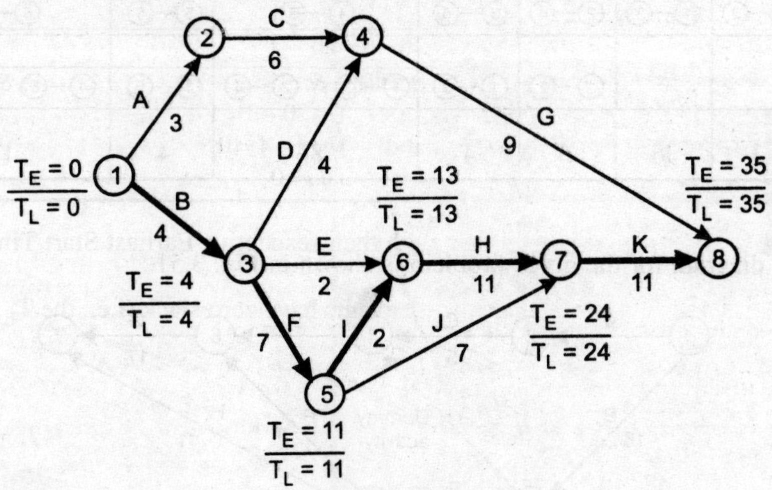

Fig. 3.50

Important Observation: An important point that we observe from the above illustration is that *"Though a critical path passes through events connecting zero-slacks ($T_E = T_L$), all the paths connecting events of zero-slacks are not necessarily critical paths".*

Under Activity Float Analysis we have seen that the Total float of activities that lie on the critical path are zero. Let us verify this statement for the above example. We shall consider only those activities for which T_E and T_L of head and tail events are equal.

Calculation of Total Float

Activity - ij	$(T_L)j$	$(T_E)i$	*t ij*	*Total float* $(T_L)j - (T_E)i - t\ ij$
B	4	0	4	(4 – 0 – 4) = 0
E	13	4	2	(13 – 4 – 2) = 7
F	11	4	7	(11 – 4 – 7) = 0
I	13	11	2	(13 – 11 – 2) = 0
H	24	13	11	(24 – 13 – 11) = 0
J	24	11	7	(24 – 11 – 7) = 7
K	35	24	11	(35 – 24 – 11) = 0

We find that activities E and J have Total float of 7 days and 6 days respectively and only the remaining activities have zero float. Therefore we can now define critical path in a more accurate manner as under.

"Critical path is that path connecting activities having Total Float Equal to zero".

Illustration 3.10

A construction project involves the following activities. Draw the network diagram and mark the critical path. What is the project completion time ?

Activity	1–2	1–3	2–4	3–5	4–6	5–6	6–7	5–7
Proceeding activity	–	–	1–2	1–3	1–3 & 2–4	3–5	4–6 & 5–6	3–5
Duration (days)	3	16	5	4	8	4	17	11

Solution :

The network diagram for the given problem is shown in Fig. 3.51.

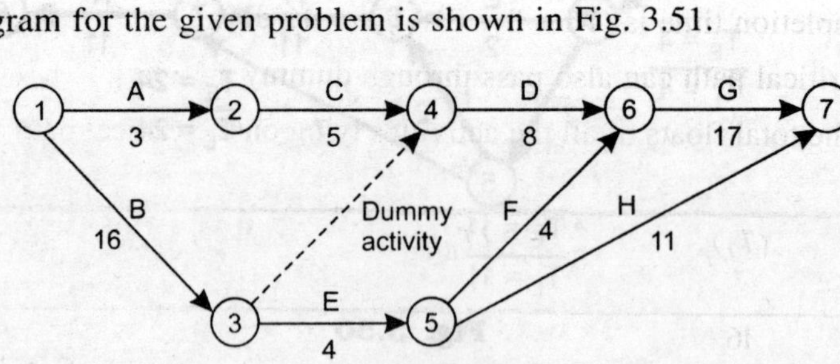

Fig. 3.51

The activities have been named A to H for the sake of convenience.

[Activity ①—② is named 'A', activity ①—③ is named 'B' etc.]

Forward pass computations			*Backward pass computations*		
Event	T_E		*Event*	T_L	
1	0		7	41	
2	0 + 3 = 3		6	41 − 17 = 24	
3	0 + 16 = 16		5	Minimum of	
					(*a*) 24 − 2 = 22
				and	(*b*) 41 − 11 = 30
					i.e., = 22
4	Maximum of		4	24 − 8 = 16	
		(*a*) 3 + 5 = 8			
	and	(*b*) 16 + 0 = 16			
		i.e., = 16			
5	16 + 4 = 20		3	Minimum of	
					(*a*) 16 − 0 = 16
				and	(*b*) 22 − 2 = 20
					i.e., = 16
6	Maximum of		2	16 − 5 = 11	
		(*a*) 16 + 8 = 24			
	and	(*b*) 20 + 2 = 22			
		i.e., = 24			
7.	Maximum of		1	Minimum of	
		(*a*) 24 + 17 = 41			(*a*) 11 − 3 = 8
	and	(*b*) 20 + 11 = 33		and	(*b*) 16 − 16 = 0
		i.e., = 41			i.e., = 0

Nodes ①, ③, ④, ⑥ and ⑦ have zero slacks. There is only one critical path, which is

$$B \rightarrow (\text{Dummy}) \rightarrow D \rightarrow G$$

The project completion time is (16 + 0 + 8 + 17) = 41 days.

[Observation: Critical path can also pass through dummy activity].

Let us find out the total floats of all the activities lying on the critical path and check up if they are all zero.

Activity - ij	$(T_L)_j$	$(T_E)_i$	t_{ij}	*Total float* $(T_L)_j - (T_E)_i - t_{ij}$
B	16	0	16	16 − 0 − 16 = 0
Dummy	16	16	0	16 − 16 − 0 = 0
D	24	16	8	24 − 16 − 8 = 0
G	41	24	17	41 − 24 − 17 = 0

As expected, the total floats of all the activities lying on the critical path is zero. Fig. 3.52 shows the critical path.

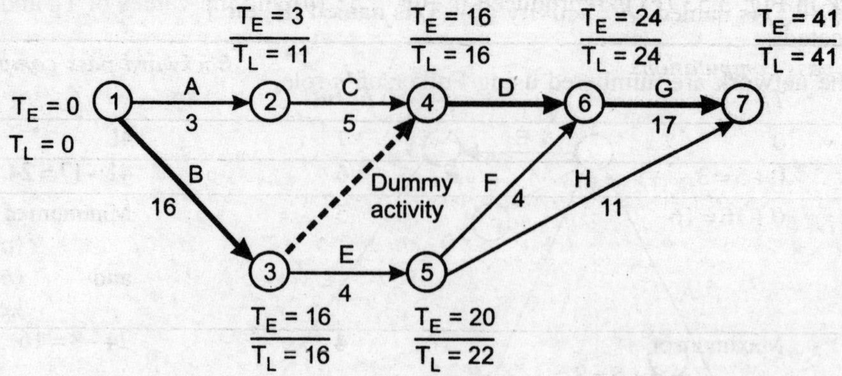

Fig. 3.52

Illustration 3.11:

Draw a network for the activity relationship given below and number the events. Make sure that there is only one initial event and only one terminal event. Ensure that the number of dummy activities does not exceed 5. Perform forward pass and backward pass computations and find out the critical path.

Activity	*Predecessor*	*Duration (days)*
A	-	15
B	-	5
C	-	7
D	-	17
E	A, B, C, D.	9
F	A, B, C, D.	4
G	A, B, C, D.	3
H	B, C, D.	4
I	B, C, D.	5
J	B, C, D.	10
K	B, C, D.	3
L	E, F.	18
M	G, H, I.	4
N	K	6
O	L, M, J, N.	10

Solution :

Drawing a network for a given set of logics is more like an art and can be learnt only by practice. Dummy activities should be used only when they are absolutely necessary. The network diagram drawn by different persons, for a given problem through correctly drawn as per the given logic, may appear to be different in view of the differences in the pattern of placing the activities.

Networks shown in Fig. 3.53 (a) Fig. 3.53 (b) and Fig. 3.53 (c) all satisfy the logic given in the illustration. However, on the face of it, these networks appear to be slightly different. In reality, all these networks are correct for the given logic.

Out of the three networks, let us choose any one (say, the network given in Fig. 3.53 (c) for the forward pass and backward pass computations and for arriving at the critical path.

The network in Fig. 3.53 (c) is reproduced in Fig. 3.53 (d) and the values of T_E and T_L of all the nodes are indicated.

Events of the network are numbered using Fulkerson's role.

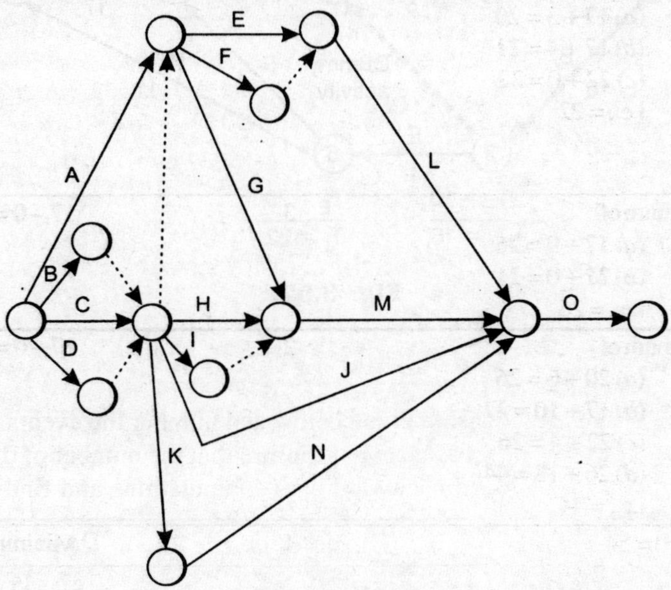

Fig. 3.53 (a)

Forward pass computations		*Backward pass computations*	
Event	T_E	*Event*	T_L
1	0	12	54
2	0 + 7 = 7	11	54 – 10 = 44
3	0 + 17 = 17	10	44 – 18 = 26
4	Maximum of (*a*) 0 + 5 = 5 (*b*) 7 + 0 = 7 (*c*) 17 + 0 = 17 i.e., = 17	9	44 – 4 = 40
5	Maximum of (*a*) 0 + 15 = 15 (*b*) 17 + 0 = 17 i.e., = 17	8	26 – 0 = 26
6	17 + 5 = 22	7	44 – 6 = 38
7	17 + 3 = 20	6	40 – 0 = 40
8	17 + 4 = 21	5	Minimum of (*a*) 26 – 4 = 22 (*b*) 26 – 9 = 17 (*c*) 40 – 3 = 37 i.e., = 17

Forward pass computations		*Backward pass computations*	
Event	T_E	*Event*	T_L
9	Maximum of (*a*) $17+3=20$ (*b*) $17+4=21$ (*c*) $22+0=22$ i.e., $=22$	4	Minimum of (*a*) $17-0=17$ (*b*) $40-4=36$ (*c*) $40-5=35$ (*d*) $44-10=34$ (*e*) $38-3=35$ i.e., $=17$
10.	Maximum of (*a*) $17+9=26$ (*b*) $21+0=21$ i.e., $=26$	3	$17-0=17$
11	Maximum of (*a*) $20+6=26$ (*b*) $17+10=27$ (*c*) $22+4=26$ (*d*) $26+18=44$ i.e., $=44$	2	$17-0=17$
12	$44+10=54$	1	Minimum of (*a*) $17-15=2$ (*b*) $17-5=12$ (*c*) $17-7=10$ (*d*) $17-17=0$ i.e., $=0$

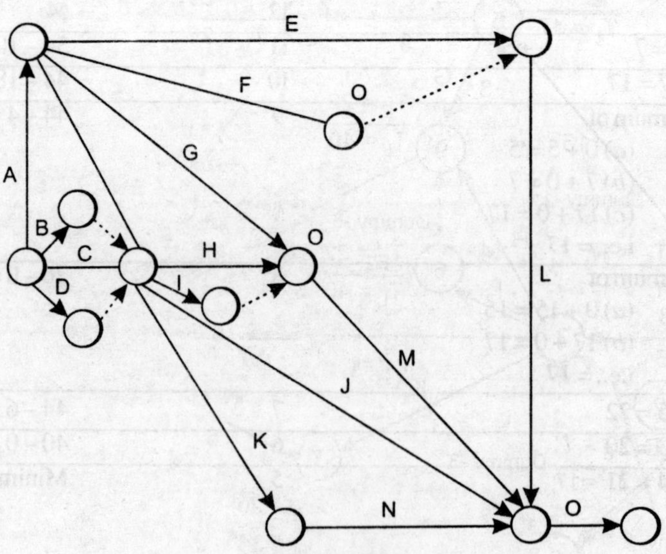

Fig. 3.53 (b)

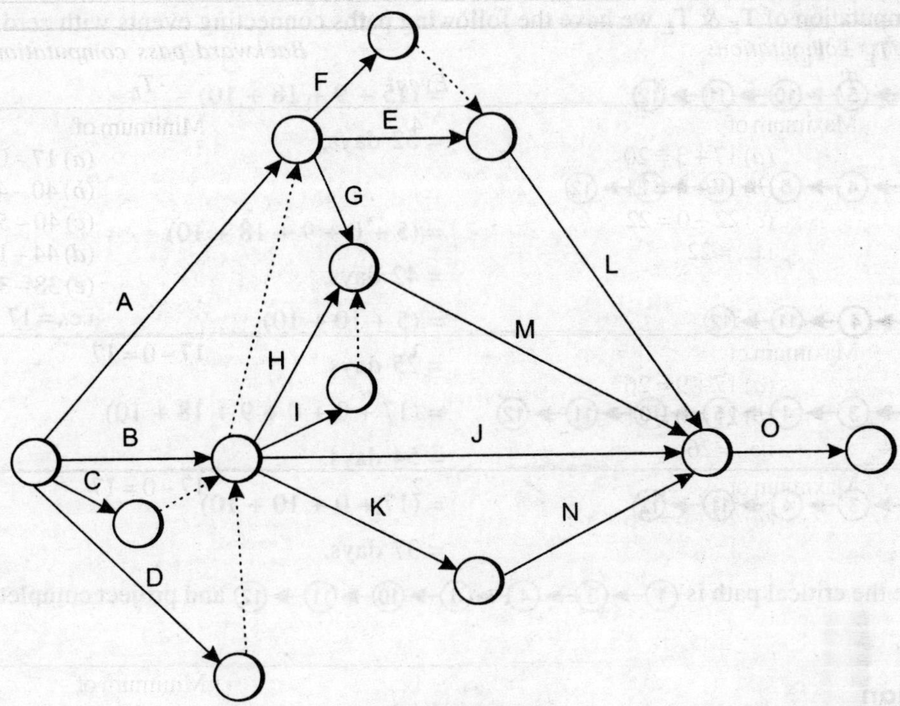

Fig. 3.53 (c)

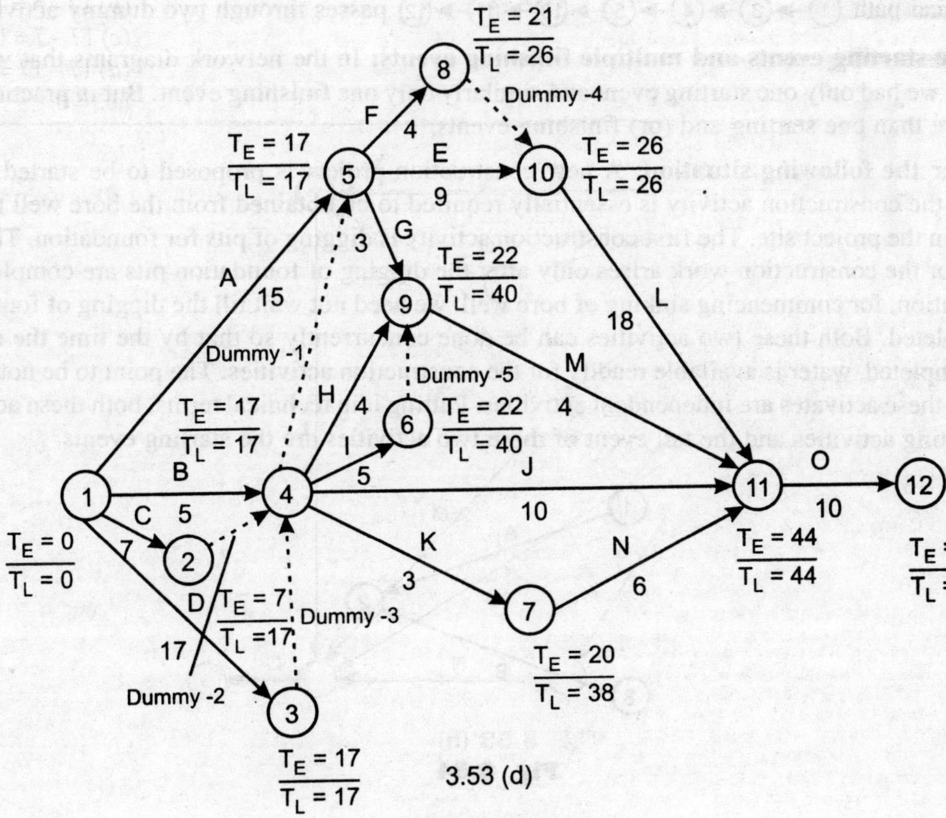

Fig. 3.53 (d)

After computation of T_E & T_L we have the following paths connecting events with zero slack (i.e., events with $T_E = T_L$).

I. ①→⑤→⑩→⑪→⑫ = (15 + 9 + 18 + 10)
= 52 days.

II. ①→④→⑤→⑩→⑪→⑫
= (5 + 0 + 9 + 18 + 10)
= 42 days.

III. ①→④→⑪→⑫ = (5 + 10 + 10)
= 25 days.

IV. ①→③→④→⑤→⑩→⑪→⑫ = (17 + 0 + 0 + 9 + 18 + 10)
= 54 days.

V. ①→③→④→⑪→⑫ = (17 + 0 + 10 + 10)
= 37 days.

Therefore the critical path is ①→③→④→⑤→⑩→⑪→⑫ and project completion time is 54 days.

Observation

The critical path ①→③→④→⑤→⑩→⑪→⑫ passes through two dummy activities.

Multiple starting events and multiple finishing events: In the network diagrams that we have so far seen, we had only one starting event and similarly only one finishing event. But in practice there can be more than one starting and (or) finishing events.

Consider the following situation: A new construction project is proposed to be started. Water needed for the construction activity is essentially required to be obtained from the bore well that has to be sunk in the project site. The first construction activity is digging of pits for foundation. The need for water for the construction work arises only after the digging of foundation pits are completed. In such a situation, for commencing sinking of bore well, we need not wait till the digging of foundation pit is completed. Both these two activities can be done concurrently so that by the time the digging work is completed, water is available readily for the construction activities. The point to be noted here is that both these activates are independent activities. Putting it in technical terms, both these activities are the starting activities and the tail event of these two activities are the starting events.

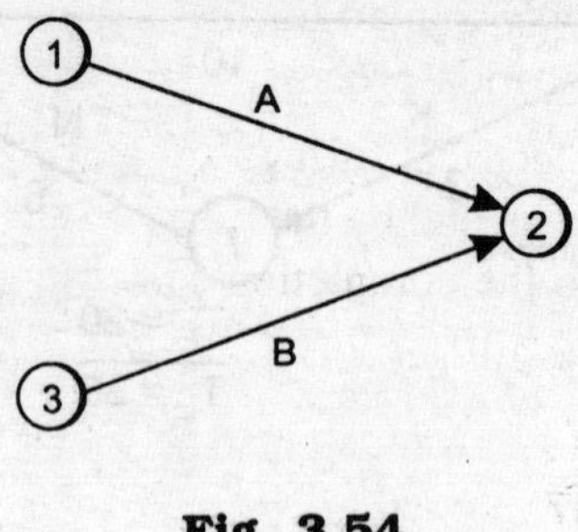

Fig. 3.54

Activity-A : Sinking of bore well.

Activity-B : Digging of foundation pits.

Event- ① :Start sinking of bore well

Event- ③ : Start digging of foundation pits.

Event- ② : Finish sinking of bore well/Finish digging of foundation pits

Both event- ① and event- ③ are the starting events. Thus we can appreciate that there can be situations in which a project network can have more than one starting events.

Consider the following situation: The Project of construction of a hostel building consists of the following major activities.

(*a*) Digging foundation pits.
(*b*) Construction of foundation.
(*c*) Construction of concrete framed structure (framework of beams and columns).
(*d*) Construction of walls.
(*e*) Plastering of walls.
(*f*) Fixing of doors and windows.
(*g*) Fixing of water supply and sanitary fittings
(*h*) Installation of elevator (lift).
(*i*) Construction of septic tank.
(*j*) Fixing of electrical fittings and wiring.

The project will be said to be completed only when all the above 10 activities are completed. As we are aware, these activities have some precedence/succession relationship between themselves (example: Construction of foundation should be completed before construction of walls etc.,)

Now, consider activity-is *viz.*, construction of spetic tank (septic tank is used for storing the effluent from toilets, water closets etc). For the project to reach its completion stage, this activity *viz.*, construction of septic tank should have also been completed. If the project completion time (as determined by the critical path) is say 120 days, the construction of septic tank should have also been completed within this period. The point that needs consideration is that there is no activity that follows the activity-i. In a sense, it is an 'end' activity. However, this is not the last activity of the project, since the project is "construction of hostel building", and "construction of septic tank" is a separate activity that should be completed for considering that the project has reached its completion stage. Since there is no activity that follows activity-i, it can be either completed on the 120th day or earlier to that. [The decision as to how to plan for the completion of activity-i is a separate issue and this depends upon the resource-allocation process, which is explained elsewhere in the book].

If the activity-j (viz., fixing of electrical fittings and wiring) is the last activity of the project, we understand that the project comes to an end by the time activity-j is completed. Activity-i should have been completed at any time prior to the completion of activity-j (or at the most by the same time by which activity-j is completed).

Refer Fig. 3.55 wherein we find two end activities.

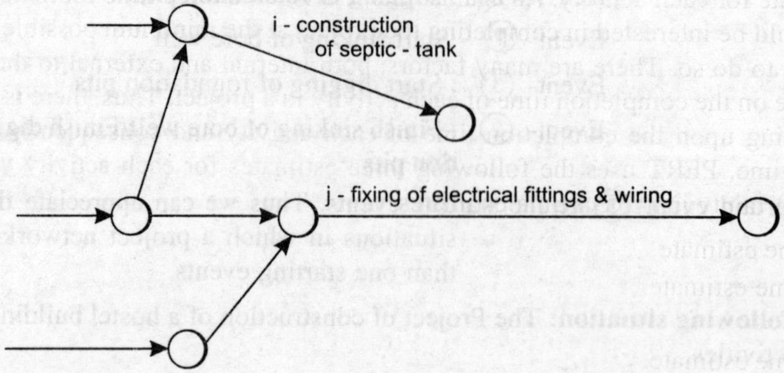

Fig. 3.55

Such instances where there are more than one end events are possible in large projects. Though there may be more than one end activity, there will be only one end activity that controls the actual project completion time and critical path will pass only through this end activity. Such a situation, where one or more activities in a network is left over as such is known as **dangling**. In Fig. 3.55 activity-i indicates 'dangling' of network; the word 'dangling means nothing but 'hanging' and we find that activity-i hangs. As per the general rules of drawing network, dangling in a network indicates error in logic and needs reassessment and redrawing of the network. However this is not a hard and fast rule and there will be practical situations (as we have seen in the example explained above) where there are danglings in a network. In such situations, it should be carefully analyzed and ensured that the activities that lead to dangling are activities that do not have any succession relationship (i.e., no activity shall be required to follow these activities to ensure logical sequence of project completion). If this is ensured, dangling of activities will not affect the network logic. However since dangling is not allowed (or viewed with suspicion!) a dummy activity may be introduced so that the network may look logical (Ref. Fig. 3.56). Without such a dummy activity, the network diagram will show dangling and one who looks at the diagram will not be able to come to a conclusion as to whether there is any activity that follows activity-i, unless he goes through the details of the different activities involved in the project.

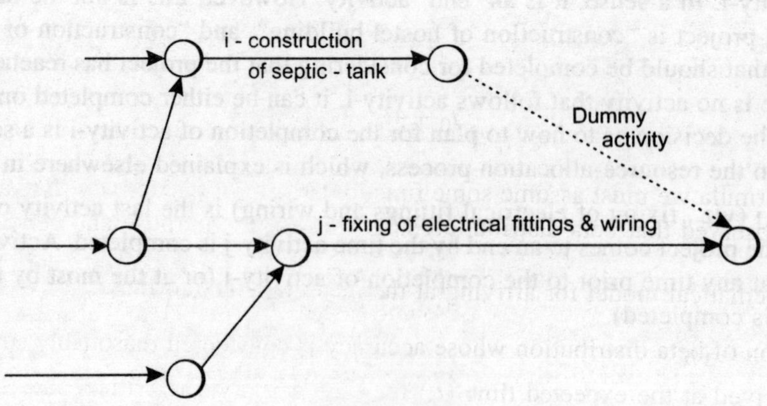

Fig. 3.56.

Programme Evaluation and Review Technique (PERT): The critical path method (CPM) uses only one time estimate for each activity. As against this, PERT uses three time estimates. Though the project manager would be interested in completing the project at the minimum possible time, it is not entirely in his hands to do so. There are many factors, both internal and external to the organisation which have influence on the completion time of each activity in a project. Thus, there is an element of uncertainty in deciding upon the completion time of each activity and consequently the estimated project completion time. PERT uses the following three estimates for each activity with a view to overcoming the uncertainty in project time estimates.

(*a*) Optimistic time estimate.

(*b*) Pessimistic time estimate.

and

(*c*) Most likely time estimate.

(*a*) *Optimistic time estimate* (t_0): It is the shortest possible time in which an activity can be completed under ideal conditions. In arriving at the optimistic time estimate, it is assumed that every thing is favourable in completing the activity in the shortest possible time.

(*b*) *Pessimistic time estimate* (t_p): It is the maximum possible time that it would take to complete an activity under worst conditions. In arriving at the pessimistic time estimate, it is assumed that every thing is unfavourable for completing the activity in time and every possible delay and difficult situation is encountered.

(*c*) *Most likely time estimate* (t_m): It lies between optimistic and pessimistic time estimates. It is the time in which an activity can be completed under normal conditions. In arriving at the most likely time, it is assumed that conditions are neither favourable nor unfavourable, but normal.

The supervisor or the foreman who is in direct charge of an activity is asked to estimate the three time estimates taking into account, favourable, unfavourable and normal conditions. In assuming unfavourable conditions, extremely unfavourable situations such as earthquakes, floods, fires, labour strikes etc., are excluded.

Expected time estimate (t_e): PERT arrives at the expected time (t_e) for an activity, taking into account the three time estimates t_0, t_P and t_m.

PERT assume that the optimistic time (t_0) the pessimistic time (t_p) are equally likely to occur while the most likely time [t_m] is four times more likely to occur than the other two (t_0 & t_p). Hence for arriving at the expected time (t_e) equal weights are assigned to t_0 & t_p while weight of t_m is taken as 4 times that of t_o and t_p.

Accordingly

$$t_e = \frac{t_0 + 4t_m + t_p}{6}$$

T_o derive this formula we must assume some functional form of the activity time as shown in the Fig. 3.57. It was observed that beta distribution suits well for the purpose and hence the same was accepted as a mathematical model for arriving at the mean (t_e). The formula $t_e = \dfrac{t_o + 4t_m + t_p}{6}$ is a linear approximation of beta distribution whose accuracy is considered reasonably sufficient.

After having arrived at the expected time (t_e) for each activity, the critical path is found out by making forward-pass and backward pass computations, calculating the Earliest Start Time (T_E) and the Latest Finish Time (T_L) of all the events, finding the slack of events and connecting the events with zero slack.

Illustration 3.12

Draw a PERT Net Work for the following data. Arrive at the critical path and find out the estimated project duration along the critical path. G & I are the last activities.

Activity	*Proceeding Activity*	*Optimistic time (weeks)*	*Most likely time (weeks)*	*Pessimistic time (weeks)*
A	–	4	5	6
B	–	4	6	8
C	A	3	5	7
D	B	1	3	5
E	C, D	2	5	8
F	C, D	3	4	11
G	E	4	5	12
H	H	4	4	10
I	F, H	5	6	13

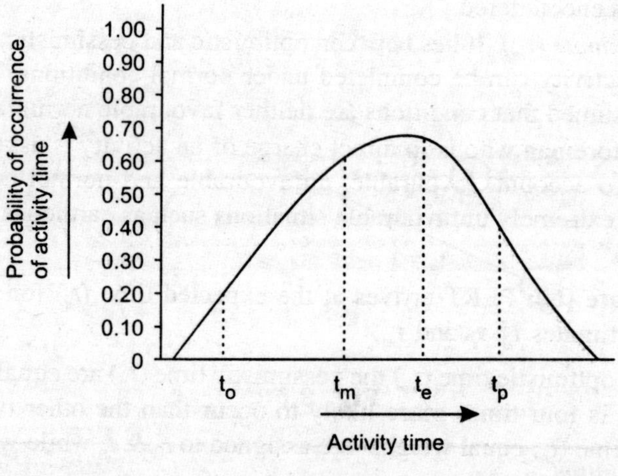

Fig. 3.57.

Solution :

The first step involved is to calculate the expected time (t_e) for all the activities from the given three time estimates, using the formula

$$t_e = \frac{t_o + 4t_m + t_p}{6}$$

After having arrived at the expected time (t_e) for all the activities, critical path is arrived at by doing forward pass and backward pass computations and connecting events with zero slack.

Activity	*Optimistic time (t_0)*	*Pessimistic time (t_p)*	*Most likely time (t_m)*	*Expected time (t_e)* $= \frac{t_o + 4t_m + t_p}{6}$
A	4	5	6	5
B	4	6	8	6
C	3	5	7	5
D	1	3	5	3
E	2	5	8	5
F	3	4	11	5
G	4	5	12	6
H	4	4	10	5
I	5	6	13	7

The network diagram for the given activity relationships is shown in Fig. 3.58.

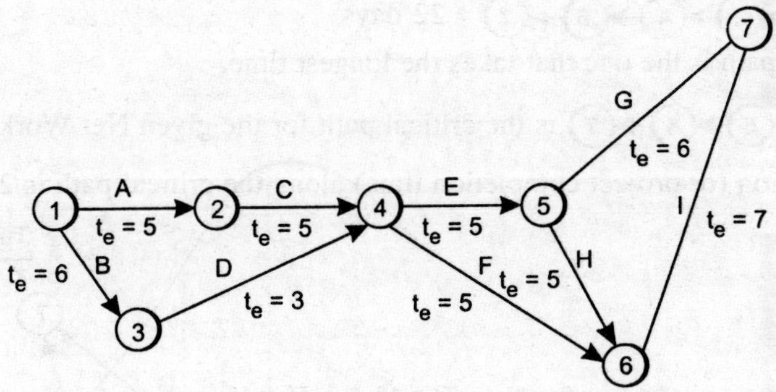

Fig. 3.58.

Forward pass computation		*Backward pass computation*	
Event	T_E	*Event*	T_L
1	0	7	27
2	0+5=5	6	27−7=20
3	0+6=6	5	Minimum of (*a*) 20−5=15 (*b*) 27−6=21 *i.e.*, =15
4	Maximum of (*a*) 5+5=10 (*b*) 6+3=9 *i.e.*, =10	4	Minimum of (*a*) 15−5=10 (*b*) 20−5=15 *i.e.*, =10

Forward pass computations		*Backward pass computations*	
Event	T_E	*Event*	T_L
5	$10+5=15$	3	$10-3=7$
6	Maximum of (*a*) $15+5=20$ (*b*) $10+5=15$ i.e., $=20$	2	$10-5=5$
7	Maximum of (*a*) $15+6=21$ (*b*) $20+7=27$ i.e., $=27$	1	Minimum of (*a*) $5-5=0$ (*b*) $7-6=1$ i.e., $=0$

The T_E & T_L for all the events are marked in Fig. 3.59. Events ①, ②, ④, ⑤, ⑥ and ⑦ have zero slack (i.e., $T_E = T_L$). Thus we have three paths connecting events of zero slack.

①→②→④→⑤→⑦ = 27 days.

①→②→④→⑤→⑦ = 21 days

and ①→②→④→⑥→⑦ = 22 days

Since the critical path is the one that takes the longest time.

①→②→④→⑤→⑥→⑦ is the critical path for the given Net Work (Refer Fig. 3.60).

The Project duration (or project completion time) along the critical path is 27 days.

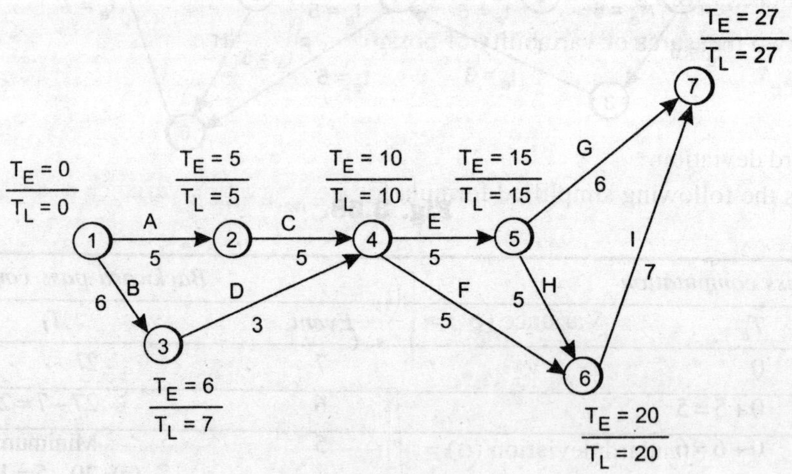

Fig. 3.59.

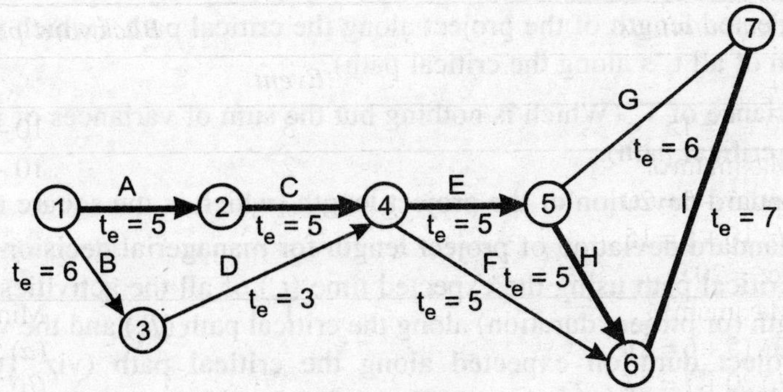

Fig. 3.60.

Variations in Activity Times: Consider the following two time estimates.

Activity	t_0	t_m	t_p	$t_e = \frac{(t_o + 4t_m + t_p)}{6}$
A	2	3	4	3
B	1	2	9	3

For both the activities A & B the expected time arrived at is the same. However as seen, the difference between t_0 and t_p is more for activity-B than for activity-A. Thus, though the estimated expected time (t_e) is the same for both the activities, there is a greater extent of uncertainty in the time estimates for activity-B. Thus the reliability of the expected time (t_e) depends upon the variability of two time estimates t_0 & t_p.

There are two measures of variability of possible activity times *viz.*,

(*i*) Variance.

and

(*ii*) Standard deviation.

PERT uses the following simplified formula for arriving at the variance and standard deviation of activity times.

$$\text{Variance } (\sigma^2) = \left[\frac{(t_p - t_o)}{6}\right]^2$$

$$\text{Standard deviation } (\sigma) = \sqrt{\left[\frac{(t_p - t_o)}{6}\right]^2} = \left[\frac{t_p - t_o}{6}\right]$$

Project duration along critical path: After having arrived at the expected time (t_e) of all the individual activities, the expected time estimates are made use of for identifying the critical path by performing forward pass and backward pass computations. The point to be noted in PERT technique is that we make use of only 'expected time' of activity durations as against the single definite time duration that is made use of under CPM technique. Thus, the time taken for project completion along the critical path is also only an 'expected length of the project'.

Let (T_e) = Expected length of the project along the critical path. (which is nothing but the sum of all t_e's along the critical path).

$(\sigma^2)_{critical}$ = Variance of T_e (Which is nothing but the sum of variances of all activities along the critical path).

$(\sigma)_{critical}$ = Standard deviation of the project length [which is the square root of $(\sigma^2)_{critical}$]

Use of variance/standard deviation of project length for managerial decisions: By now, we know how to identify the critical path using the expected time (t_e) of all the activities, how to find out the expected project length (or project duration) along the critical path (T_e) and the variance and standard deviation of the project duration expected along the critical path (viz, $(\sigma^2)_{critical}$ & $(\sigma)_{critical}$ respectively). The calculation of $(\sigma^2)_{critical}$ or $(\sigma)_{critical}$ is not without any purpose.

We will come to know the use of variance/standard deviation when it is explained with an illustration.

Illustration 3.13

Activity	t_o	t_m	t_p	$t_e = \frac{(t_o + 4t_m + t_p)}{6}$	*Variance* $\left[\frac{(t_p - t_o)}{6}\right]^2$	*Standard deviation* $\left[\frac{(t_p - t_o)}{6}\right]$
A	8	10	12	10	0.44	0.67
B	5	8	11	8	1.00	1.00
C	4	14	24	14	11.11	3.33
D	3	7	11	7	1.78	1.33
E	1	6	11	6	2.78	1.67
F	7	8	9	8	0.11	0.33

Taking the expected time of individual activities, the T_E and T_L of events are worked out and indicated in Fig. 3.61 below:

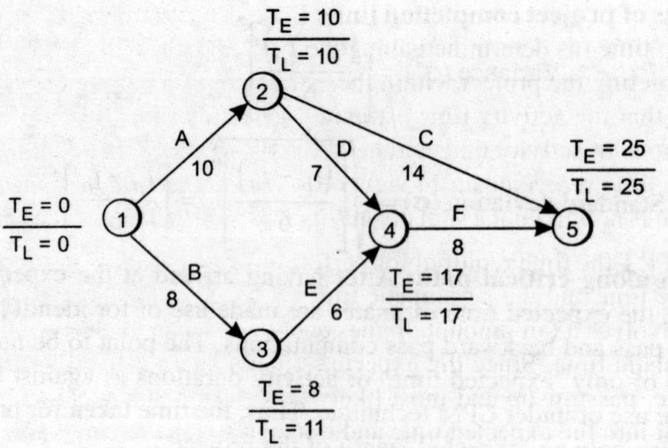

Fig. 3.61

T_E and T_L are equal for events (1), (2), (4) and (5)

Path	*Duration*	*Type*	*Variance*	*Std. deviation*
(1)→(2)→(5)	24 days	Non critical path	(0.44 + 11.11) = 11.55	$\sqrt{11.55}$ = 3.40
(1)→(2)→(4)→(5)	25 days	Critical path	(0.44 + 1.78 + 0.11) = 2.33	$\sqrt{2.33}$ = 1.53
(1)→(2)→(4)→(5)	22 days	Non-critical path	(1.00 + 2.78 + 0.11) = 3.89	$\sqrt{3.89}$ = 1.97

As seen from the above there are two paths viz., (1)→(2)→(5) and (1)→(2)→(4)→(5) which pass through events with zero slack. However, since the duration of path (1)→(2)→(4)→(5) is more, it is chosen as the critical path. The point to be noted is that since we have relied only upon the expected time (t_e) of activities, the variability of the time estimates also has a bearing. The project time along path (1)→(2)→(5) is 24 days, which is just one day short of the project time along the critical path. However, the standard deviation of project time along the path (1)→(2)→(5) is 3.40 as against the standard deviation of project time along the critical path (1)→(2)→(4)→(5) of 1.53. This means that there is more uncertainty surrounding the estimated project time along the path (1)→(2)→(5). This inturn means that the actual time required to complete the project is likely to differ to greater extent along path (1)→(2)→(5) than along the critical path. Thus, in view of the greater susceptibility to variation and also in view of the marginal short fall of one day in project duration, Path, (1)→(2)→(5) assumes equal importance as the critical path.

Thus, the project manager, apart from having a closer control over the activities that lie on the critical path, shall also have a watch over the activities that lie on the path that has a higher variance/ standard deviation.

Probability aspects of project completion time: If the activity times are definite, in all likelihood, the project completion time (as determined along the critical path) will also be definite. The question of probability of completing the project within the estimated project time arises in PERT calculations in view of the reason that the activity time estimates are not definite, but are uncertain. PERT takes into account uncertainties in activity time and hence arrives at three different time estimates based on which a mean activity time is arrived at. In view of the reason that the activity times have variances, the project time (which is nothing but a sum of activity times) also has variance and standard deviation.

We know that in PERT the time required for performing an activity is uncertain. We can at the best estimate the optimistic time and the pessimistic time with reasonable degree of accuracy. Estimating the most likely time involves a fair amount of guesswork and it can take any value with in the range of optimistic and pessimistic time. Since the expected time is again arrived at making use of the three estimates of optimistic, pessimistic and most likely times using statistical technique, the element of guesswork is also built into the expected time and it may also take on any value within a given range.

Such a measure, whose value is not certain, but may fall within a given range is called as 'random variable' in statistics.

Normal distribution. Since the expected times (t_e) of activities are random variables, the expected project time (T_e) obtained by adding the t_e's along the critical path is also a random variable. It has been observed that T_e follows approximately what is called a "normal distribution".

Before understanding what a normal distribution is, it is essential to recollect some interesting and essential topics from statistics.

The first thing to understand is 'frequency polygon' followed by 'frequency curve'.

Let us consider the example of a project, say construction of a highway connecting two cities A & B. Let us assume that a team of engineers complete the project in 30 months. Assume a hypothetical situation where in the team of engineers are asked to carry out the same project for say 100 times. (This is only an imaginary situation with the idea of explaining the underlying concept). In their second attempt, they may complete the project in, say, 25 months, in their third attempt they may complete the project in say 31 months and so on. Let the project is assumed to be repeated for, say 100 times (remember, this is only an imagination and not something that will happen in reality). Let the time taken for completing the project in 100 trails are recorded as per the table shown below.

Trial No.	*Time (in months)*	*Trial No.*	*Time (in months)*	*Trial No.*	*Time (in months)*	*Trial No.*	*Time (in months)*
1	30	26	34	51	36	76	30
2	25	27	45	52	30	77	34
3	31	28	28	53	37	78	36
4	18	29	26	54	29	79	38
5	36	30	19	55	34	80	25
6	32	31	31	56	37	81	35
7	23	32	36	57	20	82	31
8	33	33	30	58	38	83	34
9	37	34	36	59	34	84	26
10	34	35	27	60	35	85	32
11	28	36	29	61	32	86	28
12	38	37	32	62	24	87	21
13	41	38	36	63	33	88	36
14	35	39	24	64	31	89	40
15	25	40	40	65	28	90	43
16	32	41	21	66	40	91	39
17	33	42	33	67	42	92	27
18	30	43	35	68	26	93	37
19	41	44	28	69	22	94	20
20	23	45	31	70	29	95	33
21	31	46	33	71	39	96	41
22	39	47	35	72	47	97	32
23	42	48	29	73	37	98	29
24	44	49	37	74	42	99	27
25	46	50	45	75	35	100	30

As observed from the table, the time taken for completing the project varies from 18 months to 47 months. The data can be complied in a form amenable for presenting in the form of a chart. Accordingly, the data in the table are grouped as under.

(*i*) Time taken to complete the project in a span of 18 to 22 months (both months included) — 7 occasions.

(*ii*) Time taken to complete the project in a span of 23 to 27 months (both months included) — 17 occasions.

(*iii*) Time taken to complete the project in a span of 28 to 32 months (both months included) — 28 occasions.

(*iv*) Time taken to complete the project in a span of 33 to 37 months (both months included) — 31 occasions.

(*v*) Time taken to complete the project in a span of 38 to 42 months (both months included) — 15 occasions.

(*vi*) Time taken to complete the project in a span of 43 to 47 months (both months included) — 6 occasions.

Giving the above results in a tabular form

Range of the time (months)	*No. of occasions*
18, 19, 20, 21, 22	7
23, 24, 25, 26, 27	13
28, 29, 30, 31, 32	28
33, 34, 35, 36, 37	31
38, 39, 40, 41, 42	15
43, 44, 45, 46, 47	6

For the purpose of plotting a simplified graph, we can assume the central value of the time range i.e., we can assume that there were 7 occasions in which the project was completed in 20 months time, 13 occasions in which the project was completed in 25 months time etc. If we make such approximations, the results can be plotted in the form of a diagram as under. (Ref. Fig. 3.62).

The diagram shown in Fig. 3.62 is called frequency polygon.

The range of time, viz., 18 to 22, 23 to 27, 28 to 32 etc., is called in statistics as 'class interval'. Thus the class interval chosen by us is 5.

If the number of trails are sufficiently increased and if the class interval is significantly reduced, the frequency polygon will almost look like a curve and it is called the frequency curve. To draw the frequency curve, the points are joined by a smooth curve instead of by straight lines. (Refer Fig. 3.63).

Probability distribution is the listing of all possible outcomes of an experiment together with their probabilities. We can assume that the hypothetical trails that we have proposed for project completion times is a set of experiments. We have so far seen only the frequency of occurrences of different project times. The next step is to study the probability aspects of project times.

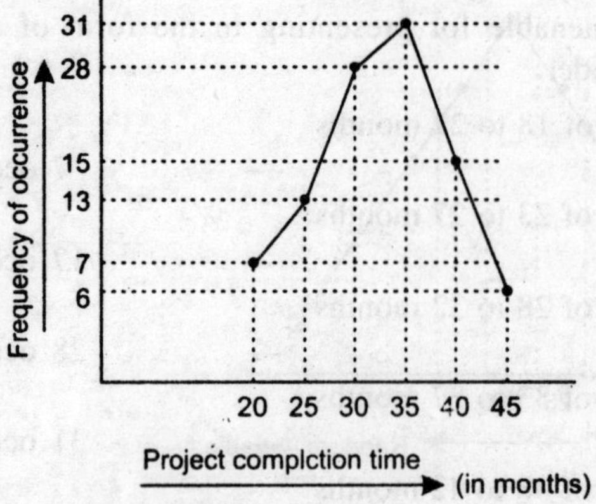

Fig. 3.62. *[Frequency polygon]*

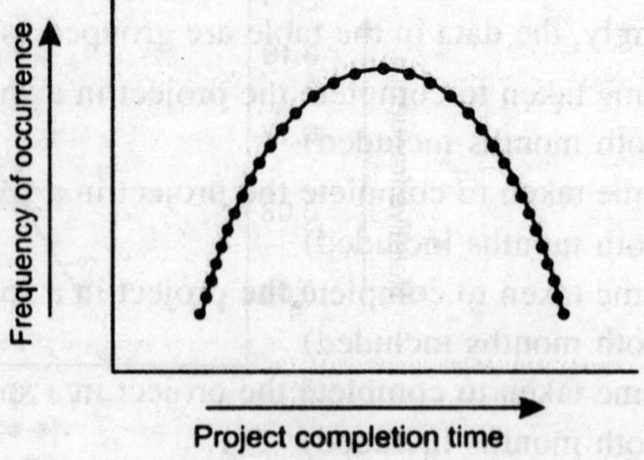

Fig. 3.63. *[Frequency curve]*

Out of the many probability distributions, the normal distribution is very important and plays a major part in statistical inference. This is because of the reason that in practice experimental results very often follow the normal distribution. In general the normal distribution results when there are a large number of independent small factors that influence the final outcome. For example, the time we take to reach home from office will be normally distributed. This is because there are so many factors which influence the time taken to reach home from office. The following are few such factors.

- Weather conditions.
- Place where car is parked and position of other cars in the parking area.
- Road signals along the route.
- Other drivers whom we come across on the way.
- Pedestrians, etc., etc.,

Another important point to be observed is that the so many factors that influence the activity are almost independent of one another. Project completion time is also influenced by many factors, which are independent. Hence the probability distribution of project completion time follows normal distribution. Let us assume a class interval of 3 and tabulate the set of data of a random experiment in a tabular form as under. The data are also plotted in the form of a graph (Ref. Fig. 3.64) which shows time on X-axis and relative frequency on Y-axis. Since the relative frequency of occurrence is nothing but the probability of occurrence, the curve shown in Fig. 3.64 is a probability distribution curve. As the curve is drawn for the data generated in a random experiment, it represents a normal distribution curve.

Range	*Mid point (X)*	*Frequency of occurrence*	*Relative frequency*
16, 17, 18	17	4	4/100 = 0.04
19, 20, 21	20	8	8/100 = 0.08
22, 23, 24	23	12	12/100 = 0.12
25, 26, 27	26	16	16/100 = 0.16
28, 29, 20	29	20	20/100 = 0.20
31, 32, 33	32	16	16/100 = 0.16
34, 35, 36	35	12	12/100 = 0.12
37, 38, 36	38	8	8/100 = 0.08
39, 40, 41	40	4	4/100 = 0.04
		Total 100	1.00

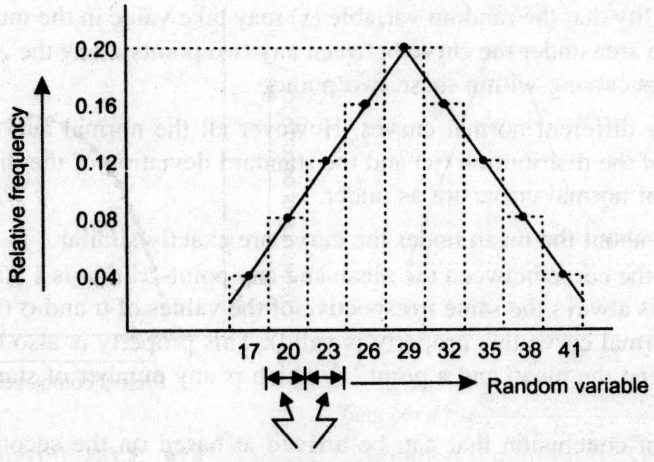

Fig. 3.64

Width of each rectangle in Fig. 3.64 is the same and is equal to the class interval (3). Let us consider any one rectangle, say the rectangle with class interval between 22 and 24. The height of this rectangle is 0.12, which is the relative frequency of mid point 23. Since the sum of all relative frequencies is equal to 1, the area of a given rectangle has the same proportion to the total area of all the rectangle. i.e., the area of rectangle with class interval between 22 and 24 would be 0.12 times the total area of all rectangles (i.e., 12% of the area of all the rectangles).

Referring to Fig. 3.65 it can be assumed without much error that the area of triangle ABC which is out side the curve is equal to the area of triangle CDE which is inside the curve. This is applicable for all the rectangles and hence it can be concluded the area of the rectangle FBDG is equal to the area of portion FAEG, bounded by the interval FG and curve AE. This relationship is applicable to all rectangles and the areas under their respective curves. This means that the area under the curve bounded by the class interval represents the relative frequency of that class. In other words the area under the curve lying between any two vertical lines passing through two points A and B on the X-axis

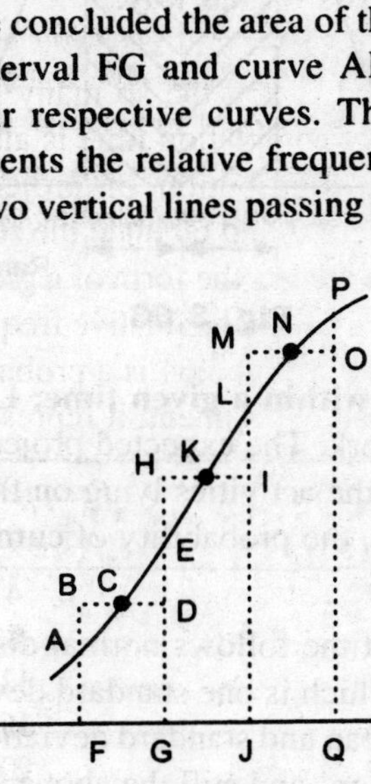

Fig. 3.65

represents the probability that the random variable (x) may take value in the interval bounded by A & B. Thus by finding the area under the curve between any two points along the X-axis, we can find the percentage of values occurring within these two points.

There can be many different normal curves. However all the normal curves are defined by two values *viz*, the mean of the distribution (μ) and the standard deviation of the distribution (σ). Certain important properties of normal curve are as under.

(*i*) The two halves about the mean under the curve are exactly similar.

(*ii*) The area under the curve between the mean and any point-'x' that is 1 standard deviation away from the mean is always the same irrespective of the values of μ and σ (i.e., irrespective of the shape of the normal curve this property is valid). This property is also true for the area under the curve between the mean and a point 'x' which is any number of standard deviations away from the mean.

Thus, the important conclusion that can be arrived at based on the second property of normal curve is that, the area under the normal curve between mean and any point 'X' on X-axis can be identified by knowing distance of the point 'X' from the mean, the distance being expressed in terms of standard deviation.

Some of the properties of normal curve are shown in Figs. 3.66, 3.67, 3.68.

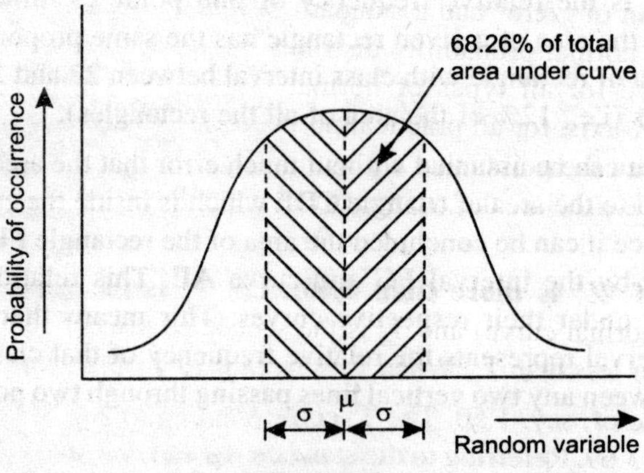

Fig. 3.66

Probability of completing projects within a given time: Let us assume that we have identified the critical path for a given PERT network. The expected project completion time (T_e) is the sum of the expected completion time (t_e) of all the activities lying on the critical path. The activity expected time (t_e) has a probability of 0.5. Hence, the probability of cumulative expected time (T_e) also has a probability of 0.5.

It is assumed the project completion time follows normal distribution. The area under the normal curve between mean and any point 'x' which is one standard deviation away from the mean is always the same, irrespective of the values of mean and standard deviation. The term 'one standard deviation' can be replaced by 'any standard deviation' and still the above statement will hold good. If 'Z' is the number of standard deviations away from the mean for an observation, Z can be represented as,

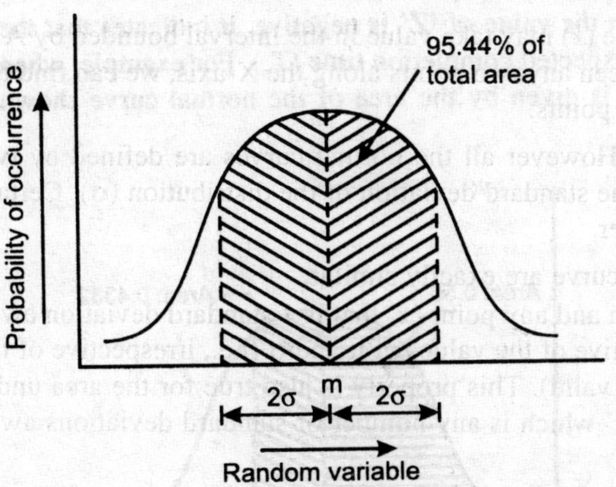

Fig. 3.67

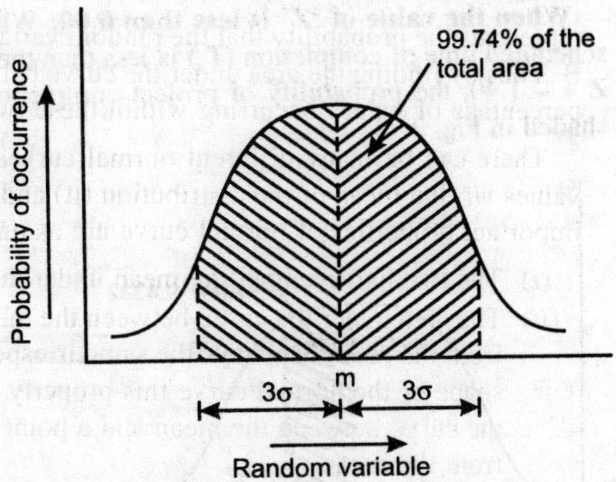

Fig. 3.68

$$Z = \frac{\text{Observed value} - \text{Mean value}}{\text{Standard deviation}}$$

'Z' is known as standardized normal deviation. The value of 'Z' also follows a normal probability distribution with a mean of 'zero' and a standard deviation of 'one'. This probability distribution is known as the standard normal probability distribution and it allows us to use a single table of areas under the normal curve for all types of normal distributions. Though the normal curve extends indefinitely along the X-axis, for all practical purposes, it can be taken that the area under the normal curve is covered between the points that are within three times the standard deviations (3σ) on either side of the mean. To be precise, the area between – 3σ and + 3σ is about 99.74% of the total area under the curve.

When the value of 'Z' is more than 0.00: Let T_e is the expected project completion time (*i.e.*, the mean of the normal curve) and T_s is the scheduled project completion time. T_s can be either equal to or more than or less than T_e. When T_s is more than T_e, the value of 'Z' will be more than zero.

Consider a 'Z' value of, say, 1.50. The T_s corresponding to Z = + 1.50, will lie to the right of the mean as shown in Fig. 3.69. Referring to the standard normal distribution table, (table 3.1, given at the end of the chapter), the area under the normal curve between Z = 0.00 and Z = + 1.50 is 0.4332. The entire area under the normal curve from the left to the point up to Z = + 1.50 gives the probability of completing the project. (refer Fig. 3.70).

Hence, the probability of project completion for Z = + 1.50 can be arrived at by adding 0.50 with the table value for Z = + 1.50.

i.e., $= 0.50 + 0.4332$

i.e., $= 0.9332$

i.e., $= 93.32\%$

When the value of 'Z' is less than 0.00: When the value of 'Z' is negative, it indicates that the scheduled time of completion (T_s) is less than the expected completion time (T_e). For example, when Z = – 1.40, the probability of project completion is given by the area of the normal curve shown shaded in Fig. 3.71.

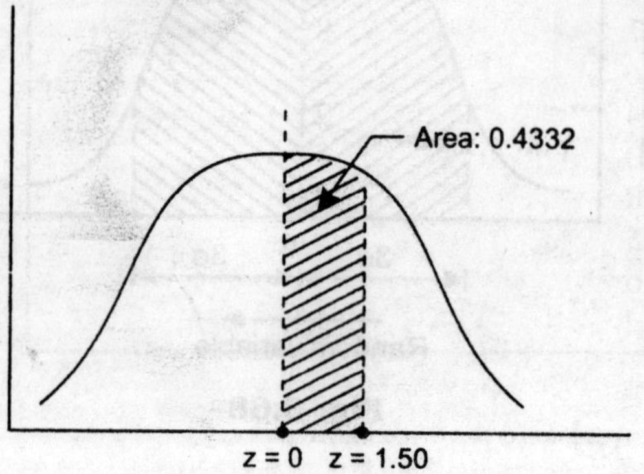

Fig. 3.69

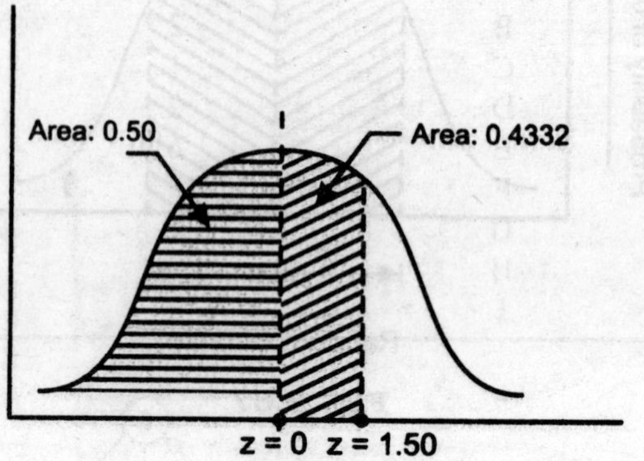

Fig. 3.70

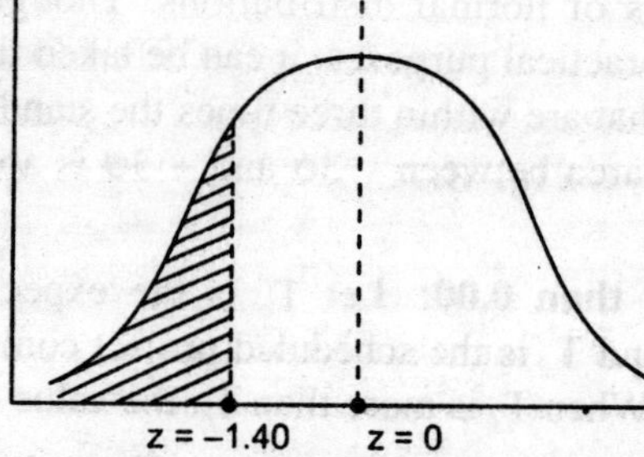

Fig. 3.71

Referring to the standard normal distribution table, we can find the area between the mean (Z = 0.00 and Z = – 1.40). For reading the table value, the negative sign of 'Z' may be ignored and the value for Z = + 1.40 can be taken. This is because of the symmetrical nature of the normal curve. Referring to the table, the value for Z = 1.40 (i.e., Z = + 1.40) is 0.4192. Therefore, the probability of completing the project for a Z value of – 1.40 can be obtained by deducting the table value for Z = 1.40 from 0.50.

i.e., = 0.50 – 0.4192

i.e., = 0.0808

i.e., = 8.08%

Illustration 3.14

For the net work shown in Fig. 3.72 calculate the probability of completing the project in 50 days.

Activity	*Optimistic Time (t_O) [days]*	*Pessimistic time (t_p) [days]*	*Most likely time (t_m) (days)*
A	4	6	4.5
B	2	17	8
C	1	6	2
D	2	4	2.5
E	6	20	8
F	12	20	16
G	6	15	9
H	10	16	12
I	1	2	1.5

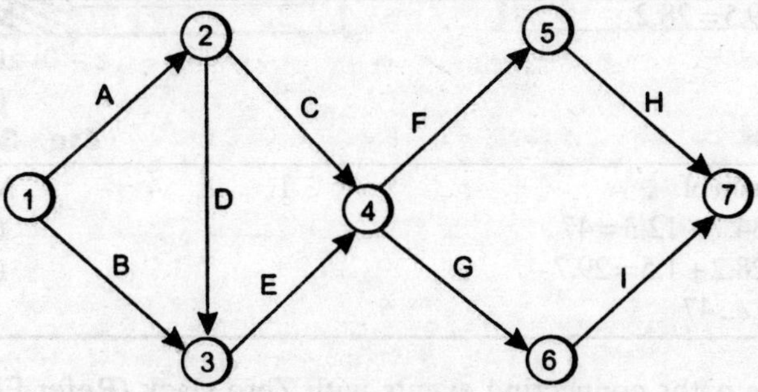

Fig. 3.72

Solution:

Let us first calculate the expected time (t_e) from the given data.

Activity	*Expected time (t_e) =* $\dfrac{t_o + 4t_m + t_p}{6}$
A	4.7
B	8.5
C	2.5
D	4.3
E	9.7
F	16.0
G	9.5
H	12.3
I	1.5

Forward pass computation		*Backward pass computation*	
Event	T_E	*Event*	T_L
1	0	7	47
2	$0+4.7=4.7$	6	$47-1.5=45.5$
3	Maximum of (*a*) $4.7+4.3=9$ (*b*) $0+8.5=8.5$ *i.e.*, $=9$	5	$47-12.3=34.7$
4	Maximum of (*a*) $4.7+2.5=7.2$ (*b*) $9+9.7=18.7$ *i.e.*, $=18.7$	4	Minimum of (*a*) $45.5-9.5=36$ (*b*) $34.7-16=18.7$ *i.e.*, $=18.7$
5	$18.7+16=34.7$	3	$18.7-9.7=9$
6	$18.7+9.5=28.2$	2	Minimum of (*a*) $18.7-2.5=16.2$ (*b*) $9-4.3=4.7$ *i.e.*, 4.7
7	Maximum of (*a*) $34.7+12.3=47$ (*b*) $28.2+1.5=29.7$ *i.e.*, 47	1	Minimum of (*a*) $4.7-4.7=0$ (*b*) $9-8.5=0.5$ *i.e.*, $=0$

The following are the paths connecting events with Zero slack (Refer Fig. 3.73)

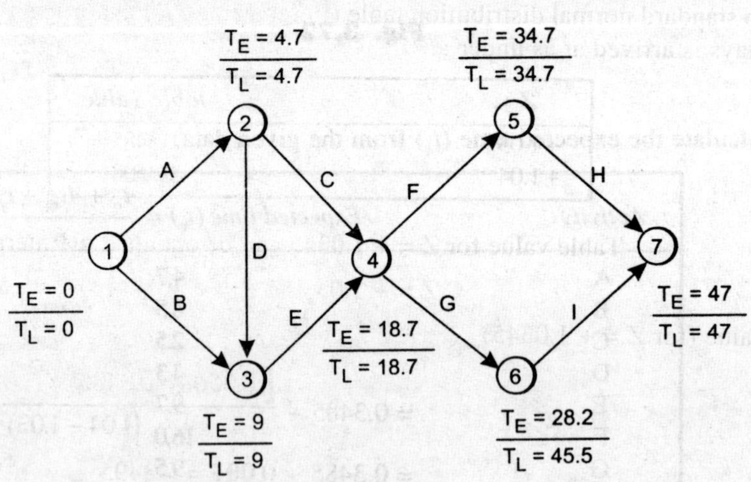

Fig. 3.73

(1)→(2)→(4)→(5)→(7) : 35.5 days.

(1)→(2)→(3)→(4)→(5)→(7) : 47 days.

(1)→(3)→(4)→(5)→(7) : 46 days.

Therefore (1)→(2)→(3)→(4)→(5)→(7) is the critical path. Let us calculate the standard deviation along the critical path.

Activity	t_0	t_p	*Variance* $(\sigma^2) = \left[\frac{t_p - t_0}{6}\right]^2$
A	4	6	0.11
D	2	4	0.11
E	6	20	5.44
F	12	20	1.78
H	10	16	1.00
			$\Sigma = 8.44$

Variance along the critical path $(\sigma^2) = 8.44$

Standard deviation along the critical path $(\sigma) = \sqrt{8.44}$

$= 2.90$

Standard normal deviate $(Z) = (T_s - T_e)/\sigma$

Where T_s = Scheduled time for the completion of project.

T_e = Expected time along critical path.

$Z = (50 - 47)/2.90$

$Z = 1.0345$

Referring to standard normal distribution table (Refer Table 3.1) the probability of completing the project in 50 days is arrived at as under :

Z	*table value*
+1.03	0.3485
+1.04	0.3508

Table value for Z = + 1.0345 can be obtained by interpolating between

Z = + 1.03 and Z = + 1.04

i.e., table value (for Z = + 1.0345)

$$= 0.3485 + \frac{[(0.3508 - 0.3485) \times (1.0345 - 1.03)]}{(1.04 - 1.03)}$$

$$= 0.3485 + 0.001 = 0.3495$$

Therefore, probability of project

Completion (for Z = + 1.0345) = 0.50 + 0.3495

= 0.8495

= 84.95%

Observation: Though the scheduled time for completion of the project is 50 days which is more than the duration along the critical path, (which is the longest path) the probability of completion is below 100% (i.e., 84.95%). This is because of the variability of times estimates in PERT.

Illustration 3.15

For the problem given in illustration 3.14 estimate the probability of completing the project in 50 days along the sub critical path and offer your observations.

Solution :

(1)→(3)→(4)→(5)→(7) is the sub critical path. B, E, F and H are the activities that lie on the sub critical path.

Activity	t_o	t_p	*Variance* = $\left[\frac{(t_p - t_o)}{6}\right]^2$
B	2	17	6.25
E	6	20	5.44
F	12	20	1.78
H	10	16	1.00
			Σ = 14.47

Variance along the sub critical path (σ^2) = 14.47

Standard deviation along the sub critical path (σ) = $\sqrt{14.47}$

$$= 3.80$$

$$\text{Standard normal deviate (Z)} = \frac{T_s - T_e}{\sigma}$$

$$T_s = 50$$

$$T_e = (8.5 + 9.7 + 16 + 12.3)$$

$$= 46.5$$

$$Z = \frac{50 - 46.5}{3.80}$$

$$= + 0.921.$$

Referring to standard normal distribution table, the probability of completing the project in 50 days along the sub critical path is arrived at as under :

Z	*Table value*
+0.92	0.3212
+0.93	0.3238

Table value for Z = + 0.921 can be obtained by interpolating between Z = + 0.92 & Z = + 0.93 i.e., Table value (for Z = 0.921)

$$= 0.3212 + \frac{[(0.3238 - 0.3212) \times (0.921 - 0.92)]}{(0.93 - 0.92)}$$

$$= 0.3212 + 0.00026$$

$$= 0.32146$$

$$= \text{say } 0.3215$$

Therefore, probability

Of project completion (for Z = + 0.921) = 0.50 + 0.3215

$$= 0.8215$$

$$= 82.15\%$$

The probability of completing all the activities that lie along the sub critical path ①→③→④→⑤→⑦ in a span of 50 days is 82.15%.

Observation

①→②→③→④→⑤→⑦ is the critical path which means that the project manager shall devote his attention to ensure that the activities lying on the critical path are not delayed to avoid time-overrun. The expected time taken to complete all the activities that lie on the critical path is 47 days and the probability of completing all the activities that lie on the critical path in 50 days time has been arrived at 84.95% in illustration 3.14. The sub critical path ①→③→④→⑤→⑦ takes 46 days to complete which is just one day short of the expected time along the critical path. However the probability of completing all the activities that lie on the sub critical path in 50 days time has been arrived at 82.15% in illustration 3.15.

Since the probability of completing all the activities that lie along the sub critical path in 50 days time is less than the probability of completing all the activities that lie along the sub critical path in 50 days time, the sub critical path also assumes significance. The activity that is contained in the sub critical path and that is not contained in the critical path is activity-B. Thus, activity-B assumes equal, if not more importance as all other activities that lie on the critical path. The project manager has to devote his attention for this activity also apart from devoting his attention on the activities that lie on the critical path.

Illustration 3.16

For the problem given in illustration 3.14, find out the probability of completing the project in 42 days.

Solution:

Referring to the illustration 3.14, the critical path duration is 47 days (T_e) and the standard deviation along the critical path (σ) is 2.90.

The project is expected to be completed in 42 days (T_s).

$$Z \text{ (for } T_s = 42) = (T_s - T_e)/s$$

$$= (42 - 47)2.90$$

$$= -1.724.$$

Referring to the standard normal distribution table, (Table 3.1) the table value for Z = 1.724 can be arrived at. (Ignoring the negative sign of 'Z')

Z	*Table value*
1.72	0.4573
1.73	0.4582

Interpolating between 1.72 and 1.73, the

Table value for $z = 1.724$ is as under :

$$= 0.4573 + \frac{(0.4582 - 0.4573)}{(1.73 - 1.72)} \times (1.724 - 1.72)$$

$$= 0.4573 + 0.00036$$

$$= 0.45766$$

$$= \text{say } 0.4577$$

Since 'Z' Value is negative, probability

for completing the project in 42 days = 0.50 – 0.4577

$$= 0.0423 = 4.23\%$$

Illustration 3.17

For the problem given in illustration 3.14, find out in how many days the project can be completed with a probability of 95%.

Solution :

For the problem given in illustration 3.14, the critical path duration is 47 days and the standard deviation along the critical path is 2.90.

Since the probability of completion has been given as 95%, T_s will be more than T_e. [Note: the probability of completion is 50% when $T_s = T_e$]

Probability = Table value for 'Z' + 0.50

0.95 = Table value for 'Z' + 0.50

Table value for 'Z' = 0.95 – 0.50 = 0.45

For a table value of 0.45, the value of 'Z' can be calculated referring to the standard normal distribution table.

Table value	*Z*
0.4495	1.64
0.4505	1.65

Interpolating between 0.4495 and 0.4505, the 'Z' value for a table value of 0.45 is as under :

$$Z = 1.64 + \frac{(1.65 - 1.64)}{(0.4505 - 0.4495)} \times (0.4505 - 0.45)$$

$$= 1.64 + 0.005$$

$$= 1.645$$

Then,
$$Z = (T_s - T_e)/\sigma$$
$$1.645 = (T_s - 47)/2.90$$
$$4.7705 = T_s - 47$$
$$T_s = 51.77$$
$$= \text{say, } 52$$

Hence, if the project scheduled time is taken as 52 days, there is 95% probability of completing the project within the scheduled time.

> ***Note:***
>
> When the cumulative normal distribution function table is available, the probability for a given value of 'Z' can be read from the table straight away. The probability for different values of 'Z', in the range of Z = –3.0 to Z = + 3.0 is given in Table 3.2.

3.4 UPDATING OF NETWORK

A network diagram is drawn before the actual implementation of the project is taken up. The project implementation may not always progress as anticipated in the network diagram. Some of the activities may get delayed beyond the expected time of completion due to non-availability of raw material in time, non-availability of required labour, breakdown of machinery, unexpected weather conditions etc., Similarly, some other activities might be finished ahead of the planned schedule due to reasons like availability of additional man-power etc., Thus, the net work diagram that is prepared before project implementation does not remain static but keeps changing. For the network diagram to remain meaningful, it must incorporate in itself all the changes that take place during the actual implementation of the project.

Once the changes that have taken place are incorporated, the original network diagram gets altered and the revised diagram becomes the one that is relevant for further control. The process of incorporating the changes that have already taken place and rescheduling the remaining activities in the form of a revised and updated network diagram is known as updating of network.

The following illustration will explain the methodology of nodes.

Illustration 3.18.

The diagram shown in Fig. 3.74 represents the original network drawn for a project. The expected time of each activity in weeks is shown in the diagram. The Earliest Start Time (T_E) and the Latest Finish Time (T_L) of all the events are also shown at the respective nodes.

The critical path is (1)→(2)→(4)→(5)→(6) as indicated in the diagram and the project completion time is 25 weeks (6 + 9 + 6 + 4).

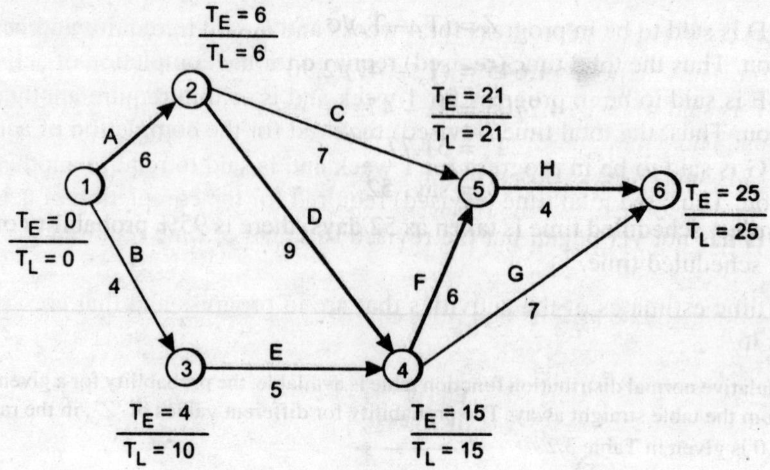

Fig. 3.74

The progress of project implementation was examined at the end of 12 weeks and the observations are as under.

(*a*) Activities-A, B and E have been completed.

(*b*) Activity-D has been in progress for 4 weeks and requires 7 more weeks for completion.

(*c*) Activity-F has been in progress for 1 week and requires 4 more weeks for completion.

(*d*) Activity-G has been in progress for 1 week and requires 7 more weeks for completion.

(*e*) Activity-C has been in progress for 4 weeks and requires 5 more weeks for completion.

(*f*) It has been reassessed that activity H needs 6 weeks for completion.

Update the network diagram based on the given data. Draw a revised and updated network as at the end of the 12th week.

Solution:

The progress as at the end of 12 weeks has been given. Let us draw a revised network diagram assuming that a new project begins at the end of 12 weeks. Activities A, B and E have already been completed and hence they do not form part of the revised network diagram.

Event-2 is the starting event for the revised network diagram (Fig. 3.75) after deleting activities A, B and E.

- **Activity-C is said to be in progress for 4 weeks and is said to require another 5 more weeks for completion. Thus the total time (revised) required for the completion of activity-C is 9 weeks.**

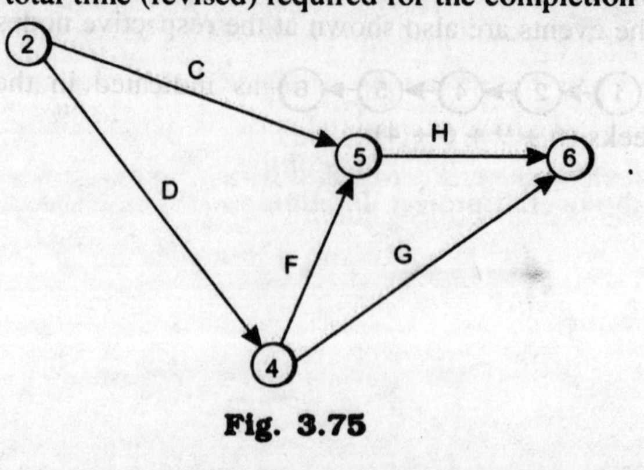

Fig. 3.75

- Activity-D is said to be in progress for 4 weeks and is said to require another 7 more weeks for completion. Thus the total time (revised) required for the completion of activity-D is 11 weeks.
- Activity-F is said to be in progress for 1 week and is said to require another 4 more weeks for completion. Thus, the total time (revised) required for the completion of activity-F is 5 weeks.
- Activity-G is said to be in progress for 1 week and is said to require another 7 more weeks for completion. Thus, the total time (revised) required for the completion of activity-G is 8 weeks.
- Activity-H has not yet begun but the revised estimate of time required for its completion is 6 weeks.

The revised time estimates of the activities that are in progress and that are yet to commence are given in Fig. 3.76.

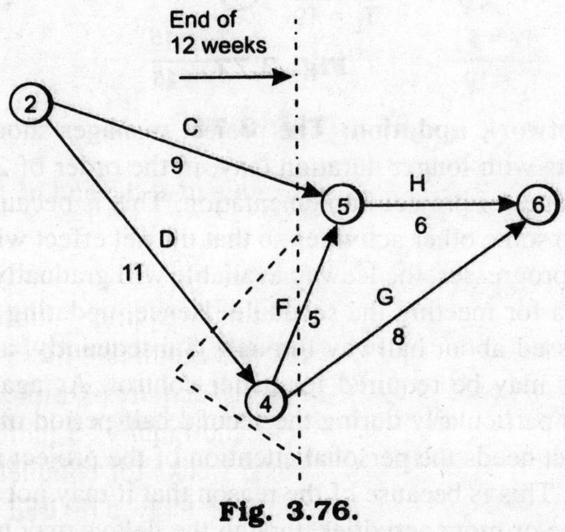

Fig. 3.76.

Reassessment of time estimates was done at the end of 12 weeks. Hence the revised network diagram should be so drawn that it starts from the beginning of the 13th week onwards. Fig. 3.77 shows the revised network diagram with T_E of event-2 as 12 (which means that from the start of event 1, 12 weeks have lapsed and event-2 starts at the end of 12th week). Since T_E for event-2 has been taken as 12 weeks, only the remaining time period required for the completion of activities C, D, F & G (after the end of 12 weeks) is taken into account.

The network diagram shown in Fig. 3.77 is what is relevant at the end of 12th week. Hence this diagram should be used for further monitoring of the project. The critical path for the revised network diagram is then arrived at by doing forward pass and backward pass computation.

(2)→(4)→(5)→(6) is the critical path and the duration along the critical path is 17 weeks (7 + 4 + 6).

Observation: The project duration along critical path as per the original network diagram was 25 weeks. At end of 12 weeks, we have revised the network diagram based on the revised time estimates and the project duration along the critical path of the revised network diagram has been arrived at 17 weeks. Thus, ineffect the overall project duration has increased from 25 weeks to 29 weeks (12 + 17).

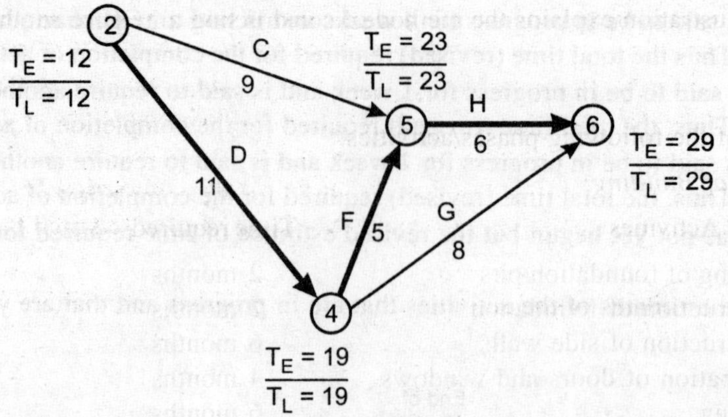

Fig. 3.77

General remarks on network updation: The project manager should know when to update a network diagram. In projects with longer duration (say, in the order of 2 or more years) updation is not required in the initial stages of project implementation. This is because, delays in some activities can be offset by speeding up some other activities so that the net effect will be minimum. However as the project implementation progresses, the leeway available will gradually get reduced and the project manager has to stretch extra for meeting the schedule. Hence, updating is required after the project implementation has progressed about halfway through. Subsequently, as the project approaches its fag end, frequent updations may be required for better control. As against a long-duration project which needs more attention particularly during the second half period of the project implementation time, a short-duration project needs the personal attention of the project manager right from the start and throughout its duration. This is because of the reason that it may not be possible to absorb all the delays that may occur in one or more activities, though the delays may be small.

Apart from the need for updating the network to study the effects of delays and early completions of a few activities on the project completion time, updating of network is also necessitated whenever the project time estimates are reassessed as the project is in progress.

The updated network offers the project manager with the latest information about the happenings till the date of updation and the revised future estimate of what is likely to happen. It is likely that even the path that is once identified as critical path may get shifted and the updated network diagram may indicate a different critical path. Updating, thus indicates that the project manager is alert and on the move.

3.5 LINE OF BALANCE TECHNIQUE

Line of balancing technique is a managerial technique for ascertaining the progress of various phases (or activities) of a project on any particular date. LOB technique is an extension of Gnatt chart.

Since LOB technique indicates the progress of various phases of a project on a particular date, it provides the management the facility of applying the concept of 'management by exception'. The LOB chart gives a pictorial view of the progress of the activities. Using the LOB chart, we will be able to identify those activities that are progressing as per the plan, the activities that are lagging behind the schedule and also the activities that progress ahead of the schedule.

The following illustration explains the method of constructing a LOB chart.

Illustration 3.19

A project consists of the following phases/activities:

A. Construction of Building:

Activities	Time required
1. Digging of foundation pits	2 months
2. Construction of foundation	2 months
3. Construction of side walls	6 months
4. Fabrication of doors and windows	4 months
5. Roofing	6 months
6. Fixing of doors and windows	2 months
7. Wall finishing	4 months
8. Flooring	6 months
9. Plumbing and wiring	3 months
B. Machinery installation:	
10. Fabrication of machine	8 months
11. Erection and commissioning of machine	3 months

The project was commenced on 1st January, 1995. On 31st May 1996, the project manager wants to study the progress of the project using LOB chart. Construct a LOB chart as on 31st May 1996 and offer your comments.

Solution:

The activities involved in the project and their durations are given. Another information required is the precedence, succession and concurrence relations between the different activities. In the absence of information on this, the following are assumed.

Digging of foundation	: First activity.
Construction of foundation	: Follows 'Digging of foundation'
Construction of side walls	: Follows construction of foundation
Fabrication of doors and windows	: This activity is independent of other activities and can start at any time. The only constraint is that the doors and windows must be ready by the time they are required for fixing. It is assumed that this activity starts after 'Construction of foundation'
Roofing	: Follows construction of side walls
Fixing of doors and windows Wall finishing Flooring Plumbing and wiring	: Follows 'Roofing'; All these four activities can be undertaken simultaneously and hence are assumed to start concurrently after the completion of 'Roofing'
Fabrication of machine	: Fabricated machine should be readily available for erection by the time the flooring work is completed.

Since the machine fabrication time is 8 months and the time taken for flooring is 6 months, it is assumed that the machine fabrication work starts 2 months ahead of the start of flooring work.

Erection and commissioning : Follows 'Fabrication of machine'

The following are the steps for arriving at the LOB chart.

(*a*) Drawing the plan of operations indicating all the phase/activities in accordance with their precedence, succession, concurrence relationships.

(*b*) Construction of the Objective chart.

(*c*) Construction of the Progress chart.

The plan of operations: This diagram is drawn to some scale using the precedence, succession, concurrence relationships among the activities. Fig. 3.78 shows the plan of operations for the given problem. Since the project is said to have commenced on 01/01/1995, the same is taken as the starting point for the plan of operations. All the given 11 activities are represented on the plan of operations following the precedence, succession and concurrence rules. The length of the line representing an activity represents the duration of the activity. Fig. 3.78 is self explanatory. As seen from Fig. 3.78, the project duration extends up to 31/12/1996. Thus, the project duration is 24 months (i.e., starting from 01/01/1995 and ending on 31/12/1996).

The Objective Chart: The objective chart for the given problem is shown Fig. 3.79. The objective chart consists of two horizontal lines. The horizontal line at the bottom represents the starting point for any activity while the horizontal line at the top represents the end of all activities. The gap between the two horizontal lines (which can be chosen arbitrarily) represents 100% completion of all activities. All the given 11 activities are drawn in the objective chart starting from the bottom horizontal line and ending up with the top horizontal line.

- Activity—1 starts on 01/01/1995 and it takes 2 months to complete the activity. Hence, this activity will be completed by the end of February 1995. This is represented on the Objective Chart by a straight line joining the two points, *viz*., the beginning of January at the bottom horizontal line end of February at the top horizontal line.
- Activity—2 starts at the end of activity — *i.e*., at the beginning of March 1995 and it takes 2 months time to complete this activity. Hence activity — 2 will be completed by the end of April 1995. This is represented on the objective chart by a straight line joining the beginning of March at the bottom horizontal line and the end of April at the top horizontal line.
- All other activities are represented on the objective chart following the above procedure. The last activity, (activity—11) starts at the beginning of November 1996 and ends at the end of December 1996.
- Though we have represented the activities by way of a straight line joining the beginning and end points, it is possible that the activity may take a curvilinear shape instead of a straight line. If so, the activity will be represented by a suitable curve.

The progress chart : The progress chart represents the progress of the activities on a particular date. Fig. 3.80 gives the progress chart for the given problem. There are 11 activities in the given project. All the 11 activities are represented on the horizontal axis of the chart at some chosen intervals. The vertical axis of the chart represents the percentage of completion of the activities. On the vertical axis, 100% completion is represented by choosing some scale.

After having marked the activities 1 to 11 on the horizontal axis and 100% completion point on the vertical axis (to some scale), the next thing to be done is to choose and the of study, *i.e.*, the date on which the progress of the activities is to be studied. The date of study has been given in the problem as 31/05/1996.

Draw a vertical line (shown dotted) on the objective chart at the point representing the end of May, 1996. The date-of-study-line intersects the activities—6, 7, 8, 9 and 10. This indicates that as on 31/05/1996, these five activities should have been at different stages of progress as indicated by the points of intersection with the date-of-study line. The stage of progress that ought to have been achieved as per the original plan for these five activities as on 31/05/1996 can be read from the objective chart by reading the percentage of completion at the intersection points. Reading from the objective chart, the following are the progress that ought to have been achieved, had the progress beeen on the lines as originally planned.

Activity — 6 : 50%

Activity — 7 : 25%

Activity — 8 : 16.67%

Activity — 9 : 33.33%

Activity — 10 : 37.50%

As per the original plan, activities-1, 2, 3, 4 and 5 should have been completed before 31/05/1996 while activity-11 would not have started as on 31/05/1996. Looking at the objective chart, it can be inferred that activities to the left of the date-of-study line ought to have been completed 100%, while activities to the right of the date-of-study line would not have commenced as on 31/05/1996.

Thus, we have the following information from the objective chart about the planned progress (or required progress) of different activities.

Activity — 1 : 100%
Activity — 2 : 100%
Activity — 3 : 100%
Activity — 4 : 100%
Activity — 5 : 100%
Activity — 6 : 50%
Activity — 7 : 25%
Activity — 8 : 16.67%
Activity — 9 : 33.33%
Activity — 10 : 37.50%
Activity — 11 : 0% (not yet started)

Line of balance (or line representing the required progress of work) can be drawn using the above data. Refer Fig. 3.80 which shows the line of balance which is drawn using the above data.

After having drawn the LOB, the next step is to draw the actual progress of different activities and hence the chart is known as the progress chart. The progress of each activity as on the date of study (31/05/1996) is represented by drawing vertical bars (shown by hatched line). The heights of these vertical bars representing the actual progress of different activities are arrived at as under.

- For any activity that has already been completed as on the date of study, 100% progress has already been achieved.

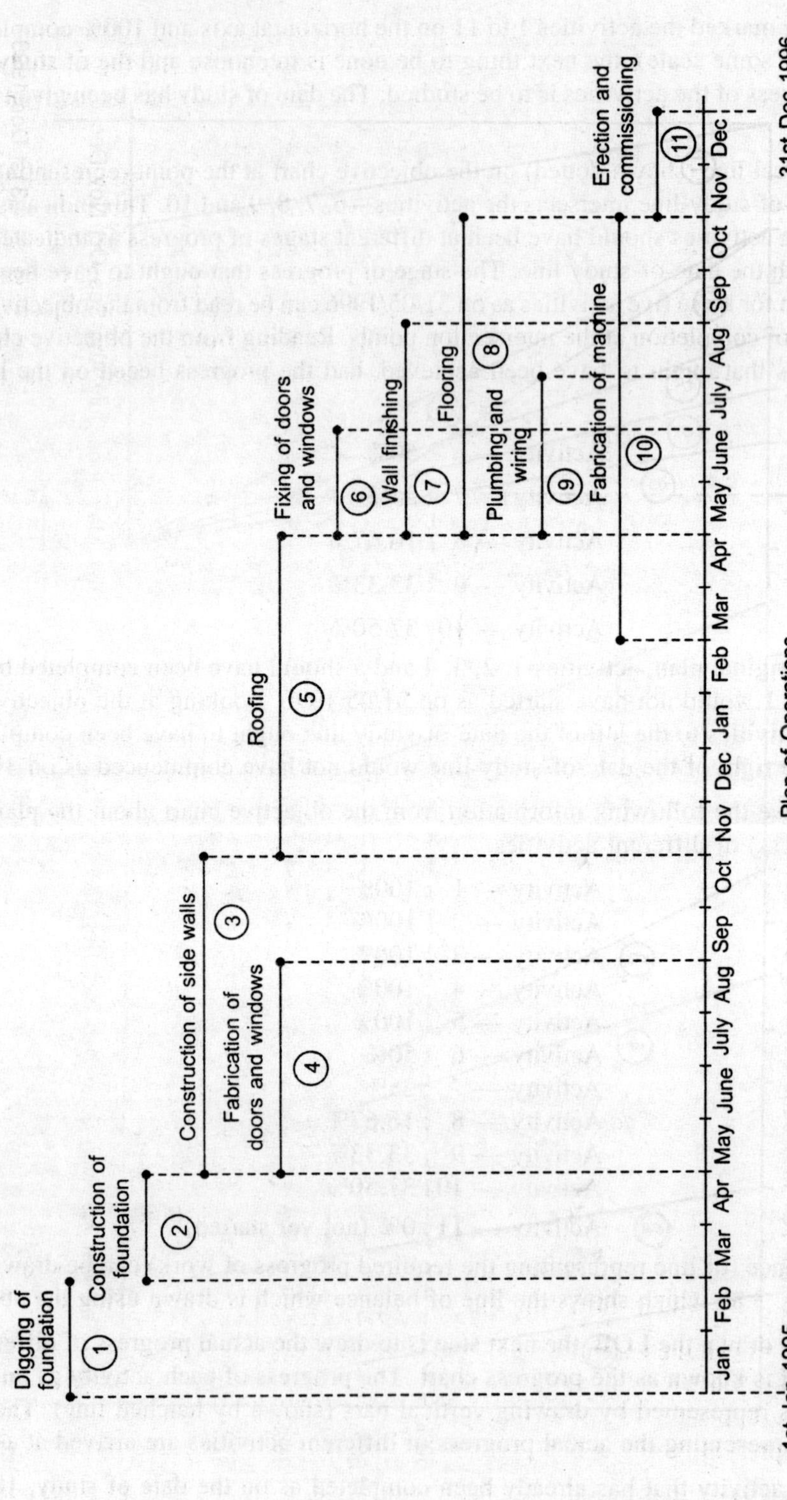

Plan of Operations

Fig. 3.78

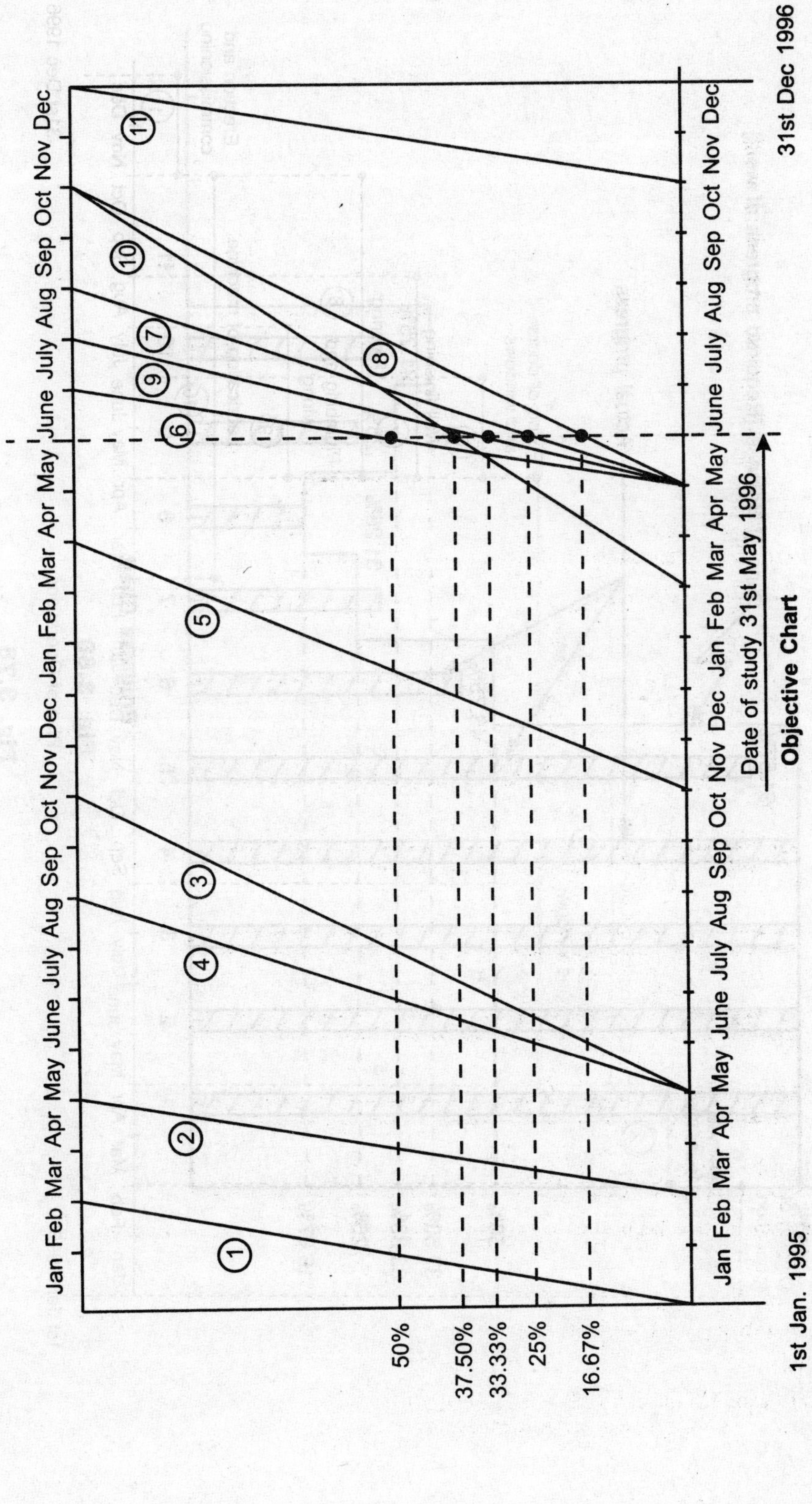
Jan Feb Mar Apr May June July Aug Sep Oct Nov Dec Jan Feb Mar Apr May June July Aug Sep Oct Nov Dec
1 2 3 4 5 6 7 8 9 10 11
50%
37.50%
33.33%
25%
16.67%
1st Jan. 1995
Date of study 31st May 1996
31st Dec 1996
Objective Chart

Fig. 3.79

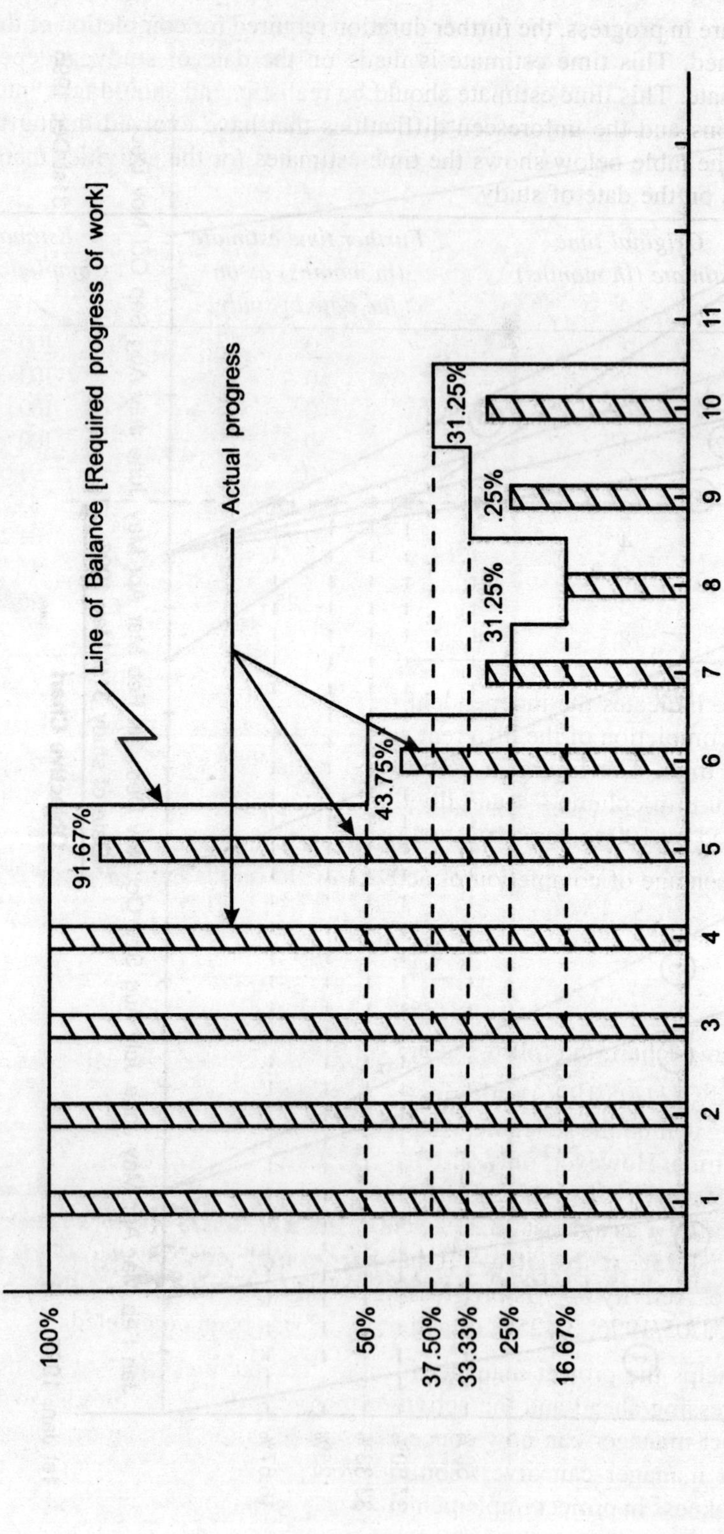

Fig. 3.80 Progress Chart

- For activities that are in progress, the further duration required for completion of these activities are to be ascertained. This time estimate is made on the date of study, independent of the original time estimate. This time estimate should be realistic, and should take into account the prevailing conditions and the unforeseen difficulties that have evolved during the course of implementation. The table below shows the time estimates for the activities that have not yet been completed as on the date of study.

Activity No.	*Original time estimate (in months)*	*Further time estimate (in months) as on the date of study*	*Estimated Completion (%)*
1	2	0	100
2	2	0	100
3	6	0	100
4	4	0	100
5	6	0.5	91.67
6	2	1.125	43.75
7	4	2.75	31.25
8	6	5	16.67
9	3	2.25	25
10	8	5.5	31.25

Column-3 of the table indicates the independent time estimate made on the date of study for the further time needed for completion of the different activities. Column—4 indicates the percentage of completion in terms of time. The figure in column—4 is arrived at by subtracting the figure in column—3 from the figure in column—4 and dividing the figure by the figure in column—2. The quotient is then multiplied by 100 to convert it to a percentage.

For example, the percentage of completion of activity—7 as on the date of study is given by:

$$\frac{(4-2.75)}{4} \times 100$$

$$= 31.75\%$$

Referring to the progress chart, the following are the observations :

As on the date of study, (31/05/1996) activities—1, 2, 3 and 4 have been completed; activities — 5, 6, 9 and 10 are lagging behind the schedule. As per the original schedule, activity — 5 should have been completed by this time. However, only 91.67% of activity — 5 has been completed. As per the original schedule, 50% of activity — 6 should have been completed against which only 43.75% has so far been completed. Similarly, as against 33.33%, only 25% of activity — 9 has been completed and as against 37.50%, only 31.25% of activity — 10 has been completed. Activity — 8 is progressing as per the original schedule. Activity — 7 is progressing ahead of the schedule. As against the planned completion of 25% by 31/05/1996, 31.25% of activity — 7 has been completed.

The progress chart helps the project manager identify the activities that are lagging behind, the activities that are progressing ahead and the activities that are progressing in tune with the original schedule etc. The project manager can now concentrate more of the lagging activities. In the given illustration, the project manager can divert some of the resources of activity—7 to the lagging activities so that the slackness in project implementation can be made good or at least controlled to the extent possible.

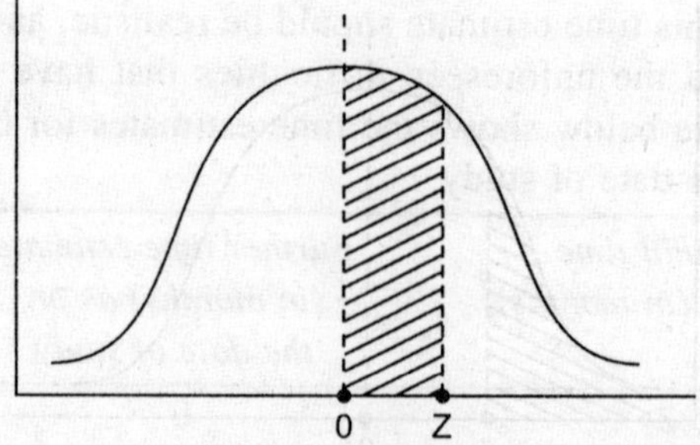

Fig. 3.81

Table 3.1 Area under the Normal Curve

Z	*0.00*	*0.01*	*0.02*	*0.03*	*0.04*	*0.05*	*0.06*	*0.07*	*0.08*	*0.09*
0.0	0.0000	0.0040	0.0080	0.0120	0.0160	0.0199	0.0239	0.0279	0.0319	0.0359
0.1	0.0398	0.0438	0.0478	0.0517	0.0557	0.0596	0.0636	0.0675	0.0714	0.0753
0.2	0.0793	0.0832	0.0871	0.0910	0.0948	0.0987	0.1026	0.1064	0.1103	0.1141
0.3	0.1179	0.1217	0.1255	0.1293	0.1331	0.1368	0.1406	0.1443	0.1480	0.1517
0.4	0.1554	0.1591	0.1628	0.1664	0.1700	0.1736	0.1772	0.1808	0.1844	0.1879
0.5	0.1915	0.1950	0.1985	0.2019	0.2054	0.2088	0.2123	0.2157	0.2190	0.2224
0.6	0.2257	0.2291	0.2324	0.2357	0.2389	0.2422	0.2454	0.2486	0.2517	0.2549
0.7	0.2580	0.2611	0.2642	0.2673	0.2704	0.2734	0.2764	0.2794	0.2923	0.2852
0.8	0.2881	0.2910	0.2939	0.2967	0.2995	0.3023	0.3051	0.3078	0.3106	0.3133
0.9	0.3159	0.3186	0.3212	0.3238	0.3264	0.3289	0.3315	0.3340	0.3365	0.3389
1.0	0.3413	0.3438	0.3461	0.3485	0.3508	0.3531	0.3554	0.3577	0.3599	0.3621
1.1	0.3643	0.3665	0.3686	0.3708	0.3749	0.3749	0.3770	0.3790	0.3810	0.3830
1.2	0.3849	0.3869	0.3888	0.3907	0.3944	0.3944	0.3962	0.3980	0.3997	0.4015
1.3	0.4032	0.4049	0.4066	0.4082	0.4155	0.4155	0.4131	0.4147	0.4162	0.4177
1.4	0.4192	0.4207	0.4222	0.4236	0.4265	0.4265	0.4279	0.4292	0.4306	0.4319
1.5	0.4332	0.4345	0.4357	0.4370	0.4382	0.4394	0.4406	0.4418	0.4429	0.4441
1.6	0.4452	0.4463	0.4474	0.4484	0.4495	0.4505	0.4515	0.4525	0.4535	0.4545
1.7	0.4554	0.4564	0.4573	0.4582	0.4591	0.4599	0.4608	0.4616	0.4625	0.4633
1.8	0.4641	0.4649	0.4656	0.4664	0.4671	0.4678	0.4686	0.4693	0.4699	0.4706
1.9	0.4713	0.4719	0.4726	0.4732	0.4738	0.4744	0.4750	0.4756	0.4791	0.4767
2.0	0.4772	0.4778	0.4783	0.4788	0.4793	0.4798	0.4803	0.4808	0.4812	0.4817
2.1	0.4821	0.4826	0.4830	0.4834	0.4838	0.4842	0.4846	0.4850	0.4854	0.4857
2.2	0.4861	0.4864	0.4868	0.4871	0.4875	0.4878	0.4881	0.4884	0.4887	0.4890
2.3	0.4893	0.4896	0.4898	0.4901	0.4904	0.4906	0.4909	0.4911	0.4913	0.4916
2.4	0.4918	0.4920	0.4922	0.4925	0.4927	0.4929	0.4931	0.4932	0.4934	0.4936
2.5	0.4938	0.4940	0.4941	0.4943	0.4945	0.4946	0.4948	0.4949	0.4951	0.4952
2.6	0.4953	0.4955	0.4956	0.4957	0.4959	0.4960	0.4961	0.4962	0.4963	0.4964
2.7	0.4965	0.4966	0.4967	0.4968	0.4969	0.4970	0.4971	0.4972	0.4973	0.4974
2.8	0.4974	0.4975	0.4976	0.4977	0.4977	0.4978	0.4979	0.4979	0.4980	0.4981
2.9	0.4981	0.4982	0.4982	0.4983	0.4984	0.4984	0.4985	0.4985	0.4986	0.4986
3.0	0.4987	0.4987	0.4987	0.4988	0.4988	0.4989	0.4989	0.4989	0.4990	0.4990

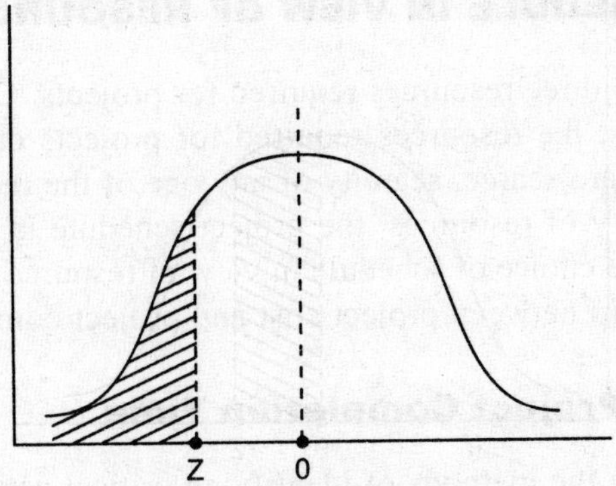

Fig. 3.82

Table 3.2. The Cumulative Normal Distribution Function

Z	*Probability*	Z	*Probability*
0.00	0.5000	0.00	0.5000
−0.10	0.4602	+0.10	0.5398
−0.20	0.4207	+0.20	0.5783
−0.30	0.3821	+0.30	0.6179
−0.40	0.3446	+0.40	0.6554
−0.50	0.3085	+0.50	0.6915
−0.60	0.2743	+0.60	0.7257
−0.70	0.2420	+0.70	0.7580
−0.80	0.2119	+0.80	0.7881
−0.90	0.1841	+0.90	0.8159
−1.00	0.1587	+1.00	0.8413
−1.10	0.1357	+1.10	0.8643
−1.20	0.1151	+1.20	0.8849
−1.30	0.0968	+1.30	0.9032
−1.40	0.0807	+1.40	0.9192
−1.50	0.0668	+1.50	0.9332
−1.60	0.0548	+1.60	0.9452
−1.70	0.0446	+1.70	0.9554
−1.80	0.0359	+1.80	0.9641
−1.90	0.0287	+1.90	0.9713
−2.00	0.0228	+2.00	0.9773
−2.10	0.0179	+2.10	0.9821
−2.20	0.0139	+2.20	0.9861
−2.30	0.0107	+2.30	0.9893
−2.40	0.0082	+2.40	0.9918
−2.50	0.0062	+2.50	0.9938
−2.60	0.0047	+2.60	0.9953
−2.70	0.0035	+2.70	0.9965
−2.80	0.0026	+2.80	0.9974
−2.90	0.0019	+2.90	0.9981
−3.00	0.0014	+3.00	0.9987

3.6 CHOICE OF A SCHEDULE IN VIEW OF RESOURCE CONSTRAINTS

Time, men and material are the three resources required for projects. Out of these, men and material can be bought for a cost. Thus, the resources required for projects can be represented in terms of cost and time. Since resources are scarce, scarcity of any one of the resources will affect the project schedule. When there is scarcity of resources, the project schedule is realigned to suit the resource availability. Before studying the choice of schedule in view of resource constraints, it would be better if we understand the relationship between project cost and project completion time.

3.6.1 Project Cost Vs Project Completion Time

We have so far discussed about the methods of identifying critical activities in a project. As we are now aware, critical activities are the activities that deserve maximum attention of the project manager since any delay in completing these activities will lead to delay in project completion time. The objective of identifying critical activities in a project is to ensure that the project is completed in the shortest possible time by proper monitoring and control of the critical activities. Why should the project manager aim at completing the project at the shortest possible time ? There are two reasons for it, viz.,

- Delay in project implementation invariably results in cost-overrun.
- Delayed project implementation means delay in getting return on the investment made.

Thus, it is the cost consideration that prompts the project manager to aim at time reduction. The relationship between cost and time is not that simple. It can not be said that time reduction will always lead to cost reduction. If a particular activity can be completed at a certain cost in a normal time, the activity may cost less or more when its completion time is shortened. This depends upon the nature of the activity and the resource used for completing the activity.

Usually, the cost of a project goes up when the project time is reduced. The reason for the increase in cost is due to additional resources required to be engaged for bringing down the project time. Such additional resources normally cost proportionately higher, which leads to the overall increase in the project cost. This fact can be verified in our day to day activities. The journey by express buses/trains costs more than the journey by ordinary buses/trains. An express bus/train takes you to the destination faster i.e., there is reduction in time. One has to pay extra fare for reduction in time, because it costs more for the transport authorities to cut short the journey time. They have to divert additional resources which will cost proportionately higher.

Another instance that one comes across is the wages offered for over-time work. An employee who works at a wage of say, Rs. 160.00 per day of 8 hour work duration (which works out to Rs. 20.00 per hour) demands higher rate of wage of say, Rs. 30.00 per hour if he works extra hours over and above the normal duration of 8 hours. Thus, on a particular day if he works for ten hours in a day, the two hours that he worked extra will cost the employer Rs. 60.00. In otherwords, the employer would have to pay additionally Rs. 10.00 for every hour of additional work done by the employee. It should be noted that the employee is not going to produce any extra output during the extra time he works in a day. His output during the extra time will remain only at the level of his normal output. (Perhaps, he may give lesser output than his normal output in view of fatigue!)

3.6.2 Normal Time and Crash Time

For any activity, two time estimates can be made, viz., the normal time and the crash time. Normal time of an activity is that time of completion, any increase beyond which is not likely to result in cost reduction. Crash time of an activity is that time of completion which can not be reduced further, irrespective of cost considerations i.e., even if one is prepared to spend additional cost towards speedy completion of the activity, it is not feasible to reduce the time limit below the crash time. Fig. 3.83 represents the Cost Vs Time relationship of an activity.

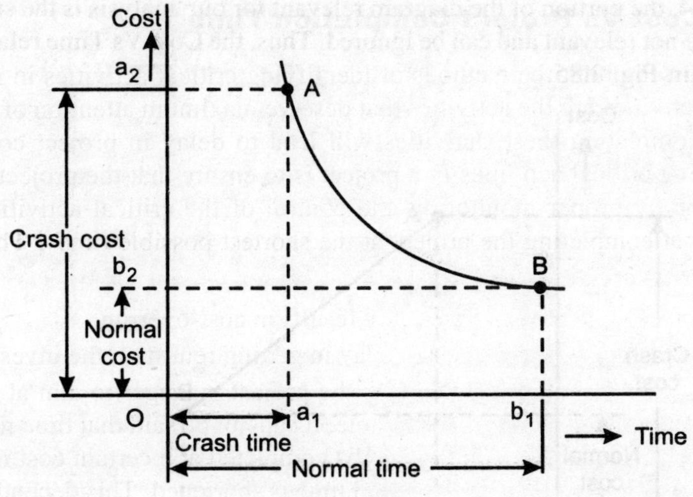

Fig. 3.83

The shape of the curve-AB (Refer Fig. 3.83) reveals that the cost of completing the activity can not be reduced below 'ob_2' even if more time than 'ob_1' is allowed. Also, the duration of the activity cannot be reduced below 'oa_1' even if we are prepared to spend extra amount towards speedy completion of the project.

The curve shown in Fig. 3.83 can be approximated to a pattern of three straight lines as shown in Fig. 3.84 for the purpose of simplifying further analysis. (line AA_1 is parallel to Y-axis and line BB_1 is parallel to X-axis).

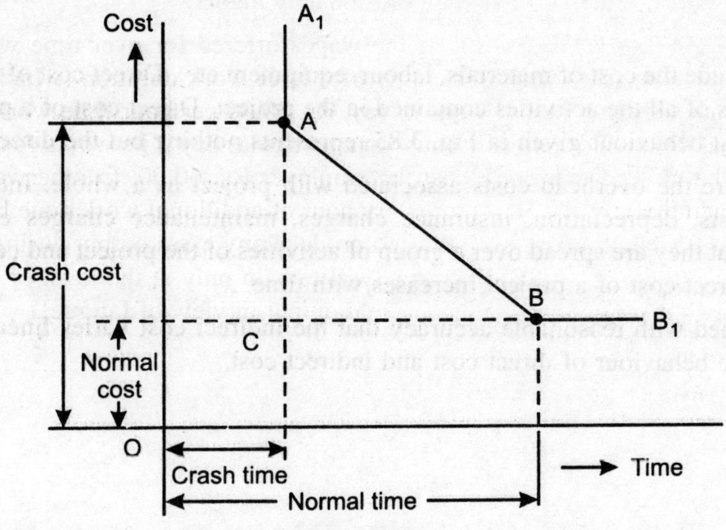

Fig. 3.84

Line-AB represents the behaviour of cost between normal time and crash time and the slope of this line is called cost-slope. Hence, cost-slope can be give by the following relation.

$$\text{Cost-slope} = AC/BC$$

i.e.,

$$= \frac{\text{Crash cost} - \text{Normal cost}}{\text{Normal time} - \text{Crash time}}$$

3.6.3 Direct Cost and Indirect Cost

Referring to Fig. 3.84, the portion of the diagram relevant for our analysis is the straight line-AB. Line AA_1 and line BB_1 are not relevant and can be ignored. Thus, the Cost Vs Time relationship will assume the shape as shown in Fig. 3.85.

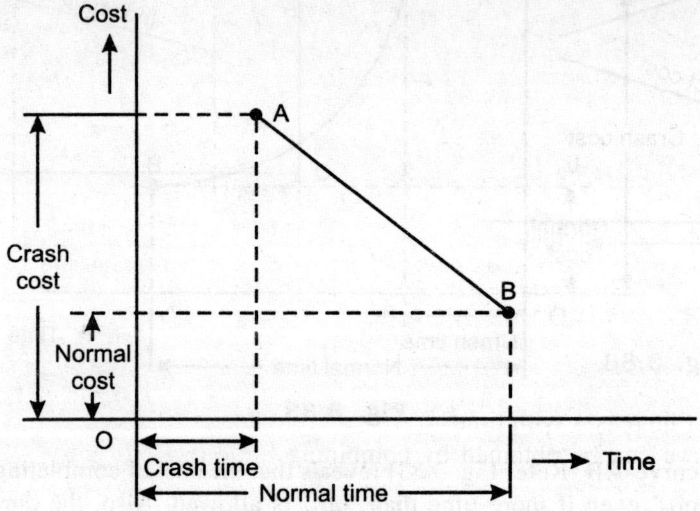

Fig. 3.85

The cost of a project comprises of two components *viz.,*

Direct Cost

and

Indirect Cost

Direct Cost include the cost of materials, labour, equipment etc., Direct cost of a project is the sum total of direct costs of all the activities contained in the project. Direct cost of a project reduces with time. The time-cost behaviour given in Fig. 3.85 represents nothing but the direct cost.

Indirect costs are the overhead costs associated with project as a whole. Indirect cost includes administrative costs, depreciation, insurance charges, maintenance charges etc., The nature of indirect costs is that they are spread over a group of activities of the project and can not be calculated activity-wise. Indirect cost of a project increases with time.

It can be assumed with reasonable accuracy that the indirect cost varies linearly with time. Fig. 3.86 represents the behaviour of direct cost and indirect cost.

3.6.4 Total Cost

The total cost of a project is the sum of direct cost and indirect cost. We have seen that

- The direct cost decreases with time

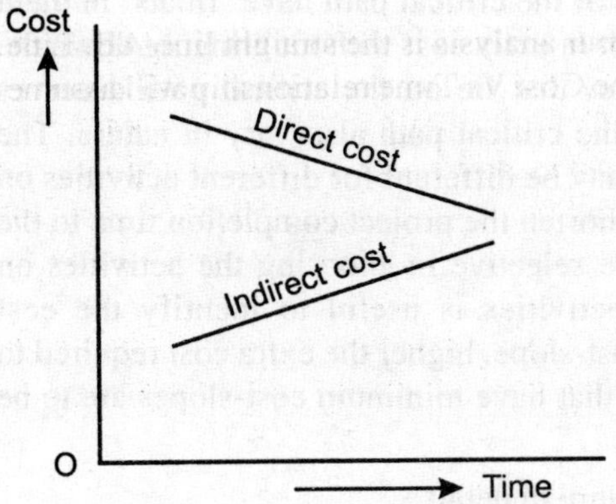

Fig. 3.86

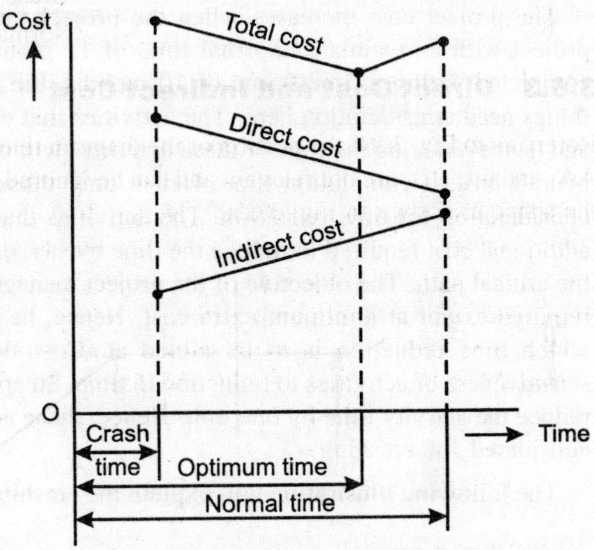

Fig. 3.87

- The indirect cost increases with time

The total-cost curve can be obtained by combining the direct-cost curve and the indirect-cost curve.

The total-cost curve takes a shape as shown in Fig. 3.87.

3.6.5 Time-Cost Trade-Off

Time and cost are the two most important resources that a project manager deals with. Both these resources have constraints and the job of a project manager is to have a judicious balance between the two. The judicious balance between time and cost is called Time-Cost Trade-Off and it can be achieved by studying the availability of these two resources and the demand for these two resources for the given project.

Every project is unique and the same time-cost trade-off rule will not be applicable to all projects uniformally. For example,

(i) The duration for a project as obtained from network calculations might be longer than the desired duration. Social, environmental or political constraints may necessitate early completion of the project even at a higher cost.

(ii) When cost is the only constraint and there is no necessity that the project should be hurried through, the project time can be extended till the total-cost becomes the minimum.

3.6.6 Crashing of Project Time

Crashing refers to shortening of project time by reducing the time of one or more activities contained in the project.

The project cost increases when the project time is reduced from its normal time. Consider a project with an estimated normal time of 12 months. If due to some reasons the project is to be completed within a time frame of 10 months, the project time is to be crashed by 2 months. Two things need consideration here. The activities that do not lie of the critical path have 'floats' in them and hence reducing the time of these activities will only result in extra cost without bringing down the overall project completion time. Hence only those activities that lie on the critical path deserves consideration for time reduction. The activities that lie on the critical path also vary in nature. The additional cost required to reduce the time by say, one day may be different for different activities on the critical path. The objective of the project manager is to shorten the project completion time to the required extent at minimum extra cost. Hence, he has to be selective in choosing the activities on which time reduction is to be aimed at. Cost-slope of activities is useful to identify the cost sensitiveness of activities to reduction in time. Steeper the cost-slope, higher the extra cost required to reduce the activity time by one unit. Hence, those activities that have minimum cost-slopes are to be considered for crashing.

The following illustration will explain the crashing procedure in detail

Illustration 3.20

For the network diagram shown in Fig. 3.88, find out the least-cost schedule using the data given in the table below.

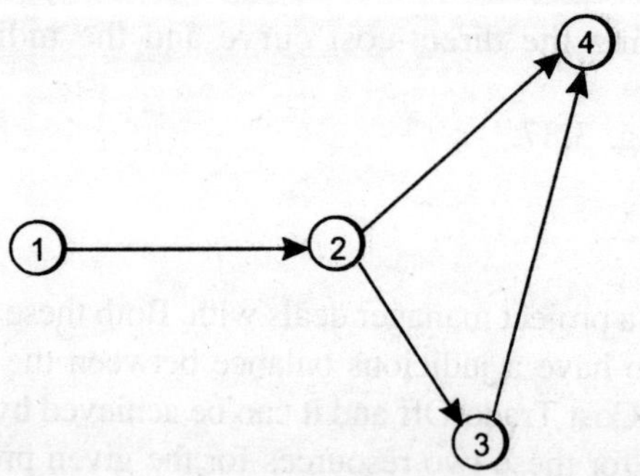

Fig. 3.88

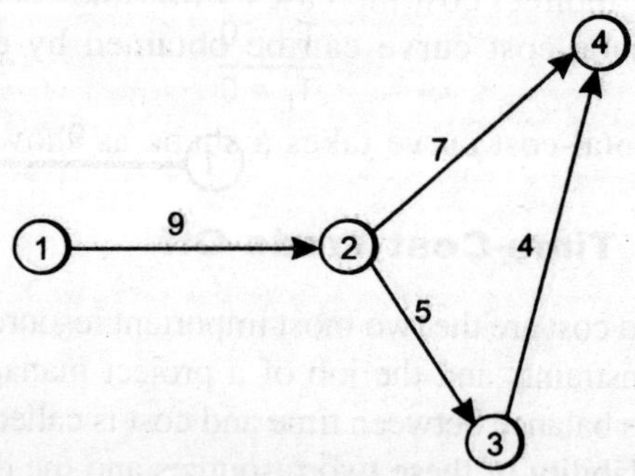

Fig. 3.89

Activity	*Normal time (weeks)*	*Crash time (weeks)*	*Cost of crashing (Rs. Per week)*
1–2	9	4	300
2–3	5	2	400
2–4	7	3	200
3–4	4	2	200

Time related overhead expenses for the project is Rs. 250.00 per week.

Solution:

Stage-1

First, find out the critical path

Forward pass computation		*Backward pass computation*	
Event	T_E	*Event*	T_L
1	0	4	18
2	0 + 9 = 9	3	18 – 4 = 14
3	9 + 5 = 14	2	Minimum of (a) 18 – 7 = 11 (b) 14 – 5 = 9 *i.e.*, = 9
4	Maximum of (a) 9 + 7 = 16 14 + 4 = 18 *i.e.*, = 18	1	9 – 9 = 0

Fig. 3.90 shows the critical path.

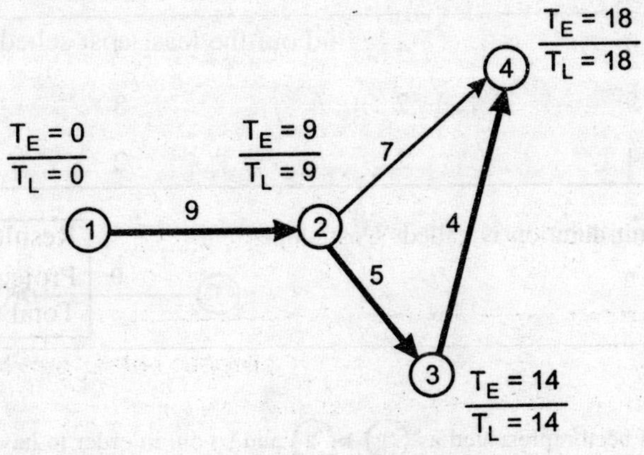

Fig. 3.90

There are two paths connecting events with zero slack. They are,

(1) → (2) → (3) → (4)

and

(1) → (2) → (3)

However, since the duration along (1) → (2) → (3) → (4) is greater, this is the critical path. Project duration is 18 weeks.

Stage-2

(The direct cost of individual activities is not given. Hence, to arrive at the least cost schedule, it is enough if we consider the cost of crashing and overheads)

Find out the cost of crashing plus overheads along the critical path. Let us call the sum of crashing cost and overheads as the total cost.

Hence,

$$\text{Total cost}^* = \text{Cost of crashing} + \text{Cost of overheads (for 18 weeks)}$$
$$= 0 + (18 \times 250)$$

* Total cost along the critical path

$$= 0 + 4500$$
$$= \text{Rs. } 4500$$

> *Note:*
>
> Critical path is the path having the longest duration. Crashing of activities is done starting with the critical path. No activity on the critical path is crashed and hence, the cost of crashing along the critical path is 'nil'. Overhead cost is calculated at the rate of Rs. 250 per week for a period of 18 weeks (9 + 5 + 4)]

Activity	*Normal time (weeks)*	*Crash time (weeks)*	*Maximum time that can be (crashed)*	*Cost of crashing (Rs. per week)**
(1)—(2)	9	4	5	300
(2)—(3)	5	2	3	400
(3)—(4)	4	2	2	200

*Cost of crashing per unit duration is called 'Cost slope'.

> Result :
> Project time : 18 weeks
> Total cost : Rs. 4500

> **Note:**
>
> Activity (1)—(2) has been represented as (1)→(2) and so on, in order to have a better 'feel' of the problem, since network diagram is constructed from left to right. This notation has been followed through out this chapter.

Stage-3

Find the sub-critical path and crash the time of critical path in such a way that the time along the critical path becomes equal to the time along the sub-critical path. In the given problem.

(1)→(2)→(3)→(4) is the critical path and (1)→(2)→(4) is the sub critical path.

Time along the critical path	: 18 weeks
Time along the sub-critical path	: 16 weeks
Difference	: 2 weeks

Hence, the time along the critical path is to be reduced by 2 weeks so that the time of both the paths become equal.

For crashing the critical path by 2 weeks, the activities to be crashed shall be so chosen that the cost of crashing is minimum.

All the three activities that lie on the critical path can be crashed by the required 2 weeks since the difference between their respective normal time and crash time is equal to or more than 2 weeks. However, the activity having the least cost slope is to be chosen for crashing.

Activity (3)→(4) has the least cost-slope (i.e., minimum cost of crashing per week) of Rs. 200.00 per week and the same is to be chosen for crashing.

$$\text{Total cost} = \left\{\begin{array}{c}\text{Cost of crashing}\\ \text{Up to the previous}\\ \text{stage}\end{array}\right\} + \left\{\begin{array}{c}\text{Cost of crashing}\\ \text{activity } (3)\to(4)\\ \text{for 2 weeks}\end{array}\right\} + \left\{\begin{array}{c}\text{Cost of overheads}\\ \text{for 16 weeks}\end{array}\right\}$$

$$= 0 + (200 \times 2) + (250 \times 16)$$

$$= 0 + 400 + 4{,}000$$

$$= \text{Rs. } 4{,}400.00$$

Result:
Project time: 16 weeks
Total cost: Rs. 4,400.00

After stage-3, the crashed network diagram appears as shown in Fig. 3.91

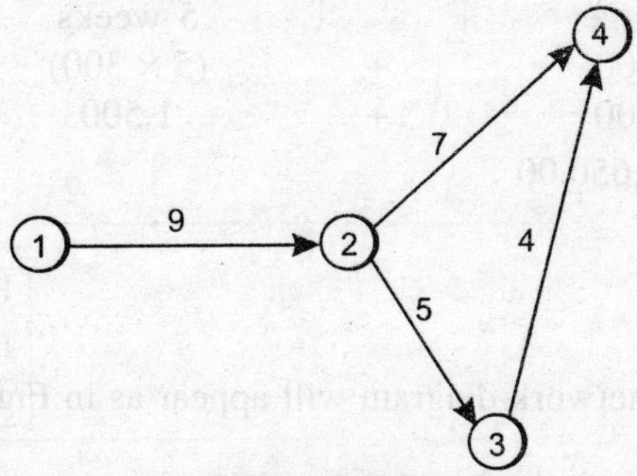

Fig. 3.91

Stage-4

Both the paths (1)→(2)→(4) and (1)→(2)→(3)→(4) are now critical paths and the time and the project completion time along both the paths is 16 weeks Each. When a stage like this is reached i.e., when the project duration along all the available paths are equal, the following are the rules for further crashing.

(*a*) If there is only one activity emerging from a node	:	Only that activity can be crashed
(*b*) If there are more than one activity emerging from a node	:	All the emerging activities are to be crashed simultaneously
(*c*) If there are more than one activity meeting at a node	:	All the activities meeting at the common node are to be crashed simultaneously.
(*d*) When two or more activities are crashed simultaneously as per (*b*) and (*c*) above	:	The cost of crashing per day is the sum of crashing cost per day of all activities that are crashed simultaneously.

Following the above rules,

- Activity (1)→(2) can be crashed independently.
- Activities (2)→(4) and (2)→(3) are to be crashed simultaneously.
- Activities (2)→(4) and (3)→(4) are to be crashed simultaneously.

Let us examine the above three options.

Crash options		**Cost of crashing per week (Rs.)**
(1)→(2)	:	300
(2)→(3) and (2)→(4) (simultaneously)	:	(400 + 200) = 600
(2)→(4) and (3)→(4) (simultaneously)	:	(200 + 200) = 400

Out of the above three options, the first option gives the least cost of crashing per week and hence can be chosen.

Activity (1)→(2) can be crashed for a maximum of 5 weeks. After crashing activity by 5 weeks, the project duration will get reduced to 11 weeks (16 – 5).

Total cost = {Cost of crashing upto previous stage} + {Cost of crashing activity (1)→(2) by 5 weeks} + {Overhead cost cost for 11 weeks}

= 400 + (5 × 300) + (250 × 11)

= 400 + 1,500 + 2,750

= Rs. 4,650.00

> Result :
> Project time: 11weeks
> Total cost: Rs. 4,650.00

After stage-4, the crashed network diagram will appear as in Fig. 3.92

Stage-5

Activities (1)→(2) and (3)→(4) have already been crashed to their maximum extent. (referring to fig. 3.92 it can noted that the time for activities (1)→(2) and (3)→(4) have become equal to their respective crash times)

Hence, only the remaining two activities (2)→(3) and (2)→(4) can be crashed further. Observing the rules of crashing explained under Step-4, both the activities (2)→(3) and (2)→(4) are to be crashed simultaneously. Activity (2)→(3) can be crashed to a maximum of 3 weeks (i.e., 5 weeks – 2 weeks), while activity (2)→(4) can be crashed to a maximum of 4 weeks (i.e., 7 weeks – 3 weeks). However, since both the activities emanate from the common node-2, they have to be crashed simultaneously for the same number of days. This condition imposes a limitation that though the difference between the normal time and the crash time for activity (2)→(4) is 4 weeks, it can be crushed only to a maximum of 3 weeks along with activity (2)→(3). This is because, activity (2)→(3) can not be crashed by more than 3 weeks.

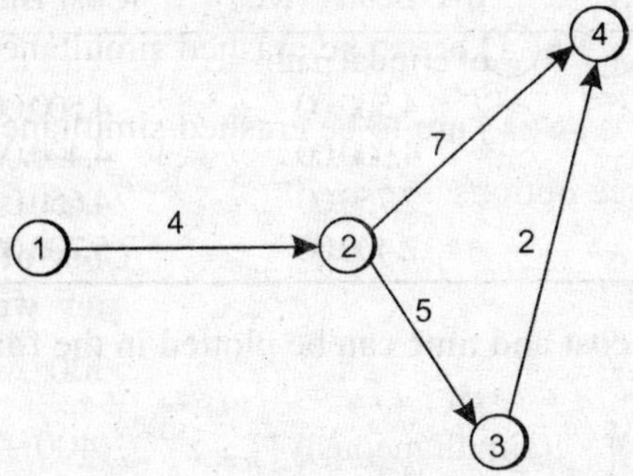

Fig. 3.92

Total cost = {Total cost of crashing upto previous stage} + {cost of crashing activities (2)→(3) And (2)→(4) simultaneously for 3 weeks} + {cost of overheads for 8 weeks}

= 1,900 + (400 + 200) × 3 + (8 × 250)

= 1,900 + 1,800 + 2,000

= Rs. 5,700.00

> Result :
> Project time: 8 weeks
> Total cost: Rs. 5,700.00

After stage-5, the crashed network will appear as shown in Fig. 3.93.

All the activities except activity (2)→(4) have been crashed to the maximum extent. Though the crash time for activity (2)→(4) is 3 weeks, it has been crashed to only 4 weeks. Further crashing of activity (2)→(4) is not possible since activities (2)→(4) and (2)→(3) can be crashed only simultaneously and further crashing of activity (2)→(3) is not possible since it has already been crashed to its maximum limit.

The relevant costs associated with different stages of crashing are tabulated as under.

	Cost of crashing (Rs.)	*Cost of overheads (Rs.)*	*Total Cost (Rs.)*	*Project duration (weeks)*
Stage-I	—identification	of critical path—		
Stage-II	Nil	4,500.00	4,500.00	18
Stage-III	400.00	4,000.00	4,400.00	16
Stage-IV	1,900.00	2,750.00	4,650.00	11
Stage-V	3,700.00	2,400.00	5,700.00	8

The relationship between total cost and time can be plotted in the form of a graph as shown in Fig. 3.94.

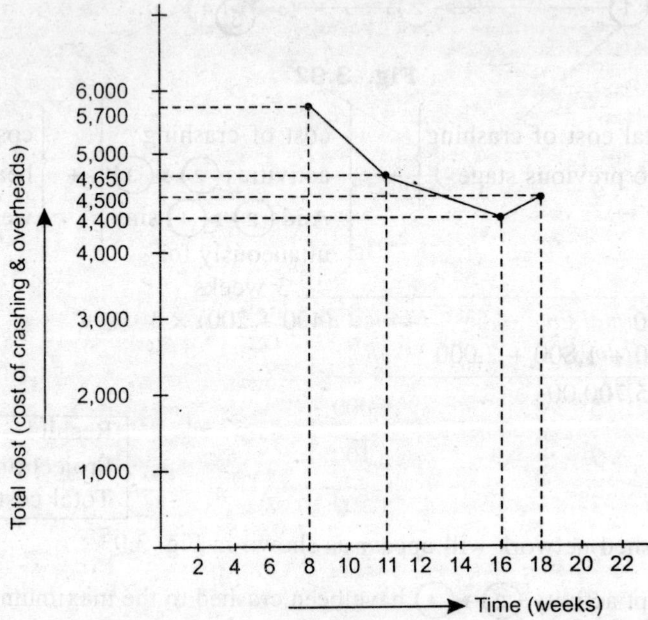

Fig. 3.94

As seen from Fig. 3.94, the least cost is Rs. 4,400.00 and the corresponding project duration is 16 days.

> *Note:*
>
> In the illustration, the direct cost of individual activities and the change in the direct cost with the change in the duration of the activities are not given. Instead, the cost of crashing of the individual activities are given. With the given data, we have arrived at the least-cost schedule (*i.e.*, the compressed network that results in minimum cost) which gives a project duration of 16 weeks for minimum cost. Reducing the project duration below 16 weeks results in increased cost. Increasing the project duration above 16 weeks also results in increased cost. Thus, the project duration of 16 weeks is the optimum duration that will be aimed at unless there are other constraints. If there is an external constraint that the project should be completed, say, within 10 weeks, the increase in the project cost can not be avoided.

If the time-cost relationship is not known, the project manager will normally try to complete the project in 18 weeks time, being the project duration along the critical path. The time-cost relationship indicates that the project cost can be reduced to the minimum if the project is completed in 16 weeks time. Thus the project manager stands to gain by way of both time and money with the aid of time-cost relationship.

Illustration 3.21

A project has seven activities and the network diagram of the activities is as shown in Fig. 3.95. The normal time, crash time, normal cost, crash cost of all the activities are given. The fixed cost is Rs. 300.00 per day. Establish the time-cost relationship and find out the least cost duration of the Project.

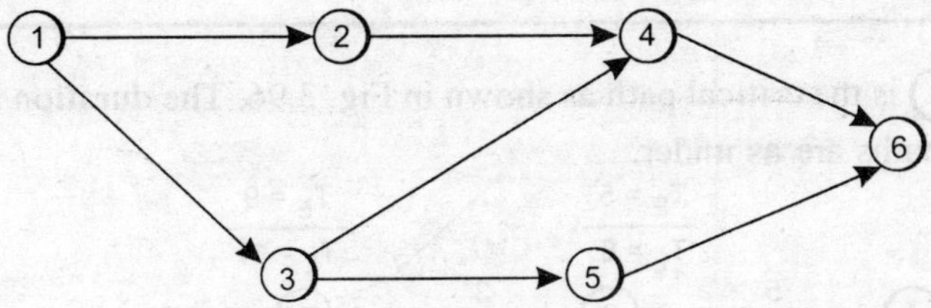

Fig. 3.95

Activity	*Normal time (days)*	*Normal cost (Rs.)*	*Crash time (days)*	*Crash cost (Rs.)*
1→2	5	1,000	4	1,200
1→3	7	2,100	5	2,300
2→4	3	1,500	2	1,700
3→4	2	1,300	2	1,300
3→5	6	1,200	4	1,400
4→6	5	2,000	4	2,500
5→6	3	1,500	2	1,700

Solution:

Stage-I

Find the critical path for the given network,

Forward pass computation		*Backward pass computation*	
Event	T_E	*Event*	T_L
1	0	6	16
2	0+5=5	5	16−3=13

(Contd.)

Forward pass computation		Backward pass computation	
Event	T_E	*Event*	T_L
3	$0+7=7$	4	$16-5=11$
4	Maximum of (a) $5+3=8$ (b) $7+2=9$ *i.e.*, $=9$	3	Minimum of (a) $11-2=9$ (b) $13-6=7$ *i.e.*, $=7$
5	$7+6=13$	2	$11-3=8$
6	Maximum of (a) $9+5=14$ (b) $13+3=16$ *i.e.*, $=16$	1	Minimum of (a) $8-3=5$ (c) $7-7=0$ *i.e.*, $=0$

(1)→(3)→(5)→(6) is the critical path as shown in Fig. 3.96. The duration along critical path and along the non-critical paths are as under.

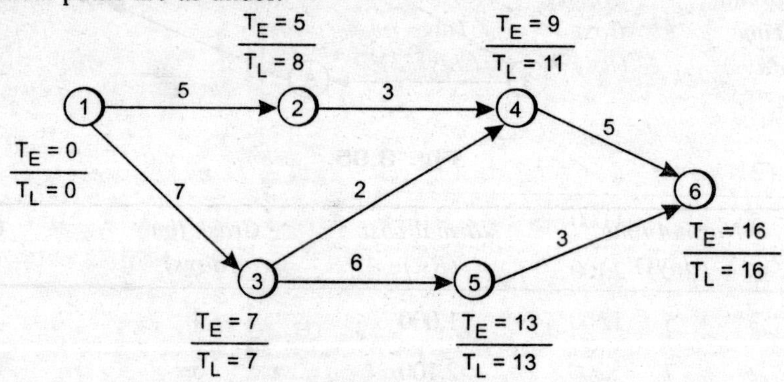

Fig. 3.96

(1)→(3)→(5)→(6)	critical path	: 16 days
(1)→(2)→(4)→(6)	non-critical path	: 13 days
(1)→(3)→(4)→(6)	non-critical path	: 14 days

For the given network, the total cost involved in completing all the activities consists of two components, *viz.*, the normal cost of completing all the seven activities and the fixed overheads for 16 days. The total cost is arrived at as under.

Activity	*Normal cost (Rs.)*	*Overheads (Rs.)*	*Total cost (Rs.)*
(1)→(2)	1,000		
(1)→(3)	2,100	At the rate of Rs. 300 per	
(2)→(4)	1,500		
(3)→(4)	1,300		
(3)→(5)	1,200	day for 16 days $(16\times 300)=4{,}800$	
(4)→(6)	2,000		
(5)→(6)	1,500		
	10,600	4,800	15,400

Result :
Project time: 16 days
Total cost: Rs. 15,400.00

Stage-2

Crash the activities along the critical path in such a way that the duration of the critical path is reduced to the duration of the sub-critical path. (1)→(3)→(4)→(6) is the sub-critical path (i.e., the path that is the second longest path, next to the critical path). The duration along the sub-critical path is 14 days. Let us try to crash the critical path by 2 days (16 – 14).

Let us reproduce the table given in the problem adding another two more columns as shown below for our easy reference and convenience.

Table 3.3

Activity (1)	*Normal Time (days)* (2)	*Normal Cost (Rs.)* (3)	*Crash Time (days)* (4)	*Crash Cost (Rs.)* (5)	*Max. no. of days that can be crashed* (4) – (2)	*Crashing cost per day (Rs.)* $\frac{(5)-(3)}{(4)-(2)}$
(1)→(2)	5	1,000	4	1,200	1	200
(1)→(3)	7	2,100	5	2,300	2	100
(2)→(4)	3	1,500	2	1,700	1	200
(3)→(4)	2	1,300	2	1,300	Nil	Nil
(3)→(5)	6	1,200	4	1,400	2	100
(4)→(6)	5	2,000	4	2,500	1	500
(5)→(6)	3	1,500	2	1,700	1	200

(1)→(3)→(5)→(6) is the critical path. Out of the three activities on the critical path, the cost of crashing per day is less for the activities (1)→(3) and (3)→(5). Both these activities can be crashed by 2 days each.

Let us choose activity (1)→(3) for crashing.

Cost of crashing activity (1)→(3) by 2 days.

$$(2{,}300 - 2{,}100) = \text{Rs. } 200$$

After crashing activity (1)→(3) by 2 days, the crashed network will be as under (refer Fig. 3.97)

The project durations along the critical path and along the non critical paths for the crashed network shown in Fig. 3.97 are as under.

(1)→(3)→(5)→(6)	: critical path	: 14 days
(1)→(3)→(4)→(6)	: non-critical path	: 12 days
(1)→(2)→(4)→(6)	: non-critical path	: 13 days

For the network shown in Fig. 3.97, the total cost can be arrived at by two methods,

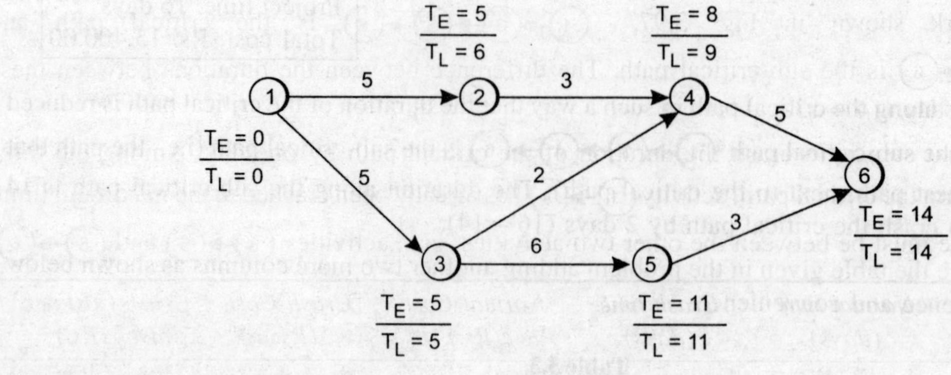

Fig. 3.97

Method-1:

Total cost for the network shown in Fig. 3.96 (*i.e.*, immediately before crashing the network by 2 days) = Rs. 15,400.00

Add:

Cost of crashing (i.e., cost of crashing activity (1)→(3) by 2 days) = Rs. 200.00

Less:

Reduction in fixed overheads for 2 days (2 × 300) = Rs. (–) 600.00

Rs. 15,000.00

Result:
Total cost: Rs. 15,000.00
Project time: 14 days

Method-2

Activity	*Normal Cost (Rs.)*	*Additional Cost for Crashing (Rs.)*	*Overheads (Rs.)*	*Total Cost (Rs.)*
(1)→(2)	1,000	—	At the	
(1)→(3)	2,100	200	rate of	
(2)→(4)	1,500	—	Rs. 300	
(3)→(4)	1,300	—	per day for	
(3)→(5)	1,200	—	14 days	
(4)→(6)	2,000	—	(14×300)	
(5)→(6)	1,500	—	=4200	
	10,600	200	4,200	15,000

Stage-3

For the network shown in Fig. 3.97, (1)→(3)→(5)→(6) is the critical path and (1)→(2)→(4)→(6) is the sub-critical path. The difference between the durations between these two paths is one day (14 – 13).

Hence, the next step is to crash the duration of the critical path by one day. Among the three activities that lie on the critical path, activity (1)→(3) has already been crashed to the maximum limit. Hence, the choice must be between the other two activities, viz., activities (3)→(5) and (5)→(6).

Activity	*Normal time (days)*	*Crash time (days)*	*Normal Cost (Rs.)*	*Crash Cost (Rs.)*	*Crash Cost per Day (Rs.)*
(3)→(5)	6	4	1,200	1,400	100
(5)→(6)	3	2	1,500	1,700	200

Though the difference between the crash time and the normal time for activity (3)→(5) is 2 days, activity (3)→(5) is to be crashed only for one day for the time being. After crashing activity (3)→(5) by one day, the network becomes as shown in Fig. 3.98. Activity (3)→(5) is chosen since the crash cost per day is less.

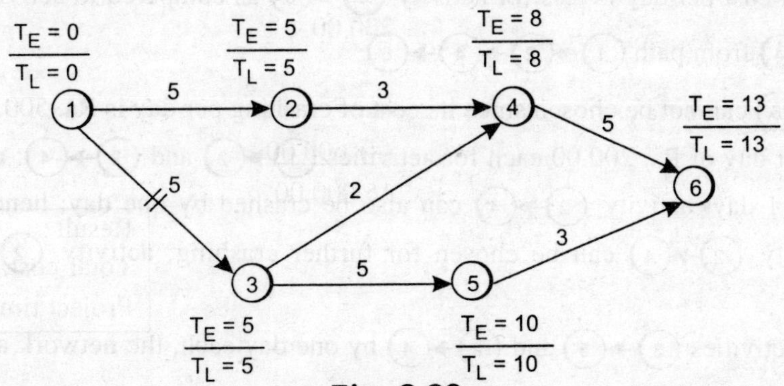

Fig. 3.98

Note:

(A # mark has been made on activity (1)→(3) to indicate that this activity has been crushed to the maximum extent and that no more crushing of this activity is possible.)

Total cost of network as shown in Fig. 3.98 is arrived at as under.

Total cost for the network as shown in Fig. 3.97

(i.e., immediately before crashing activity (3)→(5) by one day) = Rs. 15,000.00

Add:

Cost of crashing activity (3)→(5) by one day = Rs. 100.00

Less:

Reduction in fixed overheads for one day = Rs. (–) 300.00

Rs. 14,800.00

Result :
Project duration : 13 days
Total cost: Rs. 14,800.00

Stage-4

For the network shown in Fig. 3.98, the following are the critical/non-critical paths.

(1)→(3)→(5)→(6) : critical path = 13 days

(1)→(2)→(4)→(6) : critical path = 13 days

(1)→(3)→(4)→(6) : non-critical path = 12 days

The sub critical path has 12 days duration whereas there are two critical paths of 13 days duration each [path (1)→(3)→(4)→(6) is the sub critical path since it is the path whose duration is immediately next below the duration of the critical path]. Hence, the two critical paths are to be crushed by 1 day each. (13 – 12).

Referring to table 3.3, we can choose the following two activities for further crashing.

Activity (3)→(5) from path (1)→(3)→(5)→(6)

[since activity (1)→(3) has already been crushed to the maximum and out of the remaining two activities, the crash cost per day is less for activity (3)→(5) as compared to activity (5)→(6)]

Activity (2)→(4) from path (1)→(2)→(4)→(6)

[activity (4)→(6) can not be chosen since its cost of crashing per day is Rs. 500.00 as against the cost of crashing per day of Rs. 200.00 each for activities (1)→(2) and (2)→(4); activity (1)→(2) can be crashed by 1 day; activity (2)→(4) can also be crashed by one day; hence either activity (1)→(2) or activity (2)→(4) can be chosen for further crashing; activity (2)→(4) is chosen arbitrarily]

After crashing activities (3)→(5) and (2)→(4) by one day each, the network appears as shown in Fig. 3.99

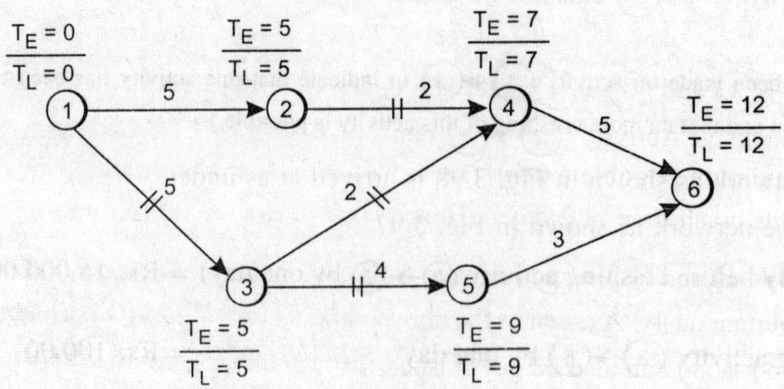

Fig. 3.99

Total cost of network shown in network 3.99 is arrived as under.

Total cost for the network shown in Fig. 3.98 (i.e.,

Immediately before crashing activities (2)→(4) and (3)→(5) by one day each)

= Rs. 14,800.00

Add:

Cost of crashing activity (2)→(4) by one day (1 × 200) = Rs. 300.00

Add:

Cost of crashing activity (3)→(5) by one day (1 × 100) = Rs. 100.00

Less:

Reduction in fixed overheads for one day (1 × 300) = Rs. (–) 300.00

Rs. 14,800.00

Result :
Project duration: 12 days
Total cost: Rs. 14,800.00

Stage-5

For the network shown in Fig. 3.99, the following are the critical/non critical paths.

(1)→(2)→(4)→(6) critical path : 12 days

(1)→(3)→(4)→(6) critical path : 12 days

(1)→(3)→(5)→(6) critical path : 12 days

All the three available paths have become critical paths. Further reduction is project duration can be studied as under :

Activities (1)→(2) and (1)→(3) emanate from the same node. Hence both these activities are to be crashed simultaneously. However, activity (1)→(3) has already been crashed to its maximum limit. Since activity (1)→(3) can not be crashed any further, activity (1)→(2) can also be not crashed.

Activities (2)→(4) and (3)→(4) meet at a common node. Hence, these two activities are to be crashed simultaneously. Activity (2)→(4) can not be crashed further since it has already been crashed to the maximum possible extent. (i.e, it has been crashed in such a way that its duration has become equal to its crash time of 2 days). Hence, activity (3)→(4) can also be not crashed further.

Activities (3)→(4) and (3)→(5) emanate from a common node. Hence, these two activities are to be crashed simultaneously. As seen in the above para, activity (3)→(4) can not be crashed further. Hence, activity (3)→(5) can also be not crashed further. Infact, activity (3)→(5) has already been crashed to the maximum limit.

We are now left with two activities (4)→(6) and (5)→(6). Since these two activities meet at a common node, these are to be crashed simultaneously.

Activity	*Normal time (days)*	*Crash time (days)*	*Normal cost (Rs.)*	*Crash cost (Rs.)*	*Crash cost per day (Rs.)*
(4)→(6)	5	4	2000	2500	500
(5)→(6)	3	2	1500	1700	200

Both the activities (4)→(6) and (5)→(6) can be crashed by one day.

After crashing activities (4)→(6) and (5)→(6) by one day each, the network appears as shown in Fig. 3.100

Total cost for the network shown on Fig. 3.99

(i.e., immediately before crashing activities

(1)→(2) and (4)→(6) by one day each)= Rs. 14,800.00

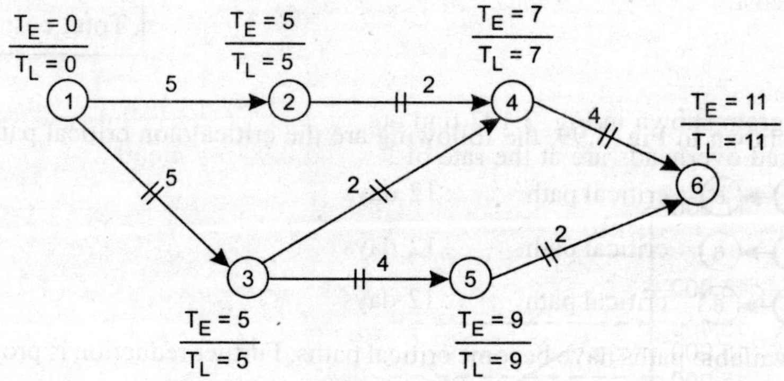

Fig. 3.100

Add:

Cost of crashing activity (4)→(6) by one day (1 × 500) = Rs. 500.00

Add:

Cost of crashing activity (5)→(6) by one day (1 × 200) = Rs. 200.00

Less:

Reduction in fixed overheads for one day (1 × 300) = Rs. (–) 300.00

Rs. 15,200.00

> Result :
> Project duration: 11 days
> Total cost: Rs. 15,200.00

All the activities in the network except activity (1)→(2) have been crashed to the maximum extent. Activity (3)→(4) can not be crashed since its normal time and crash time are the same.

Thus, the possible stages of crashing the network has been completed, the extract of which is as under.

Project Duration (days)	*Total cost (Rs.)*
16	15,400
14	15,000
13	14,800
12	14,800
11	15,200

Fig. 3.101 indicates the cost behaviour with project duration.

The total project cost is minimum at two points, viz., at the project durations of 12 days and 13 days. Hence, the schedule of activities either as per Fig. 3.98 or as per Fig. 3.99 can be chosen for ensuring minimum cost.

Illustration 3.22

For the network diagram shown in Fig. 3.102 find out the least-cost schedule using the data given in the table below. Fixed overheads are at the rate of Rs. 2,500.00 per month.

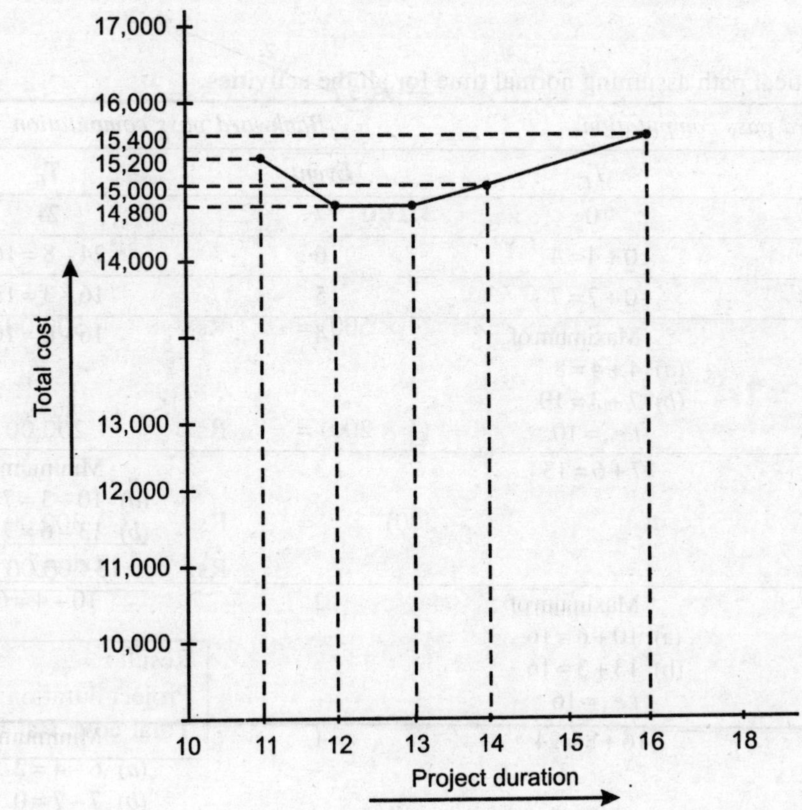

Fig. 3.101

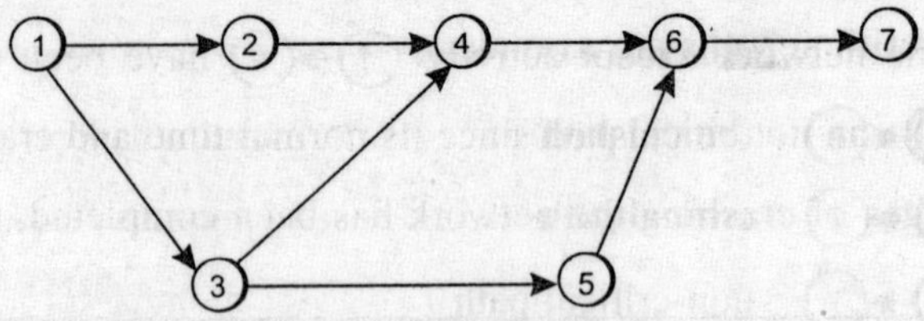

Fig. 3.102

Activity	Normal Time (months)	Normal Cost (Rs.)	Crash Time (months)	Crash Cost (Rs.)	Maximum Months that can be crashed	Crash cost Per month (Rs.)
1→2	4	10,000	4	10,000	—	—
1→3	7	35,000	7	35,000	—	—
2→4	4	9,000	4	9,000	—	—
3→4	3	9,000	2	12,000	1	3,000
3→5	6	18,000	5	20,000	1	2,000
4→6	6	12,000	5	13,000	1	1,000
5→6	3	4,000	2	5,000	1	1,000
6→7	8	16,000	8	16,000	—	—

Solution :

Stage-1

Find out the critical path assuming normal time for all the activities.

Forward pass computation		*Backward pass computation*	
Event	T_E	Event	T_L
1	0	7	24
2	$0+4=4$	6	$24-8=16$
3	$0+7=7$	5	$16-3=13$
4	Maximum of (*a*) $4+4=8$ (*b*) $7+3=10$ *i.e.*, $=10$	4	$16-6=10$
5	$7+6=13$	3	Minimum of (*a*) $10-3=7$ (*b*) $13-6=7$ *i.e.*, $=7$
6	Maximum of (a) $10+6=16$ (b) $13+3=16$ *i.e.*, $=16$	2	$10-4=6$
7	$16+8=24$	1	Minimum of (*a*) $6-4=2$ (*b*) $7-7=0$ *i.e.*, $=0$

The critical and non-critical paths are as under.

(1)→(3)→(4)→(6)→(7)	critical path	: 24 months
(1)→(3)→(5)→(6)→(7)	critical path	: 24 months
(1)→(2)→(4)→(6)→(7)	non-critical path	: 22 months

The total cost of the project for the network shown in Fig. 3.103 is as under.

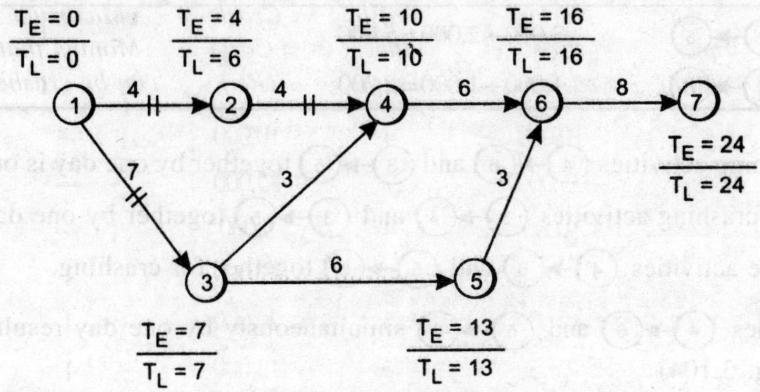

Fig. 3.103

Activity	*Normal cost (Rs.)*	*Overhead (Rs.)*	*Tottal cost (Rs.)*
(1)→(2)	10,000	At the rate	
(1)→(3)	35,000	of Rs. 2,500.00	
(2)→(4)	9,000	per month	
(3)→(4)	9,000	for 24 months	
(3)→(5)	18,000	(24×2,500)	
(4)→(6)	12,000	Rs. 60,000	
(5)→(6)	4,000		
(6)→(7)	16,000		
	1,13,000	60,000	1,73,000

Result :
Project time: 24 months
Total cost: Rs. 1,73,000.00

Stage-2

For the activities (1)→(2), (2)→(4), (1)→(3) and (6)→(7) both the normal time and the crash time are the same and '#' mark has been put on these activities to indicate that they can not be crashed.

Paths (1)→(3)→(4)→(6)→(7) and (1)→(3)→(5)→(6)→(7) are to be crashed by 2 days (24 – 22). Whenever two activities join at a node or emanate from a node, these two activities are to be crashed simultaneously.

The activities/combination of activities available for crashing are as under:

Activity/(ies)	*Crash cost per month (Rs.)*	*Maximum No. of days that can be crashed*
(3)→(4) and (3)→(5)	3,000 + 2,000 = 5,000	1
(4)→(6) and (5)→(6)	1,000 + 1,000 = 2,000	1

The cost of crashing activities (4)→(6) and (3)→(5) together by one day is only Rs. 2,000.00 as against the cost of crashing activities (3)→(4) and (3)→(5) together by one day of Rs. 5,000.00. Hence let us choose activities (4)→(6) and (5)→(6) together for crashing.

Crashing activities (4)→(6) and (5)→(6) simultaneously by one day results in the following network. (refer Fig. 3.104)

The total cost of network shown in Fig. 3.104 is arrived at as under.

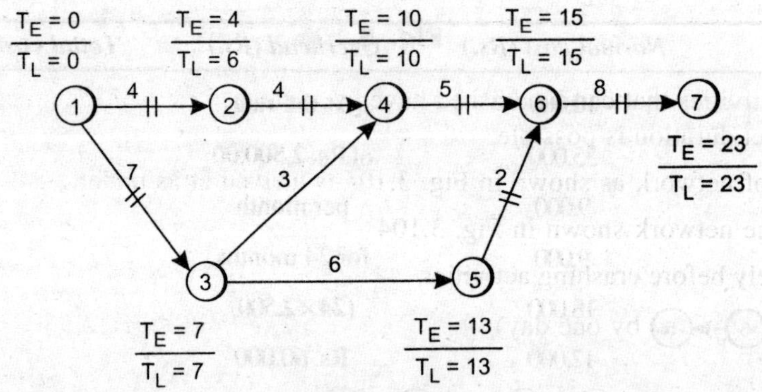

Fig. 3.104

Total cost for network shown in Fig. 3.103 *i.e.*, Immediately before crashing activities (4)→(6) and (5)→(6) by one day)	= Rs. 1,73,000.00
Add:	
Cost of crashing activities (4)→(6) and (5)→(6) Simultaneously by one day	= Rs. 2,000.00
Less:	
Reduction on fixed overheads for one day (1 × 1,500)	= Rs. (–) 2,500.00
	Rs. 1,72,500.00

Result :
Project duration: 23 months
Total cost: Rs. 1,72,500.00

Stage-3

Crashing activities (3)→(4) and (3)→(5) simultaneously by one day results in the following network. (refer Fig. 3.105)

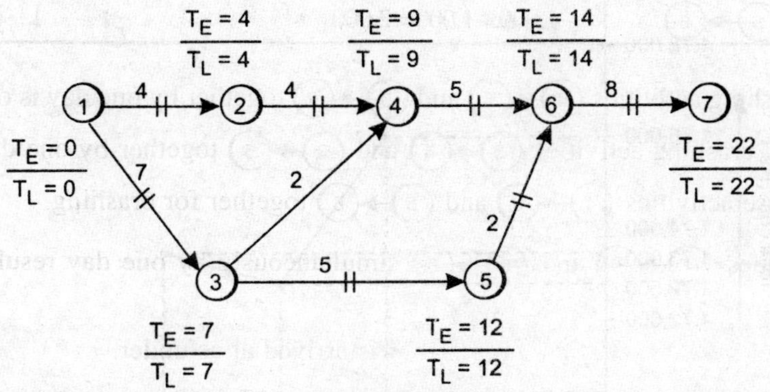

Fig. 3.105

Since all the activities that can be crashed have been crashed to their maximum extent, no further reduction in project duration is possible.

The total cost of network as shown in Fig. 3.105 is arrived at as under.

Total cost of the network shown in Fig. 3.104

(i.e., immediately before crashing activities

(3)→(4) and (3)→(5) by one day) = Rs. 1,72,500.00

Add:

Cost of crashing activities (3)→(4) and (3)→(5)

Simultaneously by one day = Rs. 5,000.00

Less:

Reduction in fixed overheads for one day (1 × 1,500) = Rs. (–) 1,500.00

Rs. 1,76,000.00

Result :
Project duration : 22 months
Total cost : Rs. 1,76,000.00

The following table shows the possible stages of crashing the network

Project duration (months)	*Total cost (Rs.)*
24	1,73,000.00
23	1,72,500.00
22	1,76,000.00

Hence, the least cost duration of the project is 23 months (refer Fig. 3.106)

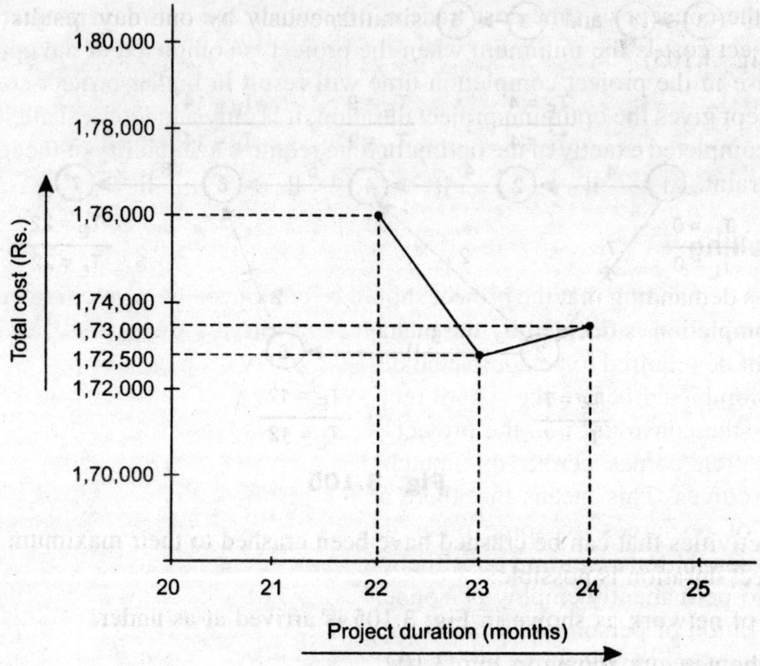

Fig. 3.106

3.6.7 Choice of Schedule due to Resource Constraint (Resource Allocation)

One of the main problems faced by a project manager is resource allocation. With the help of the network techniques explained earlier, the project manager can identify the critical activities. For completing the project in time, he must have the required resources at his disposal. Let us assume that the critical path of a given project indicates a duration of, say, 15 months. If the project is to be completed exactly in 15 months time, all the critical activities should be completed in time so that the project completion time is not exceeded. For completing the critical activities in time, there should not be any resource constraint. If the time required for the completion of a critical activity is 2 months, it means that the activity can be completed in 2 months time provided the required resources are made available without any shortage or constraint. Men, material, money are the three resources required for any activity. If there is shortage of resources, the activity can not be completed in time. If, for example, 15 men are required to work for 2 months for completing the activity, on all the sixty days the activity needs 15 men. If on a few days, the availability of men falls short of 15, the activity may take more than 2 months for completion.

A project manager frequently comes across resource constraints. There may be delay in the arrival of building materials. The available personnel may fall short of the requirement on some days and there may be excess personnel available on some other days. The job of the project manager is to plan and allocate the resources for the different activities so that the resource utilization is optimized.

With regard to resource constraints, a project manager may face one of the following two situations.

(*a*) Resource levelling

(*b*) Resource smoothing (also called 'Fixed Resource Limit Scheduling')

We have seen the concept of time-cost trade off by which the optimum project duration can be arrived at; the project cost is the minimum when the project is completed at the optimum time. Any increase or decrease in the project completion time will result in higher project-cost. Though time-cost trade off concept gives the optimum project duration, it is only a theoretical attempt and to ensure that the project is completed exactly in the optimum time requires availability of the required resources without any constraint.

Resource Levelling

There are situations demanding that the project should be completed by a specified due-date. The due-date for project completion is decided by the management for various reasons. For example, a canal lining project might be required to be completed before the monsoon sets on; a school building might be required to be completed before the school reopens after vacation. Under such situations, project completion time is the constraint i.e., the project is to be completed at any cost by the due-date. A project manager often comes across mis-match between the availability of resources and the requirement of resources. This means that there are surplus resources available on some days and there is shortage of resources on some other days. For example, in construction industry, the requirement of personnel for executing construction work varies very much from day to day. It will be uneconomical to permanently employ personnel to satisfy the peak time requirements since there will be under utilisation of personnel on many days. Hence, only less number of personnel than the peak time requirement is employed by the management with the hope that any shortfall in personnel requirement during peak time can be handled by hiring personnel on casual basis. Since the personnel requirement varies from day to day, the project manager should plan properly in such a way that optimum utilization of available personnel is achieved.

Thus, the objective of the project manager in such a situation is to level as far as possible the demand for resources through out the project execution time, keeping in view the constraint that the "specified" project completion time should not be exceeded. The "specified" project completion time may be the minimum possible time by which the project can be completed as ascertained by identifying the critical path or even a shorter duration than this as decided by the management to meet other requirements.

Illustration 3.23

A project has 7 activities. The relationship between the activities is as under.

Activity	:	A	B	C	D	E	F	G
Preceding Activity	:	—	—	—	A	B	C	D

The duration of these activities and the labour requirement for the activities are as under.

Activity	:	A	B	C	D	E	F	G

Duration (Weeks)	:	1	2	2	1	3	2	1
Labour Requirement	:	2	1	1	1	1	1	1

The project duration should not exceed beyond the minimum project schedule. Only three men are available for the project execution. Find the resource schedule with respect to labour.

Solution:

Using the precedence relationship given in the problem, draw the network for the given project.

Fig. 3.107 shows the network for the project. Forward pass and backward pass computations are calculated and the critical path is located as shown in Fig. 3.108.

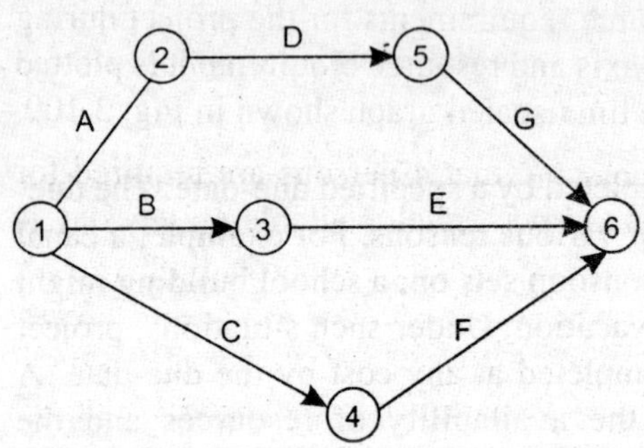

Fig. 3.107

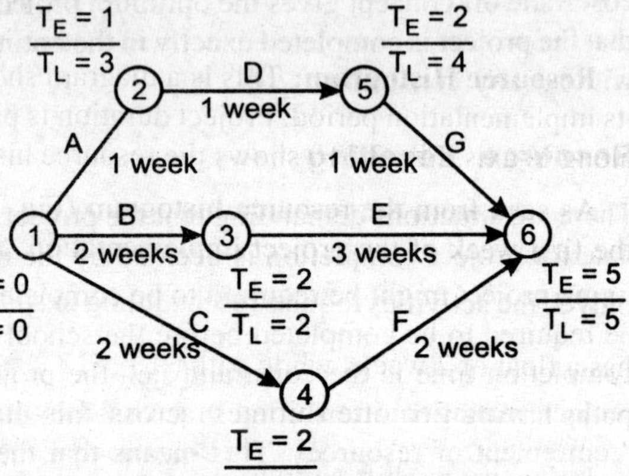

Fig. 3.108

(1)→(3)→(6) is the critical path and project duration along the critical path is 5 weeks. It is given in the problem that the project duration should not exceed the minimum project schedule i.e., the project should be completed in 5 weeks time. Since the project completion time is the constraint, this is a problem of Resource Levelling.

For solving any resource allocation problem, it would be easier and convenient if a time-scaled graph for the given network is drawn. This graph gives a clear view of the resources available on different days. Time-scaled graph of the given network is drawn as under.

The total project duration as decided by the critical path is 5 weeks. Draw a straight line to some scale keeping the length of the straight line representing 5 weeks. Mark the critical activities on the straight line. Mark the other activities above/below the straight line to scale. While marking other activities above/below the straight line, it is assumed that the activities start as early as possible. Mark the number of personnel required for carrying out each activity along the line representing the respective activities. Fig. 3.109 gives the time-scaled graph for the given network. To know the resource requirements for each week, draw a table below the time-scaled graph indicating the personnel requirement for each week. (In a time-scaled graph, the length of each activity arrow represents the duration of that activity. The location of the arrow represents the scheduled start and finish time of the respective activities. Float is indicated by dotted lines. The time-scaled graph offers visual clarity for the analysis of activities with regard to their start and finish times).

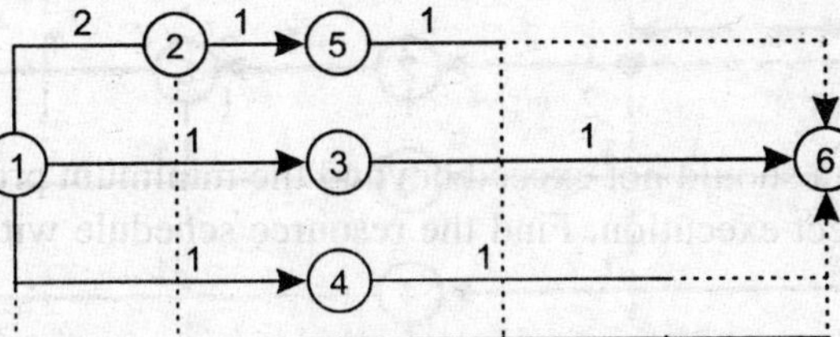

Week	1	2	3	4	5
Labour required	4	3	3	2	1

Fig. 3.109

Resource Histogram: This is a diagram showing the resource requirements for the project during its implementation period. Project duration is plotted along X-axis and resource requirement is plotted along Y-axis. Fig. 3.110 shows the resource histogram for the time-scaled graph shown in Fig. 3.109.

As seen from the resource histogram (Fig. 3.110), we understand that 4 persons are required for the first week of the project implementation. Since the maximum personnel available on any day is only 3, the activities require rescheduling to suit the resource availability. Path ①→②→⑤→⑥ has a float of 2 weeks while path ①→④→⑥ has a float of 1 week. The activities that lie on the paths having float are shifted in such a way that a peak resource requirement is smoothened out.

Let us try to shift acitivity ①→② (i.e., activity - A) by one week. The resulting time-scaled graph and the corresponding resource histogram are shown in Fig. 3.11

As seen from Fig. 3.111, though the resource requirement for the first week has come down from 4 persons to 2 persons, the resource requirement for the second week has increases from 3 persons to 4 persons. Thus, we again have a situation where the resource requirement is more than the resource availability.

Week	1	2	3	4	5
Labour required	4	3	3	2	1

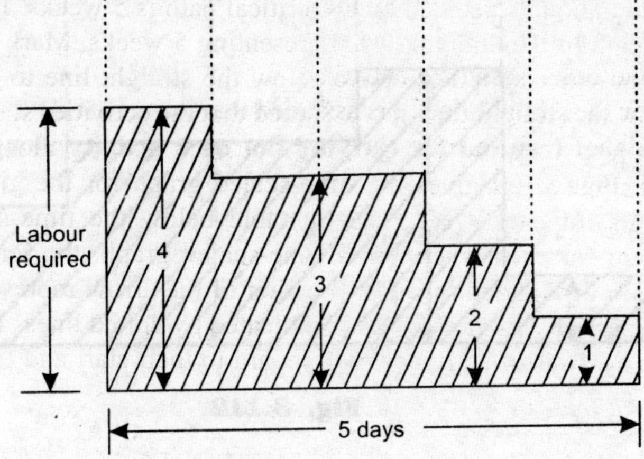

Fig. 3.110

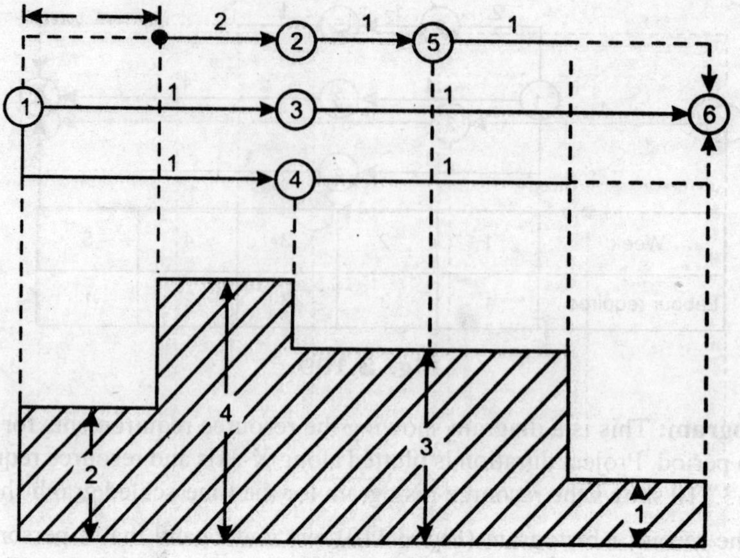

Fig. 3.111

Let us try to shift activity (1)→(4) by one week. The resulting time-scaled graph and the corresponding resource histogram are shown in Fig. 3.112. Referring to Fig. 3.112, we find that the situation has not improved since the peak resource requirement (of 4 persons) has not changed.

Let us try to shift activity (1)→(2) by one more week. The total float available along path (1)→(2)→(5)→(6) is not fully exhausted. The resulting time-scaled graph and the corresponding resource histogram are shown in Fig. 3.113.

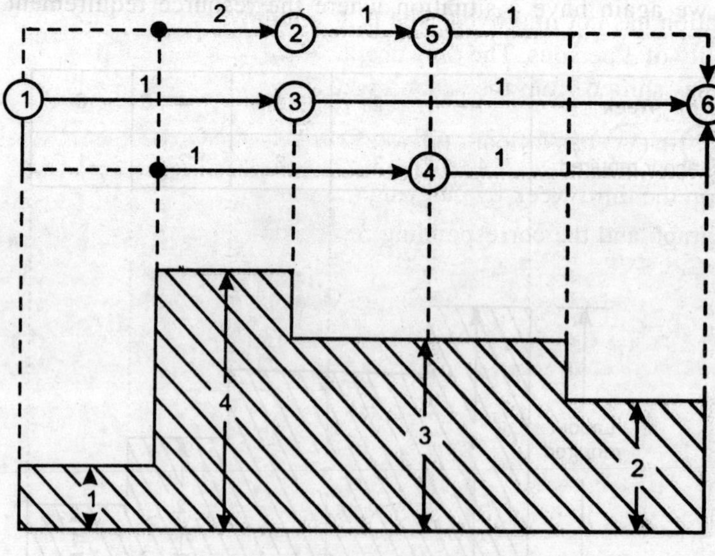

Fig. 3.112

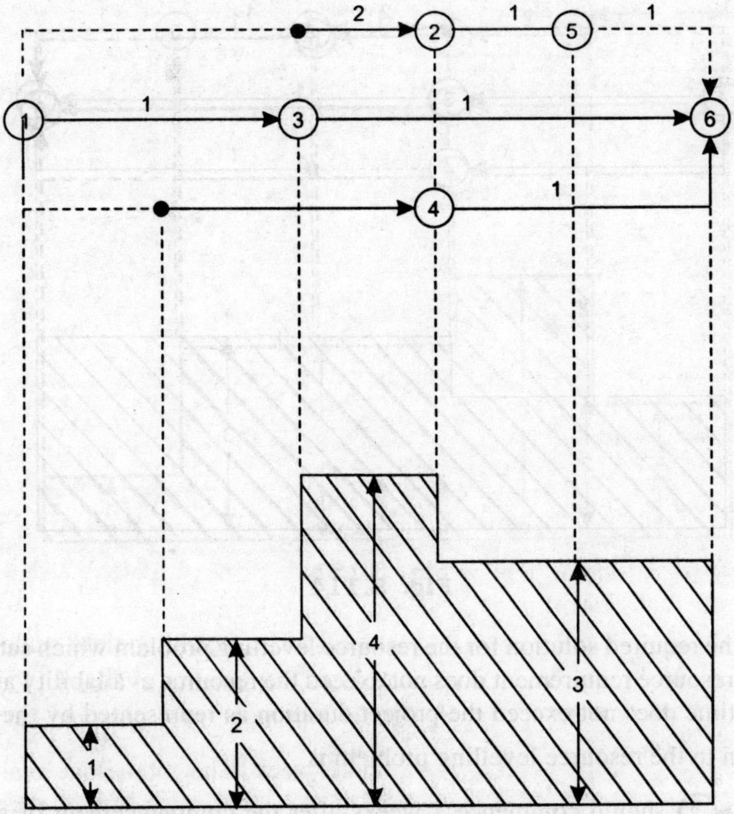

Fig. 3.113

Even now, the situation has not improved. The peak resource requirement still remains 4 persons as against the availability of 3 persons. The only change that we observe in Fig. 3.113 is that the peak resource requirement has shifted from the second week to the third week.

Since path (1)→(4)→(6) has a float of 1 week, this can be made use of for reducing the peak resource requirement on the third week by delaying the start of activity (4)→(6) by one week. The resulting time-scaled graph and the corresponding resource histogram are shown in Fig. 3.114.

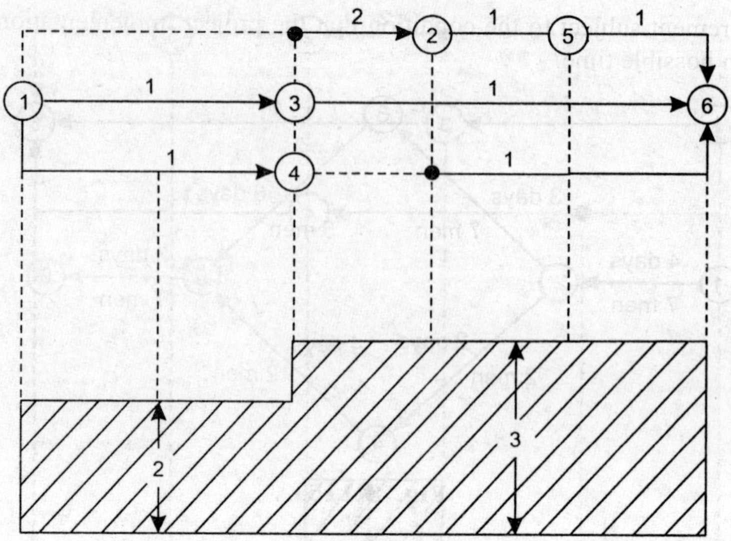

Fig. 3.114

Fig. 3.114 gives the required solution for the resource levelling problem which satisfies the requirements that the peak resource requirement does not exceed the resource availability at any time and the project completion time does not exceed the project duration as represented by the critical path.

Thus, the solution to the resource levelling problem is

- Activity (1)→(2) should commence 2 weeks after the commencement of activity (1)→(3) and
- Activity (4)→(6) should commence one week after the completion of activity (1)→(4)

> *Note :*
>
> For larger and more complex projects, resource levelling exercise as done in the illustration above by shifting/juggling of activities making use of the floats available will be a very time consuming work since there will be a very large number of alternatives available. For handling such complex problems, several heuristic type computer programs have been developed.

In the illustration explained above, the resource requirement is not uniform through out. Though the resource requirement has been levelled to the extent possible, the personnel requirement in the first two weeks is 2 while for the rest of the period it is 3. Uniform manpower requirement through out the implementation period would be an ideal situation. However, this could not be achieved in view of the time constraint, viz., the project should be completed in 5 weeks time.

The following illustration gives an example where the resource levelling exercise brings a situation of uniform resource requirement through out the project implementation period.

Illustration 3.24

Fig. 3.115 shows the network of activities of a small project. The manpower requirement for the different activities are also indicated in the network. Arrive at a schedule of activities that optimizes the manpower requirement subject to the condition that the project implementation time should not exceed the minimum possible time.

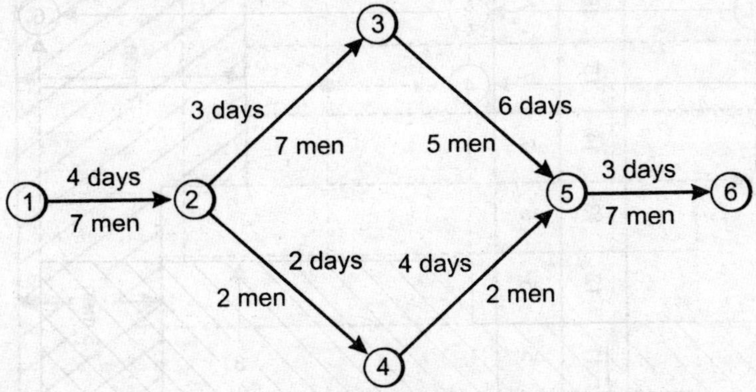

Fig. 3.115

Solution:

First, find out the critical path for the given network. Fig. 3.116 shows the critical path. (1)→(2)→(3)→(5)→(6) is the critical path and the project duration along the critical path is 16 days. This is the minimum time in which the project can be completed. It is given in the problem that the project implementation time should not exceed the minimum possible time. Hence, the scheduling of activities should be done in such a way that the project is completed in 16 days time and at the same time the resource utilisation is optimised. This is a problem of resource levelling.

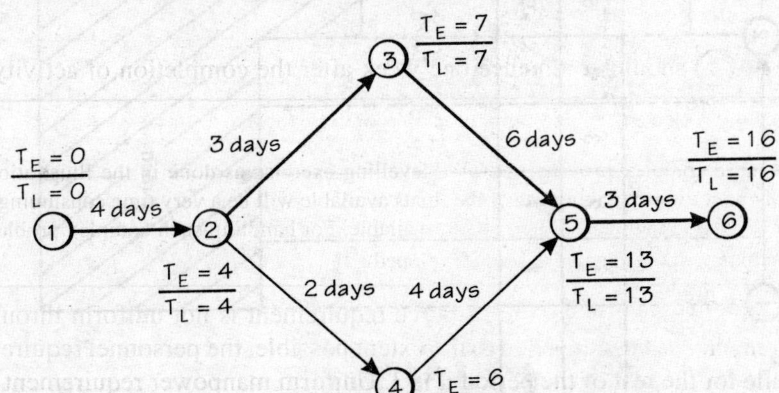

Fig. 3.116

Fig. 3.117 gives a time-scaled graph and the corresponding resource histogram assuming that the activities start as early as possible. It is observed from the resource histogram that on 10 days the manpower requirement is 7 while it is 9 for three days and 5 for three days. For levelling the resource requirements without extending the project completion time, activities (2)→(4) and (4)→(5) can be shifted towards the right as shown in the revised time-scaled graph (refer Fig. 3.118). The resource histogram for the revised time-scaled graph shows a uniform manpower requirement of 7 throughout.

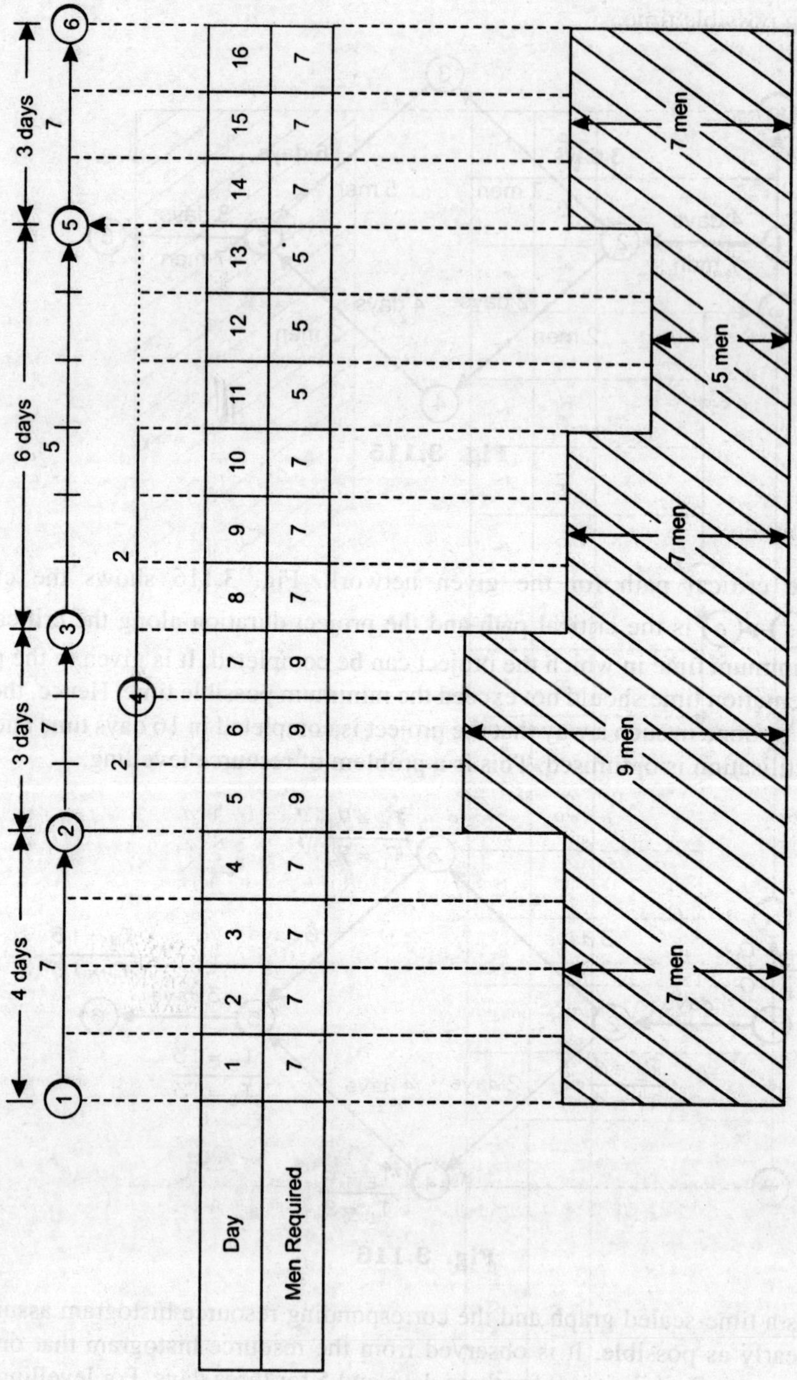
4 days
3 days
6 days
3 days
7
7
5
7
2
2
Day
Men Required
1 2 3 4 5 6 7 8 9 10 11 12 13 14 15 16
7 7 7 7 9 9 9 7 7 7 5 5 5 7 7 7
7 men
9 men
7 men
5 men
7 men

Fig. 3.117

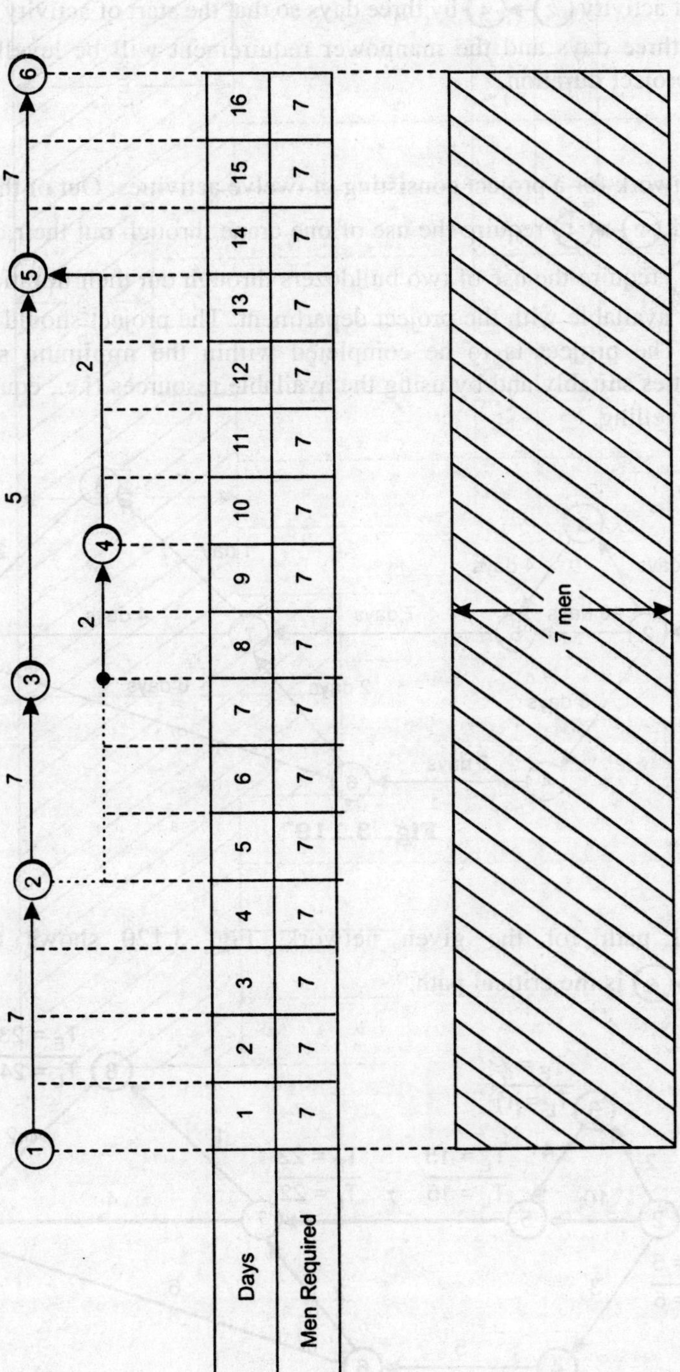
1
2
3
4
5
6
7
7
5
7
2
2
Days
Men Required
1 2 3 4 5 6 7 8 9 10 11 12 13 14 15 16
7 7 7 7 7 7 7 7 7 7 7 7 7 7 7 7
7 men

Fig. 3.118

Thus, the solution for the resource levelling problem is that

- Delay the start of activity (2)→(4) by three days so that the start of activity (4)→(5) will also get delayed by three days and the manpower requirement will be levelled uniformly at 7 throughout the project duration.

Illustration 3.25

Fig. 3.119 gives the network for a project consisting of twelve activities. Out of the twelve activities, activities (2)→(3) and (2)→(4) require the use of one crane through out their duration. Activities (6)→(7) and (6)→(9) require the use of two bulldozers through out their duration. Only one crane and two bulldozers are available with the project department. The project should not be delayed for want of equipments. The project is to be completed within the minimum scheduled time by rescheduling the activities suitably and by using the available resources (i.e., equipments). Give the solution for resource levelling.

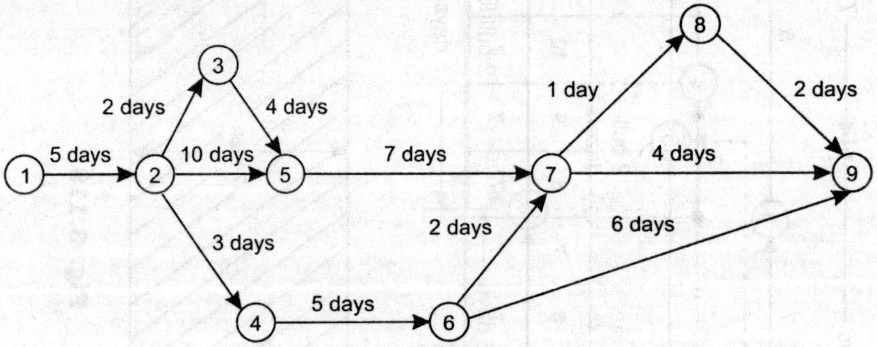

Fig. 3.119

Solution:

Find out the critical path for the given network. Fig. 3.120 shows the critical path. (1)→(2)→(5)→(7)→(9) is the critical path.

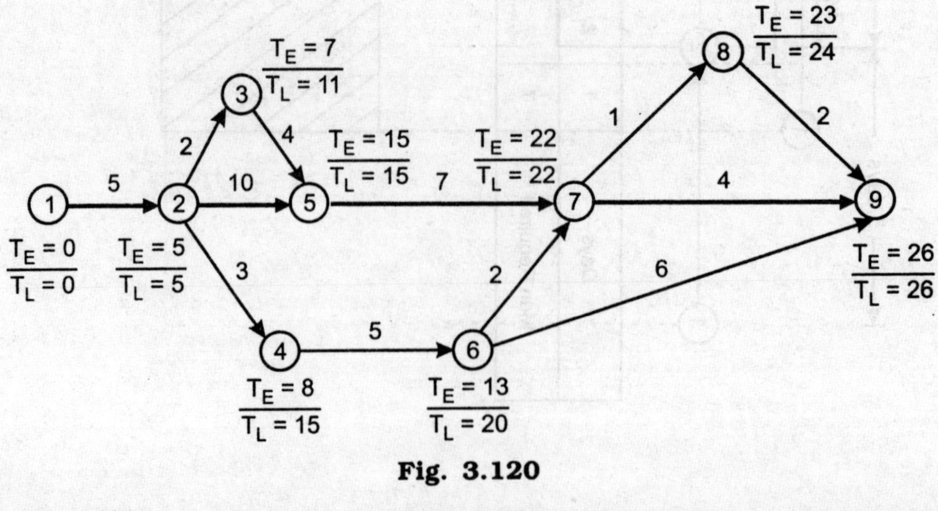

Fig. 3.120

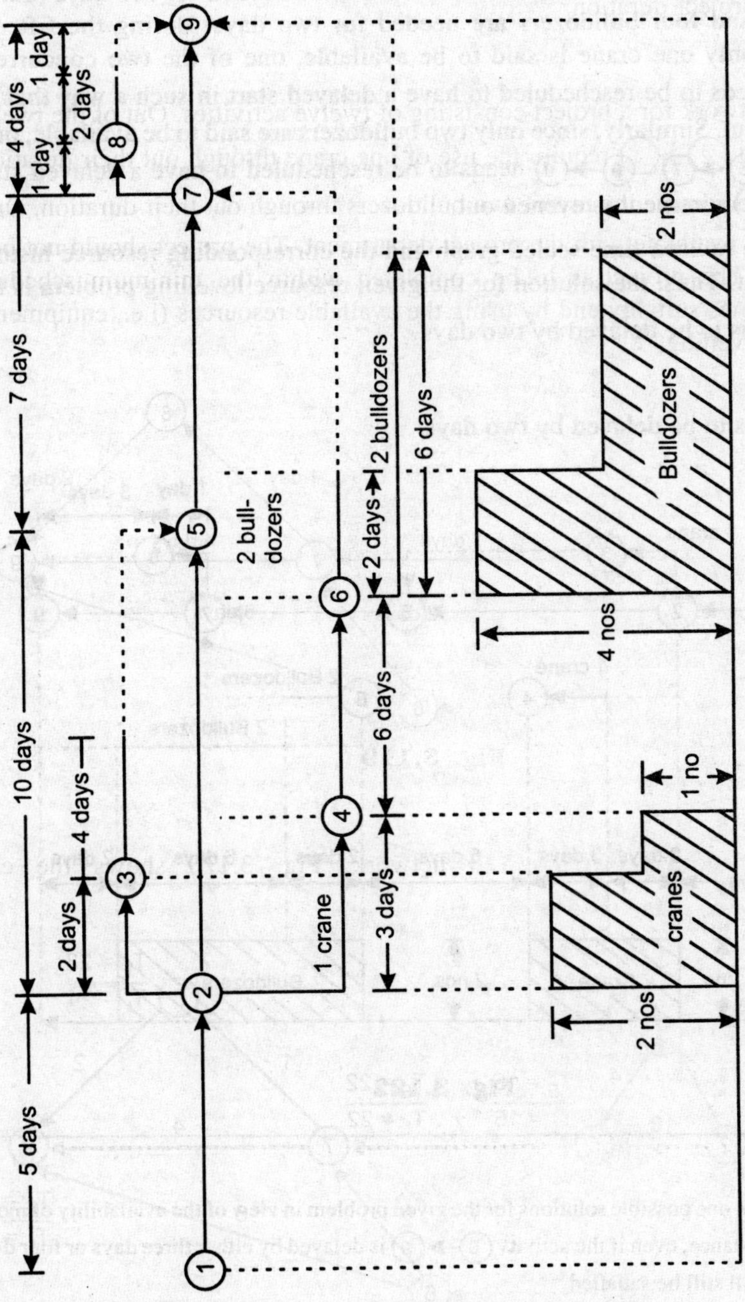
1
2
3
4
5
6
7
8
9
5 days
10 days
7 days
2 days
4 days
4 days
1 day
1 day
2 days
1 crane
3 days
6 days
2 days
2 bulldozers
6 days
2 bull-
dozers
2 nos
cranes
1 no
4 nos
Bulldozers
2 nos

Fig. 3.121

The time-scaled graph for the given network and the resource histogram for the two equipments (crane and bulldozers) are given in Fig. 3.121. As per this time-scaled graph, it is assumed that the activities start as early as possible.

Resource histogram in Fig. 3.121 shows that two cranes are needed for two days (during the sixth and the seventh day) and four bulldozers are needed for two days (during the fifteenth and the sixteenth day). Since only one crane is said to be available, one of the two concurrent activities ②→③, ②→④ needs to be rescheduled to have a delayed start in such a way that the resource requirement is evened out. Similarly, since only two bulldozers are said to be available, one of the two con current activities ⑥→⑦, ⑥→⑨ needs to be rescheduled to have a delayed start in such a way that the resource requirement is evened out.

Fig. 3.122 shows the revised time-scaled graph and the corresponding resource histogram which satisfies the requirement. Thus, the solution for the given resource levelling problem is that,

* Activity ②→④ is to be delayed by two days

and

* Activity ⑥→⑨ is to be delayed by two days.

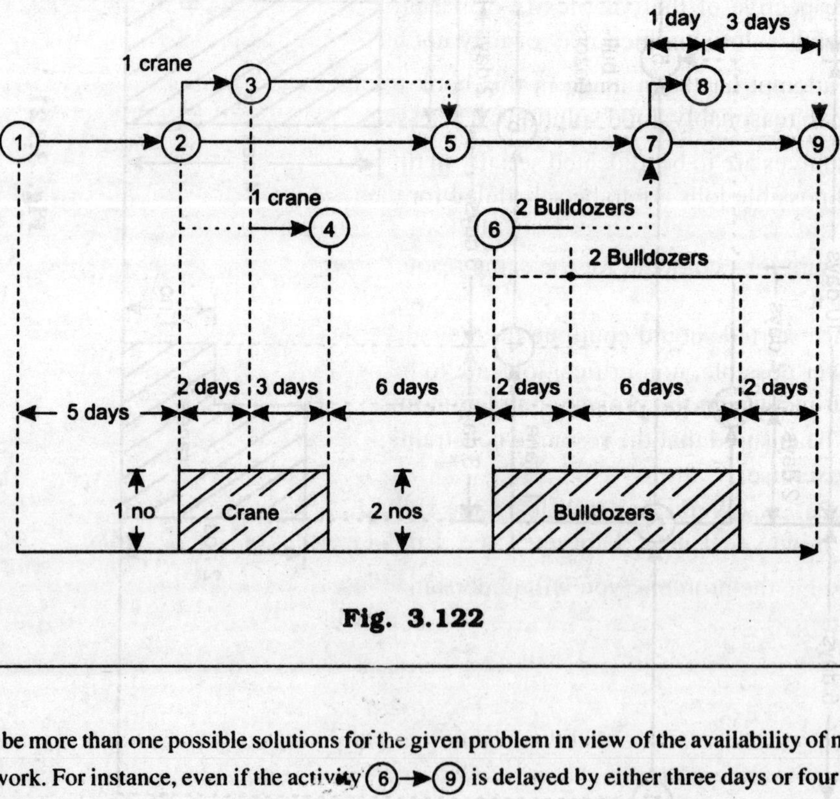

Fig. 3.122

> ***Note:***
>
> There can be more than one possible solutions for the given problem in view of the availability of more float in the network. For instance, even if the activity ⑥→⑨ is delayed by either three days or four days, the resource constraint will still be satisfied.

Resource Smoothing

(Fixed resource limit scheduling)

As explained already, the nature of problem under this head is that there is no constraint on project completion time. The constraint is only with regard to the availability of other resources. Though there is no time constraint, it does not mean that the project duration can be stretched too far. Increase in project completion time will lead to increased overhead expenses. Hence, though the project duration can be extended to satisfy the resource constraints, it shall be done in such a way that the project duration is extended to the minimum possible extent and at the same time satisfying the resource constraints.

There are many different techniques available for handling such problems. One such method that employs a heuristic (rule of thumb) which is easy to use is explained below. There are different heuristics available for resource smoothing, devised by different experts in the field. These rules vary greatly in their complexity and obviously a more complex set of rules is bound to give a better solution since it will take care of many aspects of the problem as compared to a simple set of rules. However, when the size of the project is not small, it will become highly difficult and time-consuming to apply the more complex rules and arrive at a solution manually (i.e., without the use of computers). In spite of all these, there is no guarantee that a given set of rules will always give the optimum resource allocation, irrespective of the complexity of the problem. It can only be said that heuristics give a reasonably 'good' solution which may or may not be the optimum solution.

Hence, an attempt has been made in this book to explain a simple set of heuristics which when applied will give reasonably good solutions. The essential rules are:

(*a*) The resources are to be allocated serially in time i.e., resource allocation should start on the first day; all possible jobs are to be scheduled for the first day before moving to the second day and so on.

(*b*) When more jobs compete for the same resource, preference is to be given to the job/jobs with least float.

(*c*) Jobs once started should continue till they are finished *i.e.*, breaking of jobs is not allowed.

(*d*) Whenever possible, non-critical jobs are to be postponed so that critical jobs can be scheduled with out increasing the project completion time.

(*e*) It must be ensured that the resource constraint is not violated at any stage while performing the above exercise.

(Confusing?.......... Well. You will learn the skill once you solve a problem. A Chinese proverb comes to my mind.......'I hear, I forget; I see, I remember; I do, I understand...

Once you solve the problem, you will understand the rules better and you can write down the rules in your own terms).

Illustration 3.26

A project consists of five activities. The network of activities and the duration of these activates are given in Fig. 3.123.

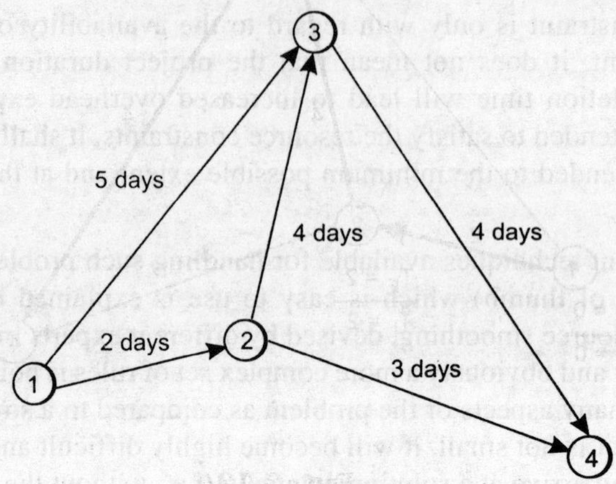

Fig. 3.123

The manpower requirement of the activities are as under :

Activity	*Manpower required per day*
1 → 2	2
1 → 3	5
2 → 3	4
3 → 4	7
2 → 4	3

The maximum available manpower is only 7 per day. Schedule the activities in such a way that the manpower requirement does not exceed the limit and at the same time the project is completed in the minimum possible time.

Solution :

Fig. 3.124 shows the critical path. [1 → 2 → 3 → 4 = 10 days; 1 → 3 → 4 = 9 days; 1 → 2 → 4 = 5 days; hence 1 → 2 → 3 → 4 is the critical path]

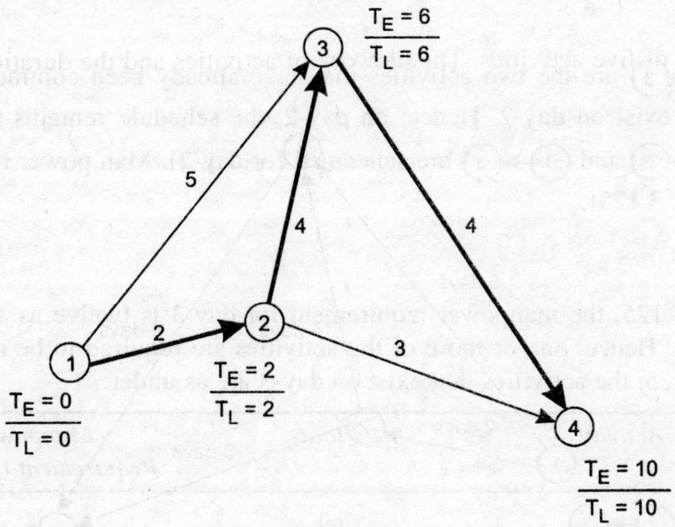

Fig. 3.124

Fig. 3.125 shows the time-scaled graph for the network assuming that all the activities start as early as possible. (Remember, that a time-scaled graph is drawn by drawing the critical activities on a horizontal line to some scale and drawing the non-critical activities parallel to this horizontal line, above or below it).

Day-1

The manpower requirement is only seven; the manpower availability on any day is also seven. There are two activities (1)→(2) and (1)→(3) that can be scheduled for day-1. Since the manpower requirement for day-1 matches with the manpower availability, the two activities (1)→(2) and (1)→(3) can be scheduled for the day.

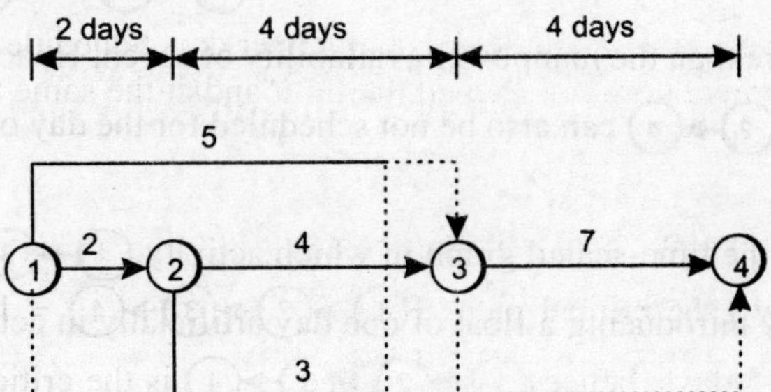

Day	1	2	3	4	5	6	7	8	9	10
Man power required	7	7	12	12	12	4	7	7	7	7

Fig. 3.125

Day-2

(1)→(2) and (1)→(3) are the two activities that have already been commenced on day-1. Only these two activities exist on day-2. Hence, on day-2, the schedule remains the same as of day-1 (*i.e.*, activities (1)→(2) and (1)→(3) are scheduled for day-2). Man power requirement for Day-2 is also 7. [Refer Fig. 3.125]

Day-3

As seen from Fig. 3.125, the manpower requirement for day-3 is twelve as against the manpower availability of seven. Hence, one or more of the activities are required to be rescheduled on day-3. Referring to Fig. 3.125, the activities that exist on day-3 are as under:

Activity	*Float*	*Manpower Requirement (per day)*
(2)→(3)	nil	4
(2)→(4)	5 (indicated by dotted line)	3
(1)→(3)	1 (indicated by dotted line)	5

As per the heuristics, activities that have already commenced should be continued till their end and for scheduling other activities, activities with minimum float should be given preference.

Activity (1)→(3) is already in progress and hence it is to be scheduled for the day. (*i.e.*, activity (1)→(3) will be allowed to be performed on day-3).

Out of the remaining two activities, activity (2)→(3) has no float. Hence, it is to be considered for scheduling. However, the manpower requirement of (1)→(3) and (2)→(3) put together will be nine (5 + 4) which is more than the manpower availability of seven. Hence, (2)→(3) can not be scheduled for day-3. Activity (2)→(4) can also be not scheduled for the day on the same logic of exceeding the manpower limit.

Fig. 3.126 gives the time-scaled graph in which activity (1)→(3) alone is scheduled for the third day. This is done by introducing a float of one day artificially in activity (1)→(2)

Day-4

On day-4, there are three activities (refer Fig. 3.126), viz., (1)→(3), (2)→(3) and (2)→(4). Out of these, activity (1)→(3) is already in progress which can not be stopped. The manpower requirements of the remaining two activities are 4 and 3 respectively. If any one of these activities is scheduled for the day, the total manpower requirement will exceed seven (5 + 4 = 9 which is more than 7; 5 + 3 = 8 which is more than 7). Hence, activities (2)→(3) and (2)→(4) need to be shifted. Fig. 3.127 shows the revised time-scaled graph in which the manpower requirement on day-4 is within the limit).

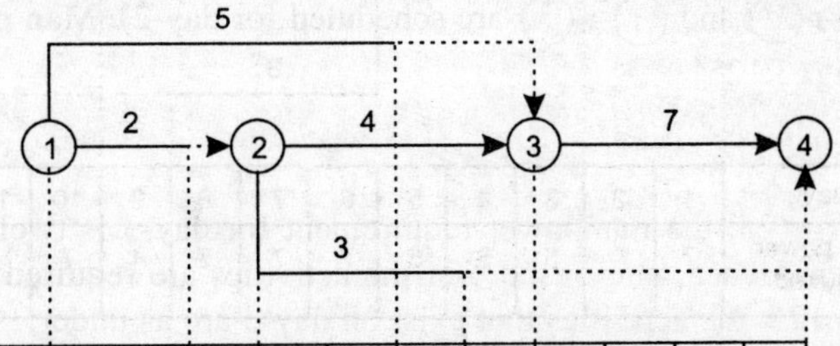

Day	1	2	3	4	5	6	7	8	9	10	11
Man power required	7	7	5	12	12	7	4	7	7	7	7

Fig. 3.126

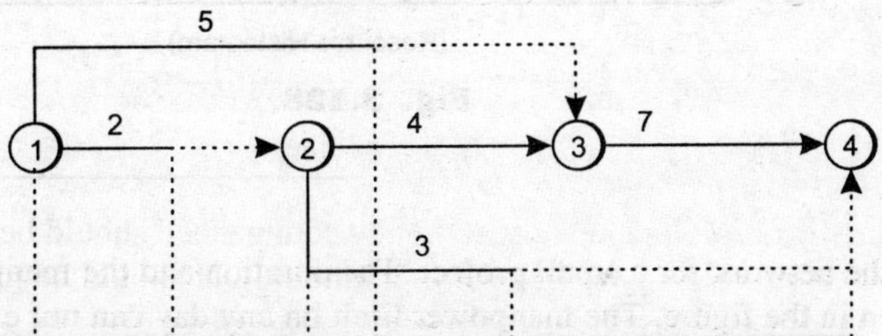

Day	1	2	3	4	5	6	7	8	9	10	11	12
Man power required	7	7	5	5	12	7	7	4	7	7	7	7

Fig. 3.127

Day-5

The logic applied to day-4 can be extended to day-5, which results in Fig. 3.128.

Day-6 to Day-13

The resource requirement on all the days is either equal to or within the resource availability. Hence, the exercise can be stopped. Thus, the solution to the problem is:

- Delay the start of event-2 (*i.e.*, activity (2)→(3)) by three days so that the manpower requirement will not exceed the manpower availability. The project duration has ofcourse increased by 3 days. (i.e., from the duration of 10 days, it has increased to 13 days).

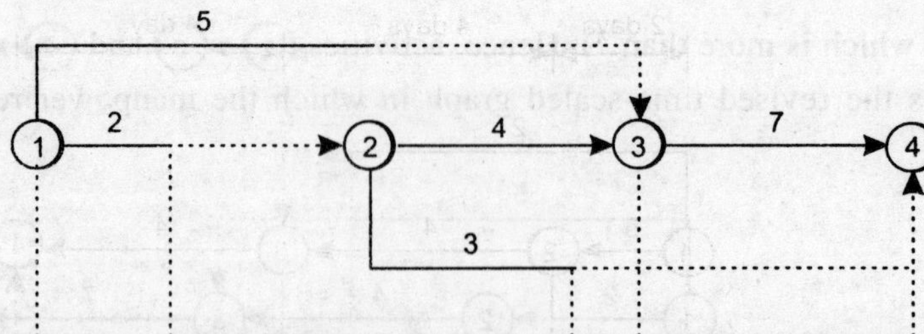

Day	1	2	3	4	5	6	7	8	9	10	11	12	13
Man power required	7	7	5	5	5	7	7	7	4	7	7	7	7

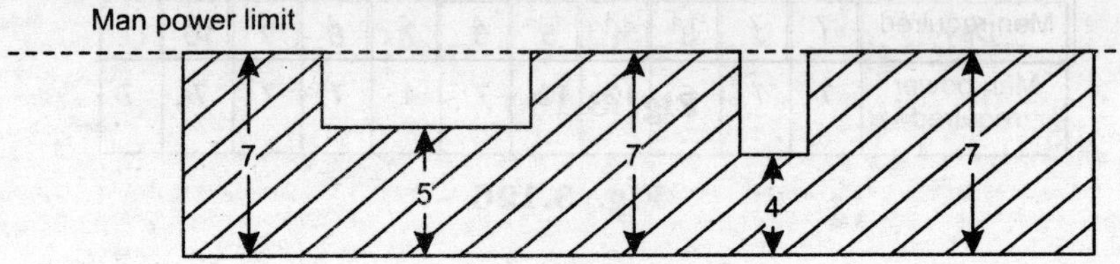

(Resource Histogram)

Fig. 3.128

Illustration 3.27

Fig. 3.129 gives the network for a small project. The duration and the manpower requirements of the activities are given in the figure. The manpower limit on any day can not exceed seven. Schedule the activities suitably.

Solution:

(1)→(2)→(3)→(4) is the critical path. (Note: the network and the activity durations are the same as given in illustration 3.26. Hence, the critical path remains the same).

Fig. 3.130 shows the time-scaled graph assuming that the activities start as early as possible.

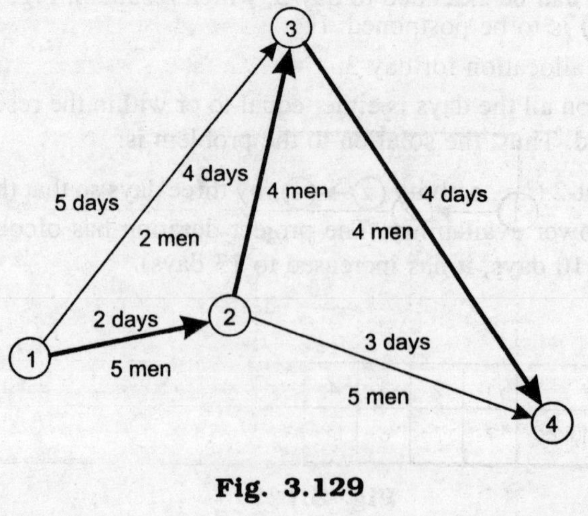

Fig. 3.129

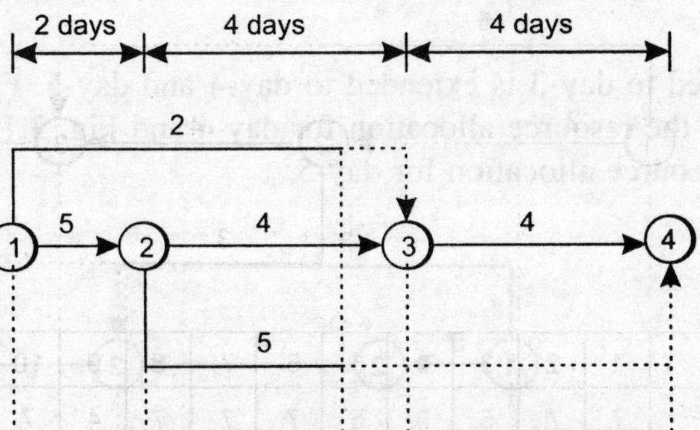

Day	1	2	3	4	5	6	7	8	9	10
Men required	7	7	11	11	11	4	4	4	4	4

Fig. 3.130

Day-1 & Day-2

The manpower requirement is equal to the manpower availability. Hence activities (1)→(2) and (1)→(3) can be scheduled on these two days.

Day-3

The manpower requirement is more than the availability. Since activity (1)→(3) is already in progress, the same can not be stopped and is to be continued for the day. Since the manpower requirement of activity (1)→(3) is 2 per day, the remaining available manpower is 5 (7 – 2). Out of the remaining two activities (activity (2)→(3) and (2)→(4)), activity (2)→(3) has no float while activity (2)→(4) has a float of 5 days (refer Fig. 3.130 which shows the float of 5 days in dotted line). If activity (2)→(3) is scheduled for the day apart from activity (1)→(3), the total manpower requirement is six which is below the limit of seven. Hence, the resource constraint is not violated. Therefore, activity (2)→(4) is to be postponed. Fig. 3.131 shows the revised time-scaled graph in which satisfies the resource allocation for day-3.

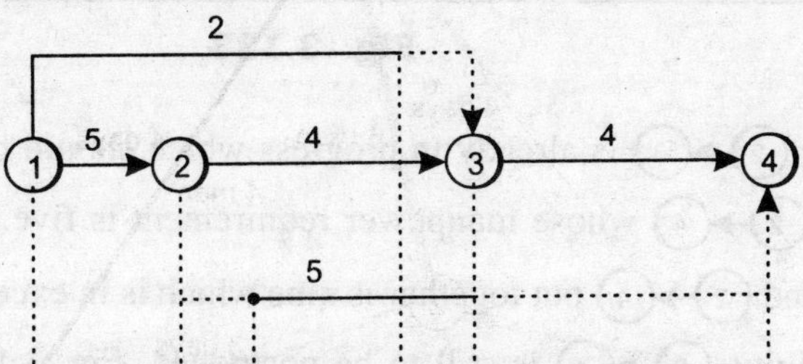

Day	1	2	3	4	5	6	7	8	9	10
Men required	7	7	6	11	11	9	4	4	4	4

Fig. 3.131

Day-4 & Day-5

The same logic applied to day-3 is extended to day-4 and day-5. Fig. 3.132 shows the time-scaled graph which satisfies the resource allocation for day-4 and Fig. 3.133 shows the time-scaled graph which satisfies the resource allocation for day-5.

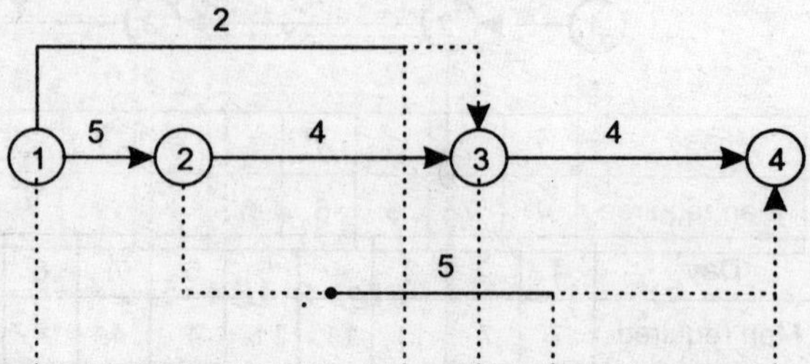

Day	1	2	3	4	5	6	7	8	9	10
Men required	7	7	6	6	11	9	9	4	4	4

Fig. 3.132

Day-6

Manpower requirement : 9 (refer Fig. 3.133)

Manpower availability : 7

Shortage : 2

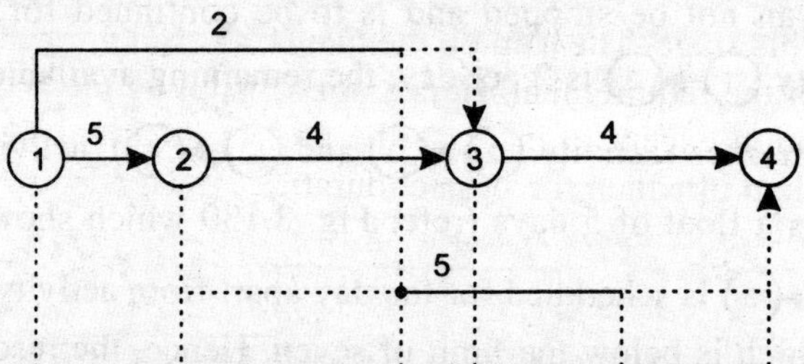

Day	1	2	3	4	5	6	7	8	9	10
Men required	7	7	6	6	6	9	9	9	4	4

Fig. 3.133

On day-6, activity (2)→(3) is already in progress which should be continued. The other activity available is activity (2)→(4) whose manpower requirement is five. The manpower requirement of activities (2)→(3) and (2)→(4) put together is nine which is in excess of the manpower availability of seven. Hence, activity (2)→(4) is still to be postponed. Fig. 3.134 shows the time-scale graph which satisfies the resource allocation requirements for day-6.

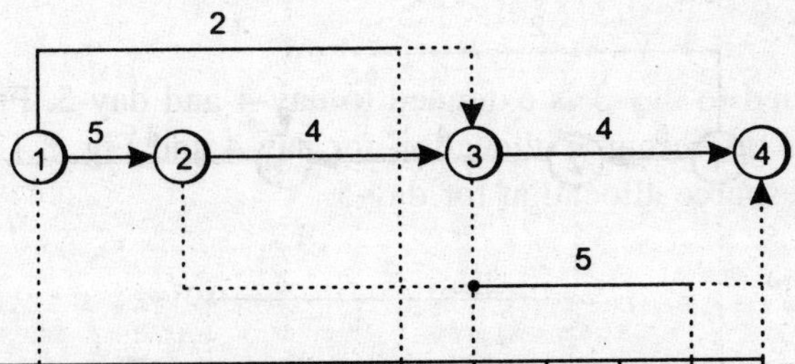

Day	1	2	3	4	5	6	7	8	9	10
Men required	7	7	6	6	6	4	9	9	9	4

Fig. 3.134

Day-7

Referring to Fig. 3.134, the manpower requirement for the day is nine, which is in excess of the manpower availability. There are two activities available ((3)→(4) & (2)→(4)) out of which activity (3)→(4) has no float and activity (1)→(4) has a float of one day. Hence, activity (3)→(4) is to be scheduled for the day, postponing activity (2)→(4) by one day. Fig. 3.135 shows the revised time-scaled graph which satisfies the resource allocation requirements for day-7.

Day-8, Day-9 and Day-10:

There are two activities (3)→(4) and (2)→(4). Activity (3)→(4) has no float. Activity (2)→(4) also has no float at this stage. The sum on the manpower requirements for these two activities is nine which is in excess of the requirement. Hence, for scheduling the activities during the last three days, there is no other option except to increase the project duration by three days. Fig. 3.136 gives the solution to the problem in which the project duration is extended by three days.

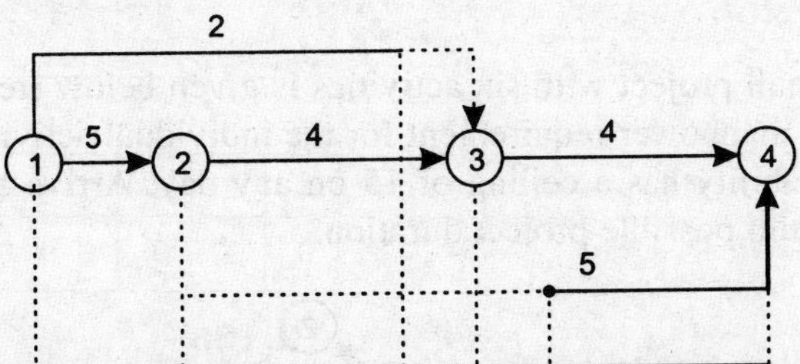

Day	1	2	3	4	5	6	7	8	9	10
Men required	7	7	6	6	6	4	4	9	9	9

Fig. 3.135

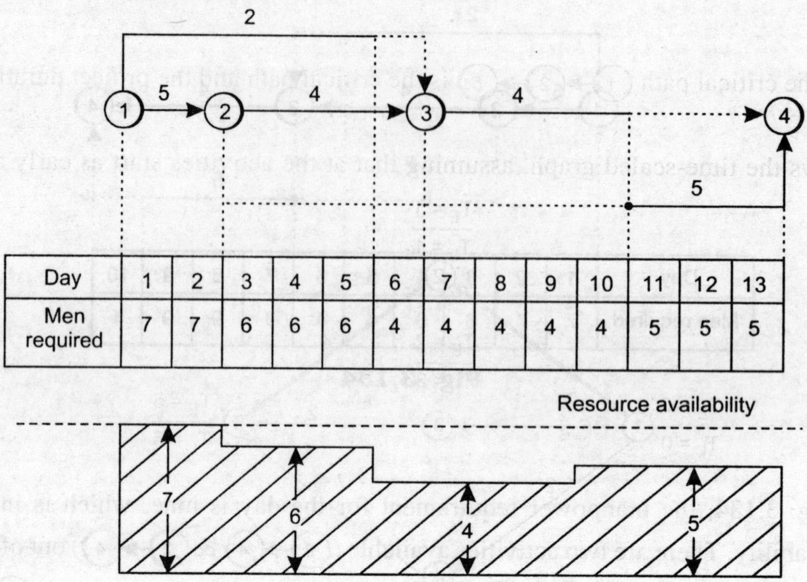

Day	1	2	3	4	5	6	7	8	9	10	11	12	13
Men required	7	7	6	6	6	4	4	4	4	4	5	5	5

Fig. 3.136

Thus, the solution to the problem is:

*Introduce artificial float of three days in activity (3)→(4); the project duration will be increased to 13 days, but the resource constraint will not be violated.

> *Note :*
>
> The resource constraint has been satisfied. Satisfying the resource constraint, the project duration has been extended by 3 days (13-10). Thus, 13 days is the minimum project duration satisfying the resource constraint.

Illustration 3.28

The network for a small project with six activities is given below (refer Fig. 3.137). The duration of the activities and the manpower requirement for the individual activities are also given in the figure. The manpower availability has a ceiling of 15 on any day. Arrive at a suitable resource allocation schedule with minimum possible project duration.

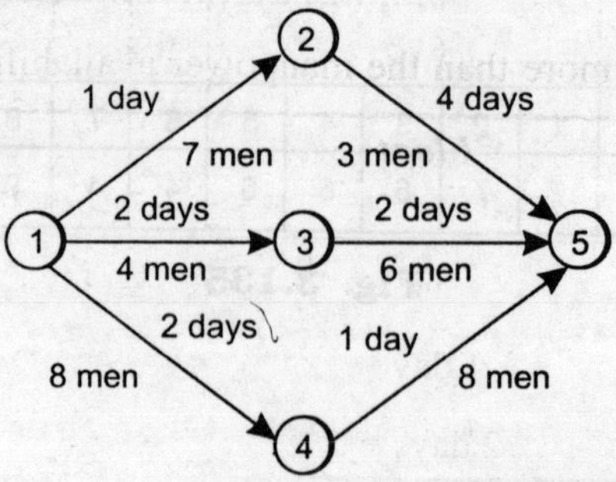

Fig.3.137

Solution:

Fig. 3.138 shows the critical path (1)→(2)→(5) is the critical path and the project duration is 5 days (1 + 4).

Fig. 3.139 shows the time-scaled graph, assuming that at the activities start as early as possible.

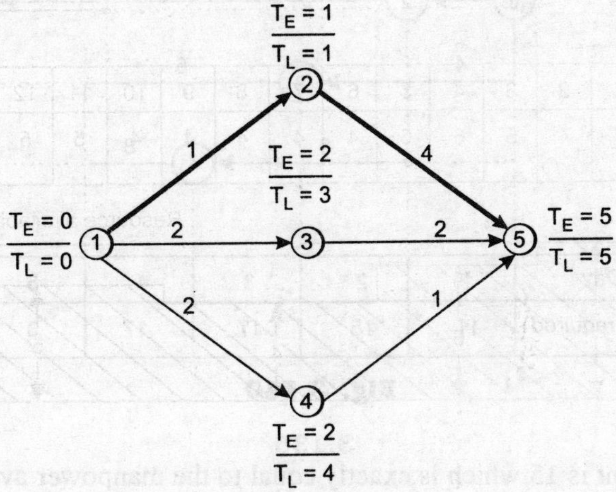

Fig. 3.138

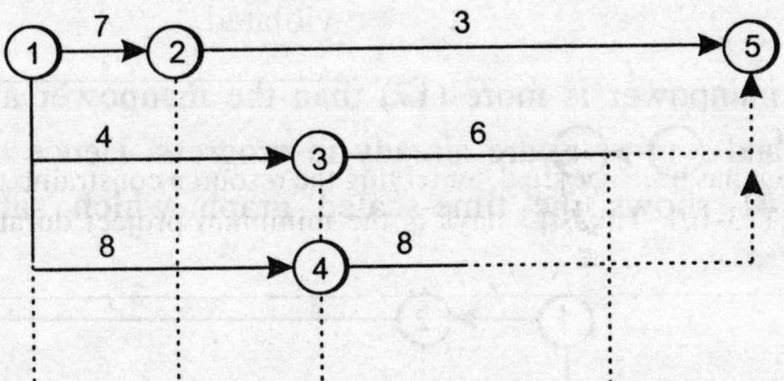

Day	1	2	3	4	5
Men required	19	15	17	9	3

Fig. 3.139

Day-1

The manpower requirement (19) is more than the manpower availability (15).

Activity	*Float*	*Manpower Requirement (per day)*
(1)→(2)	nil	7
(1)→(3)	1 day *	4
(1)→(4)	2 days **	8

* Though activity (1)→(3) has no float, the float available in path (1)→(3)→(5) is considered.

* Though activity (1)→(4) has no float, the float available in path (1)→(4)→(5) is considered.

Activity (1)→(2) is to be scheduled since it has no float. Out of the other two activities, since activity (1)→(3) lies in the path having minimum float, the same can be scheduled for the day. This means that activity (1)→(4) is left out which is to be postponed. Fig. 3.140 shows the time-scaled graph which satisfies the resource allocation requirements for day-1.

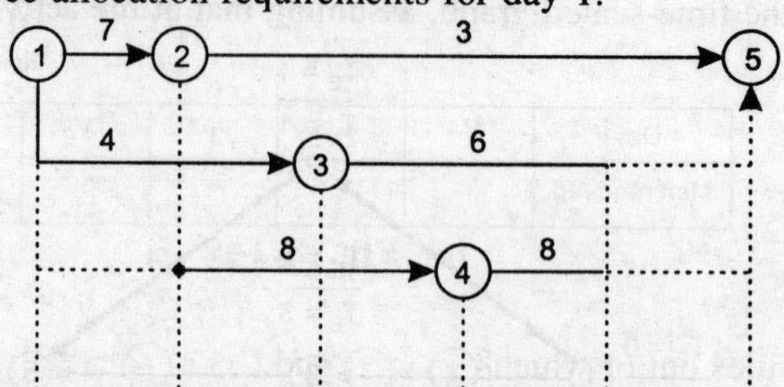

Day	1	2	3	4	5
Men required	11	15	17	17	3

Fig. 3.140

Day-2

The manpower requirement is 15 which is exactly equal to the manpower availability. Hence, all the three activities ((2)→(5), (1)→(3) and (1)→(4)) can be scheduled for the day.

Day-3

The requirement of manpower is more (17) than the manpower available (15). Out of the three activities, (2)→(5) and (1)→(4) are already in progress. Hence only activity (3)→(5) is to be postponed. Fig. 3.141 shows the time-scaled graph which satisfies the resource allocation requirements for day-3.

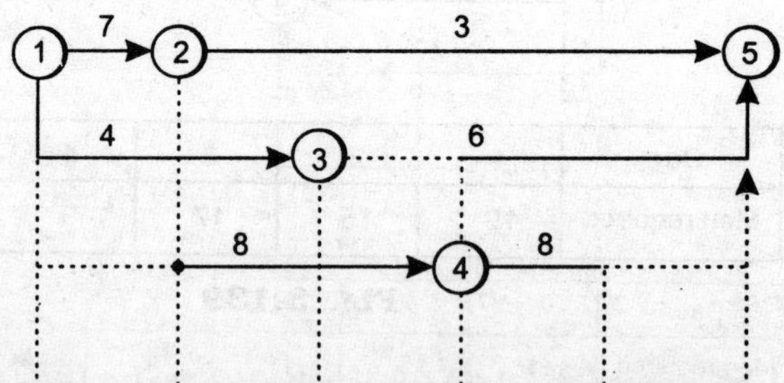

Day	1	2	3	4	5
Men required	11	15	11	17	9

Fig. 3.141

Day-4

The manpower requirement is more than the availability. Activity (2)→(5) is already in progress and hence it is to be scheduled for the day. Out of the remaining two activities, (3)→(5) has no float at this stage and (4)→(5) has a float of one day. Hence, activity (3)→(5) which has the minimum float is to be scheduled for the day. Fig. 3.142 shows the time-scaled graph which shows the resource allocation requirements for day-4.

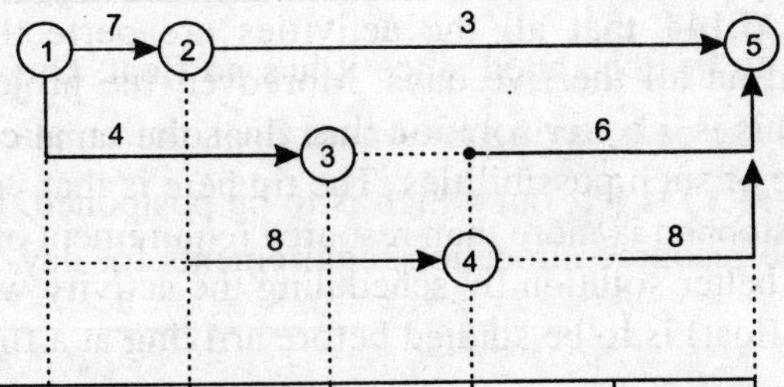

Day	1	2	3	4	5
Men required	11	15	11	9	17

Fig. 3.142

Day-5

There are three activities out of which (2)→(5) and (3)→(5) are already in progress and hence they must be scheduled for the day. For accommodating activity (4)→(5) which is yet to be commenced, the project duration is to be extended by one day. Fig. 3.143 gives the solution to the problem.

> ***Note :***
>
> It was pointed out already that the heuristics used for resource smoothing will give a 'good' solution which need not necessarily be the best solution. This can be verified by solving the problem given in illustration 3.28 by a different rule.

Whenever more activities compete for the same resource, as per the heuristics given, the activity with minimum float is to be chosen for scheduling. This rule has been followed in solving the problem given in illustration 3.28. Accordingly, for day-1, we have chosen to schedule activity (1)→(3)*. Let us try to schedule activity (1)→(4) instead of (1)→(3) on day-1 and see the result.

Fig. 3.144 gives the time-scaled graph with activities (1)→(2) and (1)→(4) scheduled for day-1.

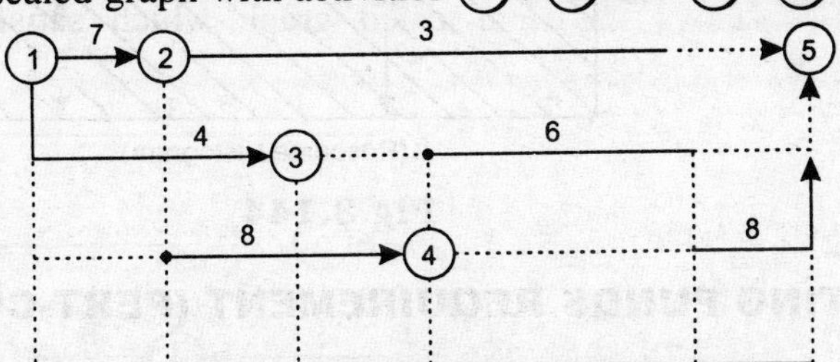

Day	1	2	3	4	5	6
Men required	11	15	11	9	9	8

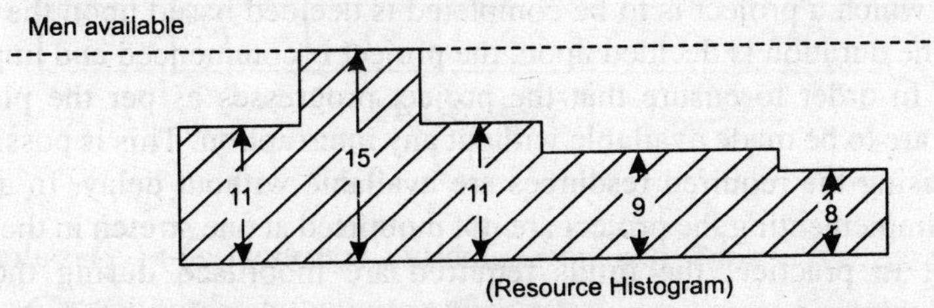

(Resource Histogram)

Fig. 3.143

* Though activities (1)→(3) and (1)→(4) do not have float, since activity (1)→(3) lies in the path having minimum float, the same was scheduled for day-1

We find from Fig. 3.144 that all the activities are perfectly scheduled and the manpower requirement is satisfied on all the five days. Moreover, the project duration is also not increased beyond 5 days. Thus, this is a better solution than the solution already arrived at. Hence, the project manager must be aware of such possibilities. The tip here is that whenever the resource requirement of an activity that is postponed is more than resource requirement of the activity that is scheduled, the possibility of getting a better solution by scheduling the activity with a higher resource requirement (though it has a higher float) is to be studied before arriving at a final decision.

Another rule that will be useful is that whenever two or more activities that compete for the same resource have the same float, the activity with minimum duration is to be chosen for scheduling (as we have chosen activity (1)→(2) for day-1).

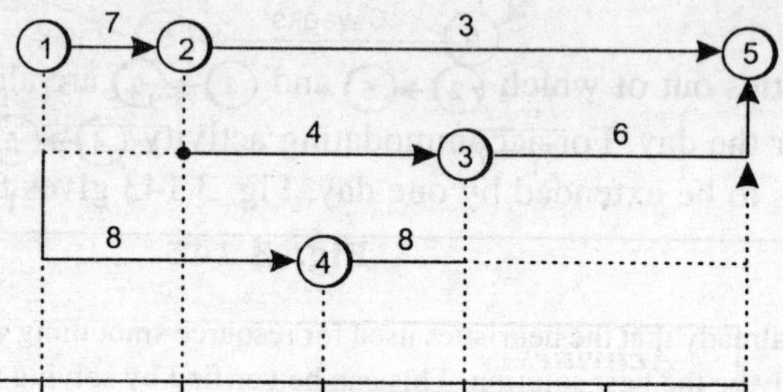

Day	1	2	3	4	5
Men required	15	15	15	9	9

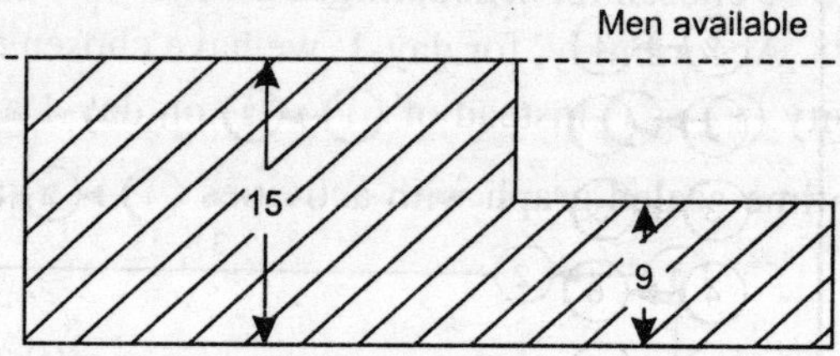

(Resource Histogram)

Fig.3.144

3.7 FORECASTING FUNDS REQUIREMENT (PERT-COST SYSTEM)

A project may be one that is required to be completed within a specified due-date (a case of resource levelling) or may be one for which there is no time constraint, but there are constraints in respect of other resources (a case of resource smoothing).

The duration in which a project is to be completed is decided based upon the field conditions and constraints. Once the duration is decided upon, the project is commenced and implemented as per the planned schedule. In order to ensure that the project progresses as per the planned schedule, the resources required are to be made available without any interruption. This is possible only if the funds required for mobilising the required resources are available without delay. In any project, the total funds required for implementing the project are not mobilised at one stretch in the beginning itself and kept as a reserve. In practice, the funds required are mobilised during the course of project implementation. If the funds requirement during the course of project implementation is forecasted beforehand, mobilisation of the required funds can be planned accordingly. Hence, forecasting the funds requirement during the course of project implementation is an important step in project planning.

Illustration 3.29

A project consists of seven activities. Fig. 3.145 shows the network consisting of seven activities. The funds requirement for each of the activities (both direct costs and overheads) are as under.

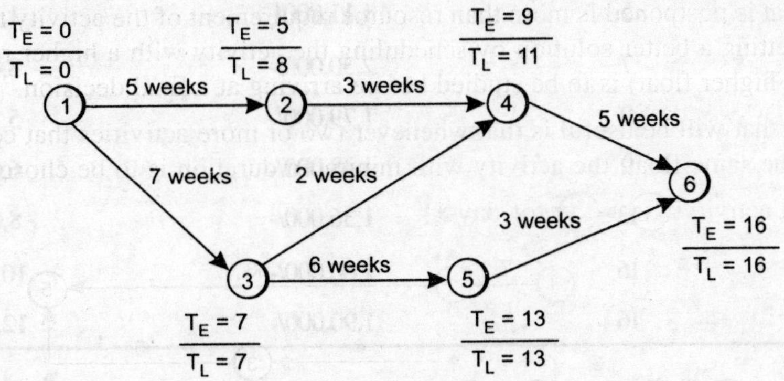

Fig. 3.145

Activities	*Funds requirement (Rs.)*
1 → 2	1,11,000/-
1 → 3	2,30,000/-
2 → 4	1,79,000/-
3 → 4	1,48,000/-
3 → 5	1,36,000/-
4 → 6	2,60,000/-
5 → 6	1,90,000/-

Prepare a schedule of funds requirement during the course of project implementation.

Solution :

As seen from the network, the project duration is 16 weeks.

The schedule of funds requirements can be drawn either on the basis of Early Finish or on the basis of Late Finish of the activities. It may be noted that irrespective of choosing Early Finish or Late Finish of activities, the project will be completed in 16 weeks.

Early Finish of Activities

If it is assumed that all the activities are finished at their Earliest Finishing times, the cost estimate (i.e., funds requirement) during the project implementation is as under.

Activity	*Early Finish (weeks)*	*Funds required for implementing the activity (Rs.)*	*Cumulative funds requirement (Rs.)*
1→2	5	1,11,000/-	1,11,000/-
1→3	7	2,30,000/-	3,41,000/-
2→4	9	1,79,000/-	5,20,000/-
3→4	9	1,48,000/-	6,68,000/-
3→5	13	1,36,000/-	8,04,000/-
4→6	16	2,60,000/-	10,64,000/-
5→6	16	1,90,000/-	12,54,000/-

[Since activities 2→4 and 3→4 will be completed earliest by the ninth week, the cumulative funds requirement by the end of the ninth week is Rs. 6,68,000/-. The cumulative figure of Rs. 5,20,000/- can be ignored since by 9 weeks both the activities 2→4 and 3→4 will be completed. Similarly, the cumulative funds requirement by the end of the sixteenth week is Rs. 12,54,000/- and the figure of Rs. 10,64,000/- can be ignored.]

Accordingly, the cumulative funds requirement assuming early finish of activities is as under.

Early Finish (week)	*Cumulative funds requirement (Rs.)*
5	1,11,000/-
7	3,41,000/-
9	6,68,000/-
13	8,04,000/-
16	12,54,000/-

Late Finish of Activities

If late finish of all the activities is assumed, the funds requirement is as under.

Activity	*Late Finish (weeks)*	*Funds required for implementing the activity (Rs.)*	*Cumulative funds requirement (Rs.)*
1→3	7	2,30,000/-	2,30,000/-
1→2	8	1,11,000/-	3,41,000/-
2→4	11	1,79,000/-	—
3→4	11	1,48,000/-	6,68,000/-*
3→5	13	1,36,000/-	8,04,000/-
4→6	16	2,60,000/-	—
5→6	16	1,90,000/-	12,54,000/-**

* (3,41,000 + 1,79,000 + 1,48,000)

** (8,04,000 + 2,60,000 + 1,90,000)

[At the end of eleventh week, both the activities (2)→(4) and (3)→(4) should have been completed. Hence, the cumulative funds requirement at the end of eleventh week has been arrived at by adding the funds requirement for activities (2)→(4) and (3)→(4) to Rs. 3,41,000/-. Similarly, the cumulative funds requirement at the end of sixteen weeks has been arrived at by adding the funds requirement for activities (4)→(6) and (5)→(6) to Rs. 8,04,000/-].

Fig. 3.146 shows the schedule of cumulative funds requirements based on early finish and late finish. The early finish and the late finish curves indicate the upper and lower limits of funds requirement at any point of time during the implementation of the project.

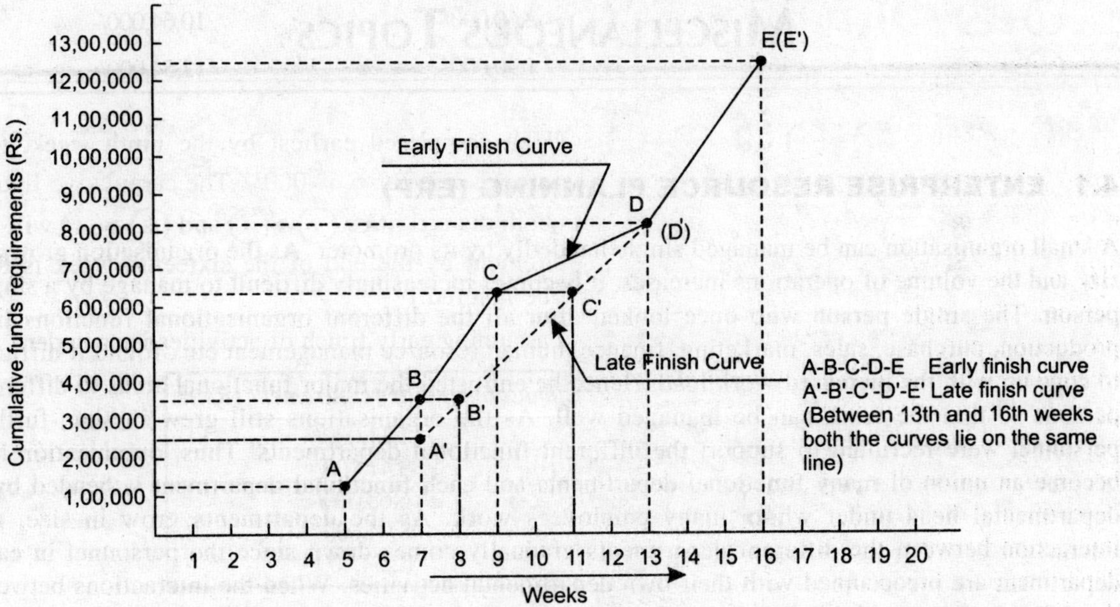

Fig. 3.146

> *Note :*
>
> The coincidence of Early finish curve and Late finish curve between 13th and 16th weeks is incidental

UNIT IV

MISCELLANEOUS TOPICS

4.1 ENTERPRISE RESOURCE PLANNING (ERP)

A small organisation can be managed single handedly by its promoter. As the organisation grows in size and the volume of operations increases, it becomes increasingly difficult to manage by a single person. The single person who once looked after all the different organisational functions like production, purchase, sales, marketing, finance, human resource management etc., found it difficult to cope up with the increased work load. Hence he entrusted the major functional areas to different persons so that the work can be managed well. As the organisations still grew in size, further personnel were recruited to support the different functional departments. Thus, organisation has become an union of many functional departments and each functional department is headed by a departmental head under whom many employees work. As the departments grow in size, the interaction between the different departments gradually comes down since the personnel in each department are preoccupied with their own departmental activities. When the interactions between the different functional departments get reduced, the flow of information between the departments suffers and a stage is soon reached when the individual departments become like watertight compartments preventing free flow of information across them. No doubt, each functional department will furnish the information sought for by the top level management. However this does not ensure flow of information across the functional departments.

As organisations grow, the volume of data/information being processed also grows. In order to handle the enormous volume of data/information computer based management information systems were developed. Though information technology (I.T.) offers wide scope for the effective handling and manipulation of data/information for the benefit of organisations, the initial Information systems designed by I.T. developers were mostly stand-alone systems. Thus, the sales department of an organisation developed an information system that was capable enough to handle its own operations. The production department had its own independent information system. Thus, though the operations of the different departments of an organisation were said to be computerised, they in fact only remained as separate entities despite the automation of their operations that took place. In such a design where the different functional departments were automated independently, it was found difficult to coordinate the functions of the different departments in tune with achieving the corporate strategy. In order to tap the real benefit from I.T. by using it for achieving corporate goals, the information system designed for an organisation should take a holistic view of the organisation.

Such an information system that takes a holistic view of the organisation will tie up all the functional departments of the organisation and will facilitate seamless flow of information across the different departments and is called as Enterprise Resource Planning (ERP) system. With such an information system the resources of the organisation can be put to optimum use.

Having seen the purpose of an ERP system, let us define the same.

The term Enterprise represents an undertaking in which a group of people work with a common goal. The term Resource represents factors like men, material, money, time and other things that are required to run an enterprise and that are consumed during the process of running an enterprise.

The term planning refers to deciding in advance about the future course of action required to achieve organisational goals. Thus, ERP can be broadly defined as the method of planning for the efficient utilisation of available organisational resources in order to achieve the organisational objectives.

The ERP system is a computer software program that supports the ERP.

The following are some of the definition of ERP / ERP software.

- Enterprise Resource Planning (ERP) is an attempt to integrate all departments and functions across an organisation into a single computer system that can serve all those departments' particular needs and also help achieve organisational goals.
- ERP software is an integrated software program that runs of a single data base in such a way that the various departments can share information easily among themselves and can communicate with each other.
- ERP software is set of programs that integrate a company's operations and operate on a shared database.

ERP is sometimes misunderstood as a mere computer system. Computer system is a part of ERP. But ERP is not merely a computer system. ERP is a system that encompasses the enterprise as a whole i.e., it encompasses the goals and objectives of the organisation that have been planned to be achieved, the system of working of the different departments in the organisation, the rules procedures, polices pursued by the organisation, the people who work for the organisation and their values, preferences, capabilities, the computer software and information technology that coordinates the activities of the entire organisation etc., figure 4.1 shows a schematic representation of an ERP system.

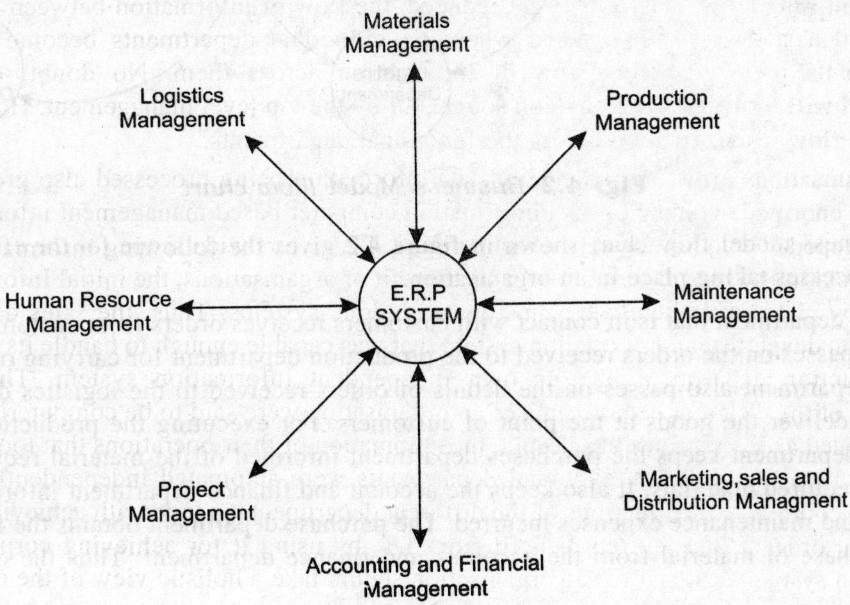

Fig. 4.1 *E.R.P. system*

The Evolution of ERP :

The seed for the evolution of ERP was sown in manufacturing organisations. Manufacturing organisations felt the need for economizing on the consumption and cost of resources. This led to the development of Materials Requirement Planning (MRP). In the beginning, MRP was used to determine the quantity and timing of the purchase of raw materials and subassemblies. Later, the scope of MRP was increased and it evolved into a priority planning system. Manufacturing Resource Planning (MRP-II) was a further development of MRP. MRP-II converted production terms (like no. of units, kilograms, etc.) into financial terms (rupees) and this helped in effectively planning for the resource of a manufacturing organisation. The next generation planning system is ERP that evolved from MRP-II and it accommodated all functional areas like production, maintenance, marketing, sales, distribution, accounting, finance, human resource etc., within its preview.

ERP modules :

Since ERP encompasses all the functional areas of an organisation, the ERP software package will contain many modules one each for every functional area. Before identifying the ERP modules, a business model is to be created for the organisation in which ERP is planned to be implemented.

A business model is a pictorial representation of what actually happens in an organisation. The business model depicts the processes that take place in an organisation in the form of a flow chart. Figure 4.2 represents the business model chart for a small organisation.

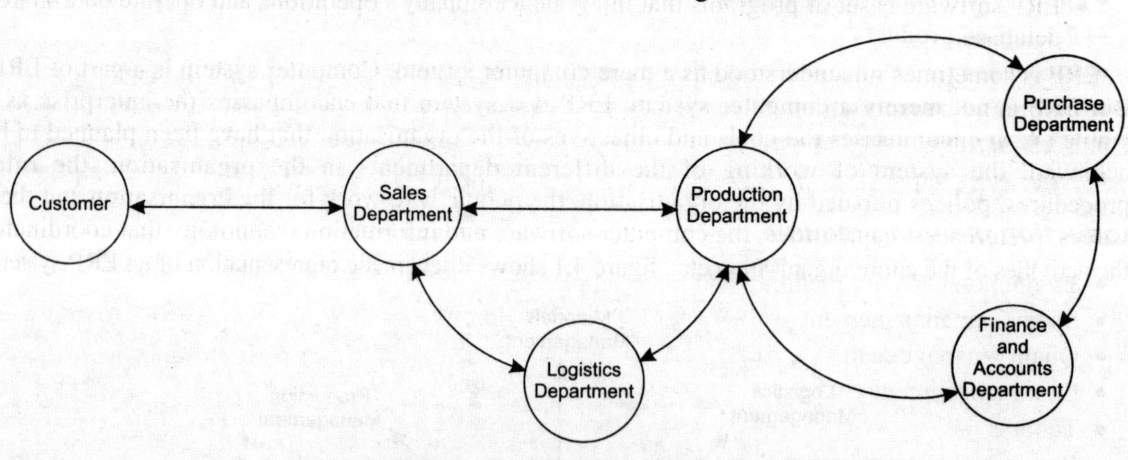

Fig. 4.2 *Business Model Flow chart*

The Business model flow chart shown in figure 4.2 gives the following information about the business processes taking place in an organisation.

The sales department that is in contact with customers receives orders from customers. The sales department passes on the orders received to the production department for carrying out production. The sales department also passes on the details of orders received to the logistics department for planning to deliver the goods at the point of customers. For executing the production orders, the production department keeps the purchases department informed of the material requirements and obtains the required materials. It also keeps the account and finance department informed about the production and maintenance expenses incurred. The purchase department obtains the funds required for the purchase of material from the accounts and finance department. Thus the order received from the customers is processed in different functional departments and finally the goods are delivered to the customer by the sales department.

As seen from the Business Model Flow chart, apart from depicting the various business functions of an organisation, it also shows as to how the different functions are related and their interdependencies.

From the Business Model Flow chart, the ERP modules required are identified. The following are the common ERP modules.

- Sales and distribution
- Production planning
- Materials management
- Finance and accounting

The above list is not comprehensive. There can be many other modules like Human Resource Planning, Logistics management, Maintenance management, Quality management, Customer service management, etc. to suit the requirement of the individual organisations.

Each ERP module will contain many subsystems some of which are given under.

Sales and distribution module

- Order processing
- Store / warehouse management
- Pricing of products
- Invoicing
- Shipping / transportation
- Foreign trade
- After sales support

Production planning module

- Production capacity planning and material planning
- Shop floor management
- Quality management
- Cost management
- Tooling
- Repair and refurbishment
- Engineering data / design management

Materials management

- Material requirements planning
- Vendor choice
- Purchasing
- Inventory management

Accounting and financial management

- Financial accounting
- Cost accounting / controlling

- Investment management
- Treasury management
- Budgeting
- Profit centre accounting

Integrated data base

Since ERP links all the functional departments in an organisation, there is no need for departmental data bases. In fact the very objective of going for ERP is to do away with independent data bases with the different departments. Such isolated data bases that cater to the needs of individual departments are no more needed. All the data in the different isolated data bases will become the data of the integrated data base used for ERP. Having only one integrated data base in ERP has the following advantages.

(*a*) **Data redundancy is eliminated :** When an organisation works on isolated data bases, the data fed into the computer by one department may not be available to another department. The other department may be required to feed the data again separately into its data bases. A third department that needs the same data may be required to feed the data separately into its data base. The same data will be available in two or more isolated data bases. Such redundant data and the duplication of work involved in feeding the same data again are avoided when we have a single integrated data base.

(*b*) **Availability of updated information :** Since a data entered into the integrated data base at any point in the organisation is made available to all those who access the integrated data base, the data available to all the users at any point of time will be the updated data.

(*c*) **Aids in decision making :** Since updated information is available to all functional departments of the organisation, all the users are able to work in real time and this helps in taking timely management decisions on many issues.

4.2 ELECTRONIC COMMERCE (e-COMMERCE)

e-commerce is a general term that is used for any type of business transaction or any exchange of information carried out with the aid of Information and Communication Technology (ICT)

e-commerce consists of three components. They are,

Electronic Markets (EM)
Electronic Data Interchange (EDI)
and Internet Commerce (IC)

As we are aware, market is a place where goods and services are traded. An electronic market is also a market for goods and services. But, this market uses information and communication technology for offering goods and services to customers. The customers can compare the prices of different goods / services offered by different vendors and their relative features and then can make a purchase decision.

Electronic Data Interchange (EDI) refers to the transfer of data from one computer system to another through a standardized system for coding the data being transferred. With the help of EDI, the need for placing written orders for buying of goods and services and the need for issuing printed invoices while supplying goods and services are eliminated. The placement of orders and supply of goods and services are done only through computers using EDI.

Internet commerce refers to the use of internet for commercial purpose. For example, internet can be use to access the web site of book sellers. Books can be chosen and ordered through internet which will be sent by the book sellers by post and delivered to the persons who placed the order through the internet.

e-commerce encompasses these three areas, viz., Electronic Markets, Electronic data Interchange and Internet Commerce. Since e-commerce became popular only after the advent of internet facilities, some experts are of the view that e-commerce exists essentially due to internet.

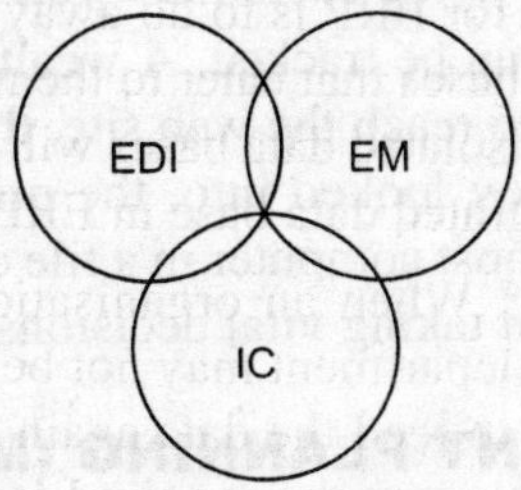

Fig. 4.3 *Components of e-commerce*

Buying of goods and services involves the following steps :

- Searching for the goods and services in the market.
- Finding the goods and services needed.
- Negotiating the price with the supplier.
- Placing of orders for the supply of goods and services.
- Delivery of goods / offering of services by the supplier.
- Raising of invoice by the supplier for the goods supplied / services offered.
- Payment by the customer to the supplier.
- After-sales service by the supplier.

All the above steps of a commercial transaction are possible with e-commerce.

'Search' facilities in the internet can help in searching and identifying the appropriate goods / services. Negotiating the prices can be done through E-mail. Placing of orders can be done either through E-mail or by making use of the readily available facilities in the web sites of the suppliers for placing of orders. EDI can be of use for the preparation of invoices. The use of EDI will help to prepare correct and accurate invoices that match with the purchase orders. With the help of EDI, the preparation of invoices can be much quicker. Payment for the goods / services received can be made by the receiver of goods and services through EDI. Banks offer an EDI payment service which can be made use of for making payment to suppliers.

Use of e-Commerce for Projects

e-commerce will be of use for organisations that handle projects, in two ways.

(*a*) The procurement of materials, equipments and services required for the execution of projects can be bought through electronic media. This will save a lot of time and also the cost of procurement will get reduced.

(*b*) When a project is meant for introducing a new product, even before the product goes to the market (i.e., during the implementation stage of the project itself), the features of the new product and the likely date by which the new product will be launched etc., can be given in the web site of the organisation. This will help customers become aware of the new products and product / trade enquiries may start coming in. Thus, an immediate demand for the product can be created by the time the product is ready to reach the market.

The other benefits of e-commerce are as under :

(*a*) e-commerce helps in reducing the cost of doing business.

(*b*) Once the needed information are entered into the system, the information are made available to customers world-wide. Thus, e-commerce helps in reaching customers in any part of the globe. Information flow from and to the customers world-wide will benefit the business a lot.

(*c*) Everything that happens on-line can be tracked. A wealth of information like who visited the web site, the route that they took to reach the web site, the locations of the web sites that have been visited, the products that they looked into, the products that they ordered / purchased etc., will all be available form the host computer in a file called log-file. These information will help in knowing the market and in taking vital decisions.

4.3 MATERIALS REQUIREMENT PLANNING (M.R.P.)

M.R.P. is a scientific technique of planning the material resources. It consists of planning for the purchase of materials, usage of materials in production and monitoring of inventories (i.e., stocks). It is a combination of inventory control and scheduling techniques. In Production Management, M.R.P. is useful when the following conditions exist.

- The demand for the end-product is known; hence the required manufacturing schedule can be arrived at.
- The input is made up of several components / sub-assemblies / raw materials.
- The procurement of components / sub-assemblies / raw materials involves lead time.
- The manufacturing cycle of the end-product is sufficiently long.

The concept of M.R.P. used in Production Management can be extended to Project Management in view of the following reasons.

The schedule of progress of activities and completion of projects are planned beforehand. This means that the first condition is met i.e.,., the demand pattern for the end-product is known. The end product in Project Management is the asset / infrastructure created for fulfilling the project objectives.

Just as in the manufacturing of a product, execution of a project involves material resources in the form of raw materials, semi-assembled components etc.,

Procurement of materials involves lead time.

The project completion time is normally long except in respect of minor / tiny projects.

Steps involved in M.R.P.

- The first step is the preparation of a Master Production Schedule (M.P.S.). It spells out the different products to be manufactured over a given span of time. In respect of projects, the M.P.S. will spell out the different project activities to be completed. (e.g., construction of foundation, construction of super-structure, fixing of roofing, procurement of equipments, erection of equipments etc.,) and the time schedule for each of the activities.
- Material Requirement Schedule (M.R.S.) is derived from the M.P.S. For example, the M.P.S. may spell out the time bound programmes for the completion of construction works for

foundation, super-structure, roofing etc., The M.R.S. converts the M.P.S. in terms of requirements of materials like cement, steel, bricks etc., and the time schedule for their requirement.

- The material requirement arrived at as above is the gross requirement. This can be adjusted for the materials already available on hand, if any, and for the materials for which orders have already been placed and the materials that are on their way to the site. After adjusting for the above factors, the net material requirement and its corresponding time schedule is arrived at.
- The net material requirement arrived at as above needs to be further refined by making allowance for wastages / rejections etc., and the actual requirement can be arrived at.
- Having arrived at the actual material requirements over a period of time, the next step is to plan for a logical schedule for buying the required materials.

Materials Purchasing

Materials required for the execution of projects are to be purchased scientifically. The factors to be considered while purchasing are as under:

- Quality
- Quantity
- Price
- Time
- Source

Quality

The quality of a product is measured in terms of its specifications. The specifications include design, materials used, physical/chemical composition and properties of materials etc., For example, the specification for the cement used for construction may be specified in terms of factors like initial setting time, final setting time, compressive strength etc., The specifications for the steel used for the construction work may be specified in terms of the tensile strength, carbon content etc., The quality of materials/products procured for a project shall be such that it meets the pre-determined quality standards. Quality that is below the standards fixed shall not be accepted since it will affect the end results. Similarly, quality above the standards fixed are also not to be accepted since it will only involve additional investment without additional gain commensurate with the additional investment.

Quantity

The quantity of purchase of materials/products at any time during the execution of the project shall be optimum. 'Hand to mouth' buying, i.e., buying in small quantities shall be avoided as it will delay implementation of the project. On the other extreme, buying in too large quantities than what is required is also not advisable. Buying in too large quantities will increase the inventory carrying cost since the materials purchased well in advance will lie idle. Economic Ordering Quantity (E.O.Q.) may be arrived at for all the major materials consumed during the project implementation. A suitable Re-order level may be fixed for such materials on the basis of lead time required for the purchase of materials from material suppliers. The quantity of purchase can be fixed at E.O.Q. and order for the supply of materials can be made once the Re-order level is reached. Such judicious planning will reduce the inventory maintenance coat and will help in containing the project cost within the budget.

Price

Since the price almost depends on the quality, the price is determined by the quality standards expected of the materials/products. However, in order to buy at the minimum price without sacrificing the quality standards, tender system can be followed to identify the potential suppliers who can quote the lowest price for the given quality. When there are only a very few vendors for the supply of some materials/products, negotiations can be made with the suppliers to arrive at an advantageous price.

Time

The materials required shall be made available at the time they are required. Delay in arrival of materials will delay the implementation of project while purchasing and stocking of materials well in advance of their actual date of requirement amounts to wasteful expenditure in the form of inventory carrying cost and also interest cost on the investment made on idle inventory.

Source

Right quality of products at the right prices can be purchased only from right sources. Materials can be purchased either directly from the manufacturers or from the dealers or from retailers in the open market. Each source has its own advantages and disadvantages. An analysis of the price quoted by the different sources and the cost of transportation from the source to the site can be done to arrive at the suitable source for the procurement of materials. The terms of warranties offered by the different sources also count while arriving at the right source.

Inventory Control

Inventory refers to those items that are yet to be consumed in the production of goods and services. Since projects consume material resources, inventory control is also an aspect that needs to be given importance during the execution of projects.

ABC analysis and Economic Ordering Quantity (E.O.Q.) are the two important inventory control techniques and these techniques are components of M.R.P.

4.3.1 ABC analysis

ABC analysis is based on the principle of 'vital few and trivial many'. ABC analysis segregates the material items that are consumed in a production process/project into three groups, viz., A-items, B-items and C-items

A-items

Any production process consumes a number of materials. If we make an analysis of the amount of money spent on the different materials, we could observe that about 70% to 75% of the total money spent is spent on a few items of materials that account for only about 5% to 10% of the total items of materials consumed. Such materials that form part of only 5% to 10% of the total items of materials consumed, but that account for a major chunk of the money spent are called A-items. In the construction of an industrial shed, for example, there may be a number of materials used, like cement, steel rods, steel angle sections, blue metal, bricks, sand, wood, asbestos sheets, bolts & nuts, rivets, paint, glass sheets, aluminium angles, exhaust fans, binding wires etc., etc., Out of these, the two items cement and steel angle sections normally account for more than about 70% of the total money spent on materials. The remaining items will account for the balance about 30% of the total money spent. Thus, cement and steel angle sections are the A-items and inventory of these items is to be closely monitored for controlling the cost of the project. As a rule, the inventory of A-items should be kept to the minimum. This can be achieved by purchasing such items at frequent intervals so that their inventory level will be minimum. Though frequent purchase of small quantities will help to keep the inventory to the minimum, a healthy practice would be to enter into a contract with the suppliers of A-items to supply small quantities at staggered intervals according to the actual requirements over a period of time. This will help avoid price fluctuations. However, for entering into a meaningful contract for the staggered supply of materials to meet the consumption requirements, a correct estimate of the material requirements at different time periods during the course of project implementation is a must.

B-items

These are those items that normally form part of about 10 % to 15 % of the total number of items and account for about 10 % to 15 % of the total expenditure on the materials. The B-items do not require a rigid control as required for A-items. In the construction of an industrial shed, for example, steels rods and Asbestos sheets etc., will be B-items.

C-items

These are those items that normally form about 70 % to 80 % of the total number of items but account for only about 5 % to 10 % of the total money spent. In the construction of an industrial shed, for example, sand, bricks, paint, wood, glass sheets exhaust fans, binding wires, etc., will be C-items. Though many in number, all the C-items put together do not cost much. Hence, the procurement policy for C-items shall be exactly opposite to that of A-items, i.e., C-items shall be purchased infrequently and at large quantities (as compared to the total requirement). For example, the entire requirement of paint may be purchased either in one lot or in two batches. Such bulk buying will also help in getting price discounts apart from doing away with the nuisance of frequently buying low cost items in small quantities.

Illustration: 4.1.

The project of construction of an industrial shed is estimated to require the following materials.

- Cement
- Mild steel sections ('L' , 'T' & 'H' sections)
- Mild steel rods (of different diameters)
- Blue metal
- Sand
- Stone boulders
- Glass sheets
- Aluminium angles
- Paint
- Rivets
- Bolts & nuts
- Red oxide
- Wood
- White cem powder
- Nails
- Fevicol (synthetic adhesive)
- Padlocks
- Rolling shutters

The requirements of different materials and their unit price are given below:

S. No	*Material*	*Requirement(in units)*	*Cost per Unit(Rs.)*
1	Cement	10000 bags	200.00 per bag
2	Mild steel sections	47 tonnes	32,000.00 per tonne
3	Mild steel rods	27.50 tonnes	24,000.00 per tonne
4	Blue metal	75 lorry loads	500.00 per lorry load
5	Bricks	100 lorry loads	2000.00 per lorry load
6	Sand	100 lorry loads	400.00 per lorry load
7	Stone boulders	20 lorry loads	350.00 per lorry load
8	Glass sheets	2000 sq. metre	100.00 per sq. metre
9	Aluminium angles	1.00 tonne	90,000.00 per tonne
10	Paint	600 Kg.	75.00 per Kg.
11	Rivets	0.75 tonne	20,000.00 per tonne
12	Bolts & nuts	0.50 tonne	25,000.00 per tonne
13	Red oxide	200 Kg.	30.00 per Kg.
14	Wood	2.00 Cubic metre	30,000.00 per Cubic metre
15	White Cem powder	1750.00 Kg.	3.00 per Kg.
16	Nails	15.00 Kg.	200.00 per Kg.
17	Fevicol	10.00 Kg.	200.00 per Kg.
18	Padlocks	50 Nos.	75.00 each
19	Door closers	9 Nos.	1250.00 each
20	Rolling shutters	10 Nos.	18,000.00 each

Carry out ABC Analysis and identify A, B and C items.

Solution:

There are 20 different materials given. First, arrive at the cost of the different materials required.

S. No.	*Material*	*Requirement (in units)*	*Cost per Unit (Rs.)*	*Cost of each Material (Rs.)*
1	Cement	10000.00	200.00	20,00,000.00
2	Mild steel sections	47.00	32,000.00	15,04,000.00
3	Mild steel rods	27.50	24,000.00	6,60,000.00
4	Blue metal	75.00	500.00	37,500.00
5	Bricks	100.00	2000.00	2,00,000.00
6	Sand	100.00	400.00	40,000.00
7	Stone boulders	20.00	350.00	7,000.00
8	Glass sheets	2000.00	100.00	20,000.00
9	Aluminium angles	1.00	90,000.00	90,000.00
10	Paint	600.00	75.00	45,000.00
11	Rivets	0.75	20,000.00	15,000.00
12	Bolts & nuts	0.50	25,000.00	12,500.00
13	Red oxide	200.00	30.00	6,000.00
14	Wood	2.00	30,000.00	60,000.00
15	White Cem powder	1750.00	3.00	5,250.00
16	Nails	15.00	200.00	3,000.00
17	Fevicol	10.00	200.00	2,000.00
18	Padlocks	50.00	75.00	3,750.00
19	Door closers	9.00	1250.00	11,250.00
20	Rolling shutters	10.00	18,000.00	1,80,000.00

Rearrange the items in descending order of cost of individual item. Arrive at the cumulative cost after arranging the items in descending coder of cost and enter the cumulative cost in the next column. Express the cumulative cost in terms of percentage of the total cost and enter the cumulative cost percentage in the next column.

S. No.	*Material*	*Cost of each Material (Rs.)*	*Cumulative Cost (Rs.)*	*Cumulative Cost Percentage*
1	Cement	20,00,000.00	20,00,000.00	40.80 %
2	Mild steel sections	15,04,000.00	35,04,000.00	71.47 %
3.	Mild steel rods	6,60,000.00	41,64,000.00	84.94 %
4	Bricks	2,00,000.00	43,64,000.00	89.02 %
5	Rolling shutters	1,80,000.00	45,44,000.00	92.69 %
6	Aluminium angles	90,000.00	46,34,000.00	94.53 %
7	Wood	60,000.00	46,94,000.00	95.75 %
8	Paint	45,000.00	47,39,000.00	96.67 %
9	Sand	40,000.00	47,79,000.00	97.49 %
10	Blue metal	37,500.00	48,16,500.00	98.25 %
11	Glass sheets	20,000.00	48,36,500.00	98.66 %
12	Rivets	15,000.00	48,51,500.00	98.96 %
13	Bolts & nuts	12,500.00	48,64,000.00	99.22 %
14	Door closers	11,250.00	48,75,250.00	99.45 %
15	Stone boulders	7,000.00	48,82,250.00	99.59 %
16	Red oxide	6,000.00	48,88,250.00	99.71 %
17	White cem powder	5,250.00	48,93,500.00	99.82 %
18	Padlocks	3,750.00	48,97,250.00	99.90 %
19	Nails	3,000.00	49,00,250.00	99.96 %
20	Fevicol	2,000.00	49,02,250.00	100.00 %
	Total Cost :	49,02,250.00		

An observation of the table shows that the first two items account for 71.47% of the total cost while the first three items account for 84.94% of the total cost. Hence, the first two items (representing 2% of the total number of items) can be termed as A-items.

The last 15 items (from item No: 6 to 20) account for 5.47% (i.e., 100 - 94.57) of the total cost, which means that 75% of the total number of items account for 5.47% of the total cost. These 15 items can be treated as C-items.

Item Nos. 3, 4 and 5 account for about 7.75% of the total cost. (i.e., 92.69 - 84.94) , which means that 15% of the total number of items account for 7.75% of the total cost. These three items can be treated as B-items.

4.3.2 Economic Ordering Quantity (E.O.Q.)

Materials that are consumed in large quantities regularly can be purchased in lots that is economical. In large construction projects, for example, cement is consumed regularly in large quantities. All the quantity of cement that is needed for the project can not and need not be purchased and stocked. It can be purchased in economic lots in such way that always the required quantity of cement is available for use and the total cost spent on purchasing and stocking of cement is kept to the minimum.

Deciding the economic lot size of purchase of any material requires consideration of two important costs, viz., procurement cost and inventory carrying cost.

Procurement cost is the cost incurred in purchasing the material. It includes the costs of stationery, postage etc., telephone / telegram / telex charges, traveling charges, inspection charges and the like. Procurement cost is expressed as cost per order.

Materials purchased are to be stored safely till they are used for the project. This storage of materials involves cost which is called as inventory carrying cost or inventory holding cost. This is the cost incurred in connection with the holding of stocks like storage charges, handling charges, insurance charges, watch and ward expenses, taxes, loss due to deterioration etc., Inventory carrying cost is expressed as a percentage of the cost of inventory.

The total cost of materials, thus consists of two components. The total cost will vary depending on the number of orders placed. If the material is purchased at frequent intervals and in small quantities, the number of purchases made will be more and hence the procurement cost will be higher. However, the inventory carrying cost will be less since only a small quantity of stock is maintained. On the other hand, if the material is purchased in bulk quantities, the number of purchase orders placed will be less which means that the procurement cost will be lower. However, the inventory carrying cost will be higher for holding bulk quantities of materials.

Total cost of inventory* = Procurement cost + Inventory carrying cost

The relationship between the procurement cost and the inventory carrying cost and the total cost is given in Fig. 4.4 (* i.e., cost of maintaining inventory)

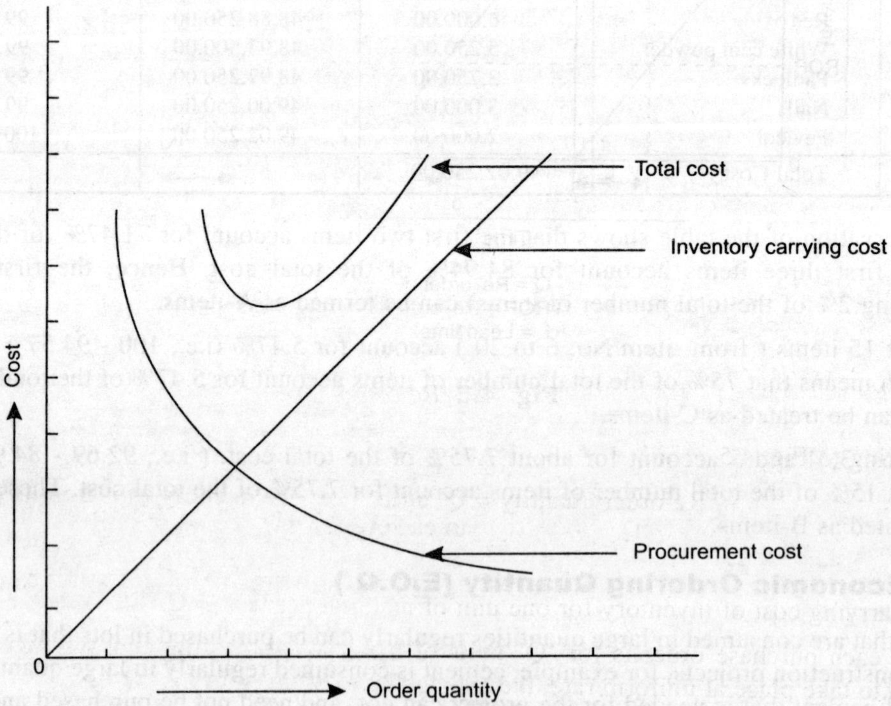

Fig. 4.4 *Relationship between costs*

Let,

Annual consumption of materials = A units.

Let us assume that the material is used up continuously at a constant rate.

Let,

Lead time (i.e., time taken for the material to reach the site from the time at which order was placed) = L time units.

If we want to ensure that the material reaches the site by the time the stock is fully used up (and becomes 'Nil'), it means that the order for procurement shall be made at such a time that the available stock of material is equal to the material required for consumption for a period equal to the lead time.

Since the consumption of material is assumed to be uniform, the Re-order level can be easily arrived at as under:

$$\text{Re-order level} = (\text{Rate of consumption of material}) \times (\text{Lead time})$$

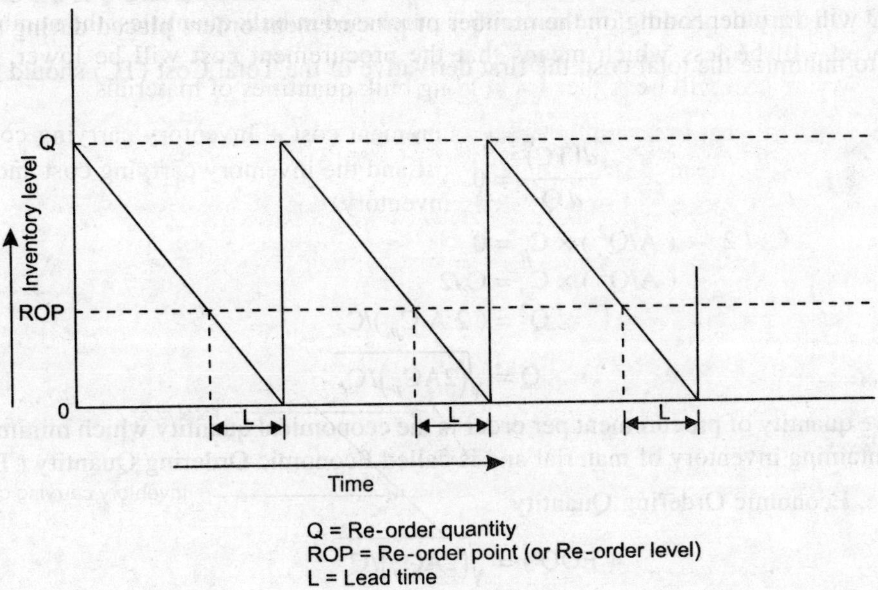

Fig. 4.5 *Re-order level*

Referring to Fig. 4.5,

Re-order quantity = Q units. (i.e., the quantity of materials purchased in each order.)

Let,

The carrying cost of inventory for one unit of material per year = C_c

Since each purchase order is for 'Q' units of materials and as the consumption of material is assumed to take place at uniform rate, the average level of inventory is 'Q / 2'

Inventory carrying cost per year (ICC) = Average level of Inventory × Cost of carrying an inventory of one unit per year

$$= (Q / 2) \times C_c$$

Number of procurement orders made

During one year = A/Q

Let,

Cost of placing one procurement order = C_p

Total cost of placing orders during one

$$\text{Year (PC)} = (A/Q) \times C_p$$

Total cost of maintaining inventory per year = Inventory carrying per year + Procuring cost per year

$$TC = ICC + PC$$

$$= (Q/2) \times C_c + (A/Q) \times C_p$$

In the above expression for the Total cost, C_c, C_p and A are constants and Q is the only factor that will vary. Q will vary depending on the number of procurement orders placed during a year.

In order to minimize the total cost, the first derivative of the Total Cost (TC) should be equated to zero.

i.e., $$\frac{d(TC)}{dQ} = 0$$

i.e., $$C_c/2 - (A/Q^2) \times C_p = 0$$

i.e., $$(A/Q^2) \times C_p = C_c/2$$

i.e., $$Q^2 = (2\,A\,C_p)/C_c$$

$$Q = \sqrt{(2AC_p)/C_c}$$

The above quantity of procurement per order is the economical quantity which minimizes the total cost of maintaining inventory of material and is called Economic Ordering Quantity (EOQ)

Therefore, Economic Ordering Quantity

$$(EOQ) = \sqrt{(2AC_p)/C_c}$$

where,

A = Annual requirement of material

C_p = Procurement cost per order

C_c = Cost of carrying one unit of inventory for one year.

Illustration: 4.2

A mega construction project of a Dam is scheduled to take four years of time for completion. Cement, which is the major construction material, is estimated to be consumed on an uniform rate and the annual requirement is estimated at 3,20,000 bags. The cost of holding inventory of cement bags is calculated at Rs. 40.00 per bag per year. The cost of placing a procurement order for cement is Rs. 1000 per order. What is the Economic Ordering Quantity ?.

Solution :

$$EOQ = \sqrt{(2AC_p)/C_c}$$

$$= \frac{\sqrt{2 \times 3{,}20{,}000 \times 1{,}000}}{40}$$

$$= 4000 \text{ bags}$$

Hence, each order should be placed for the procurement of 4,000 bags which is the EOQ.

Number of orders to be placed in a year = 3,20,000 / 4,000

= 80.

Illustration: 4.3

In the example given in illustration 4.2 above, if the lead time taken for the procurement of cement is 2 days, find the re-order level.

Solution :

Annual consumption of cement (A) =3,20,000 bags.

Assuming uniform rate of consumption, daily consumption = 876.7 bags

Lead time for the procurement of cement = 2 days

∴ Re-order level = 876.7 × 2

= 1753.4

say, 1753 bags.

(The E.O.P. and Reorder level are indicated in fig. 4.6.)

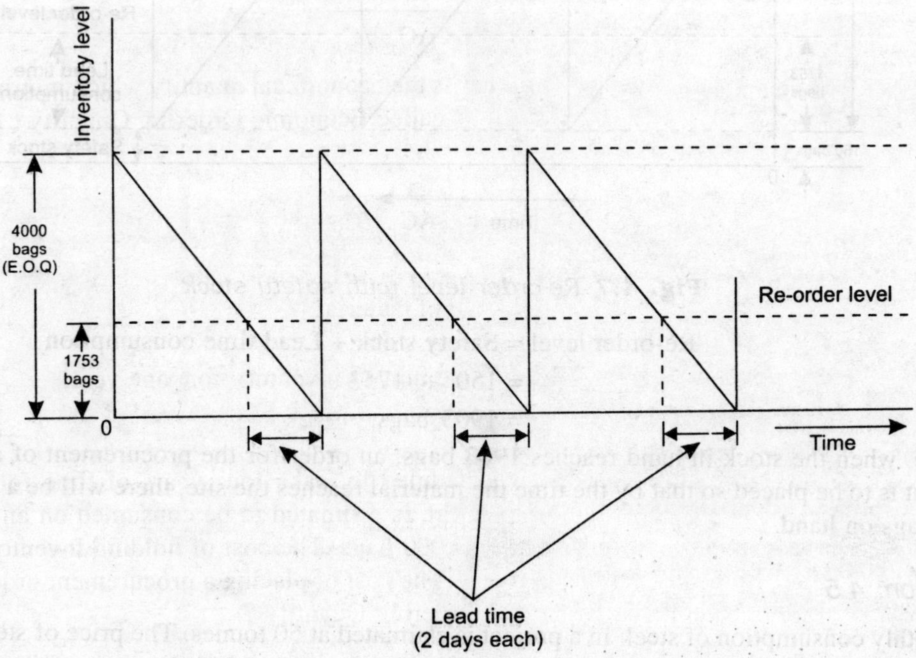

Fig. 4.6 *Re-order level*

Illustration 4.4

In the example given in illustration 4.3 above, if the project manager feels that a buffer stock of cement (i.e., safety stock) of 150 bags is to be maintained at any point of time, find the Re-order level.

Solution :

The example given in illustration 4.3 assumes that by the time the ordered batch of cement reaches the site, the stock already in hand is consumed fully. This is a situation in which the stock in hand will become 'Nil' and will be immediately replenished by the arrival of a new batch of 4,000 bags of cement. This is an ideal situation and involves an element of risk. If due to any reason, there is delay in the receipt of a new batch of cement, the project will suffer due to non-availability of cement which is not a healthy situation. To avoid such eventualities, normally a safety stock is maintained and the point of re-ordering of material is accordingly fixed, ensuring that at any point of time, 'Out-of-stock' situation does not arise.

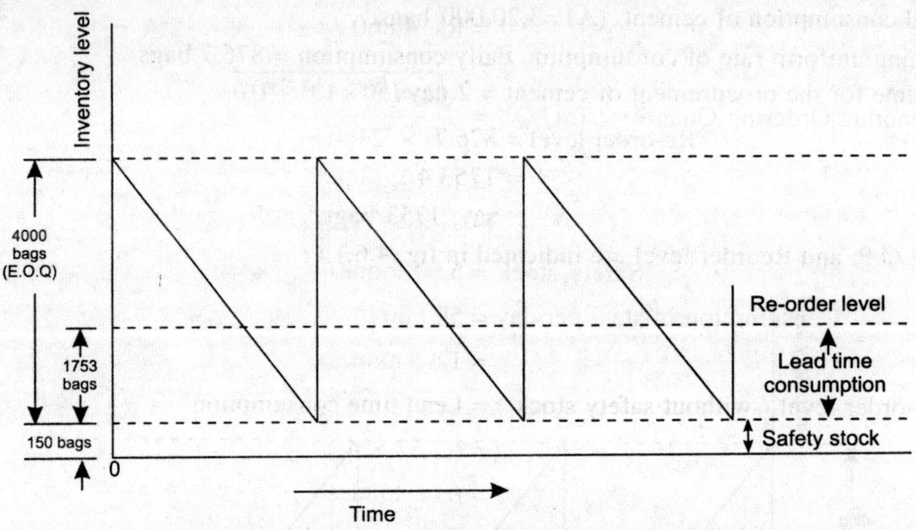

Fig. 4.7 *Re-order level with safety stock*

$$\text{Re-order level} = \text{Safety stock} + \text{Lead time consumption}$$
$$= 150 + 1753$$
$$= 1903 \text{ bags.}$$

Hence, when the stock in hand reaches 1903 bags, an order for the procurement of a new batch of cement is to be placed so that by the time the material reaches the site, there will be a safety stock of 150 bags on hand.

Illustration: 4.5

The monthly consumption of steel in a project is estimated at 50 tonnes. The price of steel is 27,000 /- per tonne. The inventory carrying cost is computed at 18 % of the cost of inventory. The procurement cost for steel has been computed at Rs. 910 /- per order. If the safety stock required is 5 tonnes and if the lead time for the is procurement of steel is 4 days, find the following:

1. E.O.Q.
2. Re-order level
3. Maximum level of stock
4. Minimum level of stock

Solution :

$$\text{E.O.Q.} = \sqrt{(2AC_p)/C_c}$$

Inventory carrying cost = 18.00 % of the cost of material

Inventory carrying Cost (ICC) per annum = 18 % [50 × 12 × 27,000]

= Rs. 29,16,000 / -

ICC annum per tonne of steel (C_c) = 29,16,000 / (50 × 12)

= Rs. 4,860 /-

$$\text{Economic Ordering Quantity (E.O.Q.)} = \frac{\sqrt{2 \times (50 \times 12) \times 910}}{4860}$$

= 14.99 tonnes

say, 15.00 tonnes.

Safety stock = 5.00 tonnes

Consumption of steel per day = 50 / 30

= 1.67 tonnes

Re-order level (without safety stock) = Lead time consumption

= (1.67 × 4)

= 6.68 tonnes

Minimum stock level = Safety stock level

= 5.00 tonnes

Since safety stock is given as 5.00 tonnes,

Re-ordering level (with safety stock) = Safety stock + Lead time Consumption

= 5.00 + 6.68

= 11.68 tonnes

Maximum stock level = Safety stock level + E.O.Q.

= 5.00 + 15.00

= 20.00 tonnes.

E.O.Q., Re-order level, Maximum level of stock and Minimum level of stock are indicated in fig. 4.8

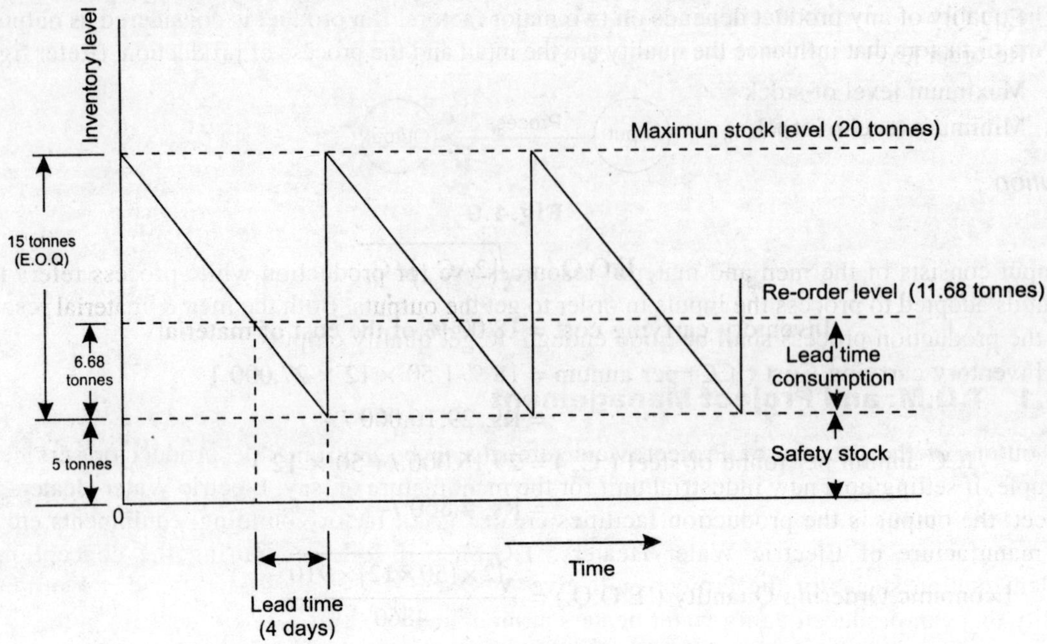

Fig. 4.8

4.4 TOTAL QUALITY MANAGEMENT (T.Q.M.)

The quality of any product can not be improved to the required extent only by inspection of the product after its production. The quality standards required should be thought of before production and the quality improvement process should begin right from the conception of the product and it should continue through out the process of production. In fact, the process of quality improvement continues even after a product is manufactured and has reached the consumers. Feed back information from the consumers about the quality aspects of a product will help improve the quality further in future. Thus, quality improvement is a continuous process throughout the life cycle of a product.

Total Quality Management (T.Q.M.) is a modern quality improvement concept that deals with a product in its totality. Quality of a product is achieved by the combined efforts of all concerned with its production. Thus, the Design Department, Research & Development Department, Production Department, Purchases Department, Marketing Department, Quality Control Department etc., all have their part to contribute for the quality improvement of a product.

There are two important aspects that are to be kept in mind while pursuing Total Quality policy. First, the quality must be consistent with the purpose. This is because, quality is sought after only to meet the functional requirements desired by the end users. If a high quality product fails to meet the requirements and expectations of end users, the efforts put up in quality improvement is only a wasteful exercise. Second, the desired quality shall be attained at the minimum cost. This is because, consumer satisfaction can be achieved not only by offering the product with the desired level of quality but also by offering the product at a minimum price as compared to the competitors. Thus, the prime objective of quality improvement is to offer maximum user satisfaction at minimum cost.

The quality of any product depends on two major factors. If a product is considered as output, the two major factors that influence the quality are the input and the process of production. (Refer fig. 4.8)

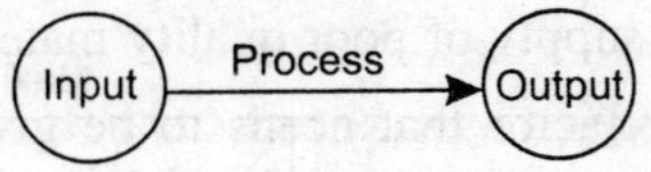

Fig.4.9

Input consists of the men and material resources use for production while process refers to the methods adopted to process the inputs in order to get the outputs. Both the men & material resources and the production process shall be good enough to get quality outputs.

4.4.1 T.Q.M. and Project Management

The output of the process of Project Management can be any tangible product or service. For example, if setting up a new industrial unit for the manufacture of, say, Electric Water Heaters is the project, the output is the production facilities created (viz., factory building, equipments etc.,) for the manufacture of Electric Water Heaters. T.Q.M. , if followed during the conception and implementation stages of the project, will give output of the desired quality, viz., a production facility that can produce quality water heaters at minimum cost. Production facilities in the form of industrial sheds, machinery and equipments form part of the output while material and human resources are the inputs and the mode of executing the project is the process.

Phases of T.Q.M. in a project

A project takes shape to satisfy some of the needs of consumers. The project will fulfill its objective only if it satisfies the consumer needs in the best possible way. Hence, assessing the consumers needs correctly is the first step towards success. Only when the needs of the consumers are correctly assessed, a product that can satisfy the consumer needs can be designed. Once the nature of the product and its special features are decided upon, the material requirements, the production facilities and other infrastructure required can be assessed.

Any project requires men and material resources. The material resources may be in the form of raw materials or finished goods. For example, cement that is used for construction activities , though a finished product from cement plants, is a raw material for concrete works used in civil constructions. Finished goods that are purchased may be used either as they are in their original form or may be used for sub-assemblies for a greater system of project components. For example, goods like air conditioners, equipments, machinery etc., are used as they are without any modifications and they need only installation and erection work; goods like water/sewage pipe lines, steel sections etc., will be further assembled / fabricated to suit the requirements of the project.

Quality control in purchasing of materials

Every project consumes men and material resources. Due importance for quality shall be given while purchasing of materials.

Before placing orders for the purchase of materials, the specifications of materials to be purchased shall be referred to the Quality Control Department of the organisation. If a separate Quality Control Department is not available, the quality requirements of the materials required are to be analysed and the specifications required are to be correctly spelt out by a team of competent persons. Specifying the quality standards required of the materials in clear terms will solve more than 50% of the problems. Vague description of the quality requirements given to the vendors while placing orders is found to be the major cause for the supply of poor quality materials.

Selection of suppliers is another factor that needs to be given attention to ensure purchase of quality materials. For traditional items, choosing of suppliers may not pose any problem since the supplier can be chosen from the panel of reputed/known suppliers on the basis of past experience. In respect of materials that are not traditional in nature and for which there is no list of reputed suppliers available with the organisation, the suppliers can be chosen by calling for quotation from a number of suppliers listed in trade directories. Though the supplier who has quoted the minimum price for the same specifications of materials is normally chosen, making the choice purely on the basis of the price quoted can not be the right approach. The ability of the suppliers to supply the desired quality of materials at price quoted and within the time stipulated are to be ensured. The supplier's premises may be inspected by personnel from the Purchase Department or Quality Control department to verify if the supplier has the required production facilities to supply the materials of the required quality and quantity within the time limit stipulated.

It is preferable to get samples of materials beforehand and check up their quality standards before asking the suppliers to supply the materials. For materials that are bought in bulk quantities (say, cement, steel, brick etc.,),an inspection plan shall be formulated. For example, a sampling inspection can be formulated in such a way that every 100th cement bag is to be tested for its quality. Even when a sampling inspection plan is formulated and operated, it is better to have 100% inspection of the first few lots of materials that arrive at the project site.

Quality Control of Project Implementation Process

At every stage during the implementation of a project, the quality aspects of the process of implementation shall be monitored. For example, in construction of structures, it shall be checked whether proper mix of mortar is used, whether proper bonding of bricks is followed, whether steel reinforcements for R.C.C. works are placed as per the detailed drawings, whether curing of cement constructions are carried out for the required number of days, whether electrical wiring works are carried out taking into account the required safety measures, whether proper lighting and ventilation arrangements are made etc., During procurement of equipments / machinery it shall be ensured that they are of approved quality and meet the specification requirements. Erection of equipments / machinery is to be done strictly as per the recommendations of the suppliers. Machinery foundations are to be constructed as per the drawings and according to the specifications given by the suppliers.

The Human Factor on T.Q.M.

The responsibility of ensuring quality is not confined to any single individual or a group. It is a responsibility that is to be shared by all concerned. A well formulated Quality Control programme may fail if the Quality Manager is not able to get active cooperation of all other concerned departments. The attitude of the top management in achieving quality standards counts a lot. If the top management does only a lip service on quality management, but thinks that quality of a project can be achieved by appointing a few quality inspectors, it will affect the project's quality severely. The awareness for ensuring quality shall run throughout the organisation, among all the personnel, right from the Chief Executive to the lower level personnel. Since implementation of quality programme needs the whole-hearted cooperation of all concerned, all the functional departments shall be involved in the planning stage itself. Better results can be achieved if all are given full freedom to offer constructive criticism and suggest methods for quality improvement. All suggestions received shall be given due consideration, irrespective of who offers the suggestions. This will help in two ways. First, this will instill confidence in the minds of all that they are part of the Quality Improvement mission and all will actively participate and offer their contribution in quality improvement. Second, the suggestions may offer useful tips, sometimes quality tips that are not thought of in the routine Quality planning exercises may come out and this will benefit the project and the organisation as a whole.

Approaches to T.Q.M. in Projects

- Avoid accepting poor quality materials that go into the project.
- Design a scientific method of inspection of materials purchased with regard to their quality. Avoid ad hoc / mass inspection.
- Don't get carried away by the price of materials. The material that costs the lowest need not be the right one. Always look for the right price. Right price is that price which commensurates with quality and which makes the suppliers supply materials of the required quantity and at the right time.
- Find out the root cause of quality problems and prevent their recurrence.
- Bring about conditions conducive for the free flow of information between the different departments; break down interdepartmental barriers and rivalry.
- Institute quality improvement programmes for the employees, train them in quality awareness and encourage them to express their views freely and frankly.
- The top management must be committed to total quality and this will bring about change of attitude among the employees in favour of improving quality.
- Build up quality improvement teams consisting of departmental heads.
- Brief all the employees on what, why and how of T.Q.M. programme and explain to them as to how they can participate in quality improvement. Also, brief the contractors about the quality policy of the organisation and advice them to act strictly in accordance with the quality policy of the organisation.

4.4.2 Quality Circles

Quality circle is a small group of employees who volunteer to meet regularly to undertake work related projects like quality improvement, productivity improvement, improvement of safety measures, cost reduction, improvement of efficiency, improvement of working conditions etc., and to arrive at recommendations for improvement.

The ideal size of the members in Quality Circles is normally between eight to ten. If the number of members is too many, the members may not have enough time to effectively participate and if the number of members is too small, the Quality Circle can not be active and may become dormant. The concept of Quality Circle evolved in Japan and it has proved its effectiveness by way of increased productivity and improved quality. The important aspect of Quality Circle is that the members of the circle are not selected or nominated by the management of the organisation, but they join the circle voluntarily.

Quality Circles are formed on the following sound management principles.

- People have integrity and creativity.
- People do not resist change; they only resist when change is imposed on them from externally.
- People love their work when they are given freedom and they derive satisfaction out of in-

volve-ment in work, when their work is recognised and rewarded.

- People are always ready to work in groups and they crave for attention and recognition.
- Only the person who does a job knows the job better and hence any remedy that he suggests for improving the job will prove good.
- Management can achieve results by harnessing human energy and this can be achieved not by coercion, but by assisting in self development, by fostering enthusiasm for work and by inculcating the spirit of cooperation.

The top management shall support and encourage the formation of Quality Circles. Functioning of Quality Circles in a project organisation can be of use in the following ways.

- It gives a sense of participation to the team members and their involvement in the project improves.
- It will help achieve project objectives of containing cost and time and maintaining quality.
- It will bring about improved working conditions and improved working methods which in turn will aid in cost and time reduction.
- It will bring about free flow of information throughout the organisation and communication gaps will be bridged.
- It will involve employees in decision-making which will improve their morale and will also improve productivity.

Quality circles, if introduced will help a lot in smooth implementation of projects, in avoiding interdepartmental conflicts in cutting down cost and time and in ensuring quality.

It is pertinent to note the distinction between Task Force and Quality Circle. A Task Force is formulated by the management to tackle a specific problem while a Quality Circle if formed voluntarily by its members. Thus, a Task Force is constituted once a problem comes to the surface. There is no need for the presence of any problem for the formation of Quality Circles. Task Force normally consists of experts relating to the problem area while Quality Circle will have employees of middle/ lower levels as its members. The life period of Task Force comes to an end once the assigned problem is solved while a Quality Circle will continue to exist. If a Quality Circle has successfully solved a particular problem, its focus will shift to some other problem and the work of the Quality Circle will continue.

4.5 BOOT (BUILD, OWN, OPERATE, TRANSFER) PROJECTS

BOOT projects have their origin in Turkey, where the formula for building up of mega projects was tried in 1980's. There are two parties to a BOOT project, viz., the principal project promoter (usually, the Government) and a private participant. The private participant arranges the finance required for the project, build the project and maintain the project during the contracted period. Finally, the private participant transfers the project to the principal at no cost. During the contracted period, the private participant owns and operates facilities and tries to recover his investment, cost of investment, maintenance expenses and earn profit on his investment.

The contract between the principal and the private participant is known as the concession agreement. All the terms of the contract, like the concession offered by the principal, the role of the private participant, the terms of financial arrangement, construction , maintenance, revenue realization, termination of the contract etc. are contained in the concession agreement. Highways, bridges, water supply lines, gas/oil pipe lines, hydroelectric power stations etc. are some of the projects suitable for BOOT arrangement. The land required for such projects are normally acquired by the Government (the principal) and offered to the private investor for the construction of the project as per the terms of the concession agreement.

The period of contract (after which, the private participant is to handover the project to the principal) is generally very high ranging from 20 to 40 years or even more, depending on the pay-back period of the project. The pay-back period of such projects are normally very high in view of the huge investment required and comparatively lower returns on the investment.

BOOT projects are useful for the development of infrastructure of a country. Without such an arrangement, neither the Government will have the required resources and inclination to build such projects nor the private entrepreneurs will take up such projects.

Some of the other variants of BOOT projects are as under:

4.6 BOO (BUILD, OWN, OPERATE) PROJECTS

The private investors execute the project, own and operate the infrastructural assets created for the whole life. Since the private investors become the sole owners and operators of the assets, they can even mortgage the assets to banks/financial institutions and arrange for the finance required to build the project.

4.7 BOLT (BUILD, OPERATE, LEASE, TRANSFER) PROJECTS

The private investors build and operate the project for a specified period of time. After the end of the pre-fixed period, they hand over the project to the Government (the principal) on lease. The Government, which takes over the project in the capacity of lessee, pays periodical lease rentals to the private investors for the rest of the life of the project.

There are also some other variants of BOOT projects like BTO (Build, Transfer, Operate), BRT (Build, Rent, Transfer), BOD (Build, Operate, deliver) BOOST (Build, Own, Operate, Subsidize, Transfer) etc.

4.8 HIRE PURCHASE

Hire purchase means hiring of an asset for a period of time and purchasing the asset at the end of the period. Pearce E.H. and Omrod R.F.G. defines hire purchase as 'a contract on hire with an option of purchase, in which the owner of the goods lets them out on hire to the hirer for a fixed term at an agreed rental to be paid at intervals mutually agreed upon as instalments, and the owner in addition to letting the goods out, further agrees that if the hirer keeps them for the agreed period and regularly pays the rent, they shall become the hirer's property'.

Hire purchase Act, 1972 defines a hire purchase agreement as an agreement under which goods are let on hire and under which the hirer has an option to purchase them in accordance with the terms of agreement under which,

1. possession of goods is delivered by the owner thereof to a person on condition that such person pays the agreed amount in periodical instalments.
2. the property in goods is to pass to such person on the payment of the last such installment and
3. such person has a right to terminate the agreement at any time the property so passes.

The general features of a hire purchase agreement are as under:

The general features of a hire purchase agreement are as under:

- The buyer takes possession of the goods and agrees to pay the total hire purchase price in instalments.
- Each instalment paid by the hirer is treated as hire charge.
- The ownership passes on from the seller to the buyer only on payment of the last installment ; till the last installment is paid, the ownership rests with the seller (Hire vendor).
- Incase the buyer (Hire purchaser) makes any default in payment of any of the installment, the hire vendor has the right to repossess the goods from the hire purchaser and forfeit the amount already received treating it as hire charge.
- The hirer (Hire purchaser) has the right to terminate the hire purchase agreement at any time before the property passes , i.e., he has the option to return the goods in which case, he need not pay instalments falling thereafter. He, however can not recover the sums already paid as such sums legally represent hire charge for having used the goods.

The two major forms of hire purchase are,

1. Consumer credit
2. Industrial and commercial credit

Consumer credit is the finance offered to consumers for acquiring consumer durables. Industrial and commercial credit is the finance offered for the purchase of equipments/machinery/transport vehicles etc.

While in actual sale, the title to the property (i.e., the ownership and possession) is transferred to the purchaser simultaneously, in hire purchase, though the possession remains with the hire purchaser, the ownership remains with the seller (hire vendor) until the last installment is paid. Though the ownership passes on to the hire purchaser only at the end of the agreement period on payment of the last installment, the hire purchaser can claim depreciation allowance.

4.9 PUBLIC SECTOR PROJECTS

As far as investment in public sector projects are concerned, various advisory and regulatory agencies like the Project Appraisal Division of the Planning Commission, the Plan Finance Division in the Ministry of Finance, the Financial advisor to the Administrative Ministry in the Ministry of Finance, Department of expenditure, the Bureau of Public Enterprises, the concerned administrative ministries etc., undertake the study of projects and preparation of feasibility reports.

Project Appraisal Division, Planning Commission, Government of India has published 'Guidelines for the preparation of feasibility reports for industrial projects'. The salient features of the guidelines are as under:

- No project can be analysed in isolation from the industry to which it belongs and from the rest of the economy. This is particularly true of public sector projects which have to be judged not merely in terms of profitability but also in terms of the general nature of public policy with respect to the industry.
- A feasibility report should include an analysis of the industry to which the project belongs. This analysis should deal with the past performance of the industry, its present status, the way the industry is organized, the problem that it faces etc. The analysis should also deal with public policies relating to the industry.
- The following are some of the questions that should be dealt with:
  Is this a priority industry ?

What is the role the public sector is expected to play in the industry ?

What is the relative priority given to the industry in allocation of investment funds and foreign exchange ?

Does the Govt. have a view about the choice of techniques in the industry ?

Does the Govt. have a view about the pattern of location of the industry ?

What are the plan provisions for the industry ?

Answers to the above questions will specify the constraints within which the enterprise preparing the feasibility report must prepare its Development plan.

- Analysis of demand-supply gap must be studied keeping in view the existing capacity, the likely production, the likely demand, capacity creation from other enterprises etc.

Demand- supply analysis

		year-1	*year-2*	*year-3*	*year-4 etc.*
I. Capacity available :					
Existing capacity	:	..	..	..	..
Capacity under implementation	:	..	..	..	..
Total	:	..	..	..	..
II. Gap between demand and Supply :					
Production	:	..	..	..	..
Demand	:	..	..	..	..
Gap	:	..	..	..	..
III. Capacity creation proposals from Other enterprises :					
Licenses issued and likely to materialize	:	..	..	..	..
Letter of intent issued and likely to materialize	:	..	..	..	..
Other projects which are likely to Materialize	:	..	..	..	..

- The various options available to fulfill the expected production target should be studied with regard to the level and pattern of production, techniques of production, location of project etc. The costs of different alternatives, both capital costs and operating costs are to be studied.
- The phasing of capital expenditure over a period of time for the different alternatives should be studied.
- The internal rate of return for the different alternatives are to be arrived at and the different alternatives are to be ranked in terms of their degree of attractiveness. The number of alternatives that should be considered depends upon the capacity creation target specified for it. Hence, the choice should move down the ranking till the capacity creation target is met. This process will help to identify the options available, which should be taken up for further study.

Economic analysis constitutes a major area in the appraisal of public sector projects. Input costs are required to be properly adjusted to reflect the true value of foreign exchange, labour and capital used. Similarly, indirect benefits are also to be correctly assessed and accounted for. Conventional feasibility reports often fail to present information on some of the side effects and, in particular, the unintended consequences of a project. Such consequences must be fully taken into account. (for example, emission of pollutants into the atmosphere, discharge of toxic wastes into water courses etc.)

Some of the indirect costs to be accounted for are as under :

Damage costs : These are the costs that society faces because of actual damage to the environment. These costs can be arrived at by adding the expenses towards additional medical care, laundry, house painting, landscape etc. which become necessary because of pollution and other environmental degradation.

Abatement costs : These are the costs for controlling the cause of environmental damage. In the case of industrial plants, the abatement costs constitute the value of additional engineering and technology needed for treating the effluents and emissions.

Avoidance costs : These are the costs paid by the public in order to avoid the effects of environmental damage.

Transactional costs : These are the administrative costs for protecting the environment.

4.10 VENTURE CAPITAL

The term 'Venture Capital' comprises of two words, viz., 'venture' and 'capital'. The dictionary meaning of 'venture' is a risky undertaking and the term 'capital' means the resources to start the enterprise. Thus, 'venture capital' can be interpreted as the investment of long term equity investment in business that has a high risk profile, but displays potential for significant growth and attractive returns on the investment made. The venture capitalist (the person who provides venture capital, i.e., equity) earns his returns primarily from capital gain in the long run. The business in which venture capital is deployed is a high risk business in view of the reason that the venture is a new one with unproven technology.

A project that has potential for substantial growth, but that has a high risk proportion in view of its technology not having been proved , will not generally attract investors since investors do not want to take 'undue' risk, however attractive the long term returns may be. Hence, the need for a venture capitalist to nurse such ventures. The concept of venture capital originated in the USA in the year 1946, when the American Research and Development Fund was founded at the Massachussets Institute of Technology. Most of the successful ventures in the SILICON VALLEY of the USA are beneficiaries of venture capital assistance.

The main characteristics of venture capital investments are as under:

- Investments are usually made in the equity capital of the enterprise.
- The venture capitalist does not interfere in the management of the enterprise.
- Apart from equity finance, the venture capitalist may also extend financial assistance in the form of quasi-equity, conditional loans etc.,
- Venture capital investments are made only in high-risk, high-growth projects.
- Risk analysis forms the major part of project appraisal.
- The venture capitalist opts to finance the venture only if he is satisfied after his extensive analysis and appraisal that the risk factors are offset by higher probability of success.
- Investment is made usually in new ventures, i.e, in 'start-ups'.

Stages of Venture Capital Financing

First stage

A small amount of capital is provided to the entrepreneur to finance his R&D efforts for product development, to prove a concept, or to go for commercial production in a small level when the product development stage has already been completed successfully.

Second stage

Once the first stage of financing has been successful, the enterprise qualifies for the second stage of financing. Second stage of financing is also known as 'expansion financing' and finance is given for initial expansion and for meeting the working capital requirements.

Third stage

This is provided for the major expansion of the company. The venture capitalist provides major finance at this stage, since by this time, he would have gained confidence about the safety of his investments and the long term returns that he can reasonably anticipate.

The Indian Scene of Venture Capital Financing

The concept of venture capital as a new area of financial service was first introduced in the fiscal budget for the year 1986-87. Venture Capital form of funding new investment proposals is still in an infant stage in India. Some of the venture capital firms incorporated in India are as under:

- Technology Development and Information Company of India Ltd., (TDICI) , jointly promoted by ICICI and UTI.
- Venture Capital division of IDBI.
- Risk Capital and Technology Finance Corporation Ltd., (RCTC) promoted by IFCI.
- Gujarat Venture Capital Limited, promoted by the Gujarat Industrial Investment Corporation Limited.
- APIDC Venture Capital Limited, promoted by the Andhra Pradesh Industrial development Corporation Limited.
- SBI capital market.
- Canbank Venture Capital Fund.
- Citibank Venture Capital Fund.
- Grindlays Venture Capital Fund.
- 20th Century Venture Capital Corporation Limited, promoted by the 20th Century Finance Company Limited.
- Credit Capital Venture Fund(India) Limited, a subsidiary of Credit capital Finance Corporation Limited.

4.11 PROJECT FAILURES

Failure of project is a costly affair and will destabilize the organization as a whole. Some of the reasons for failure of projects and the precautions to be taken to avoid failures are as under.

- The first phase of project life cycle is the project conceptualization stage. This is the stage at which the need for the project is visualized, discussed and the project idea gets crystallized. A wrongly conceived project is bound to run into rough weathers. Top managers should discuss the pros and cons threadbare before deciding upon the choice of the project. Collective wisdom of top managers will lead to correct conceptualization of projects. Hence, at this stage, difference of opinions among the top managers should be discussed in a free and fair atmosphere and consensus should be arrived at.

- The next stage is the planning stage. At this stage budgeting, scheduling, deciding on project organization structure etc. are carried out. Planning should be done after gathering the required data. Planning based on insufficient and inaccurate data will lead to project failures. Those top managers who are going to be in-charge of project execution should be included in the project planning group.
- One of the main reasons for project failures has been inadequate resource planning. The financial resources required for implementing the project should be tied up properly. If the project runs short of funds midway during its implementation, it will cause heavy damage and the project may come to a grinding halt. Apart from financial resource, availability of a personnel with special skills required for implementing the project is to be ensured. If men and material resources are not adequately tied up, the implementation will suffer leading to failure.
- Periodical evaluation of the project should be carried out. Deviations from the plan and deficiencies found if any are to be corrected by exercising proper control.
- Projects take shape only by the teamwork of personnel assigned with the task of project execution. If they fail to act as a team and if the project leader lacks the managerial ability to lead his team towards its goal, the project implementation will fail despite having adequate resources and despite having a well thought out plan.

4.12 OPTIMUM SIZE OF A BUSINESS UNIT

After having identified the product to be manufactured, the next question that is before an entrepreneur is "what should be the size of the firm?". Size can be measured either in terms of the investment required or in terms of the volume of out put. Suppose size is measured in terms of the investment required. For setting up a business unit, for the manufacture of a product, say, craft paper, the entrepreneur has to decide upon the size of the unit. It may be possible to set up a plant at a minimum investment of about Rs.5.00 lakhs. The same product can be manufactured by setting up a larger plant with sophisticated machinery at an investment of about Rs.5.00 crores. The question to be answered is as to what the size to be chosen should be.

In arriving at the size of the firm, there may be certain constraints. For instance, there may be certain restrictions imposed by the Government. Certain products may be reserved to be manufactured by small scale industrial establishments alone wherein big players are not allowed. Such restrictions automatically limit the size of the unit to the maximum investment limit stipulated by the regulatory authorities.

The entrepreneur himself may have limitations with regard to mobilization of funds required for setting up the unit. Such limitations also restrict the size of the unit. However, in circumstances where the size of the business unit is restricted only due to financial limitations of the entrepreneur, it should be evaluated carefully whether the unit will be viable at its chosen size. This is because of the reason that when a project is restricted in size due to of financial constraints and when the restricted size is very much below the optimum size, the unit cost of production will be higher and the project can not survive the competition.

Barring such limitations imposed by regulatory authorities and the entrepreneur's financial capacity, every business unit has an optimum size, which is the size of the firm at which the average cost of production per unit of production will be the least.

"By the optimum firm, we must mean a firm operating that scale at which in existing conditions of techniques and organizing ability, it has the lowest average cost of production per unit, when all those costs which must be covered in the long run are included." (Prof. E.A.G. Robinson)

For every business unit there is a minimum size. The business unit will not be feasible below this minimum size. A business unit with a minimum size will not be an economical one. As the size of the business unit is steadily increased from the minimum size, the unit will become more and more profitable. This is because of the economy of scale enjoyed by units of bigger size. Thus, as the size of a business unit is increased from its minimum size, the average cost per unit of production comes down which leads to increasing profitability. However, there is limit to the size beyond which further increase in size will become less profitable. This is because, beyond a certain limit, the law of diminishing returns will start to operate which will make further expansion of size uneconomical. The point up to which the increase in size results in decreased average unit cost of product produced and beyond which the increase in size will lead to increase in average unit cost is referred to as the optimum size of a business unit.

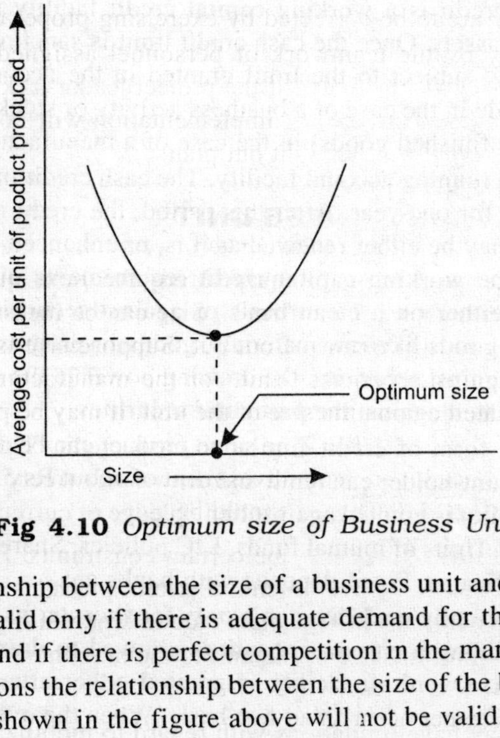

Fig 4.10 *Optimum size of Business Unit*

(Note: The above relationship between the size of a business unit and the average cost per unit of product produced will be valid only if there is adequate demand for the product so that the market can absorb the production and if there is perfect competition in the market. Under monopolistic and oligopolistic market conditions the relationship between the size of the business unit and the average cost per unit of product as shown in the figure above will not be valid.)

4.13 INSTITUTIONAL FINANCE TO ENTREPRENEURS

Capital is the major constraint for entrepreneurs. This is more so for first generation entrepreneurs. Hence, the responsibility of providing capital to entrepreneurs who have worthwhile project proposal rests with the Government if the Government wants to nurture entrepreneurial skills and to bring about balanced growth of the economy.

In India, there are many Government owned and Government sponsored institutions available for extending financial assistance to entrepreneurs for setting up business ventures. The institutions that offer financial assistance for projects fall into two major categories, viz.

1. Commercial Bank
2. Financial Institutions.

1. **Commercial Banks :** State Bank of India and its associated Banks, Nationalized Banks, Private Sector Banks, Regional Rural Banks and Foreign Banks come under this category. Banks finance both for creation of fixed assets (i.e., medium and long term loans) and for the building up of current assets (i.e., working capital loan). Banks play major role in extending working capital assistance since financial institutions restrict their lending mostly for medium / long term loans for the creation of fixed assets.

The financial assistance to meet working capital requirements is offered by banks in the following forms.

(*a*) Cash credit
(*b*) Overdraft
(*c*) Purchase / Discounting of bills
(*d*) Loans

(*a*) **Cash Credit :** Cash credit is a working capital credit facility provided to a customer for building up of current assets. Once the cash credit limit is sanctioned, the borrower can remit and drawn funds freely subject to the limit granted in the account. It is a pre-sale finance against the stock in trade in the case of a business activity or stock of inventory (raw material, semi finished goods & finished goods) in the case of a manufacturing activity of a borrower. Cash credit facility is a running account facility. The cash credit limit is normally extended for a short period, usually for one year. After this period, the credit requirement is reviewed and on review, the limits may be either renewed as it is, or enhanced or decreased on the basis of a fresh appraisal of the working capital credit requirements of the borrower. Cash credit facilities are granted either on a clean basis or against securities. The securities normally obtained by banks are goods like raw materials, goods-in-progress and finished goods. When cash credit is granted against securities, the drawing power in the account is determined on the basis of margins stipulated against the particular securities.

(*b*) **Overdraft :** This is a form of credit similar to cash credit. This is also a running account facility where the account-holder can remit and draw funds freely subject to the overdraft limit granted. Overdraft facility is granted against lien / pledge of current assets like Bills receivable, Government securities. Units of mutual funds, LIC policies, Shares / debentures of companies, National savings certificates, Fixed deposits with banks etc.
Overdraft facility is normally made available only for short terms. When a overdraft facility is granted, a customer having a current account is allowed to draw over and above the credit balance in his account. Overdraft facility is granted either after due appraisal of the credit requirements of the customer or on an ad-hoc basis. When the overdraft facility is given on an ad-hoc basis it is known as temporary overdraft and is granted to meet unexpected, immediate credit needs of the customer. Temporary overdraft facility is granted only for a very short period of about a few days / weeks / a months.

(*c*) **Purchasing / Discounting of bills :** Section of the Negotiable Instruments Act defines a bill of exchange as under. "An instrument in writing containing an unconditional order, signed by the maker, directing a certain person to pay a certain sum of money only to or to the order of a certain person or to the bearer of the instrument".

Bills are of two types, viz.

(*i*) Demand Bills

(*ii*) Usance Bills

Demand Bills are drawn against payment and they are called D.P. bills.

Usance bills are drawn against payment on expiry of Usance period. These bills are called D/A bills.

When goods are sold on credit, the seller of the goods draws a bill on the buyer of the goods for the value of goods sold. When the buyer accepts the bill by signing it, it becomes payable on demand (in the case of demand bill) or on the due date (in the case of usance bill).

When the banker lends money against demand bills, the facility is known as purchasing of bills and when the banker lends money against usance bills, the facility is known as Discounting of bills.

When the banker sanctions a "Bill purchase limit" to his client, (the drawer of the bill) the banker credits the account of the drawer with the amount of the bill (Less Bank charges) on presentation of the bill to him. Thus the drawer's account is credited immediately by the banker without waiting for actual realization of the bill amount.

For the purchase of usable bills the banker sanctions a separate `Bills discount limit' to his client (i.e., to the drawer of the bill). The banker credits the account of the drawer on presentation of the usance bill to him, by an amount equal to the bill amount less the interest on the unexpired term of the bill, less Bank Charges. The banker receives the full amount of the bill on its maturity, from the drawee of the bill. (Thus, it may be noted that only usance bills are discounted and demand bills are not discounted.)

A banker may sanction working capital limit broken up into three components, viz. Cash credit, Bills purchase limit & Bills discount limit. While cash credit limit can be used for making immediate payments for purchase of raw materials, payment of wages etc., bills purchase & Bills discount limits can be used for getting immediate money for the credit sales made.

(*d*) **Loans :** Banks extend credit in the form of loans to their customers for the creation of fixed assets and for the building up of current assets. However, loans are mainly used for creation of fixed assets (like building, machinery, equipments etc) and their use for meeting working capital requirements is limited, except under special circumstances. Loans are to be repaid over a period of time running into years. Loans may be of two types, viz., Term loan and Demand loan. Term loan and Demand loan are to be repaid in fixed instalments at periodic intervals. Loans granted with a repayment period of 1 to 5 years are classified as Demand loans while loans with repayment period excluding 5 years are classified as Term loans.

2. **Financial Institutions :** IDBI, IFCI, ICICI, SIDBI, NSIC are the major financial institutions operating at the national level. These institutions mainly offer financial assistance for the creation of fixed assets (Land, Building and Plant and Machinery) for industrial ventures. Their financial assistance is available both for new projects and for expansion / modernization of existing projects. [The type of assistance's available from these different institutions are given separately elsewhere in this chapter which may be referred to]

State Financial Corporations (SFCs) are the financial institutions sponsored by the State Governments and have their jurisdiction of operation within the respective states. They offer financial assistance for the creation of fixed assets (Land, Building and Plant & Machinery) for industrial ventures. Their financial assistance is available both for new projects and for expansion / modernization of existing projects. [The types of assistances available from SFCs is given separately elsewhere in this chapter which may be referred to]

4.14 PROJECT LIFE CYCLE

All projects have a life cycle. The duration of life cycle will vary depending on the type and nature of the project. The life cycle of any project consists of four phases. The phases in project life cycle are as under :

1. Conceptualization of project and defining the problem.
2. Planning of project activities and planning for resources.
3. Execution of project.
4. Termination of project

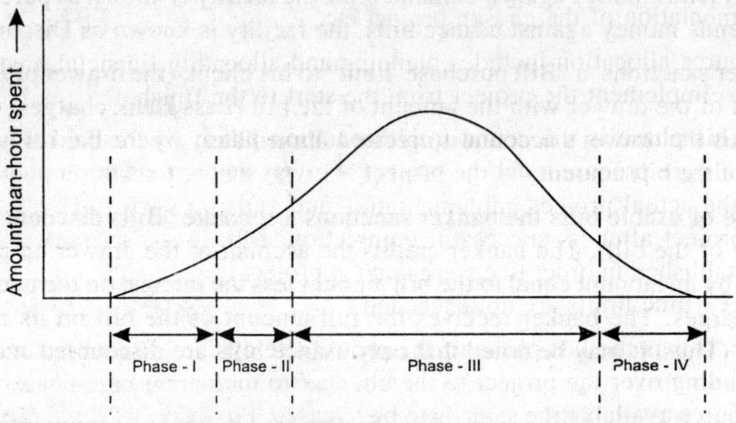

Fig. 4.11 *Project Life Cycle*

1. **Conceptualization :** Any project begins with a concept. Concept is an abstract idea. At the conceptualization phase, the need for the project has not been thought of thoroughly. Consider an existing textile industry, say a spinning mill whose profits has been showing continuously decreasing trend. There is a need to stop the declining trend in profits. The solution to the problem may lie in any one of the following strategies.

(*a*) The mill can reduce its unit cost of production of cotton yarn. For achieving this, it may have to go for bulk production which may need creation of additional production facilities by way of additional plant and machinery. Since increase in production means increase in the stock of raw material (due to the need for bulk purchases, especially at times when the raw material is cheaper) this may need the construction of raw material godown (i.e., cotton godown)

(*b*) Instead of opting for expansion of capacity in order to reduce the unit cost of production, the mill may opt for increasing the quality of yarn produced by modernizing the existing machinery. This in turn will increase the value addition to the finished product (cotton yarn) which may improve the profitability of the mill. Such an option will involve replacement of some of the existing plant and machinery with the machines of latest technology and renovating/reconditioning some of the existing machinery.

(*c*) A third strategy may be opting for either forward integration or backward integration which has got the scope for improving the profitability.

The available alternatives are to be studied and the apt one is to be chosen. In the above example, if modernization of the existing production facility is considered to be the right approach, the problem should then be defined. In the example given above the problem can be defined as one of modernizing the existing production facilities in order to improve the profitability of the unit.

2. **Planning :** Planning phase consists of the establishment of formal plans to achieve the goals of the project as defined under conceptualization phase.

In the planning phase, scheduling of project activities, budgeting of capital expenditure and allocation of resources for the implementation of the project are done.

Scheduling of project activities consists of laying out all the actual activities of the project in the time order in which they are to be performed keeping in view the logical sequence of the activities, identifying the critical activities etc., Capital Budgeting involves the entire process of planning the capital expenditure for the project which includes studying of cash flows, ranking of investment proposals, sensitivity analysis, risk analysis, rationing of capital and planning to tie up the required funds for the implementation of the chosen project etc.

Planning for resource allocation includes planning and allocating financial, material and human resources required to implement the project from the start to the finish.

3. **Execution :** This phase is the actual implementation phase where the resources tied up are made use of, materials are procured and the project is given shape. Execution phase starts from the commencement of the actual project implementation and ends up with verifying the performance parameters of the project after its successful completion. During the execution phase, necessary controls are to be established in order to ensure that the project implementation progresses as per the plan and the resource / time limits are not exceeded.

4. **Termination :** This is the last phase of the project life cycle. This phase consists of releasing of resources and handing over the project to the clients / to the parent organization. If there is any excess financial resource available the same is to be released. For example if the project is completed at a lesser cost, either due to effective cost control or due to minor modifications incorporated during the course of implementation, the excess financial resource that remains unutilized shall be released. If long term finance for the project was already tied up with a financial institution, the institution may be informed of the non-requirement of balance funds and the unutilized loan component may be requested to be lapsed. The human resources drawn from other departments may be released to their respective departments.

4.15 ENTREPRENEURSHIP

Entrepreneurship refers to the functions performed by an entrepreneur. Thus, entrepreneurship can be defined as the intangible, but very essential asset in the form of entrepreneurial qualities of innovation, organizing and managing a business enterprise, risk taking and striving to earn profit out of the business venture. Just as machinery, capital and labour are considered as factors of production, entrepreneurship can also be considered as a factor of production. Availability of machinery, capital and labour alone will be insufficient to bring about economic growth. It is entrepreneurship, which is a distinct factor of production that contributes to the economic development of an economy. An analysis of the economic development achieved by the economically developed countries would reveal the importance of entrepreneurship for economic development. Economies world over have developed only because of the pivotal role played by entrepreneurship. Entrepreneurship acts as a catalyst to bring forth economic development by the fusion of other factors of production.

4.15.1 Role of Entrepreneurship

The roles played by entrepreneurship for the development of an economy are as under.

(*a*) First of all it is entrepreneurship that brings together the other factors of production and infuses life into the economy.

(*b*) As entrepreneurship helps in building up a new business enterprise, it brings about a favorable climate for capital formulation; hence savings with the public that lie idle will be put into better use.

(*c*) As a consequence of the emergence of new enterprises, the people of the society will get employment opportunities and their standard of living will get improved.

(*d*) In the absence of entrepreneurship, the burden of economic development and providing adequate employment opportunity to the public will rest with the Government. As the Government can only set up and control only large sized business establishments, this will lead to unbalanced growth.

(*e*) Since the prevalence of entrepreneurship among the public will pave way for the growth of many tiny, small and medium sized business establishments, this will lead to balanced economic development and equitable distribution of wealth.

(*f*) When entrepreneurship prevails in a society, the entrepreneurs will be spread throughout and will specialize on ventures that are suitable and profitable for their particular location and environment. Development of such varied business establishments will be complementary to one another and will provide the backward and forward linkages required for overall and sustained economic growth.

4.15.2 Entrepreneur

Webster's Dictionary defines an entrepreneur as under.

"a person who organizes and manages a business undertaking, assuming the risk for the sake of profit".

The definition when expanded will make clear the concept of entrepreneur. It is the entrepreneur who 'organizes'. He/She organizes the resources required for starting a business enterprise. After a business idea strikes at the entrepreneur's mind, he is in the look out for the ways and means of establishing a business enterprise to give shape to his vision. To achieve this, he organizes the required resources, both men and material and builds up the business enterprise.

The objective is not achieved with organizing the resources and building up the enterprise. The business enterprise is to be managed well in order to achieve the results for which the enterprise was formed. Thus, the entrepreneur manages the business enterprise which he has built up in order to make sure that his dream comes true.

Building up a new business enterprise and managing it is not all that easy. While the opportunities available are many, there is always a scarcity of entrepreneurs. And the reason for this is due to the risk involved in starting a business enterprise 'Risk-taking' is the main attribute that a person should possess, for him / her to become an entrepreneur. If he / she shies away from taking risk, the idea of starting a business enterprise will only dwell in his / her mind and will never come true.

Why does an entrepreneur takes the risk of building up a business enterprise and managing it? Obviously he / she does so in order to exploit the business opportunity and to earn profit. It is the profit motive that induces the entrepreneur to undertake the risk of establishing and managing a business enterprise. When a person has the desire to earn profit and also has the ability to take risks, he turns out to be an entrepreneur.

Joseph A. Schumpeter, a noted economist introduced for the first time, introduced the concept of 'innovation' as an attribute required of an entrepreneur Websters Dictionary defines innovation as under.

"Something nearly introduced - new method, practice, device etc."

An entrepreneur is one who tries to exploit an available business opportunity and earn profit out of it. He can make his business enterprise a successful one only if the enterprise works on profitable lies. In order to make the business enterprise a profitable one the entrepreneur has to overcome competition from the existing players, attract new customers, offer the customers with attractive and at the same time affordable products. In order to achieve this, he has to be an innovator. He may innovate a new product or new features to an existing product economically and efficiently etc., Thus the quality of innovativeness is a prerequisite for an entrepreneur in order to make his venture a successful one.

To sum up we can define an entrepreneur as one who foresees a business opportunity takes the business risk and sets up the business enterprise by, organizing the required resources, introduces innovative products / techniques and manages the business enterprise with a view of achieving profit. It is the entrepreneur who gives life to idle resources and adds value to resources and there by brings benefits to the society. Any society needs more and more entrepreneurs in order to improve the welfare of the society and to bring betterment to the lives of the people.

4.16 PROJECT ABANDONMENT

A project may be required to be abandoned even before its completion of the project. Such a situation may arise under the following circumstances.

- When the project has lost its strategic importance both in terms of long term and short term business strategies.
- When the resources required for implementing the project have become scarce and their availability has become restricted.
- When the progress of project implementation always lags behind the schedule continuously and also substantially and when steps taken to improve the phase of project implementation do not yield favorable results.
- When completing the project has become infeasible due to the changed circumstances.

Under the above circumstances it will be wise to abandon the project and a conscious decision as to whether the project needs to be abandoned is to be taken. Abandoning the project under such circumstances will avoid throwing good money after bad money and will minimize the loss to the organization. However, it requires courage on the part of project managers / entrepreneurs to accept that the project would be a failure and to abandon it at the early stage itself, having seen the symptoms of failure. The decision to abandon the project should be taken after an objective analysis without giving room for any personal bias and without any consideration for the cost already incurred in the project. There is a tendency among the project promoters to some how try to rescue the project from danger zone in view of the heavy cost ready incurred on the project. No doubt, efforts to rescue the project can be taken when danger symptoms are visible, but the assessment should be done objectively and without any further loss of time. After all it is wise of the captain of a sinking ship to make a SOS call and to save the men and material and board instead of making vain attempts to save the sinking ship on the false hope of reserving it.

Apart from abandonment of projects even before their completion, a project that has been fully implemented may also be abandoned even before its economic life if the expected cash flows and the abandonment value point towards early abandonment. The NPV (Net Present Value) of the expected cash flows and the abandonment value are used as the criteria to judge the need for early abandonment even before the project has lived its economic life.

The following illustration will help to understand the concept.

Illustration: 4.5

The economic life of a project is estimated at 5 years. The project has been implemented and the investment made is Rs.15,00,000/-. The expected cash inflows for the first five years (i.e., till the economic life is over) are as under.

First year	Rs. 4,00,000/-
Second year	Rs. 5,00,000/-
Third year	Rs. 4,90,000/-
Fourth year	Rs. 3,20,000/-
Fifth year	Rs. 1,40,000/-

The net abandonment values (*i.e.,* salvage value) of the project for the five years are as under.

First year	Rs.13,00,000/-
Second year	Rs. 6,80,000/-
Third year	Rs. 4,80,000/-
Fourth year	Rs. 1,60,000/-
Fifth year	Rs. NIL

Make an analysis and ascertain when the project should be abandoned? Assume a cost of capital of 10% p.a.

Solution :

The investment made in the project has been given as Rs.15,00,000/-. Let us assume that the present value of cash out flow as Rs.15,00,000/-.

If we assume that the project is abandoned at the end of the first year,

$$\text{NPV} = -15{,}00{,}000 + \frac{4{,}00{,}000}{(1.10)} + \frac{13{,}00{,}000}{(1.10)}$$

$$= \text{Rs. } 45{,}454$$

If we assume that the project is abandoned at the end of the second year,

$$\text{NPV} = -15{,}00{,}000 + \frac{4{,}00{,}000}{(1.10)} + \frac{5{,}00{,}000}{(1.10)^2} + \frac{6{,}80{,}000}{(1.10)^2}$$

$$= \text{Rs.}1,61,158$$

If we assume that the project is abandoned at the end of the third year,

$$\text{NPV} = -\ 15,00,000 + \frac{4,00,000}{(1.10)} + \frac{5,00,000}{(1.10)^2} + \frac{4,90,000}{(1.10)^3} + \frac{4,80,000}{(1.10)^3}$$

$$= \text{Rs.}5,634$$

If we assume that the project is abandoned at the end of the fourth year,

$$\text{NPV} = -\ 15,00,000 + \frac{4,00,000}{(1.10)} + \frac{5,00,000}{(1.10)^2} + \frac{4,90,000}{(1.10)^3} + \frac{3,20,000}{(1.10)^4} + \frac{1,60,000}{(1.10)^4}$$

$$= (-)\ \text{Rs.}27,148$$

If we assume that the project is abandoned at the end of the fifth year, (i.e. if the project is allowed to live its economic life)

$$\text{NPV} = -\ 15,00,000 + \frac{4,00,000}{(1.10)} + \frac{5,00,000}{(1.10)^2} + \frac{4,90,000}{(1.10)^3} + \frac{3,20,000}{(1.10)^4} + \frac{1,40,000}{(1.10)^5}$$

$$= (-)\ \text{Rs.}49,504/-$$

The negative NPV from the fourth year onwards suggests that the project be abandoned at the end of three years.

4.17 JOINT VENTURES

A joint venture is an enterprise that is jointly owned and jointly managed by a local and a foreign entrepreneur. One of the parties to the joint venture may even be the Government.

Some of the advantages of a joint venture are as under :

- Each of the joint venturers may have strengths in their own line of activity. A combination of complementary strengths of each of the joint venturers leads to an enterprise that is more strong and fit to face the business challenge. The joint venturers are benefited due to the synergy of such ventures. For example, a firm may have good marketing facilities and another firm may have excellent manufacturing facilities. A joint venture between these two firms will take the joint venture company in to a formidable position and both the partners to the joint venture will be benefitted.
- Joint ventures are also sought after when the outlay on project investment is huge that it would not be possible to be contributed by only one firm. The parties to the joint venture pool their resources in order to meet the investment on the project

A foreign firm acquiring shares in a local firm or a local firm acquiring shares in an existing foreign firm also constitute a joint venture. The decision as to where should a new joint venture facility be located (i.e., whether in home town or in a foreign country) depends on many economic and other considerations.

Looking from the angle of an Indian firm, joint venture with a foreign firm may be appropriate

(*a*) when the resources available with the company are insufficient to enable it to expand in to international operations.

(*b*) when the company has resources to expand its operations beyond its national boundaries, but a wholly owned subsidiary of a foreign company is prohibited in the country in which the company wants to expand its operations.

(*c*) when the company considers it to be a strategic advantage to join hands with a foreign partner to capitalize on his marketing network and management skills.

(*d*) when the company feels that total control over the project to be set up abroad is not essential for the success of the joint venture.

4.18 LEASING

International accounting standard defines lease as '... an agreement whereby the lessor conveys to the lessee, in return for rent, the right to use an asset for as agreed period of time...'

Lease provides a person the right to use and to have control over the asset of another person without receiving the title to it and on payment of a specific consideration for such right for a specific period. The person who lets the asset to be used by another is called the lessor and the person who utilizes the asset on payment of lease rent is called the lessee.

Types of Lease

The lease agreement can be classified into two types, viz.,, Financial lease and Operating lease.

A lease is classified as a financial lease if it secures for the lessor the recovery of his capital outlay plus a return on the funds invested during the lease term. A financial lease is also known as Capital lease. In a financial lease, the lessee selects the equipment that is required for his business and enters in to an irrevocable and non-cancelable contractual agreement with a leasing company (the lessor). The lessor purchases the equipment and gives it on lease to the lessee as per the terms of the contract. The lessee uses the equipment, maintains it and pays the lease rentals as agreed upon in the contract. The financial lease agreement normally contains a purchase option, according to which the lessee has the option to buy the equipment at the end of the lease period at a pre-determined value.

A lease is called as an operating lease if it does not secure for the lessor the recovery of his capital outlay plus a return on the funds invested during the lease term. Operating lease is usually for a shorter period and is usually cancelable, either by the lessor or by the lessee. After the lease period is over, the lessor gets back the equipment which he can give on lease to another lessee.

The lessee can claim lease rentals as tax-deductible expenses while the lessor can claim depreciation over the investment made on the leased asset(since the lessor remains the owner of the asset throughout the lease period).

Leveraged Lease

Leveraged lease is employed when financing of an asset involves large capital outlay and one financial institution may not be willing to have such a large stake in the venture. In such instances, the lessor (which is the leasing company) provides the equity capital while banks/financial institutions provide funds in the form of term loans for the purchase of the leased asset.

Cross Border Lease

In this type of lease, the lessor is in one country, while the lessee is in another country. The lessor leases out his asset to the lessee abroad.

Foreign to Foreign Lease

In this type of lease, there are three parties to the transaction, viz.,

- the manufacturer (or supplier) of the asset is located in one particular country
- the lessor is located in another country
- the lessee who wants to take the asset on lease is located in some other country (Example: A leasing Company in U.S.A. might purchase an aircraft from a manufacturer in France and lease it to an Indian Company.)

4.19 PROJECT RISK ANALYSIS

In project appraisal, risk analysis play an important part. All projects are prone to some kind of risk or the other. All projects are appraised making certain assumptions. Assumptions in project appraisal are unavoidable since no two projects are unique in all respects and hence a new project cannot be compared with an identical project that was executed in the past. Though there may be similarity between two different projects, exactly identical projects do not exit. There are many elements of a project which contain assumed values. The following list of elements will give an idea of the assumptions on which any project appraisal is based on.

- Periodic cash inflows (the cash inflows are assumed by assuming the selling price of the product over a period of time and the plant output over the said period)
- Periodic cash outflows (the cash outflows are assumed by assuming the purchase price of raw materials, the cost of power, labour etc.,)
- Life of machinery
- Salvage value of machinery, etc.,

Since a project is appraised making use of such assumptions, the appraisal is very much prone to the risk of yielding results that may deviate very much from reality.

Risk Vs Uncertainty

'Risk' can be defined as the variability of return from an investment. If the probabilities of possible outcomes of a given problem are known, we can conclude that the problem contains risk; in other words, the problem is risky, On the other hand, if the probabilities of possible outcomes of a given problem are not known, we can conclude that the problem has an element of uncertainty, i,e., the outcome can not be predicted.

Kinds of Project Risks

Projects face a host of risks. Some important project risks are as under.

Project Completion Risk

Completing the project in time and within the estimated cost itself is a major achievement. A project that is delayed will result in time over-run which will consequently result in cost over-run. If the project promoters are not able to pump in additional funds required to meet the cost over-run, the project runs the risk of coming to a grinding halt. Also, delayed implementation means increase in interest commitments on the borrowed funds. When the project promoters find it difficult to meet the interest commitment during the implementation period, the lenders may not be prepared to fund the project additionally to meet the cost over-run. As the saying goes," .. .. the banker will lend his umbrella when the whether is fine, but will get back the umbrella when it starts raining…"…Hence, once symptoms of delay in project implementation surfaces, mobilizing additional funds becomes difficult which will add to the problem of project completion. There can be also technology failures, which may result in non-completion of projects. For projects with long gestation period in the fields of fast developing technology, there is risk of project not being completed due to technological obsolescence during the course of project implementation.

Resource Risk

Raw material, power, fuel, manpower etc., are the resources used by a project. Shortage of raw material may lead to reduction in capacity utilization and higher cost of production, which will make all profitability estimates wrong. Similarly, shortage of power, fuel, and shortage of skilled manpower will also jeopardize the project profitability calculations and the project may run the risk of not earning the estimated returns.

Price Risk

Price fluctuations of both inputs and outputs (i.e., raw material and finished products) affect the project. Unforeseen happenings such as Government's intentions in price fixation, ability of competitors to offer their product to customers at a comparatively cheaper price etc.,, are likely to have an adverse effect.

Technology Risk

Technology risk may appear in two forms. A project that is based on unproven technology (i.e., a technology that is proved at laboratory level but not proved at commercial level) may have hidden defects which may make the project a non-starter. Rapid growth in technology may make a project obsolete in technology due to the evolution of latest technology.

Political Risk

The saying goes . . . "Do not fight with King and God…. " The King (i.e., the Government) acts as a watch dog of the country's economy and frames rules and regulations for regulating the country's economy. The Government intervenes in many forms such as levying and regulating taxes, regulating monopolistic trade practices, imposing import duties, promoting exports, prohibiting export of certain commodities, issuing import licenses, controlling foreign exchange transactions, price controls, expropriation, nationalization etc.,

Political risk is a major risk since it can not be predicted easily.

Interest Rate Risk

Fluctuations in interest rate may bring in an adverse effect. For example, if a project is funded by way of long-term borrowings at a particular rate of interest, and if the interest rate falls down subsequently, the project that availed long-term borrowings at a higher interest rate has to service the loan only at the higher rate of interest, unless it makes alternative arrangements to mobilize funds at the prevailing interest rate and swap the old borrowings which is a difficult proposition. New entrants who set up similar projects may have access to long-tem loans at the prevailing rate of interest which is smaller. In such a situation, projects that were implemented with high-cost borrowings will find it difficult to compete with new entrants.

On the other hand, if the interest rate increases in future, the interest on working capital finance (which normally carries a floating interest rate) increases which will result in lower profit margins than estimated at the time of project appraisal. Interest rate risks can be managed to some extent by entering into interest rate hedging agreements like 'interest cap' , 'interest swap' etc.,

Exchange Rate Risk

Exchange rate risk (also called currency risk) is the risk arising from currency fluctuations. Volatile exchange rates can reduce cost and productivity advantages gained over years of hard work. Firms exposed to international economy face this risk. When a firm has already committed to a foreign currency denominated transaction (i.e., the firm has entered into an agreement agreeing to make foreign currency denominated payments or agreeing to receive payments in foreign currency), the firm is exposed to exchange rate risk. The firm will incur loss if the exchange rate of the foreign currency has moved adversely and will earn profit if the exchange rate has moved favourably .Many exchange rate risk hedging tools such as forward cover, leads and lags, currency options, currency swaps etc., are available which can be efficiently made use of to manoeuvre exchange rate risk.

4.20 BREAK EVEN ANALYSIS

The financial viability of a project is estimated by making various assumptions like the cost of raw material, cost of consumables, cost of labour, expected sales realisation, expected capacity utilization of the plant etc. The proof of pudding is in eating. After implementation, the project starts earning profit or starts incurring loss depending on the actual sales volume that it could achieve, the actual cost of inputs, the actual sales realisation etc., of these factors, the costs of inputs and the price of outputs are decided by the influence of market forces. The only thing that is under the control of the project promoter is the level of output (i.e., capacity utilization). Hence, it is very essential to know the level of operation below which the project will incur losses. Break even point (B.E.P) refers to the level of operation at which the project neither earns profit nor incurs loss. Calculation of B.E.P. for the given cost and price levels indicate the minimum capacity utilization that the project should aim at in order to be in a no-profit, no-loss situation. B.E.P. also helps in identifying the level of profit/loss for a specified level of operation and the level of operation required to attain a specified profit/ to avoid a specified loss etc.,

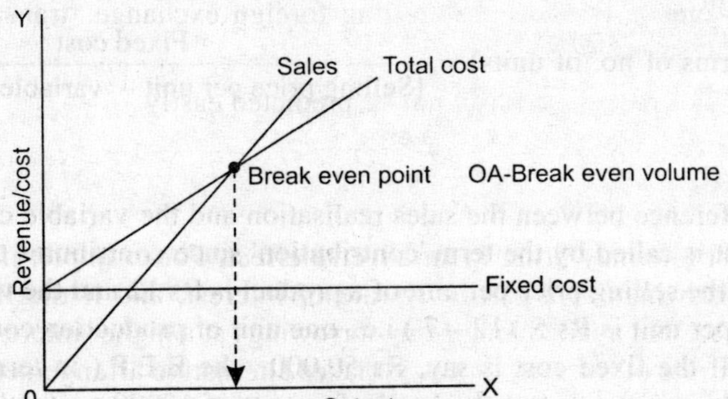

Fig. 4.12

Break even analysis starts with dividing the costs into two broad heads, viz., fixed costs and variable costs.

Fixed Costs

All projects incur certain costs that are fixed in nature. These costs remain constant irrespective of the changes in the volume of out put. Following are some of the fixed costs :

- Rent payable for land
- Rent payable for factory/office premises
- Insurance premium on fixed assets
- Interest payable on long-term borrowings/deposits
- Administrative expenses
- Annual Maintenance Charges payable for machinery maintenance
- Depreciation
- Property tax

Etc.,

Variable Costs

These are those costs that vary directly with the level of output. Raw material cost is a variable cost since it depends on the level of output. Some other variable costs are as under.

- Consumable stores
- Power, fuel, water charges
- Advertisement expenses

Etc.,

Referring to fig. 4.12

At the Break even point,

$$\text{Sales realization} = \text{Fixed cost} + \text{variable cost}$$

i.e., $$(\text{output}) \times \text{selling price per unit} = \text{Fixed cost} + (\text{output}) \times \text{variable cost per unit}$$

i.e., $$\text{output} \times (\text{selling price per unit} - \text{variable cost per unit}) = \text{Fixed cost}$$

i.e, $$\text{output} = \frac{\text{Fixed cost}}{(\text{Selling price per unit} - \text{Variable cost per unit})}$$

i.e., Break Even Point

$$(\text{in terms of no. of units}) = \frac{\text{Fixed cost}}{(\text{Selling price per unit} - \text{variable cost per unit})}$$

Contribution

Contribution is the difference between the sales realisation and the variable cost . Excess of selling price over variable cost is called by the term 'contribution' since contributes towards fixed cost and profit. For example, if the selling price per unit of a product is Rs 12 and the variable cost per unit is Rs 7, the contribution per unit is Rs 5 (12 – 7) i.e., one unit of production contributes Rs 5 towards fixed cost and profit. If the fixed cost is say, Rs 50,000, the B.E.P.(in terms of no. of units) is 10000 (50000/5). This means that at the level of output of 10000 units, the contribution covers

exactly the fixed cost. Hence, this is a no-profit, no-loss situation. Contribution first goes to meet the fixed cost up to B.E.P. and subsequent to reaching of B.E.P., contribution adds to profit.

$$\text{B.E.P. (in terms of no. of units)} = \frac{\text{Fixed cost}}{\text{(Selling price per unit} - \text{variable cost per unit)}}$$

$$= \frac{\text{Fixed cost}}{\text{Contribution per unit}}$$

$$\text{B.E.P.(in terms of rupees)} = \frac{\text{Fixed cost} \times \text{selling price per unit}}{\text{Contibution per unit}}$$

Illustration 4.6

The details of production costs and revenues of a project are as under:

Total cost	**:**	**Rs 65,000**
Fixed cost	**:**	**Rs 25,000**
Sales (8000 units)	**:**	**Rs 80,000**

Find the B.E.P. in terms of no. of units. What should be the output if the profit desired is Rs. 20,000

Solution :

Variable cost (for 8000 units) : total cost – fixed cost

: Rs 65000 – Rs 25000

: Rs 40000

Variable cost per unit : Rs 40000/8000

: Rs 5

$$\text{B.E.P. (in terms of no. of units)} : \frac{\text{Fixed cost}}{\text{(Selling price per unit} - \text{variable cost per unit)}}$$

$$: \frac{25000}{10-5}$$

: 5000 units

Output for a desired profit of Rs 20000

Let 'X' be the no. of units required to be produced for achieving a profit of Rs 20000

$$\text{Profit} = \text{Sales} - \text{Total cost}$$
$$= \text{Sales} - (\text{fixed cost} + \text{variable cost})$$
$$= (10X) - (25000 + 5X)$$

i.e.,
$$20000 = 15X - 25000$$
$$15X = 45000$$
$$X = 9000$$

Therefore, the output required for achieving a profit of Rs 20000 is 9000 units. (Refer fig. 4.13)

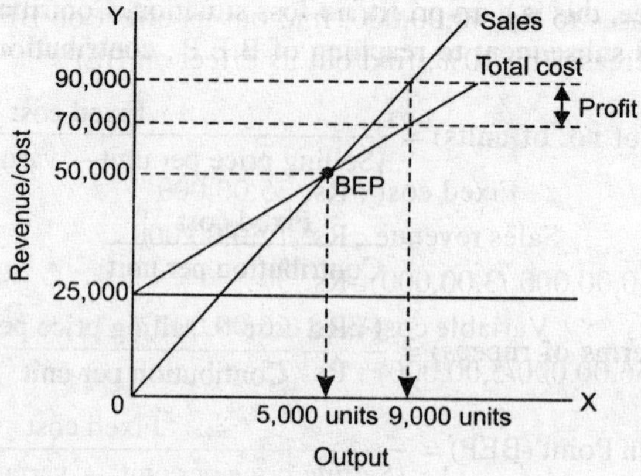

Fig. 4.13

4.21 SENSITIVITY ANALYSIS

It is a technique that measures the change in the profitability of a project caused by changes in the factors that affect the cash inflows of the project. If a small change in one factor leads to a major change in the profitability of the proposed investment, the project is considered more sensitive to that factor; in other words, the project is more risky. Other things being equal, a project that is less sensitive is preferable to projects that are more sensitive. This is because a small change in a factor will affect a more sensitive project very much and may reduce the estimated profit, or may even change the estimated profit into loss.

Sensitivity of a project is checked by observing the response of any measure of profitability (NPV, DSCR, BEP or any other measure) to changes in critical factors. For example, the sensitivity of a project can be studied as under.

- What happens to the NPV if the demand for the product drops down
- What happens to the NPV if the economic life of the project reduces
- What happens to the DRCR if the selling price for the product falls down

  Etc.

Sensitivity analysis provides the management the much needed information as to which are the critical factors that are prone to affect the profitability of the project.

Illustration 4.7

ABC Company limited proposes to start a new venture for the manufacture of fluorescent bulbs. The estimates of the new venture are as under.

Output of bulbs per annum : Rs. 3,00,000 nos.

Expected sales revenue per annum : Rs. 1,50,00,000.00

Fixed costs : Rs. 35,00,000.00

Variable costs : Rs. 66,00,000.00

(*a*) If the selling price comes down to Rs. 40.00 per unit, find out its effect on BEP

(*b*) If the fixed cost increases to Rs. 40,00,000, find out its effect on BEP
(*c*) If the variable cost increases by 10%, find out its effect on BEP

Solution :

Fixed cost : Rs. 35,00,000

Sales revenue : Rs. 1,50,00,000

Selling price per unit (1,50,00,000 /3,00,000) :Rs. 50

Variable cost : Rs. 66,00,000

Variable cost per unit (66,00,000/3,00,000) : Rs. 22

$$\text{Break Even Point (BEP)} = \frac{\text{Fixed cost}}{(\text{Selling price per unit} - \text{variable cost per unit})}$$

$$= \frac{35,00,000}{50-22} = \frac{35,00,000}{28}$$

$$= 1,25,000 \text{ units}$$

(*a*) Selling price per unit comes down to Rs. 40.00

$$\text{BEP} = \frac{35,00,000}{40-22} = \frac{35,00,000}{18}$$

$$= 1,94,999 \text{ units}$$

(*b*) Fixed cost increases to Rs. 40,00,000

$$\text{BEP} = \frac{40,00,000}{50-22} = \frac{40,00,000}{28}$$

$$= 1,42,875 \text{ units}$$

(*c*) Variable cost increases by 10 %

Revised variable cost per unit

$$(1.1 \times 22) = \text{Rs. } 24.20$$

$$\text{BEP} = \frac{35,00,000}{50-24.20} = \frac{35,00,000}{25.80}$$

$$= 1,35,659 \text{ units}$$

Results :

(*a*)

Selling price Per unit (Rs.)	*BEP*	*Reduction in Selling price*	*Increase in BEP*
50 40	1,25,000 units 1,94,444 units	$\frac{(50-40)\times 100}{50}$ = 20 %	$\frac{(1,94,444-1,25,000)\times 100}{1,25,000}$ = 56 %

(*b*)

Selling price Per unit (Rs.)	*BEP*	*Increase in fixed cost*	*Increase in BEP*
35,00,000	1,25,000 units	$\frac{(40,00,000 - 35,00,000) \times 100}{35,00,000}$	$\frac{(1,42,875 - 1,25,000) \times 100}{1,25,000}$
40,00,000	1,42,875	= 14.29 %	= 14.30 %

(*c*)

Variable cost per unit (Rs.)	*BEP*	*Increase in variable cost*	*Increase in BEP*
22	1,25,000 units	$\frac{(24.20 - 22) \times 100}{22}$	$\frac{(1,35,659 - 1,25,000) \times 100}{1,25,000}$
24.20	1,35,659 units	= 10 %	= 9 %

OBSERVATIONS

- 20 % increase in selling price results in 56 % increase of BEP
- 14.29 % increase in fixed cost results in 14.30 % increase of BEP
- 10 % increase in variable cost results in 9 % increase of BEP

Out of the three factors (selling price, fixed cost, variable cost), BEP is more sensitive to selling price.

4.22 PROJECT REPORT

A project report is a written report explaining the business plan of the proposed business venture. A project report sets out a blue print of the business plan, supporting the marketing aspects and commercial viability, detailing the production process and production requirements, giving the capital requirements of the project and the mode of tying up the required capital, arriving at financial projections in support of the financial viability and financial soundness of the project, giving a forecast of the schedule of implementation and explaining other salient features of the proposed project.

Project report serves two purposes.

(*a*) It provides the entrepreneur with a road map of the business plan and the path to reach the objectives. It gives confidence to the entrepreneur / project promoter about the success and viability of the project.

(*b*) It is useful to repose confidence among investors and to convince lenders about the success and viability of the project. Banks and financial institutions rely on project reports for making their own appraisal about the viability of projects. Banks and financial institutions look for bankable projects before committing their funds. A bankable project is one that satisfies the banker (i.e., the bank / financial institution that finances the project) about its profitability so that the banker can approve sanction of financial assistance for the project.

A project report is to be prepared with great care. Though the general format and contents of the project report is more or less the same for all projects, certain unique / special features of individual projects are to be highlighted in the report.

The contents normally expected in a project report are given below in the form of a specimen project report.

PROJECT REPORT FOR SETTING UP OF AN UNIT FOR THE MANUFACTURE OF ....

Production Plan :

(A) Product(s) proposed to be manufactured :

(B) Manufacturing Process (in brief) :

(C) Plant Capacity :

		Year							
		I	II	III	IV	V	VI	VII	VIII
i. Licensed capacity	:								
ii. Proposed capacity	:								

Marketing Plan :

(A) Major customers :

(B) Region / area where the product will be sold :

(C) Major players already in the field :

(D) Competitive advantages enjoyed by the proposed venture :

(E) Sales channels and methods :

(F) Market tie-up already made, if any (enclose market tie-up letters) :

ABOUT THE PROMOTERS OF THE PROJECT :

Name of the promoter(s)	Age	Net Worth
-------------------------------	-------	---------------

(Give details about each promoter as per format given)

SCHEDULE OF IMPLEMENTATION :

(Indicate the month and year by which each activity will be commenced and completed)

Acquisition of land	:	------------------	------------------
Land Development	:	------------------	------------------
Construction of Buildings	:	------------------	------------------
Procurement of plant and Machinery	:	------------------	------------------
Erection of plant & machinery	:	------------------	------------------
Trial production	:	------------------	------------------
Commercial production	:	------------------	------------------

Raw Materials Required :

(A) Raw materials required :

(B) Sources of supply :

(C) Minimum purchase quantity, lead time, seasonality etc., :

(D) Arrangements made for regular supply of the required quantity of raw material :

Man power Requirement

		No. of persons required	Comments on availability
Executives	:		
Production	:		
Marketing	:		
Finance & Accounting	:		
General Management	:		
Supervisory staff	:		
Skilled workers	:		
Semi-skilled workers	:		
Administrative staff	:		
Unskilled workers	:		
Others	:		
Total		:	

LOCATIONAL ADVANTAGES OF THE PROPOSED LOCATION :

INFRASTRUCTURAL FACILITIES :

(A) **Transport facilities**

(B) **Electric Power**

Power requirement :

Contracted load :

Connected load :

Arrangements made for getting

Power connection :

(C) **Water :** (*Comment on the requirement and availability of water; indicate Quality standards of water required, the quality of water available, water treatment facilities proposed in the Project, if any*)

WORKING CAPITAL ASSESSMENT :

DETAILS OF FIXED ASSETS REQUIRED FOR THE PROJECT:

(A) Land : (*indicate the extent, location, cost etc.,*)

(B) Land Development : (*indicate the type of development works required and the development cost required*)

(C) Building : *(indicate the types of construction of different buildings, built-up areas of construction and the estimated cost of constructions. Enclose approved building plan & building estimate)*

(*i*) Factory Building :

(*ii*) Raw material Godown :

(*iii*) Finished stock Godown :

(*iv*) Office & Administrative buildings :

(*v*) Laboratory :

(*vi*) Power room :

(*vii*) Pollution control facilities / treatment plants :

(D) Plant & Machinery :

Name & Specification of Machinery	Proposed Supplier	Price (excluding tax /duty etc.,)	Tax /Duty	Total Cost	Standing / Reputation of the supplier	Performance Guarantee, if any.

PROJECT COST :

Particulars		*Already incurred*	*To be incurred*	*Total Cost*
Land:				
Land Development	:			
Building	:			
Plant & Machinery				
(*i*) Indigenous	:			
(*ii*) imported	:			
Tools, spares, accessories, testing equipments etc.,	:			
Miscellaneous fixed assets	:			
Transportation & Erection charges for plant & machinery	:			
Preliminary & Pre-operative expenses	:			
Provision for contingencies				
(*i*) on Buildings	:			
(*ii*) on plant & machinery	:			
(*iii*) on other fixed assets	:			
Working Capital Margin	:			
		______	______	______

MEANS OF FINANCING :

Particulars		**Already brought in**	**To be brought in / tied up**	**Total**
Promoter's Contribution (Capital)	:			
Term loan	:			
Margin money assistance, if any from developmental agencies	:			
Subsidy	:			
Unsecured loans	:			
Other sources, if any	:			
		______	______	______

PROJECTED PROFITABILITY STATEMENT	: (To be enclosed)	
PROJECTED CASH FLOW SATEMENT	: (To be enclosed)	
FINANCIAL PARAMETERS	:	
	Promoter's Contribution :	%
	Debt service Coverage ratio :	
	Break even point :	%
	Return on Investment :	%

UNIT V

CASE STUDIES

Case studies are tools for learning which expose the reader to real world problems. The problem situations presented in a case study can be either real life problems or imaginary problems created for the purpose of case study. Cases studies require active participation of the readers so that they can learn the intricies of real-life problems and can develop problem solving skills. A case study may present a difficult situation and an unsuccessful attempt for handling the situation, thus providing the reader with an opportunity for analysing the problem more critically and for developing alternate ways of tackling the problem situations. Some case studies may present a problem with many alternate solutions and ask the reader to identify the right solution and to explain as to how the solution chosen is the right one. Also, some case studies may provide a very complex situation and ask the reader to identify the under-lying issue.

Studying cases will enable readers to practise their skills of

- Problem identification
- Data handling
- Decision making
- Analytical and critical thinking
- Interpersonal relationships
- Communication
- Judgement
- Handling assumptions and inferences

Before proceeding to find answers to the questions given in case studies, the reader should first gain an overall impression of the case and isolate key information. He should cultivate a questioning frame of mind and should develop the ability to sift through information and voluminous data given in the case study.

CASE STUDY 1

A technocrat entrepreneur, after having served in a reputed engineering industry for over a decade as a design engineer, started his own dream venture M/s. Confident Enterprises for the manufacture of industrial rough castings. The project was started with the financial assistance from a nationalised bank. The banker sanctioned financial assistance on the strength of the promoter's technical qualification and experience. The project went on stream very well with out any time or cost overrun. The promoter took pains to see that the project was implemented as scheduled.

During the first two years, the earnings from the project were good and were in fact slightly more than what was envisaged. Later on, the customers who were buying rough castings started to prefer finished castings. They started insisting castings finished as per their specifications and technical requirements. As the entrepreneur did not have the required equipments / tools for finishing of rough castings as per the requirements of customers, he got the finishing works done through other nearby engineering firms on job order basis.

Though this arrangement solved his problem temporarily, he started experiencing hurdles at later stages. Though the quality of finishing was up to the specifications, there was delay in getting the job works done. In spite of his best efforts, he could not get the job works done in time due to which he was forced to default in supplying products to his customers in time. Such continued delays in honoring the supply orders started to undermine his reputation in the field and the customers started reducing their purchase order. The entrepreneur could sense some of his orders drifting away to other competitors. Due to reduction in order position, his turnover and profit margins started showing a downward trend for about a year.

As he had taken term loan from bank for setting up his venture, he stated experiencing difficulties in repayment of the loan instalments and interest dues on the loan. The manager of the bank who has recently visited the unit was patient enough to hear the problems that the entrepreneur has been facing and promised sanctioning of additional financial assistance for setting up manufacturing facilities meant for carrying out the finishing works in-house. The entrepreneur, being risk averse, has postponed the idea of availing additional loan for the creation of additional manufacturing facilities, for the time being and has started looking for alternatives, including the alternative of entering into a contract with a nearby engineering unit for undertaking finishing work on rough castings on a timely basis instead of entrusting the work on ad-hoc basis to different engineering units which has been the cause for the delay.

Discuss the case and suggest the recommended course of action that entrepreneur should choose.

CASE STUDY 2

Mr. Venkat, a mechanical engineering graduate from Indian Institute of Technology, Madras was a promising entrepreneur. His father was owning a small scale industrial unit for the manufacture of mild-steel pressed components used in the manufacture of electrical panel boards. His father's engineering unit, M/s. Star Engineers was mainly catering to the requirements of local fabricators and electrical contractors. Mr. Venkat, after his studies, took over the management of the unit from his father. After a few years of gaining first hand experience of the trade, he decided to go in for large scale production, as he found the prospects for the industry good.

He formed a Private Limited Company by name M/s. New Star Engineers (P) Ltd., with his family members and close friends as the promoter directors. The entire investment for the proposed project was decided to be financed by share capital contribution of the directors. Mr. Venkat's dream project took off smoothly. He did not face any financial constraints as all the promoter directors were financially sound. M/s. New Star Engineers (P) Ltd., gained market recognition due to high quality of its products and within a short span of time the company became a original equipment supplier to major machinery manufacturers.

The production capacity of the plant was 10 tonnes per month. The order position was also about 10 tonnes per month and hence the plant capacity was to the requirement. Due to sudden spurt in the demand, the order position improved subsequently and Mr. Venkat found an immediate need to increase the production capacity of the plant to 20 tonnes per month.

Out of the machinery available, the power press which is a major machine could produce 30 tonnes of pressed components per month. The other engineering fabrication machines like drilling machines, welding machines, punching machines and nibbling machines have been just adequate to handle orders to the tune of about 15 tonnes per month. The powder coating machine (which is used for giving surface finish to the pressed components) could handle about 10 tonnes per month. Two of the major customers have given orders to the tune of around 20 tonnes per month and are also willing to enter into a contract for the regular supply of 20 tonnes of products per month for the next 12 months. There are also indications from other customers that their requirement would be about 10 tonnes per month and they affirm that the order position is only likely to be on the increasing trend.

In order to cope up with the orders of 20 tonnes per month finalised with two customers, Mr. Venkat went for an expansion of his production facility. He doubled the production capacity of general fabrication facility by doubling the capacity of drilling, welding, punching and nibbling machines. As the investment on powder coating machine was slightly on the higher side, he added only one more powder coating machine, thus increasing its handling capacity to about 20 tonnes per month. By the time he completed the expansion works, orders have started pouring in and orders to the extent of around 30 tonnes per month have been booked. Mr. Venkat was happy that his power press could handle the 30 tonnes order quite easily. But, the machines downstream have inadequate capacity to handle 30 tonnes per month. The production engineer suggested to Mr. Venkat to accept all the orders and to divert part of the fabrication and finishing works to outside engineering units if the entire work can not be carried out in-house. However, as Mr. Venkat was very quality conscious, he was not prepared to accept orders beyond his production capacity.

His preference is to have all the required production facilities in-house and he is even prepared to go for one more expansion plan to handle the increased orders.

Discuss the case and answer the following:

(1) Was Mr. Venkat right in his approach that all the required production facilities should be available in-house?

(2) Was the production engineer's view is a right one and will it help the company to tie-over the situation?

CASE STUDY 3

M/s. Innovative Enterprises (P) Ltd. is a company in the line of manufacture of fertilisers and pesticides. The company has a high reputation among the customers. Mr. Shyam Narayan, the Managing Director of the company is a technocrat with innovative project ideas. He wanted to diversify into a new area and got the approval of the board of directors for a new investment for setting up a plant for the manufacture of briquetted fuel using agro wastes as the raw material.

The technology for the production of briquetted fuel using agro wastes as the raw material was devised by a national level research laboratory. Mr. Shyam Narayan himself visited the laboratory to know about the technology and to get details about the financial viability of the project. He saw the prototype of the machine in operation and was also convinced about the financial viability of the project.

Being an innovative project, the banker for M/s. Innovative Enterprises (P) Ltd. also readily came forward to extend the required financial assistance for the project. The project was set up with financial assistance from the bank.

During the trial production, the machinery showed some defects and the final product could not be taken to the satisfactory level. The output was very much below the rated output. Also the machine broke down frequently due to over heating of heating elements. The engineers and technicians from the laboratory that originally designed the machine promised to rectify the defects and immediately attended for inspecting the machinery and for rectifying the defects found, if any. After two weeks of trails, they finally came to the conclusion that the machine did not function as expected because of the variations in the nature and quality of agro waste used as raw material.

Though the prototype of the machine, which when used for production using the agro waste locally available nearby the laboratory gave the rated output of the required quality, the machine installed in the premises of M/s. Innovative Enterprises (P) Ltd. gave neither the rated output nor the required quality of output in view of the reason that the nature of the raw material (agro waste) available at the site of M/s. Innovative Enterprises (P) Ltd. was different. In view of the different nature of raw material, the temperature required for fusing the agro waste into the form of briquetted fuel was more than what was designed for the machine. This was found to be reason for the frequent machinery break downs and for the poor quality of output.

Mr. Shyam Narayan got annoyed. He however did not give up. He instructed his project manager to explore the possibility of procuring the agro waste of such quality that is suitable for the machine from far off places (where they are available) and to revive the project. The project manager came out, as expected with the calculations that showed, that though the project could be revived by using raw materials procured from distant places, the financial viability of the project would suffer due to increased costs of transportation of agro wastes.

Discuss the case and offer your findings.

CASE STUDY 4

M/s. Madras Chemicals (P) Ltd. is engaged in the production of industrial chemicals. The company had plans to set up a new division for the manufacture of Precipitated Calcium Carbonate (calcium carbonated in powder form, which is major raw material for tooth power / tooth paste). The raw material for the production of Precipitated Calcium Carbonate (P.C.C.)can be either lime stone or sea shells. The company has identified two possible locations for the new plant. Location - A is nearer to sea shore where sea shells are available in plenty. This location is also nearer to lime stone quarries. Location - B is away from seashore, but lime stone deposits are available nearby. The cost of P.C.C. produced using shell lime (i.e., sea shells) as the raw material is more than that produced using stone lime (i.e., lime stone) as the raw material due to reason that shell lime costs more than stone lime. However, the increased production cost of P.C.C. using shell lime as the raw material is offset by the better price that it fetches in the market than the P.C.C. produced using stone lime as the raw material. Thus, both shell lime and stone appeared to be competitive in their use as raw material.

The quality of P.C.C. obtained with shell lime as the raw material is superior to the quality of P.C.C. obtained with stone lime. Because of the better quality and shining whiteness of P.C.C. produced using shell lime as the raw material, manufacturers of premium brands of tooth powder / tooth paste prefer that and are also prepared to pay extra price over the P.C.C. produced using stone lime. It is pertinent to note that cosmetics industry is becoming more and more quality conscious. Out of the two locations A & B, location - A is away from town and is in a rural area while location - B is nearer to town. The personnel required for unit are estimated as under.

Chemical engineer	– 1
Skilled operators	– 3
Unskilled employees	– 20
Administrative staff	– 5
Marketing / sales personnel	– 5
	34

Being nearer to town, the required labour force could be easily hired if the plant is located in location - B. Hiring the required labour force is not that easy if the plant is located in location - A, since, apart from unskilled employees (who can be hired from the local population) the others are to be hired only from the nearby town.

Having weighed the pros and cons of the two locations, the management of the company opted to choose location - B for locating its plant. Discuss the case and comment on the choice of location decided by the company.

CASE STUDY 5

Mr. U.S. Shah, a first generation entrepreneur planned for putting up a small scale industrial unit with an investment on fixed assets of Rs.40.00 lakhs, in the year 1987, for the manufacture of poly propylene bags (P.P. bags). The breakup of the investment on fixed assets proposed is as under.

	(Rs. in lakhs)
Land :	1.00
Building :	10.00
Plant & Machinery :	25.00
Machinery Erection Charges :	2.00
Electricals :	2.00
	40.00

The raw material viz., P.P. granules was to be imported from abroad. Though the raw material was available freely from abroad, it was possible to import only in bulk quantities as the foreign suppliers entertained only bulk orders. The minimum bulk quantity that could be imported would serve the raw material requirements of the unit for 6 months. As Mr. Shah was a first generation entrepreneur with only a moderate financial support, he could not afford to import the raw material in such bulk quantities. Instead, he proposed to buy the raw materials from local dealers in small quantities that are sufficient to meet his weekly requirements. The imported raw material was also available for sale in small quantities from local dealers, though the price was higher by about 20%. Nevertheless, Mr. Shah decided to go ahead with the project, as his calculations showed that he could still make a profit in spite of the higher price charged by the local dealers of raw materials.

He got a term loan sanctioned by bank for the purchase and erection of machinery and electricals and he opted to invest own funds for the purchase of land and construction of building. Mr. Shah bought the land already identified by him by investing his capital and also started constructing the building. The building was completed by about 50% and investment of around Rs.6.00 lakhs was already made. To his surprise Mr. Shah came to know that the local dealers of raw material have risen their price by another 20% due to reasons best known to them. He reworked his financials and found that the financial viability of the project would suffer due to increased cost of raw materials. He reworked his calculations on the import of raw material in bulk which proved to be a better option under the changed circumstances.

Since the construction of building was underway, he was not prepared to give up his life-time ambition midway. He approached his banker for the sanction of working capital facilities towards the import of raw materials. The banker, though reluctant at the beginning (in view of the reason that bulk import will lead to holding up a huge inventory which is not a healthy investment practice) finally agreed to finance for the import of raw materials on condition that the finance would be restricted to 50% of the import bill and that the balance 50% of the investment on raw materials should be borne by the promoter. Mr. Shah breathed a sigh of relief after the banker sanctioned financial assistance for the import of raw material in bulk. The construction of building was nearing completion and Mr. Shah was busy finalizing orders for the procurement of machinery.

One fine morning as he was glanzing through the pages of newspaper he happened to come across a news item that read: "Government contemplates banning of P.P bags as disposal of P.P. bags create health hazards". Mr. Shah was in a fix.

(1) Discuss the case and offer your comments.

(2) What is the next logical step that in your opinion, Mr. Shah should have taken under the given conditions?

CASE STUDY 6

M/s. Sofine Chemicals (P) Ltd. is a newly incorporated private limited company. The company was floated with the objective of setting up a plant for the production of detergent washing powder. The critical path for the network of project activities indicated the project completion time as 9 months. It was unfortunate that nature played havoc. There was an unexpected earthquake and the proposed industrial site also felt mild tremors. In view of the widespread damages caused by the earthquake, the overall business activity came to a stand still. The promoters of M/s. Sofine Chemicals (P) Ltd. also had to shelve their project for above six months. After the business conditions returned back to normally, they made a conscious decision to shift the location of their proposed plant to a different location as the originally proposed location was considered earthquake - prone. Identifying a suitable land in a different location and buying the land took another three months.

Thus, nine months' time, which was the completion time as envisaged originally already lapsed and the promoters have only acquired land for the project.

The cost accountant who made a revised financial projection showed an entirely different picture. The initial investment required had increased by about 25% due to hike in price of building materials and equipments. This had brought down the profit margin considerably. Moreover during the lapse of nine months, a few new entrants have already set up their plants for the production of detergent washing powder at nearby places. It has also been brought to notice that some more new entrants have been doing ground work to set up similar plants.

Discuss the case and suggest the course of action to be followed by M/s. Sofine Chemicals (P) Ltd.

CASE STUDY 7

A new bleaching & dyeing unit was started for the processing of cotton yarn and cotton fabric. Since textile processing is a highly polluting activity, consent of Pollution Control Board is mandatory for setting up such units. The units can not go for production without getting 'consent order' from the Pollution Control Board. For issuing consent order, the pollution control authorities stipulate the requirements of chemical properties of effluent and for treating the effluents the textile processing units should have necessary treatment facilities. For treatment of effluents two options were available to the project promoters. They could either set up their own treatment plant in-house or join as a member in the common effluent treatment plant. When they opt for setting up their own treatment plant in-house it would involve additional investment. Since there were many other similar textile processing units nearby they had formed an association for setting up a common effluent treatment plant. The members had to contribute their share to the association. The association would install a treatment plant away from the industrial cluster. The effluents from the member units would be transported through underground pipe lines to the common treatment plant where it would be treated and disposed off.

Though the Common Effluent Treatment Plant (CETP) was a workable arrangement, it was only in its nascent stage as sufficient numbers of members have not joined the association. The construction work of the CETP and the network of underground pipelines for carrying untreated effluent from the member units have been completed half way and the work has not been showing progress for a few months due to paucity of funds. The project promoters chose to become a member of CETP and hence decided not to set up effluent treatment plants in-house. They availed financial assistance from the State Financial Corporation and set up the manufacturing facilities in full and have been awaiting for consent order from the pollution control authorities. The consent order from the pollution control board is not expected to be forth coming as the CETP has not gone on stream. The construction work of CETP and the network of effluent pipe lines stand half way through as the required number of textile processing units have not joined as members of the association due to which the CETP association has run short of the required funds to implement the scheme.

It is more than a year since the plant was ready for operation, but could not commence its operation due to the bottleneck in not being able to get the consent order from the pollution control authorities. As the plant was purchased and erected out of financial assistance from the State Financial Corporation, though the investment remains idle, the loan availed attracts interest and the promoters are under strain to meet the interest obligation on the loan availed.

Discuss the case and offer your comments.

CASE STUDY 8

M/s. Premier Tapes (P) Ltd. is a private limited company started with the objective of setting up a new industrial venture for the production of elastic tapes used in undergarments. The unit was set up in the hosiery town of Tirupur. The company acquired land of 2 acres and constructed building measuring about 3000 sq. ft. to house the machinery. The elastic tape manufacturing machine was imported from abroad. The company had availed financial assistance form the State Financial Corporation for the import of machinery. The machinery on arrival was found to have some technical defeats due to which it was not giving the rated output. The machine gave less than 50% of the rated output. The project promoters took up the matter with the foreign machinery suppliers who entrusted the work of attending to the machinery defect with their local representative. Though the local representative attended to study the defects in the equipment, he could not set right the defects fully. He could only do minor modifi-cations due to which the output increased by another only 10%. Thus even after this, the equipment was giving only around 60% of the rated output.

The project promoters could not hold the equipment suppliers legally liable for the defective equipment that they supplied since there was no mention about the rated output in the invoice for the equipment. Nor the supplier has given any performance guarantee with regard to the output of the equipment. Under these conditions, the project promoters were hard pressed to meet their financial commitments. Since the equipment was purchased by availing loan assistance, the interest burden on the loan component started mounting. As the unit operated much below its rated production, the overheads became heavy and the project promoters could not service the loan. Default in repayment of loan and interest on loan led to attraction of penal interest and compound interest. The liability thus has grown to such a magnitude that the project has lost its viability. Tirupur being an industrial town with hectic business activity and with its export potential, the land value which was already high has grown higher in the recent past. The project promoters could find no better solution other than disposing of a portion off their industrial land and clear the dues to the State Financial Corporation on a compromise settlement formula.

Now the project has only 50 cents of lands, (the remaining 1.50 acres having been sold out) building with 3000 sq. ft. of built up area and the equipment that gives 60% of its rated output. Nevertheless, the promoters are happy that they have solved a crisis and are now looking for the purchase of new equipment. This time they are not going to buy any equipment without a written warranty from the supplier.

Discuss the case and offer your views as to whether the step taken by the promoters to avert a crisis is justified.

CASE STUDY 9

M/s. Quality Refinery Private Limited set up a new oil refinery plant in the year 1997. The project was conceived with the idea of refining sunflower / groundnut oil by procuring oil from the domestic market.

By the time the company went into production, the import of refined edible oil into the country increased since the price of imported refined edible oil proved competitive. Hence the company gradually switched over for refining of coconut oil on job order basis with a tie-up arrangement made with M/s. Mary Industries Ltd., the market leaders in cosmetic grade coconut oil. As the price of imported refined edible oil became more and more cheaper, the company relied more and more on refining coconut oil on job order basis. The compositions of sales / job order receipts for the three years were as under.

			Rs in lakhs
	1997 - 1998	*1998 - 1999*	*1999 - 2000*
Sales *	114.63	153.87	67.73
Job order receipts **	0.36	8.56	214.55
	114.99	162.43	282.28

* Sales pertain to sale of refined sunflower / groundnut oil.

** Job-order receipts pertain to receipts for refining of coconut oil.

Since the company had to depend more upon job orders, the cash generation got affected. However, the company had to necessarily undertake job orders for its survival since it could not meet the competition in the edible oil market due to the presence of cheaper imported edible oil. In view of this, the cash generation from operations reduced drastically and the company found it difficult to meet interest on borrowings from bank and financial institution.

A consultant was appointed to workout a revival strategy. The technical aspect of the plant was studied. It was found that the unit was refining, on an average, about 160 tonnes of oil per month during the year 1999-2000 as against 360 tonnes per month of plant capacity. Out of this, 150 tonnes were the coconut oil refined on job-order basis and 10 tonnes were sunflower oil refined. One of the reasons for the reduced capacity utilisation was that the refining process was required to be stopped and part of the machinery like de-odouriser and neutraliser were required to be cleaned whenever switching over from refining of coconut oil to refining of sunflower / groundnut oil. Otherwise, the odour of coconut oil got carried into the other oils.

By this time, there was a gradual increase in the import of unrefined palm oil. Hence the company visualised good scope for refining palm oil either on job order basis or by importing unrefined oil. However the company could not give up its activity of refining coconut oil on job order basis since the demand for refining coconut oil was steady and constant. Hence, the company decided to undertake refining of both coconut oil and palm oil on job order basis in future at the rate of 180 tonnes per month each. It was found that this could possibly be achieved if one set of de-odouriser and neutraliser was added, so that the plant could achieve the rated production capacity. The need for one additional set of de-odouriser and neutraliser was recommended by the technical consultant so that refining of coconut oil and other types of oils can be done continuously without stopping the plant for the purpose of cleaning the de-odouriser and the neutraliser.

The additional investment required for adding the required machinery costed around Rs.6.00 lakhs. The company was advised by the consultant to implement the above modifications in the plant by either bringing in additional capital or by way of arranging unsecured loan.

The consultant's report showed positive signs. The report projected that the company could generate adequate profit purely by undertaking jobs orders for refining coconut oil and palm oil at 50% of the plant capacity each, by making an additional investment of just Rs.6.00 lakhs which was a very small investment as compared to the initial investment on the plant and machinery of Rs.200 lakhs. On getting convinced with the report of the consultant, the financial institution rephased the repayment schedule of term loan already availed by the company. The idea clicked very well and the company went in for undertaking job orders for refining palm oil and coconut oil at the rate of 50% of plant capacity each, after investing on the two additional machinery.

(1) Discuss the case and offer your views.

(2) Do changing business conditions pose threat to industries and if so, what is the lesson that could be learnt from the case ?

CASE STUDY 10

M/s. Heavy Metal Castings Limited set up a fully automatic foundry in the industrial town of Coimbatore for the manufacture of heavy castings meant for the manufacture of textile machinery. The company was started by a leading industrial group in Coimbatore who have been running few other engineering units successfully. The project implementation period was 2 years and 9 months and the foundry commenced its operations in the financial year 1996 - 97. The project cost was Rs.

800 lakhs and the project was implemented without any cost-overrun. The company could not take off well due to slump in textile machinery manufacturing activity and the plant was operating only at 50% of its installed capacity even during its peak operation period of 1997 - 98.

As the operations did not improve, the plant was shout down during April 1999, since running the plant below its capacity would mean incurring more loss due to heavy operating expenses. Till May 2000, the plant remained closed. The plant was jointly financed by a Nationalised Bank, State Financial Corporation and State Industrial Promotion Corporation. The company could not service the loans availed from the bank and institutions and overdues accumulated. The working results of the company from the financial year 1996 - 97 to 1999 - 2000 were as under.

Rs in lakhs

	Financial year			
	1996 - 1997	*1997 - 1998*	*1998 - 1999*	*1999 - 2000*
Sales	144.54	518.26	228.50	11.98
Net loss	58.32	100.63	11.66	121.55
Current assets	170.22	253.37	203.45	143.50
Current liability (Bank)	80.64	91.33	96.41	50.25
Current liability (Others)	133.36	224.82	226.34	322.57
Current liability (Total)	214.00	316.04	322.75	372.82
Current ratio	0.80:1.00	0.80:1.00	0.63:1.00	0.38:1.00
Debtors exceeding six months	NIL	NIL	16.31	8.08

Though the operations of the plant had come to a halt due to inadequate orders for heavy castings, the company management had been exploring the possibilities of reviving the unit. In its efforts to revive the unit, the company gathered orders for small and medium sized castings meant for motors, pumps and other general engineering works. Such orders on hand was sufficient enough to meet the operating costs and to earn a marginal profit. For executing the orders for small and medium sized castings, the main automated molding section (which was meant for heavy castings) could not be made use of and would only remain idle. However, the other production facilities available could be made use of. Moreover, the company needed to invest around Rs.50.00 lakhs towards the purchase of certain equipments meant for the production of small & medium sized castings. The company approached the bank and financial institutions for a revival package.

The bank and the financial institutions showed positive response keeping in view the following facts.

- Textile industry is cyclic in nature and this has been proved beyond doubt for over five decades. Hence the plant with modern facilities could see the light of the day once the textile industry revives.
- Going in for the production of small and medium sized castings (which were found sufficient enough to keep the plant running and earning a meagre profit), will avoid keeping the plant idle.
- Though the current ratio as on 1.03.2000 was 0.38:1.00, majority of the current liability was credit supplies of raw materials from associate companies. Hence, immediate pressure from sundry creditors for repaying the current liability was not anticipated.

In view of these positive signals and as industrial economists predicted revival of textile industry in another year's time, the bank came forward with an additional term loan of Rs.40.00 lakhs towards the acquisition of additional equipments required and also sanctioned additional working capital limits. The financial institutions also decided to wait for the revival of the unit and rephased their term loan instalments and interest dues. The company also, on its part, brought in additional capital of Rs.90.00 lakhs towards reviving the unit.

The plant recommenced its operations in June 2000 and the company achieved a sales turnover of Rs.559.64 lakhs in the financial year 2000 - 2001.

Discuss the case and offer your comments on the scope for revival of the unit.

CASE STUDY 11

A project for identifying the use of unconventional fibres for the manufacture of fabric was sponsored by the United Nations Development Programme (UNDP) and a leading research institute in South India was entrusted with the task. The research institute decided to explore the scope for extracting fibre from pine apple leaf and the scope for using the fibre for the manufacture of fabric. The institute, after preliminary studies, designed machinery for the extraction of fibre from pine apple leaf and also machinery for spinning the fibre into yarn. The machinery designed for the extraction of fibre from leaf performed well and came out successful. But, the discouraging factor was that the recovery rate of fibre from the leaf was only around 2 % to 3 % Moreover, in view of the very low fibre recovery rate, the cost of pine apple leaf fibre was found to vary between 1.60 to 1.75 times the cost of cotton fibre. Since cotton, though a conventional fibre, was cheaper than pine apple leaf fibre and as cotton had all favourable qualities for making a fabric suited for man, pine apple leaf fibre was not found competitive and was found incapable of replacing cotton.

In order to improve the financial viability of the project, the research institute explored the possibility of using the wastage recovered from the fibre extraction machine for producing some other by-product. This was considered essential since the waste material constituted about 97 % to 98 % of the total raw material (i.e., pine apple leaf). Further research into the above aspect yielded encouraging results. The pine apple leaf waste was made use of for the manufacture of paper boards. The paper board manufactured using pine apple waste was found to possess the required physical properties. Since the leaf waste was used for producing a by-product, the financial viability of the composite project (i.e., manufacture of pine apple leaf fibre and paper board) showed improvement. However, even after assuming that the boards manufactured using pine apple leaf waste could be sold at a price on par with the boards manufactured using other raw materials (like waste paper, waste cloth etc.,), the composite project was found to break-even only if the pine apple leaf fibre could be sold at a price about 20 % more than that of cotton fibre. Hence, the research institute concluded that the fabric produced out of pine apple leaf fibre could not replace cotton fabric as it would not be price competitive, even if a composite project is opted for. The institute hopes that the fabric produced using pine apple leaf fibre could be exported to high-end markets by propagating it as a novel, eco-friendly, natural product and premium markets could be identified.

The institute has also received enquiries from abroad for the procurement of pine apple leaf fibre at a price that is nearly 40 times the price of cotton fibre. These are, however, initial phases and full exploitation of commercial potential is yet to be ascertained. The technology is available with the research institute. Can a promising entrepreneur opt for the composite project?. If so, what are his prospects and problems?.

DISCUSSION OF CASE STUDIES

CASE STUDY 1

Discussion of the case

The project was started by an entrepreneur who is technically qualified. The entrepreneur appears to be a sincere and committed person as seen from the fact that he took pains to complete his project successfully without any time or cost over-run.

In the first two years, the order position was good and the entrepreneur has earned profits which is a good sign that shows that his customers were satisfied about the product. The problem has started only after the customers changed their preference from buying semi-finished products to full-finished products. The entrepreneur's attempt to get the finishing work done through job-order has not yielded results since the entrepreneur could not deliver the goods in time and this delay has been the main cause for the erosion of his reputation.

As a prudent entrepreneur, he should not allow his reputation to go down further. He should take steps to set right things and to regain his reputation in the market. After all, he can not survive if all his customers withdraw their orders on one fine day. He should not allow such an eventuality to occur. The entrepreneur, being a technocrat himself, in view of his technical expertise, must be capable of producing finished products of the required specifications as demanded by the customers. The other constraint against going for additional investment on equipments meant for carrying out finishing operations, viz., the finance required is also readily available since the bank manager has already promised to extend necessary financial assistance.

Recommendation

Hence it is high time the entrepreneur went for adding the additional production facilities that would enable him to produce finished goods to meet the requirements of customers, totally in-house. It is a case of forward integration and the time for implementing forward integration is already ripe and the entrepreneur should go for it without thinking about any other alternative.

CASE STUDY 2

Discussion of the case

To start with, the unit was producing pressed components of 10 tonnes per month. It has been given that the power press could produce 30 tonnes per month. This clearly shows that the power press was underutilized. Since the unit was engaged in the production of pressed components, power press is the major machinery that would decide upon the production capacity of the unit.

By the time the unit was executing orders of about 10 tonnes per month, the production capacity of the power press was 30 tonnes per month, the production capacity of other general purpose machines like drilling machines, welding machines, punching machines, nibbling machines etc., was 15 tonnes per month and the production capacity of powder coating machine was 10 tonnes per month. Thus, there was mismatch of the production capacity of machines. In other words, the machines were not balanced. When the unit was producing orders to the tune of 10 tonnes per month, only the powder coating machine was put to full use. The general purpose machines (like drilling machines, welding machines, punching machines, nibbling machines etc.,) were used to the extent of only for about 67% [(10 ÷ 15)%] of their production capacity while the power press was used only for about 33% [10 ÷ 30)%] of its production capacity. After the first phase of expansion, the following were the production capacity of the different machinery.

Power press	:	30 tonnes per month (original capacity retained as it was)
General purpose machines	:	30 tonnes per month (original capacity doubled)
powder coating machine	:	20 tonnes per month (original capacity doubled)

Even then, the machines were not perfectly balanced. In view of the lower capacity of powder coating machine (i.e., 20 tonnes per month), the production capacity of the plant was restricted to 20 tonnes per month in spite of having higher production capacity in the other machines.

(1) Was Mr. Venkat right?

Mr. Venkat is a quality conscious person. Hence he preferred to have all the production facilities in-house and he was not prepared to engage the services of others on job order basis. In a way he was right in the sense that he did not want to compromise on quality.

But the indications were that the order position would improve beyond 20 tonnes per month and this was proved correct subsequently. Hence before going in for expansion, Mr. Venkat would have made a realistic assessment of the likely orders that he could get and based on this assessment he could have gone in for a full fledged expansion. What was additionally needed was only increasing the capacity of the powder coating machine from 10 tonnes per month to 30 tonnes per month (instead of 20 tonnes per month which he had done). The capacity of general purpose machines were already increased to 30 tonnes per month. Thus Venkat should have gone in for an expansion of production capacity from 10 tonnes per month to 30 tonnes per month. This would have helped him in handling the increased order position comfortably.

(2) Was the production engineer's view right ?

As the company has received orders to the extent of about 30 tonnes per month, it was not wise to turn down a portion of the orders and to accept orders to the extent of only 20 tonnes. It is always a difficult thing to capture the market. The company had received increased orders only because of the confidence that it had gained among the customers. Hence it was advisable to retain the customers and to retain their orders. Once a few customers shift to other suppliers it would be a difficult task to bring them back. Hence the production engineer was right in his view to accept orders to the tune of 30 tonnes and to divert powder coating work of about 10 tonnes to outside and to get it done on job-order basis. As Mr. Venkat was any way planning for another expansion (by way of increasing the capacity of the powder coating section from 20 tonnes per month to 30 tonnes per month), this arrangement of getting things done on job-order basis must have been only a temporary affair. If Mr. Venkat did not want to compromise on quality, he might have placed a supervisor at the site of the client to whom he entrusted job-order and might have supervised the quality first hand. Such an arrangement till such time the expansion of the plant was completed would have helped Mr. Venkat to retain the customers.

CASE STUDY 3

Discussion of the case

Mr. Shyam Narayan appears to be an entrepreneur with an instinct for innovation. Hence he was bold enough to venture into a new area. His visiting the National laboratory to have a first-hand information about the new project shows his curiosity and commitment to the new venture. The banker would have financed the project due to the reasons that the promoter Mr. Shyam Narayan was a known industrialist of repute and that the project proposed was an innovate one.

The project suffers from the following deficiencies.

First of all, the technology was not a commercially proven one. The technology had been proved only in the laboratory. When any technology is taken from the laboratory to the field, difficulties are normally experienced since the laboratory conditions can not be reproduced in the field. Hence modifications are invariably required to be carried out in any laboratory-proven-technology to suit the field conditions. In this case, the nature of the raw material used has proved to be a crucial factor. Since the nature of the raw material would vary from place to place depending upon the agricultural produces in those places, a machine that was designed for a particular type of raw material might not suit the requirements of a different type of raw material. Though Mr. Shyam Narayan had visited the laboratory to verify if the machine was functioning well, he had failed to observe an essential factor, viz., the type of agro waste that was used for producing the briquetted fuel in the laboratory. Unless the same raw material is used, the design features of the machine will need alterations / modifications in design and specifications. Thus, suitability of plant and machinery for the local working conditions is a crucial factor that should have been looked into.

Since the scope for reviving the project by procuring the suitable raw material from far off places also proved remote due to financial unviability, it is better to abandon the project and dispose off the machinery to some body who is interested to put up the plant at the place where agro waste suited for the machine is available.

CASE STUDY 4

Discussion of the case

The case relates to choice of location for setting up a chemical plant. As seen from the case, the end product, viz., Precipitated Calcium Carbonate (P.C.C.) could be manufactured using either shell lime or stone lime as the raw material. Though shell lime is reported to cost higher than stone lime, the cost difference is also reported to get offset since the P.C.C. produced using shell lime offers a better price. Thus, either shell lime or stone lime could be used as the raw material without much difference in the profitability of the unit. The company appears to have opted for location - B in view of the following reasons.

(*a*) Though both shell lime and stone lime are available near location - A, it did not offer any attraction to the company as the financial viability of the project is not affected by the choice of raw material.

(*b*) Getting the required work force for the plant is reported to be easier if location - B is chosen.

The choice of location - B made by the company was not a right strategic decision in view of the following reasons.

If we read the case in between the lines, we come to know about two important factors that have a bearing on the choice of the location. Firstly, the P.C.C. produced using shell lime as the raw material is of superior quality than that produced using stone lime as the raw material and hence premium customers prefer P.C.C. made of shell lime. Moreover cosmetics industry is reported to be becoming more and more quality conscious. Hence there is every possibility that more and more end users of P.C.C. will start preferring P.C.C. made of shell lime in future. Hence location - A should have been a strategic choice on this count.

Secondly, stone lime is quarried from mines. There is a chance for exhaustion of lime stone deposit in future years. There is also a chance for the variation in the quality of lime stone mined from quarries. Hence, continuous availability of lime stone of the required quality can not be taken for granted. On the other hand, availability of shell lime, being naturally available material (viz., sea shells), is not likely to be threatened. Moreover the quality of sea shells is also not likely to vary much over a period of time.

Keeping these aspects in view, the company might have made a strategic choice of locating the plant in location - A instead of choosing location - B. The non-availability of workers nearby location - A could be easily tacked by recruiting skilled personnel from the nearby towns and unskilled workers from the local area and giving them the required training.

CASE STUDY 5

Discussion of the case

Mr. U.S. Shah had proposed to start a business venture that needed imported raw material. Originally he decided not to directly import the raw material in bulk quantity as this would involve huge financial commitments which he thought he could not afford. He decided to purchase the imported raw material from local dealers since it worked out to be a financially viable proposition in spite of the fact that the price charged by the local dealers was higher by about 20% than the price of the raw material imported directly from abroad. When the local dealers for raw material hiked their price further, Mr. Shah faced the first shock. As he was committed to his project, he looked for an alternative arrangement and found that importing of raw material directly would be a right choice under the changed circumstances. His approaching of his banker and getting a loan sanctioned for the import of raw material shows that he was not prepared to give up his project midway. So far so good.

The second shock came to him by the Government's idea of banning the end product viz., P.P bags. Though the progress of the project was underway and Mr. Shah had already invested on construction of building, the Government's idea of banning the use of P.P. bags was a crucial factor to be considered carefully and cautiously before deciding upon further course of action. The project had a negative factor in that it had to depend on imported raw material which presented an element of risk. The second risk, which of course, was unexpected, was due to a macro level factor viz., the hazardous nature of P.P. bags which presented an environmental pollution due to which the Government was inclined to take a decision to ban the use of P.P. bags.

What should Mr. Shah do?

With the treat of a ban on the use of P.P. bags, it is unwise of any prudent entrepreneur to take the risk of investing in the project. Though Mr. Shah has already invested his capital on building, he has not yet borrowed money from the bank. To that extent he is safe since the borrowed money would attract interest right from day one. Since any project that is affected by macro level factors can not be revived easily, it would be a wise decision on the part of Mr. Shah to give up his idea of producing P.P. bags. He could think of some other alternate project and make use of the building already constructed for the alternate project.

CASE STUDY 6

Discussion of the case

This is a case where unexpected natural calamity has affected a project. The earth quake that affected implementation of the project was not foreseen by the promoters of the project. As the proposed factory site was later found earthquake-prone, the promoters were right in their decision to look for a safer location. But the time delay in implementing the project had made a telling impact on the project. The time over-run has resulted in cost over-run to the tune of about 25% and has affected the profit margins. Moreover, the happenings that deserve serious consideration are the new plants for the production of detergent washing powders that have come up recently and the few other new plants on the anvil by the competitors. Since the project envisaged is a small scale project (as seen from the investment planned of Rs.30.00 lakhs) the project could survive only if the demand for the end product is available locally. As a few plants have already come up in the nearby area and a few other similar plants are coming up, the availability of market is to be reassessed. As new entrants are expected to pitch their prices lower in order to capture the market, the probable selling price is also to be reworked. Thus, many factors have changed in a span of nine months. The project cost has increased. The market demand and probable selling price are to be reassessed. Hence the project needs a complete reassessment. The project is to be appraised afresh before taking further investment decisions.

CASE STUDY 7

Discussion of the case

Any project operates within an environment and if the environment is conducive, the project takes off well and becomes successful. Hence, in formulating project proposals, it must be first seen as to whether there are any bottle-necks in the environment that may stall the project. In this case, though the effluent from the plant will be polluting in nature, consent of the pollution control authorities could be obtained if the effluent is treated and made harmless before its disposal. There are two options available for the treatment and safe disposal of the effluent. Either a treatment plant can be set up in-house or the unit can become a member of the Common Effluent Treatment Plant (CETP) and get its effluent treated and disposed. Setting up a treatment plant in-house would cost higher as compared to entrusting the work with CETP. This, probably is the reason for the unit's choice of CETP for effluent disposal.

No doubt, an alternative that costs cheaper is to be chosen. But, other features of the alternative solution are also to be considered apart from cost considerations. Had the unit opted for setting up its own effluent treatment plant in-house, it would have costed higher. But, in that case, the unit can go ahead with implementing the project without depending on somebody else. By choosing to become a member of the association of CETP, the unit has made itself dependent on others. The implementation and successful commissioning of the CETP are not entirely in the hands of the unit. When the stakes of many persons are involved, the CETP project is bound to face its own problems and there is every possibility of its implementation getting delayed and this has come to reality.

The project promoters should have thought over this eventuality, especially when they have proposed to borrow funds for the project, since the borrowed money attracts interest from day one. Hence, the promoters could not afford to allow the project implementation getting delayed. A right choice should have been going in for an in-house effluent treatment plant in anticipation of the hurdles that might crop up in the successful commissioning of the CETP.

CASE STUDY 8

Discussion of the case :

This is a case where the project has suffered due to defective equipment purchased. The project promoters have failed to obtain a warranty from the equipment supplier for the rated performance (i.e., for the rated out-put). Fighting a legal battle, especially with the equipment supplier is stationed abroad is difficult and time-consuming. The problem becomes more complicated as the equipment supplier has not given any warranty for the rated out-put ; nor the supplier has indicated the rated out-put in the invoice. Hence, it would be impossible for the purchaser of the equipment to fight and win a legal battle. The maxim of "Buyer Beware" is applicable for this case. The buyer should have taken all the required precautions before buying the equipment. Having erred in the purchase of the equipment, the project promoters were under compulsion to salvage the project somehow or the other. Their decision to dispose off a portion of land and settle the dues to the institutional lender was in fact a wise decision. Had the problem been allowed to continue, the liability to the lender would have multiplied many fold and would have landed the project is an unsalvageable position.

CASE STUDY 9

Discussion of the case

The project was started with the proposal to procure unrefined edible oil from domestic market, refine the oil and sell refined edible oil. The company had proposed to buy unrefined sunflower oil or unrefined groundnut oil whichever was available at an affordable price.

By the time the company went into production, the price of imported refined edible oil came down. Thus, procuring unrefined edible oil from domestic market, refining it and selling refined edible oil back in the domestic market became more and more difficult. This is reflected by the continuous reduction in the sales from the year 1997 - 98 onwards. As the original proposal of procuring unrefined oil and refining the same did not fetch the anticipated profits, the company switched over to refining of coconut oil on job-order basis. The proportion of job-order refining kept increasing as evidenced by the increased job-order receipts from the year 1997-98 onwards.

In the year 1999 - 2000 almost 94% of the refining work done pertain to refining of coconut oil on job-order basis (i.e., 150 tonnes out of 160 tonnes refined). With continuous reduction in the price of refined imported edible oil, the company would most likely have to go for 100% job-order by the year 2000 - 2001. The availability of imported unrefined palm oil was a positive sign. As the company had already tied up with an established firm for undertaking refining of coconut oil on job order basis, its decision to retain the customer for coconut oil is justified since this option could keep the plant running to about 50% capacity. The company's decision to go for additional investment towards installation of one set of de-odouriser and neutraliser is also justified for the reason that only then the remaining 50% of the plant capacity could be effectively utilized for refining of any oil other than coconut oil. Since the additional machinery was estimated to cost only Rs.6.00 lakhs, it was worth investing this amount in order to achieve better capacity utilisation of the plant.

Lesson revealed by the case

Business conditions do not remain constant. The changing business environment can be some times predicted and sometimes not. For making a project a successful one, enormous amount of flexibility is needed. Once plans are kept rigid and changes in business environment occur, the project will get swept away and the project promoters will be doomed. Flexibility in adapting to changing situations is a prerequisite quality of any project and project managers and the top management shall be constantly aware of the changing business conditions and must infuse changes into the project to adapt to the changing conditions quickly. Only then can any project be made successful.

Changing business conditions, no doubt, offer threat to projects of all kinds. But, one need not shy away from meeting challenges. Change has become the order of the day and this is more so in the present competitive conditions in which business operates. However, the threat offered by the changing business conditions can be overcome by remaining watchful to the changing conditions and carrying out the required changes in the project as and when warranted.

CASE STUDY 10

Discussion of the case

This is again a case where unanticipated business environment has affected the project. The project idea must have been conceived when the textile industry was in boom. Since this was a reasonably bigger project with an implementation period of 2 years and 9 months and as textile industry is known for exhibiting cyclic trend, there was enough time for the trade cycle of textile industry to reverse its trend. Hence by the time the project was implemented and the plant was ready to commence production, the slump in textile machinery manufacturing industry had set in.

The promoters of the project, being industrialists with experience in running a few industries successfully, have proved their acumen by exploring orders for small and medium sized castings and were also successful in gathering reasonably adequate orders. The bank and the financial institutions came to the rescue of the company at the right time. The positive response shown by the bank and the financial institutions was due to the inherent strengths of the project like the scope for revival of Textile sector, the ability of the promoters to keep the plant operating, by producing small and medium sized castings till such time the order position for heavy castings improves to the required level and the greater share of associate companies in current liabilities.

The sales turnover for the year 2000-2001 of Rs. 559.64 lakhs was an impressive figure keeping in view that it was the highest since the company started its operations. It has not been said that the orders for heavy castings have resumed materializing. Hence, the sales turnover of Rs. 559.64 lakhs achieved during the year 2000-2001 must have been out of production and sales of small and medium sized castings.

Since the economists had predicted revival of the Textile industry shortly and as the company has reserve strength to keep itself alive till the revival actually takes place, the project showed scope for revival.

CASE STUDY 11

Discussion of the case

Cotton is a natural fibre widely used for the manufacture of cloth and it has proved its utility value by virtue of its properties suitable for cloth. The research institute has made an attempt to extract fibre from pine apple leaf and to study its usefulness for the manufacture of fabric. Though it succeeded in the extraction of fibre from pineapple leaf, it came across problems like very poor recovery percentage and high cost of fibre. These factors have proved deterrent for the pineapple fibre to be considered as a substitute for cotton fibre. The institute's attempt to make use of the pineapple leaf waste to manufacture paper board and its success in this attempt are worth noting. Thus, the research institute has identified a composite project. The economics of the composite project has showed that in spite of making use of the waste for the production of a by-product, the cost of pineapple leaf fibre still remained higher than that of cotton fibre. Thus, the composite project will also be not a commercially viable idea. The options have not been exhausted. The research institute now advocates that the cloth made out of pineapple leaf could be promoted among those end users who can afford to pay a high price based on its fancy value. No doubt, a market for fancy goods exist. The research institute's claim that it has received trade enquiries from abroad for pineapple leaf fibre at a price much higher than the price of cotton fibre proves this point. However these are only early days and there is a long, long way to go to make the composite project a commercially successful one.

It is not the right time for an entrepreneur to venture into this project. As claimed by the research institute, the project would prove to be financially viable (and highly viable too!) after a steady high-end market for the fabric made out of pineapple leaf fibre is established. The entrepreneur should attempt to tie-up his market first before venturing into the project. Another aspect to be considered is the availability of raw material. Since raw material, in bulk quantities, is to be transported from the place of availability to the place of processing, the plant shall be located nearer to the source of raw material. Else, the transportation cost will become heavy and will affect the financial viability of the project.

Review Questions

Unit I

1. Define 'Project'. What are the characteristics of a project?
2. Explain the different heads under which projects can be classified.
3. Distinguish between Modernisation project and Diversification project.
4. What is a balanced production line?
5. Distinguish between forward integration project and backward integration project.
6. What are the circumstances that necessitate backward integration projects?
7. Give an example each for forward integration project and backward integration project.
8. Enumerate the objectives of any project.
9. Give a brief note on social objectives of projects.
10. Explain in detail the different phases in establishing of projects.
11. Explain the different sources from which new project ideas can be formed.
12. What are the objectives of a pre-feasibility study? Enumerate the steps involved in a pre-feasibility study.
13. Give a brief note on support studies on projects.
14. Explain the four aspects of a project feasibility study.
15. Write a short note on 'Detailed Project Report' (DPR).
16. Explain the part played by tax planning in project investment decisions.
17. Give a detailed account of 'Zero based project formulation'.
18. What do you mean by project appraisal?
19. Explain the different factors to be considered in Technical appraisal of projects.
20. Why is commercial appraisal of projects important?
21. Explain the various demand forecasting techniques.
22. The past data for the actual demand for a consumer durable good for the period 1992 to 1999 are as under.

Year	1992	1993	1994	1995	1996	1997	1998	1999
Demand (Number in 1000's)	225	276	324	396	422	479	512	551

Estimate the likely demand in the year 2000, 2001, 2002, 2003 & 2004 using the method of least squares.

23. When is 'End use method' of forecasting useful? Explain with aid of an example.
24. Write a short note on 'Leading Indicator method' of demand forecasting.
25. Compare and contrast industry demand with firm demand.
26. What is Social Cost Benefit analysis? What are its objectives?
27. For Indian conditions, which projects in your opinion are socially desirable?
28. Explain the different types of risks that a project may have to face.
29. Explain the importance of sensitivity analysis in project risk analysis.
30. What do you mean by 'Decision tree analyses'? Explain the situation under which this technique is useful.

31. 'Monte Carlo Simulation' is technique used for decision making under stochastic situations. Offer your comments on this statement and explain the technique with an illustration.

32. Explain the importance of SWOT analysis in project appraisal.

33. What are the components of project cost?

34. Explain the need for including 'Preliminary & pre-operative expenses' and 'Contingency' in project cost.

35. Distinguish between working-capital and margin money for working-capital.

36. What are the aspects to be considered before arriving at the cost of land required for a project?

37. M/s. Royal Rubber Industries has proposed to set up a new plant for the manufacture of Rubber tyres meant for bicycle. The following are the details of the proposed project.

(*a*) The concern has identified a suitable lease-hold building for setting up the industry. The lease rent fixed is Rs.20,000 per month.

(*b*) The proposed plant will have an installed capacity of 2200 tyres per day (for 3 shifts).

(*c*) The following are the machinery proposed for the project.

(*i*) Rubber mixing machine (at a price of Rs. 15.00 lakhs).

(*ii*) Tyre moulding machines - 10 Nos. (at a price of Rs. 1.20 lakhs each).

(*iii*) Steam boiler (at a price of Rs. 8.00 lakhs).

(*iv*) Air Compressor (at a price of Rs. 2.15 lakhs).

(*v*) Scrap grinder (at a price of Rs. 4.50 lakhs).

(*vi*) Power generator (at a price of Rs. 9.00 lakhs).

(*d*) The cost of electricals is Rs. 6.15 lakhs.

(*e*) The cost of moulds and dies required for normal operation of the plant is estimated at Rs. 5.75 lakhs.

(*f*) The weight of finished rubber tyre is 0.55 kg each. The cost of raw material, (Viz., natural rubber) is Rs. 40.00 per kg; wastage of rubber during the manufacturing process is estimated at 4%.

Arrive at the estimated project cost of the proposed plant. Make suitable assumptions wherever necessary. [Note: Apart from natural rubber, other raw materials required are ignored for the sake of simplicity].

38. What is the use of thumb-rules in assessing project cost?

39. How is 'Working capital margin' calculated for a project that is going to undertake only job-orders.

40. Briefly explain non-discounted and discounted cash flow techniques of financial analysis of projects.

41. "Pay-back period method ignores the time value of money" - illustrate with an example.

42. 'Pay-back period method ignores the cash flow beyond the payback period' - illustrate with an example.

43. Explain the four factors that need careful assessment before carrying out financial evaluation of projects.

44. The estimated capital investment on a project is Rs. 20,00,000. The project is expected to be implemented in a period of one year. The operating profit expected beginning from the first year of operation is as under.

First year of operation	Second year of operation	Third year of operation	Fourth year of operation	Fifth year of operation	Sixth year of operation
Rs. 1,80,000/-	Rs. 1,95,000/-	Rs. 2,20,000/-	Rs. 2,30,000/-	Rs. 2,05,000/-	Rs. 1,95,000/-

The tax and depreciation for the respective years are as under:

Tax	Rs. 57,000/-	Rs. 62,000/-	Rs. 71,000/-	Rs. 74,000/-	Rs. 66,000/-	Rs. 62,000/-
Depreciation	Rs.3,70,000/-	Rs.2,48,000/-	Rs.1,66,000/-	Rs.1,11,000/-	Rs. 75,000/-	Rs. 50,000/-

Estimate the pay-back period.

[Hint: Since the project implementation period is given as one year, the operating profit expected from the first year of operation is to be taken as the return expected from the second year of the investment, and so on]

45. The details of a proposed project are as under:

Capital investment	:	Rs. 20,00,000
Life of the project	:	6 years
Project implementation period	:	1 year
Cost of capital	:	14%

(Rs in lakhs)

Year	1	2	3	4	5	6
Cash flow	Rs. 2.00	Rs. 3.00	Rs. 5.00	Rs. 4.00	Rs. 4.00	Rs. 3.00

Assess if the project is worthwhile to be taken up for implementation. Use NPV method of evalution.

46. For the data given in problem - 45 above, estimate the internal rate of return (IRR). Compare the IRR with the cost of capital and offer your comments.

47. Write short notes on:

(*a*) Cost of retained earnings

(*b*) Weighted average cost of capital

(*c*) NPV Vs IRR methods of financial evaluation

(*d*) Benefit Cost ratio method

(*e*) Profitability index method.

48. Two projects A and B have initial capital investment of Rs.10,00,000/- each. The cash-inflows of the two projects are as under.

Year	*Cash in flows*	
	Project A	*Project B*
1	Rs. 4,00,000	Rs. 2,50,000
2	Rs. 5,00,000	Rs. 3,50,000
3	Rs. 1,00,000	Rs. 2,50,000
4	Rs. 25,000	Rs. 1,50,000
5	Rs. 25,000	Rs. 2,00,000
6	Rs. 20,000	Rs. 1,75,000

Choose one out of the two projects on the basis of pay-back period method of evaluation. Comment on the limitation of payback period method with regard to ignoring the cash inflow beyond the pay-back period, using the cash inflow values given for the two projects.

49. The cash flow from two mutually exclusive projects X and Y are as under:

	Project X	*Project Y*
Cash outflow	Rs. 45,00,000	Rs. 54,00,000
Cash inflows (from first year through eighth year)	Rs. 13,00,000 each year	Rs. 13,50,000 each year
Project life	8 years	8 years

(*a*) Suggest as to which project can be selected based on IRR criteria.

(*b*) Advise on project selection if the life of project Y is 9 years and if the cash inflows of project - Y are at the rate of Rs. 14,00,000/- each year.

50. Do IRR & NPV methods always give the same result in evaluation of mutually exclusive projects? If not, state the reason for the deviations in the results.

51. Reliable Engineers Ltd., are considering two different investment proposals. Proposal - I has an investment cost of Rs. 10,00,000 and proposal - II has an investment cost of Rs. 28,00,000. Both the projects are expected to yield returns for a period of 5 years. The estimated income of the two proposals at the end of first year to fifth year are as under.

	Proposal I	*Proposal II*
End of year I	Rs. 3,30,000	Rs. 9,00,000
End of year II	Rs. 5,00,000	Rs. 11,00,000
End of year III	Rs. 3,70,000	Rs. 12,00,000
End of year IV	Rs. 3,00,000	Rs. 8,00,000
End of year V	Rs. 2,00,000	Rs. 7,00,000

(*a*) Which is the most attractive investment proposal considering a discount rate of 12% on the future incomes that will be generated? [Hint: use NPV method]

(*b*) Find out the internal rate of return (IRR) of the two proposals.

52. Compare the following three projects on the basis of profitability index.

	Project A	*Project B*	*Project C*
Cash outflow	Rs. 11,00,000	Rs. 23,00,000	Rs. 19,00,000
Present value of cash inflows	Rs. 14,50,000	Rs. 38,50,000	Rs. 35,00,000

53. The following is the capital structure of a newly implemented project.

Source of finance		*Amount (Rs.)*
Equity capital	:	14,50,000
Retained earnings	:	4,00,000
Preference share capital	:	3,00,000
Debt	:	12,00,000
		33,50,000

The expected after-tax cost of the different components of finance are as under.

Source of finance		*Cost (%)*
Equity capital	:	17.00
Retained earnings	:	17.00
Preference share capital	:	10.00
Debt	:	9.00

Calculate the weighted average cost of capital.

54. Discuss the provisions available for depreciation as per the companies Act and as per the Income tax Act.

55. What are the factors to be considered in estimating the capacity utilisation of plant for the purpose of financial projections?

56. What are the three major forms of organisation structures?

57. Describe functional organisation. What are its limitations?

58. Describe Product Organisation. What are its advantages over functional organisation?

59. Matrix organisation is suited for enterprises that are 'Project-driven' — Explain.

60. What are the merits and demerits of pure matrix form of organisation?

61. Describe 'Modified matrix structure' and 'Pure Project organisation structure'.

62. Explain in detail the method of choosing an organisational structure to suit a given project.

63. Write short notes on:

(*a*) Work Breakdown structure (WBS)

(*b*) Organisation Breakdown Structure (OBS)

64. 'The success of building a suitable organisational structure rests in proper intergration of WBS and OBS'. Explain.

65. What are the factors to be considered in selection of project manager and other project personnel?

66. What are the advantages of selecting personnel required for a project from within the organisation?

67. What are the skills required of a project manager?

68. "Team building is an essential factor in mobilizing the human force required for handling projects". Explain.

69. What are the duties and responsibilities of a project manager?

70. Define the term 'contract'. What are the essentials of a valid contract?

71. What is a Turnkey contract? When is it suitable?

72. What are the major types of non-turnkey contracts? Explain them in brief.

73. Write short notes on the following.

(*a*) Sub-contract

(*b*) Tenders

(*c*) Earnest money deposit (EMD)

(*d*) Security deposit

(*e*) Letter of intent (LOI)

(*f*) Liquidated damages

(*g*) First and final bill & Running account bill.

74. "Organising systems and procedures for implementing a project is essential for achieving the project objectives". Support this statement with your arguments and explain.

75. What do you mean by project direction? What are the aspects to be considered while directing of projects?
76. What do you mean by project coordination? What are the aspects to be considered while coordinating of project activities?
77. What are the three factors over which control is to be exercised in projects?
78. What is a control system? What are the requirements of a good control system?
79. Explain the use of Work Breakdown Structure (WBS) for project control.
80. Enumerate the tools available for project control explain them in brief.
81. Write short notes on:
    (*a*) Earned Value Analysis
    (*b*) PERT cost system
    (*c*) Net work simulation
82. Define project evaluation. What are its objectives?
83. Define post audit. What are its objectives?
84. Explain in brief the phases of post audit and the types of post audit of projects.
85. Give a specimen project evaluation form for a medium-sized project.

Unit II

1. 'Good communication is a must in a project environment'. Explain.
2. What is the need for a project information system?
3. What are the requirements of a project information system?
4. Explain the use of computerised project information systems.
5. What are the requirements of project management softwares?
6. Briefly explain some of the project management software packages that are widely used.
7. Explain the important facilities available in the project management software "Microsoft project 2000".
8. Write a short note on Enterprise-wide Project Management.
9. What, in your opinion, will be the trends in Project Management in the future?

Unit III

1. Define the term 'Project scheduling'
2. Describe the use of Gantt Chart. Using Gantt Chart, estimate the project completion time for the following project.

Activity	A	B	C	D	E	F
Proceeding activity	None	None	A	A	B	D, E
Duration (days)	10	8	14	7	6	8

3. What are the limitations of Gantt Chart?
4. What is the advantage of network based scheduling techniques?
5. Define terms 'Event' and 'Activity' in a network?
6. What is a dummy activity? Explain the need for dummy activity in a network with the aid of an example.
7. What are the rules to be followed in drawing network diagram for projects?

8. Explain Fulkerson's rule for numbering of events in a network.
9. What is the use of skip numbering?
10. What do you mean by 'Critical-Path' in a network? What are its characteristics?
11. Define 'Slack Time' of an event.
12. Define 'Float' of an activity.
13. Explain 'Total float', 'Free float' and 'Independent float' of activities and their significance in management decisions.
14. What are the three time estimates used in PERT? What is the relationship between the three time estimates and the "Expected Time'?
15. What is meant by updating of network? Explain its use for a project manager.
16. Explain 'Line of balance' technique with special reference to its use for project managers.
17. Draw a network diagram containing the following activities

Activity	*Immediate Predecessors*
A	--
B	--
C	A
D	B
E	C, D
F	C, D
G	E
H	F
I	G, H

18. Draw a network containing the following activities

Activity	*Immediately Preceding activity*	*Activity*	*Immediately Preceding activity*
A	--	H	D, C, G, E
B	--	I	H
C	--	J	H
D	--	K	I, J
E	A	L	I, J
F	B	M	K
G	F	--	--

[Hint: Activity-D and Activity-J are followed by dummy activity]

19. Draw a network with the following data and find out the critical path. What is the minimum time required for completion of the project as indicated by the critical path?

Activity	*Time (days)*	*Preceding activities*
A	10	--
B	12	--
C	8	--
D	13	A
E	14	A
F	18	B, D
G	14	C
H	12	C
I	12	F, G

[**Hint:** There will be two dummy activities at the end of the network.]

20. A project has the following time schedule. Construct a network and arrive at the critical path.

Activity	Time (Months)	Activity	Time (Months)
1→2	3	4→6	2
1→3	4	5→8	1
1→4	2	6→9	6
2→5	4	7→9	3
3→6	10	7→9	4
3→7	4	8→9	2

[Hint: Precedence relationship is not explicitly given since the same has been given indirectly by marking the activities with the start and end events]

21. The three time estimates of a project are given below.

Activity	Optimistic time (t_o)	Most likely time (t_m)	Pessimistic time (t_p)
1→2	4	6	14
1→3	7	11	15
2→4	6	15	18
3→4	2	5	8
4→5	6	10	14
3→5	7	16	19

Arrive at the critical path and the expected project completion time. What is the probability that the project will be completed in 35 days?

22. Draw a net work with the given data. Locate the critical path. Calculate the total float, free float and independent float for each activity.

Activity	Time (days)	Preceding activities	Activity	Time (days)	Preceding activities
A	5	--	G	8	D
B	7	--	H	5	D
C	6	A	I	7	E, F
D	9	B	J	6	G, I
E	4	C	K	2	G, I
F	11	D	L	5	H, J

23. Why should a project manager aim at completing the project at the shortest possible time?

24. Define 'Normal Time' and 'Crash Time' of an activity.

25. Explain Cost Vs Time relationship of an activity.

26. Give a brief account of "Time-Cost tradeoff".